The edition of *The Complete Works of Frances Ridley Havergal* has five parts:

Volume I *Behold Your King: The Complete Poetical Works of Frances Ridley Havergal*

Volume II *Whose I Am and Whom I Serve: Prose Works of Frances Ridley Havergal*

Volume III *Loving Messages for the Little Ones: Works for Children by Frances Ridley Havergal*

Volume IV *Love for Love: Frances Ridley Havergal: Memorials, Letters and Biographical Works*

Volume V *Songs of Truth and Love: Music by Frances Ridley Havergal and William Henry Havergal*

David L. Chalkley, Editor   Dr. Glen T. Wegge, Music Editor

Frances Ridley Havergal's formal education ended when she was 17, with one term at a young women's school in Düsseldorf, Germany, yet she was a true scholar all her life. Fluent in German and French and nearly so in Italian, she read and loved the Reformers in Latin, German, and French. Knowledge was never an end in itself, only a means to know better her Lord and Saviour and to help to bring others to know Him. The Bible was her only Book, and she studied the Hebrew and Greek texts of Scripture, memorized nearly all the New Testament and large portions of the Old Testament, and loved the Author with all her being.

Frances was brought to a saving knowledge of Christ when she was 14, and the rest of her life was consecrated to her Saviour, the Lord Jesus. Keenly aware of her own sinfulness and inability, her sole desire was to please and glorify Him alone. Very finely gifted, she was truly diligent with her gifts: her poetry is among the finest in the English language, after George Herbert; her prose works are deeply beneficial; a musician to the core, she left behind important compositions. Like her works, her life richly touched the ones near her and countless many who met or heard her. The Lord Jesus Christ was her alone, only beauty, and she glowed Him and His truth. Never wanting attention to herself, Frances' desire of her heart was for herself and for others to know her King, the Lord Jesus Christ. Her works are a gold-mine of help and enrichment. There is life in these pages: her works truly glorify the Lord, truly benefit His people, and powerfully reach those who do not yet know Him.

The Music of Frances Ridley Havergal by Glen T. Wegge, Ph.D.

This Companion Volume to the Havergal edition is a valuable presentation of F.R.H.'s scores, most or nearly all of F.R.H.'s scores very little if any at all seen, or even known of, for nearly a century. What a valuable body of music has been unknown for so long and is now made available to many. Dr. Wegge completed his Ph.D. in Music Theory at Indiana University at Bloomington, and his diligence and thoroughness in this volume are obvious. First an analysis of F.R.H.'s compositions is given, an essay that both addresses the most advanced musicians and also reaches those who are untrained in music; then all the extant scores that have been found are newly typeset, with complete texts for each score and extensive indices at the end of the book. This volume presents F.R.H.'s music in newly typeset scores diligently prepared by Dr. Wegge, and Volume V of the Havergal edition presents the scores in facsimile, the original 19th century scores. (The essay—a dissertation—analysing her scores is given the same both in this Companion Volume and in Volume V of the Havergal edition.)

Dr. Wegge is also preparing all of these scores for publication in performance folio editions.

Frances Ridley Havergal Trust   P.O.Box 649   Kirksville, Missouri 63501

This is one of the eight photographs of F.R.H. taken by Elliott and Fry on February 1, 1879, seven weeks after her 42nd birthday and four months and two days before her unexpectedly early death.

LETTERS

BY THE LATE

FRANCES RIDLEY HAVERGAL

EDITED BY HER SISTER,

M. V. G. H.

SWISS LETTERS

AND

ALPINE POEMS.

BY THE LATE

FRANCES RIDLEY HAVERGAL

EDITED BY HER SISTER,

J. MIRIAM CRANE.

AND

LILIES AND SHAMROCKS.

BY

C. W. A.

AND

FRANCES RIDLEY HAVERGAL.

"Knowing her intense desire that Christ should be magnified, whether
by her life or in her death, may it be to His glory
that in these pages she, being dead,
'Yet speaketh !' "

Taken from the Edition of *The Complete Works of Frances Ridley Havergal*.

David L. Chalkley, Editor   Dr. Glen T. Wegge, Associate Editor

ISBN 978-1-937236-23-6   Library of Congress: 2011919012

Book cover by Sherry Goodwin and David Carter.

CONTENTS

LIST OF ILLUSTRATIONS

Three close sisters. This photograph of Ellen Prestage Havergal (later Mrs. Giles Shaw) on the left, Maria Vernon Graham Havergal on the right, and Frances Ridley Havergal in the middle, was taken in 1854. That year Ellen turned 31 (February 19), Frances turned 18 (December 14), and Maria turned 33 (November 15).

Maria Vernon Graham Havergal (1821–1887) was a true servant of the Lord Jesus Christ, and a genuinely devoted sister to Frances. Very like-minded and like-hearted to Frances, Maria glowed the Lord and His truth. When their widowed step-mother died in May, 1878, Frances was free to move, and she accepted Maria's invitation to come to live with her in Mumbles, near Swansea, Wales. Neither one knew that those would be the final eight months of Frances' life. Fifteen years old when her youngest sister was born, Maria truly served F.R.H. whenever they were together, and after her death Maria was a diligent editor and publisher of Frances' completed and uncompleted works. Her desire was the same as her sister's, the glory of the Lord, and help and benefit to others. The love of Christ defined and filled both ladies. Maria's own fine volume *Pleasant Fruits* and her *Autobiography* are rich works. Her edited books of Frances' poetry and prose and music disseminated and preserved the gold-mine left after her death. Maria's biography *Memorials of Frances Ridley Havergal* is as valuable as Frances' own prose, and the volume of *Letters by the Late Frances Ridley Havergal* (which Maria prayed to be able to complete) was the final book she published of Frances' writings. On Maria's gravestone is the inscription she asked to be written: "This is a faithful saying, and worthy of all acceptation, that Christ Jesus came into the world to save sinners, of whom I am chief." I Timothy 1:15

Much love from
Maria V. G. Havergal.

The Portrait in this volume is reproduced from a Photograph taken by Messrs. Elliott & Fry.

Love for Love.

"We have known and believed the love that God hath to us."—I John 4.16.

KNOWING that the God on high,
  With a tender Father's grace,
Waits to hear your faintest cry,
    Waits to show a Father's Face—
Stay and think! oh, should not you
Love this gracious Father too?

Knowing Christ was crucified,
  Knowing that He loves you now
Just as much as when He died
    With the thorns upon His brow—
Stay and think! oh, should not you
Love this blessèd Saviour too?

Knowing that a Spirit strives
  With your weary, wandering heart,
Who would change the restless lives,
    Pure and perfect peace impart—
Stay and think! oh, should not you
Love this loving Spirit too?

F.R.H. February 12, 1879

Just When Thou Wilt.

Just when Thou wilt, O Master, call!
Or at the noon, or evening fall,
Or in the dark, or in the light,
Just when Thou wilt, it must be right.

Just when Thou wilt, O Saviour, come,
Take me to dwell in Thy bright home!
Or when the snows have crowned my head,
Or ere it hath one silver thread.

Just when Thou wilt, O Bridegroom, say,
"Rise up, my love, and come away!"
Open to me Thy golden gate,
Just when Thou wilt, or soon, or late.

Just when Thou wilt, Thy time is best,
Thou shalt appoint my hour of rest,
Marked by the Sun of perfect love,
Shining unchangeably above.

Just when Thou wilt!—no choice for me,
Life is a gift to me for Thee;
Death is a hushed and glorious tryst,
With Thee, my King, my Saviour, Christ!

F.R.H. November 3, 1874

Hush Me!

In F. R. H.'s Study, in memory of June 3rd, 1879.

Hush me, Lord Jesus! I cannot yet be still;
In vain I try to say it is Thy will;
My path is lonely, there is no one nigh
To share my sorrow, or to soothe my sigh,
    Hush me, Lord Jesus!

One voice is hushed; my sister's merry voice,
So sweet, so tuneful, as she sang "rejoice!"
From me my song-bird flew so far away—
Soft echoes leaving when she could not stay.
    Hush me, Lord Jesus!

So strange to miss my darling's footfall light,
Her smile I see not, 'twas my sunshine bright;
No tiny tokens now are brought to me—
Ferns, mosses, flowers, or shells beside the sea.
    Hush me, Lord Jesus!

O bruisèd Saviour! Thou wilt never break
The bruisèd reed, and never wilt Thou take
Thine arm from underneath Thy leaning child,
Who trusts and clings throughout the desert wild—
    Hush me, Lord Jesus!

Yes; I have proved Thy faithful word is true,
"Just as a mother will I comfort you";
"I know thy sorrow, and thy need of rest"—
Leaning I cry, upon my Saviour's breast,
    Hush me, Lord Jesus!

The hush of Heaven seems stealing over me,
The quiet haven nears in which I long to be;
My Kingly Comforter brings the sweet whisper nigh,
"A little, little while!" no need again to sigh,
    Hush me, Lord Jesus.

MARIA V. G. HAVERGAL (1821–1887).

REALITY.

"Father, we know the REALITY of Jesus Christ."—*Words used by a workman in prayer.*

Reality, reality,
  Lord Jesus Christ, Thou art to me!
From the spectral mists and driving clouds,
From the shifting shadows and phantom crowds;
From unreal words and unreal lives,
Where truth with falsehood feebly strives;
From the passings away, the chance and change,
Flickerings, vanishings, swift and strange,
    I turn to my glorious rest on Thee,
    Who art the grand Reality.

    Reality in greatest need,
  Lord Jesus Christ, Thou art indeed!
Is the pilot real, who alone can guide
The drifting ship through the midnight tide?
Is the lifeboat real, as it nears the wreck,
And the saved ones leap from the parting deck?
Is the haven real, where the barque may flee
From the autumn gales of the wild North Sea?
    Reality indeed art Thou,
    My Pilot, Lifeboat, Haven now!

    Reality, reality,
  In brightest days art Thou to me!
Thou art the sunshine of my mirth,
Thou art the heaven above my earth,
The spring of the love of all my heart,
And the Fountain of my song Thou art;
For dearer than the dearest now,
And better than the best, art Thou,
    Belovèd Lord, in whom I see
    Joy-giving, glad Reality.

    Reality, reality,
  Lord Jesus, Thou hast been to me.
When I thought the dream of life was past,
And "the Master's home-call" come at last;
When I thought I only had to wait
A little while at the Golden Gate,—
Only another day or two,
Till Thou Thyself shouldst bear me through,
    How real Thy presence was to me
    How precious Thy Reality!

    Reality, reality,
  Lord Jesus Christ, Thou art to me!
Thy name is sweeter than songs of old,
Thy words are better than "most fine gold,"
Thy deeds are greater than hero-glory,
Thy life is grander than poet-story;

But Thou, Thyself, for aye the same,
Art more than words and life and name!
    Thyself Thou hast revealed to me,
    In glorious Reality.

    Reality, reality,
  Lord Jesus Christ, is crowned in Thee.
In Thee is every type fulfilled,
In Thee is every yearning stilled
For perfect beauty, truth, and love;
For Thou art always far above
The grandest glimpse of our Ideal,
Yet more and more we know Thee real,
    And marvel more and more to see
    Thine infinite Reality.

    Reality, reality
  Of grace and glory dwells in Thee.
How real Thy mercy and Thy might!
How real Thy love, how real Thy light!
How real Thy truth and faithfulness!
How real Thy blessing when Thou dost bless!
How real Thy coming to dwell within!
How real the triumphs Thou dost win!
    Does not the loving and glowing heart
    Leap up to own how real Thou art?

    Reality, reality!
  Such let our adoration be!
Father, we bless Thee with heart and voice,
For the wondrous grace of Thy sovereign choice.
That patiently, gently, sought us out
In the far-off land of death and doubt,
That drew us to Christ by the Spirit's might,
That opened our eyes to see the light
    That arose in strange reality,
    From the darkness falling on Calvary.

    Reality, reality,
  Lord Jesus Christ, Thou art to me!
My glorious King, my Lord, my God,
Life is too short for half the laud,
For half the debt of praise I owe
For this blest knowledge, that "I know
The reality of Jesus Christ,"—
Unmeasured blessing, gift unpriced!
    Will I not praise Thee when I see
    In the long noon of Eternity,
    Unveiled, Thy "bright Reality!"

                    F.R.H.

LETTERS

BY THE LATE

FRANCES RIDLEY HAVERGAL

EDITED BY HER SISTER,

M. V. G. H.

"Sheaves after sowing,
Sun after rain,
Sight after mystery,
Peace after pain."
—F. R. H.

FOURTH THOUSAND

London:
JAMES NISBET & CO., 21 BERNERS STREET
1886

PREFACE.

"SUCH as we are in word by letters when we are absent, such will we be also in deed when we are present" (2 Corinthians 10:11). So, only those who saw St. Paul could verify his touchstone of deeds not words. And so with the beloved sister, whose letters are now unveiled; only those who saw her, could rightly estimate how truly her deeds of loving faithful labour for her Master were as golden seals to her words. Even these letters do not fully reveal all the wonderful submission of her home-life, or how the hand that takes the crown, may first be pierced with many a thorn.

It should be borne in mind that these letters were written chiefly to near and dear relatives and friends, who she knew would sympathize in the details of her service for the King.

Especial thanks are due to our eldest sister, J. Miriam Crane, for her valuable help in suggesting and revising.

Much gratitude is felt to those correspondents who now share their treasures with the ever-widening circle of F. R. H.'s readers. Attention has been given to their wishes in printing initials or names.

Her letters from Switzerland are not included, being already printed in *Swiss Letters*.

Frequent reference will be found to F. R. H.'s laborious editing of Havergal's *Psalmody*, containing her own and her father's tunes, which are now combined in one volume with the Rev. C. B. Snepp's selection of hymns, viz. *The New Musical Edition of Songs of Grace and Glory* (Nisbet & Co).

May these "Letters" cheer and guide some—

> "Footsteps weak and weary
> Through the desert dreary
> Through the valley of the night."

Again her words may be quoted—

> "Ye read *her* story,
> Take home the lesson with a spirit smile:
> Darkness and mystery a little while,
> Then—light and glory,
> And ministry mid saint and seraph band
> And service of high praise in the Eternal Land."

This closing record of the loved and loving one is laid at her Master's glorious feet, praying that interwoven with her life-story, His praise and glory may shine forth.

MARIA V. G. HAVERGAL.

August 1885.

This is a magnification of Frances from the undated photograph found on page ii.

INDEX.

There were three Appendices to this volume of *Letters* edited by Maria:

Note: The Division III "Letters to a Clerical Friend and His Wife, from 1870 to 1875" were <u>very</u> likely written to Rev. and Mrs. Charles Busbridge Snepp. The letter dated February 23, 1872, on page 36 of this book, very nearly proves this. The hymn is "The Infinity of God" (see page 365 of Volume I of the Havergal edition, hymn number 42 of *Songs of Grace and Glory*).

This magnification is taken from the photograph by Elliott and Fry on February 1, 1879, when she was 42.

Maria wrote this in her Diary (in her *Autobiography*, on page 553 of Volume IV of the Havergal edition): January 1, 1883.— "Jesus Christ, the Same yesterday, to-day, and for ever." "Able to subdue all things unto Himself"—just what I need. . . . Lord, open every life-page for me. Specially may I live to edit Fanny's letters for Thy glory.

DIVISION I.

EARLY LETTERS, FROM 1852 TO 1869.

(To E. C.)

LLANDUDNO, July 23, 1852.

How I wish you and W. H. could join us in our North Wales expeditions! There are copper mines in the Orme's Head, and as I had an intense desire to find myself half a mile from daylight, no one had any peace till my object of entering them was gained. One evening when the miners had left, Ellen, Frank, and I packed into a little truck and were pushed half a mile, till we could only see daylight as a tiny star, the tunnel being as straight as an arrow. The extreme darkness and perfect silence and the chilly air were so different from what we had left, and seemed very curious. Then we got out of our truck and followed our guide through the mine—through such curious caverns, some full of crystals and copper ore. We have plenty of walks, and great variety, but I prefer exploring alone. Oh, the breakneck places and precipices I get among. I am almost too venturesome, but my foot has never once slipped. Then, too, in such wild places I am quite alone, and I take out my little Testament and read and pray, where no human being besides myself is ever likely to be. Last week I could not do this, for I was very poorly from over-bathing, and now I must not bathe; it is very annoying, for I like swimming, and enjoy riding on the crested waves of the sea as much as on that wicked little pony. Frank went from home to Oakhampton last week to stand godfather to my new little niece "Evelyn Emily."

Now I will tell you what a capital book I am reading, Hobart Seymour's *Mornings with the Jesuits at Rome.* The style of the book is most delightful; sit down to it, and you can hardly get up again. I am so fond of controversial works. When does —— go back to school? That will be the time of trial for him; if he can stand firm on the Rock while there; if he can resist the many waves of temptation which will beat upon him there, then you may be sure all is right with him. It is more difficult to be prayerful at school than anywhere. When I went to Powick last year, I began prayerfully and carefully; but gradually, very gradually, I loosed my hold upon the Saviour, and on looking back at the end of the year, more was lost than gained. Oh, dear E., every one seems to get before me. I think I have found out my besetting sin; surely it is pride. The desire of surpassing others in everything, unwillingness to seem behind—all is pride. I never can be content to be last. But this mountain of pride must be made low before the Lord can enter my heart. I have learnt to read and speak Welsh quite easily. Some of the words are puzzling, because the initial letters are altered instead of the terminals, *e.g.* barn, mara, and fara all mean bread, but for euphony are used interchangeably in different parts of a sentence. We have excellent fun in bathing and swimming; I quite alarm our old bathing woman. Our landlady Mrs. G. is so nice and ladylike. I am sure she must be good, from many little things, and the gentle expression of her countenance. Many beautiful pieces of furniture show what she used to have.

Now I will tell you where I am enthroned. Not among green fields, or even where towering mountains rise, but by the wild sea waves; and while I am writing this, they are flowing in with softest, sweetest music, not like the deafening roar they dashed in with a few days ago. I wonder whether we shall ever be together where ancient ocean rolls his swelling tide. What a pity there are no fairy slippers which would transport you here with a wish. How bright everything is with you. I fear I shall never have such joy. Still I do not give up seeking, but there seem so many things in the way. I have been thinking a great deal about my confirmation, though it will not be yet for two years; it seems such a solemn vow which you then take upon yourself. Oh, shall I have strength to keep it? it is one of my most constant prayers, that if I am spared to be confirmed, I may never act as if I had not been so. I should so like to be confirmed with you. I have not time for much in the studying line here, and only write a lesson in Ollendoff every day, and have begun learning the Revelation, and am now in the third chapter.

(To E. C.)

TENBY, 1854.

Our lodgings look out upon the sea, and just opposite is a picturesque rocky island called St. Catherine's, with the ruins of a church on the top. There are most delectable caverns in it, quite practicable at low tide, with many lovely sea things, animal and vegetable. I have met an old Powick schoolfellow of mine here,—a very nice girl,—and we are a good deal together. She has her own horse here,—a perfect beauty,—and her father has very kindly left another,—a pretty creature (cream colour),—for my especial benefit, so we ride all over the country *ad libitum* together. The church is very large, but the pews are execrably uncomfortable. Last Sunday we had a first-rate sermon from the Bishop of Llandaff, not cram full of long words and Greek and Latin, but just what every one there could understand; it was altogether beautiful. Plainly, simply, and fully, he preached the gospel, the whole gospel, and nothing but the gospel, and his manner was captivating—so impressive and earnest; altogether I have rarely been so pleased.

The curate, tall and pale, seems as if he would not stay many years longer in this wicked world; he had such a peculiarly sweet and holy expression of countenance, that I expected great things from him. However, I was rather disappointed with his evening sermon; but yesterday he preached again, and I found I was not mistaken in my opinion of him. His text was 2 Corinthians 3:6. You would have thought him some old experienced Christian, a sort of Charles Simeon. It was beautiful, and his heart seemed full of love, not only to his congregation, but to his Saviour; and he seemed so anxious that others should enjoy God's love, and know how sweet it is. It has often struck me, dear E., that Christians scarcely think enough of the exceeding great love of God the Father. Not that they express it, but the general tone seems to give the impression that we owe everything solely and originally to Christ, keeping in the background that it was "the Father *sent* the Son to be the Saviour," that the Son makes the Father love us, and not that the love in the Father's heart made Him send the Son.

Now Mr. Smith (afterwards Bishop of Victoria) preached a good deal on this subject, not in any way detracting from the love and honour due to our Saviour, but he wanted us to see His unity with the Father, and love *God* in *Christ* more.

I am so extremely delighted and surprised that another Powick schoolfellow has come to Tenby. Did I ever tell you about Miss Threlfall, who writes such exquisite poetry? She is here too, and I am perfectly enchanted with her, my beau ideal of a Christian poetess. My sister Miriam is sketching a good deal, finishing her outlines in the evenings. Her etchings are quite artistic.

———

(Letter in Rhyme.)

1855.

My very dear friend, I fear you will be
Quite out of all patience with poor little me.
For seeming neglect, I must forthwith atone,
And meekly my humble repentance make known
By scribbling at once my epistle in rhyme,
More akin to the ludicrous than the sublime.
So little I've been with the Muses of late,
And so fearfully thick is becoming my pate,
That even a letter—of lines very few,
'Tis a dubious case, if I ever get through,

For want of a rhyme or a suitable word,
To insert where a gap in the metre is heard.
Not that the Muses will have much to do
With any epistle I scribble to you.
I shall not invoke their capricious assistance,
And keep from Parnassus respectable distance,
And only apply to my own special friend,
The goddess of scribble at whose shrine I bend.
Both gladly and oft, for she never refuses
Her aid, like the fickle and spiteful old Muses!
A little epitome seems to be due,
Dear Janey (considering our friendship), to you,
Of all the events which since I wrote last,
Like shadows, though pleasant and bright ones, have past;
Well, first on the list, on the thirtieth of June
Our hearts with St. Nicholas' bells were in tune;
Both joyous and grateful indeed they might be,
For my father (the jewel!) came home from the sea.
Returned, yes he is, but not as he went,
With dim seeing eye and his forces all spent;
For sight hath been found by the glorious Rhine,
And his books are reopened—so long a sealed mine.
So after we got up a capital dinner,
Plum-pudding and beef, at which each little sinner
Who claimed to belong to St. Nicholas' school,
Came smiling and cheering till each bench was full.
And now I transcribe, without any fear,
"The Welcome" we sang my father to cheer.

SONG OF WELCOME TO REV. W. H. HAVERGAL.

O God, with grateful hearts we come
    Thy goodness to adore,
While we our pastor welcome home
    To England's happy shore.

For Thy delivering love we praise,
    And Thy restoring hand!
Oh, spare him yet for long, long days
    To this our little band.

Thy Spirit's fulness on him rest,
    Thy love his sunshine be!
And may he still, while doubly blest,
    A blessing be from Thee.

When the Chief Shepherd shall appear,
    May he receive, we pray,
A crown of glory, bright and clear,
    That fadeth not away.

Next day I depart in infinite glee,
My heart's dearest jewel, my brother, to see,
With a couple of sisters to take care of me.
A perfect Elysium Hereford is,
A fairyland palace of pleasure and bliss;

Like some rainbow winged fay every hour flies past,
Only one is e'er mournful, and that is the last.
In this chalice of crystal, brimful of delight,
Full many ingredients mingled, but quite
The chief of them all (after Frank's conversation)
Was the music,—enchanting in my estimation,
Beethoven and Mendelssohn, Handel and Spohr,
Mozart and Corelli, with many names more,
Their harmony poured through voices and fingers,
Around me the echo most sweetly still lingers
More marvellous yet than a musical dream,
Flowed for hours together that glorious stream;
Each day as in music so happily passed,
I fancied more beautiful yet than the last,
Until when I left (with immense lamentation)
I was just in a state of complete saturation,—
The spirit of music seemed then to pervade
My very existence. That spirit has made
A firm resolution spring up within me,
That a decent musician some day *I will* be.
An army of socks in transparent condition
With which to combat, was my own special mission,
With neckties united and with shirts to affright
My latent intentions my letters to write.
This being the case, I shall hope and expect
That you will not accuse me of wilful neglect,
Since darning and visiting, walking and all,
But music especially held me in thrall.
Some ten days ago, spite of Frank's hearty grumbles
At losing his sisters, we came to the Mumbles—
For sea air is better than potion or pill,
To cure or prevent every species of ill.
This side Mumbles Head is dreary indeed,
No sands and no shells and no lovely seaweed,
No rocks which are fit to sketch or to climb.
An expanse of grey mud which is truly sublime
At low tide before you, and shingle at high,
Is the pleasant alternative greeting your eye;
And being so sheltered the water is quiet,
And hasn't a notion of making a riot.
But over the Head 'tis a different thing,
There a jubilant chorus the waves ever sing;
They seem to rejoice in their glorious might,
Their snowy plumes waving with gleeful delight.
Full many a trophy they bring from the deep,
Where forests untrodden the calm waters sleep;
Fair flowers of ocean of tropical hue,
Which glow on the sands bright with clear briny dew.
While meadow or woodland or wild heathy hill
Invite us to ramble and wander at will.
Church matters seem here in a pitiful state,
Which pains me and grieves me here to relate.
Two ting tangs set up a most pitiful chime
For church, at no very particular time.
You enter, and straight have a very fair notion
Of the nearest approach to perpetual motion.

The comma, the sole punctuation they use,
For the clergyman has not a moment to lose,—
He dashes away like a torrent of water,
And finishes all in an hour and a quarter.
The church has been whitewashed, but right long ago,
As the cracks and the dinginess amply doth show
About the same time, that a strange petrifaction
Confined the incumbent to mere Sunday action.
So many abuses in this place are rife,
The only church things giving token of life,
Are the singing within and the nettles without,
Both equally rampant, without any doubt.
But Janey, dear friend, I must hasten away,
For dinner will never allow of delay;
Entreating forgiveness for silence again,
And imploring a letter ere long from your pen,
I only will add that I ever shall be
What I now am, your fervently loving

FANNIE.

———

(*To E. C.*)

St. Nicholas Rectory, April 1854.

Our missionary meetings will, I hope, be extra good this year. The Rev. Pettitt, of Tinnevelly, and Rev. Bernau, of British Guiana, both known veterans, are our deputation. Do coax Mr. T. into bringing you over. They are warming-pans these missionary meetings; one cannot help getting some increase of mental caloric. We had a German Church missionary with us last week. We became acquainted with him in Dusseldorf, his native place, where he was taking some rest after many years' labour in Abyssinia and India, and he may return next autumn. Mr. Isenberg knows sixteen languages, and has preached and written books in most of them; he is as good as he is clever. His devotion to his work and to the great Master of his work is beautiful; it was quite a treat to have him. I have at last hit on a new device, and earned something by my brains for my pet Church Missionary Society. There are some pocket-books at 2s. 6d. which advertise so many copies gratis, as prizes for poetical enigmas sent up for insertion;[1] so last spring I wrote sixteen on different subjects, and now I have received six copies in return. I reserved one, but sold all the rest. I mean to try again next year (*D. V.*).* No one else got more than four copies, so I am well satisfied with my success.

June 3, 1854.

Last Sunday the confirmation notice was given out in our church, and this week Papa saw all the candidates at the Rectory, before beginning the confirmation lectures. July 17th is the day fixed for Worcester. Are you at all thinking about it,

[1] "Charades and Enigmas," by F. R. H., in *Life Echoes*. Nisbet & Co.
*D.V., Deo volente (Latin), meaning "God willing"

dearest? If you are, why could we not be confirmed together, and then you could have the benefit of dear Papa's nice lectures? I am not quite easy about this important and to me most solemn of any rite. Perhaps I am more fearful than I need to be. But to take that solemn vow on my lips, to answer "I do" without a really changed heart, seems dreadful. I do—oh, indeed I do—desire to live up to my profession, to be His, for time and eternity. But I am learning to see how *very* weak I am, and how easily Satan can conquer me even when I do strive against him. I do believe with my *head* that Jesus can, and will give me His grace, and I do not need to fear, yet somehow my *heart* seems to be hard and cold and not to take it in. Oh, if we were but *there*—where there is no more sin! Oh do not forget to pray for me, and don't ever doubt the love of your unworthy friend.

———

(To E. C.)

December 1856.

How quickly time does go! This is December! and our twentieth birthday! I hope God will give me grace to use this fortnight as a special season of prayer for grace to begin not only a new year, but a new *ten* years. Therefore I feel sure Satan will make it a special season of temptation; indeed, I quite dread it from experience. Will you pray for me, and with me, dear, that my faith may not fail? I have so much to humble me to the very dust—twenty sinful years! Yesterday, Papa preached a beautiful sermon from Acts 1:11. One sentence came suddenly upon me (my attention had wandered for a minute), "And the Judge on that great white throne will be *this same Jesus of Nazareth.*" Oh it made me so happy, I did not hear what followed, it seemed to *fill* me. Jesus of Nazareth, the same that said, "Come unto Me," the same who "suffered, being tempted," HE *the Judge!* how then could I fear? I wished the last trump could be sounding even then. How can it be that this never struck me *so* before? But it has passed away, like the aurora on a winter night, and all seems cold and dark again; only there seems a faint quivering gleam on the horizon, remaining, to remind me of the brightness which has been.

———

WHO SHALL BE FIRST?

'Tis nearly forty years since our first flower
Awoke beneath the fair spring's early shining;
'Tis more than twenty since a wintry hour
Filled up the wreath of home, the sixth young
     bud entwining.

That wreath, long woven, is unbroken yet,
Not one of all its opening buds hath faded,

Not one gem fallen from that coronet;
Oh, "who shall be the first" to shine in light
     unshaded?

F. R. H.

(To E. P. S.).

St. Nicholas Rectory, Worcester, 1857.

Inasmuch as I have not written for some time, I mean to give you a good long epistle to make up; and going upon the supposition that you are still a lover of St. Nicholas, shall inflict a circumstantial account of Whitsuntide proceedings on you.

Our children went to St. Andrew's. Papa's text was "Boys and girls playing in the streets," which of course produced a good many astonished looks, and caught attention,—a very pretty and interesting sermon, the text suggesting—1st, *mercies* to be thankful for; 2nd, *dangers* to be avoided; 3rd, *duties* to be fulfilled. The principal banner was, "Dear Pastor, go on in the work of the Lord," *beautifully* done in leaves. "Feed my Lambs," "None but Jesus," "We won't give up the Bible," were also conspicuous. "V. R." and "Long live the Queen." Tea as usual, and rewards. My poor scholar, dear Betsy Dyke, would have been one of *three* singled out for pre-eminent church behaviour; her father is to have the Bible which would have been hers; little Emma, too, had been marked first rate in everything. Poor little Ben looks so cut up, it is quite touching to see him; he is such a good child. The infants sang beautifully. I never saw Papa look more pleased. The others listened most attentively, and the big girls begged they might sing again, "*it was so pretty,*" they said. Our curate, Mr. James, was very cool and amusing. At last came the cheering. Mary Jenkins gave out in a clear National School voice, "The Queen," "Mr. and Mrs. Havergal, Miss H. and Miss Fanny"; then "Three cheers for Mr. and Mrs. Shaw, and the baby!" This produced first laughter, then cheers and thumping.

It was so kind of Papa, he had my little verses on 'Peace' printed and sung. We like our children to be loyal.

PEACE.

A carol for the children of St. Nicholas Sunday School.

Children, come! with grateful voice
Let us one and all rejoice:
War departs, and Peace descends;
Enemies are turned to friends.

War departs! each tuneful bell
Pealeth forth its welcome knell;
Battle shout and cannon's roar
Shall be heard again no more.

Peace descends on rainbow wing!
Thousand blessings may she bring;
Plenty, joy, and love to all,
Parents, children, "great and small."

Ne'er again may England know
What it is to have a foe;
Ever may the olive green
Shade the throne of England's Queen.

Children, come! your voices raise,
Chant the gladsome hymn of praise;
Thanking Him who reigns above,
Prince of Peace, and God of Love!

F. R. H.

In the evening, we went to the teachers' tea meeting. The President, Rev. John Davies, of St. Clements, made a very nice speech, and finished up most sweetly, and quite in character with himself and his apostolic looks.

Then a useful speech from a deputation from the Sunday School Institute; a great deal of earnest homecoming talk and practical advice; a very good man evidently, and seemed to produce considerable effect on the teachers. Then Hymn 237, to Farrant. Then Rev. W. H. Havergal! Such a sweet speech and solid withal, every one seemed pleased, and more clapping and "Hear, hear" than for any one else. He told us an instance of Sunday school teachers' work bearing fruit after a lapse of forty years—so exquisitely; then cautioned against two or three particular local evils for teachers to warn against. He just took an opportunity of congratulating them "on their singing." To our great delight, he came out so wonderfully sweet, like a first-rate Thursday evening sermon, and showed a beautiful gleam of his spirituality. I do so wish Mr. Shaw had heard him then, it was so lovely. Rev. B. Davis and W. Wright were called, but sensibly refused to speak, time being up. A few nice words from the President, then "May the grace," etc., then the Benediction. After which (9.40) every one went off in apparently a satisfied state of mind, and even Maria came to the conclusion that it had been a very profitable evening. My father gave the Irish Society a capital introduction last Sunday in the sermon; it will not be his fault if collections are small.

I am going to Germany with Auguste, when school breaks up, in two or three weeks; my next to you will be from France. The Prince of Wales is going to stay three months at Königswinter, only three miles from Obercassel, and the Countess zur Lippe is a relative of Prince Albert's and he used to spend his vacations there when at the University of Bonn; so now the Prince is sure to go there, and as I am going to spend a month there, perhaps I shall be under the same roof as the heir-apparent! Something like the comet's crossing the plane of the earth's orbit, is it not? as they said, "*if* they had only been a month forwarder, there would have been a collision"!

—— has been desperately affectionate to me of late, and more earnest and easy to talk with about better things, but I don't quite understand her. Her religion (she seems to have a good deal of it too) does not seem a very spiritual sort; it is more the "I put my trust in God's mercy" sort of thing, and savours a little of the Maurice and Kingsley notions of God's universal love, etc. And yet she *is* earnest, and thinks seriously about giving up dancing, etc., this winter. Why is it, Nelly (and am I right?), I always feel a sort of suspicious dread of there being something wrong about those who only talk about "God's mercy," "trust in Providence," etc.? If they speak of Jesus, it seems a sort of key-note, and they seem tuned to it, and you feel you *trust* them more than the other sort. I can't get over the feeling, and yet it seems almost exalting the Son above the Father; but it always gives me a sort of thrill if *His* name is mentioned, which the other expressions do not and cannot.

Papa preached from Micah 5:3. Very many at the communion. Mr. James gave us (P.M.) a pretty little commentary, simple and useful, on Luke 2:6–20. The chief peculiarity of his sermons is originality; he does not say just what you fancy is coming, but brings out thoughts and lessons which are very new and striking. He is too short and hurried in manner, and his sentences are rather abrupt. He always calls things by their right names, and does not at all mince matters in telling folks the truth, *e.g.* "there is no such thing in existence as 'a good sort of person on the whole'"; or again, mentioning something in Proverbs, "it is not only *not tolerated* by God, *not disagreeable* to Him—it is an *abomination* to Him." I like Mr. James very much; he seems in high favour with the better class and with our poor. Widow Surman thinks, "he do preach wonderful sermons, only he don't stop long enough over them; I told him of it, and he promised he'd try and read them a bit slower"!

———

(*To E. P. S.*)

Spa, October 3, 1857.

I am now almost myself again, and hope to go for a little walk to-day; but it is very strange to think that only on September 21st, I was in real danger, the erysipelas[1] having gone to my head; it seems like a new life given me, and I do hope that He who has restored it will give me grace to use it for Him. So you see, while you are all thankful for our dear father's life, I have a double cause for gratitude, my own as well as his. It is so delightful to see him walking about the room again, in his own old way; it really seems almost a miracle after what he has gone through.

I have had such a jolly summer till these last four or five weeks, and managed to get as thoroughly "ver-deutscht," *i.e.* Germanized, in manners and customs as if I belonged to them.

Home, October 16.—When will my letter be done, I wonder! Headaches always seemed to come on just when I wanted

[1] erysipelas: an acute disease of the skin, streptococcal infection causing red inflammation of the skin and mucous membranes

to write, and last Friday I left Spa for home. Dear mother travelled with me part of the way. I had a quiet journey, barring a great Sabbath argument with two young Frenchmen, who made themselves agreeable. On getting to Ostend, an English barrister, with whose ancient mother, Papa had become acquainted at Gräfrath, met me. He at once informed me that it was such a stormy night that no one in their senses would cross without absolute necessity. Then up walked Mr. H., who told me that his wife had just made up beds for me, and the lady expected with me. Mrs. H., a tall, dashing-looking person, with seven children, received me in a hearty English sort of way, and told me to make myself comfortable till the sea was fit to be ventured upon.

All this I should have enjoyed, and thought immense fun, but felt so very poorly that I almost regretted staying, under the apprehension that I might be laid up again there. A tiptop-looking lady, very pretty, was in to tea, and introduced as the "Countess Rüdiger"; she was the wife of that Russian General Rüdiger, who was killed in the war.

I went on by the Dover boat, and had a beautifully smooth passage.

The number of railway and steamboat acquaintances I have made is something amusing. I always picked up somebody. Once I fell desperately in love with a very sweet young lady, speaking almost all European languages with equal fluency; and, on exchanging names and autographs, I found she was the Princess Leonille Galitzin, of the great Russian family. I looked amazed, and said, "You see *I* have no titles." "Oh," said she, "what are titles? only empty names. I do not care for them, and should like you none the better for having one."

I left Papa marvellously better; he is going to Gräfrath by very easy stages. He was so delighted with a piano, sat down and played a few minutes, and then seemed quite overpowered, it was so touching.

He is so beautiful in illness or trouble, people don't half know him who have not seen him at such times; talk about sweet memoirs, etc., no memoir that ever was written would be good enough for him!

I have missed two weddings at Obercassel, was engaged to be bridesmaid at each. Fancy, the two groomsmen lead the bride, and the two bridesmaids lead the bridegroom up the church! Is it not funny?

———————

(*To the same.*)

December 1857.

My dear old almshouse folks are so affectionate, it is a great consolation to me that there cannot be much cupboard love in the question; it smites me rather, because I feel it more than I deserve, when I remember sometimes going round carelessly and hurriedly. They do say such nice things about dear Papa, etc.

We went to the cathedral on Christmas Eve—a very nice service. I should like to copy a piece out of George Herbert for Mr. S., about his enjoyment of cathedral services.

Thank you for remembering my birthday; it was such an unexpected pleasure to have a bit of your writing. People seemed determined to set me up in the poetry line. Miriam gave me Campbell and Coleridge, J. H. E. sent me a magnificent drawing-room table volume, all gilding and scarlet and illumination, *Christmas with the Poets,* and mother gave me a very nice copy of my dearly-beloved George Herbert. Greatly to my liking—these said books!

And, Nelly dear, I do think my best Friend sent me some of *His* birthday gifts; I had pleaded very hard for a blessing, and it was answered. I couldn't help trusting and loving Him, and could not help saying, "I am my Beloved's, and my Beloved is mine." You see Jeremiah 31:3 seemed sent me; I must admit that He had "*drawn*" me, because I FELT it, and it was with "loving-kindness" too, then that "*therefore*" showed me that He must have "loved" me "with an everlasting love," because He simply said it; for, being convinced of the effects how could I make Him a liar and disbelieve the cause? Wasn't it *kind* of Him to speak to me, Nelly dear? And then I felt so comforted about what is always my greatest trouble—my *spiritual* future; He took away all my unbelieving fear that I should not get any nearer to Him in coming years, that He would suffer me to fall away entirely, that I should after all be a castaway. He helped me there, and so I laid all *that* burden on Him. I'm not so happy now, I am so horribly wicked; but "Christ Jesus, made unto us *sanctification*," gives me *hope.*

———————

(*A City Rector's Letter to his Parishioners.*)

November 9, 1859.

My dear parishioners and friends,
　　While heartily I greet you,
I must regret to say that now
To duty's stern behest I bow,
And to a small parochial row
　　I feel constrained to treat you.

Allow me to remind you first,
　　That some few years ago,
Our worthy friend John Wheeley Lea,
(To which Esquire should added be)
The schools erected, which you see
　　When through the Butts you go.

An eligible mistress found,
    And all things else in train,
We trusted that the poor would prize
The boon aright, while kind supplies
From ready friends would soon arrive;
    We trusted—but in vain!

The children came and brought their pence,
    But pennies won't supply
The coals to fill those Tudor grates,
Brooms, dusters, door-mats, books and slates,
Insurance, wear and tear and rates,
    And salaries so high.

Though filthy lucre be a snare,
    We can't quite do without it;
And as this evil still is rife,
My precious darling little wife
Has nearly sacrificed her life,
    In teasing you about it.

For each two pounds collected, she
    One pair of boots wears out,
For every five a dress; and then,
'Tis true, though sad, for every ten
She goes and gets laid up again,
    For perhaps a month about.

Then, when at last the work is done
    And each subscription paid,
Your Rector finds himself—but nay,
I spare you—of myself I say
As little as I duly may,
    Not thus the cause I aid.

My friends, it ought not so to be,
    Your duty is most clear;
I pray let 1860 bring
Sweet charity on *golden* wing,
In every bosom may she nestle,
With every world-bound spirit wrestle,
    And make a glad New Year!

                      F. R. H.

35 Russell Square, London, 1862.

I had so looked forward to this visit to London; but the first week has brought such deep sorrow, and I am in mourning for my dear Cousin Bessie's unexpected but most peacefully-happy death; and now our dear Aunt Stratton has died also. Of course this holds me back from so much which I had anticipated; and just as I was intending to visit my dear brother Henry, I was taken ill. I have had very little actual suffering, but excessive weakness, and so a holding back from my own plans and pleasures and duties, which I see to be a most wise dispensation for me. Somehow times of check and disappoint-ment, generally seem singularly helpful to me. I think I have been enabled to rest more simply on the Lord Jesus, and His finished work, and have found peace in that, instead of the old distraction and almost despair in trying to trace out the yet scarcely-visible work within me. God has been very gracious to me,—oh, so undeservedly; for only He knows how utterly unworthy I am of all His benefits. Oh, if I might only cling always closely to Him, and never wander from Him again!

A few days ago I was much depressed,—some of my plans had failed, and —— had grievously disappointed all the warm hopes I thought I had reason to cherish of her. Then came a storm of discoveries of evil in my motives and actions, seemingly all fair. I seemed utterly helpless and weak,—bodily, mentally, and spiritually,—and utterly, oh utterly vile and sinful in my own eyes! How much more then in God's sight! I *could* do nothing; there was nothing for it but to cast myself just as I was upon the Saviour. I did so, and brought Him all my burden, even the heaviest—my deep sinfulness. Instantly "there was a great calm." I cannot express it otherwise. It gave me the strongest impression of His own merciful, immediate, and personal intervention which I have ever had. I was confident He had heard, and, while I was yet speaking, answered. For all the care and sorrow about ——, and other things, seemed taken out of my hands and safely placed in His; "the sin has been atoned for, the sinfulness shall be subdued, and He is our peace now and for ever," was my feeling rather than my thought. I could not stay to analyze the strange flow of quiet gladness and sense of relief; it was too plainly His gift just that moment when I so needed it, and what could I do but thank Him for such kindness? Vivid consciousness of this kind seldom lasts long; but Hebrews 13:8 is very sweet, and though I change with every passing hour, He is "the same."

I suppose it is because He knows how weak my faith is, that in every trial He always permits me as yet to *see* the "need be." It must seem the merest trifle to others, but it is a great trial to me to feel such lack of strength that many hours a day, especially early ones, which I would so like to spend in many pursuits for which I have no other time, must be spent in entire rest, or the very slightest occupation.

But I *know* I need this check, and am thankful, I hope, that I am stronger than a time back.

————

(*To E. C.*)

February 1862.

... "He knoweth the way that I take; and when He hath tried me, I shall come forth as gold." And He has known all along by what way you would be taken. ... Oh E., there is great comfort in the mere thought of this wonderful knowledge of our God; then add to it that He who knoweth careth too, and He who careth loveth with a love that passeth knowledge. He has indeed tried you, dearest, and the trial time is still present with you; but "*when*" (then it is not meant to last always—there is something beyond) "when He hath tried me,"—when all is over, and the storms are quieted, and the wounded heart is healing under His touch,—then you "shall come forth as gold," very precious in His sight, impressed with His own refining mark, purified and prepared for His work here, and His own safe treasury above, when that work is done. . . . To think that your sweet mother is on the very threshold of eternal rest and joy! A hush comes over me at the very thought of one so loved, being so near Christ's own immediate presence. Is it not as if the veil were growing half transparent which hangs between life and its dreams, and eternal life and its realities? Oh try, dearest, even in your deep sorrow, to lift a note of thanksgiving for the "sure and certain hope," the utter confidence which all must have in her abundant entrance. It is so wonderful to think of what we cannot conceive, that lies so close before her. And then, dearest, to think that all your sorrow is but one upward step for you towards the same bright goal!

December 13, 1863.

The eve of my birthday. I have been thinking why this year has been marked by such little advancement, while God's dealings with me have been so favourable to it; and I trust that the resolution which I have just prayerfully made may change the story of my next year's history. I find that when so late in rising A.M. as to have inadequate time for prayer and my Bible, I cannot really replace it later in the day—my mind seems unhinged. I asked Papa's advice; which was, that considering the great importance which rest, and especially sleep is to me, and the medical opinion about it, I ought not to make a point of rousing myself earlier, but rather to make a strong effort to overcome the temptation to wandering thought, and hurried formalism later in the morning. I tried to do so, and while at home partly succeeded. But now I am teaching my nieces again, I fail entirely, and have come to the conclusion that I *ought,* in this matter, "to seek first the kingdom of God," and leave health to His care meanwhile. So, God helping me, I resolve henceforth, at whatever bodily sacrifice, to rise sufficiently early to leave *full* time for reading His word, and prayer without hurry; and if I can in no other way manage it, to go to bed at nine P.M. for extra rest instead of morning sleep. And oh, may the Lord give me such increase of strength and grace, that bodily weakness and weariness may seem a little thing to me!

March 5, 1864.

. . . I consider what you call my father's Churchism to consist of—

1. *Evangelical Doctrine i.e.* Christ and His Atonement are above and before all things: Conversion, whether taking place in Baptism or subsequently, sudden or imperceptibly gradual, to be an absolute necessity; that good works follow out of and are not any means of justification, which is only by faith in Christ; that outward forms and ceremonies have no merit or virtue in themselves whatever.

2. *Loyal Church Practice, i.e.* that all things should be done decently and in order, to uphold the Church in every way, to hold fast her Articles and Liturgy, interpreting each by the other.

Now I think a "High" confession of faith would be rather different to this. They would make the "Church" their great meeting-point, rather than the Atonement of Christ. They would say that regenerating grace is always given in Baptism, and that all we have to do is to take heed not to fall from it. (I'm quite sure I never had any to fall from!) They make some sort of subtle virtue to be in the performance of rites, and so there is a sort of half-acknowledged trust placed in them. They would think as much of gaining a dissenter to join the Church as of winning a soul from darkness to light. As far as my experience goes, they have more devoutness and less devotion, more fear and less love, more feeling of duty than of desire, laying more stress on Philippians 2:12 than ver. 13, and in practice working upon the intellect and imagination rather than aiming at the heart, skirmishing among the outworks rather than assaulting the citadel.

August 7, 1864.

I ought not to let this summer pass without some slight record of God's goodness to me. All the spring was cold and dark to me, and the thanks which should have gone up for my exemption (the only one in the house) from illness were few and faint. I longed that God would speak to me, and show me the *reality* of His love and power. He answered singularly by showing me His power and His actual presence in working upon others. First He permitted me to gain the confidence of ——, and to be, by conversation and correspondence, some little help to her. And so, in April and May, I watched His hand leading her week by week out of darkness into marvellous light. Then I heard of ——'s conversion, and saw for myself in her, such evidence of His real power as left no room for doubt. And in the midst of my own dimness, it was great encouragement to see what the Lord could do and was doing. Then, having for months watched, and waited, and prayed for any signs of good resulting from my evening class, S. D. seemed touched, awakened, and in earnest, feeling a deep dissatisfaction with herself, which her outwardly blameless life had hitherto kept off. Then F. C., after my many vain attempts to get any response beyond polite assent, seemed reached at last by a little note, and earnest tears took the place of the easy smile. So I felt that God was answering my prayer, only not in my way. In June, having promised to read French with ——, I gave her a hint of my longings and disappointment. She took it up so that I told her all. She made my case the subject of her most fervent prayer, and wrote me two or three most beautiful letters. I begged her to be a candid friend, having gone so far with her, for I wanted no "smooth things." And she warned me of the spirit of worldliness. It was so, I knew and felt. How could I be delivered from the net? Even prayer seemed powerless against this paralyzation. Thus I went home, praying my holidays might bring blessing somehow.

Hannah and Janey and Andrienne V. were coming for a visit. A special impulse seemed to come upon me to pray for H., and that her visit might be blessed. She came to Shareshill reluctantly, and with a special determination not to like me, and inclination to be jealous of me. She baffled me, and knew it; no response whatever could I get. I think God poured out upon me the spirit of grace and of supplication for her, so much so that I almost lost sight of my own difficulties and depression in anxiety for her. July 2nd, Saturday evening, she broke the ice, by merely saying, "You are what I am not." "Then why not?" This led to a very serious talk the next evening; and she cried, but said, "I just feel that I don't care enough about it to be worth while to seek." I spoke of *danger* and of God's promise to give the Holy Spirit to them that *only* ask. All through the following week, she sought truly and earnestly. By Maria's advice, though reluctantly at first, I read a little with her each day, and soon was most thankful that I had been led to do so. On Saturday, 9th, I gave her Mark 10:46–52, and the first light seemed to break in. That evening we sat on the stile behind the churchyard close to our gardens; we read Romans 3, dwelling long on verse 22 and the doctrine of imputed righteousness. And God gave her faith to receive it;—"I do *believe* this, but is that *all*? Can it be all? is nothing more necessary?" I assured her it must be all, because God had said it. "Isn't it too good to be true?" was the next. But she believed the testimony concerning His Son, and was at rest. And the next day, July 11th, she sealed her faith in obedience to her Saviour's command, and came with us for the first time in her life to His table.

God seemed to help me wonderfully to read and say the right things; I felt that He did so. But while talking to her, the feeling grew stronger daily, that what was true for her was true also for me, especially when we thought over Romans 3:22. I do not think I ever before ventured to really believe that Christ's righteousness was imputed even to me; but I knew, I was *sure*, that I believed in Jesus, and so there seemed no alternative but to accept the glorious belief that "the righteousness of God" being "upon *all* and unto *all* them that believe" was upon me too. It used to seem "too good to be true" for me; but how could I doubt God's word? Then a great tide of sorrow came over me for having been so disbelieving; it seemed so very wrong to have doubted, that it threw other phases of sinfulness into comparative shade. And so that 10th of July was one of the happiest days I ever had; my own more than renewed faith, and my excessive delight at God's marvellous answer to me about dear H. I never saw such rapid work before; it was just as if God would show me what He could do, and what He was ready to do, and silence my doubts and distrust for ever. Oh that it were for ever! Why ever *does* one doubt! It seems so abominable after all He has said and done. I am so restful now; it is very sweet to yield oneself up to the belief that Christ has saved me. Yet I do not seem to realize it intensely and vividly. (I wonder whether *that* will ever come!) Still I do not doubt as formerly. Not that I feel any better or holier, much as I long to be so; but Christ Jesus came to save sinners, and as such I come to Him. My desire to be nearer to God, and unreservedly His, has deepened and strengthened.

This month at Llandrillo has been very refreshing to me, and intercourse with Mrs. G. very helpful. I think prayer has been doubly answered, for she speaks of my being a comfort and refreshment to her (which seems strange, for I cannot say much to her). Religion is so utterly real, so everything with her, and that strengthens my own faith. And some things she has said throw a new and pleasant light on thoughts which often distressed me. I hope and pray that when I return to O., the hosts of other things, both duties and pleasures, may not choke the word. I want to live more decidedly to my Master, and not to let go the confidence which He has given me, and which, feeble as it is, and easily shaken, is very precious to me. "Ebenezer."

(To F. T. H.)

Oakhampton, September 27, 1864.

I am so glad you are better; it was so dismal to know of your illness. Do stay at Breay as long as you can, and rest.

We were delighted with the Birmingham Festival. Beethoven's *Mount of Olives* went splendidly. That solo and chorus, "Prize your Redeemer's goodness," is one of the most glorious things I ever heard, and Titiens sang it wonderfully. Miriam said it was better than many sermons are. I do not know anything more spiritual in instrumental music than "The Overture to the Hymn of Praise," which we also heard with its grand theme—

'All that hath life and breath, praise the Lord'

which idea, so continually recurring in all possible forms, Mendelssohn seems determined to keep before one. I am haunted still by the strange undulating swell; and that Allegretto 6/8 movement, especially that part where there is a sort of conflict between a clear, bright, praiseful theme in steady, simple chords, and an under-current interrupting and then overflowing it, of that mysteriously pathetic minor, so restlessly rising and falling. The whole thing was to me a sort of musical picture of the inner life, and this part means Romans 7:24, 25.

How very different it is listening to oratorios, and taking part in them! Especially do I enjoy singing in Handel's choruses: one cannot but yield oneself to his broad, glad sunshine, pouring so brightly, yet so solemnly, over the mountain grandeur of his almost inspired chords. I do so delight in singing them at our Philharmonic. Never mind organ or conductor or your next neighbour; let the great ocean of sound flow in upon your soul, till you feel that it has absorbed your individual being into itself. Meanwhile sing away, because you cannot help it,—because it does you good; and, whatever the words may be, the notes will be the happy and involuntary expression of thanks to Him, who giveth us richly all things to enjoy, and especially the great and indescribable enjoyment of music. And then as we rise to a glorious climax, "Now with *one* voice," says our conductor, and truly that is a very great and noble one, and the concluding rush of sound is like a dazzling flood of light, pouring itself forth only to end so soon in silence. How quickly music passes and is gone. How one might moralize!

(To *M. V. G. H.*)

1864.

. . . I have never answered what you said some time back. Yes, dear, if I had my choice, I should like to be a "Christian poetess," but I do not feel I have ability enough ever to turn this line to much account. I feel as if music were a stronger talent, though in neither am I doing anything serious. Most of all would I like to be your ideal,—a winner of souls. But as no special path is open for me, I feel I can only and simply take any opportunity of using any talent which opens to me. I am not working now at composition; that door is certainly not now open, and perhaps never will be; cleverer persons than I have never been heard of; and I do not now care about getting into print, unless it should ever be made clear as my right way. I do not think of much beyond my present daily duties, teaching my nieces, etc.; or when at home, taking the various opportunities that arise of usefulness.

November 13, 1864.—This autumn has not been unhappy on the whole; God has been very gracious to me, in preserving me from the sort of reaction I so dreaded, after the vivid feeling of last summer. The bright side has been, that I have seldom felt prayer so much a refreshment and privilege, or been disposed to spend so much time in it; that the Bible, (especially my evening text) has often been very sweet to me; that in

two or three special conflicts in matters of conscience, the victory has been given me where before I had failed; that my desire to work for Christ has been a little stronger. When feeling overdone and languid, I have appropriated Isaiah 50:10, just to trust and cling where I cannot see.

The dark side has been, not living up to my light, and missing many opportunities of doing good, and not at all earnest in intercession, that in one struggle between a *doubtful* right or wrong, I yielded and gave the possible wrong the benefit of the doubt instead of the probable right; that I have not been truly watching for the souls of my own charge, but have taken it too easy.

I am more than ever conscious of the inward antagonism of the old nature and the new.

I want distinct guidance as to my path. I cannot help thinking I ought to be at home on dear mother's account, to help her. I hope it will somehow be decided for me. I want to make the most of my life, and to do the best with it; but here I feel my desires and motives need much purifying; for even where all sounds fair in words, an element of self, of lurking pride may be detected. Oh, that my Lord would indeed purify me and make me white, at *any* cost.

(*To the late Miss Pollock.*)

LLANDRILLO, CONWAY, 1865.

I enclose you a few of my verses. I know they are worth little in themselves, but I thought you might kindly like to have them as a remembrance of one who feels very thankful for having had the pleasure and privilege of meeting you. It does not need a long acquaintance, to love those whom we feel and know are loving the same dear Saviour. Love is the happiest feeling there is on earth, and how much more of it we have, whom He has taught to love one another for His sake. Do not you think that the "new commandment" is a singularly kind and considerate one? He knew how our hearts yearn for affection. He knows our deep need of its soothing, gladdening influence, and so He made it not a mere permission, but an absolute command. Surely this is an instance that His commandments are not grievous. We stay here (*D. V.*) till Friday, and then finish our journey to Oakhampton. I feel I ought to begin my work there, with new and holier vigour after all the refreshment and enjoyment of my long Celbridge visit, and all the pleasant Christian intercourse which I have had. One ought to be the better and stronger for it, but the enemy always seems ready with some new device, and one never feels so weak as just when one hoped to feel stronger. Yet "in the Lord Jehovah is everlasting strength," and it is very nice to know and rest upon that. Good-bye, dearest Miss Pollock. May you be very abundantly blessed in your own soul and in your work. Ruth 2:12.

May 1865.—Is there such a thing as God seeing that a seeming work for Him, is not done *purely* unto Him alone, and so sending a sort of earthly reward on the spot, and withholding His acceptance of the service, because of its sullied and imperfect motive? For the thing beyond any other temporal gift I most value is affection. I feel as if I had a perfect greed of love. Now whenever I make special effort to win a soul to Christ, or to comfort and help on some weak or suffering Christian (which last I fancy is my best, as it certainly is my best-loved form of work), I am almost invariably repaid by an amount of gratitude I had no reason to expect. The temptation follows strong and subtle, to work for this pleasant payment, instead of purely for my Master's sake. To be valued and loved by any one—no one knows its deliciousness to me. Does God give me this as a "verily they have their reward"! I long to think it is rather His kind and very gracious encouragement to me, and perhaps I am wronging His goodness in the other thought! Were my heart purer and my eye truly "single," how I should rejoice in it as a token of His love. Sometimes when walking to Yarron, praying as I go, that the Lord would give me a word in season for each, and laying their cases before Him, in comes the thought like a burglar on my peace, "How glad I am they have taken a fancy to *me*"; or what a secret gratification it is when dear old Nanna says she "would rather hear *me* talk than any one"—how horrid it is for such pride and selfishness to mingle in even one's holiest efforts. So now I oftener pray, "Lord, lead her to *Thyself*; whether I am privileged to be Thy instrument or not, grant that So-and-so's visit or words may be blessed."

Nothing has more deeply impressed upon me the wickedness and deceitfulness of my heart, than my perfect powerlessness in this form of temptation of yearning to be loved, and laying myself out to win love; my only resource is to bring again and again this impure heart of mine to the great Searcher, and ask Him to pardon and purify my motives.

October 1865.—Another summer of great mercy and loving-kindness, though far from unmingled with sorrow, has passed. The shadows which were wisely sent upon my pleasant summer sunshine have passed now. Dear, very dear ones, have been brought back from very near death, and the only remaining sorrow is partly of my own making, and moreover a cloud with a very silver lining. On the other hand, I have not for a long while had so much enjoyment in many ways as during my visit to my sister Ellen. Kindness and affection have been lavished upon me; I have been as it were *acknowledged* by Christian friends in a way I have not met with before, and altogether I have had great cause for deep gratitude. On going to Ireland, I prayed specially that I might be a blessing to Mary F., J. H. S., and A. M. S.; and I hope the Lord made me to some extent the means of strengthening them, especially in reading Scripture

with them every day. M. F. was in sore trouble and darkness; the Lord sent a glorious victory in what had seemed a hopeless struggle, not so much by my words as by agreement in prayer, and she believed God had sent me on purpose for her to Ireland, and kept me there, too, fifteen weeks instead of six. And on the 7th of September, when a heavy cloud had returned on her path, she received the Communion with Maria and me. I prayed long and intensely afterwards with her, and while we were yet speaking, He heard and sent forth His light and joy in renewed fulness. I had a very sweet consciousness and belief that He was really near, *really* with us, and pleaded His own promises with unusual confidence. I knew the Lord Jesus must be there, because He said He would be when two or three were together in His name.

The characteristic of this time was finding more and more that God heareth prayer, and specially intercessory prayer. For another, for whom I have been watching and praying for more than two years, has seen and accepted the atonement of the Cross. The simple belief in the death of Christ for our sins, has wrought what argument never could have done, and she wants no more speculative books, and is willing to be a babe and learn of Christ. I take this as a special mercy sent just now, because I have been very much tried. This trial touched me in more than one most sensitive point, and I have not often felt anything so bitterly and keenly. I tried to accept it as a needful cross; it was a very heavy one while it lasted, and I do shrink greatly from its possible renewal. I am so utterly powerless in the matter, nothing short of God's own grace can avail here. The benefit of the trial certainly was that it drove me to more earnest and continual prayer than ever before, and it is strange but true, that intercessory prayer is generally a channel of personal blessing. It will be all the greater triumph of divine grace when the Lord Himself subdues their hearts. I shall be glad to remember that it was just after this heavy cloud the sunshine broke forth on my efforts for ——. Perhaps God was preparing me for this joy by the sorrow. Anyhow I ought to thank God and take courage, and think I do.

Oakhampton, 1865.

Dearest Marie,—You see we are safe here, and though of course tired, I am not really any the worse, but wonderfully better. I imagine Mr. Crane is very glad to have us back after his lonely evenings. Connie looks as blooming as possible again. Tell M. F. that Oakhampton looks lovely in its early autumn array, and that Worcestershire looks such a *garden* after County Kildare!

My poor Parkes died two days ago, so I was just too late. She was perfectly happy in death, and I feel sure was trusting simply and joyfully in Christ. I want to thank you, Marie dear, for first putting it into my head to visit those rows of cottages.

She is a kind of first-fruits among them. God grant that many more eyes there may be opened to see His salvation.

—— has just called, very ecstatic at having me back, of course, and as eager as ever to get walks and talks with me. She is just a case in which one more especially feels the need of a wisdom not our own. I wish very much I could get her to read the Bible with me, but fear lest the proposal might do more harm than good. It has occurred to me that (as she knows a little Greek) she might not object to read the Greek Testament with me, and so arrive at the object that way—gilding the pill if pill it is! How I wish her parents had not been so vain of her cleverness and taste in books; it might save much mischief if she were not allowed to read so indiscriminately all the essays and reviews (three-fourths of them sceptical) that she can lay her hands upon.

————

(*To E. C.*)

BONN, January 10, 1866.

May this year be one of pressing onward, of clinging more simply and more closely to our Saviour, of brighter faith and warmer love for both of us. And specially do I pray that it may be a year of showing forth His praise by lip and life. Faint as our light may be, if He has kindled it at all, it must shine for Him, and this is to me one of the strongest incentives to careful walking. Only I find so often, so wearily, how self creeps in, and lays its defiling hand on our holiest desires. Oh, to be freed from the dominion of self in its most subtle disguises. One cannot track out all its winding underhandedness, and here one specially feels what an unspeakable, restful comfort it is to have "such an High Priest," all-knowing, all-seeing; because we never could confess all our sin, we do not know a tithe of it, and much of what we do dimly know of it, is so subtle that we could not fully confess it in any language. So we come, even in our blindness and ignorance, and ask to be cleansed from our secret faults, from the imperfectly-understood sinfulness of our whole being, and His blood cleanseth from all sin. I think I feel and realize this sort of thing more and more, and one's utter helplessness; "We know not what we should pray for as we ought" is not a mere generality to me, but a deeply and painfully learnt experience. Only then, this throws up into more glorious light, "He ever liveth to make intercession for us."

OAKHAMPTON, August 20, 1866.

... I have had an unusual amount of headache. I think I shall have more ultimate benefit from Ilfracombe than I found at the time. No, do not accuse —— of laying the foundation thereof. My headaches and languid feelings are the remote results of a long, long spell of troubles which made all last spring

and most of the winter, perhaps the most weary and sorrowful time for such a continuance which I ever passed.

During my week with you I had a most pleasant feeling and belief, that God was giving me the refreshment I needed with His own hand, and I took it as such, and rejoiced in it. But when I got to —— it was only natural that I should feel some reaction, after so many months of sorrowful tension. . . .

.   .   .   .

There are not many things that have made me more vividly conscious of the antagonism of the old and the new nature, as the pouring out of such prayers as may involve suffering in their answers. There is a shrinking, and shuddering, and wincing: one trembles at the possible form the answer may take, and is almost ready to forego the desired spiritual blessing for very cowardice; but yet one prays on, and desire is stronger than fear, heaven is stronger than earth, and one pleads and wrestles to be "purified and made white," even if these are to be inseparable from the following words, "and tried":—"that I may know Him and the power of His resurrection," even if this be linked with "the fellowship of His sufferings."

August 26, 1866.—I have passed a remarkably happy Easter, spent with the Boddingtons; the outward help of the services, and association with A. and E. seemed great. During April, May, and June, verily the Lord led me by a way I knew not, and never expected. I was baffled, wearied, tried, disappointed as I never dreamt I could be. I don't know that I have *ever* felt anything so keenly as the strange trial of these three months, which seemed to deepen every day, and pressed upon almost every hour. It was altogether indeed not joyous but grievous, yet I am quite clear it was good for me. It struck at pride in more phases than one, and laid bare to me a ramification of self-seeking which I had not noticed in myself. It was a trial which must be borne alone—one in which I felt so helpless, so stricken, that I felt it sent me more than ever to Jesus, and it was comfort to tell Him all. I cannot say I had any very vivid consciousness of present blessing in it, or any such spiritual sunshine as at all dispersed the clouds of sorrow. I think the Lord *meant* me to feel it, to be really tried by it. I did plead most earnestly that ultimate blessing might result, that it might *afterward* yield peaceable fruits.

July brought a different story, and a new song was put in my mouth, even thanksgiving. God Himself seemed to give me a time of thorough refreshment at Luccombe, and then a summer work for Him. And again, I must set my seal to the truth of "He that watereth shall be watered." Nothing seems to impress God's truths so freshly on my own heart, as earnest setting of them before another; nothing seems so to quicken me in His way. And so in my quiet walks with dear —— at Lynton and Ilfracombe, and with only our Bibles, I was enabled to guide her out of a very labyrinth of error (from reading Colenso and *Essays and Reviews*), and the consequent gloom and unhinging of her faith and peace—truly it was Christ's recall to safe anchorage. Was this a remote effect of my spring troubles—an "afterward" of peaceable fruit?

I think my joy and confidence rose higher than ever before, and I even lost the fear of death, a misgiving or quiver always having seemed to underlie the thought of *that*. One night, during long and fervent prayer, two things struck me—1st, the words "I will be glad in the Lord"—the expression of will in the matter, why should not I rouse my will to the same, because further it is "glad *in the Lord*"—not in anything to do with self, only in Him, and what *I* am, sinful and weak, alters not the manifold causes of gladness in Him. 2nd, I began to consider God's entire satisfaction in His Son and in His works, and the thought followed, If God Himself is *satisfied* with Christ and His work, why should not I be? And then I felt I was satisfied *with Him* and with His work, and thereout grew satisfaction and peace. And the lurking fear of death seemed to melt away in this new confidence. I know not how it might be if I were put to the test, but my impression is if I were told that this hour, nay even this five minutes, were to be my last, I should not fear, but be very thankful and glad to die. For I never feared death physically, and how can one fear it spiritually while clinging to Christ. I *know* His words are true. May He enable me ever to stay upon Him, and to follow Him faithfully.

Again I must record less earnestness, less disposition to prayer and love of the Word, which so gladdened me all the summer. Who would guess that my mind on a Sacramental Sunday morning had been continually and repeatedly distracted, by thoughts about music, and arrangements of dress! Verily I abhor myself! How much there is in me to be "purified and made white" only *He* knows. My special prayer is that He would deepen and ripen His work in me. I see that even working for God is not, by far, the whole of *living* to Him—I want to *be* as well as do, then would the working, the ministering, be true and pure work for the Master and for Him only.

I was very happy some of the time in Germany. But what I know of spiritual happiness generally, resolves itself into enjoyment of prayer. I seldom or never feel vividly; I do not know what manifestations of Christ are, I cannot say "I have seen Jesus." I have absolutely nothing of that sort to ground any confidence upon. The best and happiest times I know are when I do seem able to pour out my heart before God, when I "come boldly unto the throne of grace." But am I never to get beyond this? I speak to Jesus, and often feel very sure He hears me, but I never seem to hear Him speak to me. "This one thing have I desired of the Lord," and oh so long and so often. "I will manifest myself to Him." He has promised, and I plead it.

————

(To M. F.)

1866.

... I want to send you Psalm 77:9, 10. Are you saying, "Hath God forgotten to be gracious?" then answer yourself as David did, and "remember the years of the right hand of the Most High." There are other instances of our God's eternity and unchangeableness being taken as special comfort in dark seasons, *e.g.* Psalm 102:23–27; Lamentations 5:15, 19; Habakkuk 1:12; Isaiah 40:27, 28. It may be fanciful, but the expression "*the years,*" strikes me thus. They seem a link between His infinity and our *finity* or finiteness. They stretch over in a wide straight vista of succession, having no end to their number; and yet again, it is not an abstract and *ungraspable* thought like "eternity," for "years" are necessarily divisible into days, aye, and minutes, and so seem better to meet the need of a sorrowful spirit which wants a Father's momentary kindness and care. Not "random," you see! But it is "the years of the *right hand*." "For that He is strong in power, not one faileth"—and if that be true of stars and sparrows, is it less so of those for whom He "spared not His Son"? Look at His "right hand," His illimitable power, and rejoice, and *be glad of it*, for it is all for you, not against you. It cannot be against you, since it has been "against the Shepherd" for you. Now add the eternity to the power, the "years" to the "right hand," and then say, "If God be for us, who can be against us?" Romans 8:31. Of whom? "The Most High." Higher than your fears, high in light above your darkness, higher than the enemy. If *He* is *Most* High, most high too in wisdom, in goodness, in love, can any flood of temptation, any clouds of darkness, rise higher than the Rock, than the Sun? And now connect this with Isaiah 57:15.

Then go on to Psalm 77:11, and remember His works, not *only* creation, but see the connection in which it stands in Psalm 111:3. Or rather begin at verse 2, and see how "the works of the Lord" are traced on through the Psalm till they culminate in verses 9 and 10.

As a little corollary to the works, do not forget to include the work He did for you, on August 20th, and Sept. 7th.

I must tell you about ——. Her harp is no longer unstrung, though the strings are struck with a trembling hand, and the melody of praise is built upon solemn and sorrowful chords of deep penitence. That was given me as my summer's work this year—not that I was "sufficient," *I* had often tried before, but now it was "time" for Him "to put to His hand." A series of rather remarkable and most unexpected things led to our going to the sea, alone together, and I asked "this thing" of the Lord. She seemed to feel solemnly that it was a "Now," for her; and her return after several years of wandering after will-o'-the-wisps of reason, and "biblical criticism" and "oppositions of science," all leading her farther away from the "True and Only Light"—has been full and true and deeply penitent. I distrusted *argument;* I felt the heart was more than the head, and that the way to a "sound mind" was most surely found, by going direct to the Cross of Christ. And the felt power of *that* is more cogent than any logic, and so it proved. She has returned to her rest. I was so happy about it, as I need not tell you.

———

(*To E. C.*)

June 22, 1866.

I have lately taken to turn to the character of God for comfort. Would it be like Him the tender Father, to hold aloof from a weary, struggling, sorrowing child, and only be really near to those to whom He has given power of prayer and enjoyment. For if the power and the access and the peace are all His gifts (and who dare say they are not), it would be simply unfair if He gave most love and care, to those who have them, or when they have them. Therefore the only consistent conclusion is, that He is really just as near, just as loving when we do not see or feel anything that we want to do, as when we do. Also, that as His sovereignty and His love are co-equal and universal, they must be applying here; and He only withholds the enjoyment and conscious progress we long for, because He knows best what will really ripen and further us most. And do we not wrong His tenderness, by our distress at not being able to pray as we would when we feel weak and ill? Does He not know, not only that we would pray if we could, but also how much we are losing as to enjoyment by not feeling able, and so I do think sympathizing with us in this distress as much as in any other?

I send you a very simple text which has been to me the last fortnight, as a sort of golden key to many others, or a sort of seal upon them, "I have given them Thy Word." It never struck me so before, the Father's Word and the Saviour's gift. Now I apply this first to the word of reconciliation, the Father's message of salvation through Christ; then to the whole Bible, which this seems to make ten times dearer—(oh, we should never have had this precious gift but for Christ's coming); and lastly to every nice text, every sweet promise which comes into one's mind, it seems one's claim to appropriate it.

———

(*To E. C.*)

Autumn 1866.

I will tell you how I take Psalm 84:9, "Look upon the face of Thine anointed," linking it with "Look Thou upon me" (Psalm 119:132). It seems to me to imply our union with Christ as the Head of every member, even the least and lowest. We come to the Throne of grace, not only hand in hand with, not only hidden under the very mantle of our Mediator (the vesture dipped in blood thrown around us), but actually one with Him, so close, so united, that the look of loving complacency with which alone the Father can regard the Son, must embrace us too. How eloquent a face may be! And so it is, as if the Saviour's very countenance were full of pleading for us, and our cause. So upon this "Face of Thine Anointed" we pray our God to look, knowing that it is perfectly glorious and attractive in His sight, that its intercession must be mighty and effectual, and that it is the very face of our beloved Master "whom having not seen ye love," and upon which the great drops of blood once stood for us.

———

1867.

I have read Robertson, *carefully.* My impression I sum up in the epithet *"painfully interesting."* Though I cordially dislike discussion, yet I should wish when I see you quietly to talk over some of his positions which appear to me untenable. I think his teaching must have unsettled and clouded some minds; better for himself and his people to have remained in the evangelical views he held at Winchester. Among other parallel, though perhaps not similar teaching, I do not find those who endorse it enjoy the restful happiness, etc., which I do see among evangelicals. Only I so fear I spoke too strongly, too dogmatically, too unhumbly, in my last letter; I know so well how little I can wish to be taken as a specimen of an "evangelical," how far behind others I stand. I wish I could "adorn" more. God has taught you in many things more deeply than He has me, and I am too apt to forget this and speak to you in a tone to which I have no right. Forgive me, if I have done so.

Intellectually, I have rarely read anything more interesting than Robertson, and many of his ideas are gems and his language a golden setting of no common order. The book is far too wide a subject for letters, for I should not like merely to skim any topic. I think you could not have had my last letter before you when you wrote. Just look, and you will see that you argue for what I never denied, but distinctly admitted as a truth, the Fatherhood of God. You quote to me the very text which I quoted to you as establishing it. Ephesians 4:6, "One God and Father of all." My position was not, "Is it a fact?" but, "What is the relative prominence which, following the lead of the New Testament, we are to give to it as an admitted fact?" I think we should seek not merely to take our facts but our modes of presenting them from the great source. And what I contend for is that this is not the prominent doctrine of the New Testament, that this is not the message of reconciliation, not the "good news" (though it is good news in itself), not "the power of God unto salvation"; and so that we have no right to invert the order of God's truths any more than to tamper with those truths themselves, and I think there is danger in so doing. With the words before me, "No man cometh unto the Father *but by Me*" (John 14:6), I could not look for blessing, for conversion as resulting from the presentation alone, and in the first place, of the "Fatherhood." This truth, most blessed in itself, can be of no practical avail by itself; and I do not think your experience, or that of any one else, can furnish an instance to the contrary. And why try to ignore God's own beautiful arrangement "*but by Me*"? Is God any less our Father for being so "in Christ?" Is His Fatherhood any less wide and glorious, in that the privileges of sonship, flow through the "Elder Brother," who is *the* manifestation of the unseen Father?

I have been looking through the Epistles, our great exponents of Christianity, with an eye to the "Universal Fatherhood," and the impression left on my mind is that so far from being the special or prominent point of New Testament teaching, it is almost studiously kept in the background; I was really surprised to find how much so. Generally it is: 1st, "The Father of our Lord Jesus Christ"; 2nd, "The Father"—used in direct juxtaposition expressed or implied, with one of the names of the Son, as a distinguishing title; 3rd, "Our Father"—used by the Apostle (I am struck with this) specially as spoken by a Christian to Christians. The only exceptions which do not seem to fall under one of these three heads which I can find are James 1:27, and 3:9, both of which it seems quite reasonable to place under No. 2, the expression in Hebrews 12:9, "Father of spirits"; and strongest of all, but standing unique, is Ephesians 4:6, "One God and Father of all," on which last alone you can take your stand. Now from this I argue that "the mind of the Spirit" is not to give special prominence to this truth, in so far as it is truth. And that there is a much nearer and deeper sense, in which God is the Father of His believing children, seems plain from 2 Corinthians 6:17, 18, where the promise annexed to the command, "Come out from among them and be ye separate," is, "I will be a Father unto you." And it seems to me to be a sort of mockery to hold out, under the semblance of a gracious promise, something which is already in one's possession; I think God must mean something far more here than what is common to all. And I do think we should strive to make all our teaching as accordant as possible with the "mind of the Spirit," trying in our humble measure to give prominence, weight, and emphasis to each truth *in the same proportion*, in which we find it in God's Word. I take my stand by Romans 1:16: "For I am not ashamed of the gospel of Christ; for it is the power of God unto salvation to every one that believeth."

1867.

.   .   .   .

You will hardly understand, unless I could have a long talk, how and why that little book distressed me for you. To own the truth, it so haunted and troubled me that I lost many hours' sleep during the first three nights after I got it. I cannot think how it is you do not see that the nature of poison is to neutralize the otherwise wholesomeness of its vehicle. What is called merely "alloyed," I call Romish errors thinly enough disguised, and veiled by well-sounding language of earnestness and devotion. Their idea of "saving souls" is wide of ours,—what are outward forms, daily services, ritual and music, or even Confirmation and Communion, when they are placed so prominently as *the* things needful? If you can sympathize and fraternize with those who make no secret of restoring Confession and cognate evils, holding Romish Sacraments, giving an ostentatious right hand of fellowship to the Church of Rome (as they do at the very beginning of the book), above all, who want another than the one and only and once-offered "Blessed Sacrifice," then I can only say, How can you expect me to sympathize and fraternize with you? how can we walk together except we are agreed? Of course you may, on reconsideration, explain away some of its speciousness, but I cannot help grieving that you are so easily caught by any seeming "angel of light," and I shall fear for future temptations which the enemy will well know how to contrive for you with gilded errors, and poisoned truths, and "fair show in the flesh." I cannot think how you could expect me to take any other view of the book, and I am only glad you sent it me, because it gives me a new and very special subject for prayer.

And now God has indeed sent me a bright sunbeam, after the heavy cloud I told you of in my last letter, and I take it as an earnest that *that* cloud too, can be and will be dispersed. If you think it will please ——, ask if he remembers giving —— a little copy of *The Blood of Jesus*. For it is that identical copy which has conveyed the message of peace to two hearts—poor Parkes, who died so happily last summer, and now to ——. I had lent it in some fear and trembling; but that little book was God's messenger, and all is changed, and so wonderfully, that it seems almost too good to be true, to hear —— say the very opposite of what she used to, and that so evidently from God's own teaching, for she has never in books, sermons, or companions come under evangelical influence. She knows nothing of what is called religious phraseology, and yet she says the very things which, though so fresh to her, are old to us. I never saw such a distinct instance of the "power of the cross of Christ," and such a revolution of the whole mind by the simple acceptance of His death as our atonement. She wants no speculative books, finds no difficulty in "difficulties," and only wants to learn of Christ. There are breakers ahead as to the next London season, and, having been accustomed to look upon us, as perfect phenomena for not approving of balls and operas, I can hardly expect her to do quite as we do at once, and have said very little about it, feeling quite sure (and I have told her so) that she will find for herself that the new and old enjoyments do not and never can harmonize, and that she will have to choose between peace and pleasures, not as a matter of opinion, but of personal fact. However, of her own accord she wishes never to go to a regular ball again, but does not yet see her way on the opera question, on which, unhappily, —— is very strong.

I think you judged me a little severely last autumn; you would not quite believe what indeed was the truth, when I told you that my music with —— was not an *end* but *a means.* Indeed, my feeling in that duet-playing was very little for the music. I cared far less for *that* than you thought; I only thought it my fairest and likeliest means for getting intimate with ——, and gaining an influence over her. When she became willing to listen about better things, we gradually exchanged the practising for walks, so as to talk. Music was my grappling-iron only; it is not the first time it has been so, and as such I do desire to use it, and feel that if I neglected it entirely, it would be hiding a talent under a napkin.

And with regard to my singing, I have prayed so much and so often on this subject, and the more I do, the more I feel I should do harm to religion by taking a different course. I have prayed to be made perfectly honest with myself, but I cannot see it otherwise. I *never* sing without prayer, and I do believe that in many cases my singing has been felt as His message. I might feel differently about secular music, but *that* I never sing now, as you know. I believe that in such singing I am *speaking* for my Master. I do feel it so, and was told not long ago by a Christian what a privilege and responsibility I ought to feel it to be able to do so. If I ever saw a shade of doubt upon this, I should not hesitate to throw it up.

Ask —— to pray for me. I do so believe in intercessory prayer, and I know she would pray intensely for me if she knew what bitter tears I have shed. Tell her the ground or not; anyhow, tell her I am in what is to me great trouble. I only hope I shall be kept calm and deliberate, and kept from doing anything hastily. So I share in something of your feeling of uncertainty. Do not fear, dear ——, but that your way will be "made plain," only it may not be that you will be shown the opening till you are close upon it. I feel vividly in this most sore trial how true H. E.'s remark is, "that it is the presence of the element of evil which constitutes the real bitterness of a trial."

Do you know what it is to feel a terrible sort of temporary paralyzation of soul, coming when least expected, and when it seems full of spiritual disappointment? . . .

Autumn 1867.

What you say about prayer is just an instance of theory *versus* practice. What *have* we to do with *understanding how* prayer (intercessory, etc.) is effectual? Nothing whatever is revealed about it that I know of, so the theoretical part is undoubtedly among the "secret things which belong unto the Lord our God." I do not care to "*see* any way out of the difficulty"—the difficulty itself lies so entirely beyond the possible range of human vision that one cannot see into it. What does "belong unto us" in the matter is, an overwhelming trinity of *precept, promise,* and *experience* in the matter. We must be right, we cannot be mistaken in trusting to these. Even after Mary had asked, "*How* shall this be?" and had received a fuller and clearer response than we can presume to expect to any of our "*hows,*" I do not suppose she anything like fully understood the how, and her meek answer, "Be it unto me *according to Thy word,*" may well be ours in these most gracious revelations touching the marvellous power of prayer.

I think the "Attic salt" is not a bad idea. But in addition to that, I think I can see a subtle connection even with the "preservative quality." Let our speech be seasoned with such salt as shall preserve both itself and that, with which it is interchanged, from any taint or corruption.

I have got on so slowly with studying St. Matthew, and not at all satisfactorily as to references. Several evenings I have read without even looking for one. I felt as if I wanted only to pray it and feel it, rather than study it; and some parts I wanted to read over again.

I have somehow had plenty of odd and end work thrown in my way all this week, such as illness in various directions. Yesterday four different kinds of "ministration" turned up for me, all so different as almost to stand as types of the chief sorts, which could well fall to me. The last would have amused you. A party of Wolverhampton lads begged "coppers to get a night's lodging," last evening as I was hurrying home; they were ragged fellows out of work, and trying for harvesting. I gave them a trifle, and then talked to them. They seemed astonished, but stood round me like a class, and listened for a good while in perfect silence, thanking me, and wishing me good-night most respectfully when I had done. Three were Romanists; and two more, nominal Protestants, did not even know their clergyman's name, or ever dreamt of going to church. It was indeed seed by the wayside, but who knows— it *may* spring up.

Thank you very much for your note and birthday thoughts. I would far rather be spoken to plainly and faithfully than be made the best of, as some do to me. I hope and believe that I am not deceiving myself, but nothing seems so awful to me as the idea of false peace. Somehow I never have had any clear perception of 1 John 5:12; it does not convey the vivid and distinct realizable ideas to me, which the two preceding verses do, in connection with which, I have always taken it. Why should

I make God a liar by not believing His record? and what is His record? "That He hath given us eternal life," not that I am to carve it out for myself; only to "lay hold" of it by simply taking Him at His word and accept it. This I trust I do, feeling that such is my needy helplessness that no other salvation would have reached me, and thanking Him for such "exceeding great love." Not that I always realize this as I would, nay, it is seldom that it possesses me, as I wish it always could; but when I think of it, it seems as impossible to retract my belief in this blessed "record" as it once did to believe it. Am I unwittingly wrong? Write me a scrap if opportunity. Please practise "O rest in the Lord," "O Thou that tellest," "But the Lord is mindful," and anything you may hit upon that is low enough for me, as I so like you to play my accompaniments, dear Marie.

SHARESHILL, 1867.

I do not agree with you as to Luke 16:2, "Give an account of thy stewardship" being the key to the *primary* and *real* sense of "Not your own." The context (see 1 Corinthians 6:19, 20) is about our bodies being the temple of the Holy Ghost: "And ye are not your own, for ye are bought with a price: *therefore* glorify God in your body and in your spirit which are God's." This of course may be taken to imply the dedication of what we have, *i.e.* property, to God, as a natural deduction from it, but the primary idea is plainly the dedication of ourselves. And I do think, and all my own little experience among poor or unlearned goes to prove, that instead of being "*above* their understanding," nothing will more readily reach and touch their hearts than the story of that love which bought them with such a price; and when that is received and believed, the "Not your own" follows with a force which nothing else but this, (the connection in which God Himself has placed it) can or ever does give. It becomes, not a "highly refined," but a natural and inevitable view of it. There cannot be true and acceptable dedication of substance without dedication of self, (see Article XIII.) and dedication of self, true and unreserved, can only spring from love and gratitude for His "inestimable love in the redemption of the world by our Lord Jesus Christ." You know who first "gave their own selves to the Lord."

If on any drawing-room table you see *Lyra Britannica*, look at it. It is a capital collection of everybody's hymns from Wesley, to J. M. Neale, with little biographical notices of each writer, which are most interesting, and settle lots of doubtful authorships. Papa figures well, and the editor has also inserted me, but in the second of my hymns has made a most foolish mistake, which I wish you would alter for me in any copy you come across. I could not please myself with the last verse, and wrote two versions, asking the editor to choose which he thought best, and cross off the other. He forgot to do so, and so both verses stand, looking as if I had not an idea to spare, and was reduced to writing the same twice over in different words!

1867.

I cannot remember distinctly, except as a "horror of thick darkness" hanging over the memory of last September and October. It was a time of more than common spiritual distress, even like a flood. A letter and some verses of M. C.'s were God's chosen means to draw me out of it into peace and light. This is the first time, as far as I remember, that any quite direct *human* instrumentality has ever seemed much immediate use to me. Since then I have been tolerably happy, though far from well, and it is good for me to feel His restraining hand. It has been trying to me, this ill-health. Very humbling to be a burden and a care, where I would rather have been a help and a lightener. I prayed so much that this my last year at O. might be one of marked blessing to myself and those around me. And yet for six months I am thus held back from anything at all. Is it presumptuous to hope it is that I may myself be *prepared* to receive and give blessing before its close. I see a needs-be in this spring's trial, for I am far enough from being willing to be nothing and no one. Pride and selfishness are indeed hydra-headed, and any victory seems a prelude to a fresh battle. So it is evident this cross is just needful.

But I hardly understand another part of it: I have had to lay my poetizing aside! And yet such open doors seemed set before me. Perhaps the check is sent just that I may consecrate what I do more entirely. I have not the same temptation to vanity as years ago about this. I have a curiously vivid sense, not merely of my verse faculty in general being *given* me, but of every separate poem or hymn, nay every line, being *given*. I never write the simplest thing now without prayer for help. I suppose this sense arises from the fact that I cannot write exactly at will. It is peculiarly pleasant thus to take every thought, every verse as a direct gift; and it is not a matter of effort, it is purely involuntary, and I feel it so. This entirely precludes the old temptation when I wrote in 1860. And yet in spite of this, I trace a distinct desire to have a name. I wonder if this is really wrong in *itself*. It does not present itself to me as a sin, provided the desire is reasonable and not over-eager. And I have many reasons for it, and I do not think it is over-eager at present; possibly because it is not near and tangible enough. Still I see danger ahead in this direction, and I must pray for protecting grace.

———

(*To E. C.*)

1 ELIZABETHAN VILLAS, WESTON-SUPER-MARE,
May 4, 1867.

. . . But I do not regret this spring in the least: I am sure it was far better for me than going on in my own chosen paths.

Is it not singular that, having made it my special and continuous prayer that this year might be a marked one in blessing, I should have been entirely held back for this first half of it, from any effort whatever! But I think I can honestly say I am satisfied, and that God *has* answered my prayer, that He would enable me not merely to submit, but quite cheerfully to acquiesce in everything.

I so fear that you are overdoing yourself, and may suffer for it afterwards. How difficult it must be to have apparently to choose one's own path! But the guiding Hand *is* over it still. I was so struck in reading Deuteronomy 1 to-day with ver. 33—the Lord searching them out a place to pitch their tents in, etc. Does He care less for His spiritual Israel, for the children whom He hath given to His Son? Surely not. I had just heard of mother's having gone to Shrewsbury to see if it would do for us, and look at houses. But I think I thought still more of you, and prayed that the fiery pillar might lead you.

Pyrmont Villa, 1867.

Dear Miss Titterton,—In case I do not *see* you I must scribble a few lines (excuse pencil, as I write reclining when I can). I *write,* but I feel more inclined to give you a loving kiss. How kind of you to send me Mrs. Ashby's allegory of "The Lilies!"[1] It is touchingly sweet and true; and even had you not added to the interest by telling me about the writer, I should have felt that it was no mere fancy, but the transcript of truth graven deeply on a living and quivering, yet loving heart. "At any cost" the blessed Stranger waits patiently, and comes again and again to His children, till they can look up and say it, perhaps very tearfully, but unreservedly. How little will "any cost" seem when His work is perfected *in* us, and, by His work *for* us, we find the "abundant entrance" into His heavenly kingdom! That will be a glorious "nevertheless afterward," of the perfect fruition of His chastening; but there is a sweet and precious "nevertheless afterward," in a nearer future, linked with every trial our Father's hand sends. I think we should look out hopefully and patiently, for this corresponding light, in even the lightest and smallest shadows of life; the least trial has its own "nevertheless afterward" if we only do not miss it by wrong use of it, much more than in the really dark and heavy ones.

Did you mean that you had copied "Lilies" for me? I should so much like to keep it if I may, and it will not lie idle. I know more than one to whom I believe it will be cheering. It did *me good really,* and I thank you so much for it.

1867.

I want you to join the Saturday evening Y. W. C. A. Prayer Union. There are now more than 2000 members, including several of my own friends, whose names are written down in

[1] *Lilies and Shamrocks*, Nisbet & Co.

my Bible. The idea is this. The young women (of all classes) unite in prayer, first for themselves, *i.e.* the members, that they may be personally blessed in work among others; 2nd, for the young women of England as a class, high and low; 3rd, each one for the especial individuals for whom she is interested. The Branch Associations are where young women have prayer meetings for the same object among themselves, as well as the private Saturday evening prayers. My friend Clara Gedge, who asked me to join, has such a meeting herself.

You know how rarely I feel things vividly; but on Saturday eve, I certainly had a very sweet and singular feeling of enjoyment in the consciousness of being one of 2000, all joining in prayer for the same objects. I shall feel it an additional link with you, dear Elizabeth (if any were needed!).

I think it rather better to multiply than combine branches. I find a general reluctance to pray aloud—so I always open with a quite short prayer—ask one to pray after the requests before reading, and now and then I get another to pray after, but often have to close myself. I think the danger of pressing to pray must be judged of in each individual case or locality. I have not found one whose danger lies in the direction of being too forward or elated, but quite the reverse. Mrs. Rogers has all quite poor cottage women; some can't read. The only objection to mixing sets is that if there are fewer present, and all of a sort, one is more likely to get freedom of prayer and remarks. Otherwise I should prefer mixed and larger meetings.

(To M. V. G. H.)

Pyrmont Villa.

. . . Bishop Gobat (dear saintly man) preached twice on Sunday, and on Monday had a drawing-room meeting at Miss Rose's. The girls sang "On the mountain-top appearing," No. 871, S. G. G., to Papa's tune "Zaanaim." This tune is often sung in the English Church on Mount Zion. The dear old Bishop laid himself out to be catechized about Jerusalem, and his work there.

Your poetical request at the Y. W. C. meeting answered first-rate, it amused and interested, and has produced no end of rubbish, ribbon and scraps enough to rig out all your Wyre Hill school, I should think. You had better return poetical thanks at the next meeting—a little gratitude won't be a bad investment, and I think you will get Leamington rag-bags whenever you want any henceforth for your poor in Bewdley.

When in London, I had the greatest fun at my second singing lesson, which, by the bye, although my cold had affected my voice a good deal, was a very satisfactory one. Signor Randegger is in such amusing ecstasies over my verses ("My Singing Lesson," see *Memorials,* page 27); he said they were "so wonderfully clever and witty," and "such an embodiment of his ideas." They have been kept on his table ever since, and shown to everybody, "including nearly all the first profession-als!" That morning he had read them to Rudersdorff and Cummings, and the editor of the *Musical World.* The latter wants to have them to insert. Then the Signor had a great fa-vour to ask. My "astonishing facility" betrayed a practised hand, "Would I favour him with some verses to set to music? Could I bring him something next time?" which of course I shall do.[1] I was seized with a horrible fear after I had sent the "Notes of a Singing Lesson," lest the Signor might be touchy and southern-tempered, and fancy I was making game of him and his instructions. However, I shall be a clear gainer by it, for he is evidently disposed to take twice the pains with my voice. He says I am not a true contralto, but a mezzo-soprano.

. . . I heard Spurgeon one Sunday A.M. *Magnificent!* I don't recollect ever hearing anything finer. Heard Dr. T. the Sunday before at Westminster Abbey, P.M. Service—cold and argumentative, and decidedly unimpressive. Papa's E-flat chant to the Psalms was *grandly* chanted at the Abbey.

That "Tabernacle" is certainly one of the most remarkable sights in the world—the end of the season and London half empty, but it was *thronged,* and always is, twice every Sunday; and more than half are *men,* and intellectual-looking ones too.

I saw Doré's pictures, marvellous colouring, every sort of coloured light seems his forte, sunlight, fairy moonlight, star-light, celestial light, or infernal light! *Illustrated News* critique is most untrue and unfair—would not have given them credit for such fibs. Nothing very striking at Royal Academy.

1869.

I don't know anything that is more refreshment to me than our Y. W. C. A. monthly meetings. The last was a peculiarly nice one—never had so very many nice remarks before, and the sec-retary told me that never had there seemed to be such good and general refreshment and stimulus to the members. There had been special prayer beforehand that it might be so; I am sure I found it so myself, and all I have since met remarked the same. It was a sort of little epoch to me, for I ventured on taking the prayer for the first time! I had been specially asked and always declined; but I thought it hardly seemed right not to take my share, as I am among the older members; it was immense ef-fort to begin, but I believe God distinctly helped me. One spe-cial point I took up in prayer was *home trials*—the daily worry, and wear and tear, which every one I suppose has in some form, which generally can't be talked about and has no sympathy—

no two people have just the same—don't you think there is an immense deal of this in seemingly very happy homes? *I* do. I prayed that all this might be God's chiselling—you will easily follow out the idea of "lively stones"—the Y. W. C. A. Febru-ary subject. We reverted to it again in the reading. As I expect-ed, it was a chord that vibrated. If we pray for our own special needs, it is wonderful what echoes there are in other hearts. If one's feet are very tender and sensitive, it is as bad to walk on fine gravel barefoot as over great boulders!

I am reading the Globe edition of Shakespeare—it was for-bidden ground in my younger days. I have also made acquain-tance with R. Browning's *Paracelsus;* it is marvellous—love *alone* and knowledge *alone* imperfect life—union of both, the true thing. But he is tiring to read, and wants great attention.

I hope you will get to know Charlotte Elliott; it is an hon-our from God to have had it given her, to write what she has written.

March 20, 1869.

I wonder why, "now it is come upon thee!" Some meeten-ing[2] for the Master's use, you know not when, or where, is per-haps to be its peaceable fruit. But oh! I wish very foolishly, and ignorantly of course, that the Master would find some less sor-rowful way.

I had been thinking of you, but little guessing what our Father in heaven was leading you through. I know it is ter-rible—a sorrow from which there is no earthly comfort. But how much heavenly! All loss to you, all gain to him; and by this very grief of yours is he spared the possibility of ever feeling such, if any of his dear ones had been taken before himself, *in-stead* of his going home first. You are bearing it instead. I send you *"A Little While." He* said it, Jesus, our dear Saviour. And it is but a little while, and then He will be with you through the darkest part of that little while.

"Entered into life," how, sweet and beautiful!

I have been thinking how hard it is to realize what is yet as absolute fact as our own existence. That your beloved father has really and truly seen his Master face to face, is seeing Him in His beauty—Jesus Himself; that he has received the "Well done, good and faithful servant"; is actually, as actually as you are mourning below, entered into the joy of his Lord! A week ago with you, now with Jesus! . . .

God must mean some blessing to you by this sorrow. I am sure its "nevertheless afterward," which you do not see, and are not required to see, will be proportioned to the sorrow.

Do you remember sending me, when I was fearing a cloud that has never yet come, "They feared as they entered into the cloud," and the two following verses? You have entered into the cloud, but the voice is there, and Jesus is there. . . .

Don't you find that when one is brought into any new tri-al, it is like reaching a whole new vein of promises, getting into

---

[1] Twelve poems, *Sacred Songs for Little Singers,* were sent to the Signor. The book is dedicated to H.R.H. Princess Beatrice, music by Randegger. Publisher: Novello & Co.   [2] meeten: to render fit, ready

fresh strata altogether; it is not one or two isolated ones, but as if an entirely fresh side of the Bible were turned out towards one, which we never saw at all before. I have felt this three times in a very strong and striking way (as well as in lesser trials), so that now, if any new sort of trial befalls me, I should *expect* this to recur again. . . .

"All your need."—Sometimes that "all" seems so great and deep and varied, such an almost infinity of need; but "God shall supply" not only follows but precedes it; and it is so in our lives as well as in the wording of the verse. . . .

Are you not very conscious of the *detaching* power of sorrow? Ah! but it is *attaching* too—only the attaching to things not seen.

How utterly certain is the promise, " Shall receive the crown of life"! I have often thought that one of the joys of heaven will be to see our beloved and honoured ones so crowned.

(To (the late) J. S. Curwen.)

1869.

During the winter months we opened two nice rooms every evening, and gave free invitation to young dressmakers and others, (especially those living in lodgings,) hoping that it would prove a safe and pleasant retreat for them after work hours. Classes were arranged for each evening in the smaller room; in the other, the girls read, wrote, worked, or chatted. It was not so successful as to numbers as we expected, but the attendance on the evening on which I gave a Tonic Sol-fa lesson was nearly double. I tell you frankly that it was not for the sake of Sol-fa that I began the class, but solely because I believed it was the greatest attraction I could contribute to our little scheme for bringing them within the range of Christian care and influence. My chief reason for adopting it with them, instead of the established notation, was that all the Sol-fa songs are sound and safe; and I knew I could not give them access to anything low or bad through it, while I had no such certainty had I taught the old notation. This weighed with me more than the obvious and indisputable advantages of greater facility, cheapness, etc., which the Tonic Sol-fa system has. There was no question as to the class being attractive, and great was the disappointment when, as frequently happened, the members were kept at work too late and "lost the singing."

One evening two girls came in panting and flushed, about fifteen minutes before the close. "Why, Lizzie and Jane, what *is* the matter?" "We were kept overtime! but we thought half a loaf better than no bread, so we never stopped running till we got here." They had literally run a good mile to be in time for a few minutes' singing.

One nice girl who had just begun forming acquaintances which would have led to no good, and to sauntering about the streets, was attracted to our rooms solely by the singing-class, but soon became one of our most regular attendants at all the classes; and we have reason to hope that she is not only saved from the dangers into which she was rushing, but that good impressions have been made, and a good work begun in her heart. I have no musical results to show, for after about eight lessons, I was interrupted by illness: but I believe that my Tonic Sol-fa class has been a grappling-iron to draw many little drifting vessels close to our side, bringing them within hearing of loving and sympathizing words, and of the One name which is sweeter than any music.

DIVISION II.

LETTERS TO A YOUNG CORRESPONDENT,
FROM 1856 TO 1877.

(These Letters are printed in sequence, so as not to interrupt their progressive teaching.)

(F. R. H. to a Young Correspondent.)

1856.

I am so sorry that I have been obliged to leave your dear little note unanswered all this while; you must have thought you were never going to get a reply. I am so glad that you are not forgetting to think about and seek the Lord Jesus. But you want something more than that, do you not? You want really to find Him and love Him, and know what His great love to you is. Then if you do, you must just come to Him, and tell Him all about it. If you wanted anything that you knew your dear aunts could give you, you would go and tell them what it was, and why you wanted it, and ask them to give it you. Now, you know that our dear Saviour has great gifts for you, and gifts which you cannot do without—His pardon and His love, His Holy Spirit and His grace. Well, then, dear, go and ask Him for all these, and He will surely give them to you, and make you His own happy, loving child. You tell me about your *stones*. What would a little child do who had to go along a rough place over hard stones? Do you not think she would call out to her mother or father, and ask them to lift her over them, or at least hold their hand very tight while she stepped over them? So when you come to a great stone, you must look up to Jesus and seek His help in getting over it, and then you will find the way smoother and pleasanter. Try and remember, too, not to put any stones in ——'s way; you know what I mean. I have written in printing, so that you may be able to read it quite by yourself.

My darling, "be not weary." Is not the Lord Jesus always "the same," whatever you may be? You are looking into your own heart and expecting to find it getting better, and to find comfort and peace in that, and so, of course, you are and will be disappointed with yourself. If you were quite well pleased and satisfied with yourself, you would be all wrong. So give it up, and come back, come continually to Jesus, just as you are. Only you must come; you must not stay away, and expect Him to follow you; you must *come* to His throne of grace, and wait upon Him *there*. I think it is Satan's special device with you, to try to supply you with excuses for not spending calm and unhurried time in prayer. He knows he will not conquer you on your knees, and so he craftily drives you from them. Do not yield to him in this; make it, with God's help, your *special* effort to baffle him here. I believe that your spiritual progress will be just in proportion to your "continuance in prayer." Rouse yourself then, dear, on this point, and *so* you will grow in grace.

Sitting on the Beach, MALAHIDE, IRELAND,
September 16, 1865.

. . . .

This is the very quietest place I ever saw. The hotel stands all by itself on the river, not on the sea, so that one does not even hear the waves; all the people in the house seem afraid to make a noise, the very wind is quiet here, though blowing fresh just round the point; you have no shouting from the boats, they glide up to the harbour so quietly; and I have not heard a sound of wheels yet.

About your going to church on Wednesdays, I am very much inclined to think that you ought to embrace the opportunity, as a privilege and advantage. For you have often told me how your mind gets drawn away from holy things, when you get into full swing with your school work, and that you cannot easily secure any regular time in the middle of the day for thought and prayer. Now, if you really desire to have your heart kept from being drawn aside, and would be really glad to have opportunities of drawing near to God, it seems to me that you ought to be very thankful that there is that one hour in the very middle of each busy week when you *may* legitimately lay aside the earthly learning and seek heavenly teaching. An hour reclaimed from your studies for God's service cannot be called "neglecting" them; and if you go with your governess' sanction, it must remove every shadow of scruple on the subject. Which is most important, an hour's French, or lesson of any kind, or an hour spent in nourishing that spiritual life which is so easily deadened, yet which is so infinitely more precious to us than mere intellectual life? I do not think you would hesitate in the matter, if it were to spend the same time with some dear friend in reading the Bible, or to attend some exciting and interesting prayer meeting; but because the church service is an "old story," one is less ready to feel and acknowledge the privilege of joining in its calm sweet words of prayer and praise, which must always be full of spiritual refreshment to a really *thirsty* soul. You can hardly have a want, which is not expressed in some part of the prayers; you hear His own Word read; you have the most beautiful words of praise, which ever uninspired pen wrote put into your mouth. Only, in going to church, do not let it be a mere form; there is no magic good in your attendance, we only *receive* the blessings which we *seek*, it is "the diligent soul" which "shall be made fat." If you go desiring and praying that you may find God in His sanctuary, depend upon it you will find it good to be there, and prove the truth of His promise, "There will I meet with thee."

I have regularly joined the Rev. Marcus Bickerstaff's Friday Bible class; he questions me the same as the little ones! I like it extremely, and regret very much that I never went before. I prepare Constance for it, and find that I learn a great deal myself in so doing.

OAKHAMPTON, October 17, 1865.

. . . .

I must send you this time, "Wherefore lift up the hands which hang down, and the feeble knees," Hebrews 12:12. You must not give way to discouragement because you have failed in the rules. The prize should merely be the token of your efforts, not the object of them. I think it would be a far higher victory if, after a few failures, which have naturally disheartened you, you go on striving to keep rules, because it is right to do so, not because there is a chance of the prize. Believe me, dear, this would gratify me infinitely more, than if you had not failed at all. For if you go on now, really trying hard, although you say you have no chance of the prize, it will show me that you can strive to do your duty from principle, and without the stimulus of any other reward, than His approbation who "has chosen you to be a soldier."

You do not yet know from experience how much harder it is to do right and to *keep* right when one has left school, and has no outward rules to keep, but only one's conscience and God's Word to follow. Do not fancy that school-life is the hardest in this way; it is far, far easier than the after-life. "Lift up the hands that hang down," dearie; do not let the spirit of discouragement keep you from earnest and confiding prayer. Look up; you are very weak, no doubt, but Christ is very strong; and is not His strength yours, if you will but draw upon it? Your love may be cold, but has His love changed? You find it very hard to stand upright at all; well, that is all right, for we *cannot* stand alone. Do you remember asking me to write a hymn for you when you could not go home for your brother's coming of age? These verses have come to me for *you*.

> "Yes! He knows the way is dreary,
>   Knows the weakness of our frame,
> Knows that hand and heart are weary;
>   He, 'in all points,' felt the same.
> He is near to help and bless;
> Be not weary, onward press."
>
> —See *Ministry of Song*.

January 1866.

I am so sorry to find that I can't manage to see you to-morrow. I hope you will have a nice school half-year. Remember it is your last; so make the very most of it, as an opportunity of self-improvement which will never again be yours. Seek, my darling, to let your light shine for Him; and I am quite sure that it is by watchful, careful walking in *little* things that it must do so. For *one* little slip, one hasty, or idle, or inconsistent word or act, outweighs in the eyes of others almost any quantity of talk and profession. . . .

OAKHAMPTON, March 14, 1866.

.   .   .   .

My darling, it strikes me that you are troubled because you are looking at yourself. Give the time and thought which you are now spending in bewailing your coldness, in looking at Jesus, what He is, what He has done. I know you will think that this is "easier said than done," but here you are met by "My grace is sufficient for thee"; and He who says, "Look unto Me," is also ready to open the dull eye and brighten the dim vision. Do you tell Him all about it, dear? do you try to refer everything to Him? It does not do to sit still and lament only. Jesus of Nazareth is passing by, and therefore "*rise,* He calleth thee," yes, *thee!* "I have laid help upon One that is mighty," says our God. You have already found it true, and have received help from that Blessed and Mighty One. He is the true, the only source of help, so avail yourself of the help laid upon Him. Our only claim for help is *needing* it; you need it, therefore claim it, go to Him for it, and you will find His Word true, "Yea I will help thee." What can I do or say, dear, but point you again and again to Him? For I know that He both can and will "supply all your need," and His *only* condition is "ASK, and ye shall receive." I will pray for you, but oh! pray for yourself; that is the secret of progress, I believe.

June 1866.

I am really so sorry I have not acknowledged the photograph and your letter long ago, but you can't think how occupied my time seems, and more so than ever now the long evenings are come, because I nearly always spend them in calling on the poor people or farmer folks. But your second letter reached me yesterday, and so I must make time. You won't mind pencil for once, will you? for I am writing out-of-doors, because the afternoon sun makes my room so hot. I will begin at the end of your letter in answering it. You say, "I am not as I would be, and I am afraid I shall not till I leave school." Do you know, I can so well enter into that feeling, because it has many times formerly been a temptation and hindrance to me. One feels so inclined to look forward to some fresh outward start, as an opportunity for a fresh inward one. And one thinks one could do better, when circumstances are different, and so one rests on one's oars in the fond hope of doing better *then*. But NOW! That is the word for us, not knowing whether *any* to-morrows are appointed us. I want you to reverse your feeling, to think how only a few weeks remain of one of the great periods of your life, a period whose record will soon have closed for ever. "Gather up the fragments that remain, that nothing be lost," and He will not despise them. Try at least to close your school life, as you would *wish* to have spent it all. And oh! do believe me, dearest, nothing will be a worse preparation for a good beginning of the next stage, than a careless close of this one.

It is impossible to strive too earnestly just *now*, if you wish to start well *then*; darling, I do so hope and pray, that yours may be a steady, consistent, holy, and happy home life, but I believe it will very much take its colour from that of the last few weeks at school.

One cannot jump suddenly into warm feelings and a spirit of earnest endeavour. Was not the confirmation prayer, that you might "*daily* increase in Thy Holy Spirit more and more"?

I am afraid you must think I am always scolding you, and am very severe; but I know you like me to say just what I really think best for you.

ILFRACOMBE, August 1, 1866.

I do not know whether you are at home yet, but you will be when you get this note. And so the great step from school to home life is taken, and childhood passed for ever. I want to give you a motto for the era you are beginning; only an old common verse, but one which is always full of freshness of life and power, one which ought indeed to "work effectually in you that believe." "Ye are bought with a price, *therefore* glorify God in your body and in your spirit, which are God's." If you have, as I believe, accepted God's offer of salvation, you are "not your own." Your time, your life, your whole self are His, His by right, and if you love Him you will be so glad that it is so. And if you do but keep the remembrance of this before you every day, it will not only make you happy, but it will make you holy too. In this "seeking first" to live to Him, because you are His, how many other happy things will be "added unto you"!

You will be thus far more sure of being a happiness to your dear Papa and Mamma than in any other way, and this I know is your greatest earthly object. Is it not nice, that both lie in the very same direction—your pleasing them, and your pleasing "Him who hath called you to be a soldier"? One thing I particularly want—that you should not be "discouraged because of the way," that if you fail in being and doing what you desire, you should not give Satan an advantage over you by thinking "it's no use trying," and so forth. The first time you feel like that, look at Micah 7:8, and act upon it. If you don't mind, I should *so* like to see your examination card; would you send it me by post? It would come safely enough, and I would send it you back again directly. Do not send it if you would rather not.

August 1866.

Thank you for your letter and copy of card. I am so glad about your prize. About the word "common," all I meant, my darling, was, that I was not sending you an *uncommon* verse (1 Corinthians 6:20), that I had not chosen one, which might be quite new to you to dwell on, but one which is amongst the most familiar to every one, and among the most frequently quoted—a verse from the *highways* and not from the *byeways* of Scripture. And I am glad that such glorious words may be, and are made so "common" for us, that they are so dwelt upon and known and loved by so many; and again that they are *common to* ALL whom Christ has bought, that none need be shut out from taking them for their own, and living upon them. May they be life and power to you, dearest, from day to day.

September 1866.

I did not fully know when I wrote to you on Monday, how very poorly altogether you have been, and perhaps I should have written rather differently if I had known. Because, indeed, dearie, I do think it so very often happens that when we are mourning over lack of joy, it is only because our weak frames are holding us back from entering into the joy, which is otherwise free and open to us. And perhaps the Lord Jesus is feeling special tenderness towards you, because you are one of His weak and weary ones. For all your ear-ache and suffering must have unhinged you very much, and *He* knows it. It is very painful, very weary work to feel chilled and strengthless, to have no vivid joy, no light; but has He not made provision for this in that beautiful verse, Isaiah 50:10: "Who is among you that feareth the LORD, that obeyeth the voice of His servant, that walketh in darkness and hath no light? Let him trust in the name of the LORD, and stay upon his God"? He is too kind and too loving, my darling, to have really left you alone; perhaps He is nearer you than ever, and the clouds will some day roll away—perhaps very suddenly—and you will find that it is so. Try to trust and lean and rest, even when you cannot *see*. I send you now a second birthday text, "I will never leave thee nor forsake thee."

1868.

I have not yet thanked you for your dear nice letter. What a solemn time it has been to *me*, a strangely-mingled one of sorrow and thanksgiving. I loved dear Evelyn so *very* much. Dear ——, you have special cause to "give thanks," for you made her your special prayer (Sat. even.). Go on in the strength of this answer, dearest, and pray on for C. —— and for any others, whom God may incline you to feel interest in. Verily, He is a God that "heareth prayer."

I feel for you very much in all your varied anxieties about dear ——. I hope light is arising out of all, and that you may soon have cause for grateful praise. I am so glad that you so wish him to be ordained, and that you *see* that to be "God's ambassador" is a nobler thing than any other calling. I am very sure of it. And not only *here*, but we may remember Daniel 12:3, and wish that glory for him.

My mother wishes to have you here for a visit next autumn (*D. V.*). I do not think you will say no! Then I shall take you to one of the Y. W. C. A. meetings, and hope you will enjoy it.

1868.

I particularly wanted to have come this week to see *you*. I hope now, that having rested so long, you will prove the sincerity of all you say about wishing to improve by setting steadily to work. There are plenty of books on your father's shelves which you have not read; choose something and set about it at *once*.

Indeed, I hope you have already done so. This year or two, is the golden time of your life. Take one solid secular book, say a history, and give it a good hour; then give half an hour to some solid religious book. I hope you have some really good Sunday book in hand, (I do not of course mean any rubbish in the way of religious tales or slight memoirs); if so, better finish that first. I am going to bring a very nice French book to occupy another hour, and that will be enough for a start. I give you this outline just till you have more real assistance to fall back upon. You are a most fortunate girl to have the chance of such, and I hope you will avail yourself of it as fully as possible. But little home duties are before anything else, and *the* great point you have to aim at in improvement is to lay aside *self* in every form. Unselfishness is better than high intellectual attainments, and God's promised grace places this within your reach. And its rewards are almost infinite. I long to see you perfectly, *truly*, unselfish and humble. I shall come as soon as I feel strong enough to ride over on the pony.

August 19, 1871.

I was so glad and thankful to hear of Miss C. what certainly seems like a beginning of good work. Only I cannot quite understand the first sentence; it begins "I am very happy," and yet all the rest is anything but "happy," speaking of dissatisfaction and consciousness of being wrong and hard-hearted, etc.

Did you make a slip of the pen for *un*happy? Otherwise it seems impossible to reconcile it.

Why did you not send me another request for prayer for her? As you did not, and your letter came the day before one of my meetings, I wrote one myself, of mingled *thanks* and prayer.

Dearest, what can one say but the old, old story—*Come again and afresh to Jesus, and at once? Return* to Him, and He will return unto you. And dear one, if He keeps you waiting awhile before He sees fit to let you enjoy again the consciousness of His pardon and love, do not let the hands hang down, but seek Him in *all* His appointed ways, "go forth by the footsteps of the flock." And where are those footsteps? Where do the flock go and seek pasture, yea, seek and find the *Shepherd?*

Think and then *act*. I hope I shall soon hear again that you have returned to your rest, and are leaning on and rejoicing in your Beloved.

I am finishing this at Winterdyne, not sleeping here, but at Lower Park, with Maria.

Pyrmont Villa, Christmas afternoon 1871.

I know I have been practically defunct to all my friends and relations since the hymnal business has been on hand; but now I may be considered come to life again, one of the signs

whereof is this writing to you! Since I began the Havergal's *Psalmody* in June 1870 till now, I have been steadily and *hard* at work without intermission (except in my Swiss tour), so I think I have got off cheaply with the penalty of two or three weeks of being exhausted and tired out. I meant to have written to you on Saturday, to wish you a happy Christmas, but was prevented. But the day itself is not all, dear ——, and so I can still wish and pray that all Christmas blessings may be yours. I have been thinking a good deal of the wonderful exchange, which none but *infinite* Love would have devised. *He* made like unto *us*, that *we* might be made like unto *Him*. You will get the other Association papers for 1872, but I thought I should like to send my own New Year's Message to you myself. Will you pray that God's special blessing may go with every copy of the 5000, which the secretary is sending out to the members? It is a long time since I heard from you, and I should like to know how your are getting on, "being confident of this very thing, that He which hath begun a good work in you will perform it, unto the day of Jesus Christ."

14 Royal Crescent, Whitby, October 1875.

You will wonder at having no answer, but the fact is I have watched and waited to see what the Lord would have me say, and I seem to have *no* message whatever for you! I believe this is as distinctly His doing as if He had given me some unmistakeable word of help for you, and it may be that He thus withholds me, because He would have you give up all expectation of help from others, and say " my expectation is *only* from Him." I can tell you nothing which you do not already *know*, and therefore it can only be the "fresh springs" which are in Jesus Himself which can "revive" you. You have heard pretty well all that human teachers can say—*far* more than I; for remember, I have never been to any convention, nor any single meeting on these subjects, nor had any human word of help whatever, except those letters of Mr. W. And yet, dear, I find Jesus Himself is *enough;* and His blessed Spirit is as free to you as to me. I have been immensely struck with Revelation 3:12: "Him that overcometh will I make a pillar in the temple of my God," etc. Now a *pillar* stands *only* on the foundation, and on nothing else, it has *no* other support, it does not even lean against any other pillar; but *because* it stands thus straight and upright on the foundation only, it is the means of support to other parts of the building. Now I have long been praying that God would fulfil this promise to me, and it may be *one* reason why for nine months He did not let me have even the most ordinary means of grace; and I want you to set about pleading for it too—it is just what you want, isn't it, dear?—to be made a *pillar*, not *in the least* dependent for your spiritual life and tone upon means or influences, or helps, or friends, or meetings, or *any* thing, but to be firmly "rooted and built up *in Him*," without any more bendings or quiverings, and able to be yourself a "means" and influence and help to others.

LEAMINGTON, Christmas day 1875.

DARLINGS,—I only came home on Thursday evening, and had lots to do yesterday, and it was just a question to whom I should send Christmas greetings out of an impossible list. So I decided to send to those who have no one or very few to wish them "a merrie Christmas," and let my own pets who are pretty sure of that same (by God's great goodness) be left out in the cold as far as my postal communications are concerned. And I suppose you know I did not really forget you! and I took it for granted that sisters are not jealous of brothers, either!

I awoke this morning with, I think, a *God-sent* impression on my mind of the connection between all those five glorious titles in Isaiah 9:6 and Matthew 1:21. He could not be *the* Jesus who "shall save His people from their sins" without each one of those titles: each was necessary to His being our perfect Saviour. I can't stay to scribble all about it, but I wish you would all work it out for yourselves, it seems to me so particularly full and precious.

March 28, 1876.

I *cried* for joy over your letter—could not help it! Can it really be? After all my longing that *one* of my relatives should have the glorious missionary call, and none seemed to hear it except Clement, who I hope will follow it—that it should come to you!—My *longing* answered at last in *you!*

I too, do not wish to be hasty in counsel, yet I see not why I should not write at once, what I do not in the least believe I should alter if I waited a year! Well, then, it seems to me, that if anybody may give up home and all for Jesus, you may! It is all very well for good people to think others may go, but perhaps few "others" are really so free to go as you, except the rare cases of having no home ties at all, and really nothing to "leave" for Christ! . . . Could any one but an orphan have a more open path! So much for "free to serve." Now as to "fitness to serve." That I believe is altogether the Lord's affair. If you whole-heartedly put yourself into His hands, as a willing instrument in this great service, I think *no* Christian ought to question whether He will use you or not. He can help you over language, and everything, as much as He helps others. Why not? Only expect everything *only* from *Him,* and nothing at all from yourself, and He will undertake. Never mind about comparative supposed fitness in yourself—quite as well, nay better, that you should see none! so that you may *only* lean upon Him and His grace and *power* in and upon you. It is not as if your desire to serve Him were anything new. For a good while now, so far as I know, you have been honestly, really purposed to "let Him take all:" it is no new and sudden *principle* springing up,

untested; it is only a new opening, a new door. My own feeling rather is, Life is short, and we *owe* it all to Jesus; and if we can and may give Him *next* year, why withhold it, and say, "No, I had better not give that, but see about giving Him the year after!" I do not mean going to the other extreme and hurrying, but every year delayed is a year less devoted to His work, as we cannot add it to the other end of life. . . .

I will not write more now. I little thought what glorious news this morning's post was to bring me! it's the very, very, very best I could have. Nothing could rejoice me more!

LEAMINGTON, April 23, 1876.

You may be sure I have been thinking much about you, though I have heard nothing except the bare fact of your aunt's illness, and your being nurse. It may be that God is going to train you Himself, in ways that we do not know; you will trust Him; you can trust Him—to do just exactly what is right for you—can you not? You have put yourself into His hands, yielded yourself of Him to be His instrument, and there is the end to your present responsibility about it! Now let Him work, and "He will work, and who shall let it," and see if the day does not come that you will look back and say He has led you by the right way! Perhaps the shortest cut would not be the right way! Anyhow He knows, and will lead. I want you when that time comes, not to have the regret of looking back and wishing you had trusted Him all along, and seeing at last how you might just as well have been happy and trustful all the time! but to be able to look back in deep thankfulness to His grace, that kept your trust fixed and unfaltering. Do not fancy I think you do not trust! Only I wanted to warn you, because I rarely know any greater pang than regretting that one ever doubted His wisdom or care, when one sees how exquisitely He was working out His own purposes after all. I have been so bitterly sorry more than once, when, in the darkness, I had distrusted Him, and fidgetted, and schemed, and vexed instead of *resting.* Look the whole thing in the face. Suppose you are kept wearily nursing, with lots of other disappointments for ever so long! Even then I am sure you will say, "Jesus, I will, can, must, *do* trust Thee." And of course He will take care to make the most of His own instrument! No fear that He will let it rust and spoil! But He may put it aside, dipped in oil for a little, and then grind it afresh, and then polish it, and make it a ten times more valuable instrument than it could have been, if He had taken and used it at once! I am quite sure He will do right, and so are you!

May 1876.

I only want to send you one verse which has come so forcibly to my mind for you that I won't write about anything else to-day. Ezekiel 40:4: "Son of man, behold with thine eyes, and hear with thine ears, and set thine heart upon all that I shall show thee; for to the intent that I should show unto thee art thou brought hither." Does "hither" mean ——? I think so for you! So He has brought you there that He may "show unto thee" ("them" is not in the original, you see). Show what? Surely Himself, John 14:21; His glory and greatness, Exodus 33:18, 19; great things, Jeremiah 33:3; greater things, John 1:50. And the command is to you "behold," "hear," "set thine heart upon." It will not be a little, for the "all" seems to imply a great deal. "To the intent"—He has brought you hither purposely with distinct intention. "That I might show" then. He could not have shown you as much elsewhere. He has brought you just where He knows you can be shown most. "Art thou *brought*; does not that just fit? You did not choose or plan or go of yourself. He *brought* you hither; see ver. 1: "The hand of the Lord was upon me, and brought me thither." So far and no farther just now; but I have no doubt whatever but that in His own time, when He has shown you "all," He will go on to the following command: "Declare all thou seest to the house of Israel." Nothing could be a stronger confirmation to my own mind, of the reality of your offer of yourself to Him, and the reality of His acceptance of you, as His "chosen vessel" for service, than His thus instantly taking you apart—taking you in hand. It is so marked, and so singularly accordant with His almost invariable dealing with those whom He means to use. Oh, you may indeed trust Him, and let Him train you for what He most wants you for, just as He will.

OAKHAMPTON, 1876

. . . I have been really *ill* for several weeks, and all writing has had to be postponed. It is quite out of the question, therefore, to write a choir letter. Almost every post brings me requests which I am obliged to decline. I had just begun some little new books for this winter season, but of course have been unable to go on with them, to Nisbet's great disappointment; and when I can write, I think I ought to go through with what I felt God had laid on my own heart to do; as, if I break off and perpetually write one little thing for one, and another for another, as I have been in the habit of doing, I find I break the thread, and get my available time all cut up into patchwork, and can rarely accomplish anything but scraps, which does not seem the best investment of what little ability and less strength God gives me. You, I know, will understand me, darling, though some would not; but even you have not the least idea what numbers of requests I get to write for all sorts of causes and societies, and classes and folks in general! And here am I, just two years since I have been able to do any writing worth speaking of at all!

I have been so struck lately in reading 2 Samuel with the exquisite typical touches. Have you noticed 2 Samuel 19:20?

the *knowing* that we have sinned being the very reason for coming "the *first of all*" to meet the King. No waiting for turns in that court. Darling, how really wonderfully He is training and using you! He has done for you, exceeding abundantly above all I asked or thought for you. I did not expect all this. And more and more may "the name of our Lord Jesus Christ be glorified in you." I am so glad you gave the address. Never mind yourself at all. Just as if He would not use your lips, when you have put them at His disposal. Of course He will!

LEAMINGTON, December 29, 1876.

A very happy New Year to you! Grannie came and asked me "a *very* great favour"; it was, "Might *she* send *My King* to you instead of me, as she knew I intended?" So I resigned in her favour! She loves you very much, and wanted to send it herself. But it will say lots of little things which I should like to say or write to you; so if any chapter seems to suit you, you must suppose it headed "Dearest A.," and signed "Your loving aunt Frances." I like your calling me that so much. I always liked Frances better than Fanny, and Connie nearly always calls me by that name, and so do a good many others.

My eyes are better, but I am obliged to save them as much as possible; so M. kindly answered your dear letter to me, as we were quite of one mind on the subject. Oh, we may surely trust Jesus about it! it does not trouble me an instant for that reason.

January 30, 1877.

This is another "answer"! Being at my wits' end, so many subscribers and collectors lost by death and other causes, and efforts to replace them all failing, I had to tell the Lord that my expectation could be only from Him, and asked Him to send me something "quite unexpected"; and forthwith "quite unexpected" donations, thank-offerings, and increased subscriptions came in, and in ten days about £9 has come *thus!* I prayed yesterday that He would not stop just yet, and so yesterday He inclined you to increase your subscription! The special appeal is indeed sad, is not it? (For the Irish Society.)

I have not seen or heard of the book *High Truth*. Get hold of Mrs. Gordon's new book, *Hay Macdowall Grant of Arndilly* (Seeley); it is most valuable; his letters contain so much that is striking and practical and instructive as to dealing with souls, and the whole thing is intensely stimulating and helpful. Ditto, *Our Coffee-Room* (Nisbet), which is splendid! and especially shows how God can and does use the very simplest words. The writer, Miss Cotton, really never seems to have said a thing which you or I could not have said, and yet the power of God with it was marvellous. Both are first-rate for lending. How gracious of Him to use the trying experience you had about P. B——ism. I hope you will take the meetings, for of course

He will help you. Is not Jehoshaphat nice in this A.M. chapter, "Stand ye still, and see"? "See" how he will help you! You know I am not in the Stepney Union, but in the Christian Progress Union, which for many reasons I infinitely prefer. But we have the same morning chapter as you. I only use the "Stepney" for those whom it would be hopeless to persuade to read twice a day, and see that it rather encourages the notion, that one has done one's duty, by reading one chapter a day! All ought to be reading both parts of His Word, Old and New, every day. But many join both, and I rather think I shall also join Mr. Richardson's just for the sake of gaining any who are too far behindhand to read twice.

LEAMINGTON, 1877.

I can *most fully* enter into your somewhat complicated trials. I will hand on to you what comforted me exceedingly a night or two ago, though not a text. It is the refrain of an old *slave* hymn, "Nobody knows but Jesus"! Does it not draw one very near to feel that? Say that to yourself next time you feel troubled, and have no relief of telling it to a human ear. It *is* so sweet. Just a secret between one's own sore heart and the dear Lord's loving heart! Another thought struck me for you as to the special trial you tell me of. "Consider Him, who endured such *contradiction*"! There is a whole mine of cheer and help in that. And consider further—if it is a *far* keener trial to see— "enduring" it than if you only had it to bear. "Consider" how God the Father for His great love wherewith He loved us, saw and endured all the contradiction of sinners to His dear Son, and let them go on contradicting and never interfered, and let Him endure it to the bitter end, all because He loved us, so He "spared not His own Son" even in this. . . .

68 MILDMAY PARK, October 1877.

Fancy me laid up here of all places, and being nursed with an influenza cold! Nineteen letters this morning, and yours and two more over from yesterday. But I must try and send a line to you. I told dear Mrs. Pennefather, and she is so kind and sympathizing for you. She sends you, "Sit still, my daughter"; and "*then*," she says, "she may go on to the rest of the verse." As for "never," are you not "*ever*" in your Lord's hand, and in your Lord's service? And won't you—oh, I know you will—"let Him do what seemeth Him good"? For He will not only do what is "good," but absolutely best in you and for you and by you for His own glory. Of course, He will! Only you "*let* Him"! I don't see what you have to do with "never;" you have only to do with "*now*." "Now the tuning and the training!" If *He* says "never," He will keep you loving His Word and His will; and if *He* does not say "never," what matter who else says it? "He will work, and who shall let it?" So just leave the "never" in the dear Master's hand, and live in His "*now*," and look beyond to His "for ever" of Revelation 22:3, connected with Exodus 21:6.

Please thank Miss Holland very much for her *lovely* card, and do not I like the text!

DIVISION III.

LETTERS TO A CLERICAL FRIEND AND HIS WIFE, FROM 1870 TO 1875.

December 30, 1870.

I really do not wish any signature but F. R. H. to my tunes in Havergal's *Psalmody*. I do not want to be conspicuous as to them; every one will think it presumptuous to have written them at all, and I would far rather keep out of sight as to them, though I feel the opposite as to being recognised as editor, which is a different thing. For the public who do not know me, my full name would have been an introduction, but my initials would answer no purpose at all. Therefore, I prefer yielding my wishes, and have crossed off my name and initials from the preface altogether, and let the Havergal *Psalmody* be anonymously edited.

My mother has given me too many plain hints, for me to pretend not to know her wishes in this matter, and I have definitely set it before myself, God helping me, that whenever I *do* ascertain her wishes in anything, I will follow them *at any* cost.

But I thus forego an advantage which is not likely ever to be given me again, of gaining a musical footing of this kind, and one which I have fairly earned in all these months of musical editing and composing, and one which might have no small bearing upon my whole future path. It was with my dear father's express approval that I gave my full name to *Ministry of Song*. And I cannot say I see the difference now.

As for making the sacrifice (for such it is under the circumstances), I cannot say I have had grace enough to do it cheerfully, for I have felt naughty and vexed about it. I only do it, because it is right, and because I really wish to please my mother. Will you pray that I may have grace not to do it somewhat regretfully and reluctantly (because it will affect my own song publishing), but to feel rightly and be right in God's sight. I want to make my birthday season a "henceforth" in Christian life (2 Corinthians 5:15), and *really* to live unto Him; not merely have "a name to live."

On Sunday morning that spirit of prayer which I do so value, and for which I do so long, seemed suddenly to come upon me, and with it a special impulse to dedicate myself afresh to Jesus; and so I did, entreating Him to make me more entirely His than ever before. I brought every faculty, every gift, even every member separately to Him, to sanctify each to His service and praise. But since then, I have not been consciously much the better for it, and I have not been as much in prayer as I could wish.

There are many reasons why I like the country better than town, but one of the greatest is, that when I am walking in the country, I am often much in prayer; and in the town, where, of course, I have many home errands to do, and calls to make, I never seem able to get the quiet enjoyment.

You are one of my greatest responsibilities in this now closing year. It is no light thing to have had such prayers, such counsel, such loving watchfulness over my soul—all this ought not to leave me as it found me, and I hope it has really not been in vain in the most important respect. As to cheer and solace and comfort, it has certainly not been in vain, and God knows how much darker the shadows of this sorrowful year would have been if He had not so graciously sent you to lighten them. I am so thankful God has given me such a kind and true friend since my dear father's death.

December 1870.

Is the great darkness passed? I have been praying so much for you, and whenever I pray, that 2 Corinthians 1 passage comes again and again in connection with you. Is it not worth this great suffering if it is laid upon you for His people's sake, as I think it is? And in this sense all that you have suffered in these last few days is indeed the "fellowship of His sufferings." "Fellowship" must be, and is both-sided; and so He, too, must

have had fellowship in your suffering.

I am so glad Christmas Day falls on Sunday this year; it takes off the *edge* of the anniversary feeling.

No sad anniversaries for your little darling—*never*.

I do so pray that Jesus may be so very present to you *both*, that your great sorrow may even now be turned into "great joy." I suppose He can do it, and *so* I ask it.

Do not pray any more, or you will be the worse for it—we *have* committed (the dear sick one) to God; perhaps He would have us now leave it restfully with Him. He *has* heard, and He knoweth our frame.

I do hope you will not do anything unnecessary while you are away. You must need rest so sadly—the present "temples" are only *clay*, and you must not forget that fact, and work as if they were iron and brass. Do not write a word to me which is not actually necessary, till your eyes and head are better.

"O for a lodge in some vast wilderness!" etc. I should have enjoyed living before Caxton. Mustn't it have been nice to have no publishers?

Skating has cured me.

I am going to sing some sacred music, and my father's Christmas carols, "How grand and how bright!" "So happy all the day!" at Mr. Bromley's annual parochial tea-party to-night for 500 poor people.

On Wednesday I am to give an evening's sacred music to the patients in the Hydropathic here. Lately I sang at a large party, invited expressly to hear me; so I took it all prayerfully, and had my own way, and sang my most sacred songs, hoping some might be a "message." When I came away, our clergyman, the Rev. J. S. Ruddach, with kind and grave emphasis said, "I thank you for *your* sermon to-night."

1871.

When you pray for me, will you ask that I may use my influence *always* wisely and earnestly. I think God gives it me, for I should not know how to try to get it! Mr. Shaw said the other day, "You are a queer body, F.!" "Why?" I said. "See, here is every one making arrangements to get a *tête-à-tête* with you!"

It is queer, but a great responsibility. That is why I actually rather dread a visit to a large household; for each one separately, as a rule, seems to imagine they must pour out all their difficulties and feelings to me in private, often down to the very servants; and though I am thankful for the opportunities this gives, you cannot think what a strain it often becomes upon heart and nerves. I hope not many are the repositories of as many sad secrets, spiritual and temporal, as I am.

A dear young friend married the Rector of an immense parish, and feels overwhelmed, not merely with the vast work which might be done, and to which no young lady could be physically equal, but with the sense of being too young to "presume" to try and talk to people and influence them and so forth. She has got disheartened and tempted, and this was why she was so eager for me to come. She was one of what are called "Frances' ladyloves"; for it is a joke among my friends, what a remarkable hold I often get upon young girls. To *me* it is anything but a joke—rather a very solemn responsibility; for the influence I feel and know I do get, is often quite extraordinary and unaccountable to myself.

1871.

I do not think you ever need fear for me again as to High Churchism, for my three weeks' visit here has been about as strong a test as I could well have; and yet I feel I have not swerved a hair's breadth in my sympathies, which are perhaps more strongly and consciously than ever before on the Evangelical side. Here, I have been in contact with the best type of High Church, not merely as to exceeding beauty of musical services, without any absurdities of ritualism, but the Vicar, with whom I have had a great deal of conversation, is just one who would influence me in the matter if any one could. He is candid, gentlemanly, and kind, and I have immense respect for his intellectual powers, and no more doubt of his personal piety and real religion than I have of yours! And yet I feel I am not swayed in the least. He holds the whole High Church scheme, beginning with baptismal regeneration. I never saw before how complete each scheme is in itself. I always wondered why people did not hold some doctrines of one school, and some of the other, but I see now; and so my allegiance is given in more entirely than ever to the Evangelical side, and I never could go with the other in anything, because I now understand that it must be all or none.

We have had some delightful excursions, and yesterday, to my intense delight, spent several hours on the heights of a real wild Yorkshire moor, with nothing but moor and sky, and distant sweeps of hills and heather, and peewits and grouse and bogs and rocks! Just what I enjoy!

On the Peak of the GORNER GRAT, 10,200 feet high!
July 14, 1871.

I must write you a few lines from this grandest of all God's great mountain temples. You never had a letter from this altitude before! It is stated to be without exception the finest mountain panorama in Europe. We slept at the Riffel (8000 feet), and climbed up here for sunrise, starting at 3 A.M. It is now 9 A.M., and we have been up here all the time and alone till a few minutes ago. It is an exceptionally glorious morning, a magnificent sunrise, with all that wonderful rose-fire which I told you about in my "circular" from Bel Alp. And now there is not a cloud, and every peak stands out white, sharp,

and clear against a deep blue sky. We had to walk about a little space of three or four yards (snow being all round) till six o'clock, to keep warm till the sun got power, for all was hard frozen till then,—now it is quite hot. I have been reading and praying in this marvellous scene, and now writing. Of course our guide carried up provisions for us, as we wished to stay, and sent him down; so we have breakfasted on hard eggs and bread and wine!

Dear friend, it is utterly impossible to write hymns here—there is not the remotest chance of one unless we had some spell of bad weather! You cannot think what it is; always something to look at or do—every step needs looking at, it is not like walking along a road; then the flowers are most distracting, myriads of lovely things, then goats and cows, and our scrambling or gambolling about the rocks, not to mention the ever-changing effects of mountain and cloud; one cannot possibly concentrate thought on any subject, even in prayer—ejaculatory prayer is all that seems possible. Perhaps this is the best *possible* thing for me; I feel as if it was restoring, not merely physical but mental balance. At present it really seems as if I could neither think nor write of anything but "Switzerland;" and when I am not out and about, I generally take the opportunity of going to sleep, as E. C. and I are usually up before five and often before four.

I do so wish you and Mrs. —— would come to Switzerland, it is so utterly different from just messing at English watering-places. I cannot imagine why people who can afford it do not come.

It is very difficult to believe that *David* never was in Switzerland!

I did not forget my dear Perry Y. W. C. Association members last night—their 7.30 was 8.10 here (difference of time 40 minutes).

ZERMATT, 1871.

. . . Do you hear anything of our proceedings? I hope you do, and only wish you could *see* us at it! I am thankful I promised —— before leaving England that I would not go anywhere that *I* considered dangerous, for I am sure I have been nearly all day in places which you would think awful! The result, however, is, that I have not felt so well for years, and have quite lost that constant sense of weariness, which was so oppressive to me. Our tour has been so singularly pleasant in every way that it almost makes me tremble, and I have been wondering whether it is a gracious "nevertheless afterwards" of great sorrow behind, or whether it may be a preparation for some great and unguessed sorrows to come. Any special enjoyment is nearly always one or the other as far as *my* experience goes. I am so glad I am coming to see you, instead of going home direct; for last time I was in Switzerland, my greatest anticipation was telling my dear father all about it, knowing how exceedingly interested he would be, and I knew I should feel fresh pain and loss if I went to Pyrmont Villa, which hardly seems home now. The only cloud upon this summer is that even the very independent way in which I am going about (much as in other respects I enjoy it) constantly reminds me that I am an orphan and *alone,* and often I feel it bitterly. I do not think you could quite understand how I mean, for you as a wife have an even nearer and greater and dearer protection than a father; and yet it is a sort of relief to say out this sense of loneliness for once, just for once.

Will you ask your Y. W. C. A. members to pray for a young Swiss girl, waitress at this hotel, in whom I am immensely interested. I have been reading the Bible with her each day, and I do trust she is really awakened, though I cannot say more than that yet. She is a singularly sweet and charming girl, and has been brought up a Romanist (*no* Protestants here), and I found her, not thoughtless, but trying to earn salvation by good works; and *finding* that she "could not be good enough," she fears death; and "why should I not, when I do not merit heaven and must go to purgatory?" So the free salvation is good news to her.

OAKHAMPTON, 1871.

I do feel so much better already for the utter quiet and rest here. Glad as I shall be to see my sister return, I am gladder still to have these three days without needing to speak to any one or feeling that any one wants to speak to me, or wonders what I am about.

I am amused at your thinking my sister Miriam might not *like* me to come thus before her! The terms we four sisters are on, are simply, that each really and honestly likes nothing so much as that each should do or have *exactly* what she likes or *fancies* she likes! We understand each other so *perfectly,* it would never cross my mind "would she like it?" because if *I* liked it she would be *certain* to like me to do it. It is very nice to be thus, *all four of us* sisters.

It was a rather peculiar "need," and God has exactly supplied it. Already the wretched sense of nervous exhaustion produced by the suspense and strain of last week is *quite* gone, and though "the cross is not removed" and I am still in much uncertainty (as no letter has reached or could reach me to-day), I can feel quite trustful and restful and acquiescent in *all.*

It is intensely beautiful at Oakhampton (I always think this part of Worcestershire exquisite), and the conservatory and gardens are delicious.

The servants were delighted, and not at all astonished; it seems my sister told them it was quite likely I might drop in any day. They cannot do enough for me, and I have had quite a battle to make them understand that I really do not require five sitting-rooms! Yesterday I only went to church in the morn-ing, as I was very tired; so I only rested, and planned and prepared for my Sunday evening readings. I have decided on "The Lord's Prayer, and the Promises on which it is founded." I never worked it out entirely yet, and I think I shall enjoy doing it very much. I only took "Our Father" last night, including the (1) Means, (2) the Tokens, (3) Privileges, (4) Duties, (5) Promises of Adoption. The servants were most anxious for some singing from *Songs of Grace and Glory* and Havergal's *Psalmody,* and were greatly gratified at my approbation, which was really well deserved. My sister has gone to work in a most systematic way with both books; they learn a new hymn *and* tune every Sunday, keeping up all the old ones, and the footman learns the bass of every one! No. 642 is a special favourite hymn, and "Hermas" the pet tune. I am delighted to find that my sister is making quite a deaconess of Sarah (the nice maid); she gives the whole evening after five o'clock tea *regularly* to visiting and reading, and very often a whole morning also; she is *beautifully* humble and *thankful* to be allowed to work thus. I find she knows every cottage in the parish, and can tell me about every one; she will be charmed to help me beat up for cottage readings.

This morning I went a delicious stroll; you have no idea how beautiful some of the lanes are, and so full of flowers that I am quite consoled for Switzerland even! They are exceedingly luxuriant and *lonely* and lovely, so I stayed out till near dinner-time enjoying them. I wrote a recitative and another song for my Swiss cantata. I think you will like the latter; it is a sort of sacred mountain song. Then I called on old Mrs. Lane (see "Thankfulness for Crumbs," below) who is nearly blind, who even now recollects and quotes my dear father's texts of more than thirty years ago. I do not mean texts of sermons, but what he gave her when visiting her. She was extremely delighted at my coming, and so was another old parishioner whose cottage I passed and went in to see.

THANKFULNESS FOR CRUMBS.[1]

"Thy words were found, and I did eat them; and Thy word was unto me the joy and rejoicing of my heart."—JEREMIAH 15:16.

An old woman of ninety lives in a lonely country cottage. It is pretty enough, half-covered with roses and honeysuckle, but it is years since poor Mrs. Lane has seen them; she is blind. A few years ago ministering steps came often to her door, but now they are silent for ever on earth, and the little garden-path is never trodden by any lady visitor. While spending a few weeks in the neighbourhood, I went to see her now and then, and at each visit taught her a short text, and other young visitors did the same.

[1] Leaflet: Caswell, Birmingham.

The last time I saw her, she repeated all the texts she had thus learnt with the greatest delight. She seemed to think the possession of these little texts—only about half a dozen—a perfect treasure, and counted them over like pieces of gold.

"Oh dear, Miss, this summer's gone too quick for me; it made the time pass so pleasant, having all them beautiful texts. I couldn't tell you how it's passed away the time. There's '*I am poor and needy, but the Lord thinketh upon me;*' there's a many as don't think about a poor old blind body like me, but the Lord does; and that *must* be for me, Miss, because I'm very poor, Miss, just like it says in the verse. And then there's '*When thou passest through the waters, I will be with thee;*' that's my companion, I call it, Miss; you wouldn't believe what company that is to me, and it seems to take me through all my little troubles of every day; I don't think that's been out of my mind an hour since you learnt it me. Ah! I know what came *next*—'*Having loved His own which were in the world, He loved them unto the end;*' that was right, wasn't it, Miss? I couldn't say it rightly at first, but I've got it faster than any now, since you taught it me over again; that's always my comfort when I feel so sinking like, and I think perhaps it's the end coming near, and then He'll love me unto the end. But that last one I learnt—'*Thine eyes shall see the King in His beauty*'—that *is* beautiful; oh, it *is* a beauty! My poor eyes, Miss, that can't see you, it says they shall see Him; to think of that now! well, to be sure now!" and the dear old woman's voice lowered, murmuring on in broken exclamations of happy anticipation, till she seemed almost to forget her visitor's presence.

What a lesson of thankfulness for crumbs! Far too infirm to reach any service, no one to read to her, her only companion being a somewhat graceless great-grandson, away at work all day; no treasures of earlier teaching to fall back upon, nothing but six little texts, and these filling the poor blind woman's heart with comfort, making the lonely summer pass "too quick," and being "company" to her, night and day! What an illustration of the satisfying power of the Spirit's teaching, and what a reproof to those who, with access to all the full and precious promises of the Word, give scanty time and thought to their appropriation!

And may it not suggest the value of trying to fasten God's own words in the memories of those whom we visit? A whole chapter read and explained may leave a happy impression, but a few words actually learnt are often far more useful. Never mind if the weak or aged memory cannot at first retain them,—go over the same tiny text next time, and then add another, and by dint of constant repetition, it is wonderful how many will at last be retained, while the increasing stock is increasingly valued, and becomes not only a source of fresh, bright interest, but of true, deep influence upon heart and life.

My sister has a weekly reading with the old women of a cluster of almshouses, and has for some time pursued the plan of teaching them a short text every time. They repeat them after her, over and over, just like little children, always saying over in chorus all the previously-learnt texts; and the pleasure which this appears to give them is almost amusing. Many of the texts thus learnt have been indeed "songs in the night," cheering long hours of pain and loneliness, and giving new proof of His faithfulness, who says, "My word shall NOT return to Me void."

1871.

It was so good of you to write to me so gently and soothingly, and yet faithfully; you always do. I write pepper, and you write wine and honey. Oh! if you only knew how bitterly I grieve over my own yieldings to my peculiar temptations, I wonder He has patience with me any more. That text touches the very point. I knew it, and felt it for some time past, that I was not "keeping my own vineyard," always feeling so utterly weary at night that many nights I hardly prayed at all, and the days seemed too full to gain time for what alone can give spiritual strength,—for when I professed to go and lie down, I have nearly every day lately spent the time in writing my own letters, instead of, as I used to do, getting both physical and spiritual rest by lying down and reading the Bible part of the time. So it is no wonder that all three kinds of strength seemed to fail together. If I come back again to finish proof correcting, I must manage better, and shall aim conscientiously and plan carefully to avoid such another breakdown. But though it is so inconsistent, it always seems to me that the very fact of feeling as I do, so utterly sinful and so full of miserable failure, is just what makes me a great deal more anxious about the other vineyards, and also more eager for every help I can have for myself by the way. And it is very often when I am feeling the burden of conflict and the bitterness of failure the most, that I am most intensely anxious about others, because if the battle is so hard even *with* Christ, what must it be *without* Him; and so I could give the world to be permitted in any way to lead others to Him for safety, or *nearer* to Him for strength. And it is just because I feel so weak, and so behind what I ought to be, that such things as his Reverence's suggestions of texts seem so helpful and enjoyable. I *catch* at them, not because I feel strong, but because I feel I am such a weak Christian; and every failure only makes these desires stronger, though they must seem so inconsistent with them. I know it must seem sometimes to you, when I give way so wrongly by pen (for that is less easy to restrain than even tongue), as if my whole profession must be just hollow and unreal because I do not live up to it; but oh, how I *long* to do so! I am sure if God deals with me as I deserve, He will leave me outside all the Mission Week blessing, though I plead *"even me*, O my Father." Do you understand me? It is not easy to put it into words.

PYRMONT VILLA, December 23.

I do so hope you are better, and will be able to get easily and happily through the Christmas time.

How strange it is, the difference in one's *power*, so to speak, of prayer. Sometimes one could pray for hours, at others one's very heart seems withered up, and no prayer can flow out, even when one mourns over it and longs to be able to pray. Is this, too, another *sovereignty* which we have to learn, not merely as one grand truth, but in its every detail. How is it that you seem always able to pray?

Christmas "really come again!" Somehow I never seem to have got the full benefit out of the Holy season. I do so long to realize more of His unspeakable love in ever coming at all to save us, and of the infinite condescension of His taking *our* nature upon Him, and becoming like unto us, that we might be made like unto Him.

OAKHAMPTON.

I wonder if you were praying for me this morning, for the cloud seemed lifted, and I could pray. You seem always able to pray, and I fancy you can therefore hardly imagine the *unspeakable* relief it is, when, after long feeling as if the very tongue of prayer clave to the roof of one's mouth, it is suddenly loosed, and one can pour out one's heart freely and fully and confidingly. I did not feel well, and did not go to church (which is a long walk) in the morning. I went up on the *roof* (which is flat and very pleasant), intending only to get five minutes' refreshment of cool air; a chord had been touched of memories and trials, and, while musing over them, that spirit of prayer which I value more than I can tell you, came on me. I forgot time and walked up and down, praying intensely and with not altogether sorrowful tears, for more than an hour—more than the walk to church would have been. I am sure Jesus was drawing my heart up to Himself. And I had so much to tell Him, so very much to confess, so much to ask, and so much to give thanks for, and so much to *say* to Him which did not come under either of these. Oh, if I could only always be near and find "access"! Sometimes it seems as if I could not pray at all, even if I kneel and cry for ever so long; you can't think how miserable this is. Besides, I never seem able to speak *for* Jesus when I cannot speak *to* Him; and *then,* as I believe I have His commission, "Let him that heareth say, Come," I feel such a traitor and deserter, and I am "without excuse." I do so long to rise to a higher level of Christian life. It is not that I do not know, but that I cannot grasp the great truths to which you point me, and sometimes everything seems to melt away from me altogether, and I seem to have "no part or lot," etc. I can tell others all you tell me, but often all these precious truths seem to slip from numb fingers, and I am left with nothing, and can get no comfort at all but by beginning over again, and coming to Jesus, on the strength of His simplest and most elementary promises (so to speak), coming as a little child or an utter sinner.

February 22, 1872.

I wonder if you will recognise the answer to your prayer as sent in another hymn, "The Infinity of God," and, I think, *higher* form? Strangely enough on Sunday, not a hymn but a *poem* came to me,—certainly one, I think, of my best, and among my longest,—"The Sowers." In the course of this (which I have been giving leisure time to for three days, and hope to finish in another half-hour this afternoon) I found myself led suddenly, and by an unexpected turn, to the grandest attribute, the "Infinity of God," and wrote a few verses on that theme, which are perhaps what you would have liked as a hymn, only that they did not fall into that form, and cannot be used as such. Well now, what if that was the direct answer to your prayer, only not for your benefit, but maybe for the benefit of some who will never see *Songs of Grace and Glory* at all, but who may read this in some magazine, circulating 50,000 or more at a single blow! Can you accept this hymn as an answer?

PYRMONT VILLA.

My daily calendar!

Before 7 A.M. I was ready dressed, including making my bed (only one servant in the house). —7.30 to 8. Read Greek Testament, part of Romans 7 and 8. —8 to 8.30. Wrote to Elliot Stock about pirating my hymn. Copied new hymn. —8.30 to 9. Prayers and breakfast. —9 to 9.45. Consulted my mother about letters, calls, and house errands, and dusted drawing-room! —9.45 to 11.45. Made copy of "My Singing Lesson" for Mr. Bulloch, and wrote to him; corrected a *Fireside* proof; looked over my song, "Whom having not seen, ye love,"[1] which I am going to publish at last for the benefit of the "Female Home" here; wrote to Hutchings and Romer for estimate; and wrote three letters about the "Home" fund—a pretty stiff two hours' work. Then went to call on, and take out for a walk, a young lady whom I have been asked to visit and influence, in a very vortex of worldly society and gaiety. We walked alone, did what I could, and I deposited her at her house again, time enough for dinner, at 1.45. —2.30. Mrs. Beresford, daughter, and friend called, partly about the Irish Society, for which one of them collects. —3 P.M. Wrote to Mr. ——.

---

[1] "Whom having not seen." Sacred Song. Published by Hutchings and Romer, 9 Conduit Street, London.

—3.30. Out with my mother to pay some calls which *ought* to be paid. After these, went on alone to two poor Christian workwomen, a mile and a half from here, with a little help for them from a friend. —Home about 5.45—cup of tea. —6. Finish off two or three notes and parcels in time for post at 6.45.

When I have done this I shall *rest* for quarter of an hour, and then, if not too tired, write a little at my story till tea, 7.30.

P. VILLA, 7.30 A.M. February 23, 1872.

Here is your hymn! I have just finished copying it out, and write at once, that I may run with it to the early post, if it stops raining (it is too far to go if wet). The verses came to me almost exactly backwards, in this order—5, 3, 4, 2, 1! beginning at the end. I don't recollect ever writing dactyls before; but the magnificent words in Exodus 15 came to me *first* as a ready-made line, "Glorious in holiness, fearful in praises"! and I saw the grand swing of it, and did the rest to correspond. The poem is more akin to my Hymn 1025, "Sovereign Lord and gracious Master," than to this subject, upon which it merely *touches*.

I think you are simply tempting Providence by having gone on in this way without any rest or break. I do not believe in "*cannot*;" for it is not merely "where there's a will there's a way," but it will probably come at last to "*must,*" and the "lull in life" which you might have gained benefit by for yourself and others be enforced by illness, which will make it all time lost instead of gained. I feel very strongly about it, because it is what my best friends usually distress me by doing, and I will make no more friendships with people who *will* commit slow suicide. There must be physical retribution sooner or later.

A new idea occurred to me in the night, which I wonder I never thought of before. How would it be to have a packet of "Leaflets from *Songs of Grace and Glory,*" by F. R. H.? Parlane would do them for nothing, and *give* us probably *six dozen* packets of 50 or 60 in each.[1]

I was so sorry that I lost a special opportunity of a "word for Jesus" last night. I met some strangers with other friends. Partly because it was a splendidly *resonant* room, and partly because I knew there were some present who would sympathize vividly with me, I sang my music to, "Whom having not seen, ye love." I am conscious I sang it unusually well (so as, I am sure, you never heard me sing yet). It seemed to have an extraordinary effect on the stranger. He told me he was so unprepared for anything of the sort, and that it did not seem like singing, but something quite different (he implied preaching)—that he positively could not speak for a minute or two, and I saw that his eyes were moist. And yet, with such an

opportunity,—for I believe I might have said what I liked at that moment with *effect,*—I let some little thing break the spell and divert my attention, and let the opportunity slip. Oh, I have *so* regretted ever since that I did not at once speak of Him and for Him as I might have done!

Sometimes this losing any opportunity is overruled to make me more watchful for the next opportunity, but that does not lessen the fault.

February 1872.

There is much prayer going on now here, for a special outpouring of the Spirit. I sent a paper about it to the daily prayer meeting. It has been read out there every day for the last seven or eight days, and most warmly taken up; and this has brought out the fact that the same thing is, in a very special manner, in other minds too—simultaneous yet without communication; so we hope it preludes blessing.

We are solemnly reminded how short and uncertain our life is; for within a week two deaths have occurred, connected with our family,—Viscount Mountmorres, Mr. Shaw's brother-in-law. He goes over to the funeral in Ireland, Lady M. being his eldest sister—real and tried Christian.

Then my brother Frank travelled in wretched weather to Alloa, in consequence of the Earl of Kellie's death. Isabel was very much attached to him (they are cousins), and she feels his death much.

I have just had a curiously interesting letter from ——. He says he has formed a great regard for me, and is exceedingly struck with a poem of mine, which he has accidentally come across. I have replied in a very downright letter, speaking plainly of "Jesus," as he has given me such an opening. So possibly my visit the first day was not thrown away, though it seemed so useless. I think my having recently been over the fortifications of Belfort interested the General, and he seemed amused that I had studied fortifications generally! He is quite the courtier. After two or three calls on his sweet wife, he came and asked me to pray for and with him; it seemed such humility.

WINTERDYNE, April 19.

I was so unusually happy on Sunday and Monday, and have not yet lost the happy frame. I told my sister Ellen about Proverbs 4:11, but I got something else too. I read on Sunday some of Dr. Candlish on the *First Epistle of St. John,* and was very much struck with his exposition of the "Truly our fellowship is with the Father." I do not think I ever had any insight into that fellowship before, though I had dwelt on it as a longing outsider; but somehow it seemed on Sunday eve to be a *real* thing. I felt it was indeed "truly," and I could rejoice in it. I am so thankful to get such glimpses, for I do not have

---

[1] *Six Packets of Leaflets,* by F. R. H. Messrs. Parlane & Caswell.

many, and so I prize them all the more. But I long to be *kept* in "fellowship."

Mr. Shaw and my sister speak often and most affectionately of you; they do so really value your friendship. We have *Songs of Grace and Glory* hymns every night at prayers.

I have been wanting to write to you about a crowded meeting we had last Friday—address by Captain Neville Sherbrooke, very beautiful and earnest. An "after meeting" was held, and many stayed and "found peace." I had never been at one before; it was very solemn. I wanted to remain quietly kneeling and praying by myself, but felt a strong impulse to go and try to speak to some one, so crept away and knelt down by others and prayed and talked with them; the three to whom I seemed thus sent have all found Jesus—tears changed to thanksgiving. You would not guess who one was—dear little ———! She that night really found Christ, and came from the room so happy, and it is evident ever since that she "has been with Jesus." She has been thoughtful and in earnest on the subject for a long time, I think two or three years, but now she *knows* she is forgiven and accepted. Another was a young girl who is fatherless, and so attracted my special sympathy. Was it not good of God to give me this great joy?

Mr. Everard and Captain Sherbrooke have promised to come together in the autumn and hold a mission week at Bewdley, and the Rev. Fortescue is so cordial on the subject.

PYRMONT VILLA, June 10, 1872.

It seems a long time since I have written to you, but I have forgotten neither you nor *S. G. G.!* I have had some correspondence with Nisbet (*i.e.* with Mr. Watson) on my own affairs, and he is so extremely kind and practically obliging, not only about the *Ministry of Song,* but about my new book, that it has inclined me to hope very much that you will be guided to place *S. G. G.* in his hands.

My dear mother was very ill immediately after Frank left, and she is not getting on very fast yet. She is just able to get across into her study and lie on the sofa there. I do so long for her to be well again. Dear Miriam, L. C. has been with us; she is so lovely and so quiet and gentle that mother would not have her little visit put off, though she is not allowed to see any one else yet.

Everything seems to prosper with me as to *pen.* I see "The Sowers" is in the *Sunday Magazine* for June. I wish you would look at an article in it on "Leisure" in the same number, by Dr. John Ker, (who is rather an admiration of mine). I want you to see what he says about the quiet influence of nature, scenery, etc. I believe that is what you and all your party need, though it may not be felt or recognised; and that if you went to some grand fresh scenery, either British or foreign, right away from bricks and mortar and ordinary humdrum routine of watering-

places, you and Mrs. S. would be renovated altogether, soul and body, and E. would be rosy. There! that is my view, and long has been.

I had a little party on Friday, and quite after my own fashion, and it was enjoyed much more than an ordinary party! We had a good set-to at hymns soon after tea, and then got our Bibles and read and talked over part of Colossians 1. The hymns had done all the ice-breaking and thawing first, and so we came to the reading warmed up. I took care to have just a majority of those who were altogether "of one mind," and then threw in three or four of those whom I want to teach to like spiritual things, and I think these last were quite surprised to find how very nice it was! For it was unquestionably much nicer than the common style of evening party—just gossip and showing photographs and listening to solo music. I do positively believe that nineteen people out of twenty, even without being "very religious," would really enjoy joining in good rousing hymns, ten times more than listening to any ordinary drawing-room music. People do not know what they *do* like till one gives them the chance! They have tried soup and fish and joints and entrées and sweets and dessert and wine, but they do not try the other thing. We are to have a grand hymn spree (!) at Winterdyne some evening in the autumn, and you are to come over and assist! We did try the experiment with a party there one evening, and it was so successful that everybody hoped Mr. Shaw would invite them to "another of the same." Somebody said it was "religiously jolly"! which expression by no means displeased me, because it is just what I wish, to get people to connect religion with all that is pleasant and joyful. "Him serve with *mirth*"—do you remember my asking you to retain that old reading? I am so glad you did.

WINTERDYNE, May 25, 1872

... How strange that though we prayed so much for guidance, it should *seem* to have been withheld! Only "*seem,*" though; for surely "I have led thee in right paths," Proverbs 4:11, must follow up, "In all thy ways acknowledge Him, and He shall direct thy paths," Proverbs 3:6. "The day shall declare it." It may be *Songs of Grace and Glory* has fallen into some hands through H. into which it would *not* have fallen into through N., and been blessed "unto salvation." I quite understand *now* about your going earlier not answering the same purpose as later—thy "times are in His hands."

The day I wrote that hymn I had been particularly struck with Isaiah 13:3, and specially with the clause, "them that rejoice in my highness." I thought it a delightful expression, and one much overlooked, and so preferred it to using some expression which might be less fresh and suggestive.

On Wednesday a parochial party of 800 came to picnic here,—a special train was advertised to "the matchless grounds of Winterdyne," and a volunteer band came. The people so grateful and delightful, but heavy showers partly spoilt the day. (Whereupon Mr. Shaw threw open both the drawing-rooms, and sent for me to sing, "Tell it out," etc. Even the staircase and servants' hall were filled with these strangers.)

I fraternized exceedingly with the Vicar, who is a very hearty, energetic little man, perfectly enthusiastic about "Tonic Sol-fa," evangelical, and nice! apparently greatly attached to his people, and they to him. His wife such a worker: has a mothers' meeting, and all sorts of work among the poor women—among other things a *mending* class, which took our fancy greatly. They have a capital large choir, who sang off my "Tell it out" most spiritedly. I am quite sure, now I have heard them sing it, that it is out of sight my best musical hit as to spirit and ring—beats "Hermas" hollow!

The enclosed testimony to *S. G. G.* is nice from the Rector of Bayton and brother to "good old John Davies" of Worcester.

I have written a new song, "Thou knowest," music only, words by Rea; and another, "Singing at sunset," words only (while walking with Mr. Shaw among the beeches).

I have also written a piece for *Woman's Work,* called "A Worker's Prayer." Also two poems; but *no* hymns seem to come to me.

I enclose Mr. Sherwin's two last letters. Is not his description of the blind poetess, Fanny Crosby, delicious?

I have just written a verse-greeting to this "dear blind sister over the sea." It seems I have openings enough and to spare for my pen, now that America is open to me.

> Among Foxgloves and Ferns, DOLGELLY,
> July 5, 1872.

... I was terribly disappointed at missing the Mildmay Conference; and am praying that nevertheless, I may not miss the hoped-for blessing, but that I may find and meet the blessed Master as much alone in Wales, as in the crowd at Mildmay.

I have had so much encouragement lately, especially in my own special department,—young ladies,—that I ought to be very glad and very thankful. You, more than any one, taught me to give thanks. I had a most deeply-touching interview with K. B. before leaving. I ought to have felt quite lifted up with praise for such a miracle of change in her, but was too tired to rejoice as I ought. I also saw and had a very nice talk with A. B., to whom "Another for Christ" primarily refers.

We were detained near Shrewsbury,—a goods train had broken down on our line and rails were obstructed. After sundry signalling and red-flag runnings, we got shunted on to the other line, passing the scene of the break-down, and regaining the down-line safely. It is singular that thus, at the very outset of my journey,—just the same as last year,—I had a reminder of the need of God's protection from accident. It only delayed us half an hour, and I found Maria waiting for me at Shrewsbury, and all else was smooth and prosperous.

I enclose you the opinion of an authoress (a very successful one, too) about *Bruey.* I see my way to *Percy,* another story for children, besides *The Children of the Adoption.* But I am come to Wales for rest!

> On a Hill, near DOLGELLY,
> July 5, P.M., 1873.

How I *do* wish you and Mrs. B. were here. It would be something utterly new to you both, and perhaps would do you as much good as Switzerland, without the fatigue and expense. Summer after summer goes by, and you never get any of the restorative loveliness laid up among the hills; and I do long for a summer to come, when you shall cut the old traditions of that hot and hideous south coast, and the towns that man made, and come and drink in the beauty that "God made." But for once I am very glad you have been to Brighton, for I am so much pleased at your having asked Amy to come. I am extremely fond of her, and it will be an immense pleasure to have her with me this autumn.

I have left everything to the winds! and have told magazine editors that I am not going to be seen or heard of till my *Songs of Grace and Glory* work is done; for I mean to devote this Welsh time to getting as well as possible, and as fresh as to wits (and as to soul too, I hope), as soon as possible, so that I may do *my* best at *S. G. G.* The only things to pursue me are the proofs of my new book, and a few magazine proofs.

I hear most fervent accounts of the Conference on all hands—it must be a wonderful gathering.

Maria and I have been out since a little before 8 A.M., and are gradually making our way back to tea. We camped from about ten to one on a hill commanding a superb panorama of mountains, with Cader Idris backing up Dolgelly most grandly, and the valley opening down to Barmouth, and a shining reach of sea beyond,—most lovely lights and shadows playing over the heights and slopes, and such delicious sal-volatile air, sea and mountain both. I wish you knew the taste of it, just for once. If it continues fine weather, we think of pushing on at once to Snowdon, as fine weather is important for that. We have not seen a single human being since 9.30 this morning! though after having our hill camp we went all round by the "Precipice Walk," which is one of the finest things in Wales, and only three miles from Dolgelly. I *do* like it!

> PONT ABERGLASLYN, July 9, 1872.

I am enchanted with Lord Shaftesbury's speech, and I marked the whole report very carefully.

I do not feel (as yet) anything like my Swiss strength; still I am much better, and can walk seven or eight miles in the course of the day without much fatigue; but in Switzerland I could do sixteen or eighteen in the same way with less fatigue. No, I was not really well when you met me at the station; but I thought you had seen enough of me to know that I always flash up and look quite well under the little stimulus of any short meeting with anybody! But I am ever so much better now.

I am reading Isaiah in a "portion" the same as I read the Psalms last summer, and find it very full and beautiful. I think, thank God, I have rather given up fidgetting and doubting. I really do not see why I should go questioning the everlasting love to me which has given such proofs of my portion in it, by certainly drawing me with so much loving-kindness. So I have shelved that doubt, I trust for ever, and am just giving thanks instead for the great things He hath done for me. The trying to show these things to other doubting hearts has done me a great deal of good. I do not think I ever got so clearly hold of "accepted in the Beloved" for myself as the other day, when trying to show a dear girl who had come to Jesus, and yet was fearing and doubting, that as long as John 6:37 stood, she could not be rejected, and must therefore be "accepted." She grasped it, and so did I.

The last three evenings I have gone out alone from about six till nine, and nearly all the time have been literally talking to the Saviour. I have so much to tell Him, and ask Him about. Only (shall I ever be satisfied?) I want more from Him—I want Him to speak more to my heart. Sometimes a sweet text or thought flashes into my mind, so powerfully and so independently of any effort of memory, that I cannot but take it as His speaking to me; but then I say, "Master, say on; give me more."

When I come I will tell you some interesting things which have passed lately, too long for letters; but God has been letting me lead many to Jesus, and answering prayer marvellously. Has it ever struck you that it seems His way to send such answers chiefly and most often in cases where the interest is purely spiritual and not at all personal, and to send the delays and trials of faith in those cases which are personally nearest and dearest to us? I have noted this in the experience of many, besides my own.

I am sitting on some heather, with a most comfortable boulder for my back, just above Pont Aberglaslyn. We left beautiful Harlech this A.M., took rail to Portmadoc, and have walked from thence. Harlech really is beautiful,—a splendid sea view partly open, partly the fine sweep of a great bay, with mountains all round, culminating in a very fine outline of the Snowdon range, which is seen to great advantage. Then the castle—a real castle, not bits of old walls like Hastings—stands grandly on a prominent rock, and gives the touch of humani-ty and romance, which is all the place needs. Maria and I had quite cosy little lodgings,—a little sitting-room, and a bedroom a-piece, with attendance and all for 15s. a week! No end nicer than 4 guineas a week at that horrid Warrior Square, with nothing to see but houses opposite and a sideways squint of the sea!

On a Rock on the Side of SNOWDON.
July 27, 1872.

Your very kind letter reached me all right this morning. We liked Llanberis so much that we did not leave it sooner than we could help. I left this afternoon at three (the morning was too doubtful as to weather), and have had a glorious walk over the top of Snowdon, which was perfectly clear, and down the Beddgelert side, which is the only one of the four routes which I had not done. When resting on the Snowdon Ranger, an ascent not generally taken, I wrote a little poem, "July on the Mountains."

I am in *first-rate* trim (am writing now at Port Madoc, Saturday, 10 A.M.), and have walked without any halt straight from Beddgelert here; and though glad to sit down after eight miles' tramp, I am really not tired! It is a glorious day—it rained all night, so the air is like crystal this morning. I do not think even Anna Shipton's book, *Asked of God,* contains more marked answers to prayer in little things than I could recount—it is quite marvellous. Constant prayer meets constant answer; and I do think this is the secret of the fact that I seem able to find my way about the mountains like a Red Indian, even when there is no track at all. I do not recollect such a thing as missing my way or getting wrong by even fifty yards. I have been all over and all round and all about Snowdonia, without ever taking any guide, which most people do even for the straightforward beaten route up from Llanberis to the top. Maria is a first-rate walker; but sometimes I go alone, or she meets me on the way.

WINTERDYNE, November 13, 1872.
... I am getting on rapidly and delightfully with my volume (*Under the Surface*). I cannot write a hymn on the "Good Master," but He has just given me something else instead—

"Thou art coming, O my Saviour!
Thou art coming, O my King!"

There will be just ninety poems and hymns, and the book will be one-fourth larger than *Ministry of Song*, though I have left out heaps more. Mother is delighted with my Swiss cantata, *The Mountain Maidens.*

I have just received a letter from the author of the *Old, Old Story,* pressing me to publish my *Hints to Lady Mission Workers* (Nisbet & Co.).

I do so like your thoughts of the temple-service. I fancy it will help me over some of the hewing and chopping, which cannot be very congenial work anyhow! O yes, I do take to that view generally, otherwise I never should have stuck to this work; only, when not feeling so strong as usual, it gets over-clouded, and I only see the worry and drudgery of proofs present and to come. If I could have one week's rest altogether from proofs, I could take the young ladies' meeting; but if an extra treble quantity of proofs come every day, I simply cannot do the two things.

We were glancing over individual results of the Mission Week; and it is a very remarkable, and perhaps an unusual fact, that, so far as any of us know, there has been literally no chaff with the wheat of Mr. Snepp's work here—not one single person who gave apparent evidence of conversion has even in any degree gone back, but rather gone forward. I do not speak of those who merely attended the meetings, and seemed somewhat solemnized and impressed, but of every one, old and young, whom we had any reason to suppose really came to Christ. So much the contrary, that the number has increased instead of lessened; as we know of several who were first aroused during the Mission Week, but found no peace, and who since that have pressed on into the kingdom.[1]

Your telegram just come, dearest Mrs. ——. It is easier to pray than to write, when one would give the world to bring one touch of comfort; for one feels how helpless one is, and one knows how strong and able He is to speak comfort—even now. Oh may He be very, very near indeed, and prove His word to you as He has so remarkably done before. "When thou passest through the waters, I will be with *thee.*" I am so thankful dear —— was not away. I wish I were with you; not that I could be any good, but only that I do so feel for you in this tremendous loss and sorrow. But that precious verse has now another glorious fulfilment; for "Thou hast made *her* most blessed for ever; Thou hast made *her* exceeding glad with Thy countenance." She is *all that* to-day.

Yours very; very lovingly; and in deepest sympathy.

December 16.

How could you think about my birthday when you were in such grief? Thank you very much for the parcel—such

beautiful pheasants and flowers. It was so kind of you. Let me write to you when I feel inclined, without feeling that it is only taxing you to answer. For I know how wearying it is to have to write when one is all unhinged, and so I want you not to do it. It was such a solace to see your husband yesterday. I meant only to think of his great sorrow, and *he* was just as ready as ever to enter into ours. You both have that great gift—

> "A heart at leisure from itself,
>   To soothe and sympathize."

How *our* verse will gain in force and meaning as earthly losses multiply! "Thou hast made *them* most blessed for ever." It will be more and more to us, till He makes *us* most blessed for ever.

I send you a wee hymn, "Jesus only":—

I.

"Jesus only!" In the shadow
    Of the cloud so chill and dim,
We are clinging, loving, trusting,
    He with us, and we with Him;
All unseen, though ever nigh,
"Jesus only"—all our cry.

II.

"Jesus only!" In the glory,
    When the shadows all are flown,
Seeing Him in all His beauty,
    Satisfied with Him alone;
May we join His ransomed throng,
"Jesus only"—all our song!

With the disciples who feared as they entered into the cloud, it was "Jesus only" when the cloud was past. But don't you think that for us it is "Jesus only," *in* the cloud as well as after it?

(*To* ——)

Is it not strange? I had so feared lest I might wander or grow cold here, where there is no external help whatever, and yet God has been so wonderfully good to me (my own classes and readings being, I think, His especial means of grace to my own soul!), that I think I have never yet had a time of such *continued* peace and joy and communion with Jesus. Sometimes I feel so *near,* and nearly always able to realize Him as my very nearest and dearest Friend—more, I think, than ever in my life before. I quite marvel at it. Prayer and His Word seem just unspeakably sweet to me, and I have never before felt so much freedom and joy in speaking of and for Him.

---

[1] Many dying testimonies have confirmed F. R. H.'s words. In 1885, F.'s sister was standing by a dying bed, and repeated the text, "Yea, I have loved thee with an everlasting love." The dying voice answered, "Those were the last words Miss F. Havergal said to me in the Mission Week (1872). She had worked among our choir men and boys. It was the last night, and I shall never forget, when we rose from our knees, how she put her hand on my shoulder and said, 'Bryan, here is a last verse for you, "Yea, I have loved thee with an everlasting love."' She said more about 'that's comfort for all the way;' but I can't be sure of her words—but God's word is true to me now. I never can forget Miss F. in our organ loft."—*M. V. G. H.*

My Friday class has increased to twenty, and some of the most unlikely and hitherto careless seem the most really touched and awakened; and none of my other readings or classes seem left without blessing. I cannot tell you how I long to live more entirely to Him; yet, in the light of His felt love and presence, it seems as if one could not do other than live to and for Him.

WINTERDYNE, September 17, 1873.

May to-morrow be bright among *many* and *most happy* coming "returns of the day,"—bright to yourself and to your dear ones, a golden milestone on the homeward path. Excuse pencil—I write from bed, where I have been ever since I got back from the station on Saturday afternoon! Sudden cold and exhaustion; but I am better. We all hope that dear Mr. Snepp may not suffer from his wonderful work here last week. How strange it was that, after —— was to have had the lion's share, and he only to have *opened* the work, God should have given him the whole burden and the whole reward! It has been what I have heard of, believed in, and prayed for, but never yet *saw* in its full extent,—a real "shower of blessing," felt and seen and manifest and unmistakeable. My sister has come up just now saying, "Verily there is great joy in that city"!—in house after house greeted with tears of joy either by those who have found peace in Jesus for the first time for themselves, or who are rejoicing over dear ones, long prayed for and now brought into the fold. I cannot describe the intense, tremendous solemnity at some of the services, nor the power which accompanied the Word. I can only say, my brightest hopes and prayers as to the possibilities of a Mission Week are all fulfilled at last. I believe that the "ingathering" of this week may be deliberately reckoned as "hundreds added unto the Lord."

I am most anxious to have a very earnest, solemn, and useful hymn meeting (my last) on Thursday night. I am told it will be crowded, and I want to make the very most of the opportunity. Will you pray for special blessing on it, and also that, if it be His will, I may have physical strength for it, and freedom from pain?

October 1873.

Very many thanks from my mother and self for the most lovely flowers. They were too good to keep all to ourselves, so two dear invalid friends shared them.

... Do pray for me, that my little preliminaries at Liverpool may be blessed, even as I pray that your work may be blessed. How sad and strange it was that I felt so "far off" all the while in Switzerland! and how good it is of the Lord to have let me again come "nigh by the blood of Christ," and to have so restored to me the joy of His salvation all this summer!

I am so thankful that God has heard my prayer also in taking away all that sense of excitement which I had while in Switzerland, and the subsequent sense of anxiety and depression; so that I have not only the joy, but with it a far more earnest desire to work for Him. It was a great drawback to my enjoyment of Switzerland, that I had not the same fervent desire to work for Him that I had when there with Elizabeth Clay, nor any of the restful and quiet peace and communion which gilded my former tour. But utterly unworthy as I am of any "restoration," He has now again given it to me, and all this time I have been very happy in Jesus. I do not know how to thank Him enough for this.

I sang my hymn, "Will ye not come to Him for life?" to 150 young people and milliners last night. Some really did "come" at once.

... Will you look at my hymn on "Sanctified" in the last week's *Christian*. It completes the catena of seven in my book (*Under the Surface*)—"Chosen," "Called," "Justified," "Sanctified," "Joined to Christ," "Presented Faultless," "Glorified." You have them all for *Songs of Grace and Glory*.

As soon as I can—to-morrow, if pain permits—I shall set steadily to work at my hymn papers, *i.e.* "Specimen Glasses,"[1] for *The Day of Days*. I enclose a rough list of what I thought of taking. Some of the best of the less-known hymns in *Songs of Grace and Glory* stand alone, or nearly so, under their author's name (*e.g.* 957); so I mean to have about four miscellaneous papers, grouping writers instead of grouping hymns, and giving a specimen hymn or two of each.

I have been so happy all day, even *in* intense and incapacitating neuralgic pain.

Yours in prayerful hope of greater things.

ECCLESTON HILL, October 1873.

Many thanks for forwarding letters and for your prayers. I was wonderfully helped on Saturday evening. The people are the roughest, lowest lot I ever came in contact with, and much depended on a good start with them. So as there were going to be proposals made to them about clubs and doctors and mutual help, I began with a popular song, the burden of which is, "Do your best for one another"; and after singing a verse or two, I called upon the assembly to join in the "chorus" after each verse! This took wonderfully, and they encored it furiously! So I sang it again, with chorus. So my point was gained, and as soon as the next song was announced they cheered heartily. I am quite sure I never sang more tellingly in my life than "He shall feed His flock," and "Come unto Him." Mr. Menzies introduced it with a few nice words, and I had all that rough lot listening all through in utter stillness. I felt I had them so in my power that I could shade off into the softest notes and yet

[1] "Specimen Glasses," *Home Words* Office, 1 Paternoster Buildings.

be heard all over the great place, which holds 900. The silence and breathless attention would have been remarkable anywhere; but fancy these poor wretches, who certainly never heard anything but the lowest songs before! Mrs. Menzies got twenty-seven of them to come to her "reading" last night.

My little gospel solo, "Will ye not come to Him for life?" seems blessed. (See Appendix.)

I am so grieved, though not surprised, to hear of your suffering; only I do pray the Lord to spare you any more!

All that we hear goes to confirm the joyful certainty that the work here was indeed a very great one; and one remarkable thing is, that some who held aloof and would not go even once to hear you, are now stung with remorse at having neglected such an opportunity. Never has Bewdley been so stirred before. Mr. ——'s class last night, where he reckoned on only fifteen or twenty, was a room-full! I hear he spoke most impressively, and that the attendance is likely to keep up.

Did you know that while you were speaking in the school-room, Maria was addressing more than 100 men and boys outside, for whom there was no room inside? They stood in the dark lane for more than an hour listening to her. Mr. Shaw says he has heard her when she did not know, and her power and ability are very remarkable in that line. My sister says she will try to carry on the young ladies' class which I am hoping to form. So with new classes and a prayer meeting, that makes five new means started.

Mr. Shaw intends putting three or four new hymn books in every pew, and adding a large-type copy in each where there is any elderly regular occupant. Each book will have the number of the pew written in it for security. There are 100 pews and some extras, so he will give about 330 copies of *Songs of Grace and Glory.*

Just had such a touching letter from my Oakhampton class, with an exquisite Church Service and thimble! and all their signatures, except the young ladies, who have not been consulted! Poor dear girls, God has sent greater blessing among them than I ever saw before; and I hardly realized how great till I read the names one by one, and felt that I had full reason to hope that every one had now joined themselves wholly to the Lord,—about twenty-five of them,—and nearly all have found Jesus for the first time within the last month!

WINTERDYNE, BEWDLEY, November 20.

.   .   .   .

About Cheltenham, you know how glad I should be to be aide-de-camp to you there, but I am quite clear that I must not think of it. I am not strong enough for another Mission Week, and though I would not grudge the usual penalty of such work, yet I really do not think I am right to risk another of the series of "knockings-up" which have always followed any special work of the kind. One gets weakened, and ground is lost which I may not regain; and now that such marvellously wide doors are open to my pen, both here and in America, I have an extra motive to try to economize strength, not for myself, (at least, I don't want it to be at all for myself), but for my Master. You know how I enjoy it, and I can't tell you the self-denial it has been to refuse four such calls in the last fortnight, but I am sure He is saying to me now, "Be still." It is much harder to say, "Lord, what wilt Thou not have me do?" than the other question.

I have some more good news for you about ——. I have seen some of —— girls, and I think the fruit "remains." They are holding little prayer meetings among themselves, (young ladies' school), on the plan you recollect my telling them of; not one but several little groups meet together and read and pray! They are most eager to see "dear Mr. Snepp" again,—the work among them has evidently been most real, and apparently not one of the whole school has been "passed over" in the shower of blessing.

Then, do you recollect George ——?—that nice lad whom you spoke to on that night, who always stayed till the very last, and always in such distress? This has continued ever since. I was very anxious to see him again, but could not till Sunday. I had him alone, and again he cried most bitterly. I was sure he had really come to Jesus, only he didn't know it! So I said a little to him about "accepted or rejected," must be one *or* other if he came at all; and could Jesus have "rejected," with John 6:37 so plain? then he must be actually and truly "accepted in the Beloved!" I wish you could have seen him—he suddenly looked up, his face still streaming with tears, but lighted up with intense, eager joy—"Oh, I didn't know that before!" "But you see it now?" And I wish you had heard his fervent "Oh yes!" He went away rejoicing, and looks a different boy now the great cloud is gone. He is clearly one of your Mission fruits, for he told me he never thought of seeking Jesus at all till the Mission Week.

Mr. Fortescue says that even if he has to preach to empty benches, he should still have to bless God to the end of his days for the Mission Week! I think those who were "offended" will come back, while meanwhile their places have been much more than filled up by others; the galleries are crowded now.

Thanks, many, for your prayers for my new book. It is almost ready now. You never said whether or not you liked the title, *Under the Surface.* I don't think I shall escape a few criticisms, for some reviewers, who so approved the *Ministry of Song,* will not be so well pleased with such things as "Chosen in Christ"! However, I really think and hope that a candid literary opinion would think it rather an advance than a retrogression from the *Ministry of Song,* I mean as to literary merit; so I ought not to mind getting cut up, if it is indeed for His sake.

Mr. Shaw is going to give an account of what he saw and heard at Cheltenham, instead of his usual Bible-reading to-morrow evening—we hope it will be very useful. He has come back very full of *S. G. G.!* "more than ever convinced that it is Number One," and appears to have spoken his mind pretty freely as to the inferiority of the hymns and the singing at Cheltenham.

He says that the Rev. H. E. Bickersteth's sermon on "Thou God seest me," and Rev. C. B. Snepp's on Ephesians 1:7, are spoken of as *the* two sermons of the week, as far as he could hear. Odd that among so many, it should be the two hymn editors that should have been thus marked. How the tide seems gathering strength! Perhaps it is only beginning, and "greater things" are yet to be seen.

WINTERDYNE, December 5, 1873.

Many thanks for your note and most interesting enclosure. Poor child, surely she will not be left to wander on such dark mountains!

Is it not strange and sweet? God always gives me what I always ask for—a special "afterward," either of spiritual blessing to myself or to others, for every special little trial. And so somehow I felt that the really agonizing toothache and neuralgia[1], which lasted two or three days, would have some "afterward," and it made even the greatest pain actually sweet to bear. And this time I have had a double "afterward"—one for myself, so marked and so sweet. I cannot tell you about it now, only I have never had a brighter or more remarkable one. The other was my "hymn meeting" last night. I never have enjoyed anything so much of the sort, not only that I felt so happy myself, but that I never before was able to speak out quite as I did last night, just as if God gave me the "words for Jesus." And this morning I have heard that one who was present received such great blessing, and was enabled to rejoice then and there in Jesus as she never had done before.

Yesterday morning I had Mr. Shaw's men and my sister's boys, twenty all together, and took "Seeing Jesus" as my subject, starting from John 12:21, only glancing on the seeing by faith now, but dwelling on the future seeing Him: (1) The certainty; (2) the contrasted effects—glory and joy to His own, terror and woe to others; (3) How; (4) When; (5) Results; (6) "Seeing that these things *are* so, what manner of persons ought ye to be?" I did enjoy it so much, and all were so attentive and bright and keen in finding passages and catching ideas, and so still and solemnized when I tried to make it all real to them, as indeed I felt it myself.

I forgot to tell you my chain looks beautiful, and of course I always wear it, and always call it my *Songs of Grace and Glory* chain!

Christmas Day.—Your beautiful letter was a great pleasure; many, many thanks. God does answer your prayers for me; ever since last July things have been different with me, and this month all is even gloriously bright. I have never felt as I do now.

I have just been delighted in tracing a sort of type in Luke 5. One has so long "toiled in rowing," wearily seeking holiness, wearily striving to blend one's will really with the Lord's, yet seeming to have taken almost nothing. Then comes "Launch out into the deep," deep sea of His promises! And *at His word* we do it; and let down the net, not in the shallows any more, but into the deep of His great, grand, full, enormous promises. And one finds one's net filled. Oh, how He does fill it! Every bit of restless longing for—one hardly knew what—taken away, and instead, "satisfied with His goodness." Do you know, I deliberately thought that could not be fulfilled to me in this life; I never expected it at all, and yet He has done it for me—just "satisfied me." I do not mean that this wonderful sense of utter rest and satisfaction precludes sight of and desire for more than I even thought there was to be desired; but this is one of the paradoxes of faith which experience solves. Then, though one does not say, "Depart from me," yet oh how one endorses the rest of Peter's cry! I do not know how one could bear the clearer sight of the sinfulness without the clearer sight, too, of the Precious Blood and its full cleansing power. I had only learnt half of 1 John 1:9, but oh how precious the "and" now is! Then, "they forsook *all* and followed Him." One would like to die for Him but He has not asked that! So one wants to *live* for Him; and there seems to me a breadth and depth in that word which I never saw before. It could never be, but that we are not only to live *for* Him but to live *in* Him and He in us. And the outcome of the "in" will be the "for."

An *external* need has been wonderfully supplied. I heard Mr. Rogers, the clergyman that is to be of St. Paul's, and it was no question of merely liking him, but of very deep thankfulness for such a spiritual provision for us, after all our ecclesiastical troubles and dissatisfaction in Leamington. It was certainly more than I ever expected when I was last at home, that the next time I went to church it would be to sing out of *Songs of Grace and Glory;* so it was very nice to see the blue covers all over the church on entering St. Mary's, Rev. T. Bromley's.

I shall send you some New Year's verses, "From Glory unto Glory," which will tell you more than I have time for now. Several times lately I have felt literally overwhelmed and overpowered with the realization of God's unspeakable goodness to me. I say it deliberately, and with thankfulness and joy for which I have no words; I have not a fear, or a doubt, or a care, or a shadow of a shadow upon the sunshine of my heart. Every day brings some quite new cause for praise; only to-day He has

---

[1] neuralgia: nerve pain, sharp, paroxysmal pain along a nerve or group of nerves

given me such a victory as I never had before, in a very strong temptation, lifted me above it in a way I never experienced yet. And I believe He will "keep" me henceforth as I never before believed possible.

Will you give my love to dear Mrs. ——, and many thanks for the beautiful studs and Christmas books?

Easter 1874.

I must just write you a line, for to-morrow's early post, to tell you what a singularly and specially happy Easter Sunday I have had. Oh, it is so real and satisfying, this wonderful blessing which He has given me, this "life of faith"; test after test seems to have been sent during these last four months.

And now this day, which I thought must always be more or less a sorrowful one, (her father's dying seizure), with always a shadow upon the Easter brightness, has been one of the very happiest of my life. I awoke wondering at the sense of gladness, and I have wondered all day! For it is not, distinctly *not,* that memory has dulled, or that the loss of my father can ever be other than great, for I suppose, except husband and wife, no tie could be stronger; certainly it was my *strongest* tie, and it all seems like yesterday. And yet this depth of bright peace, and utter gladness of heart in the joy of being so consciously and closely and altogether His, and "all for Him," shone away every bit of the shade, and every vestige of "shadow" did indeed "flee away." Now, could any but Jesus do this for me? I know that nothing but Himself could have *so* filled *such* a void. Oh if, instead of arguing and reading books *pro* and *con,* folks would but seek the fulness of the blessing which is to be had!

I never had such a view as to-day of the blessedness of the "evermore" of consecration. I had asked Him to show me more of the meaning of "utterly," and "only," but I had not so much thought about "Thine utterly, and only, and *evermore* to be!"

> In full and glad surrender, we give ourselves to Thee,
>   Thine utterly, and only, and evermore to be!
> O Son of God who lovest us, we will be Thine alone,
> And all we see and all we have shall henceforth be Thine own.

Oh, it was so sweet, so *glorious* to see something of that, the being His very own, the serving Him and pleasing Him, the being utterly at His disposal, and with Him, and in Him, and all for Him, on and on through ages and ages of eternity. My whole heart said, "Whom have I in heaven but Thee? and there is none upon earth that I desire beside Thee!"

It has been such a special day, that I cannot help hoping it may have been given, not for myself only, but to prepare me for some special message-bearing, perhaps only to one, perhaps to many, while I am away. But I never feel eager even for that now; it is so much happier to leave it all with Him, and I always pray, "Use me, Lord, or not use me, just as Thou wilt." Oh, He is so good to me, I did not really expect He would do so much for me; indeed, I really did not know six months ago that such unvarying peace was possible here. I tell you all this because you said you would pray for me to-day; and if this is not an abundant answer to whatsoever you have been praying for me, I don't know what it could be! Only I wish everybody had it, and I wish good people would not think it their duty to stay in Romans 7, as I always conscientiously believed till of late! I cannot imagine how they can think that Romans 7:25 and Romans 8:2 could both describe St. Paul's experience at the same moment. They seem so clearly consecutive and not contemporaneous. So, "Thanks be to God which giveth us the victory, through our Lord Jesus Christ!"

Winterdyne, March 5, 1875.

Will you pray that patience may have her perfect work in me, and that I may glorify God in pain? It is very keen, sometimes seems almost more than I can bear, especially at night; this goes to retard my recovery considerably. I had advanced to being able to creep across the room, now I am carried again from bed to sofa.

No, dear ——, *not* "resignation!" It is brighter and sweeter than that—it is "rejoicing;" even in this terrible pain I could not have imagined that He would have made me so perfectly satisfied and really overflowingly happy in *whatever* His faithful love appoints, even such real and almost constant suffering as I have had these eleven days past,—never had such pain before except for a single day or night. "He giveth songs in the night," and all along has enabled me not to sigh but to sing, "Thy will be done." "Resignation" always sounds to me to have a shade of a sigh left in it. You can't think how glad and thankful I am that He has enabled you to say the same as to the postponement of your work. I have no doubt but that it will prove to be all right in the end; delay in such a matter may so obviously turn out to have been for the good of the work, and save another appendix!

> There is One, so fair, so bright,
>   So good, so gracious! Love, and Life, and Light
> Are His rich titles. Oh, for Him I long
>   To be my Hope, my Joy, my Strength, my Song!
> Earth's shadow melts in conquering light away
> Before the rising Daystar's earliest ray.

> Hast thou not heard, within some sacred pile,
> When hushed the swelling choir, through vaulted aisle,
> A sweet low echo lingering of the song,
> As would angelic harps the sound prolong?
> So through the silent chambers of my soul,
> In calmest melody, Thy sweet words roll.

—————— ❧ ——————

DIVISION IV.

————

LETTERS WITHOUT DATE.

YOU DEAR LITTLE THING,—I call your Bruey card quite touching, it's real right-down fag,* and I appreciate it ten times more than if you had got £5 in nothing but gold; and I have not the slightest doubt that the Master Himself takes the same view of it! The increase is delightful, and quite surprised me. I am sure you have done what you could, and I don't expect more than that! Neither does our dear Master, who knows all the difficulties and hindrances that arise in our bits of work for Him—every one of them. Do not think I have not thought of you all this while; if I had not been so very ill, you would not have had more attempts to comfort and cheer from any one. Perhaps I have only thought all the more. I think I can realize what you have felt and gone through more than you think. And you have felt more for others than for yourself, I know. It is always a little harder lesson to entrust our dear ones entirely to His wise dealing, than ourselves. But He is doing just the very best, the absolutely *right* things for every single one of you, all the time. He knoweth—He careth—He loveth, *all* of you *all* the time.

I have been worse, *i.e.* in much greater suffering, since your Aunt M. wrote, but am much easier this week. It is nearly five months since I was taken ill but it has been all light, no shadow in it, only a new test of His faithfulness, as I am sure every trial will prove to be, to *you* as well as to me.

Perhaps some day A. may be your "crown of rejoicing!" Did not you like Jeremiah 32:17, 27 ever so?

MY DARLING LITTLE THING,—It never dawned on me yesterday that it was going to be your birthday to-day! I'm *so* sorry. The twenty-first too—no longer a legal "infant," which you were yesterday! Well, darling, may you grow in grace and in the knowledge of our Lord Jesus Christ. Do not be standing still, dear; He says, "My sheep follow Me," and follow means going on, not stopping. I want you to follow faithfully, fully, and fast—all three! And of course A. says, "All very well for good

* In F. R. H.'s day, this word meant tiring, tedious work, or drudgery.

folks, but I'm different, *I* can't." No, *you* can't; but then Jesus is able—able to do it all for you and in you. Let Him.

I am writing now because I asked you to pray for my classes, and I have never had so much blessing before, so you must praise now. He "hath not left Himself without witness" in either of my four classes, but my Friday evening class is specially blessed. I have now 24 young women (of various grades), though in this country place I was told there was really no material at all for such a class. But many walk from long distances. Last Friday I had a most wonderful time of blessing; it was my fifth week, and I had tried to lead on and up to what I did. I threw off every attempt at more interest—broke off my lesson in the middle, and made it a heart to heart personal "now or perhaps never" appeal. I never in all my life so felt Christ's actual presence with us, nor saw such intense, perfectly breathless attention; nearly all were in tears. Then I asked all who really wanted to close with Christ's offer of salvation then and there to stay with me. Eleven stayed. I asked them to kneel and remain kneeling, and then I prayed for and with them—not continuously, but with intervals of silence, leaving them with Jesus. Then I went softly round to every one, so softly as not to disturb even the one kneeling next, asking my Master to give me the right word for each. Reserve seemed broken; every one, even the shyest, whispered freely what they felt; four found Him then and there with perfect joy and freedom; four more seemed no less really to have come then to Him, only did not speak quite so strongly; two more who had come before were filled with quite new peace and conscious nearness, and only *one* of the eleven went away unsatisfied, and yet even she certainly was not "sent empty away," for her desires were greatly intensified to find Jesus. Of those whom either shyness or promise to be home prevented from remaining, I have not yet seen all; but of those whom I have seen or heard from, not one seems "left out." Two or three "went out and wept bitterly" for sin; one, "never saw what a sinner she was before." Another has written most touchingly to me; another went home to pray for the very first time; and so great was the blessing, that I fully expect I shall find it the same with the remaining four or five, whom I have not yet been able to see. . . . See now how truly God does answer, and how marvellously He has answered this prayer. I have never had such full and sudden blessing before. . . . And now will you pray that still more may come,— that those who have not yet found may find, and that the new members of my class may not miss the blessing by their later journey? Will you pray that I may have special and clear guidance, what subject to take for next Friday? Will you pray that the two girls I mentioned may really be brought to Christ? because though all souls have equal value, I covet the influence of their position, and long to have it used for Christ. Will you pray that though there seems no one to carry it on when I leave, some way may be opened for them to keep together, and have at least a monthly meeting for reading and prayer among themselves? And will you ask your sister, and any other Y. W. C. A. members to pray fervently that the work may be increased and deepened? And that my other classes, Sunday morning, Sunday evening, and Monday evening, and a large choir practice on Wednesday evening (which gives me opportunity among men and boys, whom I could not otherwise reach), may all be blessed too?

Now dear, for glorious news! Dear —— has indeed given himself to Christ "in full and glad surrender!" outspoken, overflowing joy in the new and blessed service. It is enough only to see his face! Wish I could stay to tell you all about it. He told his father early on the morning of his birthday (told me at eleven o'clock the night before!), and when his father met me he could not speak for joy—he just said, "O Fanny!" and cried! They have all been so happy together, and we have had such sweet little times over our Bibles. It is so different when every one is entirely of one mind. Mademoiselle was, I think, a help, her influence is so decided and so spiritual; since you went she has shone.

And now, when shall it be "full and glad surrender" of yourself to Jesus? When shall it be, not "How much for Jesus?" but "ALL for Jesus"? "*Rise!* He calleth *thee!*" "Arise, shine!" Dearie, when?

My poor dear Little Thing,—I have *forgiven* and will try *to forget* that letter. And *He* forgives and forgets too, because He loves so tenderly. Perhaps we only feel the deep *tenderness* of that love through the consciousness of failure and sin. I don't think the angels can realize it as we do. Now one can only pray that it may be overruled for all of you. Do not vex about it. God can and does bring real good out of mistakes, and blessing out of suffering. I know He will *so* comfort and bless His own dear child E., that she will be a blessed gainer by it. But *her* suffering is perhaps a harder lesson of patience and trust for *you*, dear little thing. Pray for her and trust for

her, and *you* will have a share of the blessing that God means for her.

I have just sent off about 380 little bouquets to the Flower Mission at Mildmay, 210 of which were gathered and made up by *the servants* at Oakhampton! the rest by various nieces and young friends. The servants took to the notion with regular enthusiasm—it was quite delightful! I could not do much but set the thing going, and probably got more helped than if I had been able to gather *ad lib.* myself! Some of the nosegays were lovely, and the *ensemble* when got together ready to pack, was quite a sight.

I see *no* scriptural ground to suppose sin can ever be "eradicated," *i.e. so* destroyed that it would not instantly *revive* if the cleansing and the keeping were withdrawn, and we ran from under the wing of Jesus, as Mr. Everard phrased it.

I had not got very much out of the Word for a few days, so I asked Him to send me something special, and lit upon Luke 5:4–11. "The deep" of His promises, and the "toiling all night," and the "at Thy word,"—it is lovely.

My path would be a hopeless dilemma, but for trust in momentary guidance.

. . . This is only a scrap to wish you all good things for the New Year. For "all *are* yours," so how safely we may wish it to one of *His* dear ones. My pen has just involuntarily paused for a few moments—such a thrill came over me of thinking how He loves *you*—how He could not do without *you*—how His very glory would be incomplete not merely without you in heaven, but without the glory which you are ordained, and *made on purpose* to bring to Him here. And you will guess that *my* heart does not love you the less for this strange sudden glimpse of how He loves you! . . .

Very many happy returns of the day to you! I send you "As ye have received Christ Jesus the Lord, so walk ye in Him." Will you let that *as* and *so* often come into your thoughts through this year? It will be a test and a stimulus, and perhaps a help towards my finding much to commend and little to blame when I come again! You know how pleasant it was to me to find it so the last time! And I do not think that He who loves you and gave Himself for you can take *less* interest in your "walk" than I do!

Your letter to —— is very nice indeed, and quite the best tack to go upon with her. Singularly enough, some one of whom I had often heard has been staying here two days, and who at the same age was much such another. She was telling me deeply interesting accounts of how for years, she went off upon all these new doctrines, how utterly she believed them, fancying she had been led into them, after wrestling for whole nights in prayer and tears; and how earnestly she tried to persuade others. Now, after keen and deep trials she has fully come back to the old paths, and bitterly regrets these wanderings, only that she thinks they may help her to help others who are similarly restless. I wished you could have met her—it would have strengthened you, I think; and she is a person of very unusual power and knowledge, taking large Bible classes. I was so astonished at all this, having heard so much of her in her former phase, and not having heard of her return to quiet, steady Church of England doctrine. The enclosed may help you if you hear hasty things about the Church of England, and the Bennett Judgment—read it carefully to please me!

Yes, dearest, seek Jesus only, seek Him in His Word and in prayer, just *Himself,* and you will find it a thousand times more profitable. I was cutting out hymns the other day, and could not help cutting out this old verse with reference to all you told me of your long earnest wrestlings:

> "Were half the breath thus vainly spent,
> To heaven in supplication sent,
> Your cheerful song would often be,
> 'Hear what the Lord has done for me!'"

Meanwhile, I do so thank God that He has *kept* you, for it is indeed a "keeping."

I am delighted at your reading with ——; it will be better for both of you, and you will find it both more interesting and easier to persevere in. Only I hope you have some other book in hand to read by yourself as well. I do not think any book will seem so difficult to you after you have mastered Butler's *Analogy.*

My poor darling, do not stay away from His table, because you are feeling something of the unworthiness and sinfulness which we all have to find out in ourselves. You do want to come to Jesus, to be really His, to follow Him—I know you do. And the holy communion is just to remind us of His death, to be a *pledge* of His love, which is just what you do want to be reminded of, do you not? And feeling sorrowful and sinful is all the more reason why you may come. Not that I want to dissuade you from dealing very plainly with yourself: *anything* is better than false peace; but the Lord Jesus has true peace for you—go, to Him for it, just as if you had never gone before—lay your heart quite open before Him, "tell Him all you feel and all you do not feel," and look for the answer not in your own heart and feelings (perhaps that has been your mistake), but in His Word. *See* what He says, and take that as His answer, for His Word cannot change or pass away.

I have been waiting for days expecting my friend to send me mottoes for 1868; they are only just come—"And now, Lord, what wait I for? My hope is in Thee," and "Surely I come quickly." Will you take them for yourself, dearie? For our hope needs to be *only* in Thee, and we want to learn to wait for Him and for nothing else. And ought not the remembrance of His "*surely*" to stir us up to watchfulness and earnestness, and to lead us on to such expectant love that we may be able to give the blessed answer, "Even so come, Lord Jesus!"

———

(*To M. F.*)

Shareshill Parsonage.

If I had forgotten my promise of writing to you, the "Cead mille failthe," which smiled at me on my return home would have reminded me of it. But I did not intend to forget! Your love finds indeed "Cead mille failthe" in my heart. . . .[1]

How I should like you to see my children (nieces). Both are rather pretty and very tall; Evelyn, though only twelve last birthday, is just my height. She has been very delicate for a long time, and can seldom do regular lessons. . . . I do think God has begun His own work in her, though very gradually, and that He will carry it on. She feels her delicacy very much, specially as it keeps her back in her lessons, and occasions frequent disappointments as to little pleasures; but this training is evidently good for her, and I think she is beginning thus early to spell the great lesson, "Thy will be done."

She is very thoughtful and active in mind, and has a curious liking for any sort of theological questions, so that often I am obliged to go into things with her, for the sake of setting her mind at rest, which I should hardly have expected to converse about with girls of eighteen or twenty. Last summer, a story book of Miss S——, of very High Church tendency, was given her, which I was sorry for, but could not help. She knew I did not like the book, and asked why. I merely said, that if she read the book as a mere story, she might not notice the evil in it; and so I supposed and hoped it would do her no harm, but that she had better show me any passages which she felt doubtful about. Well, I don't think there was one error but what she discovered and showed me, perceiving the *tendency* of many fair-sounding passages with an acuteness which surprised me, remarking at the end that she thought the tendency of the whole book was to make one think that our salvation depends rather on what we can do for ourselves, or what the Church can do for us, than on what the Lord Jesus has done, which was hitting the very mark. Connie is sharp enough at lessons, but has not the same sort of development as E. She is a remarkably handy and active child, can turn her hand to anything, and has a wonderful notion of what is the right thing to do at once in any little mishap. She is very bright and merry and energetic. C. has a little class at the Sunday school, and flatters herself that she shall get the children on wonderfully, so that Minny "will see the difference" when they go up into her class. She teaches them a Bible story every Sunday out of *Line upon Line,* and I wanted her to make a point of asking them the nice little questions upon it at the

———

[1] *Cead mille failthe* (Gaelic): a hundred thousand welcomes.

end of the book; but she soon after declined them, saying "she found the children understood best what she asked them out of her own head!" She has a strongly practical turn of mind, contra-distinguished from Evelyn's poetical one; an amusing instance thereof was at the time of the earthquake, which we felt so strongly at O. two years ago: her first remark about it was, "I wonder if it has shook any peaches down?"!

————

(*To M. F.*)

Yours is a strangely tried life, dear M.; it seems wonderful that so much should be laid upon you. Somehow I always feel it so much harder to see that trouble or suffering is right, and best for others than for one's self. I think one sees one's own "needs-be" better than other people's. If yours is a pre-eminence of suffering, there must also be pre-eminence of love and care. I have thought of you lately, when our little J. was so ill, how though the others were poorly, yet a double, treble portion of thought and watchfulness was given to him, because he was more suffering than they. And I loved to think what special love must be hovering, brooding over your many trials. Join me in thinking of 1 Peter 1:5, 8 to-morrow evening at seven o'clock. Some day I will sing it you; the passage has haunted me so that I *must* set it to music. How I wish I knew all that you know of the "joy unspeakable"! What a marvellous bit that is—"the trial of your faith being much more precious," etc.

I am so glad your "joy-bells" of music definition reached me in time to add to the list; it is the prettiest of all. I wondered no one considered what music is to the blind, so I am going to put "Sunshine for the sightless." I am not good at definitions, but why did not some one speak of music as being the only universal language, understood by men of every tongue, and by the angels too? It is a sort of alphabet of the language of heaven too, not any more equal to it, of course, than an A B C book is to Milton, but a sort of introduction. At least it ought to be so. Trench (referring to a different subject) says something about the manifold provisions, which Infinite Love has made for the finer needs of our nature, and I think music is one of the strongest instances of that. Why should such a mysteriously subtle and unaccountable gratification have been provided for us? Verily, He is Love! Finally, I give you an analogy to think out—that—between light and music, or say rather between colour and music.

————

(*To M. F.*)

Your sweet and most lovely card was one of the rays, which helped to cheer an otherwise sorrowful birthday, and came as a message from the One who cannot pass away. May it come back to your heart, dear M., with its strong consolation.

Don't you enjoy *Pleasant Fruits*?[1] It is such fun, I think, as well as edification!

I am bringing out a Scotch song, "Scotland's Welcome," anent the royal marriage, which I rejoice in—don't you?

.   .   .   .

Now tell me whether you have seen *Hints on Bible-marking*, by Mrs. Stephen Menzies, because, if you have not, I will send it to you. The plan was not new to me, but I am *very* glad it is issued—chiefly thanks to Moody.

Does not His Word open out more and more, as the years go on? One feels greedy of every bit that one seems to get hold of for oneself. I so often look forward and wonder, "What next, Lord? what will be the next unexpected shining upon a text, or golden thread put into one's hand to string many upon?"

I am so glad you have our Y. W. C. A. reports. I do so enjoy our meetings. Of course when I am at home, I never write any "remarks," because I strike in with one here and there at the meetings. The outline and chief part is always by our dear little secretary, Miss M. Watson. Why don't you put in "remarks"? I am sure He does not fail to give you "new thoughts of God"—why not contribute them? I don't often get any now—the rush of the tide of life seems a little too strong and too noisy for me—I am not very strong yet, and can't quite keep pace with things in general. The "calling apart" was an enormous blessing to me, I would not have missed it for anything.

I send Ezekiel 40:4. I have been most immensely struck with it—note the *three* "*thines*," and the vaguely grand "*all that I shall show thee*," and the significance of "brought hither," and the climax of *command*. It is so full of suggestion for ourselves.

————

OAKHAMPTON.

DEAREST MOTHER,—You must have wondered I did not write yesterday, but we went to Worcester early—such a glorious day!

So grieved to hear of your suffering so much, but, dear mother, I do pray that the peace may be proportioned to the great need of it, and then I know you will not even wish it otherwise. I have wanted to write to you every day, literally, and tell you of all the various small ongoings. Most thankful to hear —— at church for the poor's sake. Such clear, ringing gospel, and, although he does ramble, I enjoy it greatly. But, alas! some are very naughty over his peculiarities. I especially regret *incorrect* reading of Holy Scripture, any alteration or

————

[1] *Pleasant Fruits*, by M. V. G. H. Nisbet & Co.

omission of words I can neither defend nor excuse. I feel quite well now, with lying down all the afternoon, and doing nothing but needlework, or reading, or croquet, or playing with the dogs and doves. Thanks for your note to me, darling mother, so kind and sweet. I don't think I quite explained, that what distresses me is not others seeing as I do, but that false statements and accusations should be so persisted in. Only let bare justice and truthfulness be kept to, and difference of opinion does not trouble me at all. . . . I do not fuss about coming to you, though heart and love would bring me this moment, only I feel it is probably better for you and Miss Nott that I should wait.

I cannot help applying my verses to *you,* mother dear :—

> Oh that the love I bear her
>   Might blossom into skill
> To comfort and to brighten,
>   And all with gladness fill!
> Ah, *helpess love*! Yet 'tis a joy
>   To turn each wish to prayer,
> And where *that* dear one dwelleth,
>   To know that God is there.

—Your loving child.

(*To the late Julia Kirchhoffer.*)

Two years ago you sent me anonymously an extract from *Our Father,* and some comforting words from the far sweeter Book! That nameless ministering was not in vain. I have never forgotten the singular solace it was to me, and now let me thank you for it. And if you live to pass through the same deep sorrow, may He pour His own sweet comfort and strength into your heart. May you have a very happy Easter Sunday, and feel the presence of our beloved Saviour, who is " risen indeed."

OAKHAMPTON.

Thanks many, indeed, for promising to pray for one so *very* dear to me, that I have no greater desire than that he may be " partaker of the benefit." There is much that is hopeful, but also much that is discouraging; but the blessing can, and I trust will, overflow all hindrances. O do pray that all prejudices and hindrances may be swept away, and that Jesus Himself may meet him there. He would be gain to Christ's cause, for he has considerable influence and natural gifts, and I do so long for these to be all for Jesus.

I want you also to pray for one I am not at liberty to name. I had a *literary* request from him two days ago, and in my reply I wrote, quite simply and without any effort, just a few lines about what Jesus has been to me in my illness, and is: his reply is almost the most touching letter I ever saw, especially coming from one who does not " wear his heart upon his sleeve"; it

seems as if the fountains of the great deep were suddenly broken up, and he says, " I would give a million-fold all I have to feel as you feel." I cannot help feeling God is doing and going to do " great things" again through these few simple words. But share my prayer, that in due time you may share my praise for him. I am better, but still very weak. What an unspeakable mercy it is to be able to trust Jesus entirely, and to leave health and everything *happily* in His dear hands! God has lately used the enclosed tiny hymn as the definite means of a very bright and decided conversion.

I do not indulge in writing to you as I would like, because writing tires me so much that I rather reserve my pencil for letters which may do a tiny bit of work for Jesus.

(*To* ——)

I wonder if you prayed for me last night? I had been feeling very " grey" all day, and had a cry at night, and then prayed a long time that I might be " satisfied with favour;" that I might know something of Christ's love, and so not feel disappointed at the denial of full earthly love all my life. And after a while I think a sort of answer came, for it seemed as if a sudden flow set in of all the texts speaking of God's love (without any effort of memory), and it was very soothing and sweet; and I went to sleep resting on it, and woke in the night praying about it. It was not exactly realization that He loves me, but a trusting Him in the dark for His word's sake, that He does love. I should tell you that before this I had, in my tears, given up and said, " Thy will be done," and meant it, with full acquiescence in His will. Do you understand me? it is not exactly or entirely feeling disappointed about ——, but more, I think, the sense of general heart-loneliness and need of a one and special love, . . . and the belief that my life is to be a lonely one in that respect. . . . I do so long for the love of Jesus to be poured in, as a real and satisfying compensation. . . . But I think I shall do better now that I have been enabled to " remember His love" for a little. I do so want Him to sanctify the whole thing, and give me spiritual blessing in and by it. " Who teacheth like Him?"

———

My heart aches for you. I can't tell you how I shrink from writing what will add to your pain, nor how glad I should be, if I could, if I dared, write what would only please and gladden you. You know I have never treated this matter lightly. I know how deeply you feel it, and I sympathize with you in proportion. But I cannot say less than what I believe before God, viz. that " only in the Lord" is His will and law. It is strange, how invariably He seems to link His obvious blessing with simple, trustful obedience to it. I never yet knew a single instance in which a Christian man or woman married knowingly one who was not really "in Christ," but what unhappiness has followed. And I never yet knew one instance of this great sacrifice for the sake of obedience to His Word, but what sooner or later, the blessing was so plain and full that it was indeed the "hundred-fold." The waiting and praying is one thing, but your taking any definite step, while you have not the evidence of her true conversion to God, is quite another. Do not think I underrate the trial; so far from that, I would even rank it as the nearest thing nowadays to the trial of Abraham's faith:—"Take now thy son, thine only son, Isaac, whom thou lovest," the very wording showing that God Himself recognised the intensity of the trial. May our Lord Himself give you proportioned faith to the test He gives you, whether that faith is exercised in long waiting or in resigning. He will guide with His eye, and will help you to look up for that guidance. "Jesus will be *more* to you than any gift of His," and yet "no good thing will He withhold" because He loves you so; and He can work in you to WILL as well as to DO of His good pleasure, so that you may wish what He wishes, whatever that may be.

The first opportunity I had, I only approached the subject sideways with ——. He probably saw what I was at, for he sheered off so very quickly and pointedly to another topic, that I thought it best not to renew the attack, but adopt different tactics next time. So then I made a full front attack, which gave *no* chance of evasion, telling him straight out my fears and hopes and prayers for him personally. He staid nearly an hour! arguing, cavilling, and twisting about like an eel. He manœuvred ingeniously to get me off Bible-ground, and entangle me in metaphysical thickets, but I know one is never safe but in standing firm on the Word and declining to use Saul's weapons—so he always found himself confronted with a smooth stone out of the brook, and thereby brought back again and again to personalities—"And what about his own soul and salvation?" But I saw no *impression;* so far I have only delivered my own soul.[1] I think I was, however, enabled to speak winningly to him, and that he was a little touched by the reality of my anxiety for his salvation. He will be a real trophy for Jesus if converted, perhaps almost more so than any one in ——. I was so exhausted after it, that I only had three-quarters of an hour's sleep the whole night, having got quite overwrought.

———

There is infinitely *more* involved in this than you seem to have the least idea of. And nothing but God's own power can teach it you. It is true my attention was called to this truth, and that set me thinking and praying (at first it was kicking!). No human word did or could open my eyes—it all came clear to me in one tremendous flash, one Sunday at Perry, when I was quite alone. I have no doubt it was the Spirit himself revealing it, even by the effects, for it is since then that all has been so different. Now will you only let your mind be open to receive *whatever* teaching He may send you? (I do not mean any words of mine). I repeat, *no* human argument can do anything, but rather making one kick the more "against the pricks." Will you for this one week, really pray that He would guide you into His own truth *whatever* that may be, and that you may be made *willing* to give up *any* "opinion" which is *not* His truth. The importance of it lies here—as long as you do not attribute all your salvation to God, so long you are defrauding Him of the glory which is His due. Who hath made you to differ? *Why* do you believe and rest in Jesus when others do not? *Is that difference your doing or His?* Could you have come to Jesus if He had not drawn you? And if He did draw you, why *you* and not everybody? If you are indeed "beloved" now, *when* did He begin to love you?

One *or* other made the choice in the first place, either *you* or *God.* If *you* did, then *you* had a share in saving yourself, and it all hinged upon your doing or not doing. If *He* did, then why deny Him the praise and thanksgiving for having chosen *you,* even you! O give glory to the Lord your God, yes, *all* the glory. At present, though you do not know it, you *are* defrauding Him of praise.

Words are often terrible hindrances, "darkening counsel,"—such is your word "favouritism"; say "sovereignty" instead—absolute, but *righteous,* though inscrutable—and then *bow* to it, and you will end by rejoicing in it. Besides you only shift the difficulty, for whose doing is it that one is born in England and another among the darkness and cruelty of Timbuctoo? *God* chose to give you English birth and Christian training, and has utterly denied the same great advantages to others. You *must* call this favouritism if anything is—I call it sovereignty. Give up that "vain word," and you will see clearer. I have been running through a Gospel of St. John for you, only because I could not find a Romans, Ephesians, or Thessalonians portion, which I should have taken in preference as to *strength* of argument. Will you accede to this most earnest request—that you will read this Gospel, *i.e.* the first seventeen chapters, prayerfully through—*willing* to receive *His* truth at *any* cost or sacrifice of "opinion" or "theory" or "idea." Oh, do not glance at it lightly, I am very anxious that you should not do so. I cannot explain all you will gain by receiving His truth as a little child; but I know it because I have felt and found it so. And will you make it a great subject of REAL prayer for light and teaching? I believe that in such things, John 7:17: "If any man will do His will, he shall know of the doctrine whether it be of God," is signally fulfilled, if we are made *quite* willing to give up our own will about theories and ideas and to follow His teaching, even if quite contrary to what we fancied or liked; then He lets us "*know* of the doctrine whether it be of God." It lies at the

———

[1] This is likely referring to Ezekiel 33:1–9.

very root of ever so many other difficulties; but once receive it, and all falls into place, while the spiritual "strong meat" *does* strengthen in a way I would not and could not have believed till His own Hand fed me with it. . . . Have you ever noticed the preposition in Revelation 5:9? I shall never forget how breathlessly I turned to the Greek, *hoping* it was wrongly translated, and found it was even *more* emphatic in the original: "Hast redeemed us to God by Thy blood *out* of every kindred, and tongue, and people, and nation." I most fully agree with you in all you say as to the lost. It will be their own fault, and they will own the *justice,* and yet the salvation of the saved will be *all* God's glory and His doing *from beginning to end.* I do not care to reconcile the paradox—both are true and revealed—the day shall declare it. This is one of the points I want you to be clear upon. Upon *what* does your *actual* salvation (not your *possible* salvation) depend? Is *the* hinge your faith? or is it *God's* sovereign and free gift to you *personally* of it? *i.e.* of the faith as well as the grace. If the former, you must have the credit of making the difference between yourself and others, and not God. Yes, dear,—that is just what I want, not argument, but the Holy Spirit's light and help—coming closer. Let us both seek that.

———

(Letter printed as a Circular.)

Dear ——,

Pardon me for regretfully resorting to this way of replying, as the continually increasing number of correspondents personally unknown to me, renders it simply impossible to send written answers to each. You will find a mark against the paragraph or sentence which contains a reply to your letter.—Yours faithfully,

FRANCES RIDLEY HAVERGAL.

1. *To those who wish permission to use or quote hymns or extracts from my writings.*—It is always a pleasure to give this freely, except in cases where I am fettered by a previously given permission or arrangement, or where "Musical Copyright" should be secured by the publishers.

2. *To those who wish a "candid opinion" as to MSS., or advice how to profit by them.*—The only "candid opinion" of any practical value will be obtained by sending your MS. to the Editor of whatever magazine issues verses or articles of the same kind; he will judge without bias, and reply accordingly. Introductions are utterly useless; everything stands on its own practical merits in an Editor's study. Payment for hymns or general verses is exceptional, and unless you already have "a name," you need not dream of it. As to larger MSS. consult a London publisher. If he says he will be happy to publish your MS., but at *your* expense, that simply means that he knows it will not

command sufficient circulation to pay its expenses. *Never publish anything at your own risk.*

3. *To those who wish a "candid opinion "or revision of Music.*—I really have not time for this. If you are a beginner, send your MS. to the nearest good organist. If not, send it to any high-class publisher.

N.B.—Composition without knowledge of harmony is totally useless for publication.

4. *To those who ask me to write for some Charitable or Religious Institution or object.*—(1.) I never write unless I have a very strong impression on my mind. A mere string of rhymes by request or on hearsay would be worse than useless. (2.) It does not follow that, because I can or do heartily sympathize in a cause, I can forthwith write a poem about it. (3.) I never write descriptions or appeals for anything with which I am not personally familiar. (4.) I am sorry to say that I really cannot find time to write letters or addresses to special Bible classes, Hospitals, etc., etc.

5. *To those who kindly suggest subjects on which they think something in prose or verse would be desirable.*—I find I have to quarry my own stones, and that it hardly ever seems possible to me to take up a line of thought suggested by another mind. At the same time, I am not ungrateful for these, as they are often interesting, though I cannot write upon them. But in several instances the result has been more surely reached by prayer that the Lord would give me the desired words, than by mentioning any subject to me at all.

6. *To those who "feel sure" of my interest or sympathy in various schemes of Christian work.*—Dear friends, I can only say that sometimes I am unable for weeks, or even months together, to cut my way through to doing any of my *own* work, because everybody expects me to take an interest in *their* work or plans! It is not want of will, but an actual physical impossibility, to respond as I would to the continual stream of such letters from unknown fellow-workers.

7. *To those who ask me to circulate or dispose of books, leaflets, work, etc.*—I am now obliged entirely and invariably to decline to do this for any one. *N.B.*—I never dispose of my own publications.

8. *To those who inquire about my publications.*—Books, Nisbet & Co., 21 Berners Street, London, or any bookseller in the kingdom. Songs, Hutchings & Romer, 9 Conduit Street, Regent Street, London, or any musicseller. Leaflets, cards, etc.: No leaflet is issued without the name and address of the publisher, who will supply them by return of post to any address. A full list of Leaflets in Verse, seventy-five in number, will be found at the end of *Royal Commandments* (Parlane, Paisley; and Caswell, Birmingham).

9. To those who most kindly write, asking for no answer, only to tell me of help, stimulus, or comfort, through some message that the Lord has given me the privilege of bearing.—I thank you most heartily, and ask you to pray that He would graciously give me His own messages for the unknown needs of His children, and to join me in thanksgiving for all His wonderful goodness.

DIVISION V.

LETTERS, FROM 1870 TO 1875.

PYRMONT VILLA, March 12, 1870.

I have been ill, or something like it—only the old story, nervous exhaustion, with more acute pain than ever before. I am round the corner now, and have been sleeping immoderately the last few days, which is more than any tonic. So "I'm not to think of going again to our young women's rooms, nor of opening my desk to any more serious purpose than an occasional letter, for I don't know how long!" So I have not been able to give away "Charley's message!"

I send you 1 John 3:2, because it seemed sent to me in the night. The phase of it which shone out was this. It (and many others) is not only a beautiful picture conveying one great subject or idea to the heart's eye—but when more closely looked at, the painting resolves itself into a *mosaic,* every word a precious and beautiful gem. The subject is the marvellous promise, or expression of confidence (which comes to the same thing), that we shall see Him and be like Him, through that seeing. But just take the words one by one, and see if each is not a jewel of many rays. "*Beloved*—*now*—*are*—we the *sons* of God—*and*—it doth NOT YET *appear*—what—we *shall* be—*but* WE KNOW that WHEN *He* shall *appear* we shall BE *like* Him—*for*—*we*—*shall*—see—Him—*as*—He is." Why any *one* is enough for a great sermon! I have double-lined those on which I dwelt most, though it does not follow that they are most full. The word "*be*" (like Him) struck me immensely—it is so absolute—not *seem,* but actually "*be*" going glorifyingly down to the very ends and depths of our whole being—no surface likeness, but entirety of transformation.

(*To E. C.*)

PYRMONT VILLA, Easter, April 17, 1870.

I must send you a line, dear E. I think Maria and Ellen will have set out on their journey hither, but *if* not, let them know.

My father still lies just the same, quite unconscious. Apoplectic fit early this morning, and he has never moved or spoken since; no consciousness of blisters, mustard, etc. Dr. Thursfield says, "humanly speaking, there is no hope whatever," and he "thinks he will not last many hours." Yesterday he was unusually well, all remarked it, and peculiarly bright and happy. He has no suffering at all, and was hardly an hour consciously ill or even poorly. And when he awakens, it will be to see Him as He is. Dear E., I did not think it possible this blow could have been sent so mercifully, all pain spared him, and that was the chief thing. And I never felt before *how* God can give peace where it seemed it *must* have been only utter grief, sudden and crushing. Pray for us.

PYRMONT VILLA, April 22, 1870.

"*Blessed* be the name of the Lord." I think He has put that in my heart, and my heart says it. I thought I should have yours to-day, and longed for it. It will be a relief to write to you, there is so much that I must write to others, and I need not to you, and therefore I want to.

It is a dream as yet—but rather solemn than terrible; and after it—"when I awake, I am still with Thee." I think He will let me prove *that.* It has been the *very* best for my father, and therefore I do not think any of us would have it otherwise. Saturday he was better than for months, was out twice, just in the sun before the house—chatting cheerily to neighbours and friends, and all day seemed quite peculiarly happy and bright. I went with Edith H. to tea at Miss Nott's, but happily was so tired that I came home at 8.30, and so was at home at evening prayers. I cannot recall his prayer, though I would give anything to remember it—all seems blotted out except the fact of it.

I never said good-night to him, never remember missing it before—but I had to go away directly after prayers, I forget what for, and when I returned he was gone up. I did not follow him, because he was tired, and I thought it would only hinder and disturb him if I did. I did not know that I should never have another kiss. Very early on Easter Sunday morning (April 19), (after sleeping fairly), he said his head was uncomfortable—got up about six, but laid down again—and became unconscious. It was apoplexy, and he never moved or spoke again—laid as in deep sleep till Tuesday at noon, and then the breathing ceased—that was all—no struggle, no pain, only gone to *rest*. Was it not merciful *so*? Not any pang for him, not a goodbye, or the possibility of a troubled thought, not an hour's conscious illness—then sleep—then glory. We could not have chosen better for him. And for us—everything that *could* soften and sustain has been given—all were in time too to see him. There was no human element, and so no evil, no bitterness; it was only GOD's Hand. Not one regret—not one of us having to wish that either he or we had done, or not done this or that as second cause. If I had loved my father less, I should grieve more, but his comfort was truly first, and that is everything. But I would have given anything *but* the inevitable cost of suffering to him for even one last word or look.

I need not tell anybody what he was to me—I have said that once for all in the *Ministry of Song*—(Our Father), and I am so glad I did.

Dear mother is—I do not know how to tell it—I never saw such grief before—and yet not one murmur.

All is in the most marvellous order—not a bill unpaid, not even one letter unanswered! He could not have done more had it been known to him. Yet we have no reason to suppose that he had any presentiment—no shadow of death fell on him at all. And now—he is "with Him," and I think that includes *all*. And I can look at that and even be glad. I did not know God could make it so easy to bow and trust, and say, "Thy will be done." He will rest in Astley churchyard, and in its loveliest spot.

April 27, 1870.

Your note to mother was just *beautiful*. Dear E., your own sorrow seems to have taught you what to say. I am so glad that it is fixed that I go out next week. I would much rather go right away than even come to Winterdyne just now! I do not think I shall get to feel comfortably well till I have more change than mere "change of air." I do not mean that I want to forget—not at all—but it will do me good to have to forget at intervals. And I have felt my father's loss even more intensely the last two days. How anxious you must be about ——, yet I am sure God will help you to be in "perfect peace." I think He does such unexpected things in that way: "perfect peace" where we ex-

pected distress, and agony where one expected peace. Yet His surprises are more often of the former kind.

(To Margaret W.)

1870.

What *grand* things Janie is permitted to do! Of course I am charmed that she sees there are advantages in "keeping rank"! I never did believe in "unattached," and never can believe the Captain intends anything of the sort, and I would sooner be a Congregationalist (always barring the great Bible-education point!) than be one of those unsubordinated (I did not say "insubordinate"!) waifs and strays.

Such a telling "present salvation" sermon last night at St. Paul's—John 6:47, and one of J. H. R.'s *very* best A.M. on John 20:29. I have been extremely struck (for myself) with the *as* and the *so* in John 6:57, so I pass it on to you and dear Bessie. I do not know how to thank her for her kind message and prayers. Can you and she find time to ask that I may be able if He will to carry out a little poem on a subject which is a good deal too grand for *me*—and yet I had a strong impulse to begin it, but stuck in the middle, not because I could not scribble on *somehow*, but because I feel utterly unequal to put the idea into any sort of adequate words, and can't bear spoiling it! We had better singing the last two Sundays than ever yet, which is encouraging. I am actually let into the choir now, to shout to my heart's content at the hallelujahs, etc.

(To the same.)

January 31, 1871.

I can think of nothing with respect to the death of dear Lucy's mother, but "Thou hast made her most blessed for ever." She was not always "glad" here, but *now* "exceeding glad with Thy countenance." Loving thanks for telling me. We are still in the *deepest* anxiety and distress—a terrible relapse last Thursday night, since which he keeps saying he *knows* he is dying. The case is *not* hopeless, and yet there is far more fear than hope, *except* for prayer. But the intense conviction of sin is an answer so far *showing* that good work *is* begun. There have been *gleams* of peace, but quickly passing again. He *never* prays for life, *only* for pardon, and will go on whispering by the hour, "*Please* do—dear Jesus, please do wash me—whiter than snow, oh, forgive me—quite, dear Saviour, do, *do!*" and so on. But the last two days he has *wandered* so much that it adds *greatly* to our trial, and he does not seem to *understand* what at first seemed to soothe him. Dear Margaret, will *you* kindly write a "request" for him for Friday, "this *only* son," and send this on to Janie?

(To the same.)

PERRY VILLA, 1871.

I meant to send an ordinary " request for praise" for Friday, but I do feel that the answer God has given about the invalid is so extraordinary, that I think it might be a help to praying ones if you would tell them in your own words what God has done in this case. I would not convey in the usual short form what a remarkable answer it is. In the last three weeks recovery has taken place, and he is at this moment, if not very strong, yet in all respects as well as usual, and running and riding about. From what I hear I have every reason to believe that the life renewed will be life henceforth consecrated, and that this illness has been indeed the turning-point. For weeks there was literally no other hope but prayer, and a most remarkable spirit of prayer seems to have been given with respect to his case, so many, not only in our own wide circle of friends, but complete strangers, having taken it up and made special request for him. Just tell your members something about it on Friday; it is stimulating to hear how gracious God is, and it may encourage them. Ask them to pray that the good work begun may be carried on, and not even temporarily hindered by temptations and snares, which his position as well as his lively disposition will expose him to, but that he may be henceforth Christ's brave and faithful and entirely devoted soldier and servant. And ask them to pray that the prayers of many years may be crowned at last by the conversion of unconverted dear ones, so that it may be another gracious instance of a "converted family." Will you send this on to dear Janie? I want her to know.

I am busy at work upon the *Songs of Grace and Glory*, having finished Havergal's *Psalmody*. My last week's work was re-writing sundry queer old hymns! It is so strange that on certain very precious subjects no hymn-writer seems to have touched. I have a most interesting servants' Bible class here, and am looking for blessing. I hope mother will join me here next week. I shall think of you on Fridays, and join you in heart. I meant to have tried my best to help you at the meetings! but as yet it has only been by prayer.

I am so delighted at the bright opening—not the least surprised that none stayed Sunday P.M. I doubt not that Monday night, which seems to have been beyond expectations, is but the beginning. You have in a special way " come near to minister unto Him" this week, Ezekiel 44:15, 16, and so Numbers 16:5 belongs to you and the 7th verse. But it begins with the being "chosen," and from that flows the "come near" and "shall be holy." Is not that for you, dearie?

(To E. C.)

Christmas Afternoon, 1871.

I must send you a line of Christmas greeting—I am so glad you are at Winterdyne. Christmas has as much of pain as of joy in it, *more* perhaps, and yet one would not blot out the memories which cause the pain. I do so utterly agree with what you wrote to Maria about widows, and the sympathy *they* have as compared with the utter lack of sympathy with those to whom the joy of union has been altogether denied, for widowhood is after all but as the shadow following a *great* light. Has it ever struck you that in this particular thing *we* have a fellowship with our Lord, which they have not? You will think this out for yourself, if you have not already dwelt upon it.

I cannot tell you how grateful I am for your sacrifice in sparing Maria to come home, I do not know when anything has been a greater relief to me. The terrible dreaded evening for poor mother of the anniversary that so recalls my father, was tided over by Maria's coming—mother's burst of agony quite startled her. But dear Elizabeth, I had no idea *you* were so suffering, or I would not have asked for Maria; so I do hope, in my own distress and anxiety for poor mother, I have not sacrificed your comfort.

I suddenly collapsed three days ago—got quite exhausted, but mercifully I have been able to sleep it off. Let me give you my special tired text: " He will *be* very gracious unto thee at the voice of thy cry." We may not *see* what He will *do*, nor be able to *hear* what He will *say*, but what He will *be*,—what He *is*, swallows up both, and guarantees *all*, no matter what we feel, " He will be *very gracious*."

(To E. C.)

. . . I feel very much inclined to send you this text: " I will never leave thee, nor forsake thee." Because that takes in *all* " the way." For if true *now*, it must have always *been* true, even when most imperfectly recognised. And we cannot get beyond "*never*." The Greek is elsewhere rendered "loose or slacken," therefore it seems very strong—" I will never loose my hold upon thee"; the "forsake," I think, includes etymologically the idea of leaving behind in a place, therefore it may be linked with "Where I am, there shall also my servant be" (John 12:26), and "I go to prepare a place for you . . . that where I am, there ye may be also" (John 14:3).

So dear E., whatever sorrows this or any coming year may bring, they cannot go beyond "I *know* their sorrows." But may He who knows your past sorrows, spare you from heavy future ones.

I do hope you will be cheered with much blessing this year, specially among your girls. We are at a disadvantage with ours as compared with yours, because we are hampered as to the coming Confirmation time, being mixed Church and Dissent, both as to ladies and girls. I hope I shall get some of them to attend Confirmation classes, whether they go on to Confirmation itself or not. I do think, and this is the experience of thousands, that it is *the* great opportunity with young persons. The

very fact of feeling themselves unfit is the means of awakening so many; for the question naturally arises, "If unfit for Confirmation, then am I not unfit for heaven?" Especially among what you call well-disposed girls, I think it is very often the turning-point, it is such a solemnly personal individual thing, that it stirs them up to decide. It used to be a time of great blessing, specially among my dear father's candidates—one of his Sunday-school teachers, Emma Shrimpton, who died lately (whom Maria knew so well), was an instance of great blessing and a consistent life. I always regretted exceedingly that —— was not confirmed; for though I believe she was a Christian before, she would have found great blessing—she says things which show she underrates it, and it has occurred to me that Satan may make use of the fact of having no personal experience of the privilege, to hinder—from making the most of it with her class of girls. For of course, merely knowing of Confirmation *theoretically* as a rite, is very different from having shared in it and found its blessing.

We are obliged to give up two-thirds of our work among the girls, and only keep the rooms open two nights, as the girls do not come. It is very disappointing and humiliating. I should have kept on, whether or no, but I was quite outvoted by the other workers.

I am so looking forward to milder weather, so that I can sit every morning in my study instead of only once a week. I have been defeated altogether in a pet scheme—you know my study is no practical use to me except in the few weeks of warm spring or autumn (as we are never at Leamington in the summer). I cannot sit without a fire, it is so extra cold under the very thin slated roof. I offered to pay for coals and fee the servant, so as to have a fire nearly every day instead of once a week as dear mother arranged—but one of our servants is invalided, so I must not propose it. I am so disappointed—one cannot have any little reading or prayer in the downstair rooms, as our callers are incessant. And it is so difficult to do anything requiring consecutive thought, with interruptions every ten minutes. If I am drawing on my brain at all, I lose the thread and forget where I was, and have to cogitate—so I produce more in my one study fire day than all the other five.

But it is foolish and selfish to grumble thus to you. I cannot think how I was betrayed into it: one would much rather dwell on mercies, which ought so infinitely to satisfy.

I thought I should not find this second return home so trying as the first after my dear father's death, but I have felt it fully as much.

LEAMINGTON, March 1812.

... I began going to the laundry girls last week, and was much interested. I *repeated* the "Old, Old Story" to a roomfull of them, and though they were *told* not to let it interrupt work, they one by one stopped, and listened in dead silence, and two or three were in tears.

I have begun giving a little series of a sort of mild "lectures" on psalmody to Miss Rose's school, with *illustrations,* which consist of practising a hymn and tune till it goes satisfactorily. For next time they are to bring me instances of the *characteristics* of *good* psalmody I mentioned and explained. Next time I shall point out some characteristics of *bad* style. They are to practise the tunes in between—for what numbers of girls can play a brilliant piece and yet cannot play a hymn tune. Miss R. has introduced *Songs of Grace and Glory,* and handed over her girls to *my* influence, which I hope to use rightly for the principles and practice of "psalmody," and while it seems to interest them extremely, gives a first-rate opening for general *anti*-High Church influence.

But I must hasten. I do so hope you will find many an evident proof at Malvern, that the angel has gone before you to choose you out a place to pitch your tent in. Not but what the *fact* will be the same, in any case, but I should like you to find pleasant proofs of it.

WINTERDYNE, May 6, 1872.

I have just written a lively little missionary song and tune, "Tell it out," which is being taken up wonderfully quickly. I will send it to you by book post, and you can make any use you like of it. I enclose you my *Plea for the Little Ones,* of which I think not less than half a million must have been in type in the last three weeks, such numbers of newspapers and magazines having inserted it. I feel *very* strongly (on the exclusion of the Bible from Board schools), and it is a perfectly inexplicable thing to me how men who *profess* to believe and value the Bible, can join hands with "infidels" and "heretics" in desiring its exclusion from Government schools; it is to me "a wonderful and horrible thing" indeed. The last verses in my *Plea* are:—

Shall those who name the Name of Christ
    His own great gift withhold?
Our Lamp, our Chart, our Sword, our Song,
    Our Pearl, our most fine Gold!

Why would ye have "no Bible taught"?
    Is it for *fear?* or shame?
Out, out upon such coward hearts,
    False to their Master's name!

With battle-cry of valiant faith,
    Let Britain's sons arise,—
"Our children *shall be* taught the Word
    That only maketh wise!"

So, dauntlessly, will we unfurl
    Our banner bright and broad:
The cause of His dear Word of Life
    Our cause,—the cause of God.

I am so glad you like *Bruey.* My dear little nieces, Alice and Bertha, to whom it is dedicated, are both stirred up by it to wish to work; and both, at their earnest entreaty, begin Sunday-school teaching in Wyre Hill to-morrow.

I have had many inquiries as to whether *Bruey* is a true story or not, so I will make an explicit statement. "Bruey," so called from the name "Bruce," was, as the children say, "a real little girl." The outline of her simple story is true; and the sketch of her character is founded on my personal recollections, and inferences drawn from them. Her Sunday-school work (in my father's school), the Irish meeting, and the collecting cards and the forty-one names, her illness and early and peaceful death, are all *fact.* If I had been writing an entirely made-up story, some things would have been very different. Probably I should have made Bruey collect for some vague and general missionary cause, in which any one might imagine they could recognise their own pet society. But my little readers (so far as I know) seem to agree with me that it is most interesting to know just what Bruey really did collect for, although there are few branches of the Irish Society in England, and none at all in America. And some of the grown-up readers of *Bruey* may think it pleasant to get a little passing view of a very quiet and far-off corner of the great harvest field in Ireland, where a silent sowing of the Word is going on by this society, which shall surely result in sheaves and singing.

Besides, the principles and motives and modes of *any* work for Christ, such as dear little Bruey undertook, apply just as much to any other branch of the same work. Bruey's card, and the list I have kept of her forty-one names, is one of my treasures. I should like any dear little unknown future readers in England to know that I have heard already of many children who have been stirred up by Bruey's example to wish to be "workers for Christ" too; and who have either found out different ways for themselves, or asked their parents to tell them of something to do, like Bruey, "for Him!"

I am so far away that I shall probably never hear such pleasant news from America; but I send my little book across the ocean with a very earnest prayer that my Heavenly Master may grant that by it many an American girl and boy may be led to become a "little worker for Christ."

[*Mem.*—By F. R. H.'s request, *Bruey* is translated into French by Mlle. Tabarié, under the name of *Lilla* (published by J. Bonhoure, 48 Rue de Lille, Paris). F. R. H. was pleased with its lively and idiomatic rendering, making it a pleasant book for the schoolroom.—M. V. G. H.]

It was kind and thoughtful of you to send Miss A.'s unexpectedly cheering letter. Ah, dear J., "even F. R. H." needs perhaps more of cheer and comfort than many who may perhaps have known less of joy, but *also* less of sorrow; and I believe this is why my tender and loving Father has of late so kindly given me so much success both in penwork and in the more directly spiritual work. So I take Miss A.'s letter as another token of this; and the same post brings me quite an *enthusiastic* note from a London firm about words for a set of six very beautiful MS. songs by Franz Abt, which they requested me to fit with English words in imitation of the original—they say, "You have done it *splendidly!*" "Rose of roses," etc. So this 1872 has been one series of little successes and great mercies. . . . Have you ever *thought out,* "The Lord will do great things" yet?

I cannot say I "miss" dear M. and E., because my one object in life at present seems to be, to keep out of everybody's way! I refuse myself to every one before early dinner, and decline every evening invitation; so people catch me if they can in the afternoon.

December 14, 1872.

This is one of the most depressed birthdays I ever had. "Sent empty away" seems inscribed on this week, both for the mission time and myself. I am certain Satan has been specially at work to spoil and hinder everything. I have not the least consciousness of any blessing or comfort whatever; but instead of it, a terrible reaction into an utter misery of numbness of soul. The whole service last night was actual weariness to me. More faith and prayer and effort and expectation there could not have been, yet the whole result seems to be, "He that is filthy let him be filthy still, and he that is holy let him be holy still." Only one case of anything like conversion (with thirty services and meetings in the eight days), and that was a girl whom I felt quite sure God was leading to Himself before. It has been a most strange and painful lesson of God's sovereignty; some parishes are *so* blessed. I heard of one where the throngs of enquirers were so great that the church had to be kept open all day for dealing with them; in others, with equal prayer and means, just nothing at all. The addresses here were so pointed and clear and direct and fervent,—just what one would think must convince and lead to Christ. Decided Christians and visitors enjoyed it immensely—to me it was all utter blank disappointment. For twelve years it has been my special wish to be in an affair of this kind, or anything like the Mildmay Conference, which I seem fated not to get to—it is so depressing, and yet it *must* have its "nevertheless afterwards."

(*To E. C.*)

February 22, 1873.

There is a little extra pressure to-day, and I can only write you a note, though I meant to write a letter. I send you these words, "He is thy Lord." You will see my comment on it in *Woman's Work* for March (see also *Under the Surface,* p. 96[1]);

---

[1] *Under the Surface* by F.R.H. (London: James Nisbet & Co., 1874), original book page 96, page 378 of Volume I of the Havergal edition.

but I shrunk from saying *all,* though if I had, it would have touched more hearts! The thought I omitted was; the restfulness of recognising the Lord Jesus as the heavenly Bridegroom,—the Husband,—meeting all the special woman's need of one to bow to and love and obey,—submitting, acquiescing, and obeying with great gladness, because with great love. You will fill this thought out for yourself, I know, darling, as I have for myself; and may He "satisfy" all the need which only He knows. I do delight in the whole of Psalm 45.

Well, dear E., may "He is thy Lord," in its fullest sweetness and solace, be your keynote for the new life.

Thank you so much for the sash; it is exactly the thing I wanted, and Amy has done it up charmingly for me.

(*To* ——)

May 22, 1873.

Your letter interested me very much, for I do so warmly sympathize with you in your longing for more knowledge and more teaching. May I say freely what I think? It may be that God means to show you the power of His Spirit, working by His Word *alone* (1 Thessalonians 2:13), and to lead you to seek and search the Scriptures more earnestly for *yourself.* Sometimes we lean too much upon outward teaching, when we have it; though on the other hand, when He does let us have it, it is most valuable and should be made the most of. But I think you may be quite sure of two things:—1*st.* That He leadeth you by the right way (Psalm 107:7); and therefore, if you really cannot go to a Bible class, it must be best so, and He means to teach you without it. 2*nd.* If God sends you to those who need teaching, He can put the right message into your mouth, just as easily as if you were a D.D. And I do feel *sure* we may look up to Him to give us the very *words* to say. Very often it is just when we feel most helpless that He uses us most.

As to the oil, I do not think it refers to Galatians 6:17. Oil is a special type of the Holy Spirit, with reference to His work in *consecrating* and *sanctifying* us. The blood came first (Leviticus 14:14), and then the oil was put upon the same members. So we need first atonement by the precious blood of Christ, every member being *defiled* and needing it; but then follows ("go and sin no more") the oil of consecration, setting apart those very members to the service of God and of sanctification throughout, down to the very lowest member and power.

I should like to write much more, but am very busy just now.—Yours in Him, "whom having not seen, ye love."

1873.

I do so wish there were more soul-winners, especially at boys' schools. Somehow many never seem to do more than pray in a general sort of way for the children, and read good little books to them. But they do not seem to aim at conversion or anything more definite than "good influence," and never speak right out about salvation. They seem afraid to aim at it, or see lions in the way. . . . And yet they are quite clear about salvation for themselves, and happy and trustful, and yet have never led a soul to Christ. I gave *Pillows* and *Bells* to a matron who had never seen them, and she quite caught at them. "Just what she wanted, often wished she could say something when she put the boys to bed, now she could read them this, and quite sure they would be delighted." She is a Christian, I have no doubt; but, oh, dear! *why* cannot Christians tell these poor dear boys a word about Jesus! and yet talk so bewitchingly to them about anything else!

I received a singularly interesting letter from a lady who picked up my leaflet, *Have you not a Word for Jesus,* in the street in Edinburgh some weeks ago. She has "always been a dumb Christian, but dare not any longer be so." She writes to ask my prayers that she may henceforth be able to speak for Jesus.

"Grant unto Thy servants that with all boldness they may speak Thy words." How grandly they did it in vers. 29 and 32 of the next chapter, and there is the same Holy Ghost for us.

May 30, 1873.

My dear Fellow-Worker (for such I am sure you are),—Your most interesting letter has been travelling about, and only reached me a day or two ago. Do not say, "If indeed a child of God at all." Let me give you a thought which has often cheered me when tempted to say the same. Can you not set to your seal that the last clause of Jeremiah 31:3 is true: "Therefore with loving-kindness have I drawn thee"? It is so, because you would not feel drawn to the Saviour, unless the Lord Himself had done it—your natural heart would not draw you, and Satan would not, so it must be His own "loving-kindnesses," "for no man can come to me, except the Father which hath sent me draw him,"—well then, if He has drawn you, WHY?

Look at the glorious antecedent of the "therefore": "Yea, I have loved thee with an everlasting love." There is no escape from this conclusion, dear friend; verily, *Jehovah hath* loved YOU "with an *everlasting love,*" and you have that absolute proof of it, "*Therefore* with loving-kindnesses He hath drawn you."

I feel very much for you in your sad story of trials, but may I send you Proverbs 4:11, "I have led you in right paths?" Does not that cover all the life-sorrows, and solve all the life-mysteries? Do not look at your trials as only sent for your own sake; see Philippians 1:29.

Who knows for what blessed service our Master is meeten-ing[1] and polishing you in your sad and lonely hours!

I am an orphan now, and have found the truth of Psalm 27:14, "When my father and my mother forsake me, then the Lord will take me up;" so I send it on to you, praying that it may be yours in your heart-orphanhood. I am very thankful

---

[1] meeten: to render fit, ready

to hear of your finding my leaflet, and shall be very glad if He will make it still further helpful to you in witnessing for Him. I cannot help an impression that there will be many stars in your crown. May He give you much grace and courage and wisdom and love, and if it be His will, success in winning souls.

OAKHAMPTON, July 1873.

I have found plenty to do here, and cannot overtake the numbers of poor people who would like me to visit them, though I give either a morning or evening of each day to it. I have the first class of girls on Sunday A.M., and my old Sunday reading P.M., for which the servants seem grateful. Thanks to Sarah D.'s information and help, I have quite a nice Bible-class on Friday P.M. of farmers' daughters, and such-like girls. On Mondays, I have a cottage reading, I should much like to begin another as well, but it seems more prudent not to begin too much, especially as there is much visiting to be done. —— is very kind and affectionate, but I see no encouragement to hope anything more—I have been crying over her to-day.

So glad you were at the Conference—strange how *that* always slips through my fingers. I quite hoped we should have been back for it this June. Well, He knows best, and perhaps it might not have been as much real help to me as I was reckoning on. I am greatly enjoying the freedom of not having pressing work which must be done. I had no variety or society or anything to make a break, and I would not like ever to have such another ten months. But for the real belief that —— is and will be an influence for God, I never could have stuck to that utterly tiring and tiresome proof-correcting and corresponding with printers, etc.

I dare not yet allow myself a free fling at any fresh head and eyes work, though there are many things I am longing to do; but I feel I need a rest from it, if ever I am to do any more telling pen-work. So the visiting and classes seem to be my work at present, and though I should probably be wiser if I gave myself a real rest and holiday, I cannot refuse to enter such an open door.

October 1873.

During the Mission Week at Liverpool, my hymn-meeting began at 7.30—opened with prayer by the Rector, who then left it to me. The hall was fairly full, and it is a capital place for sound. It took a while to get the steam up, but before long we had some very fair singing. I had made out a little programme of hymns, progressing to a climax of praise and brightness, and all seemed to enjoy it, the token thereof being that when I closed at 9.15 every one was astonished at the time being gone. There were a good many strangers and critics present, which rather awed me. It was not merely mechanical practice, and I do not think it failed in its higher objects. A lady wrote so gratefully to me next day, telling me of the new and full comfort which had come to her through a few remarks I made before singing Hymn 14, *Songs of Grace and Glory*:—

> O my Lord, how great the wonders
> Thy rich grace has wrought for me!
> On Thy love my spirit ponders,
> Praising, magnifying Thee.

We sang it to my father's tune "Zaanaim."

Friday evening was much nicer than Thursday. The singing went splendidly, and I felt as much at home as ever I did with my Sunday-school class, and somehow did not feel the least difficulty in really saying out all that was in my heart about the hymns themselves, and the great subjects of the Mission Week. Mr. Stubbs begged me so, not to refrain from freely speaking. I wondered at getting on so delightfully, but it was all explained by the Scripture reader, who came up to me after, and said, "Some of us met together to pray for you and your work this evening, and we have had the answer, for I am sure the Lord helped you most sweetly." A lady "Professor of Music" was present, and came to me afterwards most cordially, to say how delighted she was with the hymns and tunes, *Songs of Grace and Glory*. She said she intended immediately to adopt them in her classes and among her pupils.

I went to Mrs. Menzies' Y. W. C. A. house—all is so beautifully arranged and managed, and it is such a harbour of safety for numbers. Being Saturday, a good many girls were in the house, and so could come into my Bible-reading. A great many are "working bees;" but I found the idea was to bring all the young sisters or nieces or cousins that could be caught for the occasion, so I had quite a number of just the sort of girls I always want so to get at. At first I wondered how I was to find a word for *all*, as it was such a very mixed set; but I took a passage which really did seem to contain something for all, and took it almost word by word; and it was just what one wanted for the occasion, being a lovely typical passage, bringing out most clearly the three points of "Coming, Consecration, and Union with Jesus." Some told me afterwards that they had felt it to be a very precious message to themselves, and had never thought of the passage in that connection before. So again I felt very distinctly that "the Lord helped me."

Mr. S. wanted me very much to stay in the Mission Hall and address the whole gathering; but of course I refused: I would not think of such a thing—*that* is not my vocation at all!

The enormous workhouse is not far from here. One fancies little gentle Agnes Jones going into it all alone, and clearing out the Augean stable that it was; and it seems marvellous how *any* woman could do what she did in that place.

(To Margaret W.)

WINTERDYNE, December 22, 1873.

I am to-day trying to write a New Year's article for the *Christian;* it might suit your thought. It is *From Glory to Glory;* it *ought* to be the brightest thing I ever wrote, for I have had the brightest spiritual blessings I ever yet had. But positively Satan himself seems trying to prevent my writing it.

December 23, 1873.

I send you *From Glory to Glory.* It is possible it may prove to be what you feel is wanted. If, however, it does not strike you as *the* thing, will *Certainly I will be with thee* do? But, dear Margaret, you and I being the Lord's own, and *not* our own, will fully understand each other. *Neither* must be used, unless you seem guided distinctly so to do. You know I only desire His glory, and not F. R. H.'s credit; and I greatly shrink from anything of mine being used *only* as a sort of compliment to me! You know I mean this.

(To E. C.)

December 1873.

I find dear mother has already put up my New Year's leaflet *From Glory unto Glory* for you; so I only add a scrap of loving wish that even though all seems so trying and dark for you, 1874 may nevertheless prove to be in every way "from glory to glory."

I am so grieved about your hearing—I know no trial I should so shrink from as deafness—and yet I have said deliberately, verse 10, "Whatever lies before us, there can be nought to fear." I fully enter into and sympathize with all your feelings and difficulties. Perhaps altogether the Lord Jesus is about to show you how *fully* He can satisfy with Himself *alone.*

(To Margaret W.)

OAKHAMPTON, January 25, 1874.

More likely than not, I shall *not* be back for the Y. W. C. A. next meeting. I wanted so much to get you to take some extremely decided steps about the unpunctuality. I named it to two or three members, and the instant reply was that it was your fault! because you never began at eleven sharp, and there is no denying that no meetings ever are punctual unless the leader has the resolution to begin as the clock strikes without ever waiting for anybody. I should begin if only two were present, and the rest would soon learn better! Do bring about thorough reform in this. I will write a circular in my own name, if you like! And I would never admit any one during the hymn, as it is a part of our service as much as prayer, and yet it is regularly disturbed and treated as a sort of "opening voluntary," which alway annoys me intensely.

I had no idea of staying so long here, but my path is most clear, and there is special need of me here, more than at home, as Maria is with dear mother. I have had a specially precious soul given me at W. I always reap anywhere but in Leamington.

(To J. E. J.)

LEAMINGTON, February 27, 1874.

I thought often of you and your request during *the* "Week," and have no doubt there was great blessing. I wanted you to get a special personal blessing and lifting up, dear J. Did you? Only sometimes the richest blessings flow in deep under the surface, and the taking root downward is not less blessed than bearing fruit upward.

I have just been enjoying thinking out Luke 5:4–11 in a less usual way—"Launch out into *the deep sea of the promises.*" Has that ever struck you? If not, will you look at the passage and see how beautifully it bears carrying out, till it comes to "forsook *all* and followed *Him.*"

(To J. E. J.)

LEAMINGTON, March 18, 1874.

You will wonder—but I am so thankful for your letter! Because the state of mind you describe is so exactly what I have seen (and to a certain extent experienced) just before entering into the full blessing, the full rest. He brings us just to the end of our own resources, and even to the end of all hitherto tried resources, and empties us altogether (it is just a parallel to the usual state of things before conversion). And then He shows us, perhaps in one flash, perhaps gradually, that He can really do all for us, really cleanse as well as pardon, really be our sanctification as well as our righteousness, really keep us moment by moment instead of only a general kind of keeping from great or final falling. You do not limit Christ's "able;" He is able to keep, able to do exceeding abundantly, able to make all grace abound to you, etc.; but then the great question comes—"When?" Now answer Him with—"Now, Lord!" And according to your faith it will be unto you. Do just apply the very things you would say to one who was seeking salvation, and use the very same means—"Only believe," and—"Now." It is a wonderful parallel. I am not writing thus because I have opinions or have read books, but because I felt and found it all before I ever read a line on the subject.

I am praying for you. I long for you to have "the full blessing." You must have it.

(To ——.)

Yours just come. Yes, I like "Aunt Frances." You know it is Connie's name for me. I am so glad the Lord helps you to trust Him, and He *will.* I am very glad you are looking out for definite work in ——, as I think—first, it is a real means of grace, and the soul does not prosper without it unless He distinctly withholds opportunity; and, secondly, if you give up some and all for ——'s sake, you are not called upon to relinquish also the privilege and duty of work for Jesus. He is our Master, and He only—His service must be sought.

I really do think my chick took in the message of "everlasting love" the very first evening! the soil was more prepared than I had supposed, and she had very earnest desire for a blessing on this visit; and somehow she simply believed the message straight off, without any to-do! at least she appeared to do so, and says it makes her so very happy!

Dear child, she is so changed. Her mother had given her Mr. Everard's nice little book, *Nailed to the Door-post;* so the next day she went to her (of course in the twilight!) and whispered, "Mamma, I am nailed to the door-post!"

Same evening —— told her at last of his decision for the ministry. So all has been extremely happy about that; told me he had such a nice talk with his father about it, and then prayer. So the dear mother is singing Psalm 103!

So glad you like my verses, "Far more exceeding," but I never felt more miserably the total inadequacy of my attempt to touch on so grand a theme.

(*To the late Mrs. Edward Pease.*)

WINTERDYNE, March 31, 1874.

DEAR MRS. PEASE,—Will you accept my warm thanks for your lovely gift. The Tyrolean shawl is so beautiful in itself, and will be particularly useful during the semi-invalid weeks which are now before me, that thus alone it is a pleasure to have it. But it makes it a greater pleasure that it is an expression of Christian friendliness and sympathy. We cannot be really strangers when we own the same dear Master, and love the same precious Saviour. It was so kind and thoughtful of you to lend a book to read; it came just at the right time, when I was all the better for a little easy reading, but not at all able for anything needing consecutive thought. You have learnt to anticipate the little needs of invalids such as this, and I have benefited by it.

Having so often heard of you from my sister Maria, I feel as if I knew you already, but I hope very much I may have the pleasure of your personal acquaintance before very long.

May I take this opportunity of expressing what I have most strongly felt—gratitude to you for the great and real help you have been to my sister Maria by supplying her with, and supporting a nurse for, her sick poor. I do not think anything could have been devised which would more effectually help and relieve her; and we also who so love her, are most thankful for the relief which it is to her in times of much illness among

the poor; for we have often been very anxious lest she should break down. Again thanking you for the exquisite shawl, allow me to remain, dear Mrs. Pease, yours cordially.

(*To C. H.*)

April 1, 1874.

. . . Are you thus cut off from pleasant intercourse and kindness for nothing? Surely not; depend upon it, it means blessing, and will be a blessing if you seek that it may. Oh, Ceci, Jesus has been *so* much to me this winter, more than ever before. I send you a tiny book, *All for Jesus,*[1] which has been an unspeakable blessing to me, and now I want you to be "all for Jesus." It is very marvellous how God lately seems to have been stirring up thousands and thousands of Christians to consecrate themselves utterly to Him, and to seek and find more in Him than ever before. I have shared this blessing, and now I want you to have it too!

(*To C. H.*)

April 22, 1874.

I am just full of joy and praise over your letter. Oh, how I thanked God for it! You will wonder! but all you tell me shows that He has really, truly, deeply taken you in hand, that He Himself has drawn near, and though as yet your eyes are holden, He is leading you right into fulness of blessing. I am sure of it; what you describe is exactly what I expected *if* the work in you were indeed His, and exactly what He leads others through into the full blessing of entire consecration and resulting joy. Only let Him work; only let Him do what He will with you, in you, for you. He may bring you into yet deeper waters; He may show you more still of the sin and weakness; He will bring you to the point of utter self-despair, and *then*—I know what *then!* Oh, the joy of utterly yielding up to Him! But, my darling, this is a great soul-crisis—perhaps you will never pass through such another; it is a "Now" of infinite grace, and Satan will do his very utmost to keep you just out of the blessing which he knows would be the entrance upon a glorious life of power as well as of joy. Oh, do not yield to him, but yield yourself entirely to Jesus. . . .

. . . But remember nothing can be really gained in this matter without the true-hearted, whole-hearted surrender of all and for always to Jesus. This you must do; and yet for this He and He only can make you "willing," and give you power to do it. But just look straight at His promises just as they stand, and all the paradox will be solved. He "waits to be gracious" to you. Look at 2 Corinthians 6:17, 18, "I will receive," etc. With the very effort to obey, He gives the power. He gives

---

[1] *All for Jesus.* Partridge & Co.

freely strength and grace for whatever He commands. His commands are all implied promises.

(To C. H.)

May 1874.

My heart has written to you every day, though my pen has not, because I have been rather extra pressed and busy. I was so thankful to get your last letter. Oh, it is a simply glorious life that by His grace you have entered, of real whole-hearted consecration to Jesus. Now, darling, "stand fast in the liberty wherewith Christ has made you free, and be not entangled again with the yoke of bondage" (Galatians 5:1). And "by faith ye stand" (2 Corinthians 1:24), and He will give it, and increase it. And you "are kept by the power of God through faith" (1 Peter 1:5). But nothing short of the highest level will do, that is the true place of joy. . . . I am most thankful that He has impelled you to speak to ——; it is to me a test of your "gold:" you cannot keep it to yourself if you really have the blessing. Yes, "tell it out," and remember that you are responsible for what He has given you of joy and grace (1 Peter 4:10). . . . Commit your whole self to Him to be "sanctified wholly" (1 Thessalonians 5:23, 24). Look out all His promises about it, and claim them and believe them. Just see for yourself what His promises and commands are. He gives no impossible commands, for His promises and His enabling power always exceed them. Only we must believe the promises, and draw upon the power. Ask Him to teach you all about it, and to show you practically how much He is able and willing to do for those who will but trust His bare word at any cost of preconceived opinions. "Wrong thoughts" are most assuredly conscious sin, to be instantly confessed and hated and repelled, not to be excused or indulged for an instant. If you have the least wince of conscience, at any cost instantly see to it, and let there be instant confession, which surely results in instant cleansing. Recollect the glorious word "cleanseth," *i.e.* "goes on cleansing," and claim it and trust to it, and be willing to be kept under the cleansing power of the blood, leaving no place, and giving no quarter to even the shadow of a sinful thought. "Who is sufficient for these things?" God is; and your sufficiency is of Him and of Him only. See Jude 24; and let us press on in faith and hope to a really holy life. Of course, the happiness will be in proportion. Temptation is not sin; oh, no! Jesus was tempted! But parleying with temptation is sin. Satan may cast a fiery dart, and it may pain terribly; . . . but if our whole soul loathes and recoils from it as He did, the sin is Satan's, not ours. You will soon experience the difference between sinful temptation of one's own evil heart, and temptation from the Evil One in which you may claim Christ's deepest sympathy.

"Presumptuous" to speak for Jesus! My dear Ceci, is it presumptuous of a soldier to tell what a good general he has? is it presumptuous of a liberated slave to tell of his deliverer to his former fellow-captives? would it be presumptuous of me to speak lovingly and gratefully to anybody who had died instead of me? That idea was a temptation, if you like! and if you parley with that, you will be dishonouring and sinning against Him. How dare we "hold our peace"! It is "presumptuous" if through fear of man or conventionality or self-consciousness and nervousness we are cowards enough to accept all His benefits and all His love, and just hold our tongues about it, and not give Him the open praise of lip and life that should glorify Him, and yet expect Him to be pleased with us, and continue His smile upon us! That is horrible presumption!

As for ——, perhaps she will be your first soul for Jesus. Ask it! I may tell you that it is a remarkable fact that the uniform experience of those who find blessing is that God peculiarly honours the confession of what He has done for them. Look at Philemon 6. So I am peculiarly glad that you frankly told her of your *own* blessing.

"Grow?" Yes, of course, and expect that faith and love will grow day by day, and may they "grow exceedingly."

(To C. H.)

Leamington, June 4, 1874.

Your letters make me so happy! I do praise our dear Master for you and with you. I quite expected you would be made a blessing at once—it seems to be always so.

As to your choir, I think it is beginning at the wrong end to press the Lord's Table first. It is the principle of love and obedience which they want, then they will unhesitatingly "obey" the command; it will be quite certain to follow. Speak out fully and freely to them about Jesus Himself, and I believe that if He gives you grace and courage to confess to them what a blessing you have personally received, there will be fruit immediately. . . .

Be willing to take up any odds and ends of work (pen, voice, hands, feet, tongue), which the Master puts before you. And be quite sure that He will guide thee continually, so that seeming hindrances are quite sure to be furtherances. He constantly holds me back from some intended bit of work, and then gives me another instead, in a most remarkable way. . . .

(To ——.)

May 23, 1874.

You were right about the "undertone of pain," *and* about the victory. But I cannot help telling you that the wonderful and glorious blessing which so many Christians are testifying to having found, was suddenly, marvellously sent to me last winter; and life is now what I never imagined life on earth could be, though I knew *much* of peace and joy in believing before.

He has done for me exceeding abundantly above all I asked or thought,—I never *could* say that before, I say it in adoring wonder now. It seems as if a call were going forth to His own children to make a more complete surrender of their whole selves and lives, and to enter into a fulness of consecration, which I for one had not realized before. Now I want you to have this too! The Master Himself will show you how to find it, and perhaps astonish you as He did me with it. *From Glory to Glory* is the only piece in *Under the Surface* written after I found what life in Jesus could be, and that is the only piece which altogether expresses my hourly gladness,—at least as far as expression can go, which is not *very* far after all! This is overflowing "compensation" on this shore for ALL. I can set to my seal that this is true, and write "Satisfied!" upon all the yearnings you so truly touch.

(*To ——.*)

1874.

I was more glad than surprised at your letter, for I had a strong impression that this would come about. I am so very thankful that your first time after leaving school is to be with such a family. The first year or two (after school) is perhaps the most important time of your whole life; and I have long hoped and prayed that if you were not with your own dear mother, you might be where a decidedly spiritual atmosphere might be around you, and where you might learn to take such a decided stand on Christ's side, that it should never again be a doubt or even a difficulty to you to "stand up for Jesus," wherever you might subsequently be. And this you will have with ——. But remember "Paul may plant and Apollos water, but only God can give the increase;" so do make it a special prayer, that you may really profit by the privileges you will have; that you may lose none of the blessings which will be around you, but that you may be "strengthened and stablished and settled" in your spiritual life; that you may be no weak Christian, but become "strong in the grace that is in Christ Jesus." I am so glad that I shall have you with me all the autumn, and I hope that I shall be a little bit of help to you in many ways.

No teacher ever has only and altogether smooth sailing, and it would be no real advantage to have *no* difficulties, or we should never learn to overcome them, and should gain no strength of character. Your pupil is accustomed to obedience, and she has a dear little heart, and is singularly affectionate and easily touched, and that sort of material to work upon is a great thing.

Children are managed best if you show from the outset that whatever you say *has* to be done; so be rather careful in what you do say. Never say a thing is to be done, which you are not quite sure ought and must be done, so as not to have to retract or give in; but once *said* carry it out! As a rule, I always unhesitatingly advise governesses to ask to have their supper upstairs, so as to secure time to go on with steady plans for self-improvement, reading, and practising, etc.

You will, I am sure, be kind and pleasant and gentle to the maids—if they think any one is stuck up and gives unnecessary trouble, they do not like it; but speak pleasantly, and thank civilly, and consult their convenience instead of positively ordering things, and then you will be waited on night or day like a princess!

I do hope you will be a good psalmodist, so practise thoroughly a few tunes from Havergal's *Psalmody;* try "Chesalon," "Goldbach," "Franconia," "Hermas," "Claudia," "Nassau," "Sternberg," "Hobah," "Persis," "Zaanaim," "Idumea," "Sihor," "Patmos," also my father's special tune "Evan," both arrangements, 1. and 2., and "Culbach," "Iona," "Eden," "Tryphosa," etc.

You may imagine I cannot write many such long letters as this, for I have received nearly 600 letters the last six months, and of course letters must be answered.

Dear ——, do pray most earnestly in this interval that God's very special blessing may be upon this step. Nothing can prosper without that. Do not furl your colours!

I am afraid I am really more anxious about your body than your soul! but I do so want you not to be foolish, and get overdone for nothing. So that you fulfil faithfully your duties to your pupil, you have no right (as regards your positive duty to your mother and to yourself) to get fatigued and overdone, and perhaps lay the foundation of delicate health, just for want of moral courage to say "I am tired," or to face the very awful trial of any one wondering why you did retire early, or not go to the evening service; I should feel less strongly about it, if I had not split on the same rock. You must *not* sacrifice health and strength for nothing. May He give you tact and wisdom in this and all else. Never allow children to be inconsiderate, or needlessly imposing on you.

You must not be depressed, you *must* rouse out of it and go cheerily to your work again. What would you do, if you had the real causes of depression which so many young governesses have? But you are trying, and I am so glad—only you must make a real point of conscience about it, and pray vigorously and constantly for help in this thing.

I think —— is a little better, and she seemed so very bright and happy that I thought she set somebody of my acquaintance a bright example of trust and patience and cheerfulness!

"Now then do it!" See what 2 Samuel 3:17–18 says.

I am very anxious to hear how you are, but if only you are as well as I think, it will do you good in many ways to be alone awhile. Often we are least alone when most alone. Only we must not take it for granted that as a matter of course the Lord Jesus will draw near. He will be sought, and pressed to enter in and abide with us; but if we do thus entreat Him to be with us, He surely will be. Every new position is like being put for a while into a different class in His school; there will be new lessons to learn and new progress to make. So, darling, I wonder what He has to teach you now during the next few weeks—certainly *something*, so "watch to see what He will say unto you." Do not overtire yourself, because remember this is your holiday, and you must not come back fagged out. I am more afraid of your doing too much than too little. Look at Isaiah 58:11, and find out in your concordance *all* His promises under "guide" and "lead," and see what fulness of assurance He gives you.

(To ——.)

June 15, 1874.

... I do not know that I can do more than send you what cost me the greatest struggle I ever had to allow anything to be printed.[1] The way in which my Master came and astonished me by giving me, even me, a blessing, which I had hardly heard of, much less understood, was more than I could have imagined.

Now I simply and strongly believe that His hand is open and ready to give the same blessing to all who will have it; therefore to you, dear friend. And the desires which you describe look to me like a sure earnest that you will have it. Oh do not compare yourself with others—thousands are shutting themselves out from this blessing, because they will not believe it—and thus hindering others too, who argue that "because So-and-so has not experienced it, and yet is far in advance of me, therefore I ought not to expect it." Dear Miss S., go independently to the Lord Jesus and just *see* what He will do for you! Oh! believe that "able" means "able" and no less, and that "all" means "all" and no less; and taking these two words as your starting-point, go and simply search and see what the Lord *can* do for you, and what He promises to do. You will receive, He has not given you the desire for nothing, He will fulfil it. And he can do it without any human teaching—you see I had none whatever except that one single sentence of reply from Mr. W. The Lord did all the rest. Only I must own to you, "to the praise of His glory," that the blessing described in the little book not only lasts but increases. It is even having a great effect upon my health, for all touch of worry, care, anxiety, and fidget about anything earthly or heavenly is all gone. Jesus takes it *all,* and the rest of faith is more perfect and uninterrupted than I imagined it possible for any one of my own nervous, highly-strung temperament to enjoy. *All* His doing!

I was powerless,—and never saw my own weakness and my own sinfulness as I see them, now that I am finding power and sanctification in Jesus. Do not imagine there need be delay—at once, on getting this, let me beg you to break through everything—go straight and yield up your *whole* self, *unbelief* and *all,* to Jesus, and receive the blessing. I think I shall soon hear you have it.—Yours in loving hope.

(To M. V. G. H.)

1874.

I must send a copy of a note just received. See, Marie, dear! I know *my* witness does not go for much, but when one after another of old-established Christians come forward and say they have received a blessing which they have never had before, and which they had not even imagined, can its reality be doubted? It is mostly those who are looking for it who get it; but in some cases, as with myself, He seems to come and astonish His children by an utterly unexpected blessing. In answering the first letter, I felt strongly that it was due to the Lord to acknowledge what a blessing had come to me immediately after their special prayer for me, as well as the coincidences about the hymn. I hesitated much and prayed very earnestly to be guided whether or not to send *Such a Blessing.* I recollected vividly all that had been said about hindering and lessening my influence if I spoke out; and then I saw that this might be all temptation, and that I might be grieving the Holy Spirit's influence if I resisted the strong impulse to send it. So I committed it all to God, and trusted Him to send *power* with the little book and the letter I wrote with it. Now, only see! Has He not reproved me for my faint-heartedness in fearing to tell of His goodness to me? What could be more overwhelming than such an immediate result! Strangely enough, it has been so all along—in almost every instance in which I have entrusted all to my Master, and spoken or written *freely* and just as I felt He was guiding me, blessing has resulted immediately: from the day I went to Areley House till now. I still wait (in obedience), but I cannot help believing that if I had all this spring been speaking out freely and fearlessly, I should have had tenfold more blessing and result. I have had very much, but not so much as I might have had. I would give anything for all around me to enter into the fulness of "this miracle of love"—why should I refrain from seeking to lead others into this *utter* rest of heart, which I know is no fancy? For the present I will still *wait*—I will not deviate from my present nearly invariable silence till after I have been to Switzerland.

On the very same day, *while* I was praying for it, the full blessing was poured out just gloriously upon a new friend of mine, daughter of that special friend of dear mother's. They are going to have C. M. S. sermons in St. Paul's, and "Tell it out" is to be sung. (See Appendix.)

---

[1] *Such a Blessing.* Partridge & Co.

(To E. C.)

1874.

I am more thankful than astonished. . . . I am so glad for you, and feel sure that you will be increasingly blessed. I only earnestly hope that nothing of the same kind of opposition will be roused as here. It is singular that while your mouth is opened, my mouth is altogether closed! —— is more and more *strong* against the Conference, and several things connected with her make it my clear duty to *submit* and be silent.

I want you to pray specially for me on Wednesday about 12.15. It seems that some extra bold requests of mine at the last meeting, both for prayer and praise, rather startled the Association members,—the writer, of course, they guessed to be me. So Margaret is most anxious that I should use the opportunity, and at our next meeting give "personal testimony," a totally new thing in our meetings, telling them frankly what great things the Lord has done for me as to *answering prayer.* She trusts it may stimulate the whole Association. I know it will considerably astonish them if I do this unprecedented thing: then I cannot do this without going farther. I must tell out clearly upon what I believe this fulfilment of John 15:7 hinges. Once started, I shall probably, God helping me, speak very strongly upon surrender and consecration (Matthew 8:10); obedience, instant and implicit; and faith "without taking off discount,"—as it may be the *only,* as it is the first opportunity of really addressing them and speaking personally and rousingly. Of course I shall carefully avoid all shibboleths. Now, will you pray that the Lord would put His words in my mouth, and that I may say neither more nor less than He would have me say?

I am quite satisfied that God is leading me aright; I only better understand the special help I want for Wednesday. Today the words have come very sweetly to me, "Until the time appointed of the Father" (Galatians 4:2); and I shall be free to speak and act as I would like when His time comes. I know nothing I should be more glad of than if mother would invite you here. She will not just yet, I know; but when she does, do strain a point, and come.

Well, dear E., the Master knows what He has given, and what He has promised, and what He will do; and I do not expect He will disappoint me.

Mr. S. says he has had such joy in thinking, "Enoch walked with God" 300 years! Then is our life to be worse and less than his? Nay, rather, "some even better thing"! Is not that good?

(To M. V. G. H.)

The Parsonage, Bocking, June 19, 1874.

I did not mean to write any circulars, but must send one London and Bocking account. Once out of England, I shall leave all that to Connie, who will thus have a grand chance of distinguishing herself as a general correspondent.

I was consternated at finding H. had made engagements for every day! However, I felt sure I should be "cared for," and so did not trouble about it. She took me to Doré's pictures. The two great new ones are *more* striking than the others. I wish I could stay to describe the weird beauty of "The Dream of Pilate's Wife." Then I had a pleasant and long interview with Nisbet (*the* Watson of the London Board). I am delighted with him—so very kind and nice. He was called away for a few minutes, and brought me a great book of reviews, that I might amuse myself with reading up those under "Havergal"!—several capital ones which I had not seen.

I returned with ——; and at 8 p.m. we went to a party, and I was horrified at hearing carriages ordered 12.30! However, by special favour to me, ours was ordered at 11.30. I wondered what I was there for, and soon found out! For it is so strange how people drift me into actual personal religious conversation. No one could say I force it, and I *know* I do not; but, for instance, one gentleman, who began with small-talk and badinage, found himself in five minutes (we were in a quiet corner) face to face with personal salvation. I really do not know how it came about, but there it was; and he owned that he never thought of anything more than "how to get comfortably through the world," and "did not trouble himself about another just yet"—he got so sobered down, and greatly interested; promised to think it all over, and thanked me. That was by no means the only one I seemed sent to that evening. I was so glad I could sing so as to make them *all* listen; for it was a large double room, and all were perfectly silent for my music. I shall probably never *know,* but I do not see why I should doubt that seed dropped that night took root.

11th June.—I intended to have a quiet writing morning, but suddenly felt a strong impulse to go and hunt up Miss Grant, who knew my father abroad, but whom I have never met. I sent in my card, and she came open-armed; strangely enough, for an hour before I came she had been thinking and praying over something of mine which seems to have stirred her deeply, and longing especially by any means to meet me, having no idea I was in London! So she thought I was almost miraculously sent! I was so glad I went; she just wanted a bit of special comfort. She said her father, a literary man and editor, wished very much to see me; so another day I had a most delightful hour with him.

One day Rev. D. came to dinner—I wish there were 5000 more such curates—a real downright, devoted fellow, and all the sunshine in his face and over his life and work, and having the joy of winning souls. He is one who has found special joy and blessing of late, and Mrs D. too; in fact, I hear of it on all sides—Jesus of Nazareth is passing by in a most striking way among His own people with hitherto unrealized blessings for them.

16th.—Arrived at Bocking Parsonage in answer to earnest entreaty from the daughter of one of dear mother's especial friends whom I had met at home.

It is most odd how in this out-of-the-way place people know everything I write, and I was so amused to find that even the school children wanted to catch sight of me! But better than that, God Himself seemed to have given a strong expectation that if I came, it would be for blessing—and so I feel sure it was. I had the ladies for a drawing-room meeting on Wednesday, and a little gathering of young girls and women on Thursday, and I did so enjoy them. *As* I do it, it is far less fatiguing than a party. You see otherwise these ladies would have been asked to tea, and I should have been chattering to ones or twos, and singing Handel, and so on for three or four hours, and not getting so soon to rest as usual. Instead of this, they came at 7.30, and when all were ready I went straight to my place and opened with a little prayer; then—what if I did talk about Deuteronomy 33:12 for about an hour, I had it all my own way, telling them just what I wanted to tell them, and what my own heart was full of, with no tension of trying to meet remarks wisely, and trying to make the most of opportunities, etc., which would have gone on for three hours at least at a party. And then I knew they wanted this, and wanted just the blessings I was telling them of; and then I could entirely trust the Master all the time to keep guiding every word, so that it is the smoothest of smooth sailing. After hymn and prayer, I asked if any one would like to ask any questions, and two or three asked very useful and suggestive ones, which I was delighted to answer. It was all over in an hour and a half. I do not say it did not tire me last year, but I find my expectation fulfilled now, and that I can do it *quite* differently, *i.e.* without any excitement or nervousness whatever. I look to my Master to give me just what He will, and I feel He does help me, and I leave the whole thing with Him. I took a previously prepared subject, so only needed quiet thought and prayer beforehand. I felt sure God would bless these meetings, and He certainly did—several finding new light and joy. All the time I was there I had such a vivid sense of His exceeding goodness and love that I do not think I ever spent a happier four days. One cannot tell everything, but I do not think either of my visits were resultless.

20th.—I went to Bishop Stortford to see Ernest H.; he is such a dear little fellow, and was very communicative, and greatly entertained with my alpenstock. He came to see me off at the station: a pleasant man in my carriage asked me a question about the place; so I referred him to Ernest, who gave him explicit information. Then he said, "I wished to know because I hope to hold some children's meetings here." So I said, "It is

Mr. Spiers, I am sure!" And so it was! He gave Ernest some books, and promised me to patronize him specially in the autumn. I asked him about his work, which is certainly *one* of the most wonderful things going, and got a great deal of really useful material from him. Then he asked me what *my* work was, and I told him "whatever came to hand!" But as that was not definite enough for him, I offered my leaflet *From Glory to Glory* as my card; and he was so delighted. I arrived at Mrs. C.'s, who is delightful! It is a sort of dream to be at Mildmay; it is very delicious.

(*To M. V. G. H.*)

1874.

I went to tea with Messrs. H. & R. at their business house; Mr. H. was bent upon Mr. R. hearing me sing my "Tell it out" and "When thou passest through the waters." I had a most interesting afternoon, half business, half pleasure. Both of them were taken with "Tell it out," and think it "such a hit," etc., and are going to issue it at once in song form, as solo and chorus with piano accompaniment. Then they wanted more of the same, and I sang my tunes "Euodias" to "'Tis the church triumphant," and "Onesimus" to "Only for Thee," and "Hermas" to "Golden harps are sounding," and others; and they wish me to prepare a whole set. They say, "Tell it out" is safe to go. Mr. R. had never heard me play any sacred music before, and he started up, and said, "Ha! you are mistress here!" He exceedingly admires "When thou passest," and is going to publish it. Mr. H. sings splendidly himself—clear, high cultivated tenor voice.

I so enjoyed my visit to ——; was let alone, and could write in peace; then quiet pony drives with Mrs. ——. Some pleasant work opened for me. I believe one has really taken the great step this week, and three others are earnestly seeking and I am very hopeful about one of the servants.

You wanted me to write penny books. You have seen, *I also for Thee*, and Caswell will publish one for the New Year, *The Five Benefits.* Parlane is doing Packet IV. of my Leaflets.

(*To M. W.*)

All my care is upon His shoulders now! I have no burden, not an ounce. Blessed work here—one conversion and three grand blessings to tell about in this house since I came a week ago, and "more to follow," I am sure, for the Master is evidently here. So is Satan! for I never had such a pitched battle with him as last Wednesday—a soul seemed all but lost, and I never heard more distressing words. I was at it till after midnight—the battle is still pending.

I was terribly distressed for a whole day, because it seemed like living in sheer disobedience to my Lord. "In everything give thanks,"—and how could I give thanks that my poor F. had lost the blessing! I could not "thank" for a trial which was not for God's glory, but seemed all the devil's doing. Then I suddenly saw I had not been taking the literal words! It is not "*For* everything," but only "In;" so I forthwith began to "give thanks" "*in*" my sorrow, and felt *greatly* comforted. Was I *right,* do you think?

(To ———.)

October 19, 1874.

So you, too, are being stirred up by the "loving Spirit" to seek holiness and rest beyond what you have as yet found! Thank God! And I know not how to thank Him enough that though only a year ago I knew absolutely nothing of this blessed life—had not even read one word about it,—I can now tell you joyously that His own Hand has led me into it, and that for nearly a year I have not known what it is to have a shadow of care in things temporal or spiritual: all is cast upon Him, and He gives me victory and gladness in response to the utter trust (which is no less His gift); so that it is living a new life, and one which I really did not even suppose to be possible on earth. I enclose you what cost me more to lay at the Master's feet than anything ever did. You will easily understand the shrinking from allowing such letters to be printed; but He has so very *marvellously* blessed this little book, . . . it says so much more than I have time to say in letters. He is the same Lord, rich unto *all* that call upon Him, and the same fulness of blessing is as open to you as to me: only taste and see: only trust; only let Him do what He will with you; only take His promises (and His commands too) just as they stand, "without taking off any discount." . . . He will teach and lead you, and show you what He is able to do for you. And may you soon know the full blessedness of utter surrender, continual cleansing, absolute trust, and implicit obedience.

. . . I should like to tell you, as well as many other dear ones, how it has all been one song of goodness and mercy, and how I want to sing out His faithfulness, and tell all His dear children that they need indeed "fear no evil." . . .

Will you look into each clause of the sixfold promise contained in the beatitude of "trust"? (Jeremiah 17:7, 8). You will enjoy it if you have not yet gone right into those two verses.

October 30, 1874.

. . . How good He is! Oh, I am so thankful for you! And now entrust your trust to Him, and "the future is one vista of brightness and blessedness." . . . —Yours in joy and love.

. . . What you tell me of the Lord setting His manifested seal upon two of my hymns, "O thou chosen Church of Jesus," and "Certainly I will be with thee," made me feel very unworthy and very thankful, and (I cannot help saying it) sent a new thrill of love through my heart to Him who is so good to me. If you ever sing my hymns again, will you send up a prayer that I may more and more rejoice in the truths which they feebly represent; and, if it be our Master's will, that He would give me yet many more powerful messages of song, for I cannot write without Him.

(To J. T. W.)

WINTERDYNE, 1875.

This is a very suffering Sunday, and it will be a relief to write and ask you to pray for me that the Lord would let patience have her *perfect* work in me, and that I may really glorify Him in pain. I was gaining strength steadily till a few days ago, and had arrived at being able to walk across the room once or twice a day; but now I have such intense pain, especially at night, that I do feel it to be very real "chastening." He has enabled me to be quite patient so far, and it is not that I fear His grace will fail for what is yet before me; but, dear friend, will you ask that it may not only not fail, but abound. My doctor says it may pass in a few days, but that it may be a much longer affair; anyhow, I have need of patience if only for the "few days." But I am clinging, yes, and resting, all the time, and the "perfect peace" is not touched.

And now I want to tell you a bit of good news. I did mean with all my heart and soul, "Take my will, it shall be Thine," but I did not quite dare to think He *had* taken it. But now need I doubt it any more? For I am sure my will would not have been perfectly satisfied and happy under present circumstances if He had not taken it. It would not come natural to me not to feel pain. But I do lament over want of growth in grace, because that must be *my* fault. I think any other Christian would have made progress in these five months of illness, (except in the matter of trust, and perhaps of patience), I do not see that I have. I never saw so much "unpossessed ground" as now, nor more of "unconquered territory." Yet, on the other hand, I have cause to praise with joyful lips, for more possessed and conquered than two years ago I should have supposed possible.

My *Bells* and *Pillows* are such a success numerically. Your "100 acres" is a delightful illustration. But I would trust my husbandman still, even if there were no crop visible next year! But perhaps there will be! I am nearly sure I shall disappoint the expectation of my friends—as to outward fruit, writing, etc.; but so that I don't disappoint the Master, it won't be so bad. It may be very long before I write again, if ever. You had a fallow time, had you not, not long after your blessing? Were you conscious of increased blessing after? However, an "afterward" of "peaceable fruit" is *sure,* because promised in every trial.

(To J. T. W.)

I know you will be glad to hear that the fire is cooling! But for twelve days it got hotter and hotter, such terrible pain day and night, but thank God quite suddenly and unaccountably (except that —— turns out to have been engaged in special prayer for me at the very moment!) pain subsided, every bad symptom decreased, and Mr. G. was perfectly astonished, as he had reason to expect to find me worse instead of better.

Your letters always help me, sometimes directly, sometimes by putting me on the track which leads to what I wanted. In your first note of mere inquiry you *only* said, "The Lord is right!" "You can trust Him, I know." Those ten monosyllables were a volume of delight to me for days. "Right" opened out a grand view of the wise, omniscient, infallible, almighty love and faithfulness which make all that He does absolutely right—and not abstractedly right only, but right *for me*. "Can" gave a view of the difference between the time when I could not, and of His sovereign grace having enabled me to trust, and that led on to all the grand chain of "chosen," "called," etc., and so on with "trust" and "Him."

Out of your letter I got nothing direct, but a great thing indirectly. It set me into a new track; had Jesus been speaking and I mistaking His voice? Tell me, when a text comes into my mind and I have said, "I *thought* of it," may I believe that it was *not* that I thought of it, but that Jesus spoke it to me? I have almost grasped this, not firmly; but it is possibly going to be a great step in my spiritual life, it would make such a difference! Hitherto it has only been when that peculiarly strong and irresistible *flashing* of a strikingly apposite text came to me, such as only comes at rare intervals, that I have dared to hope it was His voice. But when texts rise in one's mind without any peculiar need or tension of soul, when they just "come into one's head," reminding and warning, or comforting in a quiet, gentle, everyday way,—now, is *that equally the Master Himself speaking to me?* Don't speak "smooth things" about it, don't say yes if you have any misgiving. But oh! suppose I have been mistaking His voice all this time, how I must have grieved Him! I really do not think any child of God can have more to be forgiven than I have had; "much forgiven" always comes home to me.

No! I *was not lamenting* about lying fallow! That is *His* doing, and I am satisfied, *perfectly* satisfied to be fallow as long as ever He likes. It is matter even of reason as well as faith; and if it were "fallow" all the rest of my earthly days, I should only expect the fairer and fuller harvest in heaven. For I "*shall* serve Him" there, even if ever, or very little more, here.

(To J. T. W.)

1875.

I wonder if this year is a sort of halfway house in my pilgrimage, and what the other half will be? In any looking forward (as to work), I *can* do nothing but trust and wait, for my present feeling is one of pure weakness, no sense of power for any work, whether direct soul-winning or any sort of writing. Even the plans and outlines of books, poems, etc., which I had when very ill, are all gone now. I am simply emptied—if ever there was an empty vessel it is I; and though if merely empty, one would look forward to His filling, the vessel also feels very small, and also spoutless! I never felt quite this before; I always hitherto have seen my work before me, and felt more or less ability for it—isn't it curious? Your "Ask what I shall give thee" was brought back by the second lesson this afternoon—what a wonderful *carte blanche!* I could not sing the hymn after sermon, the *favourite*

> "O Lord, how happy we should be,
>   If we could cast our care on Thee!"

and marvelled that years ago I thought it charming! Fancy singing a lament over not being able to help continual lying! But does it not come to the same thing when He has absolutely and graciously *commanded* us to "cast thy burden," etc., on Him, if we are complacently to sing about how very nice it would be if we only could obey Him in this, and pathetically and practically describe our sad life of disobedience! Well, thanks be to Him, it would have been a simple falsehood for me to have sung most of the hymn, for I *have* cast my care on Him, and have not the faintest expectation of ever carrying a care again on my shoulders. Why should I? But it made me ever so happy, because I felt the real difference between the days when I could and did sing the hymn, and *now*. Don't you think we ought to thank God and take courage when one thus sees an old landmark left far behind? It is so good of Him to lead one *on,* that it seems ungrateful to ignore it. How I should like to have a regular outpour to you of His manifold goodness to me! My heart seems too full of it to hold, sometimes! Just now I recollected Psalm 145:7; never saw it in the same light before. Just what I have neither opportunity nor power to do *now,* but which will be fulfilled with such exquisite joy in heaven (when we have the long talk!), "They *shall* abundantly utter the memory of Thy great goodness." It is very curious, but I have thought more, and with more vivid delight about heaven, since I have seen no probability of going there for a long time yet, than I *ever* did before. But the very anticipation makes me much more happy to wait patiently and *live* and work (or suffer).

WINTERDYNE, March 6, 1875.

MY OWN DEAR M.,—

. . . I am under no restrictions now . . . *any* thing I feel able to do to divert me from the pain is allowed. . . . Just a fortnight ago, inflammation came on, and has caused me the most acute suffering I ever had in my life . . . especially at night. Sometimes it seems just agony, but I have intervals of rest, and comparative, though not absolute, ease. . . . The bad nights naturally result in severe headache (also mercifully with intervals). I never get any sleep without as much laudanum as can be brought to bear on the parts, and also on my head; and more than once *no* sleep even with that. So this fortnight (considering my nerves, which the doctors say make me *exceptionally* sensitive to pain) has been more real " chastening " than any part of my long illnesses. It is more than four months since I have been at family prayers. And now for the other side!

OF COURSE He is faithful! and so I do not merely imagine *I ought* to feel, but I do most distinctly feel, that all this weakness and suffering has been, and IS, the crowning mercy of all the mercies which have been heaped upon me since the *great* blessing came to me December 2, 1873. I have been all through, and still am, not only kept in PERFECT PEACE, but I am so *very* happy that it has really seemed worth being prayed back from the very gates of heaven (which really seems to be the case!), if I may but tell of His faithfulness—*witness* to it in some way. "Not one good thing hath failed!" Nothing that I have trusted Him for has come short, and it seems to "come natural" now to trust Him utterly and for everything. The *wonderful* thing to me is that He actually does seem to have answered my prayer, "Take my will, it shall be Thine," etc., for I am not conscious of even the *rising of a wish* for even this terrible pain to be taken away one day sooner than His far-sighted love decides; nor of the *least* regret, when I was told (before this inflammation began) that I must not attempt or expect to be able to do any sort of work for at least six months more, even if I had *no* further drawbacks.

Now I am so perfectly certain that this does *not* "come natural" to me (obvious to any one who knows my decidedly "active disposition," and still more to those who know my excessive natural impatience—*fidget!*), that it is clearly altogether His own doing, and I do not know how to praise Him enough for it. For there is "no effort" whatever about it. I have never "sought to be resigned to His will;" I have just simply rested and *rejoiced* in it all along, could not do otherwise, SEEING rather than believing the marvellous love and faithfulness and wisdom of which it is the outcome. I shall enjoy trying to tell people (if He lets me serve Him on earth again) what a splendid thing it is to be utterly His own, giving Him one's *whole* trust, and then proving His *grand* faithfulness. I am quite sure if He was ready to do for *me* all that He has done, He must be even more ready to give it to others, for I should think *very* few Christians ever *distrusted* and doubted as I have done, especially with the opportunities I had, and for so *many* years!

"Forgiven *much*" is peculiarly my position; I cannot imagine any one being His child at all and grieving Him more and longer. I should like you to tell your sisters how good He has been to me, that they may see that "the blessing" stands fire. When I was taken ill I left all my small work in the Master's hands, to do as He would—and so He has taken it all up; and taking the outward success as index, which, perhaps, I am not wrong in doing, it has never prospered so much as in these four and a half months, when *I* could not touch it. . . . Nothing ever seemed to touch me more than the extraordinary way in which prayer for me in November seemed stirred up. I felt quite overwhelmed at all I *heard* afterwards, though I had a strong impression at the time that *many* were praying for me; I do not mean personal friends, but Christians in literally all parts of the kingdom, and not merely private prayer, but the number of prayer meetings at which I was repeatedly prayed for by people I never heard of, is most singular. Even special prayer meetings were held on my account, and Sankey prayed most fervently for me at the great Dublin meetings. It must be all the echo of Christ's intercession.

Friday, March 12.—I must finish in the *first* interval of comparative ease I have had for three days. The pain has *been far* worse since I began, I should not have thought a mere *limb* could have caused me so much. . . . So, darling M., *pray* for me, and ask that grace may not only not fail (*that* I do not fear), but *abound*. . . .

(*To Margaret W.*)

1875.

I have just been writing my request for praise (Y. W. C. A.). What can I do? I can't curtail it, and I might go on and add many, many details to the list. Oh I wish I could have come over to your praise meeting, and just tried to tell you all how gracious and faithful and near God has been all this summer; if I kept a diary it would be just a record of answers to prayer, and such great answers too. If you don't mind, I wish you would tell the members at your next meeting, because they would be glad to hear how wonderfully God is answering one of them, and He is the same Lord over all—rich unto *all* that call upon Him. And as some have prayed specially for me and my work, they should feel that they have been answered.

(*To Mrs. Brunot, America.*)

1875.

You must have wondered at getting no answer all this time to your most kind and interesting letter. But the Master's wise, dear hand has been upon me, and I am only now sending pencil replies to some of the many loving messages which came during my illness. I was taken ill in October with typhoid fever, but what with sundry relapses and results, it was a very suffering illness; it will be months yet ere I am likely to be able for anything beyond the little quiet opportunities of an invalid. But I do wish I could tell you how good God has been to me! It has been worth far more than all the suffering to prove His faithfulness, and to find how tenderly gracious He can be just when one most needs it. "Great is Thy faithfulness" shines out upon the past, and "I will fear no evil," on the future. And as for being held back from work, that is altogether His affair, not mine; and there is a fellowship of *waiting*, I think, in it. For He is waiting as well as I; and when it says, "And therefore will the Lord wait that He may be gracious," it is no wonder that the same verse adds, "Blessed are all they that wait for Him."

You say you would like to know what particular work I have. Had I chosen for myself, I should have *liked* some definite service on which I could have concentrated energies and time, but the Master chose otherwise; and over and above the happy certainty that His choice is best, I think I can now see that His seeming hinderings have been furtherings, and that He has really permitted me to do *more* for Him in His way than I could have done in my own, and has given me a wider influence.

Delicate health prevents my undertaking any regular or permanent work. Other circumstances oblige me to be often on the move. So I am necessarily always on the watch for what He would have me do next, just any work He sends, according to locality or strength—sometimes helping others—sometimes starting a Y. W. C. A. branch—sometimes getting temporary Bible classes or meetings—sometimes only writing, but always having ten times more openings than I have physical strength for. Perhaps my specialities are direct personal work with individuals, chiefly young ladies, and "singing for Jesus;" in these God has blessed me so abundantly that often I feel as if I could not praise Him enough, even in heaven. And now that I am quite laid aside from any work (for I am strictly forbidden to write anything involving thought), it is just marvellous how He seems to have carried on my work for me, making my books and leaflets circulate more than ever before, and sending such singular blessing sometimes upon merely a pencilled note, that I keep wondering at His exceeding grace and love. He is so good to me, that it seems worth while being sent back from the very Golden Gates, which I thought a few months ago were just reached, if I may but "tell it out."

I was extremely interested to hear of all your great work (so different to my little desultory bits!), and it seemed a special privilege and pleasure to have a sweet far-off greeting from one to whom the Lord has entrusted so much of His work. And it is a widening of one's love and interest and hopes to hear, I will not say of what you are doing, but of what He is doing by you. I had hoped to have been at the Convention, yet I can hardly say I am *disappointed,* for there seems no room for that word in the happy life of entire trust in Jesus, and satisfaction with His

perfect and glorious will. An invalid friend of mine said to me, "I think I begin to see how splendid God's will is." Was it not beautiful? How glad we shall be to see the full splendour of His will unveiled and vindicated before all the universe! What manifold joy we have to look forward to in this one direction alone!

(To the late Mary Shekleton.)[1]

April 26, 1875.

Your treasured little note was one of the pleasantest bits of outer sunshine which reached me all last winter; it was so kind of you to think of me, and your tiny note was so sweet and full. I did not get it till March! when recovering from a long and suffering illness. I am not to think of any sort of work for months yet. But this long illness has clearly been the crowning mercy of a series of varied and great mercies with which the Lord seemed almost to overwhelm me, ever since He led me into that perfect fulness of rest into which so many are entering. Every trial is but a new test of His faithfulness—a new "trial of His love"—and worth it!

Mine is probably only a temporary "calling apart" and waiting, but yours—how different! Yet even "among the shadows" of your own path, you have a splendid work for your Lord, in lighting up so many similar ones in a way only a fellow-sufferer could do. How kind of Him to give you the happy thought of the Invalid Prayer Union, and so much blessing in carrying it out! Is it not—I can't help saying *delicious*—to know that He chooses every bit of our work, and orders every moment of our waiting? What a Master we have!

I must tell you that it is quite remarkable how, during these months that I have been unable to have any communication with publishers or printers, God seems to have furthered and blessed all my writings more than previously; my *Little Pillows* and *Morning Bells,* specially, of which 8000 were sold in less than two months. It seems to me that the more completely one puts one's work into God's hands, the more He takes it up and furthers it.

May God bless the special work to which He has so clearly called you, very richly this year, and be very present all the days with you, His dear, suffering worker.

(To E. Tillerton.)

Oakhampton, June 3, 1875.

You will fully understand why I have not sent you the receipt for your kind, good work for the poor Green Islanders all this time, though dated March 24. At that date I was carried from bed to sofa and no more; and though I am now

---

[1] *Chosen, Chastened, Crowned:* Memoir, M. Shekleton. Nisbet.

convalescent, yet having had several drawbacks, I have never yet been strong enough for the journey home! But, oh, Emily, I wish I could tell it out what His gentle faithfulness is when one most needs Him. Both my illnesses have been so FULL of blessings, it seemed like everything coming true. "Great is Thy faithfulness" shines out on all the past, and "I will fear no evil" on the future. I am not supposed to be allowed to write letters, but by pencil notes I am gradually acknowledging (not liquidating) the many debts I owe of kind and loving inquiries and remembrances.

(To the late Miss Esther Beamish.)

July 26, 1875.

. . . We were close upon Midsummer, and I had gained no ground since Easter; very little improvement being followed by a relapse, though every surrounding was most favourable for recovery; and there seemed no way of preventing these relapses, which gave me no time to gain strength.

For the first time since my illness began in October, I had a time of spiritual depression, following in strange disappointment upon more than commonly fervent desire and prayer, that while others were receiving such blessing at Brighton, my Father would also bless "even me," and really confident *expectation* that He would make it a means of blessing to one of my very nearest and dearest; both which desires seemed unfulfilled, while an unexpected sorrow darkened in another quarter. He enabled me to cast the burdens upon Him; and then, during some days of literally "lying still" before Him, unable to sit up or even to read as usual in His own Word, He led me back into perhaps a sweeter, deeper rest in Him than almost ever before. On the 17th of June, the prospect of *never* being strong again came definitely before me. I looked at it very deliberately and fully—what it would be never to speak or sing or even write for Jesus, but only wait in quiet isolation and weakness, a burden to dear ones whose own burden I would like to bear, for years, perhaps for life. That this was not a mere improbable fancy is proved by my sister Miriam having written the very words "she will be a chronic invalid," on or about the same day. But as I looked, I wondered at His great goodness to me in thus proving to me that He had answered my prayer.

> "Take my will: it shall be Thine!
> It shall be no longer mine."

For I could not, *did* not feel one quiver of shrinking from the prospect,—not a fear, not a regret, not a choice in the matter. It was all "of course"—of course He would be "with me alway;" of course His grace would be sufficient; of course it would be all best and happiest, His will *must* be always sweetest and dearest. And as for service, that was altogether my Master's affair, not mine at all—He could do, and *should* do what He

would "with His own." I had the sweetest possible communion with Him about it, and felt, naturally enough, altogether light-hearted; for all that would have been too heavy for me was put *and left* in His dear hands. I seemed perfectly dead to any possible sense of anxiety or care about the future; and the present, even with fever and pain and languor, was what I would not have exchanged with any one's. Next day, June 18, was indeed much to be remembered. In the morning I was hardly so well, very weak, and with that indescribable sense of being "ill all over" which certainly does not naturally either raise one's spirits or herald a cure. But it was "perfect peace" literally passing understanding. My sister Ellen drove over to see me. In reply to her wish that I should come as soon as possible for change of air to Winterdyne, I told her it was useless thinking about it,—that no one could say when I should be able for the drive (not four miles), and that she must dismiss the idea altogether for the present. After she was gone I was again led to look at the prospect of chronic invalidism, and again, even more definitely and joyfully, "left it *all* with Jesus." After dinner I was left alone for some time, thinking I might get a little sleep, and *little* thinking what a much better thing the Lord was going to give me! Instead of sending sleep (I say it reverently), it seemed as if Jesus Himself came and *drew me out,* leading me on to tell Him what I hardly told myself. All through my illness I had never once felt able to pray for recovery, or even for mitigation of *pain.* More than once I thought I ought, for the sake of others, to *try* to ask it; but invariably it seemed as if the Holy Spirit checked my prayer and changed it into, "No! Lord Jesus! *I would rather* leave it *entirely* with Thee, and not even ask—do *just* what Thou wilt." Now, however, He seemed to say to me that the time was come to ask for recovery; but I told Him that I did not want to ask unless He *gave* me the prayer, and that *if* He did, I should expect His gracious and direct answer. Then He at once took away all the barrier, and put the prayer into my very lips. I prayed it, not as my prayer at all, but as His! Then I asked Him, "What about the answer?"—watching and *wondering* what He would graciously say next ("I will watch to see what He will say unto me," Habakkuk 2.1), and told Him I felt He had given me faith to be healed when He would. Then came, "I am the Lord that healeth thee!" with startling emphasis on "heal*eth.*" I literally started, and held my breath! Surely He Himself had said it! Then a sudden temptation, I believe from Satan himself, to think it was only a common act of recollection of the familiar words. But I did not stop to attend to this; but asked Him if He would condescendingly confirm it to me, if He had indeed "spoken to my heart." Instantly He did so; for again and again the assurance rang out in my heart, in such a way that I could not, *cannot* possibly doubt, that it was "Jesus Himself." "I am the Lord that *healeth* thee." I thought if ever He gave a marvellous opportunity for exercise of faith, here it was. So I praised Him, and told Him I would and did take Him at His word. And I did, and of course I was healed; for I saw that heal*eth* was not merely "*will* heal;" so I began to expect to find myself actually healed. This communion had been so absorbing and intense, that I had forgotten pain and discomfort; but now a pause seemed sent, that I might calmly realize the healing. It was real and complete! I examined my own sensations; it was a *total* change—no pain, no feverishness, no sense of being ill anywhere, much less "all over"! The question of restoration of *strength* had not been touched upon; it seemed quite apart from that of *cure,* and neither prayer nor faith had been given me for that. Thus I proved the more literally how *exactly* it was "according to my faith;" for though *well,* I was very *weak.* After a little while of praise, and then a sort of hushed rest, I thought, "As I *am* healed, I may just as well act upon it!" I had not intended to rise at all, unless perhaps just to have my bed made; but I got up and dressed!

When next my sister M. came into the room, she was surprised to find me dressed. I assured her I was ever so much better, and should not be the worse for getting up, but did not tell her what reason I had for saying so. I found that, half unconsciously, I had yielded to a temptation to *wait* and *see,* and not tell what the Lord had done for me till time had proved it by no relapse occurring. As soon as I detected this unbelief, I felt thoroughly ashamed of it, and forthwith "burnt my ships" by telling the whole, trusting to the Lord to "make it good." And of course He did. Next day I was down stairs, and three days after went to Winterdyne!

From that day to this, July 26, I have never had another hour's illness, but have gone on slowly gaining strength, with no greater drawbacks than a common cold and a little neuralgia.

The Lord's hand is still upon me in gentle restraining; for though much stronger, I am still *quite* unequal to ordinary physical or mental exertion, and it will evidently be a long time yet before I am able for "work."

I shall not be surprised to find that others were praying very specially for me at that time. One distant friend, I know, was led to very special and fervent prayer for me at the very time. It seems to me that "the prayer of faith" which "shall save the sick" must be "not of the will of the flesh, nor of the will of man, but of God," and that *in this direction* lies the key to whatever experimental difficulties appear to surround the promise. I think the prayer, the faith, and the healing are all equally from God—distinctly His gift, and His only.

(*To an American Friend.*)

Whitby, September 17, 1875.

I should have answered sooner, but have not been quite so well the last week or two; and if I had, I should have told you that the wise Master had not yet given me back the power of even the merest rhyme! But yesterday I read an article by a dear Christian friend trying to prove that there is such a thing as "sanctifying carefulness," and trying to make out somehow that we who testify that by His grace, we *have* cast all our care on Him, are under a sort of delusion! And then it made me so very glad to feel that it was no delusion, but that He does take every bit of my care, that it seemed as if my tongue, or rather pen, were loosed again, and I could not help a little gush of praise and testimony for the first time since my long illness. And though it is not at all the sort of thing for you to read as you wished at your Conference, I feel impelled to send this first little song of my restored life over to you ("Without Carefulness"), so that you may give it to any one to whom it might possibly be a little message of cheer and trust. It would be too great a treat to me to come over; and I do not think I shall ever be quite strong for pleasures of that kind; but I shall be with you in spirit, praying your Conference may be grandly blessed. Perhaps some echoes of the Master's voice to you and through you will reach us who cannot come over to listen with you.

> Master! how shall I bless Thy name
> For Thy tender love to me,
> For the sweet enablings of Thy grace,
> So sovereign, yet so free,
> That have taught me to obey Thy word
> And cast my care on Thee?

Curiously enough this hymn was written just *exactly* in time to be used at two great Conferences, Nottingham, and the great American Women's Christian Association at New York! I was invited to this, and if I could not come, to write a poem to be read at it and printed. I was going to answer "*Can't* write a line," when this came to me, and will reach the Committee just in time, though I did not write with the intention of sending it. Then Mr. Shaw asked for a copy the same day to send to a friend. A reply came asking permission by telegraph to use it at Nottingham Conference. Had the obnoxious Magazine article reached me just a day later, it would have been too late for both!

(*To J. E. J.*)

Royal Crescent, Whitby, October 1875.

. . . It always seemed to me harder to trust the Lord about His own affairs than about one's own! and I have chafed terribly at the strange falsehoods which have been permitted to spread and hinder the seekers after a better and happier life in Jesus, but quite lately He has taught me to cast the burden of *His* cause upon Him, and I am so glad He has. It had long seemed easy to cast all my own care upon Him, and to be utterly restful. These last two years have been a totally different life to me.

Doubt not that He is leading you by the right way, dear friend. Only give yourself up to the dear Lord, and let Him do just what He will with you, and *take all* He holds out to you. He is so gloriously gracious and " able."

. . . But *sing* my Consecration Hymn—don't *sigh* it any more!

————

" He hath done *all* things well." How sure we are of that! . . . " Thou hast *known* my reproach," and so your dear one is only having fellowship with Him. Christ said, " Reproach hath broken my heart." Think how the Lord heard every *word* that was unkindly said to ——! Don't you think he had his Master's tenderest sympathy? But I do feel very much for you both in this added pain.—In most loving sympathy.

(*To J. T. W.*).

WHITBY, October 11, 1875.

I am not nearly so strong as before my illness. I think it will have to be so literally " half-days " henceforth. But of course it does not trouble me. Not only that I know He can make a half-hour's work worth a whole day's, but more and more I am resting in His will. It is so good of Him. I ought to appear so obviously different to others after all this most precious time of chastening and waiting. Surely He will not have let it been all lost upon me. I want to bring forth fruit to His distinct praise and glory; it is " afterward " now, and He must be looking for peaceable fruit, and others will look too. I can only put this earnest desire into His dear hands, and ask Him to fulfil it in whatever way He sees best. I think the thing I most want is to have self completely crushed under the wheels of His chariot; it rises up again and again in different ways.

Of late I have found it such an odious temptation cropping up, when the affectionate deference of friends treats me as an advanced Christian, the effect of which is to make me see how very near the bottom of the ladder I am. It used to take the form of elation at public notice, reviews, etc., but that has *worn* out already. The newer form is much more horrid. I don't think I have much temptation, less than many, which is most merciful; but it is great pain to be tempted to such an entirely hateful and also contemptible disloyalty as self-gratulation. Oh! for full deliverance.

(*To J. T. W.*)

October 1875.

Somehow I think God is giving me more " power than before." I leave more implicitly every single word written or spoken to His guidance; because I don't ask Him to guide *my* words, but to give me *His*. I do not see why any should ask a lesser gift when one sees a greater one to ask for, and of course

I expect that He will do it, so the words seem more resultful with less effort, and generally with none at all. I was looking at many possibilities not pleasing to nature, and I could not really detect that I had *any* wish or choice apart from His will. I was so delighted about it, and I was so distinctly and joyously conscious that I was not only *His*, but *entirely* His, that it came nearer to " satisfied " than anything yet. The whole thing is really like living in a miracle! He has taken away now all the fear of going back into the weary old up-and-down life. Why *should* one, when He is " able to keep "!

(*To M. V. G. H.*)

November 13, 1875.

" I will direct their work in truth." So be it as to yours for this year. I have ordered Eugene Stock's *Lessons on the Life of our Lord* for you—but *why* you don't approve of Concordances is past me or Moody to imagine! He thinks them indispensable to fully getting hold of a subject! Without one (after one's own searchings) you cannot be certain you have thought of *every* text on a subject.

In answer to your question about *Reality*, I find it was written at Whitby on the very evening of N.'s prayer!

Dear mother likes *Reality*, better than anything I ever wrote! she gushed over it, till it actually made the tears come into my own eyes! I didn't see anything in the verses myself, but mother says " it's perfect "!

About ——. I have not brain-stock enough to turn out any great quantity of original writing; if I spin too much yarn, it will be proportionately weak. There will *only* be real value in anything I write in proportion to the amount and extent of *living* (" life-blood " if you like) that goes to produce it. I am only afraid my snare will be to write too much and lose weight and substance thereby. Therefore I considered it would be a most healthy and useful variety of work to arrange this Birthday Text-book (*Red Letter Days*) for Marcus Ward. I shall write perhaps a few dozen new verses, involving very little new yarn spinning, as the rest are old. I so arrange it, that for the next *ten* years, the verses will be suitable to our Church festivals or seasons. It is occupation of the easiest kind over my Bible, and all the time I am putting in rather than pouring out, and I hope I shall not select 365 texts without some mental and spiritual gain to myself.

(*To Margaret W.*)

November, 27, 1875.

God is so good to me—it is all " without effort," and has been all along, as to being *perfectly* satisfied about either suffering or waiting. *Suffering* is now *almost* past. I have very little pain now. *Waiting* will probably extend pretty much throughout 1875—but I have not one regret or quiver of longing for anything but what He appoints. It is quite curious to find how *completely* He has answered me (and at once) as to this.—Isaiah 30:18: That is for you as well as for me.

———

December 16.

I have come back into the current of life after just twelve months *under His shadow,* for such the silent and most suffering year was to me.

———❦———

DIVISION VI.

———

LETTERS, from 1876 to 1879.

43 Binswood Avenue, Leamington,
January 17, 1876.

... I have it very much on my mind, when really free, to write *Sunday Morning Bells* for the little ones, and yet I do not seem to know what to say. Of course, if the Lord means me to do it, He will tell me what to say when His time comes; but just now I am an "empty vessel" with a vengeance.

I have just heard from the Punjaub that *Morning Bells* and *Little Pillows* are going to be translated into Hindustani, and are already used in mission schools.

I do trust you are less suffering, if it be His will. Last year I got great comfort in great pain from "Thy hand presseth me sore." That *dear* Hand!

I am wonderfully better since I came home; the work at —— threw me back sadly for a while. I cannot do much without suffering for it.

Yours in Him who so loves us.

(*To M. V. G. H.*)
1876.

I was really tempted to be almost envious of your getting into quiet quarters! it does seem as if so much of my life were worn and wasted with merely "seeing people"—of course, I do try to use opportunities, but so many acquaintances are just the senior sort from whom I neither gain nor can very well give. And mother always says "nobody has such an uninterrupted life" as I, and yet I know I long for just one week without every day but one on average having engagements (services, meetings, lunches, teas, etc.) with all the calls and callers over and above. Only once since I came home have I got a real country walk alone! yet I would give a great deal to be able to secure that two or three times a week—I seem so to need it. Not that I am not sure it is right, or God would not appoint it, only it

is mysterious that I should be placed where I have so much of what tries me much more than actual work would.

I had not thought of the sea at all this year; I meant to economize, as I so want to do as much as possible towards finishing off B.'s education. If I went, I do not at all see the use of going in the height of the season, when lodgings everywhere are just double. What I should like would be to allow for finishing my books, instead of trying to clear off the MSS. before going, and then make a real holiday of a visit to Winterdyne or Ashley Moor after. In fact, if any year, I could be sure of two full months clear for writing, I would consent not even to *try* to write the other ten, and should get more done! I so want undistracted quiet—it is not merely being able to get a certain number of hours at my desk, but having the other hours undistracted by so many interruptions and controverted topics, and knowing of perpetual fresh phases of naughty and mischievous gossip and slander. I have plenty of actual time for my desk, but cannot come straight away from being annoyed about M. R., or set thinking about somebody's difficulties, and just sit down collectedly to write, the same as if I had been lying on the grass or strolling up a lane.

Sir Henry Baker's sister wrote to tell me how ill he was, and that he wished to thank me for "a deeply interesting letter"—she wrote nicely, and in replying, as she had mentioned his much pain, I "hoped it was not presumptuous to hope that the enclosed leaflet might possibly be a tiny cup of cold water."

A SONG IN THE NIGHT.

I take this pain, Lord Jesus,
From Thine own hand,
The strength to bear it bravely
Thou wilt command.

I am too weak for effort,
　　So let me rest,
In hush of sweet submission,
　　On Thine own breast.

I take this pain, Lord Jesus,
　　As proof indeed
That Thou art watching closely
　　My truest need:
That Thou, my Good Physician,
　　Art watching still;
That all Thine own good pleasure
　　Thou wilt fulfil.

I take this pain, Lord Jesus;
　　What Thou dost choose
The soul that really loves Thee
　　Will not refuse.
It is not for the first time
　　I trust to-day;
For Thee my heart has never
　　A trustless "Nay!"

I take this pain, Lord Jesus,
　　But what beside?
'Tis no unmingled portion
　　Thou dost provide.
In every hour of faintness,
　　My cup runs o'er
With faithfulness, and mercy;
　　And love's sweet store.

I take this pain, Lord Jesus,
　　As Thine own gift;
And true though tremulous praises
　　I now uplift.
I am too weak to sing them,
　　But Thou dost hear
The whisper from the pillow,
　　Thou art so near!

'Tis Thy dear hand, O Saviour,
　　That presseth sore,
The hand that bears the nail-prints
　　For evermore.
And now beneath its shadow
　　Hidden by Thee,
The pressure only tells me
　　Thou lovest me.

It is singular he made that his own last word to his people! for he wrote a short letter to them in his *Parish Magazine,* and added a *P.S.*, "the following beautiful hymn, kindly sent him by F. R. H.," and printed it in full—thus these were the last words from him as Vicar. I believe that man loved Christ personally beyond what most do.

It is quite clear why I was sent here, and why my cold got worse instead of better. *Two* dear boys, thirteen and fourteen, seem to have taken quite a decided step into life and joy. It seems so very singular that these two should be slightly invalided *just* then, both being clearly "soil prepared," having secretly *wished* to be safe. I had two talks with the elder on Friday—a most reserved boy, yet he quite opened out at the second interview to me. On Sunday I sent word he might come to me if he cared, any time while the rest were at church. Down they came, the minute the door closed on the churchgoers, and there they stopped till dinner-time! —— looked so sweet and peaceful, and told me he did "come" Friday night! Little —— seemed eager and thirsty. During P.M. service I went to them and found both at work at "Bible railways,"[1] which I had shown them how to find and make, and they had together found some surprisingly thoughtful connections. Went at once to the point, and it seemed then and there grasped by ——, who just dropped his dear little head on my shoulder and cried for downright joy! Had a most blessed time with the two, and prayer, of course.

This afternoon —— came to me (I said they would find me alone in the dining-room at 5.30), and —— was delightful, seemed overflowing with real joy, such clear sight of the "instead of me." I had talked about Christ as reigning as well as saving, so I said, finding how sure he seemed about "Saviour," "But —— is Jesus your King, too?" The little fellow seemed as if he could hardly contain himself, and said so emphatically, "Oh, I have promised Him He shall be my King, and He is!" Then he volunteered the information that he was "quite sure —— had really found Him, too," that they had been walking and talking together all the time they had been out both to-day and yesterday, and had been so happy together. My *protegés* have taken keenly to making bouquet-holders for the Bible flower mission. You see it was a definite thing which then and there could be done for Jesus. They prefer choosing their own texts, and have done some beautifully.

(*To the late Julia Kirchhoffer*).

March 1876.

Hurrah! I *said* it when I saw your £6, 18s. od. on the card, so naturally I write it also. You are a properly progressive collector. Seriously, I am so delighted. If the two or three still remaining cards come in at all, we shall pass even the £50, which seemed great things.

Well, dearie, I think you are doing the *first* duty in making home pleasant, garden included. And I have a strong idea that up to the age of twenty-four, it ought just as much to be a *preparation time* with girls, as it confessedly is with men—and that we should have more "thoroughly furnished" Christian lady-workers if it were so. Only I think the great point is,

[1] "Railways" and "railroading" was a way of studying the Bible, connecting passages together. See pages 844–858 of Volume II of the Havergal edition.

that it should be regarded honestly as preparation, not studying or drawing, etc., merely because we like it, and it is a nice way of getting through the days. Pray, dear, that you may be so wholly the Lord's that everything shall be really and truly as "unto Him," and that *He* would prepare you for whatever He is preparing for you in the unknown future of work and trial. You see you cannot possibly tell what you are really preparing for—only He knows; so how important to put the "preparation time" simply and trustfully and honestly into His hands. I am glad to hear of the Latin, and I am inclined to think that every kind of mental culture is even specially right for *you*. You know I believe in your poetry, spite of the editors! Only, "His time is not yet come." Perhaps He will keep you ten years in the shade, before He uses your pen, as I think He will use it— if it is altogether at His disposal—and all those ten years will be added power and ripeness. You cannot think how thankful I now am that He kept me back for about that space! I see as clear as daylight all sorts of reasons why it was just the wisest, best, and most really resultful thing He could have done. How I laughed to scorn as unmitigated absurdity a persistent prophecy of a literary friend that "the day would yet come when editors would have to wait their turn," and that is precisely what it *has* come to now, though I as soon expected to be Empress of China! Trust Him implicitly about it, when once we have yielded ourselves up to be His instruments, and put ourselves entirely at His disposal, it is altogether His affair to make the best of us, and bring the most glory to Himself by us.

(To the same.)

WINTERDYNE, March 19, 1876.

This is most delightful,—a grand advance! and it more than covers my own losses too, in the sum total! for had I been well and at home, I could have certainly got two or three pounds worth of new subscriptions or donations to make up for some handed over to start a new collector, and some failures.

My mother has got all my Leamington subscriptions for me, which is doubly kind, as she has been ill herself for more than a month. It seems to me that whenever I cannot do my own work, and have to leave it entirely to God, He takes it up, and does a good deal more for me than I should have done for myself. I asked Him not to let the Irish Society suffer by my illness; and here He inclines Katie B. and you to do so much extra! It has been remarkably so with all my books this winter. I have not been able to communicate with any publisher till a few days ago, since October, when I gave the MS. of *Little Pillows* and *Morning Bells* to Nisbet. Well, we boldly started an edition of 4000 each! which were *not* in time for the advantage of Christmas orders. Yet in seven weeks we had to reprint them! Also, they are going to be translated and pub

lished by the Religious Tract Society of France; and also some one in high places is going to give them to all the royal children. Caswell had to reprint my *Five Benefits* four times in as many weeks, the demand was so great! The same principle holds, does it not, dear J., in everything (I do not mean but that we are to do our very best when able)—the more entirely a burden, a care, or a work is cast on the Lord, the more entirely He *takes* it for us. It is so restful to have given up altogether to Him body, soul, and spirit—all one has and is—unreservedly. Life is a different thing thenceforth.

(To ——.)

I send you three little songs, only arranged from my tunes; but Hutchings & Romer were so taken with these from Havergal's *Psalmody,* that they commissioned me to write a set of six, with easy piano accompaniments, which I was delighted to do, as it gave me an opportunity of adding to the very meagre supply of sacred songs sufficiently tuneful and sufficiently easy for drawing-room singing. Most of the "sacred songs" extant are such very pathetic and dismal affairs that no wonder young people do not want to sing them!

Francesco Berger has lately made a *very* beautiful song of my words, "Enough." This is published by Lamborn & Cocks, London; and I greatly hope it will circulate, for the sake of setting forth the truth of the words.

ENOUGH.

I AM so weak, dear Lord, I cannot stand
One moment without Thee!
But oh! the tenderness of Thine enfolding,
And oh! the faithfulness of Thine upholding,
And oh! the strength of Thy right hand!
That strength is enough for me.

I am so needy, Lord, and yet I know
All fulness dwells in Thee;
And hour by hour that never-failing treasure
Supplies and fills, in overflowing measure,
My least, my greatest need; and so
Thy grace is enough for me.

It is so sweet to trust Thy word alone;
I do not ask to see
The unveiling of Thy purpose, or the shining
Of future light on mysteries untwining;
Thy promise-roll is all my own.—
Thy word is enough for me!

The human heart asks love; but now I know
That my heart hath from Thee

All real, and full, and marvellous affection,
So near, so human, yet Divine perfection
Thrills gloriously the mighty glow!
    Thy love is enough for me!

There were strange soul-depths, restless, vast and broad,
    Unfathomed as the sea;
An infinite craving for some infinite stilling;
But now Thy perfect love is perfect filling!
Lord Jesus Christ, my Lord, my God,
    Thou, Thou art enough for me!

(*To M. V. G. H.*)

1876.

Other workers on all sides seem doing more and more—
I less and less! I am quite content; only it is curious how I have
been held back from any work for two and a half years. Since
the Liverpool Mission and the hymn meeting at Bewdley, I
have done nothing,—not even any writing. I cannot now even
do the underground *individual* work which used to be my speciality at Leamington, for I catch cold so often on coming out
after paying a call. And now my choir work is stopped too! as
I have another bad cold, and mother wishes me to give it up.
By the bye, I think you and dear E. do not in the least understand *that*—you think it merely a "choir practice," which any
secular musician could take. It is no such thing, but the same
sort as my hymn-meeting; only that I am now much less nervous, and speak more freely and personally than in 1873. It is
to me *just* the same opportunity as having a large open Bible
class; and I am not sure that it does not give me more influence, just because it is in a less usual groove, as far as those who
attend are concerned. And then it is no trifle to aim at real
"singing for Jesus" in such a congregation as St. Paul's,—a really first-class one, both as to size and social position. The aim
I have set before them is that, as Paul and Barnabas "*so spake
that multitudes believed,*" they may "*so sing* that the same result may follow."

I believe even the few weeks I have taken it have been really resultful. The organist tries to express the spirit of the words.
I told him "I had prayed that his *fingers* might be eloquent
for Jesus." He has seemed peculiarly struck with Hymn 633
(*S. G. G.*), "I gave My life for thee"; and I have had a most
hopeful letter from him about it. Then the Christian members *pull* with me and pray with me heartily; and I hope for
real work among those of whom I stand in doubt. So I question whether I *could* better invest an hour a week than in this;
of course there is no laborious preparation, as there would be if
I had a Bible-class of thirty or forty upper-class ladies. I have
been waiting to explain this, because some remark showed that
the work was totally misapprehended. However, *now* I am to
give it up altogether, and only hope I may perhaps be allowed

it another season. Mr. Rogers has always been present; but he
is so kind, I do not mind him in the least now, though I wished
him at Jericho the first time! He leaves it quite to me; and
practises just as if he were one of the choir, setting a good example! I am told that the Rev. —— never was so meek in his life
before, and that his wife says he is "a sight to see" at the practices, keeping in the background for a whole hour! I should
not choose choir-training as my work, but it is just doing it instead of Mr. R., and so sparing him time and strength to spend
on his far higher work; and really nothing can be more important than that he should be spared for his pulpit.

(*To ——.*)

May 4, 1876.

Yes, the loss of my musical work was nearly total: a few
plates happened to be at the foundry, and thus escaped. It
has been my whole spring's work to compose several quite new
tunes to some hymns of uncommon metre; also I had most
carefully revised many others, and this work has both fettered
and fatigued me greatly. I must just patiently rewrite my own
tunes from memory, and I am hoping against hope that the
proofs may be got through by August, so that I can go to Switzerland with Maria, which would probably do us both immense good.

I heartily agree with you about "business," and wish every
Christian worker, clerical, lay, and female, could have an ap-
prenticeship to some business first! My father was eminently
business-like, methodical, and punctual, and so I ought to be!
Committees I never belonged to, and never shall, and believe
more successful work is often done by some one brave man or
woman.

I am rather in danger of being a hero-worshipper just now,
inasmuch as I never did hear any man (of course I always tac-
itly except my own dear father) whose sermons I so totally like
and enjoy as Rev. J. H. Rogers'. I have heard a few finer single
sermons, but never any one whom I am so glad "to sit under,"
to use that very horrible phrase! And while I was breaking my
neck, looking up at the pinnacle on which I had set him, he
quite startled me by coming down and seeking my friendship.
He preaches courses of sermons, which I always prefer to single
ones—his Thursday morning lectures on the First Epistle of St.
John are glorious—only it is such a responsibility to hear them.
Then we have a delicious little Saturday evening prayer meeting, and there is an excellent curate. We have *S. G. G.* hymns to
Havergal's *Psalmody,* and I have been choir-mistress! We have
just the sort of service I like best, brisk and bright, reverent and
orderly, with no single thing to fidget me; strictly evangelical,
and yet so *cheery.*

I have just been reading the report of the Church Missionary Meeting at Exeter Hall. It must have been glorious! Oh,

M., I don't believe that the former days were better than these. I cannot understand the dismal view some folks take—"Of the increase of His government there shall be no end"—certainly we seem to see the increase when we look back. Satan is very rampant, too; but what else can we expect till he is bound? I am glad you are at temperance work—I don't know details of that association, but I rejoice in any attempt to rescue from that awful drink.

I have drifted into helping the editor of *Hymns of Consecration.* It is odd what desultory work one drifts into. But oh, M., it is wonderful that He should accept *as* service such wretched scraps as are all that I can bring—one does long for the perfect service above!

(To M. V. G. H.)

I cannot tell anything yet about summer plans—I should like an outing with you, but could not go out of reach of a piano, as proofs of *S. G. G.* will be coming all the summer. If we go to Snowdon, I could perhaps arrange to have the use of one.

I have had quite a struggle with my "will"—I should *so* like the way to be opened for me to come and live with you, dear Marie. It is a very awkward position here—no freedom, always afraid to pay a call, or write a note without specifying. But I would never pain dear mother, or do anything she did not positively like. It seems most clear that I am placed here, and that without some most direct interposition of Providence, I should be doing wrong to leave, and could not expect a blessing. And again it would be bad for you, because I could not be an active outdoor helper, without really giving up what all say is my own work; and my living with you would be a mere drag, and prevent your having a real helper. I only let this out to you as my dear sister, but with the most earnest entreaty that you won't be planning or contriving or hinting in any way. If it were *the Lord's will,* He would throw the door unmistakeably open; if not, I don't want any human hand to pick the lock! "Trust you?" It's just the very greatest human comfort I have, being able to trust you so implicitly, and knowing you understand everything better than any one else does. And you never say or do anything I would just rather not!

I never make the faintest opposition, or even counterproposal, now to anything that dear mother arranges for me. I have long since determined, God helping me, there shall be no colour of excuse for saying I am inconsistent. I know I have been wrong *now,* for I was so poorly and faint, I had set my mind on a day or two's quiet and rest at home. I quite longed for it, and so was disappointed when it could not be, and was not ready for whatsoever my Lord the King appointed; so it is quite right I should learn to be invariably submissive to her. Outwardly I know I am absolutely so, but outwardly is not

enough. I need not tell you that I am seeking patience and strength, but I seem to be allowed to feel it most sensitively and shrinkingly, and I found myself praying most earnestly that this cup might pass from me, when you know bodily pain extorted no such prayer. Still "Thy will be done" does not fail in its true sweetness, and is the deepest Amen to even that prayer.

LEAMINGTON, May 31, 1876.

DEAR SISTER MARIA,—

I have been thinking and praying much about your wish, that I should come and live with you. I am wondering whether I ought to take what has just passed as an indication that I *am* in the right place, and should not be impatient of the little cross attached to it. You know part of my feeling was that I could not be of half so much real use here as I could elsewhere. Well, the last two days it really seemed as if all at once God would show me that I am of use!—it has been most extraordinary how one after another has spoken or written to tell me I have been so blessed to them this spring. M. Watson had a great outpour, and told me she felt I made so much difference in her work that she did not think she could keep on the Y. W. C. A. if I were not here at all, and that she knew my influence was felt and working beyond what I could possibly know. A young Scripture reader, who is leaving for a more important post, writes me that if my words are as blessed to others as to him, I am blessed indeed; it seems I have been let lift him up surprisingly, though with very little effort. The curate has told Mr. R. how very helpful he thinks my choir practices are. A choir member called, to tell me what great blessing she and three of her own friends have found all this spring. The enclosed note is another instance. Two other choir members have taken opportunity to thank me—all on the same Sunday.

Then yesterday I had a talk with Mr. R. and prayer, and he quite startled me by saying he was going to write, but spoke instead to tell me how he thanked God for my influence, that he was sure I was unconsciously doing a far deeper and greater work *here* than I could have an idea of; that he saw and felt it in the choir, and that it was spreading in blessing; and that for himself he had never in his ministry been so distinctly conscious of receiving help, blessing, and influence from another; that it had told upon his own life and sermons; that I was probably totally unconscious of it, but that he felt there were "streams of vitality" from me which he felt; and that many others had spoken to him of feeling the same. He spoke most solemnly and with moist eyes. You may fancy, dear sister, how *utterly* surprised and intensely *humbled* and thankful I felt, especially as it so singularly coincided with so many others saying the same sort of thing to me. I had said in speaking of choir arrangements, "*If* I come back in the autumn," and he caught at the "if;" so I told him (under pastoral confidence) that there was an " if," but did not explain details. He said he would not like to hinder what might be right, but that I could not realize what a really important sphere God had given me *here,* and that it would be intense grief and loss if I were taken away from St. Paul's. Well, Marie dear, I only write all this to you, not to stop your doing whatever you seem led to say or do—only it seemed so very *marked* that I felt another door must be very distinctly opened ere I of *myself* close this, and that the "cross" was what might well be patiently borne, if indeed God is blessing my even unconscious influence in such a place as this. If you feel inclined to write freely to dear mother about it, do so. If *she* caught at it, and it seemed that her own difficulties would be solved by my leaving, and at the same time you really wanted me to live with you, I should take the two together as outweighing the somewhat strange coincidence of the last few days. If mother negatives on *her* side, then I should consider that what Mr. R. and the others have told me was sent to encourage and cheer me in the *present* path. I am not troubling about it in the least—either way. As far as writing is concerned, I could work better with you than at L. As far as influencing individuals—I see that in a place like B.—I could not exercise as wide an influence as here. For myself there would be the set-off of sacrifice of great spiritual privileges as against the gain of having your invariable sympathy and understanding and no friction. Well, dear, the guidance is promised, and we shall have it!

1876.

I wish you had heard the singing at St. Paul's last night,—" Hermas" to my hymn "Golden harps are sounding," "With hearts in love abounding" to Papa's tune "Zoan," and "Tell it out." They *did* "tell it out," rather! A surprising difference to the feeble washed-out singing a few months ago—it was like old St. Nicholas evening singing, and the church crammed like our father's. Well, I would have done the same at Bewdley, if Mr. F. had backed me with the choir, and launched the tunes and hymns *con amore* as Mr. Rogers has done; and there was better material in the Bewdley choir than I have in the St. Paul's, where there is hardly one good voice in itself. Splendid sermons on Sunday, Acts 1:7, 8, "Ye shall receive power," and 1 Peter 4:10. I wish he would just preach some over again at Champéry! I have completely howled my voice back again in the choir!

We have had it lively at St. Paul's—"Crowns of glory ever bright" to my father's arrangement of "Lubeck," with his "Hallelujah"; "I heard the voice of Jesus say" to his tune "Evan," No. 2—both went first-rate. In "I heard" we take all the first lines in unison, which brings out what *He* says finely. At night we had "To Him, who for our sins was slain," to my "Tryphosa" (which I hear is a special favourite both here and at Mr. Bro-

mley's), and "Hallelujah" to my father's tune "Shen." Such a lovely sermon, John 20:29. Mr. Shaw would have been in raptures! for Mr. R. came out strong about the delusion and loss of blessing in craving aids external, pictures, crosses, etc., and also the subtle snare to which evangelicals are exposed, of seeking something between them and the unseen Saviour, outpourings to a pastor, seeking spiritual help from Christian friends, more than direct faith in Christ's *all*-sufficiency for *all* things.

(*To J. T. W.*)

LEAMINGTON, May 10, 1876.

I have had a wonderful week, such a lot of totally unexpected encouragements! I had no idea God was using me here half so much as it seems He has done. I have felt quite overwhelmed with His goodness, and thoroughly startled at some of it. *Not* conversions, somehow I hardly ever come in contact with unconverted folk! But very definite help and uplifting to Christians in all stages. The unaccountable fact is that I find God has not only been using me the last few weeks, while it has been so much brighter in my own soul, but even during the dimness. That is contrary to my previous experience, and I do not understand it. I am very happy now there is not any conscious cloud.

A friend wrote that I was represented as "Cordelia" in the Royal Academy, that is, it is such a likeness that she wondered if it was a real portrait introduced! So I felt curious to see what Cordelia's character was, as I never read *King Lear,* and I took down Shakespeare to inspect her. But I was not in the humour for that sort of reading, and soon turned to my Bible and felt voracious! It's almost too good to be true, to think that perhaps I shall really be at N. this day three weeks! Do pray that I may have a real great blessing, and be enabled to "pass it on" to many others.2

ARGENTIERE, July 24, 1876.

DEAREST MOTHER,—

We liked Fins Haut so much that we staid nine days instead of three (four francs a day each and no extras), and walked down here this morning: a thunderstorm in the night made it cool and lovely; arrived here in sunshine at ten; and at eleven a tremendous thunderstorm came on, continuing at intervals all day, grand and wild.

We have two bright, little, lofty rooms together on a separate landing; so very quiet for Maria, and most cosy: our view will be straight out upon Mont Blanc and the Aiguilles when clouds permit, so we can have sunsets and sunrises without stirring a step! Maria has been perfectly delighted all along, and it seems I have taken her to places exactly to her liking so far,—it is so very nice coming with her, as we fit into each other's ways precisely.

I must tell you just one thing, because it was so very original! I had been singing to myself two or three times, just odd snatches, but especially "Only for Thee" (to "Onesimus"). Our good Lonfâts, a dear, simple Swiss family, were immensely pleased, and the old mother asked me to sing again (I had not known they were within hearing); so I told her what the hymns were about, and wished I had French ones to sing, but having none, thought I might as well see if I could not roughly translate. However, on sitting down to it, I found it seemed no more trouble to write French hymns than English; so I wrote one something like "Will ye not come?" and "Golden harps," and one "Seulement pour Toi," founded on "Only for Thee," but most of it on the converse idea—"*Thou only* for me"—*i.e.* Christ *only* having done all and being all one needs, so as to meet the "Jesus *and* Mary" of these poor folks. Well, M. said this hymn was exactly what she wanted for them, and said she should like to send it to M. le Curé! who had been "on her mind" all the week! "*How* send it?" "Oh, I will take it myself!" I thought she was joking, and said then she had better ask him to see if they were all right as to rules of French verse. "Very well, so she would—it would be an excuse for calling—besides, she wanted to refer to a French Bible, and would ask him to lend her one!" So actually off she went! and had a most pleasing interview—borrowed a Bible (with Romish notes, however), got him to look over my hymn, which seems to have been respectably done, as he asked if the writer was French; and she seems to have had quite a nice opening for telling him (without controversy) of the secret of true peace and joy, and entirely relieving her mind! Now, who but Maria would have dreamt of borrowing Bibles and getting Protestant hymns revised by a Roman Catholic priest! He was most courteous and nice to her, and seemed quite interested.

Maria seems to enjoy our tour, and I never travelled with any one who has such a keen appreciation of the beautiful.

To go back—we had a specially lovely sunset from Lausanne, July 13, and ditto sail up the Lake to Montreux; there I took a mule to Les Avants to see Miss Whately, who was not well enough to come to meet me as she intended; while M. went on to Chillon, and pottered on her own hook till I joined her in train to Vernayaz. She went to see the Gorge du Trient, while I got rooms and engaged mules for the next day, 15th, when we went to Fins Hauts. Miss Whately is charming, very loving and kind to me; a wonderful linguist, and altogether mentally superior, and withal a most sweet Christian; I did not have much more than an hour with her.

One day while at Fins Hauts, we "went gipsying"—only in not quite the same way "as a long time ago"—started at 6 A.M., and went up mountain paths, resting and strolling gradually till we got to a lovely little patch of snow in a hollow, with whole beds of alpen roses all round, and big boulders and deep moss

and shady little pines, and full view of Mont Blanc, and any amount of Aiguilles. It seemed quite ideal, till we tried to go to sleep; and then we found that not having reached the line of perpetual snow, we were within the line of perpetual insects, and about ten species of flies up to the size of hornets, persecuted us (they don't bite, only buzz and fidget); so after dinner we had to seek a less ideal spot—not till after we had had "snow cream," which M. made in our tin cups, as we had a good deal more splendid cream than we wanted for tea. Later on we made tea most successfully with fir-cones—Maria making quite a clever fireplace with stones, and such a good fire.

We did not come home till after sunset, as we waited for that at a fine place, and our old Madame was in such a state of mind, and was just sending her husband to look for us. Maria made such an impression on them, they were ever so fond of her, and I believe she was really blessed to them. Though she did not set herself to work to go out of her way exactly, she seemed so to get at the root of the matter with so many to whom she spoke.

(*To James Parlane.*)

1876.

... I must tell you a wonderful bit of *Ministry of Song*, through "Whom having not seen, ye love." I was taken on speculation to call on a clever young gentleman, just an infidel, knowing the Bible and disbelieving it, and believing that nobody else really believes, but that religion is all humbug and mere profession. I was not primed at all, only knew that he was "not a religious man." In the first place, I had no end of fun with him, and got on thoroughly good terms—then was asked to sing. I prayed the whole time I was singing, and *felt* God very near and helping me. After a Handel song or two which greatly delighted him, I sang "Tell it out!" *felt* the glorious truth that He *is* King, and couldn't help breaking off in the very middle and *saying* so, right out!

Then I sang,[1] "Whom having not seen, ye love," and felt as if I could sing out all the love of my heart in it. Well, this young infidel, who had seemed extremely surprised and subdued by "Tell it out," competely broke down, and went away to hide his tears in a bay window. And afterwards we sat down together, and he let me "tell it out" as I pleased, and it was not hard to speak of Him of whom I had sung. He seemed altogether struck and subdued, and listened like a child. He said, "Well there *is* faith then, *you* have it anyhow—I saw it when you sang, and I could not stand it, and that's the fact!" He was anxious for me to come again.

When I came away, his sister, who had introduced me, wept for joy, saying she had persuaded me to come with a vague

---

[1] "Whom having not seen," Recitative and Air, by F. R. Havergal. Hutchings & Romer.

hope that he "*might* find he could tolerate a religious person," but never dared to hope such an effect as this, and that she thought I had been most marvellously guided in drawing the bow at a venture, for every word and even action had been just right. I tell you this just because you are publishing both "Tell it out" and other leaflets for me. Will you sometimes pray that God's especial blessing will go with them? I should add that it was almost a miracle in another way, for I had such a wretched cold that I doubted being able to sing *at all,* and yet I believe I never sang clearer and better and stronger. How *good* God is!

(*Extract from F. R. H.'s answer to a remark, "That death which we all dread."*)

"Not one shadow of fear."

1876.

No, not "all!" One who has seen and accepted God's way of salvation, does *not* dread death. Perhaps I shall best express myself by doing it very personally—just giving my own experience.

I do *not* fear death. Often I wake in the night and think of it, look forward to it with a thrill of joyful expectation and anticipation, which would become impatience, were it not that Jesus is my Master, as well as my Saviour, and I feel I have work to do for Him that I would not shirk, and also that His time to call me home will be the best and right time, and therefore I am content to wait.

One night I was conscious of certain symptoms preluding an all but fatal attack of erysipelas[1], I had once before, on the brain.

I knew, if means failed, it was probably my last night on earth. I let my mother attend to me, but alarmed no one, and I was left alone in bed. Then, alone in the dark, I felt it might be my last conscious hour on earth, and that either sleep or fatal unconsciousness would set in. I never spent a calmer, sweeter hour than that. I had not one shadow of fear! only happy rest and confidence in Him "in whom I have believed."

Was this delusion? Could it be so in the very face of death, that great *un-*masker of all uncertainties? I knew it was not delusion, for again, "I know in whom I have believed."

Now, *how* has this come to be so with me, for it was not always thus; and I know as well as any one what it is to "dread death," and to put away the thought of its absolute certainty, because I dare not look it in the face.

There was a time when I saw clearly I could *not* save myself—that I deserved hell. In many ways, but in one most of all, this—that I owed the whole love of my heart to God, and had not given it to Him; that Jesus had so loved me as to die for me, and yet I, unmindful of it, had treated him with daily, hourly, practical ingratitude. I had broken the first command-

ment, and as I owed all my life, future and past, to God, I had literally "nothing to pay;" for living to Him, and keeping His commands for the future, would not atone for the past. I saw the sinfulness of my heart and life. I could not make my heart better. "The soul that sinneth it shall die." So, unless sin *is* taken away, my soul must die and go to hell; anyhow I must "stand before the judgment-seat of Christ."

Where then was my Hope?—in the same Word of God, 1 John 5:10, it is written, "He that believeth on the Son, hath the witness in himself," and John 3:36, "He that believeth on the Son hath everlasting life: and he that believeth not the Son shall not see life; but the wrath of God abideth on him."

Believe what? "Whom God hath set forth to be a propitiation through faith in His blood," Romans 3:25. He must keep His word and punish sin, and He has punished it in the person of Jesus, our Substitute, "who His own Self bare our sins in His own body on the tree," 1 Peter 2:24.

Thus being "just," and having set forth Jesus as the propitiation for sin—if Jesus has paid my debt and borne the punishment of my sins, I only simply accept this, and believe Him, and it is all a true and real transaction. It is no theorizing but acting. I did it—I believed it, and cast myself utterly hopeless and helpless and lost in myself, at the feet of Jesus, and took Him at His word, and accepted what He had done for me.

Result?—joy, peace in believing, and a happy full trust in Him, which death cannot touch. Now it is a reality of realities to me—it is so intertwined with my life, that I know nothing could separate me from His love.

I could not do without Jesus. I cannot and I do not live without Him. It is a new and different life, and the life and light which takes away all fear of death is what I want others to have and enjoy.

I can say that such a light has shone upon all the dark bits of my life, that even if I was in heaven itself, I could not more clearly see why I was so led—that all the training was needed. And nothing tries me now; things that would so have disappointed me do not now. Even when I am suffering severe pain, I would not have it otherwise. And then in daily life, daily temptations, I find a victory in Jesus against sin, without any struggle.

And what was trial to me,—keen scathings, blightings,—is all taken from me, lifted out of me. It is really miraculous, I cannot say HOW; certainly it was not my own strength, but things that were such agony and bitterness—it is all gone. All was needed—and all that might have been a cloud between me and this full sunshine is taken away. Now it is utter calm and quietness, a realization constantly that—

> Life is a gift to use for Thee,
> Death is a hushed and glorious tryst
> With Thee, my King, my Saviour, Christ!

[1] erysipelas: an acute disease of the skin, streptococcal infection causing red inflammation of the skin and mucous membranes

December 18, 1876.

... "Shadowless communion,"—there you have touched a chord indeed! I too have tasted it, but I have not yet had the full, continual draughts which I believe may be ours, and which I neither can nor will rest short of! ... You will intensely interest me, and perhaps help me both for myself and for possible future writing for others, if you will tell me anything that pen can convey as to your own tasting of the "shadowless communion." Think aloud to me about it for half an hour! Tell me how much you know of it, and yet how little! Tell me what Jesus says to you, and how He says it; tell me how, *i.e.* in what way it "blends with outward life." Tell me what you see is to be had, beyond what you yet have. ... The enclosed, *My King,* has been the greatest writing pleasure I ever had! and in it I have said my say about lots of little points on which I wanted to have a say, and *My King* seemed to indicate a nice opportunity in this form. ... The title, *My King!* is in itself a very song of joy to me. ... I am afraid you will smile at some sentences in it, but I do not seem able to help saying absurd things in prose, especially when I want to hit a nail hard and square on the head!

February 4, 1877.

... I am so glad for and with you. ... Yes, that is just what I expected—"how He speaks"—always through His own dear Word. "If it lasts!" That horrible Satanic "if" crops up everywhere to hinder what our Lord would do or give. I am so glad you give that "if" no quarter! "If" any one will show me chapter and verse for "if it lasts," I'll give in; but it isn't in my Bagster in any shape or form, nor in any other edition that I know of, except Satan's own privately revised one, from which he quotes. Oh how different from "if it lasts" are God's own words, "He giveth more grace," "grace for grace," "from strength to strength," "from glory to glory," "that ye may increase and abound more and more," "go on unto perfection," etc.! If I was not very tired, and if it was not Sunday night, I should want to write a chapter for my new book against that wretched "if it lasts"! which has saddened so many hearts which Christ has not made sad. I dare say I shall to-morrow, God helping me. (See *Royal Bounty,* chap. 9.[1])

I send you His last special word to me, "The Lord shall open unto thee His good treasure." Starting with Ephesians 3:8, and ending never and nowhere, because the "riches in glory" are everlasting. Just "search and see" what He is going to "open unto thee"!

—Your loving friend and sister in Him whom we do love.

———

Deuteronomy 28:12: "The Lord shall open unto thee His good treasure."

Lesson I.—*The Good Treasure—The Unsearchable Riches of Christ* (Ephesians 3:8).

I. The Treasure itself. His, not ours, we have nothing, we are "poor" (Revelation 3:17). Consider the Riches of—1. Goodness; 2. Forbearance; 3. Longsuffering (Revelation 2:4); 4. Wisdom; 5. Knowledge (Colossians 2:3); 6. Grace (Ephesians 2:7); 7. Glory (Philippians 4:19), corresponding to our—(1) Sinfulness; (2) Provocations; (3) Repeated waywardness; (4) Foolishness; (5) Ignorance; (6) Spiritual need and weakness; (7) Immortal spirit.

How this treasure is purchased? (2 Corinthians 8:9). For whom?—1. The needy and poor (Revelation 3:17); 2. See context of Deuteronomy 28:2; 3. Christ's (1 Corinthians 3:21–23).

If Christ's, then all are yours.

II. The Promise itself. 1. Our need of the promise "shall open;" we cannot open ourselves: it is the Holy Spirit's office (John 16:14, 15). Some of us can bear witness, "I was blind, now I see," but cannot say Song of Solomon 2:16. Some can say 1 Peter 2:7. Praise Him! 2. The certainty of the promise "*shall* open." Do not say, "I hope He will;" come boldly and claim. Do not say "perhaps" when He says "shall" (Numbers 23:19). Faith is the key to this treasure; God *gives* it, it fits the lock of any promise. The Lord always responds to the claim of faith. He meets you with Matthew 7:7. There is always a promise at the back of everything: Expect and watch for the opening of the lock. (1) If opened to you it will never be shut again, "He openeth and no man shutteth" (Revelation 3:7); (2) If opened, you will never come to the bottom—the riches are "unsearchable," always "more and more" "incorruptible;" now and through eternity, they are "the fulness of the Godhead." 3. If opened, we shall not care for other things, *e.g.* as they were opened to St. Paul (Philippians 3:8). 4. If opened, draw from it, be spiritual millionaires, use it, trade with it, the responsibility is great (1 Peter 4:10). What will you do with these riches this week?

Dwell on each word "The Lord"—no human promiser, but God that cannot lie; "*shall,*" fling this in Satan's teeth when tempted to doubt or to be negligent in search; "*open,*" it is never shut up from you; "*unto thee,*" really, personally, not merely to somebody else, or folks in general; "*His,*" not yours, all his very own, you had no right or claim to it; "*good,*" recollect it is sevenfold, perfection; "*Treasure*" even Jesus Himself, the Treasure of treasures, in all His fulness as your own Saviour, Friend, and King.

Lesson II.—*The Good Treasure.*

I. His Word. *His;* the value of the gift is enhanced by the giver. It is Christ's gift (John 17:14), and the Father's gift to

———

[1] *Royal Bounty* by F.R.H. (London: James Nisbet & Co., 1877), original book pages 46–50, pages 207–209 of Volume II of the Havergal edition.

Him (ver. 8). *Treasure;* the value is relative and actual. *Relative,* "MORE than gold" (Psalm 19:10, 119:72, 127). If we really find treasure, we are glad (Psalm 119:162; Jeremiah 15:16).

A *test* to apply to ourselves in Psalm 1:2, "delight," and in Jeremiah 6:10, no delight. If there is no rejoicing in it, the treasure is not yet opened to us; this is the work of the Holy Spirit (John 14:26). The answer to the prayer Psalm 119:18 is Jeremiah 33:3. See Christ's own double opening, Luke 24:32, 45.

II. *Actual.* The value of the treasure is proved by what it will do for us. "Do not My words *do good,*" etc. What good?

1. We are born again by it (1 Peter 1:23).

2. Growth thereby (Psalm 1:2, 3) in grace and in knowledge (1 Peter 2:2; 2 Peter 3:18).

3. It gives light (Psalm 119:105).

4. It gives understanding.

5. It gives quickening (Psalm 119:50, 93).

6. It gives patience (Romans 15:4).

7. It gives comfort.

8. It gives hope.

9. It keeps from sin (outward) (Psalm 119:11).

10. It sanctifies (inward) (John 17:17).

11. It is profitable for, etc. (2 Timothy 3:15, 16).

12. It is able to save your souls (James 1:21).

13. The climax—by these ye become "partakers of the divine nature" (2 Peter 1:4).

Faith is the key of this treasure (1 Thessalonians 2:13); "worketh" all this "effectually in you that believe" (compare Hebrews 4:2: "Not mixed with faith").

Isaiah 55:11: "My word . . . shall prosper . . . whereto I sent it"—all this!

III. Responsibility attached to the Treasure. The command is Colossians 3:16 (connect 2 Corinthians 4:7). See the promise (Proverbs 8:21), "I will fill their treasures." They *bring forth* out of this good treasure things new and old (Matthew 12:35, 13:52).

February 13, 1877.

. . . You set the ball rolling; so when a few days ago the editor of a magazine sent an entreaty that I would do him a poem on "April" (very kindly furnishing me with the new idea that its smiles and tears would be a nice theme), I saw in a flash that there was another and very different lesson to be drawn—another fling at the "If it lasts"! So if you should see my poem, you will know the origin of the verses!. . . This morning's work has been a paper on simply the words, "And this is His commandment"! I wonder if you would guess how I took it? Oh pray still that I may have the King's own messages to deliver.

(*To F. C. Kirchhoffer.*)

February 20, 1877.

. . . My losses and deficiencies this year seemed more than it was possible to replace, especially when one collector after another sent much less than last year. So there was nothing for it but to pray the more; and it is perfectly wonderful how God has been answering. And now your splendid collection is a crown upon many tokens that He has most distinctly heard and answered. It is a little larger than the largest I have ever yet received; and as Miss B. gives me notice, she will have less instead of more on her card. You, as dearest Julia's representative, will stand first on my 1877 report. I cannot tell you how glad and pleased I am. Not *only* because I am so thankful that the great need of the society should be so far supplied, but I am somehow so specially glad that dear Julia's work should not be among their losses, but that if she is permitted to know anything about it (and why not?), she may see that her little share in her Lord's work is not only carried on, but increased. I am sure it must have cost you a great deal of effort and trouble to collect so much. But He knows and marks every effort, even the least done for His sake and in His cause.

(*To E. B. L.*)

March 21, 1877.

I am intensely sorry to refuse to write an article in aid of a children's hospital, but it is simply impossible, as I have already undertaken more writing than I can prudently complete before a summer holiday is necessary, and my dear mother absolutely insists on my undertaking not one thing more. I cannot tell you how many similar requests I have. I can only ask our good Master to choose for me, by flashing, as He often does, some strong impulse to write into my mind, seeming then to give me every word, in other cases giving me nothing to say. I hold myself totally at His disposal, and lay each request before Him, to give me a message to write or not, just as He will. . . .

Oh, is it not a happy life, "the life of simple trust"? One wonders how one lived at all before.

68 MILDMAY PARK.

DARLING MOTHER,—

Here I am still! I got in a draught at the Association meeting, whereby I got a regular cold. Mrs. Pennefather is the one to be positive, and so I've been kept and nursed most delightfully. It is a special satisfaction to have got over the autumn cold which I never do escape before I came home! so that you will not be vexed by seeing me sneeze and cough, and Mrs. P. thinks it is a very good thing it happened so. She does pray for *you* so beautifully. Well, I do love Mrs. Pennefather. I *see* that the more one knows her, the more one must *love* her. The workers' prayer meeting is going on down-stairs, but she would not let me come—so I am obedient! Thankful you are safe home, and that you are even occasionally a little easier—may He stay His rough wind in the day of His east wind for you, poor dear mother.

—Your loving child.

68 MILDMAY PARK, June 1877.

DEAR MISS BROWN,—

I have been detained here by a sharp influenza cold. So your dear girls' prayer that I might come again to them is very unexpectedly answered! I am still weak and poorly with a troublesome cough, so that I cannot take the Bible class, but I should be most glad to have a few more words with your dear lassies who came to me in the drawing-room, and dear Mrs. Pennefather seems to be glad I should do so. Did you know they have all written to me? such sweet, touching letters. And I do think the Lord Himself has laid them on my heart, so that I am just longing for the privilege of trying to give them a few helping words—by answering their letters in person, and I have changed my plans on purpose to do so.

And will you ask that our dear Master would give me exactly the right words for them? I do so long for an immense blessing to them, and through them to all the rest of the school. Please give my love to them, and tell them this from me.

—Yours affectionately in our dear Master.

July 21, 1877.

I have just come in from church, and two verses in the first lesson have brought to a climax the strong feeling I have had for ten days past that I must write to you. Look at verses 13 and 14 of 1 Samuel 15, see how Saul says, "I have performed the commandment of the Lord." And Samuel replies, "What meaneth then this bleating of the sheep, and lowing of the oxen which I hear?" Well, now, dear ——, this time last year you said, "All for Jesus," and He gave you a taste or earnest of the gladness of being "all" for Him, accepting your intention. But where has the fulfilment been of the words which you then said "before the Lord"? When I met you at —— in the winter, in our hurried parting words I think I must have shown as well as expressed the query weighing on my mind whether it was indeed "all for Jesus." You told me, "Yes, it is!" just as Saul said, "I have performed." But "what meaneth then" the straws which seem to show that the wind does not, to say the least, blow unmistakeably from the "all" quarter? Only straws, and yet they would blow all the same way if it *were* all! I will tell you one. Just a very casual mention of your going to —— now, and returning in time for the September ——. I know there may be a hundred fair reasons, but go deeper, which was your real heart in, which was really the thing you most cared for,—coming "to the help of the Lord" in a special effort to win souls for His honour and glory, *or* pointers and partridges? O be honest with yourself about the whole thing. It is *not* a light thing to have told your Master that you will be "all" for Him, and yet set other things before His obvious service. You have had a year now of professed "all," but how many trophies have you brought to His feet? How many souls have you even tried to win? Is the harvest, so far, "nothing but leaves"? Can Jesus say of you, "He hath done what He could"? Have you even given as much energy to "the help of the Lord against the mighty" as you ever gave to rowing or coaching your crew? and if not, are they not solemn words, "Curse ye Meroz, saith the Lord, curse ye bitterly the inhabitants thereof." Why? Not because they had done anything wrong or even inconsistent, but "because they came not to the help of the Lord."

God says, "When thou vowest a vow unto God, defer not to pay it; . . . better is it that thou shouldest not vow, than that thou shouldest vow and not pay." You can never unsay that "all for Jesus" of your twenty-first birthday. It is registered for ever; it only remains for you to make those words true or untrue. If untrue, then—! . . .

Understand me, it is not a question of any particular doing or not doing, but a far deeper one; just—have you given a true answer to the question, "How much for Jesus?" I do not want you to answer me or tell me anything about it, but I do want you to remember, "To his own Master he standeth or falleth," and He knows whether your promised service is really wholehearted or only half-hearted. If the latter, it is *not* an accepted service. He accepts all or none. There is not one measure for women, and another for young men, "My son, give me thy heart," implies no less to you than to me; the word of our God draws no such distinction, all is "all" or *not* "all," just as much in your case as in mine.

1877.

. . . Please see if you can find any syllable of mine, written, spoken, or printed, which either states or implies that "the infection of sin is or can be wholly eradicated"! It is just this supposing that people said or meant what they never did say or mean that has led to thousands being hindered from inquiring into the "way of holiness." Perhaps the very strongest expression I ever used (if indeed I have used it), would be "continuous victory." And what does that imply, but a foe that is *not* annihilated; the very fact of a continual subduing, however complete, proves a continual existence of the foe which is being subdued, and who, without being continually subdued, would be again active and conquering! The "On dit, qu'on a dit" has been Satan's fatal hindrance in this matter. I was *aghast* at being told lately that I had said I had not sinned for three years! "Oh, well, I was told so." So I investigated, as this was really a serious lie, and the succession of "They say," and "I supposed you thought the same as they did," and "I supposed they thought they did not sin," perfectly horrified me at the tissue of unintentional false witness borne and manufactured by Christians. I appeal, and so may "they" appeal to "what I have written" or even to what they have written.

September 17, 1877

. . . Had I strength and time, I should enjoy telling you much, especially of the Lord's singular dealings with me this summer.

I am here for the baptism of my dearest Miriam's *motherless* boy. She died six days after his birth, in the most *wonderful* peace, *so* perfect that *even* leaving the husband she loved so intensely, and her baby, did not cast even a momentary shadow of a shade! . . . You can imagine what a precious trust the sponsorship to "H. C. L." is to me.

. . . I have had some splendid summer sheaves, including two ——, who first gave their own selves to the Lord, and then threw law and medicine overboard as their intended professions, and will be, I hope, bright gain to His service in our dear Church of England.

. . . I am so delighted that you find you can cut off that horrible "if" and say "it lasts"! So I send you confidently "He giveth *more* grace"—more still, and more always—for *you*. I am glad you have got hold of "shall not stumble." I have a paper on that in *Royal Bounty* or *Royal Commandments,* I forget which; both will be out soon now. . . .

You may imagine how all you said of the "far better" as to your dear —— harmonized with my thoughts here. And curiously the lovely verse of B. M.'s, which you quote, "Praise God, the Shepherd is so sweet," is on the grave of little Maud Prestage, my cousin-godchild, taken not long ago to the fair country.

I am delighted with your testimony as to *One Hour with Jesus.* . . .

—— on his twenty-first birthday gave "*all* to Jesus." I had worked at him in all possible ways for two or three years,—won at last! Spent more actual "labour" on him than almost any individual soul, except ——, read with him alone daily for weeks, prayed with him, wrote to him, talked to him, and went on at him generally! "Thanks be to God which giveth us the victory"!

———

So delighted to find a few days ago that in Jude 24, "from falling," is literally "without," or "from stumbling," which, of course, makes the verse much stronger and more explicit, as the Greek usually does. Not even stumbling! isn't that a perfect keeping?

(To S. G. P.)

September 22, 1877.

I supposed I was obliged to say "Sir," because you said "Madam"! But it went against me to be formal even for once to the writer of *Never Say Die.* I made a raid into Paternoster Row yesterday. I felt puzzled what best to do for *N.S.D.,* so asked the Lord to guide me at the time, and show me *His* way about it. So, as I wanted to see Mr. M., I went there first, intending to see how the land lay; but he was suddenly gone off to Rome! So I asked to see Mr. S., and found him so full head and heart, of the Noon-Day Prayer Meeting at Aldersgate Street, which he was just going to conduct, that it did not seem the right time to distract him with my business—he had his Bible open, and was using his last half-hour for preparation. So then I went to P. and asked for Mr. P. himself, and gave him an *N.S.D.,* and told him my views; he asked a lot of questions,—I think he wanted to find whether my opinion was biassed by personal friendship! so I was glad I had not had the pleasure of seeing you!

Perhaps you would hardly guess how very much what you said about *My King* delighted and encouraged me. I never expected *men* to read or care for it,—I did not aim higher than girls of whom I have a considerable following. It is far more than I hoped,—for I am not one of those terrible "strong-minded women," but I think we have quite "rights" enough in proportion to our powers and position. And I never thought of reaching *men* by anything I might write; yet you and others are willing to listen to the little things I have to say, and I take it as an extra token for good—the more pleasant, because unsought and unexpected. I am following it up with two new books (now nearly finished printing), *Royal Commandments* and *Royal Bounty.* I am inclined to envy your special gift of heart-words to the *very* far off—it seems so much more like the Master than mine; but still it is very sweet to be allowed to write for our fellow-servants, which is what I most often seem led to do.

Do not withhold your name. Your father is so well known that the mention excites interest directly. And if the Master should lead you on further in this path (and I think He will), it is for several reasons better to give your name at once and start fair with it. Is it not a sort of little offering to Him of that which is already His own? For our names are His, and why should He not have the use of them?

(To Margaret W.)

I don't fancy somehow that I shall ever be quite so strong as I was, nor able for just the same as other people. I *did* think that I might have been even stronger, but now I think that is not likely; so the "pleasing perfectly" will have to be rather my aim than the "serving much," *i.e.* "till my change come"—

then I "shall serve Him"—and won't it be delicious? (Ezekiel 44:15, 16). So Numbers 16:5 belongs to you, and the 7th verse. But it begins with the being chosen, and from that flows the "come near" and "shall be holy."

Did you ever think that our Lord must have had a great deal of such refraining from what He would have done? It must have been *very* hard not to make greater displays of His love and power; for surely, if that had been His Father's will, He could just as easily have done His personal work and ministration on a far larger scale, even during the last three years, much more during the thirty years of such closely-veiled glory.

October 1877.

Dear M., will you pray for me, that I may have "the patience of Jesus Christ," however long this lasts, and that He would graciously help me over what must be a very weary and probably suffering journey? I will enclose you some verses, which came to me on the words, "*ONLY for Jesus.*" Make the printer put the very biggest and fiercest ONLY he can! People will emphasize any word but that in their lives, and it is just being "*Only for Jesus*" that makes all the difference. They are ready enough to emphasize "Jesus," if they may only drop the severe, uncompromising "Only" into the shade. Do you see?

> ONLY for Jesus! Lord, keep it for ever
> Sealed on the heart and engraved on the life!
> Pulse of all gladness, and nerve of endeavour,
> Secret of rest, and the strength of our strife!

———

I have enclosed a parcel for you. It is a present which you won't care twopence for at present, so you needn't profess to! But I believe you *will* care for it if, please God, this time ten years or so, you are bringing forth out of His treasure things new and old for some flock committed to you. It is a set of *Goodwin's Works*—one of the grandest and oldest of the 17th century writers—much too deep and solid for modern taste, but full of Christ and of "the deep things of God." Some day if you are going to preach out of Ephesians, you will find, I should think, everything that could be said on every single word of the first, and part of the second chapter. He is called "that peerless divine, and star of the first magnitude"!

November 15, 1877.

If I wait till I can write you a long letter, I may never write at all! so I will just send you a few lines, chiefly to tell you how glad your letter made me. For I think I see in it that Jesus is more of a reality to you than before. And after all, it all hinges on that; it is the old question, "What think ye of Christ?" Is He nothing, or something, or *everything?* It is a help to pull oneself up with plain questions now and then.

I had a really beautiful letter from —— lately; I think he will get less reserved by being at College. What I most want to hear of you is that God has given you the great joy of winning some soul for Christ. When once you have had that, you will never rest without more, I think. It is like a tiger tasting blood! I am so very glad you have had an opportunity of seeing an ordination. May every day be preparing you for your own solemn vows. I have got lots of new C. P. members. How beautiful the estimate of Christ in our chapter this morning is! "Chiefest"! Link it with Philippians 3:8–10.

(To M. J. W.)

November 5, 1877.

I hope you will not mind my *not* fulfilling your request to write an answer to the letters you send me from Plymouth sisters. The fact is, I am so utterly startled and entirely shocked at them, that I cannot think it worth while to write *seriatim.* The cool ignoring of the clearest Bible commands and teaching, the un-gospel spirit of judging, condemning, and want of the gentle charity which should be learnt at the Master's feet, are to me most saddening. I do not mean so much of the writers personally, but of the principles they lay down, and the inevitable results of following out those principles. From a merely critical and intellectual point of view, I see it would be waste of time to argue; as a mind which can in all good faith base its arguments and build its conclusions on the merest assumptions, and never even see that it is doing so, must be left to its own inverted pyramids!

If the writer of the three-sheet letter had but spent the same energy on seeking to set forth Jesus and His salvation to some one who does not know His preciousness, as she has spent on trying to unsettle one who does know Him, surely it would have been much more like the Master's own work! Instead of writing, I can only pray that she may be delivered from what her letter additionally convinces me is one of the special devices of the enemy for hindering the Lord's real work and the real unity of the Spirit. It is "strong delusion," and God grant that deeper searching of His word with the light of His Spirit in the clear atmosphere of greater humility, may show her that it is so.

1877.

A very strong light has come to me about this almanack! Do you not believe that remarkable coincidences are not chance, but God's leading? I need not tell you I do! Well then, was it not striking that you should have been troubled about these opinions, and that immediately after I should have been led to suggest what may and will (probably) at least help to keep others from being unsettled, 2 and 2 make 4!

I believe we are punished for a sort of half-cowardly shrinking from acting up to our own light, and fearing to tell others frankly what we believe to be the more excellent way. How many young Christians might be saved from drifting off to the P. B. S. if Church members were not so dreadfully afraid of showing their colours! So far as I am aware, my father never through all his ministry had any one single member of of his flock go off to them, nor even nibble at it, because he never shrank from showing them why we should value our Church. And yet he never had the least trouble with dissenters; they always cordially respected him and understood him, far more so than many who were less loyal to their Church principles.

December 14, 1877.

Pray for me, darling E., for I am passing through some of the *strangest* as well as the *keenest* trials I ever had, which is saying a good deal!

OAKHAMPTON, January 31, 1878.

I determined I would "never say die" till somebody published your book, and also that I would not write to you till I could tell you I had succeeded about it!

Now it is your turn to act, and I hope you will find time to set to work immediately, and put the whole into shape, *i.e.* into short chapters, and short paragraphs, and short sentences. And if you can invent lively little titles for each chapter, so much the better, and the queerer the better.

I have never thanked you for the exquisite card, quite a treasure—it is so totally uncommon, and the colouring so rich. I am busy trying to get all or most of a new book (into which I am putting my very heart), done during a very restful and quiet visit here, while my sister relieves guard at Leamington—so I have not time for a proper letter.

A beautiful photograph hangs close by the drawing-room piano here, and I look at it while I sing; but it never occurred to me to ask whose it was till a few minutes ago. "Ah," says my sister, "that's a photograph of a picture of St. Ouen by your friend, S. G. Prout!"

(*To S. G. P.*)

OAKHAMPTON, February 8, 1878.

The "Grey Raven" must allow me the privilege of a little contribution towards the "bread and flesh." If only you had not written such very awful Sanskrit, I should have shown your letter right and left! but nobody could be expected to read it second-hand! I wish you would send that story of the poor hungry woman to the *Times*, not touched up a bit, but just as you wrote it to me. Who could resist it? It is terribly bad taste to quote oneself, but I cannot help it this time, so you must forgive; but thinking of your present work, the lines kept humming in my head—

"The King will stoop to crown it
With His gracious Inasmuch."

Of course, I read *Down the Steep*—you have something of the poet [1] in you (as well as of pretty nearly everything else, it seems!), but I was not so personally struck with it as with *N.S.D.* But it is a poem and not mere rhyme. Will the specimen page of *N.S.D.* do? You might give your mind sufficiently to say yes or no to that!

And don't, oh don't, write Sanskrit to ——, or he will send me your letter to decipher, and I shall have to write it out for him.

My new book is *The Royal Invitation*—distinctly and entirely for outsiders; I have long wanted to have a full fair shot at those who are *not* the King's children. Can you spare two minutes to pray that I may have special help in this?

Believe me, there is real spiritual power in what you have written; as I glanced over your specimen page I felt inclined to envy you,—it throbs with life and warm reality. Oh, may you have the joy of bringing the living water to thousands by it! And then, as I share in praying for this, I shall have a share in the praise for it! It is a good investment, I consider! So you might put a little prayer about that—please do! I do not feel sure of their accepting it, because so few will sing such very "out and out" words, unless Sankey had first taken it up.

—— is lingering just "outside the door." I have given him as strong personal pulls as I know how, but he is not inside yet.

I mean your book to "go;" I have got a large Scotch bookseller to start *Never Say Die,* and I promise you a start in Dublin too. Wonder what else the Lord is preparing you to do by keeping you in the shadow.

I do so feel for your dear sister.

(*To Leonard Bickerstaff.*)

February 7, 1878.

I have a request to you, for which yours to me gives opportunity. Will you take it up as a little bit of special praying work during the next few days? I have written twenty-two chapters of my new book, *The Royal Invitation; or, Daily Thoughts on coming to Christ,* and I do long for very special help for the nine chapters which remain to be written. I want the Lord to give me every word, and not let me write a word without Him, nor a sentence that is not a message from Him. I do so want to win those who have never yet come to Jesus. Will you ask this for me every day till about next Thursday, by which day I shall about finish, please God.

Why not join both the Scripture-reading Unions? Ever so many are members of both. Both are good solid bread, but I prefer the whole loaf to the half one, both for myself, and more especially for the sake of the many whom I thus induce to read twice a day, who otherwise would read only once. I have often said to others, "Join Mr. Richardson's Union for the sake of your personal friends, but join Mr. Boys' for the sake of work among others." The one chapter a day is a pleasant *link,* but the two chapters are a *lever* to raise those who need raising to fuller feeding on the Word. I myself have joined both.

—Yours affectionately in our dear Master.

February 14, 1878.

The twelve o'clock prayer to-day was commuted into thanksgiving for completed work; so I write at once to tell you that the good Lord has given it me all, and fully answered the prayer that it might be done without difficulty or strain. I have now merely to put it straight for the press, fill in the references, and send it off. But the last sentence is written! I shall write no preface; the title is, *The Royal Invitation; or, Daily Thoughts on Coming to Christ,* and I prefer leaving it to the reader to find out who I am aiming at.

I shall next see about a re-cast of the *Ministry of Song,* and *Under the Surface* for one volume, *Life Mosaic.* This will be an opportunity of dropping out a dozen or two of the weakest pieces, and I must ask clear guidance to do this judiciously. Next, I want to arrange *Daily Melodies for the King's Minstrels.* I am reserving MS. poems for a still future book.

———

Wish I knew, Marie dear, if you are sacrificing yourself very much for me. You tell me when I had better propose to return home. I do feel most grateful to you, and certainly I am in greatest possible clover of quiet and luxury at Oakhampton. I have not had such rest since the farmhouse at the Highlands (Herefordshire). Please order *Spanish Brothers* for a present; it is a book I much admire.

1878.

Tell Mr. Shaw, Parlane sent me some time ago a letter from the widow of good Duncan Matheson. He had owed P. about £20 for printing his hymn-book. Mrs. Matheson paid it, and Parlane generously returned the whole to her. She says: "When you sent the account, it came the day after my beloved husband died. You enclosed a leaflet by F. R. H., the text at the heading was, 'My God shall supply all your need,' and the last line of each verse was, 'God shall all your need supply.' I cannot tell you the blessing I got in reading it, and each day it has been in my mind, and I have felt its sweetness, and now your returning the money is another proof of His faithfulness." I am so glad I had thus unwittingly the privilege of comforting Duncan Matheson's widow.

(*To F. T. H.*)

The letter you delayed was not of any consequence, only one of the usual gushing sort; thanks for my writings, which seem spreading in America very fast. They reprint my books there with no reference whatever to me or Nisbet! Yes, dear Frank, I often feel how I need counterbalancing trials (of which, in more ways than one, I have had more than you know of) with all this singular success. I do want all my work to be *purely* and *only* for our dear Master, and not to work even for work's sake, much less as pleasing men or myself. But it is very curious that the very amount of expressions of pleasure, gratitude, etc., which I get, deadens their effect, just like opium! You see when one gets half-a-dozen a day at least of such letters as would have elated me for a week a few years ago, they come to be almost a bore! and really I have to watch against the opposite temptation not to be grateful for all this—not to think *enough* of it. However, I certainly was extra gratified by your telling me that the good Bishop of Hereford cared for anything I wrote, and placed the card on the mantel-shelf. ("No rose without a thorn.")

And I was much more grateful, dear Frank, for your thoughtful and brotherly words of warning, than I am for several dozen of the gushing letters I get!

I have several times thought I should like to buy your harp-piano—it would be at times of very great use to me for composing in my own room without being overheard, the consciousness of which I am foolishly sensitive about, and never can compose if any one is in the house! But just now I could neither pay for it nor use it, lest it might disturb dear mother. She is far worse than when you were here, Nurse says so—not that there is any immediate danger, but that she is worse is evident.

May 13, 1878.

My poor mother is very ill, the end may be very near. It is an exceptionally distressing and trying illness in all respects—God has had many special lessons to teach us by it, and "who teacheth like Him?" Pray for us, dear friend.

I don't suppose I ever sent you *Such a Blessing.* I cannot but see what I *have* seen, and do see. And if "all" in 1 John 1:7 does not mean "all," how much *does* it mean? and if "cleanseth" only means "cleansed me when I said my prayers last night," what force is there in tenses? And I know that such a blessing is to be had, and that life is a different thing then. And I know that it is *not* perfection, *nor* perfectionism, because if it were, I should not *need* and *desire* and *claim* that wonderful perpetual present tense—"goes on cleansing;" I cannot do without the precious blood of Jesus one hour or one moment.

Many thanks for your sermon, it is so nice; I am going to send it on to the Baroness; I know she will like it.

(*To E. T.*)

May 26, 8 A.M.

A line to ask you all to pray that if it is His will, He would, in very pity, release our poor unconscious sufferer. My sister, who professes to be able to stand anything, broke down a few hours ago after so many days' incessant watching with our good nurse Carveley. Again, all yesterday, we were watching, expecting every breath to be the last, and the whole night as three times before has been one long struggle. Poor mother is still unconscious—it is most distressing. I want you to ask for me that I may be enabled to trust quietly about my sister, that is the greatest strain upon my trust, knowing by previous experience the results of overstrain, but I did not think she would break down now; I have been entreating Him not to let me quiver about this, and am so thankful for, "I have prayed for thee that thy faith fail not."

TO NURSE CARVELEY.

I have no photograph to give,
And so I do not ask for yours;
But I've a picture that will live
As long as memory endures.
The faithful word, the pleasant face,
The skilful hand, the watchful eye,
The "sunshine in a shady place,"—
This photograph will never die!

May 29, 1878.

(F. R. H.'s tribute to the nurse of her stepmother C. A. H.)

(*Post Card.*)

May 31, 1878.

Our poor sufferer entered into rest on Sunday afternoon. The last fortnight has been trying and distressing beyond anything I ever heard of, let alone saw. Eight days and nights of literal dying and every distressing concomitant imaginable. God has been answering my eager prayer for more teaching, by "terrible things," according to Psalm 65:5. But it is over now, and my text for to-day is, "He hath done all things well." I see it as clear as daylight.

I am so thankful that my poor mother's last smile, a startlingly bright and sudden one, after weeks without a smile, was turned on me fully and consciously.

(*To* ——.)

June 1878.

I quite agree with you in preferring the exact Scripture in Isaiah 53:6, although I have no doubt "us all" means "the Church of God." I should not myself have so paraphrased it, but as I was quoting Rainsford, I thought I must keep to him. Had it been a new MSS., I might have asked him to alter it.

But I do not agree with you in giving verse 24 instead of 22 of Genesis 5. I expect it never struck you what it implies.

"Enoch walked with God," is usually quoted from verse 24, and therefore kept in connection with, "and was not, for God took him," as if walking with God were rather an older-aged experience, approaching the end. But do not you see how telling it is to take it in the other connection? "Enoch walked with God three hundred years!" nobody quotes that! and if he walked with God three hundred years, may not we walk with Him "all the days of *our* life"? It was Mr. Snepp who showed it me, and I thought it such a find. It is but the difference between the dismal must be always sinning, teaching, and the brighter hopes I laid hold of, but which are an old story to you.

By the bye, it is "Christ our example of *trust*, not truth," that has long been a favourite thought to me, and I was glad to see Rainsford bring it out. I think we get Christ as our example of three things in John 17. —1. Of coming to the Father; 2. Trust; and 3. Consecration.

Many thanks for calling my attention to "having no part dark."

I have never dived into its meaning, but am greatly struck with it now you mention it.

(*To* ——.)

July 25, 1878.

Here is your programme. Saturday "do" Gloucester, reaching Worcester in the evening. *N.B.*—Sit on the left, for view of Malvern. Stay Sunday at Worcester; hear cathedral bells, about the finest peal in England; twelve bells, No. 10. is exceptionally rich. The only clergyman I know is Rev. W. Wright, of St. Peter's, Evangelical. At cathedral, ask to see my father's memorial brass (designed by brother Frank) in an arcade of the southeast transept. St. Nicholas was his own church: a marble tablet to my sweet mother (Jane Havergal, died July 5, 1848), and a memorial brass to my father, are in the chancel.

On Monday, leave by earliest train for Bewdley station; in approaching Bewdley, sit on the left, and you will see Winterdyne,—a large white house alone among trees on the height of the ridge of rocks above the Severn. Then walk up to Winterdyne, where you are invited to breakfast, and will be welcomed for the Master's sake. You will get there a little before nine—just between prayers and breakfast. Mr. Shaw, my dear brother-in-law, will show you his beautiful grounds, and you will see how Bank holiday is improved there! If possible, Mr. S. will drive you on to my sister's, Mrs. Crane, Oakhampton; but it is a heavily-engaged day, and I have told them that on emergency you can walk the four miles. Mrs. C. invites you to dinner, and to stay the night. Then I will take you leisurely to Astley churchyard in the evening. If you cannot stay all night, Mr. C.'s carriage can drive us to the churchyard, and then drive *you* on, say half-way, to Worcester in the cool of the evening.

I hope it will be a fine day, and if it is, I shall be very glad to have been able to do you a small " good turn " after the *very* good turn you have done me.

(*To the same.*)

OAKHAMPTON, Monday A.M.

The coachman is to take you round by Ribbesford Church (unless you have already been there this A.M.)—look at the singular 11th century carving over the porch,—an old Saxon legend. I hope the rain will cease.

There are some visitors at W., whose relatives are very " high " and rather prejudiced; tell them you have been to Jerusalem, and hope to go to Gaza, or anything in that line, and perhaps after you are gone, I may tell them you are a Wesleyan after all! that they may see some good *can* come out of Nazareth!

At Winterdyne there is no treading on eggs,—a real, wide, hearty " grace be with *all* them that love our Lord Jesus Christ," even as I say it!

[F. R. H.'s correspondent says: "This little note was neatly done up with her peculiar beauty as she wrote it in the early morning at Oakhampton, and drove over herself with it to Winterdyne, and put it into my hand. And on the afternoon of that day, F. R. H. drove with me to Astley churchyard, and showed me her father's grave (now her own)—that time will always live in my memory, in whatever part of the world my lot may be."]

August 8, 1878.

Mr. L. came Monday, was delighted and grateful—writes that " if you did not build the Palace Beautiful, at least you showed it to the Pilgrim, and once more he thanks you for pleasure which grows with keeping." Neat! Results of my going to W. to fetch him was that Ellen saw with me how papa's parish was being cared for, and his own grandsons left out in the cold! W. and A. came the same afternoon to fetch their cousins, and the upshot is, they stay till Saturday, and are at the tent every night! I had the waggonette, and took the servants last night—capital—tent nearly full—probably 500—but shoals were listening in the dark outside! The evangelist Cauker, very nice on Isaiah 59:2, on " separated," but now " put away." Giles got up after, and spoke for two minutes most beautifully—set to *his* seal—told of his own experience—" God says it—I believe it—that's enough for me!" Then Thomas Wales, from the Evangelization Society, on " The Master is come and calleth for thee." I never heard such an enormous voice—can be heard on the bridge just as well as in the tent, *and* all up Load Street—a man one instinctively honours and loves on the spot for the Master's sake. I took the harmonium—Frances was quite leading the singing—good thing for younger ones to be thrown on their

own resources—" put out to swim!" Alice *so* sweet and hearty, and *in* it all. W. and A. had been canvassing Sandy Bank and Wyre Hill all the morning! and had the management of seats, hymn-books, tent ropes, etc. Twins *at it* too. Nellie looked *radiant!* Well she might, all her children heart and soul in such work, and with her nephews too!

1878.

I must not refuse my friend's entreaty to send the enclosed request on to you. The letter will explain itself. Many, many thanks for prayer for ——. Well, now I think you may praise! I have had no chance of gauging the work myself, and do not know why I am not feeling so confidently exultant as I might be over the account of them. I do not know whether it is only want of faith by looking on to all the ritualistic hindrances which they are returning into, and which must choke the Word except by most special grace,—or whether it is that the work is less deep than the ——'s hope. Anyhow, it is no small thing to thank God for that they have had that week, and have intelligently heard the truth as it is in Jesus, and have most certainly and evidently liked it, if no more!

Now I am with ——. They are exemplary to a degree, but I saw collision must come, and it came an hour ago. We were singing that hymn,—

> " Christians dost thou see them
> On the holy ground?
> .   .   .   .   .
> Smite them by the virtue
> Of thy Lenten fast!"

Whereupon of course I " struck "! stopped, and would not sing it, and said, " No, no!—no victory that way—they overcame by the blood of the Lamb," and so forth. Whereupon they argued and opposed very courteously, but very determinately. So you see the sort of work I now have—much more difficult than if they were not so wrapped up in their blameless conduct and fasts and efforts. Do pray for them. Oh, if my visit here might but be a blessing! I am so tired that I do not feel as if I had my usual energy, or could rise to the work.

(*To* ——.)

Not a drop of any special blessing here till to-day, and now—who, though converted, has often caused me anxiety from lack of consecration, has given herself over wholly (with her fine voice and musical talent). A real blessing—but when the ice once thus breaks, it is seldom only for one—and I am intensely longing for —— to be touched. Somehow I have watched in vain as yet, never can catch him alone, and conversation in the presence of others is no use. I have just been praying for him with two of the others. I leave on Tuesday, so time is shortening—not even a beginning made yet—oh, if God would but call him and rouse him. So the one who is rejoicing to-day is great gain, but —— is out in the cold. To-day's blessing makes me treble my fervour for him. Jesus has passed by to-day, and surely He will be gracious to one more? I got hold of a most interesting case at a garden party two days ago (where I had a series of bits of direct work all the time), and am just off to get another interview with her by her own wish. But oh for my bright lad ——!

They have dessert here on Sunday afternoon, after they return from Sunday-school teaching; so —— took the opportunity of calling for "order!" and took me by surprise by making a regular little speech in the name of his brothers and sisters—so very prettily done, thanks and gratitude, etc., and affectionate welcome and thankfulness to have me with them at last. You cannot think how nicely he did it, and of course it was vehemently applauded, and there was a general uproar of affectionate fuss!

(*To Margaret W.*)

August 15, 1878.

I can't possibly advise *now*,—being no longer on the spot. "*His* Name shall be called, Counsellor."

I have just sent off my *Almanack* to Mr. Bullock,—subject for this year is "The Words of our Lord Jesus Christ" (1 Timothy 6:3); 365 texts spoken by His own "gracious" lips—somehow I do think this will have *power* and be much blessed. I have grouped into a little piece (for insertion) the texts which show *why* He spoke them, and what we may expect from the daily feeding on this fruit of *His* lips. Edith and I both think it would be so nice if the future *Reports* contained a blank page headed "Questions," especially if it is to be more especially an "Isolated Members' Branch." Many would insert a "question," who would not venture on a "remark," and these would elicit answers. Just as the "Corner for Difficulties" is to me usually the most interesting part of *Woman's Work!* Put a little word about it to begin with—*inviting* members to ask any "question" which occurs to them in the course of studying the subject. Edith is eager for this, and thinks she would *always* have a "question," though she could not venture on a "remark"! *Do* try it. I think it would be a practically valuable feature of the new series.

Does not your brother want old gold and silver for his tabernacle things? I enclose two bits to throw in, if so. I found them in clearing out. I have shipped off all my jewellery to the C. M. S., chain and all, so of course I never enjoyed packing a box so much. Fifty-three articles! But I have reserved my portrait brooch of dear Papa for daily wear, and Evelyn's portrait locket. I really only want one brooch.

(*To the late Miss Esther Beamish.*)

THE MUMBLES, 1878.

It seems like standing afar off, beholding with solemn and fresh sense of the reality of the things unseen, as you tell me of this strange "trial." No, I never had that sort of sifting,—it seems to me, however, all a token for good. First, that it is a case of "The strong He'll strongly try." Such honour have not all His saints. Satan allowed to try His hardest, and defeated! Then surely it is a prelude to special blessing of some sort. When the devil has had his turn, then I think Jesus is sure to have His! He does not speak to me like He does to ——; yet I think it is from Him that words have kept coming to me about it, "He shall appear to your joy." Then in connection with this comes 1 Peter 1:7, taking the appearing as a present one. Just think of this trial of your faith being precious to Jesus, dear friend; for of course it means what it says. I know sadly plenty about times when I cannot pray, but do not get the fiery darts you tell of; I expect it is that Satan thinks I am not worth them, and God knows I am too weak to stand them; for oh, if you only knew how really far behind I am—my feeling always is that I can hardly keep you and —— in sight at all! I ought to be much further on with all the discipline I have had.

I could *not* write to you this A.M. somehow, and now it's late, and Maria will be anxious if she hears the typewriter going, so I finish this in pencil!

———

Thanks for Lord Radstock's speech, which is very interesting. But I cannot think the Lord would have made such wonderful provision of medicine and *means* for our use, if He did not both intend and sanction the use of them. And I do not see in the least why there may not be just as perfect and God-honouring trust while accepting and using *them* as His means, and doctors as His exponents of means, as when refusing them. It is a dangerous principle to admit, or at once it may be followed by queries as to using means of grace! as the same arguments or *seeming* arguments apply to that.

THE MUMBLES, October 7, 1878.

Oh M., it is such gracious leading to have been guided here, *just* the place! Maria has been so ill nearly all the time in Switzerland, and looks fearfully bad—it will be a long time ere she regains tone and sleep, etc.; she has never had what other folks would call sleep since that terrible time in May. *So* thankful to be here. I am very tired—could not have gone on much longer visiting—am weary to death of *lionessing!* Yet have had no end to be thankful for—only so overdone. I hardly ever had a text more sweetly and powerfully given me than Exodus 15:13 on Sunday week. Hope Association affairs all subsided and settled. We are in the midst of carpets and curtains and suchlike gear—settling in takes time and strength! I suppose I shall get rested *some* time! Anyhow, there is heaven to come!

THE MUMBLES, October 1878.

. . . I must send a line to tell you I have had a very happy time. The Lord " dealt wondrously," and caused ―――― to throw herself (metaphorically) right into my arms, not waiting for me to open fire! Conscious that the Lord has given me something which she, as yet, has not got and is groping for. Of course I did not mince matters—full consecration is the point. How many know and love Jesus, and yet are not " all " and *"only"* for Him, and they cannot see that He is able to keep them from stumbling, so the goal is not reached.

I do think we Church of England are more conscientious about Sunday post than Nonconformists generally. Those excellent ―――― had their letters, to my grief, on Sunday. So I was delighted in another house to see a notice on the post box in the hall, with the post times, and " No delivery or despatch on Sundays." *"No manner of work"* must include postal delivery, and it is not right to ignore God's commands.

I have met " B. M."!* Never felt more interested in any one yet, and never met any one yet who just knew and understood all my special mental and poetic experiences in thinking and writing; and as she is the only *real* poetess I ever met, I am beginning to fancy I must be a bit of one too.

(To S. G. P.)

October 10, 1878.

" All right " did not include the picture—that arrived two days ago, to my great delight; it was just in time for it to be rightly placed: I was just going to arrange my pictures. My especial favourite is a large engraving of " The Martyrs in Prison: Cranmer, Ridley, Latimer, and Bradford,"—a saintly picture linked with my earliest good memories, and it was my father's: so this is centre of the best piece of wall in my little study. Your Spanish prison view hangs most curiously appropriate on one side of it, so you could not be in better company.

As to *Never Say Die,*[1] I do not much wonder you shirked it! for a more puzzling little editorial work I never undertook! I cannot decide till I have gone twice through at least, how to chapterize it! But, dear friend, time spent on it is overpaid,—it brings to me all the sweetness and freshness of the old, old story as nothing else ever did; I keep reading it all for myself.

Two or three evenings ago my sister Maria and I went out to see a superb sunset just beginning. I gave her *N. S. D.* just before, and she had it in her hand. In about half an hour I came back, having gone a little way on—the sunset was over,

and she had forgotten all about it, never saw it at all! She is so peculiarly alive to natural beauty, that I could not have believed any book could have so " riveted " her, as she herself said. I am glad she so endorses my deliberate convictions, for she is very independent as well as decided in her judgment; and she has *far* more experience than I have among poor people, so it is worth a good deal. We agree that it is exceptional, and in fact unique, and that we know nothing in the evangelistic line to equal it. When I have done putting it straight for press, I will write again, and shall also tell Nisbet what M. says! A good proof of her sincerity as to its real value as work for God is, that she is ready to anathematize anybody and everybody who gives me *anything* to do at present, and wants me to send everybody's else little requests straight back with a refusing P.C., but is " quite agreeable " to my giving my mind to *N. S. D.*

Yes, I do trust that you may have, or rather that the Master may have, a very harvest of souls from its circulation.

(To the late C. H. Purday.)

THE MUMBLES, October 14, 1878.

Your note has touched and interested me most deeply. " Heart answereth to heart." I do trust that ere now you are still further on the way to recovery. Yet there is, I *know,* so much real blessing in the touch of our Lord's hand, even when we have to say, " Thy hand presseth me sore," that somehow, ever since a very long and suffering illness of my own, I have hardly been able to say sincerely to any really Christian friend, " I am *sorry* you have been ill." And the " afterward " is surely promised. Every time of calling apart leads us to know and understand a little better " Him with whom we have to do." How much these words imply! . . .

I am so glad you like my *Royal Commandments,* though I should not have expected you to like it so well as *Royal Bounty.* Mr. Snepp is charmed with your tune to " Yes, He knows the way is dreary," and would be very glad to include it in his new edition.

Possibly the enclosed tiny books may give you some pleasant thought—I shall be so thankful if they do. (*Precious Things,* and *I also for Thee.*)

(To the same.)

THE MUMBLES, October 30, 1878.

. . . I am so glad to hear you are raised up again. It is curious that in the night I was thinking so much of the promise, " Thou shalt glorify Me," specially in its connection as following deliverance from trouble (Psalm 50:15). And then your letter came in the morning, speaking of your desire to do something for His glory! Whatever He has promised, surely we may and should claim and expect, however much better and

---

[1] *Never Say Die.* S. G. P. Nisbet & Co. * This was Barbara Miller McAndrew.

greater it may be than we should have thought of asking. Oh yes, if one may but do anything for Him "who loved us and washed us from our sins in His own blood," it is worth coming back from the very golden gates to do it. If He has made us for His glory He will surely "be glorified in us." That He will even *now,* and there is 2 Thessalonians 1:10 to come! It is so wonderful.

(*To* ——.)

December 19, 1878.

. . . Yes, I have noticed the text you send; it is most solemn and striking. But because I happen to have got this one, please do not hesitate always to tell me of any that strike you as "*finds*"—I am always glad and grateful to have a share in the spoils of others, and sometimes even, when *not* new to me, it brings a text with new force or freshness. Christians might help each other in this way far more than they do.

I must send a line to say how delighted I am that the Church Missionary Society has taken up the Gaza Mission, which I had already heard of. You need not trust (!) "that it will be faithful and do the work in the proper way!" You may just *rejoice* that it *will!* If there is faithfulness and soundness to be had in the Church on earth at all, it is in the C. M. S.—the grandest and most uncompromising of all evangelical societies—except that one may bracket the Bible Society with it. Not one *touch* of any evil leaven has been permitted by God's great mercy to enter it from any side. Just *go,* and you will find all I have said true, and you will be under the best and safest auspices any human organization can furnish. God speed you!

(*To the late C. H. Purday.*)

December 30, 1878.

I have been on the shelf,[1] or should have replied sooner. And now the few days' illness has thrown me all behind with letters and work, so pardon haste. The only tune I do not like, and cannot possibly sanction, in your *Songs of Peace and Joy,* is the setting of my Consecration hymn, "Take my life," to that wearisomely hackneyed kyrie of Mozart. It does not suit the words either, and I was much vexed with Mr. Mountain for printing it with it in his *Hymns of Consecration,* and it would just spoil your book to let it pass. I *particularly wish* that hymn kept to my dear father's sweet little tune, "Patmos," which suits it perfectly. So please substitute that, and your book will be the gainer. You have rather taken the wind out of my own sails by your book, as Hutchings & Romer have for a good while wanted me to set *Loyal Responses* to music (now published by them); but I have so many irons in the fire, that I can barely find time to heat a musical one. However, I could not find it in my heart to hinder you in your wish, with which my whole heart sympa-

thizes, to do this thing for God's glory. I do so very much like many of your tunes.

"Therefore, being justified by faith, we *have* peace with God." Dear friend, why say, "May that peace be mine," when it is yours already, purchased for you, made for you, sealed for you, pledged to you—by the word of the Father and the "precious blood of Jesus"! Forgive me for touching up your words, but I have recalled them so many times since you wrote.

(7 7, 7 7.)   PATMOS.   Rev. W. H. Havergal.

Take my life, and let it be Con-se-crat-ed, Lord, to Thee; Take my mo-ments and my days, Let them flow—in cease-less praise. A-men.

(*To M. V. G. H.*)

THE PARAGON, BLACKHEATH,
February 7, 1879.

Send by return of post our dear father's words, "God save our widowed Queen," which he arranged in the minor key. Mr. Bullock is bringing out a capital little book about our Royal Family, and would like to insert it.

I have been photographed! Mr. Elliot himself came for me, Saturday, and they tried eight times, and hope one will do! Elliot and Fry both superintended in person; such a fuss! And I forgot to put on tidy frill and cuffs!

I hope you and Ellen will not go saving the fur things I send—will disappoint me entirely if you don't wear them for garden.

(*Memorandum.*—My sister F. had intended buying a sealskin jacket for herself, *instead* of which she bought these fur cloaks for her sisters!)

Mr. and Mrs. Bullock ever so kind and pleased to have me here—she is such a nice friend.

February 12.

Will Miriam undertake to write out some biographical notice of our dear father for the *Dictionary of Musicians?* You see I have barely three months to do my new books for next season, and cannot do the odds and ends that pour in.

Interesting lecture last night by the Rev. H. Lansdell on a Bible-scattering scamper to Archangel, etc. 25,000 "por-

---

[1] In the 20th and 21st centuries, British people widely understand the phrase "on the shelf" to mean a woman who would never be considered for marriage, a woman certain to be a spinster, never to marry. This is not at all Frances' meaning of this phrase: here she meant the idea of a tool or utensil set on the shelf

tions" and tracts given! Proceeds of lecture to Irish Church Missions.

I called at the Church Missionary House—Mr. Eugene Stock most delightful!

Glad I have had the opportunity of making friends personally with my publishers. Dear Mr. Watson is still so ill, but he came down in the evening and seemed cheered with talk and music, asking me to play again Beethoven's Moonlight Sonata for Mr. Robertson. Mr. Watson is almost, if not quite, as heavenly as Giles! His prayers most beautiful, and lovely grace before meat. He will not live long, I am sure, so feeble and so ripe. He gives me plenty of good advice—I do *love* him, he is so fatherly. His partner, Mr. Robertson, a pleasant Christian—much younger and very energetic. I think he took a liking to me, which is important, as I may have all book business to do with him in future years.

Mr. Hutchings was quite struck with "Loving all along" (*G. S. P.*). Dr. Waugh accepts his verses for (*The Sunday Magazine*) "Abercane," and calls it "splendid poetry." Mr. Watson read them out one night magnificently!

(*To M. V. G. H.*)

CHARING CROSS HOTEL,
February 17, 1879.

Singular and sad instance of not knowing what a day may bring forth! Case of small-pox, and poor dear Mr. B. so overwhelmed. Doctor ordered the house cleared at once. I saw my way in an instant—not right to go to any friend's house, and so shall give up my invitation to Mr. S. Blackwood's. It seemed horrid to come away from the dear B.'s in their trouble, but I could do no good; and though I have not a vestige of fear of infection, they were eager to see me safe out of it. So I had fire in a cosy little room here all the afternoon, and quiet rest, as I could not venture out to church, my cough teazing me. You see this involved only *one* bit of Sunday travelling, and I leave direct for Mumbles by express this, Monday, morning.

Tell dear Giles and Ellen they need not be afraid of my putting my neck into any nooses. I am much too snug at the Mumbles!

(*To M. V. G. H.*)

THE MUMBLES, February 18, 1879.

It was quite delightful getting in here last evening (from my sudden flight from London and change of plans), although you had not returned. It felt so really coming *home*, and I had such a comfortable journey. Mary helped me unpack, and it was delicious to be all straight the same night. Oh, the sunshine here! hot and brilliant in my study. Such a pile of letters this A.M., only one worth sending on for you to answer. Mr. Shaw will be amused with dear Mr. Wright's explanation,

which of course I answer. When I called at the Church Missionary House, I thought him kind, but a little bit stiffer than I expected; so his not knowing who I was, explains it. I had no idea he did not know me, but it seems he did not catch the name from Mr. Eugene Stock, and as he says, "We are not in heaven yet!"

Elliot & Fry will send you proofs of my photos. Remember nothing ever will induce me to have any sort of likeness-taking again. So you make up your minds once for all! Please send me the address of the Church Pastoral Aid Society and the secretary's name, as now I can do what I wanted.

(*To M. V. G. H.*) PARK VILLA, MUMBLES, February 21, 1879.

If you are writing to E. Clay, please give her my love, and I shall not forget to-morrow. You will get the photos to-day; I was wretchedly poorly, and shivering with cold the day I was taken. I thought I looked more of a lady, which these certainly do not give me the idea of!

I had such a spree last night! I got the whole household to sign my Temperance Pledge-book, Tucker himself down to little Johnnie! and Mary F. I am so delighted.

I did so want to send to the Church Pastoral Aid Society, but I don't like halving things, so I will not do that; but to please dear Giles, I will postpone my gift to C. P. A. till next year, and send to the Bible Society instead, so he may reckon that is his getting for it! Tell Ellen I will be sure and take care of number one, and that I have not found Philippians 4:19 to fail yet, and moreover the Lord always does at least as much, and generally more than He promises, so she need not be alarmed as to my future.

I have set really to work. I am re-writing part of the *Kept* papers: the first chapter is quite new; there was so much to say. It is a very serious thing to set about work which goes to tens of thousands. I felt I must set apart a day entirely for prayer, etc., which I did yesterday, instead of setting to work, and I do not think it was time lost.

I found old Mrs. Phillips sitting up, and no end delighted to see me back. A dear little girl died yesterday in the village from heart disease, the sister of that lovely little heathen who comes to me for books. The little dead child looked so exquisitely beautiful.

Snow here the last three mornings, but it melts, and as usual brilliant sun, when not actually snowing. My cough is less, and I feel much better than before I went to London. Mary is most devoted, and it will be an immense addition to my comfort to make her save my eyes; as finer weather and longer days come on, I shall try to be out of doors as much as I possibly can, so as to be fresher for real work at my desk.

I have just sent £100 towards clearing ——'s premium; I do want that millstone cleared off, and then I can easily do

when not being used, on the shelf awaiting use, in F.R.H.'s case caused by illness. The current meaning of unattractiveness and certainty to be a spinster was not at all true of F.R.H.

more next year. It is so tremendously nice earning money to give away; I had no idea it was such fun!

(*Post Card.*)

March 29, 1879.

I know it is fanciful, and not the real meaning, but I like applying verse 8 of Ezekiel 10, "The form of a man's hand under their wings," to the thought of the Divine wings and hand. "Under the shadow of His wings," there is *still closer* the form of a Man's hand—the pierced Hand. Perhaps pressing sore, but certainly encircling and holding fast. Or again, taking the cherubim in their, I suppose, *real* meaning, as the Church of God, while the sound of their wings (ver. 5) is "heard even to the outer court" (cf. Romans 10:18), the Man's hand, "Christ the Power of God" (1 Corinthians 1:24) is under them as they "run and return" (Eze. 1:14), not *their* hand, but "Thy right hand" (Psalm 44:3), "working with them" (Mark 16:20). Do you like this thought? I have only this minute hit on it.

The Mumbles, April 2, 1879.

My dear Collectors,—

God has given us one of the most splendid answers to prayer I ever knew. He has prospered our Bruey Branch ever so much beyond what *I* asked or thought, and so, maybe, it is beyond what you asked or thought either. So those of us who have been faithfully remembering to pray for our work on Monday mornings, may have the joy of hearty thanksgiving for answered prayer; and if those who have been forgetting all about it will nevertheless join in thanking Him for doing what they did *not* ask, I think they will be glad to join in our prayers after this.

Two years ago we started with eight collectors, and sent up £20, 9s. 1d.; last year we had eighteen collectors, and sent up £41, 9s. 3d.; and this year we have seventy-eight collectors, and have sent up £108, 19s. 1d.! Is not this grand? And this is not nearly all. Mr. Roe, one of the Association secretaries, tells me that he has "hundreds of cards out, and is appointing 'Twig' secretaries in all directions," so that dear little Bruey's work is bearing most wonderful fruit, and it looks as if there would be a great deal more next year than this. We have five "Twigs" in the Bruey Branch, besides the senior and junior divisions; but it seems we shall have a *great* many more soon.

Now, as our faithful God has heard our poor little prayers so far, I want you to pray still more, and especially that He would not only help us in our collecting, but that He would send a very great spiritual blessing on the work done in Ireland by means of the money collected. Will you join me in asking four things? 1. That God would give His Holy Spirit to all the Irish teachers and their pupils. 2. That very many may, during this year, seek and find Jesus. 3. That those who find Him, may be filled with love, and that the joy of the Lord may be their strength, especially in bearing persecution for His sake. 4. That every one who finds Christ, may begin at once to bring others to Him. I wish you would just copy these four things out, and put them in your Bibles, so that you may be reminded every Monday morning *what* to pray for, and we shall see what gracious answers God will give us. "The Lord *hath* done great things for us," and it seems as if He were saying, "Thou shalt see *greater* things than these," so "be glad and rejoice, for the Lord *will* do great things." Find these three texts out, and mark them in your Bibles.

Now for some business remarks. I wish you would all learn to be business-like. Some of you did everything right, and I herewith offer my best thanks, as secretary, for their having saved me a good deal of trouble by doing *all* I asked. But how was it that I had to write to seven or eight of you, because the 1st of March went by, and you did not send your card in? Some of you even then kept me waiting, and thus I was defeated in a very nice little plan I had, which I meant to have written to each of you about, to reach you on St. Patrick's day, March 17. I will see if I can do it next year.

Do you remember my asking you to pray for a dear little girl? Her mamma writes as follows:—"I enclose £5, our darling Nony's collection for the Irish Society, and which in all probability will be her last, as the doctors say she is now past recovery, and that it is only a question of *time*. What an unspeakable comfort and perfect rest it gives us to feel that our *times* are in His hand whose way is *perfect!* so that we cannot for one moment wish anything otherwise than as *He* orders it. The work sold was not *all* her own doing, but she worked a few minutes at a time as long as she was able. She has had two operations during the last month, and has a large wound in her thigh. Her sufferings have been terrible, but I have never heard a murmur. It was so kind of you to ask prayer for her, and seemed to please her much." Please remember poor dear little Nony, and ask the Good Shepherd to deal very tenderly with His little suffering lamb. Surely He will send a special blessing on *her* work, "the few stitches" done "as long as she was able."

I am sending a copy of the February number of *Day of Days* to each collector. If any one does not receive it, please let me know. I particularly want you *all* to take the little magazine in, and recommend it to your subscribers—it is only a penny a month,—for now we have arranged to have something about the Irish work in it every month, so that all collectors and contributors will be able to get fresh accounts, besides a great deal else that will be nice to read. The one I send contains a paper called *Novel Kind of Schools*. The March number (which I do hope you will get) has been called *How very Irish!* April will have ——. Well, you get it, and see what! Next June I hope, please God, to go to Ireland myself, on purpose to go to the parts where our Society is at work, and then I shall write all about what I saw and heard, and have it printed in the magazine, which will be better than these short circulars, and I hope much more interesting. That's another thing I want you to pray for; ask that if it is God's will I should go and do this, I may be both blessed and made a blessing in doing it.

And now I will give you a text for your next year's work: "Be not weary in well-doing." Perhaps some of you *are* a little bit weary in it; some have owned that they are, as they sent up a card not quite so full as last year.

However, I do trust the loving Saviour will lay it on their hearts with enduring power, that they may work for Jesus' sake only, and not get weary now the novelty has worn off. This is just what I pray for every one of you, dear ones, whether I know you personally or not. To that loving Saviour I commend you and your work for the coming year.

—Your very affectionate secretary,

Frances Ridley Havergal.

On receiving the £5 with the news that dear Nony had been very, very ill for some months, my dear sister sent her this sweet little note:—

My Dear Nony,[1]—

I had no idea you were suffering so much all this time. I think Jesus must have been carrying you in His arms all the while, because you see when anybody can't even walk, they *must* be carried. And I am quite sure He must be loving you ever so much; I mean with a very special and tender love, because it says, "Whom the Lord loveth He chasteneth." I thank you so much for the violets. I have such a number of new Bruey collectors that I hardly know how I shall manage them all. We shall have a famous report for next year, I hope.

Very much love from your loving friend.

The Mumbles, February 25, 1879.

Yours is just such a letter as it is real self-denial to me not to sit down and answer *seriatim*. I resolutely take only a P. C., because I have set myself to a bit of work which I find requires very careful thought; and as writing tries me, I am going to write post cards till it is done, as I do want to keep fresh and free, that I may give my *best* to the Master in doing it. (*Starlight through the Shadows*).

Very much obliged for the books, and for your sister's charming letter. And believe me that my full sympathy followed *all* you told me; instead of answering by pen I will, God helping me, answer by prayer!

I cannot understand how any Christian can stand still and sing such a misrepresentation of His service as—

"If I find Him, if I follow,
What His guerdon here?
Many a sorrow, many a labour,
Many a tear!"

Is not that too bad? Do we not know it to be unfair to our Lord and His happy service? Where does *He* say that is "His guerdon[2] here"? Let us just think for our service what He *does* say: "Work; for I am with you, saith the Lord of hosts." That alone is the grandest, richest, sweetest "guerdon here" that any loving heart can ask. Now for another promise, which certainly does not look like that wretched linking of "labour" with "many a sorrow, and many a tear." That is what the old Greek hymn-writer says. But God says, "Mine elect shall long *enjoy* the work of their hands."

The Mumbles.

. . . The one thing strongly on my mind to say to you is, Do not let your mind dwell at all on any attentions you may receive. If it is to come to anything, your thinking about it will not make any difference; but if it is not, then every thought you have spent on it will have to be, as it were, unthought—you will be preparing pain and disappointment for yourself just in proportion to how much you have allowed yourself to dwell on this. I know well enough by experience, that one cannot help it of one's self, but I do know also what power our Lord has over our thoughts when committed to Him, and how wonderfully He can make a way of escape for us. See, dear ——, I want you first thing to go and lay the matter very simply before the Lord. Tell Him all that is in your heart, every bit of it. And then ask Him to undertake for you. Ask your King just to order everything if it is His will, and to keep you very calm till His will *is* clearly shown, and very willing that He should take His own way with you and with your future life. But ask the Lord, if it is not His will you should marry, to make you perfectly content, and then to *take away* all the wish out of your heart, so that you may be "free to serve" with your whole mind undistracted by it. And then ask Him, in His great kindness, that He would interpose in some way to make this easy to you, He has such wonderful ways! I think this is very important, for I am sure one does not serve quite so freely and fully when one has possibilities of marriage in suspense. Of course I have gone through all this years ago, and even just now have had to say "No," though to a decided Christian, being perfectly clear it was right to say so; I need hardly tell you I shall, God helping me, pray about it for you. I will ask that if it is God's will you may not be kept in any suspense, whichever way it is. I should so like you to have the happiness of human love and care for you; it would make me extremely happy, if it does turn out to

[1] See *Memorials of Little Nony.* Nisbet & Co. [See pages 899–925 of Volume IV of the Havergal edition.]

[2] guerdon: reward or recompense

be a real and right step. But you are in the hands of your own dear Master, and He will do the *best* thing for you, I have no doubt of that!

(Memorandum by M. V. G. H.)

March 20, 1879.

"H. converted and O. P. consecrated." This extract shall be briefly explained.

F. R. H. had promised to take most needed rest from her desk-work on the breezy cliffs that afternoon. The hour passed by, and still her door was shut. Then she came, beaming of course: "Marie, I've had such a tussel with Satan! I had my hat on and was going to the cliffs with you when I saw O. P. on a ladder painting my study windows. I was so tired, that it was quite a battle to talk to him *then*, but I threw the window open to ask how he was getting on. Directly he said, 'O, Miss Frances, I've been longing for weeks for a chance to speak to you.' Then came such an outpour of his desire to be quite out and out on the Lord's side; so I saw the time was come, as I expected it would from our last conversation. So I told him to come in through the window; and after reading and prayer, I asked if he would *now*, in his own words, say to Jesus Himself, 'Thou art my King.' And so he did, so fully and really; and the answer, 'I will be Thy King,' seemed to fall with hushing power as we knelt. And afterwards he told me how differently he left my study than when he came in, so glad that Jesus was henceforth his King as well as his Saviour. My verse seemed just to express his desire:

> "'Reign over me, Lord Jesus!
> Oh make my heart Thy throne;
> It shall be Thine for ever,
> It shall be Thine alone!'"

(Post Card to Mrs. Morgan, Vicarage, Swansea.)

Good Friday Night.

I am still better, and though of course not myself yet, I hope now to be able for Thursday (Y. W. C. A. meeting). Was so ill Tuesday, that it seemed quite hopeless to think of it, but I should think you have been praying! Should have been so sorry to disappoint you, knowing your difficulties. Do pray that I may have a real message to some.

Monday, April, 14, 1879.

DEAREST MRS. MORGAN,—

God has been so very gracious in making me better so very much quicker than usual after such a turn, so it is all right for Tuesday as far as that is concerned. I took a sort of turn and got rapidly better just after my first note went—but I was *so* ill when I wrote it, that judging from previous experiences it did not seem likely I should be out of bed, let alone out of doors,

in time; and it seemed as if God were intending to say "No!" to my coming. However, I was mistaken in that! I wish I had your and my sister's gift—because I know I must disappoint you and all who know me as F. R. H. Gifts do differ—and mine is not addresses. Still I will just simply try to say whatever God may give me at the time. I feel too *done up* somehow to prepare properly—I tried and could not! So must just leave it and ask God to use a *weak* thing, and you will ask too for blessing, in spite of my incapacity.

(Memorandum by M. V. G. H.)

My dear sister Frances went to Swansea on Thursday, 17th. I sent our good maid M. Farrington with her, as she did not wish me to go; she says that on the way Miss Frances talked so humbly, and that she "felt as if she had no right to go teaching others—such a sinner as I am; but then Mary, I am just trusting for every word." The room was quite full. Mrs. Morgan, not knowing F.'s subject, had chosen a hymn that did not suit it, and my sister always thought it important that hymns should be suitably chosen. As her subject for the evening was from Hosea 3, "I also for thee," (See *Starlight through the Shadows*), F. said she wished to sing "Precious Saviour, may I live, only for Thee." Mrs. Morgan said they did not know her tune to it ("Onesimus," *S. G. G.* 257.) F.: "No fear! Do let me just sing one verse alone, and I know they will join." Going to the piano and turning her face to them, she sang with her own bright ringing cheeriness one verse, and then all joined most heartily with her. Mary told me of my sister's soft pleading voice—that her words were intensely tender and entreating. At the close of the meeting, my sister gave to each one a card with her Consecration hymn, "Take my life and let it be Consecrated, Lord, to Thee," specially prepared and printed for this evening (Messrs. Parlane, Paisley, still supply them). Her own name was omitted, and a blank space left for signature. As she gave the cards, she asked them to make that hymn a test before God, and if they could really do so, to sign it on their knees at home. Then the hymn was sung to our dear father's tune "Patmos" (No. 145, *S. G. G.*).[1]

It seems to have been a great night of decision to many present. The next morning, before ever her breakfast was finished, one and another came for conversation with my dear sister—a French governess was specially impressed. My sister returned very much exhausted—meetings seemed to take away her little physical strength, and yet she always cheerfully took up any work for her King.

---

[1] This tune was invariably sung by my sister to her words, and it certainly grieves us that such a very *mournful* unsuitable tune is substituted for it in Sankey's *Solos*.—Messrs. Parlane, Paisley, supply this and many others of F. R. H.'s *own* tunes, as also the only *correct* version of "Tell it out." [See page 230 of this book.]

(7 4, 7 4, D.)   F. R. H.

ONESIMUS.

Precious Saviour, may I live Only for Thee! Spend the powers Thou dost give Only for Thee! Be my spirit's deep desire Only for Thee! May my intellect aspire Only for Thee! A-men.

(To S. G. P.)

May 1879.

I will tell you the *worst* first! It's all up about Mr. Sankey singing "Loving all along" in England. He has asthma or something worse; is forbidden to sing at all; is giving up all his engagements here, and going back to America next month. So he only tinkles on the piano. Then the very day he came, I started a feverish attack which threatened to get serious, but mercifully is diminishing this morning; but when I shall be able to sing again I don't know! as I am in bed of course. However, I did sing "Loving all along" directly he came, as I knew I might get no other chance, though it was a poor chance enough to sing it with a splitting headache and an icy chill down my spine. And the first thing Sankey said was that "it wouldn't do for America at all"! because, "Tramp, tramp" is their most popular war song, and it would never do for him to sing it!

Now for the other side.

Next morning he said, "That song of yours abides with me, that *big one!* I woke up with it. There's two or three points that *haunt* me." "That's all right," said I, "for *I* woke up with a way out of the American difficulty. '*Far, far* on the downward way,' etc., instead of 'Tramp,' if the author does not object." Then he looked very serious (which he generally does not), and said, "It's my belief that song has *got* to go. And that *I'll have* to sing it! It's kind of taken a *hold* of me"! So then we looked carefully through the song, for as I have not heard him sing, I could not tell if it would suit his voice, and was ready to alter and

carve as much as he liked, but oh, dear no, he would not have a single note touched. I was "*just to go right ahead,*" and write it out for press, exactly as it stood.

I hope you won't feel it needful to give thanks *under protest* for the answer to your prayer under protest! The Baroness von Cramm is extremely struck with the music, which she says is "so dramatic and so beautiful," and I know you won't be sorry to hear this! All the same, I do not think the song will be popular, because it is just one of those which is utterly ruined if stumbled over, or even if well played by one who does not DASH off the recitative-like style with real *spirit*, and bring out the *sharp* contrasts which give effect. But if nobody else *ever* sings it but Sankey and the Baroness in their different spheres, those two are worth thousands of ordinary singers, and if not a copy sells, the two copies that go to them, may do more real work for God than a dozen editions. So we will *thank God* and take courage. Besides, though I cannot sing like them, I know I can make some listen to "*Loving*—ALL *along*!" and perhaps God will give *me* a little fruit thereby besides what they will get.

I go off to Ireland on my mission station tour on June 4 (*D. V.*). Have been "marvellously helped" in total abstinence work here, and got 120 to sign in this little village of Newton— at least, chiefly in the village and a few around—mostly children, but it is spreading upwards. I am quite astonished at what God has wrought. I never dreamt of asking for so many as He has given me for my "Newton Temperance."

(F. R. H. to C. H. Purday.)

May 1, 1879.

Glad it is all straight now for Nisbet! Shall leave form and style and everything to you and Mr. N.

Thanks, I rarely have anything the matter with me except what arises from over-pressure. God has given me an exceptionally healthy set of organs, so all doctors tell me, only they add, "Your physique is not equal to the brain and nerves." "If you could live as an oyster, you might be a little Hercules," said one to me! But *I cannot* live as an oyster! I have always more to write and do and talk and attend to than I *can* get through in the day without just so much fatigue and pressure as keeps me nearly always more or less suffering or exhausted. It is the little things that do it—"only just" this note and that letter, and the other ten minutes' interview, and so on—all day long! And I cannot live near a poor village (Newton Mumbles) and not get doing anything for the people—and one thing always involves and leads on to another, and the very success that God gives to really everything I put my hand to, wears me out. A special branch of work for the Irish Society, which I started only two years ago, thinking merely to have about a dozen juvenile collectors in tow, forthwith grew, so that there are now more than

100, all in my own hands, and this will ere long be multiplied and be kept organized with lots of other things growing out of it. I only name this as one out of many similar *growths,* and your kind interest deserved an explanation of the state of things once for all! Then every time I pay a visit, I always get a whole following of fresh friends, and readers and correspondents! I can't imagine where into it will grow! And sometimes I look longingly to the land that is very far away just for *rest.*

THE MUMBLES, May 9, 1879.

I leave this (*D. V.*)[1] on June 4. Then for two months I shall be touring about the Irish Society Mission stations, with a few visits to friends near Dublin at the end. Of course, it would be very inconvenient to have proofs pursuing one on a carpet-bag tour in the backwoods, but equally of course they cannot stop altogether, so I will get the Society to keep forwarding them from headquarters.

I have just finished a little book for children, *Morning Stars; or, the Names of Christ for His Little Ones.* Please say truly whether your hands are so full, that if you were to read over my little book, it would cause you any extra trouble; for in that case I would forego the advantage sooner than you should be burdened. It is just a size larger than the *Bells* and *Pillows.*

I have had it much on my mind to write something for children. It seems time I gave them a turn, but I was waiting for my orders!

I think my sister is as grateful as I am to you, for the way in which you have saved me fatigue.

THE MUMBLES, May 1879.

DEAR MR. WATSON,—

You did not answer one part of my question, whether I should print the enclosed little book with the *Kept for the Master's Use,* as it is all part of the same subject? I should be glad to know what you think, because it will make a little difference in my rewriting the first chapter of *Kept* whether I include *I also for Thee* in the same little volume or not. If I do include it, I shall of course alter the opening, rewriting it so as to fit on to the other and complete it. I should *rather* prefer thus putting the two into one, for the sake of getting greater completeness of the subject; but if you see any objection, I will not do so. Of course, I can easily do it at once, and have it out for Easter; but would you like to risk my having nothing but the invalid book for October? Had I not better wait? I'll tell you just how it is. I have been very unhappy since I left you about the whole thing, and I don't think I have got any *real* commission to write anything at all for next season except the invalid book. You see,

I found I was looking at it all in a different light, thinking rather of what would be most successful, and keep up the run, than simply and only, "Lord, what wilt *Thou* have me to do?" And it won't be the least use my attempting to write to any purpose if that element comes in, and I simply dare not write at all if I find it there. It is a totally different thing with you. I quite see all you said, but then God has given you a definite calling, and therefore it is your duty before Him to fulfil it from a business point of view, but He has not given *me* any duty of the sort at all, and I believe I am going off the lines of my especial calling altogether if once I begin thinking of it as a matter of business and success and cheques and all that, and I can't expect the same blessing in it. And so, though of course it stands to reason that the invalid book must have a very limited circulation compared to the others, I shall be much happier doing that, and I believe I shall have more real, *i.e.* spiritual, results from it than if I set myself to do those I subsequently thought of, because I do think God gave me the thought and the wish to do the one, whereas the thought of doing the others this season seemed to me to arise rather out of having got that big cheque. No one can be more delighted than I am to get those same cheques; but so far as I know myself, I have never yet taken them into consideration when thinking of writing any one of my little books, and finding myself doing so, made me just miserable. I don't know if I have explained myself, only I have felt so very strongly and sweetly hitherto that my pen was to be used *only* for the Master, that I am very fearful of getting the least out of the course in which I have felt His blessing.

The upshot is, I don't think I shall write *any* general book for October, nothing but *Starlight through the Shadows,* and possibly one or a pair of books for children; and this being the case, had I not better reserve *Kept* to come out along with *Starlight?* Then I should still have a pair of books apparently, though not really a pair. I did not mean to tell you all this, but if I did not, you might think I was fickle and perhaps idle, and that it was no good giving me advice. I hope you won't be vexed and disappointed with me; you don't know how really grateful I feel for all you have said and done.

Will you tell dear Katie that if she has not already sent the photographs to Winterdyne, I should be glad if she will address them to Elm Row instead? How glad I should be if the reports of you were better.

—Yours affectionately and gratefully.

————

[This was one of F. R. H.'s last letters. She passed into the presence of her King, June 3, 1879.]

————

[1] *D. V.*: Deo Volente (Latin), meaning "God willing"

APPENDIX I.

THE APPROACHING MISSION SERVICES, BY F. R. H. [1]

Edited by A. W. Thorold, D.D., Lord Bishop of Rochester.

A WEEK OF SPECIAL MISSION SERVICES is proposed. The movement, which has spread so rapidly in all parts of the kingdom, has reached your own doors. Energetic preparation is being made, earnest prayer is being offered, and warm expectation is already awake.

What is it all about? Why do people talk of "expectation"? Why should clergymen give themselves so much trouble? And how will it affect the readers of this paper?

We will answer the last question first, and say to every one who reads this: Perhaps it will affect *you* for ever and ever and ever! Perhaps, ere that week closes, you, who know and love the Lord Jesus, will be sealed anew with a fresh baptism of the Spirit, blessed with richer manifestations of Christ's presence and love, filled with deeper joy, and stirred up to holier zeal and more single-hearted devotedness than ever before. Perhaps, ere that week closes, you, who earnestly desire to be saved, and yet have never dared to lay hold of Christ's full and free salvation, will be rejoicing "with joy unspeakable and full of glory." Perhaps, ere that week closes, you who have "no hope, and are without God in the world," will be made "new creatures" altogether, will know the terrible danger in which you have been living, and the hitherto unguessed joy of having a "sure and certain hope," and an Everlasting Friend to love and lean upon. Such are the effects which we hope for, pray for, and expect.

It is a thrillingly grand and glorious thing to stand on the eve of such a season, looking forward to such blessings, and to an actual share in them. It is a thrillingly solemn and awful thing to remember that one may be taken and another left; that a day of doom may follow close upon a day of grace, and that if the blessing is despised or neglected by any heart, that heart may be left dry, dead, untouched, while showers of blessing fall on all around.

But WHAT IS A MISSION WEEK? It is a means of grace which, more than any other of late years, God appears to have used for the conversion of sinners, and the raising of His own people to a higher, holier, and happier life.

Many important towns have followed this plan. The whole week is set apart for one object. Special services, not long, but intensely fervent, are held in every church every day; the usual order of services being shortened, and earnest, striking addresses given by special preachers, specially qualified for this work. These are preceded and followed by meetings for prayer—for pleading and wrestling with God for His blessing, and the outpouring of His Spirit. Arrangements are made to bring the glad tidings to those who will not come to any place of worship, and to those who cannot attend the special Church Services. Meetings and addresses are planned for all classes—rich as well as poor. Short addresses are given in factories, workshops, and railway sheds; gatherings of different callings and classes are held; cabmen, policemen, servants, young shopmen and shopwomen, poor mothers, young ladies in boarding-schools, gentlemen in business—all are considered and arranged for.

It may not be advisable to mention names, but we could tell of many places where great and abiding blessing has rested upon the Mission Week. In one small town, the number of those who were not merely impressed at the time, but have become decided and steady Christians, is estimated at 1200! In a manufacturing town, the numbers added to the church in one parish were so great, that the Incumbent had to procure an additional Curate, on purpose to take up the work arising out of the Mission Week! In another, it was the working men who seemed to obtain the greatest blessing; and such congregations of these have perhaps never been seen as in a large church in that town on the Sunday evenings after the Mission Week. In the same place, the railway men, to whom short daily addresses had been given, have requested the Vicar to continue them regularly; and the results have been such as no scoffers could ignore or explain away.

It has been remarked that the greatest blessing, in nearly every place, has been among those who have already had serious impressions, and in whom the soil was in some degree

[1] Re-issued as Leaflet. Messrs. Nisbet & Co.

prepared, rather than among such as have had no previous care or thought about their souls. Is not this a very important note of encouragement and of warning? To those who are seeking Jesus, but have not found Him, it gives encouragement to pray very earnestly that this coming Mission Week may be the great turning-point of their lives, and the coming out of doubt and darkness and indecision into "marvellous light" and "glorious liberty." To those who care for none of these things, it gives a warning, lest this great opportunity should only add to their condemnation, if they refuse to "prepare their hearts to seek God."

Our God may work above reason, but He does not work against reason. So we may fairly ask, WHY SHOULD WE EXPECT GREAT THINGS FROM A MISSION WEEK? And the answer is no mystery, to those who know the secrets and the power of PRAYER. For months beforehand, many faithful hearts have been pleading, constantly and intensely, for a blessing. As the time approaches, more and more are stirred up to join in these prayers. Their fervency and earnestness deepen day by day, till at last one great cry is ascending day and night, unheard by the sleeping souls around, but strong and loud in "the ears of the Lord God of Sabaoth." How is this? Do our own evil hearts prompt to such prayer? Does Satan set us praying? How else can it arise, but from the promptings of the HOLY SPIRIT? The God in whose hand the blessing is hid, waiting to be gracious, pours out "the spirit of grace and of supplication" upon His people, because "He will be inquired of" for the good things which He purposes to give. And the coming shower of blessing, of which this spirit of prayer is the earnest, will be all the sweeter and more powerful for being thus, as it were, drawn down by their prayers.

"He that watereth shall be watered;" and it seems that these prayers for those around generally receive a double answer, returning in a wonderful gladness,—a very reaping-time of joy, upon the hearts of those who have been, it may be, sowing these supplications in tears. Let no Christian heart lose its share in the blessing, by neglecting or delaying to join in the prayer. Let every one resolve at once, by God's help, to make it a subject of daily prayer during the coming weeks of anticipation.

BUT WHY DO THE CLERGY TAKE ALL THIS TROUBLE? They are not paid for it; they will get nothing by it; they will only be wearied and worn outs after days of work, and perhaps night-hours of prayer. Why? It is because they love the people around them, and because they believe that God means what He says, when He speaks in His Word, of sin, death, judgment, eternity, and of pardon, life, salvation, and glory. Months of prayer and preparation, and a week of labour to the utmost, are a very small thing to those whose whole lives are being spent for

their people, and who know that in a few years every soul under their care will be in heaven or in hell.

If so, shall it be a great thing to those for whom they toil, to give a few hours to the affairs of millions of years beyond imagination? What does it matter about any business or engagement in comparison? "What shall it profit a man, if he gain the whole world and lose his own soul?"

The Mission Week will be a golden opportunity; perhaps the very last for some who read this. Loving voices will say to you, "Jesus of Nazareth passeth by! Rise! He calleth thee!" Oh, will you not come to Him, that you may have life?

A word with those who talk about "excitement," or who throw cold water on that zeal for God, which one longs to see kindled in every heart. Do any perish through religious excitement? But are not thousands perishing of religious apathy?

There is much foolish parrot-talk about this, by persons who, having no real means or power of forming an opinion of their own, catch up clap-trap phrases of irreligious cant (and for every phrase of religious, there are ten of irreligious cant!) and talk grandly about the "danger of excitement." What *is* the danger of it? Confessedly this, that if the feelings are touched and excited, without real change of heart, they lapse into greater coldness and deadness than before. Then the danger obviously is—not of going too far, but of not going far enough! None are so illogical as those who try to argue with God. See to it, you who would hinder others by talk about the danger of "excitement," but shut your eyes to the danger of death and hell,—see to it that God does not take you at your word, and leave you, untouched by "excitement of feeling," cool and easy, outside the gate, while others are entering in. What will you feel, when the last hour has struck for you, when the door is shut, and you are outside, left to "the blackness of darkness for ever"? Will there be no "excitement" in the moment of *that* discovery, think you?

But some real Christians look a little doubtfully upon new efforts, and hold aloof, and do not see why ordinary means should not be sufficient. Have they proved all-sufficient? *Do they reach all the unconverted?* And if not, why not try other means, in the spirit of our Heavenly Father, who doth "*devise means* that His banished be not expelled from Him;" in the spirit of our Master, who said, "Go ye out into the highways and hedges, and compel them to come in;" in the spirit of His follower, who said, "If by *any* means I might save some." Let us not, then, hinder the Gospel of Christ by our chilling half-heartedness.

While praying for "showers of blessing" upon our country and our Church, surely it will be both right and pleasant that Christians should join their pastor in seeking and expecting a special blessing on their own parish. God's order appears to be, "The more prayer, the more blessing."

Again, the approaching Mission Week seems a new call to pray for our own home circles, that if any who are near and dear to us are not yet "on the Lord's side," they may then be brought to Christ, and thenceforth live unto Him. And, drawing the circle still closer, shall we not each, whatever be our state or need, whatever be our age or position, seek a personal blessing upon our own souls? *"Bless me, even me also, O my Father!"*

Hymn 839 in "Songs of Grace and Glory for Mission Services." (London: Nisbet & Co.)

"LORD, I HEAR OF SHOWERS OF BLESSING"

PERSIS   Music by F. R. H.

Lord, I hear of showers of blessing
  Thou art scattering full and free;
Showers the thirsty land refreshing:
  Let some dropping fall on me,
            even me.

Pass me not, O gracious Father!
  Sinful though my heart may be;
Thou might'st curse me, but the rather
  Let Thy mercy light on me,
            even me.

Pass me not, O tender Saviour!
  Let me love and cling to Thee;
I am longing for Thy favour;
  When Thou comest, call for me,
            even me.

Pass me not, O mighty Spirit!
  Thou canst make the blind to see;
Witnesser of Jesu's merit,
  Speak the word of power to me,
            even me.

Have I long in sin been sleeping,
  Long been slighting, grieving Thee?
Has the world my heart been keeping?
  Oh, forgive and rescue me,
            even me.

Love of God, so pure and changeless,
  Blood of God, so rich and free,
Grace of God, so strong and boundless,
  Magnify them all in me,
            even me.

Pass me not, this lost one bringing;
  Satan's slave Thy child shall be;
All my heart to Thee is springing;
  Blessing others, oh, bless me,
            even me!

ELIZABETH CODNER

"WILL YE NOT COME?"

LUCIUS.   Words and Music by
                                      F. R. Havergal.

Will ye not come to Him for *life?*
Why will ye die, oh why?
He gave His life for you, for you!
The gift is free, the word is true!
Will ye not come? Oh, why will ye die?

Refrain, after any or each verse.

Will ye not come? Will ye not come,
Will ye not come to Him, to Him?
Oh, come, come, come to Him!
Come unto Jesus, oh, come for *life.*

Will ye not come to Him for *peace,*
Peace through His cross alone?
He shed His precious blood for you;
The gift is free, the word is true!
He is our Peace—Oh, is He your own?
Will yet not come, etc. . . . for *peace?*

Will ye not come to Him for *rest?*
All that are weary, come:
The rest He gives is deep and true,
'Tis offered now, 'tis offered you:
Rest in His love, and rest in His home.
Will ye not come, etc. . . . for *rest?*

Will ye not come to Him for *joy?*
Will ye not come for this?
He laid His joys aside for you,
To give you joy, so sweet, so true:
Sorrowing heart, oh, drink of the bliss!
Will ye not come, etc. . . . for *joy?*

Will ye not come to Him for *love,*
Love that can fill the heart?
Exceeding great, exceeding free!
He loveth you, He loveth me!
Will ye not come? Why stand ye apart?
Will ye not come, etc. . . . for *love?*

Will ye not come to Him for ALL?
Will ye not "taste and see?"
He waits to give it all to you,
The gifts are free, the words are true:
Jesus hath said it, "Come unto Me!"
Will ye not come, etc. . . . to HIM?

In compliance with a request from Sankey for a Gospel Musical Call, my dear sister F. R. H. wrote these lines at Winterdyne, December 21, 1873. The same morning, I met her with the MS. in her hand, toiling up to the Wyre Hill school-room. She said, "Maria, will the children be out of school?" "Yes." "Then I shall lock myself in and fancy the room full for a mission service! I have been praying that the *music may be sent me,* to fit His message, 'Will ye not come?'"

Soon I heard these chords on the harmonium and her ringing voice. She called the tune "Lucius," and often sang it with pleading tenderness at mission and other meetings.

Thus in poetry, in prose, in music, in life, and in death, her silver refrain was, "*Will ye not come?*"

"Still shall the key-word, ringing, echo the same sweet '*Come!*'
Come with the blessed myriads safe in the Father's home;
Come—for the work is over; Come—for the feast is spread;
Come—for the crown of glory waits for the weary head."

MARIA V. G. HAVERGAL.

"TELL IT OUT!"[1]

Leaflet, Parlane, Paisley.   Words and Music by
F. R. Havergal.

Tell it out among the heathen that the Lord is King! Tell it out! Tell it out! Tell it out among the nations, bid them shout and sing! Tell it out! Tell it out with adoration that He shall increase; That the mighty King of Glory is the

[1] This is F. R. H.'s own arrangement—that given in the *Christian Choir* is incorrect. M. V. G. H.

Tell it out among the heathen that the Saviour reigns!
  Tell it out! Tell it out!
Tell it out among the nations, bid them burst their chains.
  Tell it out! Tell it out!
Tell it out among the weeping ones that Jesus lives;
Tell it out among the weary ones what rest He gives;
Tell it out among the sinners that He came to save;
Tell it out among the dying that He triumphed o'er the grave.

Tell it out among the heathen Jesus reigns above!
  Tell it out! Tell it out!
Tell it out among the nations that His reign is love!
  Tell it out! Tell it out!
Tell it out among the highways and the lanes at home;
Let it ring across the mountains and the ocean foam!
Like the sound of many waters let our glad shout be,
Till it echo and re-echo from the islands of the sea!

[Note: The Nisbet "Third Thousand" printing of *Letters* (dated 1885) ended with the previous "Appendix" of F.R.H.'s "The Approaching Mission Services." The Nisbet "Fourth Thousand" printing (dated 1886) had after that the next two Appendices of "Additional Letters" and "Hinderers and Hindrances."]

APPENDIX II.

ADDITIONAL LETTERS.

Since the publication of the First Edition of F.R.H.'s Letters, correspondents have supplied these additional ones. A fragment from my sister's MSS. is also given.

M. V. G. H.

Dec. 10, 1885.

(*To Hannah . . .*)

Llandrillo yn Rhos.

I am writing now on a seat at the bottom of the garden just above the beach, and not two yards from high tide mark, which the sea has just now nearly reached, the morning sunlight trembling and quivering most dazzlingly in a broad band before me. . . . I am trying to help Mrs. Gillman with the choir, but the language makes it such a difficulty, they do not always understand what one wants them to. I play the harmonium for her on Sundays at the English service, and at one of the Welsh services; and find the little Welsh I picked up years ago very useful, for it would be nearly impossible to keep time in chanting (Te Deum, etc.) unless one understood and could read it. I understand enough of *book* Welsh to follow the services quite well, and to make out a little of the sermon. Last Sunday, I stayed to the Welsh communion, and very much enjoyed a return of my old German feeling of "*one* Lord, *one* faith," etc., which used to be very vividly present to me when with foreigners, and in a foreign country, where it was particularly nice to feel that union with all those who love our Lord Jesus Christ in sincerity, which difference of language and race seems to throw up into brighter relief.

You speak of Satan being very busy; I could *almost* say, I am glad to hear it! Because if he thought he could lull you into a *false* peace, he would be only too ready to do so, and to leave you to yourself unmolested; he does not attack and trouble his own children, and you would have no conflict with him if you were not fighting under another banner. And anything, oh anything, to keep us watching; it is better to be painfully awake than fatally asleep. The very consciousness that he is busy about you will make you cling to the Mighty One, and will help you not to fall into that comparative carelessness which so often follows the earnestness of our first adherence to the Redeemer, and which must in its turn be followed by many a bitter hour of repentance. Let faith be your shield in every assault; faith, not in what you are, or in what you have felt or attained to, but in the Lord Jesus and His unchangeable word. The more closely you cherish the remembrance of His death, His infinite atonement, His *absolute* faithfulness to every word He has ever spoken, the stronger you will be against the enemy. We are never so safe and happy as when our hearts are filled with this. Then there is no room in them for doubts and worries. Of course God has given us secular duties which it would be wrong not to give full attention to; but then we should be always ready to "return unto our rest," and He who knows what work He has given us will always be ready to meet us again.

(*To Hannah.*)

I was so glad to hear that you are so much better, and more glad still that you can tell me so happily, "He seems always so near." How very tender He is in not overwhelming His children when He sees needful to send trial of some sort, that just *then* He sends more peace, more spiritual brightness than at other times. At least, it is very often so. Sometimes one has to walk in darkness as well, and that is dreary indeed, but even then He *is* leading. You and I have had pretty much the same path for the last few months, having to lay everything aside and suffer instead of trying to do His will. I will give you a text which seemed to float on my heart a great part of the time I was ill. "He will be very gracious unto thee at the voice of thy cry." Somehow it is even more precious to me than promises of answering our cry. For His infinite and loving wisdom may see best to withhold the answer we want for a long while, or may send it in such a different form that we hardly recognise *as* an answer, but this *covers* all, "He will be very gracious;" this is something always the same, a very *present* promise and quite unlimited and absolute, and unconditional and invari-

able. And "*very* gracious" not only what we might think so, but what He Himself calls *very* gracious;—how gracious that must be, only Himself knows. It is His own account of it, not ours. And while He *is* and *will be* very gracious, it seems to make one content to wait for anything and everything else.

(*To Hannah.*)

I am so sorry that you are distressing yourself about staying to the Lord's table, for I think it is one of Satan's devices to hinder you from a means of strengthening and refreshing your soul. We do not come because we are strong in the Lord, but because we are weak and need strength; we do not come because we *are* full of love and faith, but because we feel our lack in both, and draw near to Him in His own appointed way to have these renewed. He said Himself that He came not to call the righteous but sinners to repentance, and perhaps we are never so welcome as when we feel our intense unworthiness, and come to Him as *empty* vessels longing to receive of His fulness. That hymn is so true:

> "All the fitness He requireth
> Is to feel your need of Him."

Would it be like Him, our own most tender and gracious Saviour, to turn us away just when we feel sad and sinful and unworthy? Was it not His glory on earth that "this man receiveth sinners, and eateth with them." Do not grieve Him by misjudging His kind heart, but come trustfully to His table, and He will not reject you. . . .

And now I send you, *Grow in Grace, and in the Knowledge of our Lord and Saviour Jesus Christ.* He who gave this precept will Himself ensure its fulfilment to those who long for that grace, and thirst for that knowledge. Yet we must not forget that it *is* a command, that we ought not to be standing still in the heavenly way, but pressing toward the mark daily and hourly.

(*To Hannah.*)

I cannot let your birthday pass without a word of loving remembrance. It falls in what always seems to me a very beautiful and sacred time, the interval between the Ascension and Whitsuntide. For as the disciples spent those days in "waiting for the promise of the Father," waiting and praying, so I think our Church in the sweet collect for this last Sunday gives us the hint that we should do the same. For have we not an equally sure promise of the blessed Spirit ("how much more shall your heavenly Father give the Holy Spirit to them that ask Him," Luke 11:13, and others), and is not our need as great as theirs in reality even if our sense of it is not as deep! So I think our spiritual attitude in these days should be special waiting and praying for this great gift which our Master has to bestow on us. Will you join me during the remaining days till Whitsun-tide in seeking it for each other? I am praying that the great and glorious Whitsuntide gift may be sent you anew in a measure not according to what we ask, but "according to His riches in glory by Christ Jesus." How confident the disciples must have been in their Master's promise, when they could return to Jerusalem *with great joy* though He had been parted from them. And to think that we have just the same ground for joyous anticipation, "the promise is to us," also; an abiding Comforter for us as much as for them. I so enjoyed taking the subject with my Bible class on Sunday morning, putting it thus—they had often, continually heard me beg them to pray for the Holy Spirit, now we would put all the things together which were included in that one gift, all His gracious offices to our souls, and see whether it was not *worth* pleading for. And as we took these things one after another, contrasting each with our deep need of it, and regarding each as sealed with His free promise, it did seem such a glorious accumulation of blessing as if one could not care for anything else in the world. Papa and mamma have lately gone from Bonn to Pyrmont, which lies thirty to forty miles from the boundary of Hanover, in the little principality of Waldeck. The waters were so strongly advised for papa in preference to those of Nassau, that they resolved to go. It is more of a foreign watering-place (or rather bath-place), not many English resorting thither, but numbers of Danes, Russians, etc. But for those who do go, no spiritual provision has ever been made. Papa hears that he is the first English clergyman ever seen there, so as the coast is clear, he hopes, strength permitting, to be a minister of spiritual health to some who come in search of physical health.

[This was the commencement of Church of England services during several summers by F. R. H.'s father, and now carried on by the Colonial and Continental Church Society.]

(*To A. H.*)

OAKHAMPTON, September 7, 1864.

. . . I have thought continually of you, and prayed that the gift for which you so long, might be given you soon, if it be God's holy will. I thought much of what you said—"that you had not the witness of the Spirit, and that you so desired it." Now I do not think that even that precious witness should be made a ground of confidence, we are not to trust to what the Holy Spirit has done in us, but to what Christ has done for us. Still we can hardly be right in ignoring the former, and therefore I wish you would consider wherein, after all the "witness of the Spirit" consists; is it not possible that you may be under some misapprehension about it? I think this "witness" is the *consciousness of the presence of His power* in our hearts.

And when we find in these our "desperately wicked" hearts, a conflicting current of heavenward desires, of longing after holiness, of shrinking from sin—either God's testimony concerning our hearts is not true, or we must believe that the Holy Spirit has implanted in them that, which never could have sprung up from such utterly evil soil.

Dare we believe that our natures are good enough to have originated these holy desires? is it not presumptuous to think it? And *if* we believe in our own deep sinfulness and entire depravity, how else *can* we account for such strong *upward* yearnings but by ascribing them to the work of the Holy Spirit? Oh, do not rob Him of the credit (so to speak) of what can only be His own blessed work; the truest humility lies in acknowledging it to be His, and therefore not ours.

Think this out, and I feel sure you will be obliged to *admit* that God *has* given you the earnest of the Spirit, even if the adversary should still be permitted to hinder you from finding comfort in it.

Among the fruits which confirm the witness in our hearts, we find *faith* specified. (Ah, this is too good a fruit gift to be anything of our own producing!) Now this fruit you undoubtedly have. For faith does not consist in being able to speak with the confidence of the aged Paul, and in being persuaded that our names are in the book of life. Thank God that faith and assurance are not identical! I have thought much about it, and cannot find anything at all to prove faith to be anything more than simply believing God's testimony about Himself, His Son, and ourselves, simply believing that He means what he says, when He tells us that "all have sinned and come short of the glory of God," and that "the Father sent the Son to be the Saviour of the world." Now this simple testimony *you know,* you believe in your inmost heart, you do not doubt it at all. And what but this, is God's condition of everlasting life? I know of no other. "He that believeth"—believeth what?—"on the Son,"—*i.e.* believeth that He came to save sinners,—"hath everlasting life." Now the benefit of Christ's redemption is co-extensive with the human race. He died for *all,* 2 Corinthians 5:15, and *all* cannot mean a *few.* Therefore it must be that He has died for you, *unless* you willingly exclude yourself by rejecting His message as *untrue,* or by neglecting His great salvation. And you know that your whole heart recoils from the bare idea of either rejecting or neglecting; you cannot, by any stretch of language, admit that you do either. Consequently, not excluding yourself, you must be *in*cluded, if the glorious declaration is worth anything at all. This train of thought is my key to my favourite 1 John 5:10, 11. Because "He died for all," eternal life is given to all, except those who will not have it. "And this is the record, that God hath given to us eternal life." There is no limitation and no exception, God *has* given it. There is nothing in ourselves to tell us so, and no arguments are supplied to convince our reason, only God's own bare word about it, set against all our doubts and fears. And is not His bare word enough? Would it be any surer if an angel came to tell us, or even if the inward voice for which one yearns, whispered it distinctly to our hearts? *Must* it not be sure and true now, only because God has said it?

Then comes the terrible alternative. We make Him a liar, if *we do* not believe that He has given us eternal life. You saw and felt all that it involved when you said so earnestly, "No, I cannot make God a liar."

One shrinks from the bare thought, as from a fearful blasphemy, not to speak of the treachery of heart which can make the "Faithful and True" a liar. Yet the Lord has left you no escape from the alternative, but to believe the record, that He has given you eternal life. Trust your soul upon this promise, and if you are lost, then, *God* must be untrue and be a deceiver.

What grieves a friend more than refusing, or even hesitating to take him at his word? And is not our distrust one of the sorest wounds with which He is wounded in the house of His friends. For very love to Him, strive to take Him at His word! He would *not* have said that He has given us eternal life, if He did not mean it, or He would never let it stand in His word to deceive and mislead us. Do not wait dearest —— for some special conviction or inward voice about it; the woman who came to be healed by our Saviour, came *in the press,* waiting for no personal and special call, and the remembrance of all this has often been strangely sweet to *me.*

(*To the same.*)

We have some beautiful leaves in the Oakhampton conservatory, which are merely a dull green marked with white, if they are allowed to be in the light, or when any sun can get at them, but if they are kept in the shade, they have a rich deep purple tint and come to be one of the most lovely plants.

I have connected you with this, ever since your last note. God would not thus keep you walking in the shadow, if He did not know that it was your best training. For there seems to be no element of sin in your present darkness, you do love, you do believe, only you are mysteriously held back from rejoicing in the light which you so value and love.

So I do think most strongly that it is only that you may be secretly all the more beautiful and sanctified, that the Lord leads you through this singular discipline. Perhaps He sees that you will be thus far better fitted for His work, better able to sympathize and help others than you would have been without. Perhaps you would not have been so patient with the spiritual difficulties of others, so gentle and forbearing and persevering in watching for souls if your own training had been different.

Yet see how the Lord keeps drawing your heart to Himself, how He has made you feel that there is none upon earth that

you desire like Him; is not this a sweet and sufficient proof that He must indeed have loved you with an everlasting love? If we run after Him, it can only be *because He draws us,* and if He draws us, it can only be *because He loves us.*

(*To the same.*)

Would it be like our God, the God of the Bible, to put all those glorious promises in if He did not mean them? Would it be like Him to tantalize longing souls by letting them hunger for what He never meant for them? Would it be like Him to say "all" and "whosoever," and then to refuse your claim? *Could* the Lord be so cruel, so untrue? Is not His word worthy of fullest credit? "He died for *all*," is wide enough to include you and me, and we have no warrant to wait for a special revelation that "He died for *you* and *me*." Not but that assurance is sent later on, but the Lord would have us quite satisfied with His revealed word first. You do not reject Christ's death; and what would the Bible be worth if, after putting in your claim (which you know you have done), and do continually do, by owning the death of Christ to be your only ground of hope, if after that it proved that His precious death was not for you! It would be a very simple proof that we had utterly mistaken God's character, and that He is *not* the Faithful and True which He says He is, but the very opposite. Do not grieve your Saviour by fearing to trust Him with your soul, with your eternity. Is He not worthy to be trusted?—He, our own gracious and long-suffering and faithful God? "He died for all,"—do go upon that *broad* ground, for it is firm enough for you, as well as for "*all*."

(*To ——.*)

RUNNYMEDE HOUSE, ILFRACOMBE,
July 24, 1866.

The first topic of your letter number one and the last sentence of to-day's letter must be taken together, for the text I want to send you belongs to it. "My people shall be satisfied with my goodness, saith the Lord." This is the bright side to the "disappointment" you speak of as arising from the immense demands your spirit makes. The more immense one finds these demands to be, the more it says for the immensity of the promised satisfaction. Just in proportion as one finds oneself anything *but* easily satisfied, the value of absolute satisfaction rises and magnifies. Satisfaction is most restful and sweet to those who know most of dissatisfaction; and thus even an infirmity and a trouble is made a stepping-stone to a deeper happiness, and "out of the eater comes forth meat." How God meets all our need with such wonderful provision and prevision! "I shall be satisfied when I awake with Thy likeness." "We shall be satisfied with the goodness of Thy house." "He satisfieth the longing soul." And my special favourite, which I have given you, Jeremiah 31:14. And the deeper the dissatisfaction which the heart *can* feel, the greater must be the satisfaction, because it must *fill* those depths. But "satisfied with my goodness"!—somehow I feel as if I never could say or write one word about His goodness, His love. It "passeth" words. And one's very soul seems hushed into a sweet and most solemn silence by the feeling. If what one knows of that goodness and love in this dim twilight of existence, if what one apprehends of it with these weak, cold, half-awake hearts and these imperfect faculties, *is* what it is,—so wonderful, so unspeakable,—what must the unveiled and unhindered manifestation of it be! Oh! "abundantly satisfied" will be far too pale to express it! . . .

. . . As to the Sunday writing,—my feeling is that it is a mere Pharisaism to object to *write* about what one would be happy and thankful to talk about on the Lord's day. I only place two limits to such writing. First, it depends on the amount of Sunday leisure; and I rarely, if ever, write at Oakhampton on a Sunday (we have such long walks to and from church), because I think one ought to reserve as much time as one can profitably use for reading, thought, and prayer. But on a wet Sunday, or if not well enough to go to church, I sometimes do it. Second, I never give servants or children the opportunity of thinking I "write letters on Sunday," because they would not distinguish "things that differ," and the example might therefore do harm. . . .

"Blessed are the pure in heart." Oh, yes! But for myself, feeling something of that "stain and impress of sin," I like rather to turn from the sad side of the subject to our beloved Master's own connection of much love with much forgiveness. You will say, "That is a different thing!" Perhaps so—metaphysically; but perhaps *not* practically. Oh, that love to the Forgiving One may neutralize the dark impress of the past! I think it ought to do, somehow; but it is a point on which I *feel* more than I can clearly *think.*

I do hope and think that God is blessing this stay together, and that my summer holiday will not have been without the "pleasant fruit" I prayed it might bear. I feel so strongly that doubts and difficulties spring so much from the heart, even more than from the head, that I have aimed far more at keeping our minds fixed upon Christ and His love and His truth, than at mere theological discussion. A full and simple and penitent and loving return to Him as the only Saviour, is the truest remedy for the ills of unbelief in all its ramifications of difficulties, paradoxes, and uncertainties. And this path I really do think is being entered upon, and already some of the fog-wreaths are vanishing. I have a very happy feeling that "the power of the Lord is present to heal," for many reasons. One is, that we seem so constantly to come upon the very thing we want. We spend a good deal of time every evening, and nearly every morning, in reading the Bible together; but we read straight on

in course, not picking and choosing, and yet the chapters seem full of such startlingly appropriate passages. Besides, I am *asking;* and He says, "Ye shall receive."

(*To* ——.)

August 28, 1866.

. . . What you say about "good to the souls of others unknown to us," has struck me very much. . . . One does try to sow seed often where one does not expect to see it spring up; but I never thought of making a special prayer of it—I am too eager to see the fruit *myself,* and rejoice in it. This is a bow drawn at a venture to *me*—thanks for it. I wish you would always send me a text when you write; you cannot think how much I need help. . . .

I think I will tell you one little regret which hangs over my happy—visit. I have *wished* since, that we had read the Bible together. I did not propose it, because I know some persons do not like to do so, and until the last three or four years I never liked it myself; but I have really found by experience that it is not only pleasant but helpful, and conversation springing directly out of God's word generally seems more profitable than what one drifts into at random. However, until the last two or three days I hardly felt intimate enough with you—do you understand? Tell me what you think on the subject in general, and also about prayer together; for I am passing through a sort of transition, and hardly know what the result will be.

By the bye, I made use of you on Sunday night with my class when reading Acts 27:6. "A ship of Alexandria sailing into Italy," ver. 38; "they lightened the ship, and cast out the wheat into the sea." I told them about the Alexandrian wheat, and about *your* "going down into Egypt to buy corn," which seemed to make the thing more tangible to them. Jacob, and St. Paul, and *you!*—the intervals balance so well!

I must tell the fulfilment of my special hope and aim in that Lynton visit (see pp. 156–157[1]) . . . Oh, how wonderfully gracious God is to hear and answer as He does! And, really, the more one asks, the more one does get. I do so like the old verse:

"Thou art coming to a King,
Large petitions with thee bring," etc.

And generally one does distinctly get more than we ask in cases of intercessory prayer; for does He ever leave one without a reflex benefit upon one's own soul? I feel inclined to say, "Rarely, if ever." I am asking that you may have a double blessing in "unknown good" question,—that watering, you may be watered; that the good to others may return in showers upon your own heart. . . . Shall you be tired of reading this, I wonder? . . . I like writing to you; but I am very thirsty for a letter from you.

[1] *Letters by the Late Frances Ridley Havergal* edited by her sister Maria V. G. Havergal (London: James Nisbet & Co., 1886), original book pages 156–157, pages 48–49 of this book.

(To the same.)

August 30, 1866.

. . . I have told you how very much I liked your thought about John 17:23. It has repeatedly struck me since then how entirely our Lord seems to share everything with His people,— how He seems to think of them *with* Himself. Sometimes this seems to be under the surface, as comparing Matthew 5:14 with John 8:12; also Matthew 13:43 with Malachi 4:2 and 1 John 3:2; and plenty more such. Sometimes it is fellowship of sufferings, as Matthew 10:25; sometimes of joy, as John 17:13: "The works that I do, shall ye do also;" "All things that I have heard of my Father, I have made known unto you;" "They are not of the world, even as I am not of the world;" "For their sakes I sanctify myself, that they also might be sanctified;" "The glory which thou gavest me, I have given them;" "That the love wherewith Thou hast loved me," etc.; "My Father and your Father;" "As my Father hath sent me, so have I sent you." Then Hebrews 2:11–17 carries on the subject. So we are not only partakers of Christ, but partakers *with* Christ—"joint-heirs" even here.

(To the same.)

September 1, 1866.

I was so glad to get your letter that I must begin an answer forthwith. But first I will give you a text, one that has been floating about me all day: "My meditation of Him shall be sweet: I will be glad in the Lord" (Psalm 104:34). I have been connecting it with a specially favourite sentence of mine, "We give Thee thanks for Thy great glory," and with David's magnificent ascription of praise in 1 Chronicles 29:10–12, and his conclusion of it in verse 13. That "therefore" (in verse 13) has struck me very much: one's thanks and praise are so generally on account of benefits received, or on account of what He is to us and for us. That is glad work enough, but this is higher, grander, even more satisfying, and its vibration far less liable to be damped and stilled by contacts of earth. This "meditation" of Him must be "sweet," because there is no infusion of self at all to embitter it. It is a wonderful relief to leave on one side just for a little while all one's own needs and infirmities and lownesses and shortcomings, and dwell only on what He is *in Himself.* It is such utterly unalloyed glory, such utter perfection of every attribute, one cannot help being so glad "that our God is so glorious, so great, so holy." (And I think we find out that we certainly do love Him because we are so very glad of it, though this is only a pleasant parenthesis in our "meditation.") The revelation of His glory so that all must see and acknowledge it, has for some time been my *special* anticipation for the future, outweighing somehow even the personal joy of seeing Him as He is. Then comes the "I will be glad in the Lord;" and here the "I will" was not long ago a

great help to me. It is not a mere future tense, but an expression of resolution and intended effort. May it not be that instead of merely waiting for joy to flow in upon us, we ought to arise and bend the whole strength of our wills to the matter. I took it *so* one day, when being "glad in the Lord" seemed a thing beyond hope almost, and I cannot tell you the help the idea was: it seemed as though the Lord gave it the sanction of His enabling blessing. This is very much to me because I think I know so *very* much less than most do of "rejoicing in the Lord." I never seem to have the bright happy views which others have of their realized acceptance, being chosen, etc. I have been ready to give up ever expecting it; and so to have a way of being "glad in the Lord," with which no consciousness of sinfulness and weakness, no cold shadow of *self* can at all interfere, *is sweet;* but it is only while it is purely "of Him" that it is so. Further, I think we ought to be "glad." I do not think a mere negative peace is all we are meant to have; and it is "whoso offereth *praise,*" Psalm 50:23, the expression by lip or life of grateful joy that "glorifieth," not whoso is at *peace*— precious as even that is. I don't know what I can ask for you, dearest—more helpful for both inner *and* outer life, than that your "meditation of Him may be sweet," and that you may be "glad in the Lord." . . .

Your meditation of Him was sweet as to the *diversity* of treasures, quite a new thought to me in the connection you give it. I suppose one effect of believing His knowledge of each one and their needs, etc., ought to make us calmly satisfied with His dealings, with all His spiritual dealings with us, which are often much harder to acquiesce cheerfully in than His temporal leadings. Is it not nice that He knows how much we want more grace, more faith, more of Himself? for the wisdom and the love are as infinite as the knowledge.

Thursday, September 13.

We have been to the Worcester Festival—two days—and oh how I wished for you! . . . The whole Mount Carmel scene winding up with "Thanks be to God," sublime enough to stir the coldest heart. Can you imagine that the result of my Festival enjoyment has been a "vanity of vanities" impression? Perhaps it is because I am very tired! But when one comes to think that the very essence of music is *passing,* it can't be continuous, you cannot stop it any more than time itself; hold the loveliest notes to contemplate them (if it were possible), and it would be like singing a bubble—it would cease to be music. No enjoyment is so *essentially* transient. It is oppressive to me, and even the succession of beauty seems too much, too rapid.

On the other hand, I never was so comforted by music before. I did not think that what I was so familiar with could have come so freshly into my heart as did "Cast thy burden," and "O rest in the Lord." . . .

... I should not have minded if you had said what you did before I told you the result. For, dear ——, I do not think I have *that* sort of faith which positively expects *the* very answer it asks at the very time. And I do not feel that it would have been any blow to it had the answer been withheld. For answers tenfold more earnestly desired, tenfold more earnestly sought and eagerly looked for, have been and are withheld—withheld for more *years* than this was for *days*. Only on the other hand God has often given me such very distinct and full answers, that it is as if He would encourage me always to "make known my requests." And so I do I know, with a very clear happy confidence that He hears, and so that if it is His own time He will answer. If the answer is delayed, I know it is not that He did not hear, nor do I ever feel that He has rejected my prayer, only He knows best, and I would not dictate as to time and means. Still additionally to this I have a sort of feeling that, as all "good desires" come from Him, so when one does seem to feel a special earnestness in prayer for any one, it often is a sort of token that the Lord is waiting to be gracious in that particular case. The very speedy and full answer so manifestly sent at L. and I. was peculiarly *gracious,* for I needed some such encouragement, and so could take it as a sort of double boon, both for her and for myself. Oh! He *is kind.* ...

This leads to the question (allusion to a previous letter and reply to it) of prayer together. I have not for a long time felt any difficulty or hesitation about it with my Sunday class, with children, or poor sick people. But I could not ever do it with equals. I thought I never could divest myself of self-consciousness, that I never could simply and purely "draw near" if any other ear were following. —— said a good deal to me about it, but I simply *could not.* This time last year a poor invalided girl, whom I saw nearly every day, was in terrible distress of mind. Nothing seemed to avail, the gloom deepened month after month, till it told fearfully on her already feeble and diseased frame. One day I found her in bitter darkness, and stayed long with her. And at last she said, "Oh, Miss F., if you would but pray *with* me, now!" What could I do but consent. I have never felt the same consciousness before or since,—the intense vivid consciousness that the Lord Jesus Himself was there; *must* be, because of that verse, Matthew 18:20, it came upon me and intensified with every petition; and I pleaded with Him as if He were standing before me, and only waiting for our prayer to give the desired blessing. How long I do not know, one does not think of time at such times, but, *while* yet speaking, the answer came. I rose, and saw it in poor ——'s face; it seemed almost a reflection of the light of His countenance, and indeed He was "shining in her heart." She could hardly speak for very joy but to ask me to change the prayer to praise, and to kneel again to thank and bless Him, the Saviour, who had so revealed Himself anew to her. Life cannot have many such

happy hours as that was. The effect of this as regards the question was to make me wonder whether I had not been wrong in my shrinking,—whether I was not foregoing unknown blessings by it,—whether this ought not to be a stronger lesson on the subject than any argument. And there it remains. I have not often since had the opportunity, and I have by no means lost my shrinking from it; but I could not refuse when, for instance, dear —— begged me to pray with her. My present feeling is that I absolutely could not make it a frequent or general thing, but that one ought not to hold back under special circumstances.

(*To* ——.)

June 29, 1867.

"Able to do exceeding abundantly above all that we ask or think." Why I send you this is because it suddenly shot into my mind in the midst of a buzz of general talk on most opposite subjects, that we, at any rate I, had had a singular fulfilment of it, and that it ought to be an earnest to us, so as to expect more, to believe it more. Now I am going to set my signature to it, believing that to some extent you can do so too. I asked that—coming to O——might be a mutual benefit, that we might "strengthen," etc. (1 Samuel 23:16), that God's blessing might be with us, etc. I do think the Lord Jesus Himself drew nigh when we read and talked together. It was in His name, so there was His promise to go upon; but besides that was there not something of "our hearts burning within us"? something more than was to be accounted for by our love to each other? could we so have enjoyed His word without Him? I asked for benefit, and He added enjoyment. I do not remember ever being quite so happy as the night you talked to me about John 14:23. And though I have not the thing I desire, and though such a feeling is not continuous, yet it seems as if the high wave had not gone back so far as usual, as if allowing for fluctuation my tide had risen a little higher, and covered some of my dark and terrible rocks. ...

Of course, as usual, I don't seem able to receive all the comfort I yet think I might from this fact, still I have been linking it with Joab's words: "To-day thy servant knoweth that I have found grace in thy sight, my lord, O king, in that the king hath fulfilled the request of his servant."

I am intending to begin a little book of *Answered Prayers.* One forgets one's mercies so. We could not record all our mercies, for often we do not recognise them. But I do think a record of every definite answer might be helpful, and I shall try it. ... I rather wish you would try it too.

I must go back to your note about John 4:10. ... Yes, I would not shrink from being kept in store for this, *if* it may be so. I read it almost nervously lest you should go a step beyond what I could follow, but because you only took ground that I can stand on, it seemed all God's message to me. For oh! I have felt the urgent necessity of coming again and again to Him, etc. And oh! it made me so hopeful that He really has given me a "*silent* answer." I cling to that idea now so much. I wondered at what you felt about me, and yet it was *great* comfort, for I cannot account for your feeling except that it may be the true instinct of a Spirit-taught heart recognising the Spirit's work through all the veiling clouds of infirmity and sin in another. . . . I tacked your thought in yesterday's note on to last night's text. I never somehow thought it out just as you have put it, "because He will *not let you leave off coming to Him.*"

I have been reading Whateley's *Commonplaces,* so amusing and suggestive. He has a rather full article on writing in magazines, etc., as to responsibility—the very thing I wanted to be clear about. He holds that a magazine is like a public conveyance—you use it because you want a vehicle for your opinions, and you take your chance of fellow-passengers. But a joint volume—*e.g.* "Essays and Reviews"—is quite different, and you are fairly open to be interpreted by the others, and share the responsibility of the general bearing of the book. . . . Now goodbye; will you remember me next Sunday? For then even if it is "sent empty away," I feel as if I could better wait on and trust on. He must have good reason if He denies united prayer.

[The next letter, June 30th, "Sent empty away—just empty," is given in the *Memorials* of F. R. H., p. 85.[1]]

(*To the same.*)

WINTERDYNE, July 11, 1867.

It was not "sent empty away"! I can wait now for a fuller answer. Your letter came on Saturday afternoon, while I was sitting with ——, in a lovely bit of the grounds. I told her my longings, and read her some of your letter. She said, "Oh, Miss F., can you not trust His *silent love?*" On Sunday, it fell to me to take her to church, the first time she had been for eight years, and we sat alone in a small high pew close to the door. During the ante-communion, she was very faint, and the attending to her seemed a singular boon, for I was just beginning to feel as usual that the strain of the service was too much (especially as I was enjoying it more than usual) and the break was like unstringing one's bow, so that I was fresher for the rest than usual. Then her joy was something marvellous—it seemed almost to *awe* me. "He is here," she whispered; it is more like *going home;* "oh! can even the joy there be greater!"

Then I thought of "Thou art the same," and felt that He really was the same Jesus for me as for her—only that I did not see Him as she did, and that helped me to cling and trust. The service seemed to contain so much more for me than usual. Did you know that your text came in the Psalms for the day? . . . The second lesson, Luke 19:7, struck me as just the very thing, especially followed up by ver. 10. It seemed a strange sacramental service, for except *at* the Table, I could not kneel at all, because I was supporting poor ——. I hardly knew what I thought, but I had an *unusual* sense of quiet and rest and gladness all the time, just what I thought I should not have expected considering the unusual distraction of my care of ——. At the Table it went away, and all the old clouds returned. I could see nothing but darkness; but I looked up to Jesus almost agonizingly just as it came to my turn, and then "Who loved me and gave Himself for me" flashed into my mind, and close upon it my own *seal,* "I have given them Thy word." In spite of feeling half or three-quarters afraid to take it, I caught at it in a drowning sort of way: "I *must* have it, Lord." Of course there was some shadow of misgiving over my gladness—there always is more or less, but this time it was *less* than others. Is that sense of gladness really from Him? I do hope so. "In Thy word do I hope." Oh! I *do* care more for His words, His people, His cause, than *anything.* And if the whole thing were a dream and a myth, which is one of the fiery darts launched at me by the enemy sometimes, why then I am simply a monomaniac! An odd argument is it not? but I like it! Well now I am going on my way, not exactly rejoicing, but I think and hope "strengthened and refreshed." . . . Poor dear ——. Her Sunday joy was preparation for many hours of absolute agony. . . . You must excuse pencil. I am sitting in an ideal nook of green shade with a peep of the Severn deep below me, through oaks and Scotch firs and tall ferns.

MORECAMBE, July 29, 1867.

After this I must give up writing long letters to you for some time, but this is to reach you on your birthday, so I must indulge myself. . . . I want to be paid in my own coin, so send you Part II. of my poem *Threefold Praise!* You perhaps remember reading Parts I. and III. with the gap between. I wanted a strong contrast in style and metre with Haydn, whose praise—

"A praise all morning, sunshine,
        And sparklets of the spring
O'er which the long life-shadows
        No chastening softness fling."

"Handel" is in a strict iambic metre, breaking for the final trochaics. I don't believe there is any *regular* metre invented that would do for the *Elijah,* and so I did as I have done, contrary to my usual principles. If you don't know the *Elijah* well, or have no copy of it to refer to, it is nearly useless your reading my poetry—you could not see the reason for a good deal of it. It was very difficult to condense it at all. I wanted to write a thing as long as the oratorio itself, only then it would only have been for my own private edification—nobody else would

---

[1] *Memorials of Frances Ridley Havergal* by Maria V. G. Havergal (London: James Nisbet & Co., 1880), original book pages 82–84, page 25 of Volume IV of the Havergal edition.

have read it! Send it me back with annotations and criticisms, as many as you can.

You need not condole with me as to Morecambe. I have found *work,* and am happy in it, and thoroughly glad on that account to be here. I had an odd impulse my first Sunday morning in church to go to the Sunday school (at risk of M.'s wrath!) *not* for the children's sake, but fancying I might do some good to the clergyman's young pretty-looking daughters whom I saw at church. I went and found fifty or seventy children—girls under *one* teacher, a lodging-house keeper's daughter—she toiling quite alone except such rare and chance help as mine, neither clergymen nor family ever coming near or taking the slightest notice on account of some inexplicable quarrel with trustees of the building. The teacher thinks I have been *sent* here for her; a young but true Christian, so wearied and depressed about this school and other troubles. So I have taken her up while here. Also I have found a girl in consumption, who is very eager to hear, and I do trust the Master may have sent me to her too. Also at M.'s suggestion, I am carrying on a little system for my Irish Society collecting card, etc. . . .

I am reading Whateley's *Annotations on Bacon's Essays.* I like it immensely—so racy and shrewd, and much so really valuable. Also I have Wordsworth—have just finished the "Excursion." I see much to admire, but I can't rave about him! I send you "My Teacher," which I fancy you will like better than "Threefold Praise." It is partly old, written in 1859, with a lot of personal history—now omitted—ver. 4 owes its existence to your sending me Wesley's Hymns. Please cut it up well. First verse is vile!

And now I have asked God to give me a verse for your birthday: "He hath said, I will never leave thee nor forsake thee." If true now, has it not been true all along? Therefore may not this improve one's view of life retrospectively? And for the ever faster on-coming on-*rushing* years, can you get beyond "*never*"? See how it embraces one's whole existence. I have been looking whether the Greek gives any light on the seeming repetition. I am not quite sure, not having a Lexicon, but I think ἐν καταλείπω, *forsake,* contains the idea of "leaving behind in any place." If so, link it with John 12:26 and 14:3. And the ἀνῶ means in other places *loose* or *slacken;* so it seems more than merely "never leave on one side," rather, never loose hold of us, never slacken the grasp with which He holds us. Now seal it, dearest, with "I have given them Thy word!"

(To the same.)

OAKHAMPTON, August 24, 1867.

. . . Ever since your Morecambe letter, I have reserved a text out of it for *you.* It was one of the many stepping-stones you laid down for me. "As for thee, the Lord thy God has not suffered thee to do so." You quoted it in passing; but it struck

me a good deal in a wider application, wider than one can possibly think out. We give thanks—often with a very doubtful, tearful voice—for our spiritual mercies *positive;* but what an almost infinite field there is for praise for spiritual mercies *negative.* We cannot even imagine all that God has suffered us *not* to do, not to *be.* Partly by circumstance, partly by grace, we have been withheld from—we know not what, but He knows; and there is no depth of sin, and consequently of misery, in which you and I might not at this moment have been, but that "He suffered us not." . . .

27th August.—I am better this week—feel *numb,* and the stormy-petrel is asserting itself. So good of you to write again. Your hymn, Isaiah 41:17, came in nicely for me. . . . My Lakes' visit was very pleasant. I first saw Grassmere (drove round from Red Bank). I saw Keswick—rowed round Derwent Water; scrambled up the face of Lodore; saw Barrow Fall, Skelwith Force, Stock Ghyll Force, Dungeon Ghyll, Coniston, Esthwaite, Rydal, and Thirlmere; and boated no end on Windermere: had every possible variety (I should think) of effects, from grey lake mists and rain to silver and gold and crimson, and rosy transparent purple, and olive and amber, and soft dreamy hazes, and marvellous clearness, and veilings and unveilings, and—everything that is lovely except snow. . . . I have a singular difficulty in alterations. Most of my verses have been published exactly as they were first written on the backs of old letters or on a slate. I never make a rough sketch—can't do it. . . .

(To the same.)

OAKHAMPTON, September 14, 1867.

. . . Thanks so many for "Be still, and know that I am God." It was *just* what I wanted. I could not rise to take comfort from other things.

. . . So, after all, I shall not have my fling in the *Messiah!* And I dare say this is a little bit of the "right way." For I *can* sing those solos in the Hall in a fashion which would make it a greater temptation than common, (though how HORRID that it should be so with that holy music!); and I could not have cut off that right hand for myself, so I believe God has sent circumstances to cut it off. I have had a good many pleasant things lately, and am very thankful (at least I hope so) for them. I was glad of your suggestion about God sending comfort and relief through little ordinary channels. . . . I send you only, "The LORD reigneth." Are you not GLAD that it is so!

(To the same.)

GREAT MALVERN, October 10, 1867.

. . . Is it not odd? After all, I have been singing, "Oh, thou that tellest good tidings" in public! I was asked to take the contralto music in a *Messiah* selection at Bewdley, under circumstances which gave me no reason for hesitating; and did so. Dr. Marshall, hearing I was to sing, actually offered to come and accompany *my* songs, which was most kind and advantageous. The " secular " puzzled me; but I chose Blockley's *Storm*, which has a good tone, and the gist of it is, a little child's prayer answered. Of *course* I sang it as I never can sing in private—all manner of lights and shades occurred to me at the moment: (it is mere waste of time to practise beforehand, and I did not). It is really curious how a large audience inspires me; and the result was,—a good deal more fuss than I expected! . . .

. . . I particularly dislike all this unsettlement, and had been longing for the rest of being in a settled home; but " I know whom I have believed " as to His word about " the right way." The " pleasant things " I referred to were little things which yet make up great mercies, and entwine our cross with flowers: pleasant walks and drives and visitors, and going over to Winterdyne, and kind things said of me and to me, and lovely sunsets, and nice letters and such like. . . .

Sunday Evening.—I send you " Faithful and True." What a keystone to the grand bridge which His promises have made for us over the abyss of despair and misery! Faithful, as regards us; True, essentially and inherently. I have been thinking that experience of life is a great commentary on the Bible, and a sort of realization of it. At first it is a sort of detailed map which we study and admire; but as one goes along, one finds on the road exactly the very things one had noticed, but not realized in one's map. And of course one values it more accordingly. I can't tell you how many of the hills and valleys I read of (and only read of) in the Psalms, I seem to have come across in my own journey of late. It has been so to-day with the verse I send you, Isaiah 26:3, which is rather like sitting under the shadow of a great rock, which one knew was marked in one's map, and knew the name and description of quite well, but which was not in sight a few days ago. It has been a very peaceful Sunday somehow, in spite of a certain nervous dread about this undertaking, which has impelled me to pray that it might be prevented, though I recalled the prayer and changed it for " as Thou wilt."

(*To the same.*)

I have been rather struck with part of Habakkuk 2:1: " And will watch to see what He will say unto me." It came to me as another motto for Bible-reading. Not " whether " He will say anything; but " *what*." This surely ought to be our feeling on opening His word. *Watch*, because it may be so easily overlooked, mistaken, unrecognised. " He " and " me "! " Master, say on." " Speak, Lord, for Thy servant heareth." And not only as to His word; but it bears a daily application, " what He will say," or teach, by everything that befalls us, great or small; by impulses given to our own minds.

It has haunted me a good deal, and of course falls in with my own special longings, though by no means confined to them.

Thanks for your birthday text. " For Christ " is the longing of one's heart, but impatient waiting is not true " waiting for Christ." How much of one's life is made up of *waiting!* It must be a needful lesson, indeed, seeing He is at so much pains to teach it us. . . .

I very particularly like your reversal of 1 Peter 2:7. I think Jesus *is* precious to me,—at least the *thought* of Him, prayer to Him, the very mention of His name, are precious and sweet to me. Is that the same thing? Sometimes one is a mere chaos of feelings " without form and void," and one does not know which are the shadows and which the realities in one's heart. But especially in trouble, prayer seems to quiet and order the chaos; and *He* is the centre and object of prayer.

I shall not send you a text this time. I don't seem to have been getting anything *given* me lately. I never like sending you anything but what is fresh and true to myself. Oh, if we did but " follow on " more " to know the Lord " and all that that knowledge includes!

I shall have a very pleasant visit here, I think (Hilton Park). I very much like grand houses! Should you have thought it of me?—rejoice in magnificent staircases and all that sort of thing! Dear Mr. Fisk (Vicar of Great Malvern) is so charming and kind. He is going to read with me and M. V. every morning. I do not know whether it is to be Greek or English yet.

February 9.

I send you " More than conquerors through Him that loved us." Perhaps you do not, but I find myself fighting *alone* sometimes; and oftener fighting, not alone exactly, but not giving full weight to the " Him that *loved* us." How frequently " *abundant*," or some equivalent, occurs in spiritual promises! It would be much to be merely " conquerors "—but " *more than* "! . . .

March 10, 1868.

Your account of your visit is so interesting. Work of that sort is most valuable, because of the further influence an educated person has, specially a clergyman's wife. And I do not think we ought to undervalue *building* work as compared with foundation work, as so many are apt to do. Yes, " an inverse ratio," truly. If all the " requirements " which we afterwards meet, crowded upon us at the outset, we should be appalled, or perhaps rise up in despair of ever meeting them. But " He giveth more grace." . . .

I should have written to you yesterday, but wrote a poem instead,—" Life Crystals." The world full of crystals, so is life;—soul chemistry going on where we little guess. *Song*

Crystals,—from what ingredients produced—their effects—analyzing light—telling star secrets—prismatic radiance, etc.

Sorrow Crystals,—now formed, found, and treasured by other mourners. *Love Crystals,*—*He* pouring His own love into an *empty* heart, shadowing and silencing, then setting the crystals in His own crown. . . . Do you like the fancy?

"Righteousness and peace and joy in the Holy Ghost. For he that *in these things* serveth Christ is acceptable to God and approved of men." I send you this, which was suggested to me in thinking over a question given out for written answers at our Association meeting. It is a wonderful view of service,—all this imparted work,—the mere reception of such great gifts. And they "approved" is very striking, and not just what one would have expected. I take it to be the involuntary recognition of spiritual beauty by outsiders which really one often sees. But what do you think? The question given us is, "What are the characteristics of service for Christ?" . . .

(To the same.)

Leamington, March 21, 1868.

The bare idea of *not* going to the Handel Festival, or any part of it, when you have a fair opportunity, is so utterly beyond my comprehension, that I am afraid I have no sympathy with your hesitations. I can only say, Go! and be *thankful!* It is as near one's ideal as anything earthly can be—at least such is my impression of 1859, the year I went, a thing not to be missed if God gives the chance of it during the pilgrimage through this mostly untuneful earth. I shall *certainly* not be there, so shall neither help nor hinder your enjoyment! If you go, I'll tell you sundry things to watch for. If you do not go to all, and have a choice of day, secure the *Israel in Egypt.* The *Messiah* I would as soon hear in a cathedral, but *not* in Exeter Hall, where there is a lack of resonance—which to me destroys some of the finest effects, especially one in the Hallelujah Chorus. But the *Israel in Egypt* cannot be heard anywhere so well as at the Crystal Palace. The magnificent massive choruses need a gigantic orchestra to give a scope for their great swing of grandeur. The mighty flinging of sound from side to side in some of the great double choruses, is what you can't get anywhere else, until the notion is carried out of Handel having Salisbury Plain for his concert room, cannon for his basses, an army for his tenors, and angelic legions for his sopranos. I had better drop the subject—I get excited and crazed if I begin thinking about it! . . .

I send you Judges 6:14: "And the Lord looked upon him and said, Go in this thy might." What is *this?* Was it the power of Jehovah's *look?*—as divinely strength-giving as another look was heart-awakening? I suddenly saw it so while it was being read as 1st Lesson at a weekday service, and liked it. Link it with "Look Thou upon me," and "Looking unto Jesus," for by so looking only can we expect to *receive* such a look. . . .

(To the same.)

Kilmarnock, July 16, 1868.

. . . As for the externals of my visit, take Black's Guide and see what the principal lions are, and take it for granted that I have seen them! We had a grand tour to the Hebrides, Staffa, and Iona, etc. I started, first the Doxology, and then "God save the Queen," in Fingal's Cave, and it was taken up *splendidly* by most of the excursionists—such a concert hall. Then, by request, I sang part of "Let the bright seraphim!"

Oh—I have met with so much kindness and appreciation, and downright homage, that I sometimes felt quite overwhelmed. What am *I* to have such things poured into my cup? "I am not worthy of the least of all Thy mercies." It was a strange effect, *not* elating, but often almost depressing from its contrast with what I know I deserve. On the other hand, I am conscious that it gave me a sort of impetus, and I fancied I *rose* to meet it in some extent both in music and talk. Can you understand this? . . .

I send you "The exceeding greatness of His power to usward who believe." It struck me very much, for that POWER is *active,* and *systematic,* and *sure,* and He wields it in us and for us. He is "on our side."

(To the same.)

Kilmarnock, August 5, 1868.

. . . I have an *unusual* birthday text for you, but it is strongly on my mind, so I won't try to find another—"Even so Father, for so it seemed good in Thy sight." For what does not that "*it*" apply to! Surely to "all things," and they are working together for good to us, and therefore seem good in our Father's sight. You know I would not apply a text thus, but that there are others to bear it out; and then I like to *extend* the application sometimes. "Even so" would so often be hard to say, but it is "even so *Father,*" and that makes it easier. Still it is *not* easy to say about everything—yet it might be said, and at last will be said. The "it" often does not seem good in *our* sight, but that's not the question—"in *Thy* sight." Oh, how much further He sees than we do! I am so glad He does, are not you? Well, I hope this year may bring no very heavy strain upon *your* "even so." . . .

I am made a musical wild beast of to be exhibited! so I have less and less pleasure in music which has no element of "ministry" in it. I may go away on the 12th, and get a week alone at some seaside place. I have a craving for it, which I believe indicates need, physical and mental.

Mrs. —— wished me so much to come and join their communion last Sunday that I went. We had a most happy day together—perhaps the happiest communion I have ever yet had; (not that I *prefer* their *form* by any means, the sermon was about the sweetest I ever heard, John 15:19, 20, and the communion addresses carrying on the same subject, Mr. L. taking the whole service. I know that both Mr. and Mrs. —— had prayed that it might be a specially blessed day to us all, and I believe we all three felt it so. In the evening we sat in the garden, ... and then I sang them "Comfort ye," and "Whom having not seen," etc. I have struck up a thorough friendship with Mr. L. He told —— that I had done him great good. I *can't imagine* how—it was most *unconscious* ministry, but it is very sweet to me to bring any little cup of cold water or wayside flower of pleasure to any one of God's *true* ambassadors. . . . I have had a headache, and shirked a large musical afternoon party (which was to have been expressly for me), including a really superb cornet accompaniment to my "Let the bright seraphim." The G——'s are really kind, and have left me to myself, so I have sauntered out of reach of Kilmarnock smoke and am writing in a plantation. I have written as much as is good for me, and rather more. . . .

(*To the late Rev. C. B. Snepp.*)

Pyrmont Villa, April 20, 1870.

My beloved father entered into God's rest at noon yesterday. Early on Easter Sunday morning he was seized with apoplexy, and consciousness never returned. So he went home without any suffering, only ceased breathing and was with Jesus.

I write to ask if you would give me what would now be a very precious treasure, his last tune. He wrote it before breakfast that last Saturday morning, and gave it to me, as he *always* did all his music to look over in case of slips of the pen (from his eyesight), and I gave it him back with one trifling suggestion as to inner parts. It was the last tune too that my father played to me Easter even. Will you give it me? I shall be so grateful for it. Of course you will keep a copy, but it is his own dear last writing that I so long to have that I cannot help asking you for it. (This tune F. R. H. named "Havergal," see No. 163 in Havergal's *Psalmody.*) My father seemed peculiarly bright and happy all Saturday. God has mingled every possible mercy with this deep sorrow, and it is not the least to be permitted to *see* it. No one but my mother and I could imagine what the sunset light of this winter has been—his perfect patience and sweetness—he did indeed glorify the Master whom he loved and followed. Pardon my request. I know you will.

(*To the same.*)

Oakhampton, July 1870.

. . . How very, *very* kind your thought of a wreath for that dear spot (her father's tomb). The very thought deserves and *has*

affectionate gratitude from me. My dear mother bore the visit to it better than I feared. To me it was *unmitigated distress*—hers seemed to be added to mine,—I seemed to have no time to think or pray or *seek* comfort, much less receive it, for I was supporting her, afraid to leave her for a minute and dreading her fainting, etc., trying to whisper verses of peace and consolation which seemed only *words* to me in my occupied distress. I could not bear for that to be the only memory, so I slipped away alone on Monday evening to Astley churchyard. And *then* it was mercifully different. God sent such peace that I *wondered.* I was hardly even sad whilst I knelt where I had felt actual agony two days before. Verily this was "tender mercy." But it is selfish to draw upon your sympathy thus—forgive me. Ruth 2:12.

October 1870.—Home life is very different now, and in spite of my pleasant work *very* sad. No one guesses how much I miss my dear father, because I can flash up and talk and laugh when spoken to, and some think, of course, that because I do this, I do not feel it much. But God knows how intensely I miss him and how desolate and fatherless I do feel, and how there are no smiles and often enough tears when I am *quite* alone.

(*To the late Rev. C. B. Snepp.*)

Hastings, August 24, 1870.

I have been thinking about what you say as to the name "Master." Somehow with me it is quite different, I mean that this is the name which rises when I love *most.*

When I feel very far off and in danger then I cry "Saviour," but when I love Him vividly, and only long to fall at His very feet and tell Him so; then I always say, "Jesus, *Master.*" For is it not when one loves most that one longs *most* to prove love by obedience and service? I think women generally would feel this about the name, but men *generally* would feel it differently. For a true woman's deepest love is in its very essence a reverencing, looking-up love; a love which craves obedience as its expression, a love to which submission becomes joy. And this is the love which says "Master." "Master," from whom one would learn, at whose feet one would sit, in whose will one would acquiesce, whose service is one's ambition and honour. I am never so happy as when I say, "Jesus, Master," really with my heart. But I like the combination because that makes it not "master" only, but the "Master" to whom we *owe* the love and gratitude and service, *because* He has *saved* us. No other name ever seemed so much to me as this. I think I should feel just the same, or rather, even more strongly about it, if I come to see *more* of the preciousness of His other names, "Beloved" and "Friend," etc. For then I should still more desire to bow, and worship, and obey, and serve. Excuse this scrap written on the beach.

(To the same.)

Ascension Day 1871.

... Yes, I have for several years *specially* delighted in this day, and I wonder that it is not more generally rejoiced in. For it seems almost selfishness that we can make so much of Good Friday which is all for *us,* and yet so much less of the Ascension, which (though also "for us" in one sense) is specially commemorative of *His* own joy and glory. It seems as if we were *not* ready to sympathize with Him in anything but His sufferings for us. And when one feels so much of sadness and weariness oneself and sees so much around, it is a *great* solace to think that our beloved Master has entered into *His* joy. I am so glad when I think that the Lord Jesus is *really, truly* "exceeding glad." I often think about it—not merely of His *glory* but of His *gladness*. ...

I was brightened up yesterday, although feeling so exhausted, because I had two unexpected opportunities of trying to speak for Jesus, and I do not think anything is so refreshing as that, it always seems such a means of grace to one's own soul. This makes it more strange that one should hesitate and shrink from it as I so often do. ...

I am so delighted at your wish to print more of my dear father's hymns, it will give the book (*Songs of Grace and Glory*) a special value in the eyes of so many who loved him. I hope you will insert his lovely Harvest hymn—

> "Our faithful God hath sent us
> A fruitful harvest tide;
> He summer boons hath lent us,
> And winter wants supplied."

Also his Sunday hymn, "Hallelujah, Lord, our voices," and his Missionary hymns.

Do you know my father's tune "Evan"? It has been claimed as a Celtic air by some of those Celts who want to appropriate anything that can add to Celtic glory! The Andersonian Professor of Music at Glasgow has recently inserted a challenge to all Highlanders on the subject in the Scotch papers, and the result is, that it is finally and incontestably proved to be my father's own, entirely and only, and neither Celtic *nor* Lowell Mason's, to whom he once played and sang the melody,—which the Doctor much admired, and took it with him to America,—reducing it to a common metre tune, with only my father's initial "H." All my dear father's own tunes are wonderfully suited to large congregations.

I wish my own tunes could be put in the corner of an appendix! though I am greatly relieved about them by Mr. Goss of St. Paul's. He recommends an alteration or two in St. Barnabas, but none in the others, and there were no actual errors in *any*. And as he is Professor of Harmony and Examiner at the Royal Academy, it was as safe a test as I could have. He says, "You are less fastidious in your choice of chords than your father, but not on that account the less happy in your results." I also sent six of my tunes to a friend whose critical and musical taste I have great confidence in, and he is quite delighted with them. He likes "Claudia" best—"an exquisite little melody of most symmetrical construction," and "Hermas" next best, and "St. Silas."

(To the late Rev. C. B. Snepp.)

24 WARRIOR SQUARE, August 1870.

I shall trust you more than ever, because you tell me candidly my hymn won't do! I am afraid it is no use hoping that I shall be able to write a better. I will tell you why; I cannot write, and never yet have written *beyond* my own personal experience. I need to have *felt* a theme and *lived into* it before I can write about it. And the better a hymn or poem of mine is, the more the feeling from which it arose generally exceeded it; it is only when anything is *burning* in my heart that I write my best, though I can express but little of it. Now this great theme of God's electing love is one into which I have not thus personally entered. I am, I hope, approaching it, but the view is pale and distant as yet! How then *can* I write rightly about it? *If* it would please God to reveal the glory of the subject to my own soul, then, and *only* then, I could write what you want. I do not feel as if my heart were now in a truly receptive state for such a revelation, even if I dared to hope now for what I have prayed for (often very long, and I think I may say agonizingly) for so many years. I am far too much preoccupied—I am always tired at night, and though 1 rise early I am always in a sort of irresistible hurry to get down-stairs to my *S. G. G.* work. I might be better if this were a quiet nice place, where without the fatigue of a long walk one could get into a quiet lonely spot and feel alone with God by His beautiful sea.

... I cannot resist sending you another letter of C. Tennyson Turner's, because *you* will be pleased with his commendation of my poems. But how strange it is that sometimes God should *give* me thoughts and poems which can so delight and satisfy a man of that calibre, and at another leave me just powerless to write a simple hymn on a requested subject, with a whole outline ready drawn out for me. Is not this sovereignty? One half of me *feels* this, and feels humble, and dependent, and unworthy, and (yes, I think I *can* say) "chief of sinners," "a worm," "vile," etc. And the other half of me is always so delighted and elated when I get real appreciation of men (not women and girls!) whose own powers and works *I* appreciate and admire, that it militates against the other. Yet how can I help being pleased, and it would be ungrateful *not* to be so—can it be wrong?

(*To* ———.)

Pyrmont Villa, April 24, 1872.

I wonder what you will think of me! only do not think me either ungrateful or unloving! But I have come to the conclusion to decline your kind offer and live in hope of the chance of a sight of you later on. What has decided me to let the C. P. alone is simply this; I have not strength to do all I would like to do "for Him." I profess to economize it for the sake of being able to do a little of His work. Well, now I know certainly that the Handel Festival would be quite as fatiguing as many a bit of mission service which I have felt it my duty to decline. It would be only for my own pleasure if I went, because it is not like recreation of a kind which would (like Switzerland) be setting me on a better working level, nor is it what would give new intellectual or poetical impressions which would tell upon that part of my work. And I do so entirely feel that myself and my life not merely ought to be, but is and shall be "all for Jesus," that nothing weighs in the scale on the other side, not even a Handel Festival! Then secondly, if I do go to the Conference, it will be distinctly to seek spiritual blessing and strength, and I would not like to feel that I had risked this by going just before to what might as likely as not unhinge me physically, and make me less likely to be up to the mark of capability for the Conference. If I go on to Switzerland with Connie, as seems most likely, it would have to be immediately after the Conference, as she is tied for time at the other end, so that I should thus be precluded from coming back to you after the Conference, which I should otherwise have delighted in doing.

I earnestly hope that my not going will not stop you, because I want you to go extremely. "Zenith" I had written part of, and it would have been one of my best poems if completed, but I unaccountably lost the MS., and have never been able to find or recall any of it. . . .

God is blessing "Such a Blessing" quite wonderfully; no end of people have said that it has been "such a blessing" to them, and it has roused many in L——— to seek, and a few to find, the same.

May 7, 1874.

Dear Mrs. Simpson,—

I wonder why? But we never have a "why" without the Lord's having a full "because," whether He sees it well to tell it or not to us. So there must be a "because" in this seeming denial to our prayer for you. *Is* it an answer that now in this matter it is *definitely* given to you to suffer for His sake? May you have all the sweetness and hidden blessedness of that gift, and a special and gracious "nevertheless afterward" as well! I do think your present suffering is most definitely *for His sake,* for I am sure you would not have risked it for any other consideration. All the same, I can't help feeling a bit remorseful at hav-

ing been the proposer of your staying! I hope Mrs. Barbour will forgive me!

I have just heard that a French Wesleyan pastor in the south of France has been so roused by "Such a Blessing" to seek *more* for himself, that he too has got "such a blessing," and has gone among his people with new power, and God has used him already for the conversion of many members of his flock and the quickening of others. Isn't that nice! What shall I send you? What "He had promised, He was able also to perform."

(*To* ———.)

It is surprising and often actually painful to me how Christians speak of the Old Testament, forgetting that "*All* Scripture is given by inspiration of God," and they will hardly accept its authority in argument or statement, saying, "Yes, but that is only Old Testament," which seems to me to come perilously near Revelation 22:19.

Do not be vexed with my saying that I wish you had left out those words in your "Questions,"—"apart from Old Testament." You might not mean it so, but such things help this spirit of disparaging *part* of His precious word.

And you will hardly wonder at my saying that I regretted your note very much, and I will tell you why. Such "Questions," flinging little stones at grand old institutions (which, though you may crash the windows, you *cannot* overturn!) all help to foster this terrible spirit of restlessness and overturning and radical principles. *Because* the greatest form of Christian worship has been abused, and has fallen in many places into a lifeless form, is it therefore for us to smash the candlestick which was meant to give light? Our cathedrals are a *great standing protest* against godlessness and the modern spirit of expediency and utilitarianism, and *God* is witnessed for by them.

I fully expect that when millennial grace and glory come, they will be as they ought to be, the great centres of the *beauty of holy worship,* and standing types of the yet more grand and glorious worship of the heavenly temple. Meanwhile, questions like yours can do no possible good; they won't pull down a single cathedral, nor stop a single service,—but they may do harm; they will foster that carping dissatisfaction, that spirit of innovation and irreverence and destruction which is easier fanned than checked, and which may and perhaps will end in a deluge of fiery trial in which not merely the Church of England, but those outside of her pale have "cast stones" at her, may have to suffer very terribly. This may seem strong, but I am only following out the little "bud "of the overturning spirit to its fruit.

(*To* ———.)

January 25, 1878.

I meant to have set to work this morning at my new book,

The Royal Invitation, but instead of that, I give the time to *prayer,* and requests for prayer about it. *To-morrow* I hope to begin.

Now I ask you most earnestly to pray about it, and to pass on the request to any other friends who, though unknown personally, will kindly do me this GREATEST service of "helping together by prayer." I never felt such need of it. The thing is so on my mind, that I can better understand than ever before, what the old prophets meant by "the burden of the Lord." I must write it—I must set aside other things for it; and yet, most strangely, I have not two ideas as to *what* to say! all I know is that the title must be *The Royal Invitation,* and the keynote must be "COME!" I can't see beyond that! But I entirely expect that when I sit down to-morrow, the Lord will give me what He means me to say.

You see, I have only written for Christians as yet (with the exception of a few leaflets), and so I have not fulfilled the great commission, "Let him that heareth, say, *Come,*" in writing, though of course I am often at it in speaking. So *now* I want to peal out a "COME!" that shall be *heard* and followed; a "Come!" especially to those who are not reached by tracts or little books in paper covers, but who would not reject a pretty gift-book of daily readings, not too long and not too prosy.

It will want special tact and power, and all that I have *not* got, and must therefore look only to the Lord for! The other books have opened a wide door for it; and if I am enabled to do it at all, it will probably go by *tens of thousands,* and so it is an immense responsibility to dare to write it. I feel as if it were hardly less than preaching to one of Moody's enormous congregations!

Now won't you and your good friends help me mightily about it? Ask that He would give me EVERY SINGLE WORD from beginning to end, that I may leave *nothing* unsaid which should be said, and not say one word which is not really from Him. One may as well ask much as little, while one *is* about it! So please ask that it may be FULL OF POWER—that every chapter may be a channel of converting grace—that it may be more really and definitely blessed to souls than anything I have yet written—that it may be a sort of condensed Mission Week to every reader. Have you faith enough to ask all that? . . .

There! Have I asked too much? I don't mean of the Lord, but of you? What, if this time next year, I am writing to ask you for help in praise for an immense answer? WE SHALL SEE.
—Yours in our dear Master.

THE MUMBLES, October 1878.
DEAR MRS. SIMPSON,—

It is *worth* knowing something of under-the-surface sorrows if one may thereby have the privilege of bringing a drop of God's comfort to others—the *same* comfort, and yet each has such different sorrows. I did not know you had had such a heavy one; but if the Lord uses your little book to comfort many, I know you will be praising Him. I am glad you can tell me Dr. S. *is* better after your anxiety about him. I hope it is only temporary illness.

I have just begun an *entirely* new life-era; since my poor mother's death last May, our old home has been finally broken up, and now my very dear elder sister and I have just settled into lodgings here for the winter—partly for economy, partly to be well out of reach, as both of us were very worn and weary and sorely needing rest and quiet. All the "changes and chances of this mortal life" seem to bring one into view of fresh promises—don't you find it so too? There are so many which one *can't* get the full preciousness of till one is brought into some specially corresponding position of need or sorrow. And as one after another lights up, one wonders what next!

THE MUMBLES, October 23, 1878.
We have been most graciously guided here, and really if loving-kindness shines in little things, it is simply resplendent in this case, for God has not only supplied our need, but our notions in a most wonderful way in the details of our little lodgings and their surroundings. We came the beginning of October, and consider it "home" till next June, and so far as we see at present, this arrangement is likely to last our lives! for I do not see how anything could suit us better. I never did see why those who could choose their abode should not live where they have something beyond lanes and fields—not to say rows of houses—to look at. (Description of view from the house, etc.)

. . . I am actually settled here with dear M., with a possibility of rest before me—I was getting so worn out. I have cleared off all my own work for this season, *i.e. Royal Invitations* and *Loyal Responses,* and have just done the last proof of the illustrated edition of *Ministry of Song,* under the title of *Life Mosaic.* I have also done with editing *Christian Progress* for the invalided editor, and now am steadily clearing off, etc.

. . . (After alluding to a Bible Reading Union to which she belonged, she continues)—Just finishing reading Exodus—so strange and tantalizing that I never get the spiritual enjoyment out of that set of types that I really do out of the historical ones, though I know all the typical points. But Joseph! I am so sorry I touched that type in one or two chapters of *Royal Invitations,* for when reading Genesis four or five weeks back, I thought I should so like to do a little book like *My King* or *Our Brother,* and work that aspect of Christ with Joseph rather prominent, as David is in *My King.*

(*To the same.*)

THE MUMBLES, December 21, 1878.
I am mixed up with so many workers and works; and my own books and cards and leaflets seem always involving more and more correspondence, and the requests I get are simply a steady daily stream. I am so utterly weary in mind and body that I hardly seem to know where I am drifting to—only I do know the drifting is really only being steered in the dark.

APPENDIX III.

HINDERERS AND HINDRANCES.

BY FRANCES RIDLEY HAVERGAL.

PART I.

HINDERERS! Whoever set to work in real earnest without finding them? Yet they act like centrifugal and centripetal force, producing a tolerable equipoise—the ice and the steam resulting in lukewarm water, in which you can wash your hands very comfortably. Some temperaments need a little cold water, yet the world is the warmer for them. Some are of the wet blanket nature, and they are useful when the chimneys are on fire.

All who bend their minds to the attainment of some object soon find out the existence of hinderers. There are few who do not at some time or in some way hinder some one. The men hinder the women, the women the men, and children hinder both. Yet, in society as a whole, the various and mutual hindrances so fit into each other that they act like the opposing forces of gravitation and attraction.

Perhaps workers for God, and those who are longing to work for Him, longing to win souls and advance the glory of their Lord and Master,—these know vividly, and often bitterly, what hinderers mean. There are hinderers from *without:* world-loving friends, secret or open opponents, false reasoners, and many others, which one's own life-experience supplies.

There are hindrances from *within:* restless and ambitious thoughts, weary doubts, and down-heartedness; coldness of spirit, darkness of vision, impatience and overanxiety. Do we not know these and thousands more?

And are there not hinderers from *below?* Yes, grim legions,—dark-winged opposers, hovering around both work and workers. But they cannot pierce the invisible shield, they cannot efface the invincible prayer and promise, "I have prayed for thee, that thy faith fail not," and, "Thou shalt have good success."

There are no hinderers from above! only blessed helpers, holy watchers, a cloud of witnesses, and One who ever whispers, "In me is thy help." The garrison may be shut in on all sides, but the free, bright sky will always be open above.

But all *these* hinderers are as a matter of course, a thing to be taken for granted; as soon may the soldier be astonished at encountering an old and well-known enemy as expect to be exempt from these.

There are other hinderers than those without, within, and below: the unintentional ones, well-meaning ones, hard-working ones, affectionate, ay, over-affectionate ones; and it is these classes of hinderers we shall now consider, and by a few conversations illustrate and enforce our meaning.

"Mother, dearest, I have a favour to ask you. Are you too busy to listen?"

"What is it, Alice?"

"I think you will grant it, mother; but I am half afraid, too."

"If it is anything right and reasonable, you know I shall be glad."

"I have been thinking about it all the week, mother, ever since last Sunday's sermon about, 'She hath done what she could;' and I am wondering if you would mind letting me go to the Sunday school with Lizzie, and taking a little class,—I should like it so much." And Alice drew closer to her mother, and laid her arm along the back of her chair.

"My dear Alice, I think you are quite too young—not sixteen yet. It will be quite time enough to teach when you are seventeen or eighteen. Besides, you have a great deal to learn yourself; and your Bible questions take up all your Sunday afternoons, and I like you to read before morning service."

"But, mother dear, if you would only let me go once a day, say in the morning, I could easily do part of my questions on Saturday, and so get time for reading."

"There are plenty of older people to teach besides you, Alice. You will be able to do it much better when you leave school."

"But, mother, this is the only thing I could think of; and I don't know what else I could begin with."

"You have a great deal to do, Alice, a great deal that is very important,—your own education, your own heart and mind to improve. You can set a good example to your sisters out of school-hours, and be kind and helpful to them, and other ways in which you can earn the commendation, 'She hath done what she could.'"

"But can I not try to do all this, mother, and yet undertake just this little class? May I not, mother dear? It seems so long to wait till I am eighteen; and I might not live till then," said Alice thoughtfully.

Her mother looked up from the table, which was strewn with tracts, carefully sorted, and in process of being supplied with neat brown paper covers. For Alice's mother was an energetic and useful district visitor, and hoped in due time to lead her children to follow in similar paths of usefulness.

Alice was an impulsive girl, and required to be rather held in check than otherwise. Yet she had given many evidences of such care for her own soul that might have encouraged her mother to let her undertake what she might have done faithfully and perseveringly. But Alice was little for her age, and childish and merry in her ways, so that few gave her credit for ever being thoughtful, and possessing some tact and brightness when talking to her younger school-fellows.

Her mother did not know how Alice had thought and prayed over this seemingly sudden request, nor how her child longed to "do something for the Lord Jesus;" so she could not measure the depth of disappointment, the crushing out of the loving desire, as she replied:

"Alice, dear, if God has work for you to do, He will spare your life to do it—that is in His hands, not yours. Wait two or three years, and then I promise you we will see about it. But just run and fetch me the ball of string out of the dining-room."

All these objections were perfectly true, and the mother thought she was acting rightly in restraining her child, though sorry to disappoint what she thought only a momentary fancy. But did she pray that God's will might be known and done in this matter? Was she not her child's *hinderer*?

An elder and a younger sister's conversation will be our next illustration.

"Ada, it's no use your thinking of going to the night-school; it will be pouring with rain before we get back,—it's beginning to spot now." And the speaker turned from the window, where she had been scanning the clouds.

"I don't much think so, Mary. I can put on goloshes and waterproof, and then it is no matter if it does."

"There is no occasion for you to run the risk of catching another cold. Jessie White can look over the writing; and as for the Scripture, your class can join mine."

"But, Mary, dear, it never answers to put so many girls together. I would rather go. Please, don't say any more. If we don't attend regularly, how can we expect the girls to come?"

"There's a difference between going regularly and going imprudently, Ada; and you look tired to death now, and nothing comes of over-exertion. You really must not be so foolish as to go. I shall just have to nurse you with a cold."

Ada felt annoyed; but Mary's manner was determined, and to save further fuss she gave up her wish.

However, things did not go smoothly at the night-school. Mary found a note of excuse from Jessie, and the hope that the day-schoolmistress would take her class. But the mistress was gone out to tea, and Mary found herself with three or four classes on her hands. She was clever and energetic, but had some difficulty in getting so many girls to attend to the Bible lesson, and certainly the thought half intruded, "I wish I had not hindered Ada from coming!"

Shall we glance in a curate's home, that centre of struggle and devotion, where burning zeal and loving labour are often sorely unpaid and unrequited?

"Charlie! it's all very well for you to undertake one thing after another, but I know what the end of it will be—breakdown, doctor's bills, and next to nothing to live upon."

The said Charlie was a hard-working curate, with a wife whose affection was most devoted to him, and to his parish, to a certain extent, for his sake. The immediate subject of attack was a cottage-lecture, voluntarily undertaken, but involving a long walk. He had already walked five or six miles that morning, visiting from house to house, besides a good set-to at his sermon and taking a funeral in the afternoon.

"I am perfectly well and strong, Agnes dearest, and so long as God gives me such powers, why should I not use them?"

"Perfectly well and strong! Oh, Charlie! Who had such a headache last week that he couldn't bear to have the fire poked, and who had such influenza and had to pay two guineas for a Sunday's rest?"

"But I have neither headache nor influenza, and when I had I omitted the lecture. Walking really does me good, and the lecture is quite a refreshment to me. You must not grudge your husband his parochial pleasures," and he put his hand caressingly on her shoulder.

"Oh, yes, I know it's very nice, and the people listen, so it's encouraging, but that's no reason you should wear yourself out."

"Would you have me give up the lecture, and disappoint those who are just beginning to value what they hear?"

"I wish you would distinguish things that differ, Charles. I never wanted you to give it up (you'll be late if you go on talking), only I do think it very wrong to go on work, work, work. You don't consider what it will be to me. if you are ill for weeks, like Mr. J——'s curate, and then I shall break down too."

This was not a pleasant view of the subject for a man who loved his wife as men *should* love their wives, and as Charles did. An expression of endurance came over his face. "Dear Agnes, don't talk so!" was all he said.

"Talk how, Charlie? You know it's true, and you can't deny it. Why, there's another hole in your glove! If you mean to be in time, you must start, and please don't step into those ruts in that dark lane. I shall have you brought home with a broken leg, I expect, for you dash on so!"

Charles departed; but the discussion had an irritating effect upon him, and he felt dispirited, and almost disheartened, and almost disinclined for his usually loved work.

His subject was, "Bear ye one another's burdens, and so fulfil the law of Christ." But the practical commentary upon the precepts which he had just experienced was unfortunate. He felt that his burdens had been momentarily at least added to by one who would have given her life to lighten them. And, like a sudden gust of wind, his wife's remarks had utterly blown away many of the thoughts which he was intending to give his waiting people, and so ruffled and disordered the rest that he thought it best to give up that subject and take some other.

Was it any marvel that his lecture was less full of the powerful simplicity of gospel truth which drew and kept that little congregation together? Yet who would have thought that the help-meet had been the *hinderer*?

Again, and let our illustration warn the unconscious hinderers.

It is night, and the candle is almost burnt down in a double-bedded room shared by two brothers. The elder is still intently reading—he had read in that book an hour ago, and since then has knelt long by his bedside, and now he has returned to its pages again. There was a reason for that return. He had been walking many days in darkness, without light or comfort, almost without sensible love to the Saviour whose service both brothers had chosen. That evening Edgar had striven hard, with wandering thoughts in prayer which often well-nigh overcame him, and, after long wrestling, something of the old fervour of spirit had returned, and he thirsted to read again the words of pardon and comfort, which had been as a sealed roll to him. How could he wait for morning hours? He rose from his knees and sought out the passages which had been as living waters to him in days past, and oh! that they might be so again.

"Edgar, my good fellow, are you going to sit up all night, and be frozen to death?"

"I shan't be long," he quietly replied, without raising his eyes.

Two or three minutes elapsed.

"I say, when are you going to come? What would father say if he sees the light?"

"Oh, don't chatter, John, please; I'm coming directly."

"But just see the time—twenty minutes to twelve; why can't you read after tea?"

Edgar did not answer. He knew his father wished them to be in bed early, but as they had come to years of discretion he had issued no special rule, and only too gladly would he have seen his boy over the open Bible; but seeing that John had set his head upon enforcing "regular hours" that night, he shut up his Bible and put out the light.

When spiritual realities are trembling in the balance, it needs but little to turn the scale to the wrong side.

Edgar's train of thought and prayer was broken by this little cloud. Was it not unkind of his brother to interrupt him, and how could he think out that chapter? The wheels went heavily enough already, now they were still more clogged. John would not knowingly hinder his brother from the heavenward way, and yet his few impatient, though well-meant words, had done so, and the step so nearly gained was for that night lost.

Shall *all* hindrances prove to be furtherances? Some there are which seem as if they could not so be resolved. Our whole life may have hinged upon some well-meant yet not the less fatal hindrance; a shortsighted pointsman may have turned our train on to the wrong line, we may have travelled far from what seemed our true terminus, and there is no possibility of return ere "the night cometh." It was no doing of ours—why should we and the Master's work suffer loss by it? There are life-enigmas of this kind which admit of *no* solution, hindrances which remain such in grim reality unsoftened by past or future as far as our eye can reach, and beyond. What are we to think of these? Turn the others, the minor ones, the solvable ones, into so many arguments for the *probability,* to take the lowest ground, that these also have their solutions, quite as clear when once revealed, only a little farther to seek.

Last May we stood on a hill and looked down into the valley just flushing out into its early summer smile of leaf and blossom. The opposite slope was wooded, but the foliage was late, and did not hide the ground below. That ground was covered with a soft blue mist, pale and lovely, melting and thinning away towards the summit, and showing the wild undergrowth of spring greenery. We gazed long—it was surely mist. After awhile we went down into the valley and crossed the stream from which the blue haze must have arisen. As we and gained the other side our feet stepped upon beds of wild hyacinths, delicately blue, paling with the advancing season into tenderer tints and stretching away up the bank, and along the brook till, in the distance, the blossoms blended again into the semblance of blue mist.

But we knew then that as far as we could see, and farther, it was only flowers. We cannot expect all blue mists to resolve themselves into flowers *here. But* there is a hill to be descended, a valley beneath, and a stream to be crossed, and *Then!*

So much for analogy. But there is more certainty to go upon. We come back to the grand old pillar Promise, which shall stand without a quiver "though the earth be removed, and though the mountains be carried into the midst of the sea." "*All* things work together for good to them who love God." Or, to change the figure, that "work together" makes one think of a mighty current, far too strong for mortal engineer to turn or dam, steadily and grandly rolling on to the ocean of perfect ultimate good—hinderers and hindrances dash noisily down from the hill-sides to meet it, their course at right-angles to the current, but do they impede it? does the splashing torrent counteract one inch of its flow? do its little sticks and stones delay it for one moment? Not one inch, not one moment! They only join the great stream, and the larger they are the more they swell it and add to its force and volume. Yes, they too, *hinderers* and *hindrances,* are among the "all things," and therefore, whether within sight or beyond sight, they never work *against,* but only and always "work *together for* good."

"The ills we see,—
The mysteries of sorrow deep and long,
The dark enigmas of permitted wrong,—
    Have all one key:
This strange sad world is but our Father's school;
All chance and change His love shall grandly overrule.

"He traineth so
That we may shine for Him in this dark world,
And bear His standard dauntlessly unfurled,
    That we may show
His praise, by lives that mirror back His love—
His witnesses on earth, as He is ours above.

Part II.

Are our illustrations exaggerated? We appeal confidently to any one placed in close contact with fellow-workers. But what if your own conscience replies, "I have been a hinderer?"—that is, consciously to yourself, for who may tell the "secret faults" in this particular? Who may tell the unknown times that word or example of yours has hindered the soul's work? Seek to amend the habit, if habit it be, of impeding those around you in efforts for good, and hold out a helping, not a hindering, hand.

It is not to be denied that there are people who will go out district-visiting for hours at the expense of being laid up for weeks; others who will act in diametrical opposition to medical and parental advice—who will go out in east winds, who will sit up for hours in their bedrooms after the household are asleep instead of early rising, who, in fact, seem bent upon annoying their friends and shortening their usefulness: of such extremes we do not speak. But how many needless anxieties arise about infections and colds, and long walks! How many worrying and useless objections are started regarding undertakings which the objectors have no intention of seriously opposing! How many lions in the way of others are seen by those who tread on fierce ones themselves! How many a nervous semi-invalid is kindly prevented from working off his or her nervousness! How many a dispirited one is still further discouraged by gloomy remarks and prognostications! How many an ardent one damped and dulled by the same! Let us consider one another to provoke unto love and to good works, that the crown of no beloved one may be the less radiant for our hindrances!

The previous illustrations affect only passing circumstances, but we must not forget those more serious hindrances, which may embitter a very lifetime, or thwart the purpose of some heaven-sent aspiration. Parental ambition may check some high resolve of dedication to God's service. It may be some of England's daughters who are startled from their silken dreams and homes of peace and joy, where truth and light are shining fair as the stars of night, and they long to rise and go,

"Laying their joys aside,
    As the Master laid them down,
Seeking His love and lost in the veiled adodes of woe,
Winning His Indian gems, to shine in His glorious crown!"

And so some hasty home decision quenches the bright flame. Or may be some son, with no definite opening, no call of home duty, hears the Master's call, and his true-hearted response is, "Here am I; send me," and he is ready to go and—

"Tell it out among the heathen that the Lord is King,
     Tell it out, tell it out!
Tell it out among the nations, bid them shout and sing!
     Tell it out, tell it out!"

A letter from Ernest at last! And the sister eagerly gives her father the morning budget at the breakfast table. Her mother watches, for gloom gathers on the father's face as he reads it. Silently the letter is given to the mother, and he passes through the open window to the pleasant terrace-walk beneath. The sister guesses in vain, "What can Ernest have written?" The father paced up and down, thinking of the position he himself had won, and which he had hoped would be a steppingstone for his son to one far higher, in which his many gifts of mind and heart would shine with no common effulgence. He had hoped his son would carry out and develop many schemes of benevolence he had set on foot. But that morning's letter was as a mighty crucible, wherein the man's devotedness to Him who had given him that darling son was to be tested and analyzed. What was that letter?

"—— COLLEGE, CAMBRIDGE.

"DEAR FATHER,—Will you listen to your son's request for your consent, your blessing, your prayers? Father, there is a burning impulse within me, a new life-pulse seems beating in my soul, a still deep voice ever sounding in my ears, 'Go ye into all the world, and preach the gospel to every creature.' Years ago that same voice called me, when I first heard stories about the heathen and their idols, and when standing by my mother I looked at the Church Missionary Society's green picture-book (*Juvenile Instructor*), of white men preaching to the heathen. Silently, but surely, has that call followed me. I have cried earnestly, 'Lord, what wilt thou have me to do?' and again the heavenly whisper comes, 'Go ye.' Therefore, though never before breathed to any but God, this is no sudden thought, no unconsidered plan. Father, let me go, let me take the cup of living water to him that is ready to perish. I should like to tread the very footsteps of Him who came to seek and to save that which was lost, to search in His name for the 'other sheep, which are not of this fold.'

"I know the hopes and intentions which you have cherished for my future; but is not a missionary's joy a nobler gain, the missionary's crown a nobler ambition than any other? And what if the time came when, among the multitude out of all nations and kindreds and tongues, I might be permitted to recognise some who first heard a Saviour's name from my unwor-

thy lips. My own dear mother! her heart will be with me in this; I know she lent me to the Lord.

"Dearest father, I believe Christ has called me, will you not let me obey His voice?—Your loving son,

"ERNEST."

Reader, what would *your* answer have been? Would you have hindered? The father could not brook that the talents of his son, the pride of his ancestral hall, should go forth into the gloom and obscurity of distant shores. But who can tell how bitterly that question, "Father, will you hinder me?" returned to his mind when the bell tolled for the early death of that loved and devoted son!

"Man's hindrances may be God's furtherances." Not that this is any excuse for the "hinderers" we have described. No thanks or praise to them that medicine is distilled from their poison, heavenly sparks struck from their cold steel and flint. We have no consolation for "hinderers," in their thoughtless jarrings upon the strings tuned for God's music. But for the *hindered* there is honey out of the rock, honey upon the ground; sweet and abundant and ever-flowing. Put forth the end of the rod that is in your hand, ye hindered ones, weary and discouraged with the rocks, the boulders, the stones in your way, perhaps merely the grit of a fairly smooth path, which others do not see, but which you feel and wince at, because your feet are sensitive and bare. Dip your rod in the honeycomb of God's own ruling gentleness and love, and, like Jonathan, your eyes shall be enlightened, and you shall no more be faint.

It is a wide subject, that of hindrances. Even a catalogue of the varieties known to any one person's experience would occupy too much time and patience to write or even read. They fall into two classes, God's hindrances and man's hindrances. On the former we need not dwell. It is more easy to see that they are furtherances; it is easier to say, "Thy will be done" with regard to that which is unmistakeably and directly God's will, and which has not to be painfully traced back to it through some distorting human medium, and therefore more easy to open the heart to receive comfort at first, and profit afterwards; more easy to weave them into the web of our work, and to believe that the design will be all the richer for the troublesome insertion of a dark thread. In these hindrances from God the element of bitterness is wanting, even when the trial is otherwise deep and heavy. For bitterness can only grow out of evil, evil that has sin for its essence or foundation, and this cannot be from God; this cup, though divinely *permitted*, must be humanly *presented*. The heart knows the difference, the essential difference between a trial which comes only and purely from God's hand, in which we say, not only "Himself had done it," but Himself *only*, and the trial which comes through a human medium, which treachery faithlessness, ingratitude, heartlessness have brought about. There is a sting, a gall, a smart in the one which appertains not to the other. Let us fall into the hand of God, and not into the hands of man, said David, and he knew the depths of both.

In God's trials, moreover, the chief earthly alleviation of sympathy is enjoyed to the full, and its ministration is almost invariably co-extensive with the circle of our friends—often far wider.

Not so with the trials of man's hindrances; often we have but partial sympathy or none at all, and we bear them in smiling but heartbreaking silence.

Take the case of illness *simple,* by which you are laid aside for a few weeks or months. (We speak not of excruciating agony or consequent poverty.) You are hindered from all work, rendered utterly useless and helpless, debarred from ordinary pleasures; you lie in uncertainty of the issue, and you seem a very hinderer and drag to the willing and kindest friends.

And so you are driven to trust, and lean and rest on the bosom of the Father. You are drawn closer to Him; even if you cannot think continuously, nor read, nor listen to reading, you have far more communion on the whole with the Invisible but felt Presence than was possible in your busy days and sleepful nights. You know it *is* the Lord's chastening, and so you look for a "nevertheless afterward" of blessing. You cannot struggle against the trial; by no planning, no wakeful contrivings, can you slip away from His hand, and so you lie still under it; and there are no rankling regrets, no struggles to forgive and forget anything or any one who has caused pain.

The Master's voice does not bid you "Enter the thick of the conflict," but "Come ye yourselves apart into a desert place and rest awhile." It *is* a desert place, and you leave all the pleasant fruits and fair flowers of life behind, but you leave its turmoil too; and is there not *enough* to make you glad when you are alone with Jesus, so utterly weary that He lays your head upon His bosom; is that not rest?

Contrast this with any trial from the hand of man—some one great wound or succession of blows from one whom you trusted and loved. You are withdrawn by it from none of your ordinary work or calls, these are superadded; you cannot speak about it; you cannot speak about your trial, it would not be half understood, or it might injure and even exasperate the listener if you sought the solace of sympathy. You puzzle yourself vainly and wearily; you torture yourself with suppositions as to what might have been, if this or that had not been said or done. If you have any cause for self-reproach, you are miserable; if you have none, you almost wish you had, that the matter might be less wrong, less unreasonable. There is *evil* in it that you are sure is not God's will; how are you to say, "Thy will be done?" You grieve over your friend's sin, and you grieve over the evil it stirs up in your own heart, and you lie wakefully with worse than pain. And perhaps you get letters alluding to some of your blessings,—your happy home, your pretty study, and "nothing to do but write poetry!" and other felicitations on your supposed unclouded lot. You sigh over the kind, ignorant letter, and say, "How little they know!" Or you must keep an engagement to sing, and it is for your King, and strangers shall not misjudge your loyal love. You sing sweet words of "Comfort ye!" but they little ween the tight tension on your own heart as you sing, "Whom having not seen ye love … though now for a season if need be, ye are in heaviness through manifold temptations";—and yet, oh yet, you do trust in Him, whose love seems more precious still in the fires.

F. R. H.

[These thoughts on Hinderers and Hindrances were written some time ago by my dear sister, F. R. H. By experience she keenly felt for many a young disciple, whose first desires to follow Christ are often checked instead of being cherished and encouraged. Unconsciously F. R. H. lifts the veil from some of her own life-enigmas most patiently borne, till shone for her—

"Light after darkness,
   Gain after loss,
Strength after suffering,
   Crown after cross.
Sweet after bitter,
   Song after sigh,
Home after wandering,
   Praise after cry."

M. V. G. H.]

Manuscript letter of F.R.H. to her sisters Maria and Ellen. See the explanation on page 125.

[This manuscript letter was given to the researcher by Dr. Jonathan Havergal Shaw in 2002. Dr. Shaw is the son of Rev. Vernon Graham Havergal Shaw and the grandson of "Willie," Rev. William Henry Shaw. The hand-written notes above and below the manuscript letter are by Rev. Vernon Graham Havergal Shaw. Rev. V. G. H. Shaw was born August 20, 1887, two months after Maria's death, and his father (Maria's nephew, William Henry Shaw) named the son after her. He lived from 1887 to 1985, aged 97, and he and his cousin Cynthia Havergal were diligent stewards of original Havergal manuscripts and papers. David Chalkley]

Note from FRH to M (aria) & E (llen) at Winterdyne, probably by hand.

Bewdley mission. Sept 1873.

Dearest M & E

    Rejoice with us -- the first-fruits of the week are here, Willie -- oh so rejoicing & decided, yesterday was indeed his spiritual birthday, he has so fully come to Christ & found joy. I never saw a more decided case. I hope Alf. too, but not so sure. I will see about Miss Parsons & her girls this morning, so you need not have that on your mind.

I am rather used up, for last week & the week before were just one continued strain, but it was well worth the work -- there are many "new-born" at Astley.

    Haste

    Your loving

      F.

Memorials page 122 [page 35 of Volume IV of the Havergal edition] tells of F's stay at Oakhampton, July & Aug. 1873
Poems p 518 [*The Poetical Works of Frances Ridley Havergal*, original page 518, the poem on page 397 of Volume I of the Havergal edition, F. R. H's sonnet "How Wonderful!" copied at the end of this] dated Aug 30 is re answered prayer: '4 Bible classes weekly', 'unwearied exertions', 'crowded attendances'.   After this, (i.e. Sept.) 'preparatory work for a mission at Bewdley.' F. 'gave much help'. M. 122-3 [*Memorials of Frances Ridley Havergal* by her sister, Maria V. G. Havergal, original pages 122–123, page 35 of Volume IV of the Havergal edition, early in Chapter 8] "The family at Winterdyne will ever have reason to thank God for F.'s visit" no doubt refers to the news in this note, when W. was 16, A. 14: they [the two nephews, William Henry Shaw and Alfred Havergal Shaw] would be on holiday from Repton [school] Aug-Sept. Both were confirmed at Repton in Nov. '74: & were students at T.C. Dublin when M. wrote in 1880 re FRH [*Memorials* by Maria V. G. Havergal]. [William and Alfred were] ordained in 1881 & '82.

"How Wonderful!"

He answered all my prayer abundantly,
    And crowned the work that to His feet I brought,
    With blessing more than I had asked or thought—
A blessing undisguised, and fair, and free.
I stood amazed, and whispered, "Can it be
    That He hath granted all the boon I sought?
    How wonderful that He for me hath wrought!
How wonderful that He hath answered me!"
O faithless heart! He said that He would hear
    And answer thy poor prayer, and He hath heard
And proved His promise. Wherefore didst thou fear?
    Why marvel that Thy Lord hath kept His word?
More wonderful if He should fail to bless
Expectant faith and prayer with good success!

Frances Ridley Havergal, August 30, 1873, Oakhampton

[The manuscript of this sonnet is shown on page 126.]

These two quotations of two letters by F.R.H. are given by T. H. Darlow in his *Frances Ridley Havergal A Saint of God* (London: James Nisbet & Co., 1927), "Extracts from Letters," the first quotation on pages 136–137, and the second quotation on pages 138–139 of Darlow's original book. These two quotations have not been found anywhere in the Havergal edition, and apparently were quoted by Darlow from an original manuscript letter. Darlow was given much access to original manuscript materials by F.R.H.'s niece and nephew, Frances Anna Shaw and Alfred Havergal Shaw. See page 1096 of Vol. IV of the Haveral edition.

I do so hope that God will mercifully soon give you some special interest; it would so help the great wound to cicatrize.[1] You can't cut one out for yourself, and He may see fit to withhold it for a long time yet, but this is the special thing I wish for you just now. . . . It would be such a valuable means of comfort. I do not think there is any means, short of God's own direct comfort, which does so much towards helping one over a great trial as some new interest, if strong enough to be really such.

[At the end of this brief quotation, Darlow wrote, "Written in 1878."]

Yes, I will be one to give thanks for the super-abounding consolation; but it is so much harder to rejoice in the tribulation of others than in one's own, that I must own to grieving a little that there should be such need of these consolations. I could choose a smoother path for you, dear friend, and then, what an amount of blessing I should make you miss!

[At the end of this brief quotation, Darlow wrote, "Written in 1878."]

Note: Though there is an abundance of true riches in the edition of *The Complete Works of Frances Ridley Havergal*, yet this is only a part, the whole of which is known only by God. There were letters and other written items, spoken words, and deeds of love, of which we are completely unaware, now either no longer extant or unavailable, not found and made available. These two quotations by Darlow of letters are a glimpse of so much that we do not have now. Like any true work, F.R.H.'s life, and her written poetry, prose, and music, are solely the Lord's doing alone: a book which He wrote, and which He alone fully knows and understands. D.C. August 27, 2008

[1] cicatrize: to form a scar, to help or heal a wound by causing a scar to be formed

Fair copy autograph of "How Wonderful" in F.R.H.'s Manuscript Book No VII. See page 125 of this book.

Dear

Pardon me for regretfully resorting to this way of replying, as the continually increasing number of correspondents personally unknown to me, renders it simply impossible to send written answers to each. You will find a mark against the para=graph or sentence which contains a reply to your letter.

Yours faithfully,

FRANCES RIDLEY HAVERGAL.

1. *To those who wish permission to use or quote hymns or extracts from my writings.*—It is always a pleasure to give this freely, except in cases where I am fettered by a pre-viously given permission or arrangement, or where "Musical Copyright" should be secured by the publishers.

2. *To those who wish a "candid opinion" as to M.S.S., or advice how to profit by them.*—The only "candid opinion" of any practical value will be obtained by sending your M.S. to the Editor of whatever Magazine issues verses or articles of the same kind, he will judge without bias, and reply accordingly. Introductions are utterly useless; everything stands on its own practical merits in an Editor's study.

Payment for hymns or general verses is exceptional, and unless you already have "a name," you need not dream of it. As to larger M.S.S., consult a London publisher. If he says he will be happy to publish your M.S., but at *your* expense, that simply means that he knows it will not com-mand sufficient circulation to pay its expenses. *Never publish anything at your own risk.*

3. *To those who wish a "candid opinion" or revision of Music.*—I really have not time for this. If you are a be-ginner, send your M.S. to the nearest good Organist. If not, send it to any high-class publisher. N.B.—Composition without knowledge of harmony is totally useless for publi-cation.

4. *To those who ask me to write for some Charitable or Religious Institution or object.*— (1.) I never write unless I have a very strong impression on my mind. A mere string of rhymes by request or on hearsay would be worse than use-less. (2.) It does not follow that, because I can or do heartily sympathise in a cause, I can forthwith write a poem about it. (3.) I never write descriptions or appeals for any-thing with which I am not personally familiar. (4.) I am sorry to say that I really cannot find time to write letters or addresses to special Bible-classes, Hospitals, &c., &c.

5. *To those who kindly suggest subjects on which they think something in prose or verse would be desirable.*—I find I have to quarry my own stones, and that it hardly ever seems possible to me to take up a line of thought suggested by another mind. At the same time, I am not ungrateful for these, as they are often interesting, though I cannot write upon them. But in several instances the result has been more surely reached by prayer that the Lord would give me the desired words, than by mentioning it to me at all.

6. *To those who "feel sure" of my interest or sympathy in various schemes of Christian work.*—Dear friends, I can only say that sometimes I am unable for weeks, or even months together, to cut my way through to doing any of my *own* work, because everybody expects me to take an interest in *their* work or plans! It is not want of will, but an actual physical impossibility to respond as I would to the continual stream of such letters from unknown fellow-workers.

7. *To those who ask me to circulate or dispose of books, leaflets, work, &c.*—I am now obliged entirely and invariably to decline to do this for any one. N.B.—I never dispose of my own publications.

8. *To those who enquire about my publications.*—Books, NISBET & Co., 21, Berners Street, London, also J. T. ADKINS, Leamington, or any Bookseller in the kingdom. Songs, HUTCHINGS & ROMER, 9, Conduit Street, Regent Street, London, or any Musicseller. Leaflets, cards, &c. : No leaflet is issued without the name and address of the publisher, who will supply them by return of post, to any address. A full list of Leaflets in Verse, seventy-five in number, will be found at the end of " Royal Commandments."

9. *To those who most kindly write, asking for no answer, only to tell me of help, stimulus, or comfort, through some message that the Lord has given me the privilege of bearing.*—I thank you most heartily, and ask you to pray that He would graciously give me His own messages for the unknown needs of His children, and to join me in thanksgiving for all His wonderful goodness.

This is the printed letter found on pages 51–52 of this book. A significant amount of her time and effort was given to answering many letters, taking away hours to work on books.

This is an account written by Frances Ridley Havergal (apparently completed July 26, 1875), a manuscript telling of the Lord's gracious healing of her. Much of this was written in a letter to Esther Beamish dated July 26, 1875 (near the end of Division V of *Letters by the Late Frances Ridley Havergal,* on pages 70–71 of this book), with important changes by F.R.H. Apparently this manuscript account, which was not addressed to anyone, was written and signed by F.R.H. for her own use, and she made important changes in the text when she wrote the letter to Esther Beamish.

Very likely or almost surely this has never been printed before now, and likely few have read this since she died. Ones who do not know her well or who for other reasons distort what she said and meant, could take "Such a Blessing" to be a claim or recommendation of sinless perfection in this world, though that is not remotely what she clearly said and meant, and similary with this manuscript account others may try to portray her as charismatic or pentecostal: she did not try to "make" or "persuade" God to do her way, but earnestly sought and wanted His will alone, and she was truly Biblical. What she describes here only the Lord alone can do, and in this He—Himself alone—is truly glorified. Her final words are, "the faith and the healing are all equally from God—distinctly His gift and His only." After this account, her poem "What Thou Wilt" is given: written November 29, 1878 at Caswell Bay (a little more than six months before she died), this true prayer was the desire of her heart, given to her by the Lord.

This account is transcribed from a ten-page manuscript document written by F.R.H. The manuscript was written on three single-fold sheets of paper. There is no person named as the addressee, and at the end she signed her name Frances R. Havergal. The way she began a number of new paragraphs unindented and other paragraphs indented, was followed in this transcription. In the section or unindented paragraph that begins "After dinner I was left alone for some time," in the fourth sentence, the word "No" is underlined twice, double underlined. David Chalkley

June 17, 1875. I was in bed all day. We were close upon midsummer, and had gained no ground since Easter; every little improvement being followed by a relapse, though every surrounding was most favourable for recovery, and there seemed no way of preventing these relapses, which gave me no time to gain strength.

For the first time since my illness began in October, I had had a time of spiritual depression following in strange disappointment upon more than commonly fervent desire and prayer

[this next part she crossed out] that while others were receiving such blessing at Brighton my Father would also bless "even me" and a really confident <u>expectation</u> that He would make it a means of blessing to one of my very nearest and dearest; both which desires seemed unfulfilled, [here the crossed-out part ended and she marked to resume here]

while an unexpected sorrow darkened in another quarter. He enabled me [here a line of words was very heavily covered over and is not transcribed here] to cast the burdens upon Him, and then during some days of literally "lying still" before Him, unable to sit up or even to read as usual in His own Word, He led me back into perhaps a sweeter, deeper rest in Him than almost ever before. On that 17th of June the prospect of <u>never</u> being strong again, came definitely before me. I looked at it very deliberately and fully—what it would be never to speak or sing or even write for Jesus, but only wait in quiet isolation and weakness, a burden to dear ones whose own burden I would like to bear, for years, perhaps for life. That this was not a mere improbable fancy is proved by my sister Miriam having written

the very words "she will be a chronic invalid"—on or about the same day.

But as I looked, I wondered at His great goodness to me in thus proving to me that He had answered my prayer:

"Take my will: it shall be Thine.

It [here the next words are covered over, possibly by a mistake or by the crossing out of words on the last line of the first page] shall be no longer mine."

for I could not, <u>did</u> not, feel one quiver of shrinking from the prospect, not a fear, not a regret, not a choice in the matter. It was all "of course"—of course He would be "with me always," of course His grace would be sufficient, of course it would be all best and happiest, His will <u>must</u> be always sweetest and dearest. And as for service, that was altogether my Master's affair, not mine at all—He could do, and <u>should</u> do what He would "with His own." I had the sweetest possible communion with Him about it, and felt, naturally enough, altogether <u>lighthearted</u>, for all that would have been too heavy for me was put <u>and left</u> in His dear hands. I seemed perfectly <u>dead</u> to any <u>possible</u> sense of anxiety or care about the future; and the present, even with fever and pain and languor was what I would not have exchanged with my one's.

Next day, June 18, was indeed much to be remembered. In the morning I was hardly so well, very weak, and with that indescribable sense of being "ill all over" which certainly does not naturally either raise one's spirits or herald a cure. But it was "perfect peace," literally passing understanding. My sister Ellen drove to see me. In reply to her wish that I should come as soon as possible for change of air to Winterdyne, I told her it was useless thinking about it, that no one could say when I should be able for the drive (not 4 miles) and that she must dismiss the idea altogether for the present.

After dinner I was left alone for some time, thinking I might get a little sleep, and little thinking what a much better thing the Lord was going to give me ! instead of sending sleep. (I say it reverently,) it seemed as if Jesus Himself came and drew me out; leading me on to tell Him what I hardly told myself. All through my illness I had never once felt able to pray for recovery, or even for mitigation of pain. More than once I thought I ought for the sake of others to try and ask it, but invariably it seemed as if the Holy Spirit checked my prayer and changed it into—"No! Lord Jesus! I would rather leave it entirely with Thee, and not even ask, do just what Thou wilt with Thy child—just what Thou wilt." Now however He seemed to say to me that the time was come to ask for recovery. But I told Him that I did not want to ask unless He gave me the prayer, and that if He did I should expect His gracious and direct answer. Then He at once took away all the barrier, and put the prayer into my very lips. I prayed it, not as my prayer at all, but as His! Then I asked Him "What about the answer"—watching and wondering what He would say next—("I will watch to see what He will say unto me." Hab. 2:1) and told Him I felt He had given me faith to be healed when He would. Then came—"I am the Lord that healeth thee!" with startling emphasis on "healeth." I literally started and held my breath! Surely He, Himself had said it! Then a sudden temptation, I believe from Satan himself,—to think it was only a common act of recollection of the familiar words. But I did not stop to attend to this, but asked Him if He would condescendingly confirm it to me, if He had indeed "spoken to my heart." Instantly He did so, for again and again the assurance rang out in my heart, in such a way that I could not, cannot, possibly doubt that it was "Jesus Himself"—"I am the Lord that healeth thee." I thought if ever He gave a marvellous opportunity for exercise of faith, here it was. So I praised Him and told Him I would and did take Him at His word. And I did, and of course I was healed—for I saw that "healeth" was not merely "will heal," so I began to expect to find myself actually healed. This communion had been so absorbing and intense that I had forgotten pain and discomfort, but now a pause seemed sent, that I might calmly realize the healing. It was real and complete! I examined my own sensations—it was

a total change, no pain, no feverishness, no sense of being ill anywhere, much less "all over"! The question of restoration of strength had not been touched upon, it seemed quite apart from that of cure, and neither prayer nor faith had been given me for that; thus I proved the more literally how exactly it was "according to my faith," for though well, I was very weak. After a little while of praise, and then a sort of hushed rest, I thought, "As I am healed, I may just as well act upon it!" I had not intended to rise at all, unless perhaps just to have my bed made—but I got up and dressed! The very first thing I did was to go to the glass and look at my tongue, which had been very bad, expecting to see it look all right! And so it did! It was not that I went to look whether it was so, but simply to see that it was so! When next my sister M__ came into the room, she was surprised to find me dressed. I assured her I was ever so much better, and should not be the worse for getting up, but did not tell her what reason I had for saying so. I found that half-unconsciously, I had yielded to a temptation to wait and see and not tell what the Lord had done for me till time had proved it, by no relapse occurring. As soon as I detected this unbelief, I felt thoroughly ashamed of it, and forthwith "burnt my ships" by telling the whole, trusting to the Lord to make it good." [A quotation mark is missing in the manuscript, in this sentence.]

And of course He did. Next day I was downstairs, and three days after went to Winterdyne!

From that day to this, July 26, I have never had another hour's illness, but have gone on slowly gaining strength, with no greater drawbacks than a common cold and a little neuralgia.

The Lord's hand is still upon me in gentle restraining, for though much stronger I am still quite unequal to ordinary physical or mental exertion, and it will evidently be a long time yet before I am able for "work."

I shall not be surprised to find that others were praying very specially for me at that time. One distant friend, I know, was led to very special and fervent prayer for me at the very time. It seemes to me that "the prayer of faith" which "shall save the sick" must be "not of the will of the flesh, nor of the will of man, but of God," and that in this direction lies the key to whatever experimental difficulties appear to surround the promise. I think the prayer, the faith and the healing are all equally from God—distinctly His gift and His only.

Frances R. Havergal

Note: F.R.H.'s manuscript of this letter is given on the next three pages.

What Thou Wilt.

Do what Thou wilt ! Yes, only do
    What seemeth good to Thee:
Thou art so loving, wise, and true,
    It must be best for me.

Send what Thou wilt; or beating shower,
    Soft dew, or brilliant sun;
Alike in still or stormy hour,
    My Lord, Thy will be done.

Teach what Thou wilt; and make me learn
    Each lesson full and sweet,
And deeper things of God discern
    While sitting at Thy feet.

Say what Thou wilt; and let each word
    My quick obedience win;
Let loyalty and love be stirred
    To deeper glow within.

Give what Thou wilt; for then I know
    I shall be rich indeed;
My King rejoices to bestow
    Supply for every need.

Take what Thou wilt, belovèd Lord,
    For I have all in Thee !
My own exceeding great reward,
    Thou, Thou Thyself shalt be !

Frances Ridley Havergal, November 29, 1878.

---

page 4

all over" which certainly does not
naturally either raise one's spirits or
herald a cure. But it was "perfect peace",
literally passing understanding. My
sister Ellen drove over to see me. In
reply to her wish that I should come as
soon as possible for change of air to
Winterdyne, I told her it was useless
thinking about it, that no one could
say when I should be able for the drive
(not 4 miles) & that she must dismiss
the idea altogether for the present.
After she was gone I was again led to
look at the prospect of chronic invalidism,
& again, even more definitely & joyfully,
"left it all with Jesus".
After dinner I was left alone for some
time, thinking I might get a little
sleep, & little thinking what a much
better thing the Lord was going to give
me! instead of sending sleep. (I say it
reverently,) it seemed as if Jesus Himself
came & drew me out; leading me on to
tell Him what I hardly told myself.
All through my illness I had never once

page 1 of a 10-page document by F.R.H

June 17. 1875. I was in bed all day.
We were close upon Midsummer, & I
had gained no ground since Easter;
every little improvement being
followed by a relapse, though every
surrounding was most favourable
for recovery, & there seemed no way of
preventing these relapses, which gave
me no time to gain strength.
For the first time since my illness
began in October, I had had a time
of spiritual depression following in
strange disappointment upon more
than commonly fervent desire & prayer
that while others were receiving such
blessing at Brighton my Father
would also bless "even me" & a really
confident expectation that He would
make it a means of blessing to one
of my very nearest & dearest; both
which desires seemed unfulfilled,
while an unexpected sorrow darkened
in another quarter. He enabled me

This is the manuscript account written by F.R.H. See the caption on pages 131–132 for the explanation of the arrangement of the pages.

to cast the burdens upon Him, & then during some days of literally "lying still" before Him, unable to sit up or even to read as usual in His own Word, He led me back into perhaps a sweeter, deeper rest in Him than almost ever before. On that 17th of June the prospect of never being strong again, came definitely before me. I looked at it very deliberately & fully — what it would be never to speak or sing or even write for Jesus, but only wait in quiet isolation & weakness, a burden to dear ones whose own burden I would like to bear, for years, perhaps for life. That this was not a mere improbable fancy is proved by my sister Miriam having written the very words "she will be a chronic invalid" — on or about the same day.

But as I looked, I wondered at His great goodness to me in thus proving to me that He had answered my prayer.:

"Take my will: it shall be Thine

~~It shall~~ ~~be~~ ~~no~~ ~~longer~~ ~~mine~~

for I could not, did not, feel one quiver of shrinking from the prospect, not a fear, not a regret, not a choice in the matter. It was all "of course." — of course He would be "with me alway"; of course His grace would be sufficient, of course it would be all best & happiest, His will must be always sweetest & dearest. And as for service; that was altogether my Master's affair, not mine at all — He could do, & should do what He would "with His own". I had the sweetest possible communion with Him about it, & felt, naturally enough, altogether lighthearted, for all that would have been too heavy for me was put & left in His dear hands. I seemed perfectly dead to any possible sense of anxiety or care about the future; & the present, even with fever & pain & languor was what I would not have exchanged with any one's.

Next day, June 18. was indeed much to be remembered. In the morning I was hardly so well, very weak, & with that indescribable sense of being "ill

look all right! And so it did! It was not that I went to look whether it was so, but simply to see that it was so! When next my sister M— came into the room, she was surprised to find me dressed. I assured her I was ever so much better, & should not be the worse for getting up, but did not tell her what reason I had for saying so. I found that half-unconsciously, I had yielded to a temptation to wait & see & not tell what the Lord had done for me till time had proved it, by no relapse occurring. As soon as I detected this unbelief, I felt thoroughly ashamed of it, & forthwith "burnt my ships" by telling the whole, trusting to the Lord to make it good."

And of course He did. Next day I was downstairs, & three days after went to

felt able to pray for recovery, or even for mitigation of pain. More than once I thought I ought for the sake of others to try & ask it, but invariably it seemed as if the Holy Spirit checked my prayer & changed it into — "No! Lord Jesus! I would rather leave it entirely with Thee, & not even ask, do just what Thou wilt with Thy child — just what Thou wilt." Now however He seemed to say to me that the time was come to ask for recovery. But I told Him that I did not want to ask unless He gave me the prayer, & that if He did I should expect His gracious & direct answer. Then He at once took away all the barrier, & put the prayer into my very lips. I prayed it, not as my prayer at all, but as His! Then I asked Him "What about the answer" watching & wondering what He would say, nolet — (I will watch to see what He will say unto me." Hab: II. 1.) & told Him I felt He had given me faith to be healed when He would. Then came — "I am the Lord that healeth thee!" with startling emphasis on "healeth". I literally started & held my breath! Surely, He Himself had said it! Then a sudden temptation, I believe from

This manuscript account was written on three sheets of paper, each sheet folded once in the middle. Thus on the first sheet, pages 4 and 1 are on one side, and pages 2 and 3 on the other side; on the second sheet, pages 8 and 5 are on one side, and pages 6 and 7 on the other side; on the third

Satan himself, — to think it was only a common act of recollection of the familiar words. But I did not stop to attend to this, but asked Him if He would condescendingly confirm it to me, if He had indeed "spoken to my heart". Instantly He did so, for again & again the assurance rang, out in my heart, in such a way, that I could not, cannot, possibly doubt that it was "Jesus Himself" — "I am the Lord that healeth thee." I thought if ever He gave a marvellous oppa= =tunity for exercise of faith, here it was. So I praised Him & told Him I would & did take Him at His word. And I did, & of course I was healed — for I saw that "healeth" was not merely "will heal", so I began to expect to find myself actually healed. This communion had been so absorbing, & intense that I had forgotten pain & discomfort, but now a pause seemed sent, that I might calmly

realize the healing. It was real & complete! I examined my own sensations — it was a total change, no pain, no feverishness, no sense of being ill anywhere, much less "all over". The question of restoration of strength had not been touched upon, it seemed quite apart from that of cure, & neither prayer nor faith had been given me for that; thus I proved the more literally, how exactly it was "according to my faith", for though well, I was very weak. After a little while of praise, & then a sort of hushed rest, I thought, "As I am healed, I may just as well act upon it!" I had not intended to rise at all, unless perhaps just to have my bed made. But I got up & dressed! The very first thing I did was to go to the glass and look at my tongue, which had been very bad, expecting to see it

Winterdyne!

From that day to this, July 26, I have never had another hour's illness, but have gone on slowly gaining strength, with no greater drawbacks than a common cold & a little neuralgia.

The Lord's hand is still upon me in gentle restraining, for though much stronger I am still quite unequal to ordinary physical or mental exertion, & it will evidently be a long time yet before I am able for "work".

I shall not be surprised to find that others were praying very specially for me at that time. One distant friend, I know, was led to very special & fervent prayer for me at the very time. It seems to me that "the prayer of faith" which "shall save the sick" must be "not of the will of the flesh, nor of the will of man, but of God"; & that in this direction lies

Valley of Lauterbrunnen with the Staubbach.

This is the frontispiece color print with Frances' handwritten caption, and to the right is a page in which she drew an alphorn and wrote the notes played on the alphorn, in F.R.H.'s handwritten Swiss Journal "Encyclical Letter, specially for the benefit of Maria, Ellen, & Frank 1869." These were her sisters Maria V. G. Havergal and Ellen Havergal Shaw, and her brother Francis Tebbs Havergal. See page 149 of this book.

F.R.H. travelled to Switzerland five times in the years 1869–1876, wonderful visits for her. She was utterly fluent in French and German, and nearly fluent in Italian, and she could communicate very well with those whom she met. Her letters back home while she was there are so rich, true gold, and many of these were posthumously published by her sister Miriam in *Swiss Letters and Alpine Poems* (London: James Nisbet & Co., 1881), reprinted on pages 277–366 of Volume IV of the Havergal edition. She wrote an "Encyclical Letter, specially for the benefit of Maria, Ellen, & Frank 1869" in a bound journal volume, with several prints or photographs pasted on pages, and flowers and ferns taped on several pages, a very beautiful journal. She wrote *The Mountain Maidens*—"A Mountain Cantata"— for her family (see pages 1059–1062 and 1183–1190 of Volume IV of the Havergal edition for more context). Francis (Frank) Romer (1810–1889) was a partner of Hutchings and Romer, the primary publishers of Frances' own music scores (see pages 1484–1485 and 2315–2393 of Volume V). This was published in 1874 or possibly earlier: this music score was advertised in the periodical *The Musical World*, in the issue for October 17, 1874.

PENSION WENGEN.

See page 334.

This was the frontispiece to the original book Swiss Letters and Alpine Poems. See pages 220–222 of this book.

Swiss Letters

and

ALPINE POEMS.

BY THE LATE
FRANCES RIDLEY HAVERGAL.

EDITED BY HER SISTER,

J. MIRIAM CRANE.

London:
JAMES NISBET & CO.
21, BERNERS STREET.

pages 328-329 of Swiss Letters and Alpine Poems by Frances Ridley Havergal (London: James Nisbet & Co., 1882)

Seulement pour Toi.

Only for Thee, only - solely, wholly

Words and Music by F. R. H.

Que je sois, O cher Sau - veur, Seulement à Toi!

O that I be - May I be, O dear Saviour, only (wholly) Thine!

Soit l'amour de tout mon cœur Seulement pour Toi.

Be the love of all my heart solely for Thee.

Je re - viens à mon Père, Seulement par Toi,

I come back to my Father only through Thee,

Ma con - fiance en - ti - ère Veut être en Toi, Seulement en Toi.

my confidence entire wants to be in Thee, only in Thee. solely in Thee alone.

Le péché, Tu l'as porté
Seul, seul pour moi ;
Et Ton sang Tu l'as versé
Seul, seul pour moi.
Toute gloire, toute joie
Sera pour Toi ;
Et l'espérance et la foi
Seront en Toi,
Seulement en Toi.

Aujourd'hui, mon cher Seigneur,
Acceptes-moi !
Toi seul es mon grand Sauveur,
Toi seul mon Roi.
Tous mes moments, tous mes jours
Seront pour Toi!
Jésus, garde-moi toujours
Seulement pour Toi,
Seulement pour Toi.

Que je chante, et que je pleure,
Seulement pour Toi !
Que je vive et que je meure
Seulement pour Toi!
Jésus, qui m'as tant aimé,
Mourant pour moi,
Toute mon éternité
Sera pour Toi,
Seulement pour Toi !

The sin you bore
alone, alone for me
and Thy blood Thou hast shed
alone, alone for me:
All glory, all joy
will be for Thee,
and the hope and faith
will be in Thee,
only in Thee.

Today, O dear Lord,
accept me.
Thou alone art my great Saviour,
Thou alone my King
All my moments, all my days
will be for Thee.
Jesus, keep me always
only for Thee,
only for Thee.

May I sing
O that I sing and that I weep
only for Thee!
that I live and may I die
only for Thee!
Jesus, who hast so loved me,
dying for me,
All my eternity
will be for Thee,
only for Thee.

July 23, 1876

Jesus only, Jesus ever, Jesus all in all. Luke 7:36-50

Matthew 4:1-10 Proverbs 3:5,6 Matthew 22:37-40

par Frances Ridley Havergal
en Suisse; écrit pour et chanté par
les Suisses pauvres à lecture de Bible
de l'après-midi Dimanche, 23 Juillet 1876

By Frances Ridley Havergal
in Switzerland; written for and sung by
some Swiss peasants at a Sunday afternoon Bible reading.
July 23, 1876

329

328

See page 218 of this book.

PREFATORY NOTE.

THE world-wide interest excited by the writings and "Memorials" of my lamented sister, FRANCES RIDLEY HAVERGAL, has led her family to think that such of her letters as I have been able to collect, written to her home circle from Switzerland, will be acceptable to her many admirers.

Some willl feel pleasure in mentally revisiting the sublime scenery she describes with such vigour and simplicity; and others will be interested in observing how unconsciously these letters illustrate her enthusiastic nature, her practical ability, and her ardent desire that every one should share her earthly pleasures and her heavenly aspirations.

JANE MIRIAM CRANE.

OAKHAMPTON, NEAR STOURPORT,
October 20, 1881

CONTENTS.

These images were imprinted on the hard cover of the original Nisbet edition of Swiss Letters and Alpine Poems.

SWISS LETTERS.

I.

ENCYCLICAL LETTER,

SPECIALLY FOR THE BENEFIT OF MARIA, ELLEN, AND FRANK.

May 31, 1869.

AFTER raining and roaring all Friday, and nearly all Saturday, the weather smiled out on Sunday, and promised for a beautiful passage on Monday, so we started from Dover this morning in good spirits. I have no notion of waiting till I am too ill to stir, before making myself comfortable; so I made a regular nest in the lee of a deck cabin with a shawl for a mattress, carpet bag for pillow, pile of tarpaulin for back rest, hat off, and cape of waterproof over my head and pinned under my chin in sister-of-mercy-looking style. Then I lay down, and as rain seemed imminent was covered with a tarpaulin all but my nose. "You will be walked over, Fanny," says M. L. C.; "you don't look like a human being!" H. C. did not look much more like one I opined, for he was cased in a tarpaulin coat down to his heels, with a hood which stuck up in two stiff points, leaving little of his physiognomy visible but his venerable beard.

So we joked each other for the first half hour, which was in all senses smooth sailing; then sleep was suggested; then kind inquiries were exchanged; after that, silence; after that, well, we won't talk about it, as it does not belong to the pleasures of memory.

Poor J. M. C.! "Is that lady going to die?" asks H. C. of the steward.

"Oh dear no, sir; not yet awhile," says he; "but you'd much better have all sat still up here."

"In ten minutes, sir," says the steward. That keeps up our spirits; sea trials can be borne that long. But a quarter of an hour passes, and we ask again. "Not much longer now, sir; ten minutes or so will take us in." So we get unbelieving and give up asking. At last we *are* in, and happier in mind and body, rather!

A most uninteresting rail ride, leaving Calais 1.15, arriving at Brussels 6.30. Hotel de l'Europe, in Place Royale. Table d'hôte speedily, at which we chattered with a Swiss gentleman, who "could afford to be generous," as M. said, and praised the Rhine astonishingly, far more than I could, who have only Scotland to compare it with.

After this, the lady who was "going to die" in the morning proposed going out to see what could be seen in the lovely evening light; so the three went, and I stayed to rest. For this piece of prudence I had a reward. Very soon a pleasant Belgian maid came in, with her white frilled cap tied under her chin. She asked if I was not well, seeing me on the sofa. I explained that I had had a long journey from England. She asked how it was that England was all surrounded by water, she had heard so, but could never understand it. My explanation led on to more talk, and she told me of a fearful illness she had last year when "la maladie" was raging in Brussels. This was a nice opportunity to speak of Him who "healeth all our diseases." She seemed thoughtful, and so interested that she stayed talking half an hour. She told me how near death she had been; she did not know it at the time, but when she had since thought of it, "that one must die, and all alone,—" and she finished the sentence with a most expressive shuddering gesture. Evidently she felt the ceremonies of her church were not enough to give peace in death, nor in life either; for when I appealed to the feeling, certain to exist even if denied, that the heart is not filled, that it has a craving for *something* that is always at the bottom *unsatisfied,* even when things are smoothest and brightest, she looked almost startled at hearing her feeling put into words, and said most sadly and earnestly: "*Mais oui, mais oui, mademoiselle, mais c'est vrai, cela!*" She promised me that she would pray for the Holy Spirit. Poor girl! she will have no earthly teacher. After she was gone I marked all I most wanted her to notice in a French St. John's Gospel, and gave it her next morning. She seemed pleased, and promised to read it. In marking it I was struck with what I have so often felt, viz. that when one reads any part of the Bible with anything special in view, it is wonderful how much seems to bear on the particular subject, as if written on purpose. So it was that every chapter seemed full of just the very teaching poor Victorine needed, the satisfied thirst, the promise of eternal life, the teaching of the Holy Spirit, and all through "Jesus only," all pointing to Him and to none other for peace and salvation.

June 1. FROM BRUSSELS TO OBERCASSEL.

We had no sunshine for the lovely Verdre valley, but the evening was exquisite. H. C. and the others stayed to see Aix and Cologne, while I went on to see Fraulein Krämer, at Bonn, where papa stayed the winter. They were heartily delighted to see any one who could bring news of him, "the best man in the whole world, so through and through good, who had left a blessing which had rested on their house ever since." Then I walked down to the Rhine; the stream was very full and strong, and the colouring vivid as we left Bonn; the Rhine a delicate silver blue, the east bank golden green, houses and walls almost scarlet in the evening glow; then beyond the low sunny shore rose the Seven Mountains in deep cloud shadow, soft dark blue sharply outlined against the pale clear sky. As we neared Obercassel, the red rocks of the Rabenlei caught the last of the sunshine.

The pastor was waiting for me, and in a few minutes I was besieged by eight of his olive branches (by way of mixing up peace and war!). I went to bed at ten; but we had talk enough to fill a book, so as I cannot record all, I shall record none.

June 2. OBERCASSEL.

Of course I have had the whole history of the war from a Prussian point of view.[1] The gist of it is that Prussia had no alternative but to allow itself to be *put upon* and *sink,* or to *put upon others* and *rise,* and that it was only natural to choose the latter. Denmark was a naughty obstinate child, which must be punished; Hanover, ditto. Pastor S. says that all the strength and patriotism of Prussia lies in its Protestantism; that the Catholics are an absolute drag upon both, sympathising openly when they dare, but secretly always and everywhere, with Austria.

In the afternoon we drove to Heisterbach, a lovely ruined apse of a monastery in a little glen on the south side of the Seven Mountains. It was quite warm enough for the usual German plan of taking coffee under the trees. Here we had a talk over church matters. The pastor's impression is that the great rationalistic vein is being rapidly worked through in Germany, and that the ferment is nearly over; that in this respect the English are a few years behind, and are now giving more weight to German theology than the Germans themselves are doing. Then we had a stroll through the beech woods, poor Theodor keeping up with us on his crutches. He has had a year of terrible suffering, ending in amputation; he is expecting his new leg this week, and hopes to return to the university in the autumn. He is a first rate *student-specimen,* full of fun, and no end of snatches of all sorts of songs *apropos* of everything, yet with abundance of talent and sense and feeling beneath it. His father read me a touchingly beautiful little poem which he had written on his last birthday in the midst of his suffering.[2]

The girls sing all day long, with various fraternal accompaniments. I heard Agnes singing simply magnificently, and on going to her found her preparing some young potatoes in a basin on her lap all the time, while Theodor was playing for her! It was characteristic. She sings very like Sarah Conolly, and with great spirit and expression. My godchild, Adelheid, has not yet had lessons, but sings numbers of duets and trios very nicely.

After supper the pastor read us "Otto von Schütz," a Rhine poem by Kinkel. We worked, and Theodor, Paul, and Franz sat in great delight, listening to their favourite poet. These young Schulzeberges all follow their father's tastes, and enter into everything poetical, musical, and intellectual, most eagerly. They are exceedingly attached to each other and to home; in this respect they are a perfectly ideal family. Agnes told me that Hermann's distress at spending his first Christmas away from home was something grievous, and Paul is already dreading his own possible absence next Christmas.

June 3. OBERCASSEL TO BINGEN.

Coffee at 7.30, then the household assembled for prayers. First we sang my favourite chorale of years ago, "Ach, bleib mit deiner Gnade";

then all sit with folded hands and slightly bent heads while the pastor reads a verse or two and a short comment, something like Bogatzky. This is generally all, only on special occasions,

---

[1] This was the Austro-Prussian war of 1866, which terminated at Sadowa.

[2] Dear Theodor fell asleep in Jesus after several weeks' great suffering, in January 1870.

birthdays or festivals, is it followed by prayer. But this morning the pastor closed the book and folded his hands and prayed; we all remain sitting, only the head is bent a little lower and the eyes closed. Such a sweet, loving, earnest prayer it was, specially asking abundant blessing both for the present journey and for the whole journey of life, "for her who has again filled our house with grateful joy": these dear Schulzeberges are one and all most loving and kind. Then we all went down to the Rhine to meet the boat coming up from Bonn. The pastor, Agnes, and Adelheid came with us to Königswinter, to make acquaintance with the rest of our party.

It promised well for a fine day, the sun shining through a soft mist that suggested more beauty than it hid. But that only lasted till we had passed the Seven Mountains, and the rest of the day was grey, so that we had only form and not colour; the difference between this and my last view of the Rhine was just that between an engraving and a painting.

There were very few people on board, the season has been late and cold. We got into talk with a most queer looking, keen eyed, elderly man, who spoke English with a strong strange accent. He was German, but had lived many years in London, and was going for a holiday to Frankfort. He seemed to know "all about everything," and was an odd mixture of shabbiness and gentlemanliness. Presently he brought his daughter, and introduced her, I think with a little pride. Oh such eyes! neither English nor German, dark, soft, beautiful, a perfect picture. She was very quiet and retiring, all the more fascinating on that account, with a gentle, sad expression, lighting up when she spoke into a very sweet smile. We decided they must be Jews; and later in the day, when better acquainted, I asked her if it were so, and was almost sorry I did, for she coloured deeply and answered "Yes!" in a shy, reluctant tone. So I made haste to tell her what an interest it was to me to find that she was of that noble race, and said I could wish that I too were of Jewish blood! That seemed not only to relieve, but to astonish both her and her father; and he said, in a bitter tone, "You stand alone; other Christians feel very differently towards us." Then we had a long talk in German. He said he honoured Jesus of Nazareth: "He was a wonderful man, and a very beautiful character, and had wrought a wonderful work in the world through His marvellous insight into human nature and adaptation of His teaching to the times. But as for His being God!" and he finished the sentence with just a look, which spoke more contempt for the idea than words could have done. I replied that I saw no alternative between His being all that He claimed to be, that is *God,* and being a liar and impostor. We argued frankly for some time, and not at all unpleasantly; he was quite willing to listen fairly, and never replied captiously. The girl was listening with her soft, sad eyes, so I broke away from argument and spoke to the hard old Jew what I wanted *her* to hear, just about the love, and tenderness, and sympathy, and all-sufficiency of Jesus; tried simply to carry out:

"Tell them what you know is true,
Tell them what He is to you!"

Afterwards the old fellow was very anxious that I should come to Frankfort. I was "a friend of Jews," and as such would be heartily welcomed by himself and his friends, and he would like to show us all he could, especially of the Jews' quarter. As we were not going there, he gave me his London address, and a most cordial invitation to call if I possibly could.

We also made acquaintance with a German-American, "travelling scientifically," and a Prussian soldier with a Königgrätz medal, overflowing with national pride.

The vineyards rather spoil than improve the scenery at this season, they are in the potato garden stage. Still the Rhine is the Rhine, and it is very lovely even under a dull sky. As we came on shore at Bingen, about forty schoolgirls went on board and instantly formed on deck and struck up "Am Rhein," the very pretty Rhine song, singing it right well in three parts.

Oh the luxury of sitting out in the hotel garden to write! We are close to the river, and the garden is full of roses, and has a long terrace entirely arched over with green; it is so delicious to sit here and rest, and not be in a town! I have (with permission) gathered splendid roses and white syringa, just for the pleasure of gathering them. H. C. and the M.'s are gone to the vineyards.

June 4. Bingen to Heidelberg.

We have come into full summer at once, a hazy heat, just relieved by an occasional light river breeze. After breakfast we went up to the Burg Klopp, a scrap of a ruined castle commanding a grand view of the Rhine valley. M. sketched, and we loitered about and enjoyed ourselves. Then we came down into the town, and hearing music went into a church. It was the Feast of the Heart of Jesus, and there had been high mass early, and now service again at 10.30. A fine solemn chorale was being sung, the congregation joining lustily. Oleander trees were set down each side of the church, and the whole altar end was decorated with flowers, both growing and gathered. While we stood just inside, relays of children, led by uncommonly pleasant-looking sisters of mercy, came in, dipping in the holy water and crossing themselves as they passed. One lot of toddling wee things could hardly reach the holy water, so the *sœur* made a dash at it and sprinkled it over them all, and hurried them in, cutting the ceremony short.

We left Bingen at 12.20. The rail to Mayence is not striking, but one gets some nice peeps of the river. At Darmstadt we had half an hour to wait, so ran into the town, which is cheerful and pretty, with wide streets and wonderfully long avenues. We passed a guard-house, so H. C. walked up to the soldiers and began making signs and talking English to them to their great amusement, till I came up to interpret. We asked if their helmets were not very hot and heavy, so one instantly took his off and handed it to him with great politeness, and another or two had medals to show. We had just time to see the Grand Ducal Palace, which looks like a great hotel, and then got back to the train. The rail to Heidelberg is extremely pretty, running under the range of hills which bound the Odenwald. To-day the sun added all its charm to the green and gold and shadow on the wooded heights and tempting ravines which broke the range at intervals. At the entrance of these valleys a picturesque village generally lay, with gardens and gable and a church tower all complete.

At Heidelberg we put up at the Prince Charles. Being much too late for table d'hôte we had to dine separately. M. left dinner ordering to us. H. C. would not say what he would like, so I told the waiter we wanted "*dinner*," and to bring anything, whatever they happened to have. So in about three quarters of an hour we sat down and *dinner* began. When it would have ended I don't know; but after having soup, salmon, roast beef, tongue, cutlets, and a queer preparation of duck and olives, we thought we had had enough, and declined with thanks the couple of fowls we were to have eaten, and the salad and stewed cherries, and ditto three remaining courses. The waiter was afraid we were not pleased, but we explained to him that our capabilities were not unlimited; he said some English were not satisfied when they had gone through the whole menu! I shall not hear the last of this dinner; when they want to do it in style "F. shall order,"—they will say.

We had an evening stroll over the bridge and along the Neckar, not far, for we were tired, and M. L. and I go upstairs at 8.30, and potter about and write our journals.

June 5. Heidelberg.

A most delightful morning, spent at the castle. The way up is steep enough, but all overhung with green, which would beguile any ascent for me. The castle has a rich sunny look, being built of red stone, which is warm and full of colour without the least brickish effect. It was altogether beyond my expectations, whether as to extent, beauty of detail or of whole, or as to the lovely situation. It is a perfect combination of far and near, the splendid ruins and luxuriant foliage close at hand, the quaint town below with river and bridge, the vineyards and wooded heights opposite, the Neckar valley with its sharp turns soon closing the view to the east, and then the wide reach of plain to the west, green softening into blue distance and bounded by the dimmest grey outline where the mountains of France are *hinted*.

We sauntered about *ad libitum,* and simply enjoyed ourselves; tonics and salvolatile are nothing to lying under a tree with nothing to disturb one but birds and pretty beetles, and knowing that there is absolutely nothing to do for the next two hours but look at the green and the blue around and above. In the afternoon M. was done for and decided not to stir; so H. C. took M. L. and myself in a carriage up the valley of the Neckar among lovely wooded hills, reaches of cornfields, steep red rocks quarried here and there, and the river constantly winding and forming new pictures. We went past Neckargemünd to Neckarsteinach, where while the horses were watered we did the correct thing, and took coffee in the garden overlooking the river, for which we paid twopence each! I asked the driver many questions, and he was civil and communicative, and recommended an excursion to Schönan to-morrow. I said "No, not to-morrow!" "Ah, yes," he said, "I had forgotten, you are English, and the English do not go excursions on Sundays." I was glad to hear that this is an understood thing.

Of all the noisy places I ever was in, this is the worst. Certainly till two a.m. the natives kept up chattering, whistling, shouting, and singing, and when I looked out at five a.m. the market place was all in a buzz, and buying and selling had begun again. "Do the Germans ever go to bed at all?" I said. "*Some* of them do I think," said H. C. very gravely and rather doubtfully.

June 6. Sunday at Heidelberg.

At nine a.m. I went to German service in the large church close by the Prince Charles. The Catholics have the choir, and the Protestants the nave; but there is a division between the two, so that it is almost the same as separate churches. The sermon was from the gospel for the day, "And they all with one consent began to make excuse"; it was not remarkable. But the singing! When after a short prelude the first chorale burst out, it went through me, and I only wished all my Leamington friends could have been there to hear: dignified, solemn, grand, massive, the very antipodes of some of the flimsy rattling church music at home. It was just the difference between a cheap ball dress and coronation robes, or better, a musical embodiment of the mighty world-upheaving Reformation as compared with the effervescence of a revival in its least hopeful form. The organ is played full, and all sing, so it is very slow, and a gallop would be impossible; but then each chord is so rich and perfect that the ear requires time to enjoy it, and the general effect is most elevating, the very majesty of praise. I can hardly imagine what my German friends would say if they heard the Te Deum raced through, presto, to the tune of "The heavens are telling," the utter barbarians they would think us, and the profanity it would appear to them!

It was very hot in the afternoon, and M. L. and I found a

quiet corner in the castle grounds, where we rested a long while and enjoyed being away from the clatter of Heidelberg, where we shall never recommend any one to take a *rest*.

We went to the one o'clock table d'hôte, and speculated as to what Maria would have done! For had we dined apart it would have made extra work, and yet the table d'hôte was as un-Sunday an affair as possible, with a band playing most of the time in very good style, beginning with the overture to "Tancredi"! A little girl came round with flowers, a young gentleman sitting next M. L. took a tiny bouquet of roses and pinks and laid it by her plate. He did not speak English, and we had quite a talk in German. He was of Italian parentage (though of German abode), and had all the proper accompaniments of dark handsome eyes, musical voice, and courteous manners. He wanted to arrange some excursion for us in the evening, but yielded politely at once when we declined. Presently he offered me his card, "Romeo Ghezzi"; I had not mine at hand, but what did much better, my Leaflets. So I chose out "To whom, O Saviour, shall we go!" and gave it him, saying that was my card, having ascertained that he could read, though not speak, English. He read it slowly all through, asking me the German of two or three words he did not know, and then put it in his pocket book. He seemed a little taken aback at the style of thing I fancy, but was too polite to make himself less agreeable for it, and for the few words with which it was followed up.

June 7. Heidelberg to Freiburg.

Oh, we were so glad to get out of Heidelberg in spite of its surrounding beauties; it seems to possess some peculiar acoustic properties whereby all sound is magnified. Every footstep reverberates, every voice echoes, and a passing carriage might be a pack of artillery or a fire engine at the least. We started by the Baden railway, our route being south with a wide plain to the west, and wooded ranges on the east, all day. Finding we could get three hours at Baden-Baden, we turned off the main line at Oos. The heat was intense, and we took a carriage at once to the Trinkhalle. In front is a splendid open saloon, the inner wall covered with paintings on large panels. Within is a superb hall exquisitely decorated, in the centre a fine column with a base of flowering plants, from among which the waters hot and cold come out in little fountains. We passed on through shady gardens to the maison de conversation; the tastefully decorated ballroom has the most superb chandeliers I ever imagined, their masses of crystal festoonery glittering with prismatic hues even in this subdued light. Through an opening in the mirrored wall we came upon a novel scene, a large green table surrounded by perhaps sixteen silent players. The banker or leader rapidly laid down cards, flung coins to various parts of the table, swept them in with a little money rake, now and then

saying "Le jeu est fait," which was followed by a sweep of the money; there seemed no play in it. In another room we saw the roulette table; only men were there, no ladies.

After a lunch of chicken and ices we ran up a little height above the Trinkhalle, and got a good general view of the place, which is pretty enough; lying among these wooded hills. At three p.m. we left for Freiburg, and the country became more beautiful as we neared it; but the dust neutralized the enjoyment. Surely there could have been no dust in Eden! it must be part of the curse.

After our arrival at the Zähringer Hof, we sauntered out, and thought Freiburg charming. Half way round the town are forest-clad hills, broken by lovely valleys, stretching away into the Black Forest. On the other side the soft purple outlines of the French mountains told grandly under the sunset. A rapid mountain stream, alternately flooded and dried up (as we heard), crossed our path, making white noisy dashes over little rocky barriers. It comes from three sources in the hills above, and so is named the Dreisam.

It is an additional interest to this tour that H. C. travels agriculturally; I shall get quite up in comparative crops, and so forth. We stopped to talk to a pleasant honest-faced man working on his own ground, and he gave information about lucerne, and fodder, and Indian corn with apparent pleasure, especially when I told him that Mr. C. had an English country estate and liked to know how a German one was managed. He had vines too, and we noticed the difference in foliage; some vines, having large plain leaves with only three divisions and hardly serrated at all, bore the Johannisberger grape. They were in blossom. "Smell it" he said, and verily "the vines with the tender grape give a good smell."

H. C. is very amusing to travel with, he throws himself so thoroughly into everything. It is great fun interpreting for him, not that he always waits for an interpreter; he talks English to the natives quite complacently, and they make very good guesses as to what he wants, and signs go a long way.

June 8. Freiburg to Basle.

Soon after breakfast we went to Freiburg cathedral or münster, in 12th and 13th century architecture. The spire is 380 feet high, of most delicately beautiful openwork, the airiest tracery imaginable. The variety of gothic pattern in the parapet work is quite a study in itself. We had intended going to Steiz, a splendid drive through the Höllenthal (Valley of Hell), issuing in the Himmelreich (Kingdom of Heaven), so I wonder it was not called Valley of Purgatory instead; it is a sort of circumstantial evidence that the aborigines were not Papists. From Steiz we were to drive next day to Schaffhausen, but as thunderstorms blew up we went on by train to Basle instead. Our window in La Croix Blanche at Basle looks on the Rhine, which is here a beautiful blue green, inclining to silver in the light and emerald in the shade; it is flowing swiftly, and breaking white against the piers of the bridge. Opposite are quaint, many windowed, steeple roofed houses, the cathedral and other towers, and gardens and trees overhanging the river; above these, grey and purple folds of cloud-curtain, within which lightnings are playing and thunder is growling. But, once for all, let me remind you that I do not intend to write what Murray gives much better; and that my journal is only a prattle of individual reminiscences, of no interest to any but amiable and affectionate friends.

June 9. Basle to Neuhausen.

I had just time to stroll over the bridge and set foot on Swiss soil for the first time, and then off by rail. For two hours it was the prettiest line we have yet seen, constantly close to the Rhine, and the valley was wide enough to allow of a fair view on both sides. The river grew gradually narrower, and at Rothenburg it was compressed into a narrow gorge, down which it thundered dark, and white, and mighty. Actually the station was placed exactly where we had apparently the best possible view of the cataract, with some old towers on the opposite bank, a quaint bridge just above, and a background of lovely wooded hills. From Waldshut the scenery was tame, and one could rest one's eyes without compunction.

At Neuhausen, three miles from Schaffhausen we went to the Schweizer Hof, and asked for rooms fronting the Rhine, but hardly expected the *vision* when the waiter opened the glass doors and ushered us on to our tiny balcony. It was a full front view of the falls of the Rhine, 380 feet wide by 50 or 60 feet high, the hotel grounds alone intervening between us and the river. The falls are a mass of sparkling white, broken by two or three tree-covered rocks; about four we set out to see them, by winding, shady paths to the railway bridge above the falls, which has a footway. It was fascinating to look down at the wild rapids, sheets of glasslike transparency flowing swiftly over rock tables, then a sudden precipice below, water which might go down to any depth, only that you are not looking down into darkness, but into emerald and snow, mingled and transfused marvellously, and full of motion and power and almost life. Then we went up to the castle of Laufen, and saw some fine Swiss paintings by Jenny, a pupil of Calame of Geneva (now dead), the greatest Swiss landscape painter. But the view from outside was unapproachable by any artist; and we descended from point to point, getting new impressions of what a waterfall *can* be, at each. At one we had a rainbow in the highest spray, arching the whole fall; at another a new rainbow hung over the lower part, seeming to rest upon the utter restlessness behind it. I felt it was perfectly impossible for

any words to convey a tolerable idea of the falls, as seen from the rocks close beside them. The rocks beneath them are not a smooth ledge, but broken and varied, and thus the water is thrown into a chaos of magnificent curves and leaps infinitely more beautiful than any single chute could be, water against water, foam against foam. You look up and see masses, mountains of white, bright water hurled everlastingly and irresistibly down, down, down, with a sort of exuberance of the joy of utter strength. You look across and see shattered diamonds by millions, leaping and glittering in the sunshine. You look down, and it is a tremendous wrestling and sinking and overcoming of flood upon flood, all the more weirdly grand that it is half hidden in the clouds of spray. Only one cannot look long, it is so dazzling, so intensely white, every drop so full of light, that the eye soon wearies and memory has to begin her work. Oh, if one were only all spirit! We came across the Rhine in a little boat just below the falls, and were thankful to rest in our charming hotel.

June 10. Neuhausen to Zurich.

After breakfast I could not resist a fling upon the piano, and among other things played the Wedding March. Presently after we were told there was a wedding breakfast in the hotel that morning, the last unmarried lady in Neuhausen, said our informant; there were sixty not long ago, but the fifty-nine were already married and done for. We saw the wedding party come in, from church I suppose; the bride, a handsome dark-eyed girl, looked radiant, and beamed out smiles with the kisses she was bestowing most graciously on a bevy of lady friends. It was great luxury to sit on the terrace overlooking the falls, and scribble my journal under a shady tree; and, when that was done, I jotted some verses which have been haunting me. The text was sent me lately; I never noticed it before. How strange it is what treasures we miss every time we read!

DARKNESS AND LIGHT.

"What I tell you in darkness, that speak ye in light."—Matthew 10:27.

He hath spoken in the darkness,
　In the silence of the night,
Spoken sweetly of the Father,
　Words of life and love and light.
Floating through the sombre stillness
　Came the loved and loving Voice,
Speaking peace and solemn gladness,
　That His children might rejoice.
What He tells thee in the darkness,
　Songs He giveth in the night—
Rise and speak it in the morning,
　Rise and sing them in the light!

He hath spoken in the darkness,
　　In the silence of thy grief,
Sympathy so deep and tender,
　　Mighty for thy heart relief.
Speaking in thy night of sorrow
　　Words of comfort and of calm,
Gently on thy wounded spirit
　　Pouring true and healing balm.
What He tells thee in the darkness,
　　Weary watcher for the day,
Grateful lip and life should utter
　　When the shadows flee away.

He is speaking in the darkness,
　　Though thou canst not see His face;
More than angels ever needed,
　　Mercy, pardon, love, and grace;
Speaking of the many mansions,
　　Where in safe and holy rest
Thou shalt be with Him for ever,
　　Perfectly and always blest.
What He tells thee in the darkness,
　　Whispers through time's lonely night,
Thou shalt speak in glorious praises,
　　In the everlasting light!

We left at 1.15, and came on to Schaffhausen and had a run into the town; the cathedral is the plainest barn that ever bore the name, "A Methodist meeting!" opined H. C. The rail from thence to Zurich was very pretty, giving glimpses of the Rhine, which seemed to get greener and greener. We drove through Zurich in an open carriage, and H. C. remarked on its very prosperous appearance. I reminded him that it is Protestant. Presently we passed a private carriage with some very sleek well-to-do looking steeds. "Protestant horses, I suppose!" said he.

Not wishing for the dawdle of five o'clock table d'hôte, we dined alone in a side saloon tastefully decorated, and set off with a few paintings of Swiss scenery. As we sat in peace and silence, a band commenced in the large saloon to my intense delight, the effect softened by the closed doors which barred the table d'hôte clatter, and only let sweet sounds through. It was very superior to the Heidelberg band; I never heard better light and shade, or more gradual and delicate diminuendos, except at the festivals, and to have it all to ourselves in such quiet was something delicious.

Then we walked in the garden, which stretches down to the lake, our first Swiss lake! It was too hazy for the distant mountains, but the nearer scenery was soft and lovely, the lake very still, and delicately tinted with green and purple, while the dipping sun caught the scarlet oars and *really* snowy sails of numbers of bright little boats. I intend systematically to let the towns alone and reserve myself for the beauties of nature; one

gets knocked up if one tries to do everything; so I shall always rest (as now) while the others are gone into any town. I am always better for a rest, and enjoy the views all the more for sacrificing the architecture.

June 11. Zurich to Berne.

M. L. and her father went for a walk at 6.30 a.m. The whole day was cool and hazy. We left at ten and reached Berne at two by a still more beautiful line than the last; and though we have seen no snow yet, we passed near a group of sharply peaked mountains unlike any we have yet seen in our lives. I had a talk with an old Swiss gentleman from Winterthür, chiefly on music. He had been in England several times, and knew a very musical set personally, Joachim, Piatti, Benedict, and others. He was evidently really musical. He had been to some of the English festivals; but catch any one speaking the German tongue giving a good word to any English music! "Yes, they were pretty fair, but the English were all infatuated for large orchestras," which he considered a great mistake; "it was impossible to get perfect light and shade from five hundred performers." And the Handel Festival itself had made no other impression on him. I am glad I have not arrived at that pitch of musical cultivation! We went to see the bears in the afternoon, and had great fun with them; the largest literally laid himself out for our amusement, catching the cakes lazily as he rolled about on his back.

Berne is quite the most novel and utterly foreign town I have seen, the streets arcaded like Chester, with bright red or orange cushions in every window seat, which touch up the grey stone effectively and complement the bright green venetian shutters. We ought to see the Alps from our windows at the Berner Hof, which command a fine view even without them; but it is hopelessly misty.

June 12. Berne to Thun.

At last! About five a.m. M. L. crept quietly to the window, and I woke as she passed. "Anything to see?" "Oh yes, I really do believe I see them," she said quite solemnly. Of course I was up in a second. The sun had risen above the thick mist, and away in the south-east were giant outlines bending towards him as if they had been our mighty guardian spirits all night, and were resigning their charge ere they flew away into farther light. Anything less ethereal and less holy they could scarcely be; the very mist was a folding of wings about their feet, and a veiling of what might be angel brows, grand and serene. It is no use laughing at "fancies"; wait till you have seen what we did from the roof of the Berner Hof! The effect was the more striking as we had scanned the southern horizon the evening before with glasses, and not a vestige of mountains could be seen; and now these lofty, shadowy sentinels stood where our senses had told us there was nothing but sky, not even cloud, tall and majestic, far out-topping the green hills in front. The vision did not last long; it seemed to melt into light rather than into mist.

We took a morning train to Thun, and got letters and luggage, and rooms with the very perfection of a view, at the Belle Vue, rightly named. It was the pleasantest hour I ever spent in a train, for the Alps were visible soon after leaving Berne, and every minute we were seeing more and more of them, and of the marvellous glisten of the glaciers. In the afternoon we took a boat for a two hours' sail on the lake, and saw the Jungfrau and Mönch and Eiger in delicious restful leisure; and the mountains looked at leisure too, so still and mighty and unapproachable by any human bustle and hurry and ferment. So now the dream of all my life is realized, and I have seen snow mountains! When I was quite a little child the idea of them took possession of me; at eight or nine years old I used to reverie about them, and when I heard the name of the snow-covered Sierra de la Summa Paz (perfect peace), the idea was completed, and I thenceforth always thought of eternal snow and perfect peace together, and longed to see the one and drink in the other. And I am not disappointed, not in the very least; they are just as pure and bright and peace-suggestive as ever I dreamt them. It may be rather in the style of the old women who invariably say "it's just like heaven" whenever they get a comfortable tea meeting; but really I never saw anything material and earthly which so suggested the ethereal and heavenly, which so seemed to lead up to the unseen, to be the very steps of the Throne; and one could better fancy them to be the visible foundations of the invisible celestial city, bearing some wonderful relation to its transparent gold and crystal sea, than only snow and granite rising out of this same every-day earth we are treading, dusty and stony.

June 13. Sunday at Thun.

And rather an ideal Sunday too, calm and bright and quiet, and with "beauty all around our path." I went to the German, or rather Swiss, service, guided by the "sweet bells jangled," though not "out of tune," only out of all order and rhythm, as continental bells always are.

The Swiss punctuality, which so far we have found perfect, extended to the service, for though I was in full two minutes before the organ began, not half a dozen came in after me, and the church was full. More than half the feminine part were in costume; I looked over the hymn with a velvet bodiced, white sleeved maiden. It was an old favourite of mine: "Praise ye the Lord, the mighty King of glory." Then the preacher read the eighth Psalm, which was his text. The first part was on God's glory in creation; he worked up a rather eloquent rhapsody into the climax: "And who of all on the face of the earth should so

praise God for the splendour which He has poured out upon His works as we Swiss, in this our blessed and beautiful fatherland!" The old man said it with a patriotic emphasis worthy of a son of Tell. After service the whole congregation lingered for quite half an hour in the churchyard, which commanded a magnificent view on all sides up and down the valley, for the church crowns a little round hill standing alone. Many went to different graves and gathered a flower or adjusted a creeper. The inscriptions were chiefly on little brass plates, brightly polished, on neat iron standards three or four feet high; the greater part were verses of affectionate remembrance, or passages of well known chorales, but there were many Scripture ones too. On one side were several English graves: one was to Frances Hatfield, aged 15; it had been beautifully arranged, but now the little railing was rusty, and the rosebush was straggling, and the weeds were rank at its foot. Perhaps there are sorrowful hearts in England, to whom that little foreign grave is very dear.

The English service in the evening was very pleasant and quiet, a nice little sermon on "When ye pray, say, Our Father," etc., from the chaplain, Rev. E. Venables, son-in-law of Frank's godfather, to whom M. introduced herself next day.

June 14. Thun to Interlachen.

A day of considerable variation as to plans, the morning being stormy; but as the sun came out in the afternoon we took the three o'clock steamer to Interlachen. But before we were two miles down the lake it commenced pouring, and soon the steamer seemed to be charging a rampart of fog, any view being hopeless, and we continued rushing through the wild storm till we landed at Interlachen, and were safely omnibused to the Jungfraublick, the highest hotel in Interlachen (which has the reputation of being hot and close and sleepless). Here we are perched on a terrace looking down into the valley, with the Jungfrau looking down upon us between two steep wooded hills, shining out of grey clouds every now and then like a sudden smile, with that wonderful intensity of whiteness which to me gives a totally new force to "whiter than snow." And I see too how perfectly the evangelists complete each other's description of our Lord's transfiguration raiment (St. Matthew says it was "white as the light," St. Mark "exceeding white as snow"), for this Alpine snow is light materialised and snow etherealised, it is a combination of the impressions of each. I came across "solidified hydrogen" the other day, which rather astonished me; but now I seem to have seen solidified light.

June 15. Interlachen to Lauterbrunnen.

We looked out upon a morning view of grey driving cloud, where mountain summits ought to have been, with glimpses of snow on heights which were certainly bare the evening before. But a wet morning enables one to pay off arrears of scribbles and stitches, so we wrote letters and sang duets and chatted with an agreeable English lady who was pedestrianising with her brother. Table d'hôte in a superb saloon, every chair carved, and all else in proportion. We sat next four Germans. Foreigners call the English unsociable, but not once as yet (except the Italian at Heidelberg) has a single foreigner addressed us for the sake of sociability; we have always spoken first, and so to-day. One gentleman was evidently superior and cultivated, with a positively brilliant flow of language; he was discussing the various construction of different languages, and then varieties of German construction, and gave fluent and clever illustrations of each. After rain, sunshine; so we set off at four in an open carriage to Lauterbrunnen in a perfectly transparent atmosphere. Fancy nine miles' drive up a deep valley, hills six or seven thousand feet high on each side, wooded wherever trees could get root, and where not, rocky and precipitous, between them at each opening views of snowy mountains glittering in brilliant light; below, a wild stream, the Lütschine, rushing in one perpetual downhill of rapids and little falls; every now and then a silver thread of a waterfall gleaming out on the farther side of the valley, or a broad riband of one dashing down the nearer side to our very feet, to be crossed by a little bridge, then the whole picture "grounded" with all shades of the freshest, brightest green, still wet with the morning's rain and canopied with vivid blue. And at every turn coming nearer to the Jungfrau, "Queen of the Alps," which fills up the valley in front, and only hides herself again when we get too close under her silver throne! Was not this "something like"?

It struck me again here, as in Scotland last summer, what marvellous lavishment of beauty God has poured upon the details of His works. For here, in the presence of these culminations of earthly magnificence, scenes beyond what we ever saw before, if the eye dropped and rested on the very ground it was just as beautiful in its proportion as if there were no other loveliness for us far or near; ferns, and flowers, and grasses, and mossy boulders, and tiny streams, every square foot being a little world of beauty. One item in these minor charms was the luxuriant way in which the firs had sown themselves, thousands of wee fir trees springing up on banks and among rocks, some standing alone in green tiny gracefulness, others growing in the prettiest little miniature groves you can imagine. I never saw firs growing this way anywhere else; they were like kittens to cats, so very pretty and petable.

Near Lauterbrunnen we passed under tremendous bastions of rock as the gorge narrowed in; and then saw the long waving veil of delicate white mist, and needed no telling that it was the Staubbach. We walked on to its foot, and H. C. irreverently suggested what a firstrate shower bath it would be! I should not mind trying, it comes down so temptingly and fairly, not nearly so substantially as in its picture. We walked a mile or more up the valley, enjoying the evening sunshine on the Jungfrau, and its shining and most pure Silberhorn and other white peaks before us. And just as we returned, and the valley was darkening, lo "the afterglow," which I so much wished to see. Rosy gold, or golden rosiness, comes as near as I can give it; but words of any sort are not much use. One more effect was still in reserve: when we came up to our room, the crescent moon was shedding a pale holy glimmer over the snow, and the sky behind it was no invisible purple or neutral tint, but a most ethereal blue, which I never saw *at night* before and do not understand.

June 16. LAUTERBRUNNEN TO MÜRREN.

To open our eyes upon the Jungfrau itself before one even raised one's head from the pillow was very like a dream! At nine we started, all on horses; the creatures had lively heads, and were very knowing and cautious in picking their way. "Mine is a most stupid beast," says H. C., "and a great deal more afraid of breaking his knees than I am." We did not consider this conclusive as to his stupidity, and think it must be rather advantageous to ride such "stupid beasts" up and down such break-neck places. The road to Mürren was to take us over the *top* of the Staubbach, which was rather incomprehensible, as the sides of the valley look nearly perpendicular, and a good part is *absolutely* so. But a path developed itself by degrees up an unnoticed ravine, a series of tremendously sharp steep zigzags and shelves over precipices, and crossings of wild little burns, about one-fourth torrent and three-fourths waterfall. When we got to the Staubbach we dismounted, and scrambled to the very edge from which it takes the one leap of 925 feet sheer down into the valley! The guide was a little anxious, and kept warning us to hold fast by the small trees; a slip on that "mossy bank" would have been too awful to think of.

After this, though still very steep, the path was easier, lying chiefly through fir woods, the slope being so great one wondered how they could grow at all, and the *tops* of tall trees were close below us. At every turn, as we rose higher and higher directly opposite the Jungfrau, she seemed to grow grander and grander, and we began to realize her stature. Tremendous precipices rise like Titan walls out of the valley, then rock and snow struggle for predominance, then snow prevails, and the Silberhorn rises in one smooth curved cone of pure unbroken white, and the real summit towers still higher behind, dazzling even against the dazzling sky. "It will be finer yet," said our guide, Perther. "How can that be?" "You will see!" It was true; when we finally came out of the forest the Jungfrau was still the centre, but only the centre point of the grandest of even Alpine amphitheatres. On her right the white Monk and the Eiger with its perpendicular side in full view, on the left the

Rothhorn, Breithorn, and Sparrenhorn, in stately range; glaciers, avalanche tracks, snowfields, snow-walls, and everything Alpine that ever one heard of, all in one view. And all the while "the grass of the field" was as lovely as ever at our feet, sheets of flowers around us, all delicate and tiny and exquisite, just the other pole of the world of the Beautiful.

M. seemed to know them all, though there was an immense variety. We gathered gentianellas large and small, and it is heresy to have no raptures for them; but for a perfect eye-delight of blue, commend me to the Alpine forget-me-not, I never saw anything prettier in shape and colour; and they grew as buttercups do with us, by millions, like turquoises, only alive and positively smiling.

We reached Mürren at eleven. It is a little village to which there is no nearer or easier way than that by which we came, and all the people want has to be carried on mules. "But they don't want much," said the guide; "they have wood and cows, and they don't need anything else except coffee and flour and a little cloth." There are too few for a church, so they come all the way to Lauterbrunnen on Sunday, except in the winter, when they are entirely snowed up for weeks together, and even Lauterbrunnen is in pretty much the same predicament.

We set off on foot to get as much higher as we could by goat paths, and soon came to little patches of snow which did not seem in the least to interfere with the flowers, but glittered on in a "happy family" sort of way among the forget-me-nots and saxifrage. But clouds were gathering on the heights and coming lower rather suddenly, so we were all in very good time for the table d'hôte at one o'clock; we thought we ought only to have feasted on goat's milk and such like, at 5465 feet above sea level! Before we rose it was sleeting fast, and beyond ten yards nothing was visible. The next hour or two was decidedly lively; there was difference of opinion as to weather, so some started and others waited, but everybody had taken atmospheric champagne, and was in the best possible spirits, and all crowded to the door to see each departure and get as much fun as possible out of it. Two good tempered and most plucky English ladies actually set off to the Stachelberg, some miles farther and a good deal higher, and did not care whether they saw anything at all, so that they went. Our German acquaintances from Interlachen were there, and rattled away most amusingly. One of them, a sweet looking girl, reminding us a little of Emily B., took H. C.'s fancy greatly and made herself most agreeable in pretty broken English. One of the gentlemen said both his ladies had fallen in love with him, and he must have shared in the fascination, for he offered H. C. two tickets, freeing a great deal of Italian travel, including fare from hence, to use, if he would do him the honour to accept them! In the midst of it two Liverpool gentlemen came down from the Schilthorn, for which they had started at three a.m.,

leaving their wives to amuse themselves with watching them through a telescope, and it was rather fresh and interesting to hear them talk of being dug out of the snow only two hours before, and other small adventures of the kind. We waited longer than most, and at last set off in heavy rain and sleet. We looked down on formless cloud and fog, with no outline and no colour, filling an indefinite abyss, now and then shapeless openings disclosing darker cloud. We intended walking down all the worst places, but it was so wet and dirty, and the guides were so reassuring, that we stuck valiantly on till we reached the Staubbach again. Here we dismounted and raced down the hill. The guides having pronounced H. C. "a right good rider," he had been allowed to go forward alone, and we found him comfortably settled at the hotel. "Why, papa!" said M., "did you ride down all those staircases?" "Why not?" said he; "the horse had got to come down, and he might as well take me on his back as not!"

June 17. Lauterbrunnen to Grindelwald.

A very lovely but uncertain looking morning, which finally cleared up radiantly. We got photographs from Yakob Huggler, a clever peasant carver, at his stall of alpenstocks and knick-nacks close by. The drive to Grindelwald was much such another as that to Lauterbrunnen, with the Wetterhorn instead of the Jungfrau before us and the valley rather wider. The twin Lütschinen streams meet at its entrance, and we followed the black instead of the white Lütschine. On nearing Grindelwald, the driver told us we should see the lower glacier round the next corner, so we looked eagerly and saw—a dirty mass of stones and grey mud, among which peered out dirty ice and snow, worthy of the Black Country itself. So we concluded it to be a delusion and a snare, and went to the upper glacier instead, which is much purer. We had a lovely walk and ride to its foot, which is like a very wild and wide sea beach all barren and desolate. We scrambled a little way up the sloping ice, but the man in charge urged us not to go on, for the edge of the glacier itself, high above us, was constantly breaking away and it was very dangerous, so we came down after inspecting a snowball big enough to have killed half a dozen people, which had fallen only a few hours before; we attacked it and ate avalanche, and found it very refreshing. We went into an ice grotto, blue and glistening and transparent, but too evidently neatly hollowed out and not natural, so I did not feel frantic about it.

It is immense fun meeting all sorts of people over and over again. Already we have so many acquaintances that we meet some everywhere whom we had met before. To-day the amusing heroines of the Stachelberg came to our inn, and on our way to the glacier we saw our German friends coming down a bank upon us; one instantly hoisted his cap on his alpenstock and waved a merry welcome. Last night some Thun friends walked in to Lauterbrunnen, and we improved the acquaintance. The chambermaids are a speciality of mine, and interest me; they are always pleasant and obliging, and generally very intelligent girls. They all say they can never go to church, as Sunday is usually the busiest day; they always seem extremely pleased to be chatted with.

June 18. GRINDELWALD TO INTERLACHEN.

Thick and threatening all day, and we drove to Interlachen early. On the way we passed an alpenhorn played by a small boy not nearly so tall as the horn was long. It is fastened on a pivot, so as to command different echoes. The alpenhorns are best at a little distance, which softens the tone and assimilates it more nearly to the flute-like sweetness of the echo, which seems a sort of fairy answer coming out of some magical hall in the rock. The strain oftenest repeated, and perhaps the most telling, was this:

The tone is very powerful, and the middle notes extremely mellow.[1]

We had aspiring ideas as to the Scheinige Platte, the nearest height to our hotel, 6000 feet; but clouds hung heavy all round, so we came down to a walk across the valley to Hohbühl. The afternoon also was not fine enough to be worth an excursion, so M. and I rested, and M. L. and her papa had a walk.

June 19. INTERLACHEN.

The weather settled our plans for us, as it rained nearly all day. In the morning, curious long soft white clouds went slowly creeping along the Scheinige Platte, "like great white Persian cats," said M.; and in the evening they assembled in force on the top, and came down in a heavy snowstorm. So we had a quiet day. Before settling to letters and work I wrote

EVENING TEARS AND MORNING SONGS.

"Weeping may endure in the evening, but singing cometh in the morning."—*Marginal reading of Psalm* 30:5.

IN the evening there is weeping,
Lengthening shadows, failing sight,
Silent darkness, slowly creeping
Over all things dear and bright.

In the evening there is weeping,
Lasting all the twilight through;
Phantom sorrows, never sleeping,
Wakening slumbers of the true.

In the morning cometh singing,
Cometh joy, and cometh sight,
When the sun ariseth, bringing
Healing on his wings of light.

In the evening cometh singing,
Songs that ne'er in silence end,
Angel minstrels ever bringing
Praises new with thine to blend.

Are the twilight shadows casting
Heavy glooms upon thy heart?
Soon in radiance everlasting
Night for ever shall depart.

Art thou weeping, sad and lonely,
Through the evening of thy days?
All thy sighing shall be only
Prelude of more perfect praise.

Darkest hour is nearest dawning,
Solemn herald of the day;
Singing cometh in the morning,
God shall wipe thy tears away.

June 20. SUNDAY AT INTERLACHEN.

The service for the Queen's accession was used at the English church with the Communion service. Text, Matthew 22:21, "Render unto Cæsar," etc. All was orderly and nice; moreover we had reasonable chants and no galloping. The evening service was at six; text from the first lesson. A showery day ended in a splendid evening, and when we came out of church the Jungfrau was glowing with that indescribable tint, golden snow with a touch of rose, shining out between two dark heights magnificent in purple and green and bronze, with a coronet of the fresh snow lingering on their summits, and the shadows of the western mountains darkening the fir woods of their base and sides. I overheard a little girl say, "Mamma, I think the Jungfrau would do to form the great white throne of God." *That* expresses it. Later we had quite a treat: an American lady, one of two couples who have sat next us at dinner, came down at my entreaty to sing. She gave Mendelssohn's "Oh that I had wings of a dove" very beautifully, and "But Thou didst not leave," and "Come unto Him." I was positively thankful for her music, as the news had just reached us of that horrid wicked bill having passed the Lords, and one needed a little soothing after that.[1]

Mutual acquaintances always do turn up; so, though I only know two people in all America, she knew one of them, Dr. Lowell Mason, and was distantly connected with him by

---

[1] The bill for the Disestablishment of the Irish Church.

[1] This is reminiscent of a postcard letter by Johannes Brahms in 1868 to Clara Schumann, in which he described hearing an alp horn (aplenhorn) melody in the Rigi area of Switzerland, used by Brahms at the start of the final movement of his Symphony No. 1.

marriage, and had been in his singing classes. She had greatly enjoyed English cathedral services, but thought it a great mistake to introduce anything of the sort into parish churches, or indeed into America at all; they belonged to the real old cathedrals, and should never be separated from them.

June 21. WEATHERBOUND AT INTERLACHEN.

Certainly the shortest longest day I ever spent! It poured from morning till night, but we resigned ourselves to it, and had a very pleasant day. A German gentleman asked H. C. to play chess, which he did; and I had two games also, and found him the best player I had ever met, and the most rapid; it was quite a treat to see his instantaneous pounce on the right man, and his unhesitating setting of it in the right place. He played again in the evening with H. C., and then with M. L. He also plays the flute, and I accompanied him for an hour or more. We had a good deal of music and talk in the evening. Mr. and Mrs. Fane, whom we met at Thun and Lauterbrunnen, make themselves very agreeable. Some German ladies, including a nice little girl, seemed delighted with the music and thanked me warmly. After I had sung "O rest in the Lord," a Scotch lady came and talked to me most refreshingly. She had just met Dr. Guthrie at Lucerne, and talked about the *Sunday Magazine*; and we got on so well that after a while I introduced "F. R. H." to her, whom she knew perfectly well, and gave me a hearty invitation to visit her at Falkirk.

The "portier" at the Jungfraublick is quite a character; he superintends arrivals, letters, and money matters, and sits in an office in uniform. I left my "Ministry of Song" downstairs one night, and in the morning I found the portier reading it. When we came again M. had put a *"pro bono publico"* copy in the reading room, and this he carried off likewise, and asked me if he might keep it till we left, as he could read English, and was so fond of poetry, and thought mine "most beautiful!" He said his wife had a pension near Geneva, at which Russians stayed; also he knew Longfellow personally and poetically, and admired him extremely in both respects, and knew many of his poems by heart, and quoted part of the "Psalm of Life," to prove his words I suppose.

June 22. INTERLACHEN TO GIESSBACH.

A bright though threatening morning, so a general exodus seemed to take place. We steamed down the lake of Brienz to Giessbach, and as my Scotch friend was on board we had another talk. She gave me a pretty thought: we spoke of cloud-shadows; "Yes," she said, "but they are the shadow of His chariot, for 'He maketh the clouds His chariot.'" We went to see the falls, which are very lovely, a whole series one above another, at least a dozen, and each a picture in itself; but just as we passed on a little wooden path *underneath* a splendid curved leap of

water, I became faint and had to turn back and go to bed. The others went to see them illuminated at 9.30, and seemed to think the effect very fine.

June 23. GIESSBACH TO MEYRINGEN.

A lovely morning, and I was able to get up in time for the eleven o'clock steamer to cross the lake to Brienz, and then we had a nine miles' drive along the valley to Meyringen. Although M. and I had both been invalids, curiosity and excitement seemed to do us good, for we ventured down a horrible and wonderful place, the "Finsteraar Schlucht," or "Black gorge of the Aar," which strangely enough none of our guidebooks mention, though we thought it worth going miles to see. It is a sharp descent, mostly by little wooden steps, into what at first looks like a lofty cavern, very narrow, the rock on each side hollowed out in most curious round or oval sweeps, with sharp jagged edges all bending over, and quite or nearly meeting overhead. It is full of the sound of rushing water, but we saw none till near the bottom, and then the witch-hole opens out upon the Aar, tearing along apparently from nowhere to nowhere, shut in by two awful walls of rock five hundred feet high, with just room enough below for the narrow strong river and a beach like the sea, three or four yards wide on one side, and the rocks overhanging so much that there is the merest little slit of sky. Said M., "We have got into Dante!" How we ever got up the stones and steps again I don't know; but we revivified with some red wine at a little auberge close by, and so got home; and I had a delicious sleep of nearly ten hours.

June 24. MEYRINGEN TO ROSENLAUI.

At last M. yielded to a chaise à porteur, inasmuch as the guidebook describes the first of the ascent to Rosenlaui as a "ruined stair two thousand feet long." We rode, and these Swiss horses would go up St. Paul's or the Pyramids apparently. After some time the ascent was less stiff, the path leading along the side of an upland valley, with the Reichenbach roaring below, and fine precipices rising straight from its edge on the other side; the last part of the way was level, and might have been any English valley with a brook at the bottom, but for the sight of the Wellhorn rising in front, with a glimpse of glacier through a cloud at its side. The Rosenlaui glacier is diminishing so rapidly that an immense basin of rock, which took us nearly half an hour to skirt, was full of ice only twelve years ago. As we returned we thought we should like a canter, and told the guide we would wait for him before the descent began; but he scorned the idea of being waited for, he liked a run as well as we, any pace was all the same to him. Whatever H. C. rides is sure to *go,* and my pretty grey four-year-old pony was quite of our mind as to a canter; but our guide was equal to anything, and raced and laughed and leaped the boggy bits with his alpenstock without regard for his limbs or lungs. We went round by the Reichenbach falls; and now for a piece of unmitigated heresy. I am inclined to class waterfalls among the good things of which one can have too much! I calculated on silence among these mountains; and instead of it, one has to shout to be heard above the noise. Every valley has its roar and rush of water, with a cataract every two or three hundred yards, leaping to join the chorus of torrents below, from the chorus of torrents above, and making one appreciate Wordsworth's line, which I used to think far fetched:

"The cataracts blow their trumpets from the steep."

All night long you hear it, and clearer and louder than by day. From our window at Meyringen five separate waterfalls were within sight and sound. It is a sad case of nerves versus poetry, and will go far to prove the truth with which a chaplain hereabout took my measure, his conclusion being that I was "very matter of fact, and had no poetry in me!"

June 25. Meyringen to Lucerne.

We chartered a return carriage from Meyringen to Lucerne with four horses, and built to carry ten persons, so we had room enough! This was again a fine morning, though hazy, and the passing magnificence of that drive over the Brünig, with the valley of Meyringen at our feet and the Oberland giants beyond, is one of the scenes least likely to be forgotten. Our midday halt at Sarnen and the glimpse up the Melchthal took one back into the old days, or rather into Schiller's revivification of them. The last ten miles lay along the lake of Lucerne, round the base of Pilatus; but it was not a clear evening, and my first impression was one of extreme disappointment. It was lovely no doubt, but on such a small scale compared to the Alps behind us, and I had given my allegiance so utterly to them, that I could not instantly transfer it to anything so different. Snow mountains are not less to me now than in my child dreams, and Lucerne is a town! so I did not take kindly to it.

June 26. At the Schweizerhof Hotel, Lucerne.

The weather seems settling at last, and it is fine and even hot. We were to do nothing to-day, and unhappily it occurred to me to go and assist at the practice in the English church, so we utterly wasted an hour and a half's sunshine in trying over tunes and listening to remarks of the usual calibre of amateur choirs. Somebody tried over a "new tune," melody meagre and entirely secular, running chiefly in thirds, and spiced up with absurd and unnecessary accidentals; and this was pronounced "simply exquisite"! And the rest to match.

Our table d'hôte was accompanied by a very charming string quartett. I subjoin the "Menu Musicale."

Soupe royale: to potpourri from Donizetti.

Salmon trout with Dutch sauce and potatoes: to a lively and pretty waltz.

Roast beef and lettuce: to a fine solid thing of Mendelssohn's.

Calf's head *en tortue*: to a set of rubbishy quadrilles.

Mutton and green peas mashed: to—silence.

Spinach and eggs *à la crème*: to Gounod's Berceuse.

Chicken and salad: to a plaintive and sweet violin air.

Lemon pudding: to Soldier's March in Faust.

Gateau Pithiviers and *compôte de pommes*: to a waltz by Strauss.

Dessert: to another waltz by Strauss.

We had a hot walk above the town, and a lovely soft view of the lake. Then we went to find the Lion of Lucerne, and when we came upon it I stood fascinated; not merely with the wonderful sculpture, but with the perfect effect of the whole thing. You come suddenly from the glare above, or the clatter of the road below, into a deep quiet nook, shut in by large shady trees with a wide opening in their foliage through which the afternoon sun falls upon the lion cut in the living rock. Close below is a dark pool in which it is reflected beautifully. The grey rock rises perpendicularly some little height above, and ends in a crown of acacias and drooping bushes and creepers.

A photograph of the lion gives no idea at all of the sentiment of the place, which is sacred and still, and almost solemnly beautiful. It is a memorial of Swiss fidelity, and a worthy one.

June 27. Sunday at Lucerne.

The English chaplain proved a great stick, or rather a *little* stick, so in the evening we went to the Scotch service in a Roman Catholic church. We had a nice sermon on John 15:27, and the simple, full evangelical truth we heard contrasted strangely with a great gold-lettered shield above the altar ("*Hilf, Maria, hilf!*") (Help, Mary, help!).

The cathedral bells here are grand, filling the air with confused thundering resonance, massive and almost awful, yet magnificently beautiful; a fit accompaniment to the majesty of snow mountains, in presence of which any other sounds of human production would be puny and impertinent.

One part of the Lucerne cemetery was most touching, it was set aside for the little children. Row after row of tiny graves, with loving sorrowing inscriptions, some with little white marble crosses simply twined with ivy, all with carefully tended flowers and shrubs proportioned to the size of the little graves.

June 28. Lucerne to the Rigi.

What could promise better? All the natives prophesying settled fine weather and a regular sunrise glow over mountains and lake, moreover the little cloud upon Pilatus which is supposed to make all safe!

We had a pleasant hour's sail to Küssnacht, and struck up with a clever and amusing man, a friend of Prof. Tyndall's, who travels with his eyes open as to physical science, and gave us a good deal of desultory but interesting information and observation in that line. The ride up was very pleasant, with a grandly widening horizon with occasional fine views of the picturesque outline of Pilatus. On this (north) side of the Rigi we see several lakes, especially Zug, blue as a harebell. For the last twenty minutes we change sides, and have the south view. The panorama from the very top is immense, but I do not count it among the impressions of my life; however our afternoon was delightful, strolling at leisure all about the top, gathering flowers and enjoying the views and the air. Heavy clouds hung over the distant mountains, but the sun was bright, and the general haze hardly made it less beautiful. Towards seven p.m. every one began to move towards the top, probably about two hundred people. Then came an excitement of hopes and fears for the sunset; would it clear, would the clouds rise, should we see the afterglow? No! The sun went down into a bank of clouds, and the Bernese Oberland did not reveal itself. I stayed a long while after, part of the time alone. Suddenly a cloud rushed up from nowhere and hid everything; in a few minutes it was gone again like a grey spirit, leaving no trace or trail, gone nowhere! Tremulous lightning was playing in a far-off low cloud towards Zurich, and once a quiver of light over the Alps gave hopes of a display; but all gradually calmed and darkened away.

June 29. Rigi Kulm to Lucerne.

At 3.30 a.m. a queer horn, woefully out of tune, played up and down the stairs and passages. We had arranged everything over night, to save every possible minute in the morning, and so were almost the first on the top, looking down upon an arctic sea, white downy undulations of cloud about two hundred feet below us, covering hills and lakes and plains in one billowy sea, out of which rose a few rocky islands, of which the Rigi itself was one, and Pilatus the most noticeable. The Alps bounded it like a shore, but hazy and clouded. The sun rose from a cloud, and was far too late in appearing to effect anything in the rose-tint line upon the mountain coast, but it did cast a stream of faint pink for a few moments upon the silent polar sea at our feet. In the bedrooms was a notice to "Messieurs les voyageurs," praying them not to take out blankets and bedclothes for the sunrise, which was not unlikely to put it into their heads. In spite of this there were three or four barefaced blankets, one worn by a lady. All the wearers, as I expected, spoke the German tongue.

The beds were not luxurious, notwithstanding spring mattresses and down quilts, for the sheets were cold and clammy, and horrid to a degree. "No wonder," said M. L., "when they dry them in the clouds; I saw them at it!" And when we passed the neat little hotel, Rigi-Staffel, at eight a.m. in a dense cloud they were hanging out sheets on lines for the benefit of the next comers. We had a three hours' walk down to Weggis entirely through cloud, with a chaise à porteur between us. Yet there was the lake below and mountains before us, and all sorts of beauty around us. Only we could not see!

June 30. Lucerne to Altdorf.

A very threatening morning, which gradually developed into a tolerable day, with pretty gleams on the shores of the lake; the higher summits were invisible. We walked through the two covered bridges, which have paintings in the roof of scenes from Swiss history, and then took the 9.40 steamer.

It is a very lovely three hours' sail by Brunnen, the Grütli meadow, and Tell's Chapel to Fluellen; then we drove two miles to Altdorf, and saw the fountains where Tell and his child stood, and went to the entrance of the St. Gotthard pass, returning to Lucerne by the same route; but I have not time for detailed description. I had my little "Wilhelm Tell," and read a few scenes, especially the Grütli one; but actually found it too exciting, and was obliged to give it up. I had no idea before what power that sort of poetry possesses.

July 1. Lucerne to Langnau.

A little sunshine early in the morning and evening, but otherwise gloomy and grey. We drove nearly forty miles through the Emmenthal, said to be the most fertile part of Switzerland, a very pretty country, but nothing distinctively Swiss except the houses with their enormously overhanging roofs and curious wooden coat-of-mail walls, little bits of wood nailed over each other with rounded ends. This is an unusual cross country route, and the Hotel Emmenthal was in striking contrast to the palace we left at Lucerne. The waitress looked amazed when we asked for extra spoons to attack our cupless eggs, and returned with one spoon for all of us! I like an out of the way place, and specially rejoice in not having to dress up for the evening. The Schweitzer Hof was too grand for me, and where there are so very many people one is far more isolated; moreover there was a tantalizingly good piano in a splendid saloon with just the right resonance, but it was too much even for my audacity to sit down to it, before fifty people at least.

July 2. Langnau to Fribourg.

A journey by rail, not specially interesting; and being cloudy, we could not see the Oberland as we ought to have done.

A very enthusiastic Swiss lady (an acquaintance of the Malans) raved about her Swiss mountains most charmingly. I like to find the Swiss appreciating their privileges. Our guard from Langnau to Berne appeared also quite alive to the beauties of nature. He came into the carriage on the way, and held up an awfully cut thumb, appealing to me for the chance of getting doctored. He had just had an accident with the brake; luckily I had a sponge and rag at hand, and made a tidy job of it for him. He was very grateful, and kept coming to us all the rest of the way to point out views and any places of interest. At Fribourg we had a fine evening, and a curious view of the deep gorge containing the old town, spanned by two long suspension bridges. These vibrate even to the tread, and a passing vehicle makes them almost swing.

A little before eight p.m. we went to the cathedral. M. had brought papa's "Forty Specimens of the Grand Chant" to give to the organist. Two years ago, when papa was here, he sent up his "Morning and Evening Hymn" (the one which is played backwards *or* forwards, and turns upside down) to M. Vogt, who introduced it forthwith into his extemporizations, and rendered it very appreciatively. So having received the little book which M. gave the verger for him, he very politely came to us and thanked M. for it. He looks about sixty, is short and stout, with a remarkable forehead and keen and full dark eyes. I asked him what he was going to play. He said: "First something from Mendelssohn, then a toccata of Bach's; after that," he added, with a look of scorn and wave of his hand, "something, more for the public" (*Etwas, mehr für das Publikum!*) Mendelssohn was a strange plaintive minor piece, a wailing of voices far and near, very striking. Bach did not come next, but a soft piece, I think extempore. Then came the Bach, unmistakably grand and masterly; and Vogt played it as if he revelled in it, as if he mastered it and it mastered him, which is a necessary paradox in true musical rendering. Then came the sop to the "Publikum," first Rossini's "Prayer of Moses" and then extemporization, introducing some astonishing thunder and showing off the ninety-seven stops, including a good deal of singing from the vox humana. The *power* of the organ is astonishing, and the pianissimo contrasts hardly less so. Still on the whole the Lucerne organ performance does not seem so very far behind, especially in the more perfect illusion of the vox humana, and in its more complete and natural thunderstorm. On these points we gave the palm unhesitatingly to Lucerne. There the thunderstorm was almost real, first the far off growl among the mountains, then the gradual approach, the moaning gusts of wind, the nearer rumble, the distant echo, then the sudden awful crash overhead, and the burst of rain, suddenly ceasing again; then, as the peals receded, a most perfect quartett was heard singing "Hanover," beautifully harmonised and in perfect chorale time, one could hardly divest oneself of the idea that it was really a vocal quartett, only just too far off to catch the words, which *must* be Psalm 104, "My soul praise the

Lord." As one listened the voices came a little nearer, the thunder died away into the faintest peals, seeming to come from behind the mountains, the wail of the wind ceased altogether, the voices died into a sweet lovely close, and then a most exquisite flute stop predominated in a concluding symphony of perfectly enchanting sweetness. We had nothing to compare with this at Fribourg; but, on the other hand, we had nothing at Lucerne to compare with the Bach toccata, either as to organ or organist.

One never gets perfection, or if one approaches it, it vanishes; and so here: we were rejoicing in the dreamlike, ideal effect of darkness falling upon the cathedral while the music was going on, shadows growing deeper, roof and aisle darkening into mysterious grand gloom, no light but a faint paleness through the tracery of the windows, one tiny lamp like a star near the altar, and a sort of veiled glimmer from the organ-loft just quivering up to the great pipes and suggesting a hidden source of life and power somewhere among them; it was precisely what one imagined as the right scene for such sounds,—when up stalks an odious old verger, with creaking shoes and a horrid flaring lamp, and lights two vile great candles, one on the pillar just over our heads and the other just opposite, right in our eyes! Such is life.[1]

July 3. FRIBOURG TO VEVEY.

Heavy rain and fog all day, through which we went by rail to Lausanne, imagining the Jura to the north, and Alps to the south, and the Lake of Geneva where the fog hung thickest, excellent practice for the imaginative faculty! At Lausanne we drove to the cathedral, a plain, awkward affair, but said to be the finest in Switzerland. (The Swiss have natural temples, and have troubled themselves little about architectural beauty in contrast with the Belgians, who have cathedrals instead of mountains.) It is fitted up with plain wooden benches, and must accommodate a large congregation. The sacristan said the attendance entirely depended on the preacher. There are five pasteurs, who preach in turn at this and the other churches, but there is only one service, and that at nine a.m. We came on to Vevey to the Hotel Monnet, which seems to combine the attractions of our previous favourites; and, as it left off raining for an hour, we had a little walk by the lake, and concluded it must be a perfectly delicious place in anything like ordinary weather.

---

[1] This was poor old Vogt's very last thunderstorm. A few days after we heard of a grand musical funeral service for the organist of Fribourg. We heard him on Friday evening, July 2; on Saturdays there is not any performance; on Sunday he played the usual services in his usual health; on Monday he died suddenly.

July 4. SUNDAY AT VEVEY.

To Swiss (French) service at 9.30 with M. The church commands a splendid view. The service commenced with the commandments read by a deacon or elder from the pulpit, followed by the gospel epitome of the two tables, Matthew 22:27–40. Then the pasteur went up and read a long string of banns, each written on a separate sheet, which he deliberately unfolded and folded again into envelopes, with all their family history on each side. No more Scripture was read except the text, "Thou art the man!" and the sermon was like most foreign ones, rather an oration than an exposition. The singing was in the old Scotch fashion, a precentor standing up in a little box under the pulpit, and roaring the tune just half a note ahead of the congregation. The tunes themselves were probably good old Genevan ones, very old church psalmody in style. The afternoon English service was quick and quiet; not remarkable.

Though a lovely day, the mountains were clouded, and the Dent du Midi never appeared till nearly sunset, and then the St. Bernard and Sugar Loaf appeared and vanished. Hotel Monnet has a flat roof with seats; it is five storeys high, so no one seems to think it worth while to mount. *Tant mieux pour moi!* It is delightful, and I spent most of my Sunday evening alone on it.

July 5. VEVEY TO MONTREUX AND GLION.

A splendid morning, and the white clouds so bright and soft that one would hardly quarrel with them for veiling the mountains, though as H. C. said, "they *were* obstinate." We took a boat to Clarens, three quarters of an hour over the *pearly* blue water, then walked up to the cemetery for the view. Here we remarked, as at Lucerne and other places, the very large proportion of comparatively young persons, more than fifty years being quite exceptional. Among the English and Russian graves the ages were still lower, and told of consumption; so many between 17 and 25, who probably came here for the mild winter and never saw another summer. From Clarens a lovely road took us to Montreux, where we again made for the fine view from the churchyard. After a rest and some cherries, we mounted the hill to Glion, a little village three quarters of an hour higher, and the view proportionally finer. We walked down and returned to Vevey by steamer. At the 5.30 table d'hôte I had a long conversation in French with a Swedish countess, handsome, polished, and very agreeable. She talked of Jenny Lind and her retirement from the stage; and said it was thought that Christine Nilsson might possibly follow her example. She described her as being like Jenny in firmness and high principle, and said that the Parisians thought her "trop sage et sérieuse," and that she better suited the English idiosyncrasy. Later in the evening I was playing in the nice little salon de conversation, when my countess came in and recognised the "Song without Words," and asked me for more. So I sang "Comfort ye." "That is fine music," she said; "whose is it?" I answered and explained. "Really! so that is from the 'Messiah'! I never heard it. The English are *passionnés* for Handel's music, are they not?" So then I played the overture to "Samson," and sang "Let the bright Seraphim." She admired both extremely; it was totally new to her; she had never heard Handel before, and thought he wrote chiefly church music! Yet she was thoroughly "up" in Mendelssohn and Mozart, and knew all the operas that ever were written apparently. And never heard Handel!!

July 6. VEVEY TO ST. GINGOLPH AND VILLENEUVE.

A spree! H. C. could not realize the fact that the opposite shore was seven miles off, and its mountains eight thousand feet high, and thought it would assist his realization to row across. But M. and M. L. don't like boats, so they decided to rest for the day, while I had no objection to anything and volunteered to go anywhere. Our little boat sported an American flag, and a pretty striped awning, which we were glad of as the sun was hot.

The mountains grew and grew, and seemed to get larger, much faster than they got nearer; so we began to take in the idea of the seven miles and the eight thousand feet. St. Gingolph is made no fuss about in the guidebooks, and consequently is not prepared for tourists as yet; but we have not seen many things more beautiful than the Gorge de la Morge at the entrance of which it lies. Our inquiry for saddle horses or mules or donkeys rather astonished the natives at the inn; but they were polite, as all the Swiss are, and sent post haste to a butcher who owned one donkey, and to somebody else who was supposed to have a horse. The messengers returned in a depressed state of mind; the horse could not be found at all, and the donkey was gone to the mountains. So we were obliged to walk, and set off up the gorge to a certain village *somewhere,* named Novelles, which we should reach if we had patience and perseverance.

The said virtues were exercised for about two hours and a half, and then were rewarded by a village and a most welcome auberge. At least that was the ultimate reward, but there were plenty of proximate ones. The valley winds up between mountains, wooded below, and grand precipitous rocks above, snow-wreathed and ice-creviced. The Morge, a wild, leaping, racing torrent, rushes down to the lake, forming the boundary between Savoy and the canton de Vaud. The path was steep but very lovely; visions of the lake at every turn to the left, and visions of the mighty rocks above at every turn to the right, both seen in a framing of luxuriant foliage. But it was dreadfully hot, and no vestige of human life appeared turn after turn.

At last the coming event cast its shadow before in the shape of a chalet, and some haymakers whom we hailed. In their musical-toned civility they told us the auberge was only ten minutes farther; and a good humoured Savoyard ran up and told us he was the "maître de l'auberge," and encouraged us along, chatting most cheerily. He introduced us to his domains in great glee through a rugged yard, and up what looked as if it led to a henroost, saying "Entrez, mademoiselle!" to a little dark kitchen with a pot hanging over a gipsy-like fire of sticks on a great hearthstone; then another and quite triumphant "Entrez!" to a "salon" beyond, with three little tables and six little benches. He scampered about, getting necessaries together, with the aid of his equally good-tempered but quieter helpmeet. First he produced a bottle of Swiss wine, then a loaf of capital black bread, and a plate with three funny little cheeses and one knife. On second thoughts he ran away and returned with a sharp-pointed pocket knife, which he deposited most engagingly before me. "Pour vous, mademoiselle; un *joli* petit couteau!" He offered an egg; and while it was boiling sent round the village for butter, *hoping* he could get some, but the butter was made half an hour higher up the mountain. H. C. seemed satisfied now that the eight thousand feet were no myth, for he "should have thought that walking three hours straight up hill we should have got to where they make the butter!" Presently my egg appeared in a little brandy glass, but a spoon had not occurred to him, and a cupboard had to be rummaged to find one. In course of time the butter arrived, quite superlative and only just churned, so we were in clover.

I catechized him next as to whether there was any mode of descent other than our tired feet. On this subject he was sanguine but mysterious. Mademoiselle might trust him, he would arrange, "tout irait bien," only a little time was necessary, his horse was gone to pasture. We were not particular I told him, a hay cart would do. He danced in and out to keep us quiet; it would soon be ready, mademoiselle would be charmed, she would laugh at his beautiful new carriage, she would remember it, etc. After one of these intervals he appeared in a clean white shirt, and told us in immense glee that the *horse* was nearly ready except a little glass of wine! He rushed into a dark lumber room and drew a glass from a little cask, then danced into the salon and filled his mouth with the remains of our bread and cheese, while his wife sewed a button on his wristband.

Outside the door stood, or rather lay, our conveyance. Its foundation was a hay sledge, two little wheels behind with two thick runners, joined by rough crossbars. On this our host had tied with ropes an old wine chest; across it was a plank, with a manifest bolster on it as cushion. Two long crooked sticks were tied to the runners for shafts. "Montez, monsieur, we will go like the chemin de fer, vous verrez!" So in we got; the plank and bolster being wider than the box, there was room enough to sit, while our feet converged to a focus of about twenty inches in the narrow bottom. He waved his cap to his wife, with whom he was evidently on the best of terms, and set off full tear, downhill. It was no use shouting "Doucement!" he only looked round and laughed, and tugged away at the shafts, over boulders and holes, and swinging round corners on the very edge of the deep gully, till really if we had not been incapacitated by laughing from either thinking or doing anything else, we should have been seriously frightened.

On retrospect, I can't think how we escaped with whole bones. I never felt anything like the jolting; our cheeks shook like jelly. H. C. said it was complete electrification. Our "horse" only stopped when quite out of breath and steaming with perspiration, eager to know how many minutes he had been, and pluming himself on his speed, and still more on his invention. He would have it patented, and send it to the next *Exposition* and make his fortune, and so forth, joking away his breath so that his next start was a trifle more moderate. As for admiring the valley (which *he* found time to do, waving one hand and giving an extra tug with the other, "Ah que c'est un beau pays, mais que c'est magnifique!") it was out of the question, all we could do was to laugh and hold on, and try to balance the machine.

About a quarter of a mile from the bottom, just as we were getting used to the said balancing, and our steed perhaps getting more careless, we were swung round a corner and over some unexpectedly large stones, when suddenly we felt a most queer giving-way, earthquaky sensation, and roared for a halt simultaneously. Just as the man contrived to stop, the whole concern came bodily to grief, *all to pieces at once* in a most surprising style, cords yielded, shafts broke, nails came out, and boards subsided into one shapeless heap, from which we extricated ourselves with nothing more than a bruise or two, laughing more than ever, for it made the thing so very complete to have such a proper and thorough break down, it was the only finishing touch it wanted. It was no use reconstructing the machine, so H. C. paid the man and wanted to dismiss him; he knew well enough the five francs for which we agreed before we saw the concern was more than the job was worth, so he proposed to go down to St. Gingolph to have a bottle of wine with us at his own expense, as a wind up of accounts! He seemed rather hurt at his kind invitation being declined, but soon got over it, and made his adieux, begging us to make his compliments to all at Vevey, and inform them what a firstrate carriage would be at their disposal if they would make an excursion to Novelles.

We got to Vevey just in time to cram our things together and set off by the evening steamer to Hotel Byron, another of these Swiss palaces between Villeneuve and Chillon.

July 7. Hotel Byron to Chillon and Bouveret.

Very hot and very hazy. Walk to Chillon, dungeons, oubliettes, hall of justice, and everything *à la carte;* every one knows it all. But no one told me one little thing, a surprise of colour. In the dungeons, at first seemingly quite dark, one's eye soon accustomed itself to the faint light through the tiny slits in the enormous walls, and then one perceived a most singular reflection from the blue lake on the grey vaulting, tremulous and delicate and curiously metallic, an effect impossible to convey in words.

After a broiling walk to the landing place near Montreux, we boated across to Bouveret on the other side of the lake, crossing the mouth of the Rhone. Leman lies in azure peace, utterly tranquil and innocent; all at once you are in the midst of a mighty wild brown roaring current. The boatmen say, "Don't be afraid, only sit still," and they pull with all their might. In a minute or two you shoot into uncontaminated, still, blue water again. The current is so impetuous, it flows thus unmingled for a mile and a half. It suggested plenty of analogies, but I have no time for them here. We landed and took a stroll at Bouveret, returning by boat to Hotel Byron, landing on our way upon the Ile de la Paix, the "little isle" in "The Prisoner of Chillon." Three poplars grow on it; I send you a specimen spray.

July 8. Hotel Byron to Martigny.

We went by rail thirteen miles up the Rhone valley to Bex, and I rather wished George Stephenson had never been born as we whisked through the grand scenery; however, it was a very hazy day, and perhaps but for railroads I should never have come to Switzerland at all! At Bex we took an open carriage, past St. Maurice and the Gorge du Trient, nine miles. The view up the valley must be magnificent, but the heat haze almost hid it; the side views were superb, of the Dent du Midi, 10,000 feet high, and of the Dent de Morcle, 9000. This Rhone valley, at least up to St. Maurice, is the grandest thing we have seen, next to my glorious Jungfrau.

In the afternoon we went up the Gorge du Trient, at each turn different and wonderful. The sun never penetrates some parts, and only touches any for about an hour. We came, said the guide, "juste au bon moment," sunshine bringing out the strange curves and angles in strong relief, and contrasting the exquisitely brilliant green of the ferns and bushes wherever they *could* cling, with the depth of shade of the caving rock, and the cold grey rushing torrent of the Trient. This gorge is nine miles long, but only passable by gallery for half a mile. After a scramble on the rocks outside, and a rest in cooler air above, we drove to Martigny.

July 9. Martigny to half way through Tête Noire.

Hot and hazy again; but we discovered that the haze belonged to the valleys, and the higher we rose the clearer it became. We took mules, and had a three hours' ascent to Col de Trient; then one hour's descent to Tête Noire, where we dined; then another hour's descent to the Hotel des Cascades, a little white inn facing a waterfall down a wild rocky gorge, close to the junction of two wild streams. This glacier water is a peculiar colour, which no word describes so well as Job 6:15, 16: "The stream of brooks which are *blackish* by reason of the ice, and wherein the snow is hid." You never see the same "blackish" look in any other water but these glacier streams; and "by reason of the ice wherein the snow is hid" is a wonderful touch of true and poetical description.

M. and I both heard the curious *latent music* of the water when our ear was pressed on the pillow, "just like a piano," she said, and truly! It really was like a distant piano playing a monotonous yet sweet melody, always nearly but never quite the same key of G, and harmony merely tonic and dominant in turn, a move of the head occasionally producing the subdominant!

July 10. Tête Noire, Col De Balm, Chamouni.

A day after my own heart! Breakfast at six, and start on foot at half-past. A lovely fresh morning, making the rather sombre valley bright and beautiful. After twenty minutes' walk the road took a slight turn.

"There is Mont Blanc!" shouted M. L., pointing to a little shoulder of white peering between the near hills and the Aiguilles Rouges, which closed the view ahead.

"Nonsense!" we exclaimed, but we hoped we were wrong.

"It is," she persisted; "clouds can't deceive *me; that's* Mont Blanc. I know it!"

A few yards farther settled the question; in the opening shone the monarch himself, up to his very crown, distant but majestic, clear and dazzling. And I knew that my allegiance must be transferred from the Jungfrau, that henceforth she was only second. Every half mile gave us more of the snow glories for which I have been absolutely hungering, more aiguilles, more shining whiteness. Mountains, real ones, are more to me than any other created thing; the gentle loveliness of lake scenery or forest, or pastoral picturesqueness, is delightful; but nothing sends the thrill all through one's very soul that these mountains do. It is just the difference between the Harmonious Blacksmith on a piano, and the Hallelujah Chorus from a grand orchestra. One day among the mountains is worth many of other beautiful scenery; I say *among* advisedly, for a far off view is not the same thing; it is the difference between *antic-*

ipation and *possession,* future and present. However beautiful a distant view may be, one wants to be nearer, to be *there*. It would be well if all instinct of anticipation were as true and as truly to be satisfied as this!

A rapid descent fronting the glacier of Argentière brought us to the village of St. Pierre at 9.30, after a walk of seven miles and a half with occasional rests.

After a decidedly severe déjeuner we set off on mules to the Col de Balm, which is just seven thousand feet high. Though clouds were thick on the mountains, and a haze filled the valley, the view toward Chamouni was magnificent. I might as well have sat backwards at once, for my head felt nearly wrenched off with turning it behind. About half way up we had perhaps the grandest idea of Mont Blanc, towering with an inconceivably majestic sweep of outline above everything else.

From the top of the Col de Balm, which is a *pass* over the lowest dip of the great mountain wall, we ought to have seen the Rhone valley and away to the Great St. Bernard; but on that side we only looked down and away into mist. After refreshing ourselves at the chalet, we wandered to some great snow patches just for the pleasure of walking into it on the 10th of July. M. said she should "eat some snow and then go to sleep on the gentianellas," which I literally did. The sun was blazingly hot, though the air was cool, and our cloaks were only needed for pillows.

After our rest H. C., M. L., and I went up a summit above the Col de Balm, which commands one of the most sublime and perfect panoramas in the world I should think. Here the grandest mountains in Europe are pressing close around you, a perfect abyss into the Tête Noire on one side, the perfectly graceful sweep of the valley of Chamouni on the other, aiguilles that defy the Alpine Club, glaciers between and below them, linking the winter above with the summer below, all one ever dreamt of alpine splendours crowded into one scene and oneself in the very centre of it, far above the waterfalls and the noisy torrents, far away from the chatter and clatter of tourists; what if one did see it at some disadvantage as to the list of peaks which ought to be visible? even with the cloud veil on her forehead, it was the most glorious revelation of Nature I have ever seen. And what was our *seat* here, up above more snow than we saw all last winter? A regular carpet of flowers, chiefly forget-me-nots, gentianellas, brilliant potentillas, violets, pansies, and daisies, and many lovely flowers I did not know. The grasses too were various and pretty. What an addition to the enjoyment of the *great,* the *small* can be! And there I wrote these lines.

Sunshine and silence on the Col de Balm!
  I stood above the mists, above the rush
  Of all the torrents, when one marvellous hush

Filled God's great mountain temple, vast and calm,
With hallelujah light, a seen but silent psalm.

Crossed with one discord, only one. For love
  Cried out and would be heard: "If ye were here,
  O friends, so far away and yet so near,
Then were the anthem perfect." And the cry
Threaded the concords of that Alpine harmony.

Not vain the same fond cry, if first I stand
  Upon the mountain of our God, and long
  Even in the glory, and with His new song
Upon my lips, that you should come and share
The bliss of heaven, imperfect still till all are there.

Dear ones! shall it be mine to watch you come
  Up from the shadow, and the valley mist,
  To tread the jacinth and the amethyst,
To rest and sing upon the stormless height,
In the deep calm of love and everlasting light?

It seemed a pity to lose the chance of a sunset behind, but it would not do to be benighted there and on Saturday evening too, so we rode quickly down[1] and took a carriage at Argentière for Chamouni, which we reached when the twilight was deepening into dark. From our window in the Hotel de Londres we looked out and saw the mountains marvellously beautiful with just the same sort of pale solemn light we saw on the Jungfrau at night. It was quite dark below except for the lights in the village; but up above against the dark sky, Mont Blanc, the Dome du Gouté and the Aiguille du Midi seemed robed in that singular holiness of light, utterly calm and pure, entirely celestial, which to both of us is more than rose tints and gold; there is nothing like it except the smile of holy peace on the face of one asleep in Jesus. Presently we saw a little twinkling on the edge of the glacier, and wondered what it was. On Monday we knew more about it. While we watched it, another little light, but purer and clearer, rose into the intense depth of blue between the Aiguille du Midi and the Rochers Rouges.

---

[1] As we came down the Col de Balm we heard a chorus of cow bells rising from the valley. Our guide said there were two hundred cows in the invisible herd, all wearing bells. The confused, pleasant, *quick* sound was very novel; and though the bells are various in pitch, all melted into one general musical effect, without any clashing of tones just as the song of many birds does:

  "The tintinnabulation that so musically swells
  From the bells, bells, bells, bells!"

                          —Edgar Allan Poe.

A little farther on we neared a tiny hamlet, and up above us came a wonderful tinkle, tinkle, tinkle. Presently a goat peered over the edge of a ridge and ran down followed by one hundred and twelve companions; they were not the least timid, and passed close to us, each one looking curiously at us, as if aware we were not *"du pays."* They were going home, and knew the way quite well.

You will know how a star can rise when you have seen it on a clear night, when a snow mountain seems its stepping stone to its place in the sky.

July 11. SUNDAY AT CHAMOUNI.

M. L.'s birthday, which she began by seeing Mont Blanc crested with sunlight before five o'clock in the morning. The services in the little English church were most refreshing. The clergyman, Mr. Cripps, of Nottingham, led the chanting and hymns without accompaniment, and every one seemed to join heartily, with an unusual proportion of men's voices. Both tunes and chants were judicious, such as all must know and all could sing. The morning sermon was on Isaiah 33:17: "Thine eyes shall see the King in His beauty, they shall behold the land that is very far off." The evening from Revelation 3:20: "Behold, I stand," etc. Both were extremely interesting and useful, with loving encouragement and earnest warning, such as one does not hear from every pulpit. The evening was radiant in rose tints, and when they had faded away we came in from the balcony and sang hymns with the clergyman and others.

July 12. PIERRE POINTUE AND PIERRE À L'ECHELLE.

A real fine clear day at last! We inquired about the twinkle on the mountain, and found it was the lamp at the little auberge at Pierre Pointue, the first stage up Mont Blanc; this was attractive, so we went. A remarkably steep ride through the forest, and then far up above it, brought us to Pierre Pointue in three hours. H. C.'s mules always *go*, though he does not appear to use any extra means, so he was there long before. M. L. and I have taken pains to acquire the mule language and its correct intonation; but all our Hu! Allez! Hupp! Carabi! Hui, hui! Allons! *Arrrdi!* is lost on them, and they pursue the even tenour of their way. Pierre Pointue commands a fine view of the Glacier des Bossons (a very fine one) and the snowy shoulder of Mont Blanc. We dismounted, and I had a real *bonafide* scramble an hour and a half higher up with H. C. and M. L. across the ends of snowdrifts, and right through torrents and up rocks and places you would not think feasible anywhere but in Switzerland. We rested and lunched with immense satisfaction on the rock called Pierre à l'Echelle because the ladders for the ascent of Mont Blanc used to be kept there before the Grands Mulets were set up with a hut. We were now about eight thousand six hundred feet high, and I at least was proportionately happy. It was marvellous how far up the lovely rhododendrons grow, but the forget-me-nots were almost as daring, and the Alpine ranunculus grew higher still, the special glacier flower, said Joseph Dévouassoud. It was a wild scene, the grim Rochers Rouges and Aiguille du Midi just above, the whole Dome du Gouté shining close beyond the great glacier,

an awful slope of snow and stones below us, and ever so deep down the Chamouni valley, which we must have seen as the birds see it.[1] On our way down our youngest guide, Aristide Couttet, proved himself a true boy in spite of his learned name, shortening his route by sliding down all the snow slopes anywhere near the line of march; it looked such fun I envied him; but though I "take kindly" to mountaineering, I am not advanced enough for snow slopes. We walked nearly all the way down from Pierre Pointue, as it was so steep for riding, visiting the Cascade du Dard on the way. So we really have been more than half way (in height) up Mont Blanc, and would have gone to the Grands Mulets had we been prepared for it.

July 13. LA FLÉGÈRE.

It was intensely hot, so we had a quiet morning for writing and resting. La Flégère was selected for a nice little afternoon excursion, only five and a half hours, starting at 3.30. See how we have improved! This is an hour more than our first mountain ride to Mürren, and that we thought a very trying day's work. The ascent is on the opposite side to Mont Blanc, and the whole chain should be visible, but unfortunately it clouded over long before we reached La Flégère, and we could only imagine how grand the scene would have been with the evening light full upon it. Still it was worth going, and we gained a better idea of the real height as we rose; it is impossible to realize the height of mountains from below, the higher we are the grander they look. Is it not so in other things? A certain proportionate elevation is essential to appreciation. We climbed above La Flégère, eagerly watching for the expected break in the clouds above the monarch, which did not come. Suddenly we heard a low roar ending in a grand crescendo, with a character of its own quite distinct from thunder, echoing along the whole chain, so that we did not know where to look for our long hoped-for avalanche! M. L.'s eye caught it just in time, rushing from the cloud upon the Aiguille Verte; we only saw a rising of white snow-spray where it rested. Twice more we heard the same curiously impressive sound, but not so loud or near. Barring the avalanche we reckoned this our least interesting mountain excursion.

July 14. MONTANVERT AND MER DE GLACE.

Our last *Alpine* day! Always excepting Mürren, the five days from Martigny to the end of Chamouni were the very es-

---

[1] If there were any birds to see it! But there is a curious paucity of them in Switzerland. We hardly ever saw or heard a bird of any kind. If we did, it was quite a thing to be remarked upon to each other. H. C. was always on the look out, he seemed to miss the birds and living creatures generally. Nature has devoted herself to the inanimate instead of to the animate; one never sees a wild living thing except insects, which quite make up as regards numbers and beauty; no game, no rabbits, nothing!

sence of our whole tour; getting up to Pierre à l'Echelle was the centre and culmination, but Montanvert was a capital wind up.

We started at 6.20, breakfasted at the auberge more than six thousand feet high, and then, with H. C. and M. L., I went across the Mer de Glace. We did not slip once, though we had the gratification of seeing two gentlemen tumble down. It feels queer for the first few minutes, but one soon gets one's balance and one's glacier feet. Only near the farther shore there are some decidedly interesting bits, where one has to walk along a ridge just wide enough to tread, with beautiful blue crevasses yawning on each side; if you slipped, on the right side you would go down a house-roof slope of ice first, and then into the crevasse, and on the left you would go straight down at once perpendicularly. Where the ice is blue at all, it is wonderfully blue, shading into an intensity and depth of colour no painting could exaggerate. But on the whole the *dirt* is annoying, and I cannot entirely respect the glaciers in consequence. The correct thing is to send the mules round to Chapeau on the farther side, but this seemed rather extensive, and involved the Mauvais Pas, so M. and the mules waited our return at Montanvert. But, once across, it stood to reason I wanted to go on, and bit by bit we approached the Mauvais Pas to my intense delight. It is a way, half staircase and half shelf, about a foot wide, round the face of a perpendicular rock overlooking the glacier, and at some height before reaching Chapeau, and looks most charmingly awful. It is not really dangerous unless one is disposed to be giddy, for there is an iron rope fastened to the rock all the way within reach of one hand, and with a stick in the other you cannot well come to grief if you step cautiously.

Of course this was quite irresistible, so down I went and back again, leaving Dévouassoud with M. L.; he had long ago given up looking after me, but presently a gentleman came up and wanted the guide to go with him, which he did by H. C.'s permission. We were rather amused at this. It was a pull to get back again to the crossing point, but it was worth coming, for we saw the pinnacles and pyramids of ice at the lower end of the glacier, and heard the constant fall of blocks and stones. "Always movement here," said the guide.

In re-crossing we diverged to see a bottomless-looking hole in the ice, from which rose a tremendous roar from the hidden river three hundred feet below, raving like an imprisoned giant. We had a shower during our walk, but this was all right, for we got some "effects"; it was specially fine when a few minutes' sunshine lit up the whitest part of the glacier near the ice needles, and a heavy cloud threw the opposite side of the valley seen just over the ice into the deepest violet shade. Just as we got back to the auberge it began to rain, and we waited two hours till it cleared.

On our way to Chamouni, I got Aristide Couttet to tell me the rules and arrangements about guides, which is all code and

tariff here, and he explained clearly and intelligently. But do not visitors sometimes go to the mountains without a guide? He answered just what I wanted him to say. "Oh yes, madame: but it is very foolish; they only lose their way, and it is very dangerous; accidents happen when they *will* go without one, but if one has a guide all goes well" *(tout va bien)*. "We have a Guide, Aristide; do you know who I mean?" "Oh yes, madame; you mean Jesus Christ, He is the best Guide." He seemed quite delighted to go on with the subject, which we did for some time. "One does not fear death if one has that Guide," he said; "He gives us salvation" *(Il nous donne le salut)*. I gave him some little Scripture papers; he glanced over them, and putting his finger on some verses about the Saviour (John 3:16 was one), he said *"C'est bien joli, cela!"*

The storms must be awful here in winter; we passed hundreds of great pines broken short off at the roots, or torn right up. Dévouassoud said it is most dangerous to pass the forests when they are laden with snow, if a storm rises. The evening was cloudy but pleasant, and we spent it on the flat parapeted roof. I gathered several flowers on the Mauvais Pas, and the guide gathered a plant he had never found before, but it had once been shown him by another guide. It is a little green thing, and as M. does not know it it must be rare.

Jos. Dévouassoud has been four days' excursions with us, and he asked us to write him a testimonial in his book, so I wrote:

> CAREFUL and gentle, respectful and steady,
> Always obliging and watchful and ready;
> Pleasantly telling, as children say,
> All about everything on the way;
> Good for the glaciers, strong for the steeps;
> Mighty for mountains, and lithesome for leaps;
> Guide of experience, trusty and true,
> None can be better than Dévouassoud!

I gave him a free translation which pleased him amazingly.

July 15. CHAMOUNI TO ST. GERVAIS (15 miles).

A brilliant morning after the showers, and Mont Blanc far too dazzling to look at steadily. We thought we had left it all behind, and so were astonished and delighted, when about half way, to find perhaps the most perfect single view we have had at all, even allowing for an exceptionally clear atmosphere. The whole drive to St. Gervais is a succession of beauty, both near and distant, and I was really sorry that, for the first time, we had a dashing driver. H. C. was exactly suited, but wanted to know how often he had to get absolution for breaking Protestant necks! St. Gervais aux Bains is an enormous mineral water establishment, partly hotel, partly medical pension. It is built in a narrow wooded gorge, and has a fine waterfall just beyond it. The visitors' rooms occupy two long wings with open galleries running along the front of each storey; it is like streets of bedrooms, and the view of the same as you pass to your own is comical. It was not full, but there were two hundred and twenty visitors. In the afternoon we went to the village of St. Gervais, a stiff walk up zigzags out of the gorge; the view at the top was indeed a lovely upland dip below Mont Joli (8000 feet) with a glimpse of the Mont Blanc chain at one end, and the fine valley of Salenches, bounded by jagged purple hills against the evening sky, on the other. We went to see Cheminées des Fées, most curious pillars of gravel, with roofs of the same, standing straight up, separate from the side of the rock against which they are seen.

Our Alpine work is really over, and I had a token thereof. I had made quite a small idol of my alpenstock, with its long spiral of names beginning with Lauterbrunnen and ending with the Mauvais Pas; it was so handy and helpful; but having served me up to the last day, it closed its account by falling out of the carriage and getting smashed. I have enjoyed the Alps exceedingly, not less than I expected, and yet it has been in rather a different way. When one hears very perfect music, pleasure overshoots itself into pain, the exquisite thrill is just too much, one longs to dare to let it all out in tears, the cup of enjoyment overflows as the hand trembles with delight, and the nectar is lost through its very abundance. But if one has a share in the performance of the very same, the enjoyment is *more* complete because less intense and concentrated; the physical action of hand or voice is the safety valve, and just takes off the too keen edge, just keeps the thrill of pleasure from rising, yes *rising,* into pain. It is exactly thus with these mountains. The strange unique solemn beauty would be too oppressive, the sense of it would weigh one's soul down into awe, would be like a mighty hand upon one's breast, stopping the very breath of one's soul. But the physical exertion is just the needed balance; one is in motion, there is effort, there is even the sense of inhaling a different and most exhilarating air; one is thus kept within the region of real enjoyment; one has not time for the snow silence to fall on one's heart. The pleasure is more perfect for one's whole being, just because it is more imperfect for the higher part of that being. If one were borne on an angel's wings up to Pierre Pointue, one would hardly dare speak in the sudden presence of the snow glory; but as one comes up on a mule and grasps an alpenstock, one is more inclined to shout and laugh with delight, and hasten to scramble higher.

July 16. St. Gervais to Geneva.

A splendid morning, but oh such a hot drive; none the cooler for leaving the snow mountains farther behind. But they are beautiful to the last, even at Geneva, where they edge the horizon like bright clouds, rather golden than white. On this hot day even the enormous Hotel de la Métropole was a most welcome refuge from the heat, welcome actually to *me!*

July 17. Geneva.

A morning's shopping and strolling. In the evening a drive to the cemetery at Petit Sacconnex, where, after some search, we found the tomb of (Mrs.) Maria Vernon Graham, with the text 1 Thessalonians 4:17; also Dr. Barry's tomb. We called on Mrs. Pennefather (S. A. de Montmorency). Major Pennefather said it had been a most exceptional summer, and that, till the last few days, Mont Blanc had not been visible for six weeks!

We went to an open air concert on Rousseau's Island at 8 p.m. It was very un-English, but very pretty. The little island lies just in the point where the Rhone rushes out of the lake, and is connected with the city by a bridge. On it is a wooden café and several trees. A little semi-circular orchestra, roofed but open in front and brilliantly lighted, was faced by about four hundred chairs placed under the trees. The lake and river, dark or glittering, reflected the bright rows of light from quays and bridges and hotels; and the moon, after two months' absence, shone through the branches and lit up a reach of the Rhone.

The music was rubbish, mostly from French operas, but very prettily played. One piece, a string sextet, was of higher order and a real treat. The conductor stood facing the audience instead of the orchestra, though he occasionally turned to the instruments which led off any special point. It was not the least like English conducting; the time seemed less marked than the expression; a soft passage was given with the slightest little movements of the hand, down, down, down, no right, left, etc., at all; then you saw the crescendo coming, by the stronger motion.

Between the parts we did "as they do at Rome," or Geneva, and had coffee and ices at one of the little round tables in the moonlight.

July 18. Sunday at Geneva.

We were told we should hear a very superior preacher at the Temple de St. Gervais, so M. and I went at 10 am. We were early, but the large church was already crowded; it is one of the oldest in Geneva, and it was pleasant to think that many of our Reformers had worshipped in it. All the windows were darkened with red curtains to keep out the glare of heat. M. Tournier gave out Romans 3:22, 23, but as usual it was "an oration and not an exposition." He opened by saying, "What is Christianity? What is the church?" A pause. "This is the great question on which men's minds are divided." The first part of the sermon, an answer to the first question, was singularly eloquent and forcible, the answer being that it is the religion of

Jesus Christ, and *that* is "the religion of redemption." He alluded to the rationalistic controversies of Geneva, and implied that there is much present agitation on the subject.

After service we had passed a little figure in the crowd; I turned back, it was Andrienne Vignier. She is staying two miles off, but had walked through the heat to hear M. Tournier. She only came from Naples a few days ago, and her accounts of it were sadly amusing. We remarked on Switzerland being so noisy. "Noisy! go to Italy, *alors!* There it is all noise. Music? *Mais oui!* the people all sing. To be sure, ha, ha! Imagine the roaring of wild beasts let loose, and you have it. They have three notes in their voices, and those three come through their nose. The donkeys are far better; they bray in a long melancholy note, quite sentimental, as if they mourned the wrongs of the country. But when the people fight it is more lively; they always fight when they have nothing else to do. They throw things at each other, generally their wooden shoes; and they take such good aim, *olà!* they never miss." Then she described the family to which she has devoted herself, body and soul and purse, for three years, all for love of the mother, her old schoolfellow, for a nominal salary. "There are ten of them, and they all have *dispositions volcaniques.* You hear such a noise" (here she makes sundry illustrative and most unearthly sounds), "it is an eruption, each is a little Vésuve in herself, and when it is over in one quarter it begins again in another."

"Talking of Vesuvius, did you see much of it?"

"We saw the whole proceedings of the mountain day and night, without putting on our shoes."

"And what impression did it give you? What was it like?"

"Hell! just hell, *précisement!* But the whole country is its portal; one must not think of being happy there, it is all misery and wretchedness. These three years have been just agony, and I am completely imbécilified!"

She came with us to the hotel, just her old self, as rapid and as funny as ever, only spicing her accounts with more French words and idioms. In the evening we went to English service, but it was almost too hot to listen.

July 19. Geneva to Neuchatel.

Andrienne came early and took us to the Musée Rath, a public collection of statues, pictures, etc. A poor Swiss woman found her way in, and was like a child among the pictures, full of interest and delight. I told her about some of them, and she followed me all the time for the chance of more information. I stood some time before a beautiful copy from Carlo Dolce, "Christ with the crown of thorns," and she liked to hear about the "old, old story."

In the heat of the morning I went to the Rhone swimming bath, which was delicious. At one end the river comes in in a regular waterfall three feet high, through which you can see the light, blue and shining; fancy sitting under this azured crystal. It was such fun to swim down the long bath, it was one's beau ideal of bathing, and the cool, transparent, exquisite blue is so much nicer than salt grey waves.

We left Geneva by two p.m. steamer for Morges, and, though hazy, the view was very beautiful, especially with the assistance of M. L.'s ex cathedra announcements as to *which* were mountains and *which* clouds, among the dim golden-white horizon fringings to the south! We reached Neuchatel about ten, after more than an hour on the very edge of the lake by moonlight, a very pretty line of rail.

July 20. Neuchatel.

Simply broiling! The rest shopped all the morning; gifts for home, etc., I stayed in the comparatively cool and very pleasant Hotel Bellevue saloon, close to the lake and public gardens. Mr. and Mrs. Maynard are here; which is a great treat; his chaplaincy is now over, so we were only just in time to meet them. We wished to go to Chaumont in the afternoon but all the carriages were engaged, so we had a row on the lake instead. We tried to make out Mont Blanc and the Jungfrau, but it is tantalizing to try to identify those majestic presences among far, faint, shadowy cloud outlines, after one has stood face to face with them.; it was looking at the wrong side of the tapestry. The moonlight was perfect; what would we not have given for an hour of it at Thun, or Lucerne, or Chamouni, or Vevey?

July 21. Neuchatel to Dijon.

What would Frank have said? I was coward enough to decline going with the others to the cathedral on account of the heat, and had a luxurious morning of writing and chatting with Mr. M. The heat was intense. Mr. M. said he "wished last Sunday that he could have preached *in* the lake!" Fancy preacher and congregation up to their necks! it would have been emphatically "a refreshing service."

Our afternoon train saved us much heat, for after sunset it was cool and pleasant, and we did not get to Dijon till nearly eleven p.m. The first hour and a half from Neuchatel till near Pontarlier is right across the Jura chain, not grand but extremely beautiful, especially at first, when the line rises steeply along the side of a splendid gorge, wooded, except where the limestone rocks are too precipitous to give any hold for firs. And it is wonderful how little hold seems necessary for tree roots in Switzerland; they cling to rocks where one would have thought not a bush or even a plant could find footing, and shoot up straight and stately, vegetable aiguilles.

As we left Neuchatel we looked out for the possibility of a definite farewell to the Alps. What a strange, sad fascination there is about a *last* glimpse! Above the hazy horizon were some little, pale whitenesses, was it to these that our good-bye must be said? So we called in our mountain oracle, M.L., who answered authoritatively "that they *were* Alps certainly, Mont Blanc *probably*." So we watched on till they were lost: all silent.

But is it not then that thoughts talk loudest?
    Shall we ever see them again?

"The works of the Lord are great, sought out of all them that have pleasure therein."

———— ✥ ————

II.

THE MOUNTAIN MAIDENS,[1]

(Zella, Dora, Lisetta.)

A CANTATA.

————

PART I.—SUNRISE.

(1.) DAWN CHORUS.

THE stars die out, and the moon grows dim,
    Slowly, softly, the dark is paleing!
Comes o'er the eastern horizon-rim,
    Slowly, softly, a bright unveiling.

The white mist floats in the vale at rest,
    Ghostly, dimly, a silver shiver;
The golden east and the purple west
    Flushing deep with a crimson quiver.

The mountains gleam with expectant light,
    Near and grandly, or far and faintly,
In festal robing of solemn white,
    Waiting, waiting, serene and saintly.

————

Lo! on the mountain-crest, sudden and fair,
Bright herald of morning, the rose-tint is there;
Peak after peak lighteth up with the glow
That crowneth with ruby the Alpine snow.

Summit on summit, and crest beyond crest,
The beacons are spreading away to the west;
Crimson and fire and amber and rose,
Touch with life and with glory the Alpine snows.

(2.) CHORALE.

Father, who hast made the mountains,
    Who hast formed each tiny flower,
Who hast filled the crystal fountains,
    Who hast sent us sun and shower:
Hear Thy children's morning prayer,
Asking for Thy guardian care;
Keep and guide us all the day,
Lead us safely all the way.

Let Thy glorious creation
    Be the whisper of Thy power;
New and wondrous revelation
    Still unfolding every hour.
Let the blessing of Thy love
Rest upon us from above;
And may evening gladness be
Full of thanks and praise to Thee.

[1] The music to this cantata, for treble voices, by Frank Romer, is published by Hutchings and Romer, 9 Conduit Street, Regent Street. [This music is published on pages 2315–2393 of Volume V of the Havergal edition.]

(3.) Recitative.—*Dora.*

Our pleasant summer work begins. You go,
O merry Zella, with the obedient herd
To upland pastures, singing all the way.
And you, Lisetta, to the sterner heights,
Where only foot of Alpine goat may pass,
Or step of mountain maiden. It is mine
To work at home preparing smooth white cheese
For winter store and often needed gain;
And mine the joy of welcoming once more
My loving sisters when the evening falls.

(4.) Song.—*Dora.*

The morning light flingeth
  Its wakening ray,
And as the day bringeth
  The work of the day,
The happy heart singeth,
  Awake and away!

No life can be dreary
  When work is delight;
Though evening be weary,
  Rest cometh at night;
And all will be cheery
  If faithful and right.

When duty is treasure
  And labour a joy,
How sweet is the leisure
  Of ended employ!
Then only can pleasure
  Be free from alloy.

[Repeat v. 1.]

(5.) Song.—*Zella.*

Away, away! with the break of day,
  To the sunny upland slope!
Away, away! while the earliest ray
  Tells of radiant joy and hope.

  With the gentle herd that know the word
    Of kindness and of care,
  While with footsteps free they follow me,
    As I lead them anywhere.

Away, away! with a merry lay,
  And the chime of a hundred bells;
Away, away! with a carol gay,
  And an echo from the fells.

  To the pastures high, where the shining sky
    Looks down on a wealth of flowers;
  To the sapphire spots, where forget-me-nots
    Smile on through lonely hours.

Away, away! while the breezes play
  In the fragrant summer morn;
Away, away! while the rock-walls grey
  Resound with the Alpen-horn.

  To the crags, all bright in the golden light
    With floral diadems,
  As fresh and fair, as "rich and rare,"
    As any royal gems.

Away, away! while the rainbow spray
  Wreathes the silver waterfalls;
Away, away! Oh, I cannot stay,
  When the voice of the morning calls!

(6.) Recitative.—*Lisetta.*

Adieu, my Dora! Zella dear, adieu!
The quick light tinkle of the goat bells now
Reminds me they are waiting for my call,
To follow where small flowers have dared to peep
And laugh, beside the glacier and the snow.
I shall not go alone, your love shall go with me.

(7.) Duet.—*Zella and Dora.*

Adieu, adieu till eventide!
  The hours will quickly pass,
The shadow of the rocks will glide
  Across the sunny grass.
We shall not mourn the lessening light,
For we shall meet at home to-night.

Adieu, adieu till eventide!
  The hour of home and rest,
The hour that finds us side by side,
  The sweetest and the best.
For love is joy, and love is light,
And we shall meet at home to-night!

Adieu, adieu till eventide!
  'Tis but a little while!
We would not stay the morning's pride,
  Or noontide's dazzling smile;
But welcome evening's waning light,
For we shall meet at home to-night!

———

Part II.—NOON.

(8.) Song.—*Lisetta.*

It is noon upon the mountains, and the breeze has died away,
And the rainbow of the morning passes from the torrent spray,
And a calm of golden silence falls upon the glistening snow,
While the shadows of the noon clouds rest upon the glen below.

It is noon upon the mountains, noon upon the giant rocks;
Hushed the tinkle of the goat-bells, and the bleating of the flocks;
They are sleeping on the gentians, and upon the craggy height,
In the glow of Alpine noontide, in the glory of the light.

It is noon upon the mountains. I will rest beside the snow,
Glittering summits far above me, blue-veined glaciers far below;
I will rest upon the gentians, till the quiet shadows creep,
Cool and soft, along the mountains, waking me from pleasant sleep.

(9.) Noon Chorus.

Rest! while the noon is high,
   Rest while the glow
Falls from the summer sky
   Over the snow.

Rest! where the alpenrose
   Crimsons the height,
Piercing the mountain snows,
   Purpling the light.
Rest! while the waterfalls,
   Murmuring deep
Far-away lullabies,
   Hush thee to sleep.
      Rest! while the noon, etc.

Rest! where the mountains rise,
   Shining and white;
Piercing the deep blue skies,
   Solemn and bright.
Sleep while the silence falls,
   Soothing to rest,
Sweetest of lullabies,
   Calming and blest.
      Rest! while the noon, etc.

(10.) Recitative.—*Lisetta.*

Where am I? I was sleeping by the snow,
Upon the alpenroses in the noon.
But am I dreaming now? The sun is low,
'Tis twilight in the valley, and I hear
No music of the goat bells. Oh, I fear
It is no dream; but night is coming soon,
And I am all alone upon the height;
And there are small faint tracks, too quickly lost,
That need sure foot and eye in fullest light;
And crags to leap, and torrents to be crossed!
I go! may Power and Love still guard and guide aright.

(11.) Song.—*Lisetta.*

Alone, alone! yet around me stand
   God's mountains, still and grand!

Still and grand, serene and bright,
Sentinels clothed in armour white,
And helmeted with scarlet light.
   His Power is near,
   I need not fear.
Beneath the shadow of His Throne
Alone, alone, yet not alone!

Alone, alone! yet beneath me sleep
   The flowers His hand doth keep;
   Small and fair, by crag or dell,
   Trustfully closing star and bell,
   Eve by eve as twilight fell.
   His Love is near,
   I need not fear.
Beneath the rainbow of His Throne,
Alone, alone, yet not alone!

Alone, alone! yet I will not fear,
   For Power and Love are near!
   Step by step, by rock and rill,
   Trustfully onward, onward still,
   I follow home with hope and will!
   So near, so near,
   I do not fear.
Beneath the Presence of His Throne,
Alone, alone, yet not alone!

———

Part III.—SUNSET.

(12.) Sunset Chorus.

It is coming, it is coming,
   That marvellous up-summing
Of the loveliest and grandest all in one;
   The great transfiguration,
   And the royal coronation,
Of the Monarch of the mountains by the priestly Sun.

   Watch breathlessly and hearken,
   While the forest throne-steps darken
His investiture in crimson and in fire;
   Not a herald trumpet ringeth,
   Not a pæan echo flingeth,
There is music of a silence that is mightier far and higher.

   Then in radiant obedience
   A flush of bright allegiance
Lights up the vassal summits and the proud peaks all around;
   And a thrill of mystic glory
   Quivers on the glaciers hoary,
As the ecstasy is full, and the mighty brow is crowned.

   Crowned with ruby of resplendence,
   In unspeakable transcendence,

Neath a canopy of purple and of gold outspread,
    With rock sceptres upward pointing,
    While the glorious anointing
Of the consecrating sunlight is poured upon his head.

    Then a swift and still transition
    Falls upon the gorgeous vision,
And the ruby and the fire pass noiselessly away;
    But the paleing of the splendour
    Leaves a rose light, clear and tender,
And lovelier than the loveliest dream that melts before the day.

    Oh to keep it, oh to hold it,
    While the tremulous rays enfold it!
Oh to drink in all the beauty, and never thirst again!
    Yet less lovely if less fleeting,
    For the mingling and the meeting
Of the wonder and the rapture can but overflow in pain.

    It is passing, it is passing!
    While the softening glow is glassing
In the crystal of the heavens all the fairest of its rose;
    Ever faintly and more faintly,
    Ever saintly and more saintly,
Gleam the snowy heights around us in holiest repose.

    O pure and perfect whiteness!
    O mystery of brightness,
Upon those still majestic brows shed solemnly abroad!
    Like the calm and blessèd sleeping
    Of saints in Christ's own keeping,
When the smile of holy peace is left, last witness for their God!

(13.) Song.—*Dora.*

    The tuneful chime of the herd is still,
      For the milking hour is past,
    And tinkle, tinkle, along the hill,
      The goat bells come at last.
    But sister, sister, where art thou?
    We watch and wait for thy coming now.

    The crimson fades from the farthest height,
      And the rose-fire pales away;
    And softly, softly, the shroud of night
      Enfolds the dying day.
    But sister, sister, where art thou?
    We watch and wait for thy coming now.

    The cold wind swells from the icy steep,
      And the pine trees quake and moan;
    And darkly, darkly the grey clouds creep,
      And thou art all alone.
    O sister, sister, where art thou?
    We watch and wait for thy coming now.

(14.) Duet.—*Zella and Dora.*

    We will seek thee, we will find thee,
      Though the night winds howl and sweep;
    We will follow through the torrent,
      We will follow up the steep.
    Follow where the alpenroses
      Make the mountain all aglow,
    Follow, follow through the forest,
      Follow, follow to the snow!
    And our Alpine call shall echo
      From the rock and from the height,
    Till a gladder tone rebounding,
    Thine own merry voice resounding,
      Fill us with a great delight.
        Lisetta! Lisetta!
    Hush and hearken. Call again!
        Lisetta! Lisetta!
    Hearken, hearken. All in vain!

    We will seek thee, we will find thee,
      In the wary chamois' haunt;
    Toil and terror, doubt and danger,
      Loving hearts shall never daunt!
    We will follow in the darkness,
      We will follow in the light;
    Follow, follow till we find thee,
      Through the noon or through the night.
    We will seek thee, we will find thee,
      Never weary till we hear,
    Over all the torrents rushing,
    Joyous answer clearly gushing,
      Thine own Alpine echo dear!
        Lisetta! Lisetta!
    Hush and hearken. All in vain!
        Lisetta! Lisetta!
    Hearken, hearken. Call again!

(15.) Trio.—*Zella, Dora, and Lisetta.*

Lisetta (*pp*). I am coming!
Zella and Dora (*f*). She is coming!
Lisetta (*p*). I am coming. Wait for me!
Zella and Dora (*p*). She is coming!
Lisetta (*mf*). I am coming!
Zella and Dora (*f*). Come, oh come, we wait for thee!
      Nearer, nearer comes the echo;
        Nearer, nearer comes the voice;
      Nearer, nearer fall the footsteps,
        Making us indeed rejoice.
Lisetta. I am coming, wait for me!
Zella and Dora. Come, oh come, we wait for thee!

ZELLA, DORA, and LISETTA.

We { have sought { her, / me, } we { they { have found { her, / me, }
They
they

Fear and danger all are past,

Now with joyful song { we lead her / they lead me }

Safely, safely home at last!

(16.) CHORUS—*Finale.*

Safe home, safe home!
Fear and danger all are past,
We are safely home at last!

Oh, the lovelight shed around,
  In a rich and radiant flow,

When the lost and loved are found,
  Is the sweetest heart can know.
Fairer than the dawn-light tender,
  Fuller than the noontide glow,
Brighter than the sunset splendour
  Purer than the moonlit snow.

Now let the wild cloud sweep,
  Let the wild rain pour!
Now let the avalanche leap
  With its long, grand roar!
Now let the black night fall
  On the mountain crest!
Safe are our dear ones all
  In our mountain nest.

Safe home, safe home!
Fear and danger all are past,
We are safely home at last!

III.

EXTRACTS FROM LETTERS WRITTEN TO J. M. C.[1] IN 1871.

LETTER I.

June 29, 1871. Sitting in an arbour outside the
station at Belfort, the only strong place left
to the French in this region.

DEAR MIRIAM;

We have had a most interesting journey, and I feel quite
historical. We crossed from Newhaven with a crowd of returning French, and reached Dieppe about 9.30 a.m., had coffee,
and went on *viâ* Rouen to Paris. H. C. would be charmed with
Rouen, and I bracket it with Edinburgh and Berne as the three
most picturesque towns I know. We had just time to go, *viâ*
rue Jeanne d'Arc, to St. Ouen, which is a crystallization of all
one's floating visions of lovely architecture. E. Clay had laid
in a splendid stock of little French books and tracts, which we
were to divide between us; and as we thought Rouen was not
a usual place for tract distribution, we gave away many, and
you cannot think how delighted people seemed. One tall grave
man, of superior rank, watched us, and came up to E. ask-

ing if she had many. We were afraid he meant to interfere, as
he looked very official; however, he only wanted to ask "if we
would kindly give him one for himself, two if we could." He
took them, and thanked us as if we had given him some great
thing.

We left Rouen at 2 p.m., and made friends with two very
taking French girls returning to Paris after the war; one of them
had immense lovely eyes. They told us all sorts of war experiences. One had an uncle in La Roquette who escaped by brib-
ing the guard the night before he was to be shot; her own house
left standing and untouched, but houses on each side burnt to
a shell. The other had a brother who had three horses killed
under him, but escaped unwounded; a cousin was killed in the
first battle, an uncle escaped from his chateau two minutes before the "Communistes" entered and killed three men instead
of him; this girl said her family had lost nearly all their property, the other had fared better. They both reviled the Emperor,
and said it was all his fault; that he was resolved on war in order

---

[1] This was Jane Miriam Crane (1817–1898), F.R.H.'s eldest sister.

to preserve his dynasty; but they would not own that the Communists were French altogether, "it was the bad of all countries who constituted the *Communistes* and they disowned them as *compatriotes*." As we neared Paris they pointed out where the line had been broken up, and soon after we crossed the Seine by two bridges (an island being in the middle) of the most fragile and temporary looking appearance, at about two miles an hour, with awful squealings of the engine all the time. The ruins of the broken bridge were about fifty yards higher. Then we saw war effects visible and terrible; for some miles all through those bright looking suburbs it was one succession of desolations, great ragged holes in the roofs and walls of some houses, and others mere shells, gutted entirely, and others laid open like the front of a baby house, a whole wall having fallen, and showing the skeleton of the storeys.

It was far worse than I expected to see, and the two poor girls were sadly distressed and flushed, and their pretty eyes full of tears. We were so sorry for them.

At Paris, 4.20, we could not get a cab, and walked with a porter about a mile and a half to the station for Basle (*viâ* Troyes). Most of the way was just Paris of old, gay and clean and lively, but here and there houses were pitted with bullet marks, and over nearly all the churches we saw the mark of the Communists in large-lettered "*Liberté, Egalité, Fraternité.*"

At the rue Strasbourg station we decided to go by the night train, and meantime set off to see the more special ruins. We walked nearly two miles before we could find a vehicle, and then drove to the Tuileries; the principal walls are standing, but through the burnt out windows I noticed especially the superb rooms I went through with you, not a floor or a cross wall was left. Then the gardens looked so knocked about, and soldiers' tents looked queer and ominous. The Palais Royal seemed much the same, and the stumpy pedestal of the Colonne Vendôme looked most melancholy.

Our driver was a Communist, I fancy, and a lively one. We bemoaned the Tuileries.

"Ah!" said he, laughing, "it's all right, that makes work for the labourers."

He showed us the Colonne Vendôme that *was*, with absolute glee, saying, "We have taken it down that another may be put up!"

"Where is the money to come from?" I asked.

"Oh, there is always money enough forthcoming when we want it!"

"Were you in Paris during the siege?"

"Surely! it is my country, my Paris."

The unsubdued care-for-nought look of the man gave me a notion of French levity. He showed us the rue de la Paix, where the awful massacre began, and the bullet marks on the houses. In contrast to all this the boulevards looked just as gay as

in 1869, crowded and bright; no end of people drinking coffee and wine at the little tables under the trees, theatre placards in all directions, and all just as usual; *only* it was less *coloured,* for we took special notice that at least seven out of eight women were in mourning; no crape, perhaps they can't afford it, but plain black; this was most striking, and a great contrast to the colours of 1869. We saw a good many dirty and dismal looking soldiers, and were told that these were returned French prisoners coming in by every train.

We left Paris by eight p.m. train, and arrived at Belfort at nine a.m., nearly an hour late. All beyond this (Belfort) is in Prussian hands, so the French officials don't or won't know anything about it, and show no timetables, and give no answer but shrugs to any question, or they refer one to "those Germans" at the other end of the station. It is quite sadly comical.

We both vote a night journey a great success; after 9.30 we had the carriage to ourselves, and were quite luxuriously comfortable. Mrs. Snepp gave me a hood which was a great comfort, and E. admires it extremely.

The guard was most polite, and, though he did not resort to the simple expedient of locking us up, he took trouble in warning people off as if they were *canaille* compared with English ladies, there being no other specimens of the article on this route, One unadvised individual opened our door, and the guard rushed at him with "*March-t-en! il y a deux mesdames banquées; march-t-en! hui!*" Is not *banquées* a good word? We don't know whether we slept much, because we seemed to be aware of the stations, at most of which there was tremendous hullabalooing, occasioned by soldiers returning from Prussia. We quite roused up at 3.30, and fell upon gingerbread and biscuits, and then subsided till after six, when we got up for good, and found ourselves nearing and then crossing the lovely Vosges mountains.

I forgot to say that between twilight and moonlight, about nine p.m., we passed a most desolate and scathed region, and were told it was the battlefield of Champigny. Anything grimmer and gloomier you could not imagine; ground broken and scarred, nothing but weeds growing, a few deserted cottages with great gaps in roofs and ball marks with great cracks radiating from them in the walls, and many, terribly many, irregular shaped mounds at irregular distances, where heaps of dead were buried just where they fell. It was so ghastly, and made war seem so real.

After we had breakfasted here, we sauntered towards the fortifications, and distributed little books as we went along, and never had such a time of it! The people were so eager after them, we only wished we had hundreds more; several superior people came and asked for them, though we only offered them to the poor. Some asked for "another to give to a friend"; one workman at the fort seemed delighted, and begged us to give him some for his fellow workmen; there were a great many at work above, he said, and they would be so glad of them. We went into a place where some wounded soldiers and some women at work were sitting; they spoke most gratefully, and rose, and bowed. "Merci infiniment, infiniment!" said one man. We exhausted our stock, and after having pottered about the fortifications we parted, as E. wished to go farther, and I came back to write. As I passed through the town I found lots of people on the look out for me, to ask for more little books; at one point at least thirty people clustered round me, begging for more. I had only three French hymns left, and they were so disappointed that, after talking a little to them, I told them they might come to the station for some. We took the opportunity; for plenty of people give tracts on the Swiss routes, but here they are evidently a novelty.

Belfort is terribly battered about; the large church is just a ruin, not a square yard of roof whole; the houses nearest the fort are simply heaps of ruins. The weather is just warm enough to be pleasant for sitting out of doors without wrap. E. and I are mutually satisfied with our equipments, which are nearly alike; and having nothing but what we can carry ourselves on emergency is most delightful, and we have been "first come first served" several times already. The "unprotected female" line answers first rate; every one is civil and attends to us. I hope somebody will write to us at Zermatt; I ought to get some encouragement to write my circulars. Love all round in general.

Your loving sister,
F.

P.S.—Mrs. S.'s maid supposed, of course, we should have a courier; did you ever! I think E. and I could train a courier if wished; but the idea of *our* being taken in tow by one!

LETTER II.

Beyond ERSHFELD. June 30.

E. and I were in such a state of felicity that it went beyond talking, and we walked in a silence of delight. We are (for siesta) encamped under two trees and a huge boulder, a little more than half way from Altdorf to Amsteg (nine miles), at a most lovely bend of this valley which the "Practical Swiss Guide" well describes as "solemnly beautiful," the Bristenstock towering close in front of us, a cone of snow. Can't you imagine me perfectly suited! But I will go back to where I left off. When E. came back to me at Belfort, she said she was convinced no one but an "unprotected female" would have been allowed to go where she did, up among the fortifications and on the top of the walls! The sentinels merely looked at her, but no one spoke to her. She had found a whole street in entire ruins.

We left the Belfort station at two, and arrived at Basle at five. I must own to having been a little nervous at crossing the broken and only partially repaired bridges and viaducts; we crossed one great breach at an immense height, on what seemed merely temporary beams, so that we looked out of the window into the valley below, without any apparent thing under the carriage! At one station we passed an ambulance train very slowly, so that we could see well into each "doktor's wagen," full of all sorts of surgical looking things, and a "kitchen carriage," full of stoves and pots and pans, and others evidently for the wounded with beds in them.

Had we ordered special trains, we could not hitherto have done better; and at Basle, where we thought of sleeping, we had just time for a comfortable meal at the station, and then a train was going direct to Lucerne; this was irresistible, and we did not feel tired, so on we went. It was a most exquisite evening, brilliantly clear, and the rail from Basle to Olten one series of changing lovely views. Just before Olten we had a sudden revelation of Alps; for about five minutes a distant range of snow mountains shone out with sunset full upon them, perfectly golden. It would have suited John Bunyan; you know what those visions suggest, as nothing else on earth ever did or does to me. Except the lake of Sempach, which we skirted, there was nothing else special till about 9.30, when E. announced Pilatus! which was just ahead, delicately outlined in the moonlight, and looking very spiritual and holy! We went to the Cygne at Lucerne; I was in bed at eleven, and slept like a dormouse for eight hours. It was delicious! Fancy our not having been undressed since Monday night! When I awoke I looked out on the most glorious morning view of the lake and mountains. Last week there was rain and snow here; now all is in perfection; very clear; the green vivid and fresh, waterfalls full, and all the near mountains with extra snow, Pilatus all capped and streaked, and looking finer than ever in consequence. Again boat departure was just right, 9.30, giving us time to get money changed, etc. Our sail down the lake was simply perfection, and we saw the Bernese Alps, Jungfrau, and all as distinctly as possible; you remember we never saw them at all in 1869. To add to it, a school came on board, going to Fluellen for a treat, and struck up some uncommonly pretty Swiss national songs in three parts; and seeing our interest, the children lent us their books to follow the words, which were also very pretty. The effect of one in particular was quite upsetting, it was so sweet and charming.

You remember H. C. suggesting a "lift" on the steep side of the Rigi. Well, they have outdone him, for they have actually got a railway to the very top! on the Mont Cenis principle of a toothed line in the centre, and a wheel to catch, which continually locks itself, so that the carriages cannot run back, but regularly climb up; they told me that at one part, which we could see, the incline is actually one in four!

We omnibused from Fluellen to Altdorf, being a hot flat two miles, and then sent on our bags by diligence, and walked up the valley.

N.B.—I am writing now at Amsteg, 7.30 p.m. It is grander at every turn all the nine miles, and we are so glad we walked it; don't fancy we overdid it, for we took six hours, resting two hours half way, besides shorter rests; and this Swiss air is atmospheric salvolatile. We dined half way at a tiny village quite unknown to guidebooks, and the affair was charming. A nice girl of twenty waited on us, but thought it part of her duty to entertain us, and came and sat down all the time, making herself most agreeable. "Yes, plenty of English passed by, but none ever stayed there." She was greatly entertained with *us* evidently, and watched everything like a child. She and a younger sister had never seen indiarubber bands, and were quite delighted when I gave them a few. E. gave them some Gospels, and they promised to read them.

July 1. We were in bed at nine last night and up at five this morning and off a little before seven. Morning superb, and the pass just magnificent; we took it easy and did not get over the seven miles to Wasen till nearly noon. But then how could we hurry! There were gorges to look up, and high bridges to look down, and snow summits through every opening, and lights and shadows playing over all. Not having cut out too much work for to-day we had time to take any number of mental photographs. At Wasen we went to the inn, a real Swiss one, and dined at 11.45 on cold kid and ham and Italian wine, and were charged tenpence each. (I will always quote English money.) Though Belfort is obviously the most direct route to Switzerland, it must be rarely used by English, for at the station we had coffee, eggs, *and* ablutions, for tenpence each, and a dinner of cold beef for elevenpence each. Our whole expenses from London to Wasen have not been £5 apiece, and here we are in the very heart of Switzerland. Yet we have had everything we wanted, and the only difference is that we are waited on by the most obliging Swiss girls at these small inns, instead of by napkined waiters at the great noisy grand hotels.

Amsteg, where we slept, is most picturesque, at the junction of the Maderanen Thal with this grand pass, but we did not get a good night owing to the roar of the Reuss, which equals that dreadful Arve at Chamouni for noise, and I dislike this as much as I did in 1869, and am longing to get up above it. We are now camped out. It is very hot, and E. is gone a little way from me, I think sketching. E. is an unexceptionable companion for me, and we agree precisely in all our ways and fancies in this expedition. Tell H. C. the hay is being cut, and it is the fashion here to set it up in most queer cocks about six feet high and two broad; they are put on stakes with four crossbars, rather crooked and not at any particular angle to each other, so it seems to *stick* and let the wind blow through it most "convenient."

7.45 p.m. Geschenen. Here we are in immense clover! Soon after we moved on from our camp, a storm came grandly down the valley; we took refuge in the outside gallery of a chalet, and watched it in comfort. It was so fine to see it rush past and leave us in the sunshine, while it swept like great dusky wings down the pass. We soon got on to this place, which is *ideal,* of a different kind to the exquisite loveliness of the lower part of the pass. It is a wee village, shut in by the wildest, most savage looking heights, mostly topped with snow, awful rocks and a great avalanche gorge on one side, a wild valley narrow and solemn on the other, shut in at the end by what looks like a very large glacier, which they say no one has ever yet crossed. We are close to a bridge over a very deep and narrow gorge, and about a hundred yards off can get back into the great St. Gothard pass, which is very grand both up and down. And here we are going to spend Sunday! Don't think us heathens, but we could not possibly get to an English service to-morrow, and I really think it will be as good as going to church just for once! Our inn is very simple, but spotless; the host is very young and very eager to oblige; and the hostess must have taste, to judge by the way she has set off the deal furniture with pretty white netting and crochet. We are the only visitors in the place, and consequently receive the utmost attention.

We are three thousand five hundred feet high here, having risen nearly two thousand feet in our nine miles' walk yesterday, but we are not at all tired, and having Sunday to rest we are planning greater things for next week. We are quite early enough; the diligence only ran today for the first time over the Furca pass, there was so much snow; and now it is so warm I am thankful for cool attire.

Monday, 11.45 a.m. Hurrah! Seven thousand eight hundred feet high, and going to stay all the afternoon and night here! E. and I are quite shocked at our giddy and exhilarated state of mind. We feel just like children, and except a little undercurrent of general thanksgiving, we don't feel solemn at all, and have been in the wildest spirits, especially since we got over seven thousand feet level. But I go back to yesterday; it was the very perfection of a day, clear sunshine with enough cloud floating about to give most satisfactory effects, the temperature delicious. E. and I strolled up a valley finished up with a weird looking, half veiled, and very precipitous glacier, made ourselves cosy nests among boulders and moss, and had a small service on our own account, after which we separated for the rest of the morning, coming back to dinner at three.

Geschenen is the most picturesque place I ever *stayed* at, four gorges opening from it, and most emphatically *gorgeous* as to scenery. Our hosts are so devoted to us that we might be personal friends paying a visit! Our bill from Saturday afternoon to Monday morning, beginning with a meat supper and including quite a good Sunday dinner of trout and beef, was altogether 14*s*. 4*d*. for both of us. We generally only have one course, which saves time as well as money.

LETTER III.

Furca Pass (7,800 feet). Monday,
July 3rd, 1871. 6 p.m.

We have had a real proper day, and finished up by having to get into bed (while sundry garments are dried), where I am now writing! After yesterday's rest we started this morning at 5.30, having sent on our bags to Viesch, carrying our few necessaries. We walked the five miles and a half by 7.30. The pass from Geschenen to Andermatt is savage and grand beyond description; the Reuss is a succession of cataracts, so that any fifty yards of it would make the fortune of any English place. The Devil's Bridge is simply awful, rocks tremendous and overhanging, the depths below grim and terrible, and the river coming down in furious leaps.

The road is marvellous engineering; in one place it is strongly roofed over to protect it from avalanches. The weather was quite suitable, stormy and gusty, with sudden and fitful gleams of light breaking through wild grey clouds. We had a foretaste of climbing, for we made various interesting short cuts, and were just in time at Andermatt (4,500 feet) to catch the diligence for the Furca.

This road was only opened last summer, and most of the way lay along the edge of precipices; and the latter part had been injured by avalanches, and was cleared out between walls of snow. You can hardly imagine the wildness of the place, utter desolation of snow and rocks all round, and grey depths to peer down into; the Rhone valley in front and the wild pass behind, the most utter contrast to the *rich* magnificence of our walk from Amsteg.

The inn here was very small, but is being enlarged. We have a very comfortable little room with a table and sofa, and are royally lodged, for here the Queen slept when she was in Switzerland, in this very room!

Hitherto, being the only English, we have been taken into the best rooms at once. After a good feed at 11.45 we both went sound asleep, and awoke up quite fresh at two. It looked tolerably fine, so we took a guide (which is absolutely necessary) up the Furca-horn, a peak just above. It was the best climb I ever had, beat our Pierre à l'Echelle experience. There is no vestige of a track, and most queer places and snow slopes to cross; the latter were most entertaining. The guide went first, feeling every step lest he should get a plunge; we following exactly in each step, occasionally up to our knees. I enjoyed the

scramble exceedingly, and got on capitally. The view was sublime, nearly a panorama of the very wildest Alpine scenery, and the Galenstock, a lovely shaped peak of 11,000 feet just above us, the Rhone glacier deep below, and on the other side the Maienwand, an awful precipice at the top of which in a dip is the Todten See (lake of the dead); the Grimsel, and Zitterhorn, and Finsteraarhorn beyond. But we only stayed a few minutes, for most awful looking clouds were gathering and we heard distant thunder. It soon began to sleet violently, and our guide took us down a longer way but safer for descent, in a cloud which rushed up and enwrapped us. I was not sorry when we got down safe and sound. We enjoyed some coffee, and I am now writing most luxuriously in bed. It is snowing and raining alternately most furiously, but this is a pleasing variety in our experience! They are closing the outside shutters of three of our windows as it will probably be a rough night; the other window is sheltered and can be left for light. Have we not speedily got into the real thing?

The Alpine flowers have had the boldness to come out actually right among the snow; wherever a patch is thawed there they are, forget-me-nots and gentians, and most lovely lilac and yellow anemones, both all fringed and furred with curious soft hair; also some tiny bells of delicate mauve, the prettiest little things imaginable. These and the anemones are true ice flowers, the guide said, growing where not a blade of grass has started yet.

I have been reading this over to E., and she is afraid I shall have frightened you by my account of to-day, and that you "will be sending some one to look after us!" This would be an undesirable arrangement, as we don't wish to have any one *to look after!* Seriously however, I do not consider we have done anything dangerous, and I mean to keep the promise I made to that effect.

At the Æggischhorn Hotel, 7,372 feet high.
Wednesday, July 5. 3 p.m.

Yesterday morning the storm was past, but the Furca was all in a cloud, so though we were up at 5.30 we did not start down till 8.30, when it cleared rapidly and the rest of the day was bright. The first six miles took us close by the side and to the foot of the Rhone glacier, which is an enormous *precipice of icebergs,* with a comparatively flat foot beneath. We had what the aborigines call dinner at 11.30, then we strolled on about another six miles down the Rhone valley. As we got down to about 4,400 feet the hay region begins; it looked beautiful, but will not be ready to cut for a fortnight. It seems more than half flowers, but they say that is good for the cattle. In the afternoon we got some goat's milk, which is horrid stuff but very refreshing.

We arranged to reach Obergesteln about three, for the diligence to Viesch (twelve miles), but a cute Swiss waylaid us, and proposed taking us in a little carriage which would be much pleasanter. I had some misgivings as to whether it might be anything in the same style as our spree at Novelles, (tell H. C.,) inasmuch as the man candidly owned it would take him an hour to catch his horse, which was "somewhere" on the other side of the valley "at play." We were in no hurry, and the view was pretty, so we waited for him and trusted! It turned out to be quite a nice little carriage with a most lively horse, and H. C. would have appreciated the driving, which was like the spin we had down from Chamouni to St. Gervais. The drive was delicious, and the evening lovely. Viesch lies in a charming hollow, just below the Viescher glacier and the Viescherhörner, which are over 12,000 feet. Its own level is 2,800, so we had descended five thousand feet in the day. Our bags were waiting for us as usual; sending them on by "post" is most convenient, and saves all trouble and porterage; the average expense is about tenpence a day.

The Viesch hotel is primitive, and the maid scampered out to fill our ewers and water bottles at a general village spring and large trough formed of half a hollow tree. The morning was lovely, and we were up before four, and off at 5.15 for the Æggischhorn, and by 5.30 the sun was over the shoulder of the opposite mountain, and struck us with such power we were glad to get into the pine woods and be sheltered. This was the hardest walk we ever had in our lives, the steepest possible track nearly the whole way, rising straight up to 7,372 feet. It took us exactly four hours, including one half hour's rest and several odd minutes' halt. We had some refreshment, and then lay down and went fast asleep for two hours and a half, waking up quite jolly, and as if we had had another night, just as we did at the Furca, but are just in the same fix as there! It clouded over when half way up, and since we got in has been raining heavily, just clearing suddenly once, giving us a grand view of the other side of the valley entirely filled up with rolling grey clouds far below us. So we have no alternative but to take a day's rest, a day in the ordinary sense, as we got here at 9.15, but we had done enough for one day before that, for though not seven miles of actual distance it is more real work than over twelve down hill yesterday. We shall not get our letters till Tuesday, and shall have been a fortnight entirely cut off from communication; but we find it so much best to plan only a day in advance; the local information we get as to what is before us is much better than guidebooks, and we can also do more or less as we feel inclined.

We have not come in contact with a single English tourist, nor heard a word of English yet. The winter on the Furca would be too lonely even for us; they say two men and a big dog stay up there all the seven months' winter, and only come down once or twice, so that they are often three months without seeing any living thing, except hares, which sometimes stray over. On the St. Gothard pass, which is not nearly so high, there is regular sledge traffic all the winter, and men constantly employed to keep a track open.

In coming down from the Furca we passed in many places between great walls of snow through which the road had been cut; in one place the wall was at least fifteen feet deep.

I find letters are going to be sent at 5.30, but I pity the bearer, for we are in a dense fog and we see no sign of clearing for to-night.

LETTER IV.

July 7, 4.30 p.m. Sitting on the rocks above the Bel Alp Hotel, about 7,500 feet high.

Hitherto we have gone on in a grand crescendo; and have not finished it yet. Yesterday, Thursday, we jumped up at four a.m. for the sunrise, but seeing nothing but fog retired again. From six to ten it was great excitement to watch the cloud possibilities; they seemed to be going head over heels just below us, whirling and drifting and breaking and closing in the most chaotic way, in every shade of grey from nearly black to dazzling white. Just before ten they rolled off altogether, and as we were quite ready for this we set off for the Æggischhorn. There is a guide here, Fischer, who is famous, and the best in the district; but he was pre-engaged; however, we got Alexander Binner, a very fatherly and watchful specimen, quite a ladies' guide. He insisted on our starting slowly, and consulted and patronised us in general. We have to learn by experience; we thought we were excellently got up for the work by wearing waterproof dresses with a flannel jacket underneath, but we soon found it necessary to *peel,* and actually went up in our petticoats! You can't think how hot one gets in climbing, even among the snow. A little way up we heard a great yell (guides here make a point of yelling if they spy one a mile or more away), and presently we met a young Alpine Clubbist, whom E. found she knew by name as a distant connection of hers! The guides rushed at each other most affectionately, and to my delight I found they were the celebrated Ulrich and Christian Lauener, whom I have often seen mentioned in books. The young fellow had been sleeping with them in the cave of the Faulberg, in order to go up the Jungfrau at two a.m., but the fog prevented.

I cannot in conscience say I kept my promise that day, because in one sense there was "danger," for had we slipped in some places it would have been no trifle; but I never feel giddy, and I have a sure foot I am certain, and never feel the least nervous. Alexander told us *after,* that when he heard we were new to real mountain work he made up his mind we could not reach the top, but after he had seen us get over the first snow and rocks he was quite satisfied! Fischer told Alexander I "went like a chamois," and that he was astonished how quickly and easily I got up a very difficult climb where he watched me from above. I tell you this because I always had an instinct that I should find myself a rather extra good climber if I ever had the chance of really proving it. The "P. S. G." calls it "a severe climb" in any case, and the snow makes it now far more difficult and interesting. We crossed and ascended some great snow slopes like those awful looking things one sees in Swiss photos; one crossing was quite a third of a mile along the middle of a slope of steep unbroken snow, about six hundred feet high. The guide goes first, treading down the snow over soft p!aces, and we follow *exactly* in his track; but each step is a separate business, you stand firm and take time to plant each foot, not the least like walking, and as long as one does this there can be no danger, for if there are hidden holes the guide of course tumbles in first, and we stand still while he gets out and tries for a better footing. E. got one plunge into soft snow up to her waist, but that sort of thing does not hurt, and getting wet is no consideration at all! Near the top it is very precipitous, and we climb with hands quite as much as feet.

The top itself is 9,649 feet high, and commands one of the very finest views in Switzerland. You look sheer down on the Aletsch, the largest Swiss glacier, fifteen or twenty miles long, with great ice tributaries. Above it, close beyond, N. and N.W., the grandest heights of the Oberland, Aletschhorn, Finsteraarhorn, Jungfrau, Mönch, Eiger, etc. South-west rise the Weisshorn and the Mischabel, a many-peaked giant and the highest Swiss mountain, and between them, quite lonely and most grim looking, the Matterhorn. South-east lies the whole Rhone valley, bounded by Monte Leone, a superb snow ridge, and other half Italian mountains. The St. Gothard range follow, and the Viescherhörner quite near, and between 12,000 and 13,000 feet high, fill up the circle. Just imagine! Col de Balm is nowhere compared to this! We stayed an hour on the top in brilliant sunshine, seeing the view as favourably as possible short of a sunrise, and devoured hard-boiled eggs, red wine, and bread enough to last one a week at home. Of course we were in an awful pickle when we got down, about 3.30, and went to bed and to sleep while our clothes dried! For the first time we went to table d'hôte, and were lucky, for there were only two besides ourselves, and they Alpine Club men, and it was as good as a book to hear them. E.'s friend had such an escape two days before, that even Lauener turned white; the largest avalanche the guides ever saw, four hundred feet wide, came upon them "like a flash"; they saw it, and were just in time to clear it, in three seconds it was at rest, 1,500 feet below. He said "one half minute later on the path, and they must have been all killed."

In the evening we strolled out and saw an exquisite sunset; Weisshorn and Mischabel especially splendid in golden rose light, not the least speck of cloud, and the sky all flushed with wonderful tints like an aurora. You can't see these things unless you sleep up high; the finest valley sunset is quite a different article.

July 8.—Yesterday we were greatly disgusted at oversleeping ourselves, so that we started at six instead of four a.m. We got Fischer for this walk, one of the noted guides; such a nice fellow, has been up the Jungfrau seventeen times, five times in one summer. Though it was a good five hours walk to Bel Alp, not counting any stoppages, we were not at all tired, it was so delightful. The first two hours lay through the high summer pastures, and we passed some fine herds of lovely cows, so much prettier I think than ours, especially those which look like soft fawn-coloured satin; all had bells of course. We stopped at a chalet on the Riederalp, and had milk, rich and sweet, and Alpine strawberries. Then we crossed the ridge between the Rhone valley and the Aletsch, and had a long descent to the glacier through pine woods with little glades and vistas, and no end of flowers and *perfect* peeps of the snow mountains. It was too good to hurry through, so we sat down, and Fischer sang us a Swiss song with jödeln *ad lib.* I got him to dictate me the words, and then I learnt the tune, the "jödeln" is harder than Handel, and most awkward to get into. The glacier was absurdly easy to cross, being rough and dirty, and we did not even go near any big crevasses. The last hour was more fatiguing than all the rest together, as it was fearfully hot, and a very steep shadeless path up the sunny side of the glacier bank; so we rested repeatedly but got to Bel Alp at noon.

To give you an idea of the sun's power among the snow: I went up the Æggischhorn without gloves, this gives a firmer grasp of the alpenstock; but it resulted in my right hand being so burnt that I have worn a wet handkerchief on it for two days, it is just as if it were badly scalded. What dark ones we shall be in complexion when we come home!

Bel Alp is after the fashion of the Rigi, only more than two thousand feet higher, and snow peaks are much nearer, indeed close. People *pension* here a good deal. Summer chalets are dotted about all round; there are plenty of cows, and to my great entertainment goats, who climb most charmingly among the rocky bits behind the hotel. Again we had a lovely sunset, and the whole day not one speck of cloud; it is very hot by day, but gets deliciously cool and refreshing at night.

To-day, July 8, has been the best of all! We had secured Anton Walden, the best guide here, for the Sparrenhorn, which is nearly ten thousand feet high, right above the hotel. Another lady, a Miss Anstey, wished to join us, her mother, an energetic elderly lady up to a good deal, but not to *this*, making a great favour of it, as she was so very glad for her daughter to have the opportunity. So we chummed, and made all arrangements over night, ordering coffee at 3.30 a.m. We made our actual start at

3.54. Now I have seen it at last, a *real* Alpine dawn and sunrise to perfection! When we came out we saw the "daffodil sky" which Tyndall describes, in the east, a calm glory of expectant light, as if something positively celestial must come next, instead of merely the usual sun. In the south-west the grandest mountains stood white and perfectly clear, as if they might be waiting for the resurrection, with the moon shining pale and yet radiant over them, the deep Rhone valley dark and gravelike in contrast below. As we got higher the first roseflush struck the Mischabel, and then Weisshorn and Monte Leone came to life too; real rose, with something you had to persuade yourself was rose colour, only it was rose-*fire,* delicate yet intense. The Weisshorn was in its full glory, looking more perfectly lovely than any earthly thing I ever yet saw, when the tip of the Matterhorn caught the red light on its evil-looking rock peak. It was just like a volcano, and looked rather awful than lovely, and gave me the impression of an evil angel impotently wrathful, shrinking away from the serene glory and utter purity of a holy angel which that Weisshorn at dawn might represent if anything earthly could.

The eastern ridges were almost jet, in front of the great golden glow into which the "daffodil sky" heightened. By 4.30 it was all over, for as soon as the sun was up the colouring all changed to ordinary daylight hues, and thenceforth we devoted ourselves to getting up the Sparrenhorn and that alone! I think one cannot take in overmuch beauty at once; I hardly looked at anything for a long time after this great dawn splendour was over.

Now we found the practical advantage of starting early. The Sparrenhorn is a little farther, a little higher, and a little more difficult than the Æggischhorn, and yet we did it in about the same time, with much less fatigue, and without getting into any pickle as to raiment. For the snow was quite hard frozen, and, being very uneven, was quite easy walking, except when very steep, and then Walden picked out little steps with his ice axe almost as fast as we cared to mount them. Coming down I had the felicity of two real good glissades, which were immense fun, besides some sliding. One glissade I did quite alone; the other was a capital long one with Walden's hand, and it was such fun, *he* caught his foot and was all but down, and I held *him* up; he laughed no end at this, and gave me full credit for it. The view from the top was much the same style as from the Æggischhorn, not so panoramic, but *very* fine. There was plenty of rock climbing, quite to my mind. Miss Anstey is sister of an Alpine Clubbist, and seems very strong and up to mountaineering; but E. and I agree that we have no personal acquaintance, at least in the lady line, who would do to make a third with us, all things considered! However, no one can judge of what they can do here by what they can do in England, as to strength. We got to the top at 6.30, and were down again

by 8.45, just as most of the folks here were breakfasting.

I fully meant to go to sleep all the morning, but did not feel the least tired or sleepy, only a little stiff; so I have had a general lazy day out of doors by myself, getting flowers, reading and writing, and have postponed my lying down till after dinner.

I had some little talks with Anton Walden, who is superior and intelligent. In response to some remark, he quoted a verse from Hebrews to my surprise. He explained this by telling me that an English lady visitor here had sent him a beautiful New Testament; "it is forbidden to read it, but I read it nevertheless." I told him I did not know it was forbidden in Switzerland. "Oh, yes!" he said, "it is entirely forbidden. The one end and aim of the priests here is to keep the people in stupidity and ignorance, so that they may do what they like with them. They cannot bear that any one should read the New Testament for themselves, they know that would not do; but there are a few *free spirits* among us who read notwithstanding." I spoke to him about asking for the Holy Spirit to teach one whenever one read the Testament (which is all he has), and he said: "Yes! that was just what he thought too; he had found that out of his book, and had prayed for the Holy Spirit." Was it not nice?

This hotel is the best placed I ever saw, it is corner-wise somehow, so that every window commands a fair view of something fine; we have a corner room with windows looking two ways, both beautiful. It will be a delightful place for Sunday. There is a chaplain, Rev. Mr. Phillips and Mrs. P.; but I am disappointed to find that he is not C. C. C. S. There are about fifteen people in the house, not more, it is such a late season.

LETTER V.

Hotel des Alpes, Zermatt, July 11.

Rain always comes conveniently for us! So now having got here all right without a drop this morning, and being comfortably housed entirely to our mind, it is raining, furiously, and the edges of the clouds are, I think, literally not more than twenty yards off, up the mountain side. You wished that "the Angel might go before us," and certainly the prayer seems to have been answered, for anything more entirely *hitch-less* than our whole progress has been could not possibly be; even the little bad weather we have had always comes when it is rather agreeable than otherwise, and it is quite extraordinary how every little decision as to where or how or when to go, or do anything, invariably turns out to be apparently the best and pleasantest we could have done: really far too uniformly so for us to attribute it to anything but the "good hand of our God upon us." The Furca-horn adventure was the only seeming exception, and that was rather fun after all!

Sunday at Bel Alp was splendid: quite different mountain effects, grand but distant tempest clouds massed in great castles and towers and peaks over and among the mountains, always giving more grandeur and beauty than they ever hid, while all continued serene and sunny at Bel Alp till quite late evening, and deliciously warm without being oppressive. About nine p.m. a thunderstorm came over, which laid the dust and cooled the air for Monday's hot transit over the Rhone valley, and ensured a brilliant morning.

The services were the most rapid I ever was at, just one hour and twenty-five minutes in the morning, including sermon and Communion, and forty minutes in the evening, including sermon. Rev. J. E. P., of W., gave us about ten minutes of commonplace and stiff sermons. Mrs. P. chose hymns, very nice ones, out of S. P. C. K.: "How sweet the name" and such like; went the round of the few ladies in the hotel to get some one to start the singing; no one would, and she came to E. last of all, who of course referred her to me.

Monday, the 10th, we ordered coffee at five but did not get off till nearly six, which we now consider a sadly late start! H. C. ought to come to Switzerland again on purpose for Bel Alp, it combines so many things. Beside the superb views and excursions, one gets such a charming bit of Swiss pastoral life. The hotel stands alone, with grass and heather and flowers all round; and dotted all about beyond are numbers of the summer chalets, with no end of funny little children. In the middle of the day we see only a few odd cows and goats, but in the evening the creatures come pouring in from the bits of high pasture in all directions. They all come of themselves, are never fetched, and never miss or come late. In the evenings we could hardly pay attention to anything but the goats; they came trooping down the rocks, generally gambolling, and most amusing in their ways. They are most inquisitive and very tame, always came up to look at us in a most comical way, and often let us pat and play with them. There were numbers of pretty little kids and calves too; all this was so new and amusing.

Bel Alp is the best place I have yet seen for combining real mountain life with most comfortable accommodation and very moderate charges. It only cost us exactly £1 each for three whole days, including wine and everything; we were quite sorry to leave.

We walked or scrambled all the way down to Brieg, nearly five thousand feet lower; and did not halt, unless for a minute to look at a view, for three hours and twenty-five minutes, and were not a bit tired! Then we indulged in diligence six miles to Visp, an odious place in spite of the mountains around, all marsh, and flies, and heat, and malaria. We had dinner and a short rest, and then walked up the first stage of the Zermatt valley to Stalden, about five miles and a half, a lovely spot at the junction of the Zermatt and Saas valleys. Here we had coffee and rest again, and I got a native shoemaker to arm my boots with immense rough square Swiss nails, which do not slip either on ice or steep grass slopes.

We intended staying the night, but felt so very lively that we actually set off again by six p.m., and walked to St. Nicholas, another six miles and a half. Altogether we must have done over twenty miles walking in the day. Of course we went to bed when we got in at 8.15, but I did not feel at all used up, and we walked a good seven miles this morning just as if we had done nothing. We could not possibly have done it but for the very opportune weather, for a most handy thunderstorm came on while we dined at Visp, which cooled the air; I can do nothing in heat, but almost any amount if cool. Our long early walks are what enable us to get over the ground so well. We are both disappointed with Zermatt at first sight, but then the Matterhorn and Monte Rosa have not been visible yet. We took a carriage from Ronda after our early walk, so as to get in here fresh, and speer about for quarters to suit our views, which we soon found. "Hotel des Alpes" is unpretending but very clean; we have a little room each, close together, deal furniture, but all new and sufficient; we have two windows each, commanding three different looks out, and are higher up than any other hotel here, and have the most charming Swiss waitress. We are to have everything, for excursions or not, for four shillings a day each, and we thought this was to be the dearest place of all! We drank some milk, and told them to give us anything they liked for dinner at one. Whereupon we had five courses all to ourselves; we told them three would do in future. (Oh if you could but see the rain!) We have no definite plans, as we cannot cross the St. Théodule except in settled weather, nor do the Allée Blanche, but we shall call for letters at Aosta not later than the 21st. E.'s uncle and cousin are at a large hotel here; they have come nearly the same way as we have, but their journey has been a succession of mishaps and the most complete contrast to ours, yet *they* are travelling *en grand seigneur*. Their story made us realize how much we have to be thankful for.

LETTER VI.

July 13, 10 a.m. Sitting above the
Riffel Hotel (8,000 feet).

I am intensely hoping Miss Anstey may be here to-day (which is not unlikely), as, if so, I go at once to the very top of all my Alpine ambition. She and I are wild to go up the Cima di Jazi, 13,000 feet! and yet the safest in all Switzerland for anything that height. We should sleep at a chalet two hours and a half up, for the ascent to take only four or five hours in the morning. E. will not attempt it, as long ascents try her breath, and I am not so demented as to go without a lady companion, so if Miss A. does not turn up I shall resign the idea. Wednesday was too doubtful a morning for any serious excursion, so we went for a walk, and E. turned off to call on her uncle, and I found an old woman knitting and tending goats in a lovely dingle, so I sat down by her and read out of the German Testament, apparently to her intense delight, and had a most interesting talk with her. After that I had nothing particular to do; the Görner glacier was looking most bewitching, hardly three miles off, so what could I do but walk towards it and to it? I did not meet a living soul, and enjoyed immensely being so utterly alone in a most wild and beautiful spot, where a seemingly full-grown river rushes mightily out of a great dark-blue ice cave, with great ice pinnacles up above, and the full catalogue of Alpine beauty all around.

I am so desperately cautious, that being alone I did not attempt to go upon the glacier itself, although one part looked perfectly safe and easy, but only scrambled a little about the terminal moraine. I gathered a white lily, only one, most lovely and lonely, like our yellow garden lilies. Zermatt is in a different zone of flowers; yellow globe flowers, large campanulas, two very bright rock pinks, and some intense crimson rock flowers preponderate. On my way back some little white clouds, which looked far too innocent to be hiding anything, suddenly broke off, and there was the Matterhorn right above; the weirdest, most unreal looking spectre of a mountain you can imagine. It is unquestionably the most striking single object I ever saw or expected to see. How it ever entered any mortal brain to think of scaling it I cannot understand. It stands quite alone, no connection with any other mountain or range, and seems not simply peaked and perpendicular, but actually to hook over. Why it does not tumble over bodily seems a mystery!

In the afternoon we took a horse between us to the Z'mutt glacier, the path thither being the object rather than the glacier, which, though curious, is very ugly, covered with reddish stones. It took us about four hours and a half, but we did not get the full benefit of our nag, as the path was so atrocious that the guide actually did not let us ride more than twenty minutes of the way back. Part of it was so narrow that two people could not possibly walk abreast, with a precipice at least a thousand feet straight down from the edge. But it was a most paying excursion as to beauty, and totally changed our ideas of Zermatt; it is considered only a second rate excursion by many, and yet it is one of the very finest things either of us have seen. We went close under one side of the Matterhorn, which looks unique from anywhere; its base there consists of extraordinary square cut snow terraces, one above another, perfectly perpendicular. We waited for a cow to be milked for our benefit at a pitch dark chalet, where the poor people live without either window or chimney.

This morning we walked up here, handing our waterproofs and knapsacks half way to a luckily met baggage mule. Every ounce seems to make a difference to my walking powers up hill; I have even cut up my "Practical Guide," and carry three leaves at a time to save weight. Sometimes we catch a small boy and charter him to carry these wretched waterproofs, which are never anything between an unmitigated nuisance and an absolute necessity. We are camped out now for the rest of the morning; there are patches of snow round us, but the sun is hot and the air fresh and delicious.

Friday, July 14, 8.30 a.m.—10,200 feet high at this moment! on the Görner Grat, said to be simply "the finest mountain panorama in Europe!" Not many letters are dated from here I fancy, for it strikes me we are doing a rather original thing in spending a morning and writing up here.

To go back; yesterday afternoon we merely took a general scramble to see what we could, and had no end of fun in jumping little snow torrents, and contriving how to get across melting snow and round snow beds. You can't think what a *boy* I feel; it does so entirely occupy my mind where to set the next step or take the next jump; no need to tell me not to think or talk; why we should sprain our ankles if we gave our minds for two minutes to anything. Mr. Snepp wanted me to write hymns, but, dear me, he has not been in Switzerland! My only chance for that would be if we got entirely shut up in the clouds for two or three days.

We made all arrangements over night; our guide was to call us (it seems to be the guide's duty, not at all the chambermaid's!) if it was fine, not otherwise. We ordered coffee soon after 2.30 a.m. They were not punctual, and we had the aggravation of waiting till 3.5 before we could get fairly off. However we had the consolation of breakfasting with a party of gentlemen starting for Cima di Jazi, and a gentleman who with two guides was off for Monte Rosa. There was a faint clear light in the east, and the snow mountains glimmered like ghosts; but otherwise it was quite dark, though it rapidly brightened. We made a great effort to go fast, and succeeded in gaining the first Görner Grat just before the very first touch of rose came. It is really exciting and wonderful and thrilling, beyond almost anything, to see that *first* marvellous rose-fire suddenly light up peak after peak. I think it beats the Hallelujah Chorus! We waited half an hour till the sun was fairly up, as we should have lost by going on. Everything was frozen, and a great deal of hard snow to cross, so odd on the 14th of July!

About five o'clock we got up here; it is an exceptionally glorious morning; at first a few tiny clouds floating about and waving like streamers from the highest peaks; now it is absolutely cloudless, unbroken deep blue above, and a perfect circle of the highest mountains in Europe enclosing enormous glaciers around us. Monte Rosa, the nearest of all, looks a stone's throw across a glacier valley. Till just now, when some tourists came up, we have not heard a sound except a very distant waterfall several thousand feet below, and one adventurous little bird that must have lost its way. We sent our guide off, so as to stay *ad lib*. There is a little space at the top here, partly rock and partly stony, where we walked like hyenas backwards and forwards (about three yards) to keep up circulation till the sun got power, which it did soon after six. Then we read a little, and then I went to sleep for three quarters of an hour, then another hyena promenade, then breakfast on hard eggs and bread and red wine. Then some German tourists came up as hungry as wolves, and were quite thankful for a bit of bread we could spare. It is quite hot now, and not a breath of wind; had there been we could not have stayed so long; the clearness is extraordinary, so different from yesterday, when the peaks kept up a sort of sublime bo-peep among the clouds. An avalanche somewhere towards the Matterhorn has just fallen with a long deep solemn roar; no one saw it, only heard it. There is snow all around us, *i.e.* on three sides; on the fourth there is none, because it is a precipice.

Monday, 11 a.m.—Up atop of the Hörnlein, a sort of impudent sucker sprouting from the root of the Matterhorn. I could not finish half I had to say on the Görner Grat, as some Americans came up and made an awful clatter and quite broke the spell of the place. We consequently started down soon after ten, and entirely lost our way, got into a sort of labyrinth of snowdrifts and rocks; you see this unprecedentedly late snow makes everything unusually difficult. We got into no *danger*, only a little extra delay and fatigue.

In the afternoon we came leisurely down from the Riffel to our pet hotel at Zermatt, where we had an amusingly gushing welcome, as we are in great favour, especially with two particularly nice Swiss waitresses, who simply worship us. It is quite odd the fancy they have taken to us; they watch for our return from every walk, and run to meet us and carry up our things.

Saturday we really kept our resolution to be quiet, and only camped out all the morning a mile off in a pine wood, and had an ordinary walk in the evening. Sunday was just brilliant all day; a nice little church, Chamouni style, but very few there. Chaplain Mr. A., a young curate; sermon no harm, but very young and mild. Service otherwise very nice; good reader. E.'s uncle and cousin staying over Sunday; the latter a warm hearted little thing and a recent Young Women's Christian Association member.

This morning, Monday, brilliant again. When I came down to breakfast about 4.40 a.m., the Matterhorn looked like an obelisk of solid gold, a most peculiar effect, for on that side we see no other snow peak, and all below it was still in shadow, deep green and brown, and nothing between this and the one immense golden rock.

We have come in for a piece of peculiar good fortune. We had no intention of doing anything grand to-day, but took food and went without a guide to the Schwarzee, a lovely little lake, perhaps seven thousand feet high, reflecting the snow summit exquisitely. By our host's directions we found the way easily, and got there at 8.30, having started at five. On the way we fell in with cows and goats and a boy, so we made him milk a goat for us into E.'s tin cup, while we held its horns!

We only got one little cupful apiece, and wanted the child to catch and milk another. He declined entirely, saying the others were not his own, and therefore he could not; only that one belonged to him. Was not this wonderfully honest? Of course we took care he did not lose by it. We camped at the Schwarzee, but very soon saw Mr. Whitwell (E.'s connection) coming near with two guides and a porter, on his way for five hours up the Matterhorn, intending to do the worst part early to-morrow. He had never been up this Hörnlein, which is not much out of the Matterhorn route, so we had the advantage of following him and his guides all up here to my great delight.

We are in such good training that we did it easily enough, especially as there was very little snow to cross; but I don't think you have the least notion of the sort of places we get up now. Tell H. C. we should not now count Pierre à l'Echelle at all among our proper good climbs! Anything under nine thousand feet does not count at all! Mr. W. and his party are gone, and we have been some time quite alone; and there will be no more tourists, as it is too late for early birds, and it is far too much for an afternoon excursion. The view is nearly as fine as from the Görner Grat, but not so panoramic, because we are close under the Matterhorn.

Tuesday, July 18.—We stayed a good while on the Hörnlein, and when we did come down we found we had the hardest work we have yet done; we clambered up so delightedly that we never took in what a complete precipice it was, and infinitely harder to come down than going up could be. However, we got down without the least slip or nervousness. It is simply a question of making each foot sure before you remove the other or replant your alpenstock. We find the Hörnlein is about the height of the Görner Grat, and anywhere else it would be a very grand rocky peak; but as it juts out in front of the Matterhorn, it seems part of it, and does not interfere with the unity of the enormous single peak.

We were out from five a.m. to 6.30 p.m., pretty well of oxygen for one day, and we did not feel over tired.

To-day we are really taking it quietly, as we must be off at two a.m. to-morrow for the Col de St. Théodule, the highest of all the passes, 11,000 feet. All the telescopes in Zermatt are at work upon the Matterhorn. This morning Mr. W. was visible not very far from the top, *i.e.,* three moveable black dots supposed to be himself and the guides. We have done all the excursions here except Cima di Jazi, as Miss Anstey has not turned up. Zermatt itself is not equal to Chamouni on the whole, but some of the views when one gets to them (the mule paths and others are the worst I ever saw) are as grand, and much wilder and more astonishing. The contrasts are very great, some of the loveliest quietest little dingles imaginable. You might be in England or Wales, all green and ferny and shady, little tumbling brooks and stepping stones; and then you look up and see something fifteen thousand feet high through the branches!

LETTER VII.

July 20. Noon.
CHATILLON, *in the Val d'Aosta.*

We are safely and pleasantly over our grand affair and one great extravagance, the Pass of St. Théodule, and after floundering in snow yesterday morning have been eating ripe figs, apricots, and pears *this* morning. We ordered coffee at 1.30 a.m., and got fairly off by two, with a most gushing farewell, the host insisting on presenting us with a bottle of some special red wine for our journey as a token of regard! We had quite a cavalcade, a guide *en chef,* Schaller, and another engaged as porter, but who did not think fit to carry my carpet bag, and transferred it to a sub. Also a man with E.'s horse, and another with my mule. It was clear cloudless starlight, and therefore not dark, when we got away from the lights of the hotel. It was very curious, this silent march under the stars, and quite novel, along a roaring glimmering white river and over a little foot bridge, and then up into the blackness of the pines, and at last out above them just as a little quiver of paleness began to show where the dawn was to be looked for. We saw some shooting stars, and then E. saw a meteor, and towards three a.m. I saw a splendid meteor in the north-west, as large and bright as a crescent moon, but lasting only two or three seconds. The progress of dawn was most interesting, so gradual and lovely; but the sunrise itself was not so fine as some we have seen, being golden only and not rosy. But we had to perfection that pale, clear, saintly, expectant light on the great white mountains, which I think so peculiarly beautiful, before any colour comes upon the world, and some singular reflections of gold clouds upon snow slopes, themselves in shadow.

We did not ride all the way to the foot of the Théodule glacier as a few do, for Schaller said it was really dangerous, and very little saving of fatigue, being sheer scrambling over rocks; so, though the creatures had shown themselves astonishingly knowing in picking a way over most dreadful places already, we dismounted and dismissed them. Most of the path had been just a track creeping along and up the side of tremendously

steep slopes; with the great Görner glacier down so many hundred feet below. Even I submitted to have my animal led by a little chain, a thing I never gave in to before. How horrified you would have been at my attire! for on alighting we took off every possible thing, even the skirts of our dresses, and I proceeded with simply my grey linen unlined body on, and not even a necktie, between four and five a.m., and over ice and snow. It is experience that it is the best plan, one walks lighter, and the exertion keeps one warm enough, while if one wears jackets, etc., one only gets hot, and then runs risk of getting a chill. I believe girls catch more colds than boys, because they have so much extra on to go out in, and consequently get warm and thereupon get chilled. I remember my own agonies at being "wrapped up" when I was a little girl, though I was not extra coddled in that way.

The almost unprecedented snow here greatly diminished instead of increasing our difficulties, for the upper glaciers are firmly snowed over, crevasses and all, so that our grand affair turned out less difficult than some smaller-sounding things we have done. Schaller was very wroth on reaching the glacier to find that the rope had been forgotten by Biner, but the snow was in such good condition that it proved to be not at all necessary, though usually an essential for this pass. It was a long pull of nearly three hours up the snow, never steep enough to need steps cutting with ice axes, as on the Sparrenhorn, and not in any way exciting, except for the wonderfully wild snowy scene all round, right up among the enormous heights of Monte Rosa, Matterhorn, etc. We were surprised how little fatigued we were, but this was probably owing to Schaller's determined management of us; he would not let us go beyond a very quiet pace, said we should get palpitation at that height if we did, and insisted on our eating a little and drinking red wine. He says it is a great mistake in mountaineering to go on *till* you get a little exhausted.

On the top of the col we halted (and then was the time to put a shawl on!): such a strange wild scene, a vista into a great misty depth, was Italy; but otherwise it was all grand and solemn and pure, snow summits far too high for either dirt or noise. There is a hut on the top, the walls of which were built by De Saussure nearly a hundred years ago for his scientific experiments, *now* the guides went and smoked in it! It is the highest dwelling (so called) in Europe. In ordinary seasons a man would be found here, and wine, but no one has come yet this year, and the floor was ice, with the old straw for beds frozen into it. I picked up a feather very near the hut, which I send as a relic to Johnnie; can he tell what bird it belongs to? I don't think many of his relations will send him feathers from eleven thousand feet high. We only stayed about twenty minutes, for the snow softens every minute, and in the afternoon might be even dangerous. It was about eight when we started down on the Italian side, and we were soon plunging and floundering in soft snow. I found I had a great advantage in being so much lighter than the others, though I got let in sometimes.

About eleven we got to Brend, a nice little inn below the snow and above the first chalets. Here we went to sleep, guides and all; and to my extreme astonishment, when we fairly roused up and felt like *morning,* it was nearly three p.m. So we had made up for our short night, and felt quite fresh, and as if another day had begun. After dinner we had a lovely evening walk down through magnificent gorges to Val Tournanche, only five or six miles more; and we were perfectly ready to start again at 5.30 this morning, and walked more than thirteen miles down to Chatillon, dined there at eleven, and have had an hour's siesta after it.

It was "like a book," only a great deal better, to watch the gradual development of vegetation during our uninterrupted descent of ten thousand feet. On the col not even a lichen, then down through Alpine lichens and mosses to gentians and glacier anemones, every mile bringing us into a different zone of flowers: then pines, then birch and hayfields, then ash and standing corn, then walnuts and chesnuts and reaped corn, and now vines and every kind of Italian greenery and fruit. It was more than passing in a day from January to July, for the extremes are greater than English winter and summer; perhaps from Spitzbergen to Italy represents it better, without seven-league boots. It was well that it was quite cloudy part of our way, or we should have found the snow more trying than we did, even with veils and dark spectacles; we had a few showers, but nothing to hurt or hinder. Down here they have had none, and it is as hot and dusty as can be, with flies equal to Visp or Egypt. It is a very picturesque place, rather like Freiburg, only Italian in character; a beautiful bridge of one high arch spanning a tremendous gorge close to the hotel, and peeps of snow mountains over an almost tropical valley.

> July 22, 7.30 A.M. Perched on rocks just above
> Courmayeur; Mont Blanc, aiguilles, and
> all, glorious before us!

I hated Chatillon, could not settle; hotel dusty and awfully hot, just what I dislike; so we left at 4.30 by diligence, and reached Aosta at 7.30. We were obliged to go inside; however I was consoled by getting an opportunity of airing my Italian with some Turin people; I got on better than I expected, and think I should soon get pretty fluent. I am disappointed to find that in this Val d'Aosta they speak almost entirely French; and if not this, Piedmontese, which is a hideous patois, as ugly as Welsh, and not at all like Italian. Next morning we did Aosta pretty thoroughly before 9.30 a.m. First we had a superb walk up to a church, St. Marguerite, which commands a magnificent view of the whole valley (weather magnificent too; always is when we want it!). It is very beautiful indeed, wide and grand, with two rivers winding below three separate sets of grand snow mountains in the openings of the lower ranges, town itself a picture, with towers and bridge, and plenty of walnut and chesnut trees and vineyards, to fill up.

We were in ecstasies with a little village perched on a green shelf of the mountain, every separate house a picture with galleries and gables, and the spaces between, one mass of arcading of vines trained on stone pillars and wooden trellises above, surpassing the prettiest Italian pictures you ever saw. It is literally "sitting under his vine"; and the natives did look so cool and picturesque in the shade, quite enviable. This expedition took us about two hours, and then I actually went all about the town. This is the first time we have slept in one since Lucerne, and the first time we have slept below three thousand feet; but then Aosta is really uncommon, not merely Italian, but full of such fine Roman remains as I did not know could be seen out of Rome, massive arches and towers in wonderful preservation and most interesting. We gave a fruit woman twopence and my bag to put what she liked in. I thought she would never stop, and on counting for curiosity there were thirteen plums, fourteen apricots, and five large pears! Walking along this valley does not do after seven a.m., so we went by diligence at 10.30 seventeen miles to Morgex by about three o'clock; some folks could have "walked backwards" quite as fast. We heard a great deal of talk about the king, who is now "in the mountains" hunting a beast of the chamois kind, but peculiar to one mountain district south of Aosta. He seems immensely popular here; they told us with great satisfaction that he always speaks Piedmontese "*en famille,* and to *us,* though he can speak all the other languages," and that he is "*un vrai montagnard,*" and enjoys above all things getting away to the mountains, and that he camps out quite near the snow for three days at a time, and is "a wonderful shot and never misses," and various other items of praise.

Morgex was very lovely, but horribly hot, and I have had quite enough of Italian valleys and am delighted to be nearer the snow again at Courmayeur, which was about seven miles farther. I must have been either a ptarmigan or a chamois, if I transmigrated, before turning up as F. R. H.; mountains do suit me, and no mistake. At Morgex I tumbled about on a mattress all the afternoon; it was too hot to sleep, and too hot to go out, and even too hot to have the windows open. However, the enormous shadow of Mont Blanc brings early evening, and soon after six the whole valley was in shadow and we had a nice walk.

Owing to a fortunate mistake, we have had the most exquisite sunrise of all. We ordered coffee at 3.30, and to be called at three, thinking, as these Italians are unpunctual, we might get off at four. They did call us, and we thought it a very dark morning; and when I had finished dressing, I looked at my watch, and it was just 2.20. We were not sorry, for a Mr. Wade we met at Aosta (brother of the ambassador at Pekin) warned us that it would be an awfully hot walk if once the sun got over the shoulder of the mountain. So we set off at three under the stars again, with a delicious breeze coming straight down from Mont Blanc to meet us. The dawn was perfection and cloudless, except some fairy flakes of pink and gold, and one little pale bell of cloud half way up the monarch. *But*, when the rose-fire touched Mont Blanc itself, and spread down to meet the little cloud, the glory of it was entirely indescribable. E. said, "the most heavenly thing upon earth," and there it must rest, for one can't say more. I always thought people coloured these sunrises a little, but that is simply impossible; even Ruskin will not over-paint them. "Fade into the light of common day" has great significance; for though the splendour lasted longer than usual this morning, it is only a matter of fifteen minutes at most; and if one misses *that*, one may just as well not get up till eight. Had we started at four, we should have had little if any view of Mont Blanc, owing to the bend of the valley; as it was, we reached the very finest point of view at the right moment.

Courmayeur is most charming, grand and lovely combined, decidedly beats Zermatt. Fortunately Mr. Wade recommended us to Hotel Mont Blanc, which we never should have found for ourselves; a quiet hotel-pension half a mile away from Courmayeur, and on the grandest site, quite to our liking; we are pensioned at about 5s. 3d. a day. We are camped out for the morning; there are no goats to play with, but pretty little green and brown lizards scampering about the rocks, which do as well, and make a change!

A wrinkle for Maria, which seriously I should think worth introducing for poor people at Wyre Hill! At our pet hotel at Zermatt we had *hay* duvets! of course too hot for July, but must be most comfortable in winter, and quite as much warmth as a good blanket. Just a large doubled square of coloured print, neat and clean, lightly filled with loose hay! What a boon they would be in hard winters, and they could be made of any old stuff for almost nothing. I shall try it myself for very poor people, if it comes a hard winter.

The bread on this side the Alps is most queer; the waiter brings a small clothes basket full of bread, and puts a handful like a little sheaf by each party on the table. It is in strips about two feet long, size of my little finger, very crisp and nice. They give other bread or roll, but these sticks are evidently the leading idea.

The hours here are most original. We are supposed to have coffee early, when we like; then at 10 a.m. a déjeuner table d'hôte; this was, first a white grainy compound with grated cheese supposed to be soup, then sliced German sausage and bread and butter, then very good cutlets and fried potatoes, then stewed pears, then cheese, then apricots, etc. The second table d'hôte is at five. There are about thirty-two Italians and Piedmontese in the house, no English; they are rather noisy, but very amusing to watch. After breakfast we strayed into the salon de lecture, and found a tolerable piano, the first we have had; so naturally I sat down, there being only two ladies in the room, played a bit, and finally sang. I was rather startled after the latter performance to hear a vehement round of clapping. I had no idea of it, but the room had filled quietly; I had my back to them, and found I had a room full of Italians as audience, quite a new thing for me! and they seemed amazingly pleased. Actually the waiters brought more chairs in, seeing the concourse, to my great amusement; so what could I do but yield to the requests, and sing two more songs! We are not the least tired as yet, but mean to have three hours' siesta; we always make up our short nights.

LETTER VIII.

Courmayeur, Wednesday, July 26.

We could not have beds in our pension, and the hotels were full, so we slept in a pigsty of a cottage where nothing was clean except the beds. It was too late to make a fuss, but we made up our minds to live out all day and decamp on Monday morning.

Sunday was tolerably pleasant. Services quite delightful, though there were only seven English and a few foreign *spectators*. Chaplain Mr. Phinn, from Dorsetshire; two lovely little sermons, all one could wish, and not stiff and unappropriate like some others we have had. The hymns went so capitally in the morning that Mr. P. put on four hymns in afternoon service; he is almost a match for Mr. Snepp at it! And really we seven English, Mr. P. included, made the little Vaudois chapel ring again, and did a good deal better than many a congregation of ten times as many. Mr. P. knows many of dear papa's own tunes well, and his especial favourite is Zoheleth, which he says every one is struck with who hears it, as far as his experience goes.

We were to have gone early on Monday to Mont de Saxe, but a really tremendous thunderstorm came on with torrents of rain, so we got up late, and did not finish breakfast till nearly seven. It was fair then, but too late for Mont de Saxe, which is a special sunrise affair, so we walked off to the Pavilion de Mont Blanc, which is exactly parallel to Pierre Pointue on the opposite side, and about the same height. Not having slept properly for three nights, we found it rather a pull, and clouds came down on the aiguilles, and Mont Blanc might have been in England for all we saw of him, and an old Swiss farmer told us there would be "*le vent et la grêle et la pluie* and all that was bad." So we raced down again and got to the hotel before two. Thereupon it cleared up and was a lovely afternoon, and we wished we had stayed. Next morning we started with a mule and guide for Mont de Saxe; it was fair enough till we were near the top, and then it began to snow, and snowed all the time till we got down to rain level, and then it rained all the day in such a style that you would not think it could go on like that for ten minutes longer. We gained our hotel by eleven.

My proofs had come late the evening before, so I sat down to make the best of it in the salon de lecture (as we had no room), but did not get on at all well, as the Italians fidgeted in and out and played cards and piano. We had decided we could not go on this way any more, so poor E. went off to Courmayeur in the rain, and after going everywhere, finding all full, to her great delight got a comfortable and fairly quiet room, only very dark and no look out, at the Hotel Royale. Still we hailed this and departed as to a sort of refuge, and had a very good night.

The Italians made a great fuss at our departure, and want me to come back and sing again. Each time I touched the piano the whole company flocked in from all sides, it was most amusing! All are staying *en pension,* which is why we could have no room. At table d'hôte at Hotel Royale Mr. and Mrs. Phinn's places were next ours, and Mr. P. talked most interestingly; such a nice man. They had called on us at Hotel Mont Blanc, which is what a chaplain ought to do I think, so I was gratified.

This morning proved perfectly magnificent, which was tantalizing, but I determined to buckle to and had a good steady five hours' work on my proofs in an open air gallery without any distracting view except a brilliant sky.

Friday, July 28.—Still at Courmayeur! So far I had written in a delicious den, a discovery of E.'s, a shallow cave under a rock a little way up Mont de Saxe, cool and shady, and commanding a grand front view of Mont Blanc, with a little white pillar of cloud on the very top.

Yesterday I had a very satisfactory proof morning. In the afternoon we had a stiff climb up the shoulder of Mont Chétif, whose Courmayeur face is a striking precipice, and whose top is a curious cone of rock; there is a tolerable path up a gorge which leads to a ridge below the cone, from this you get an astonishing face to face view of the most precipitous side of Mont Blanc (too steep for any snow to stick), and the immense ice-fall of the great Glacier du Brenva. The summit of Mont Blanc was almost entirely veiled, but that seemed almost to enhance the weird sublimity of the view.

Mr. and Mrs. Phinn asked us to come to tea to meet Costabel the Vaudois missionary pastor, stationed at Courmayeur. This was very interesting. He is a simple, good man, very cordial and communicative, and he told us a good deal about Vaudois work, etc.; the talk was all in French. Costabel is very isolated here, and has only a few poor Christian friends, and never any superior society unless English find him out. Mr. P. has thoroughly taken him up, and they go long walks together. He told us the fear of death among the people here is awful, that he is frequently present at the most painful death scenes. During life and health they leave everything to the priest, and believe that he will make it all right for them, and except complying with certain forms do not think or trouble themselves about religion at all. Then when they are dying they get alarmed, and see that this natural shifting of their religion upon the priest will not do, they lose confidence in him, and have no other; they want peace and have none; they would like to feel assured, but they have no assurance, and die in the agonies of terror. It was terrible to hear Costabel's description of what he says is the rule as to death-beds. "Unto the poor the gospel is preached," and he says it is so here, that only the poor will listen to him and those in the outlying villages where no priest resides.

We find the people here quite different from the Swiss, and not so ready to accept Gospels, etc. It is the first place where on offering one we have been asked "if it was a Protestant book." However they always end by taking them.

We did so hope to have got away this morning, and now I fear we cannot get to Chamouni at all. The Allée Blanche is a route which is worse than lost by going in bad weather, and Courmayeur is in such a hole that you cannot get out of it without going over some great pass, unless you do two days' diligence to Torca and round by Turin, or go back to Aosta and over the Great St. Bernard to Martigny. Although Courmayeur has been the scene of our only mistakes and misfortunes, I more than ever think that either for strong or weak folk it is the very best place I know of for making a long stay; the walks and excursions are inexhaustible, grand ones for mountaineers and lovely little easy ones for invalids. Valleys and gorges fork in all directions. It is totally different from Chamouni, which is one grand valley, and even better than Zermatt in this respect. It is on a gentle slope, some height above the noisy foaming Dora, and so has not the perpetual roar which is such a drawback to Swiss enjoyment. If the rivers would but go to sleep at night, what a relief it would be! I shall take your advice about not overdoing oneself the last thing before coming home; I found my broken nights took down my strength to English level, and I was quite fagged in getting up Mont de Saxe, but one good night set me up again. I certainly have not been so well for years, and I am so sunburnt it will take two winters to bleach me.

CHAPIU. Saturday, 5.30 p.m.

We have got off at last; the weather was not hopeful, but we ordered a mule and provisions, and set out at five a.m. in the highest spirits, and there was the most transparent dawn-sky imaginable, not a cloud, and a delightful north wind, which is an infallible sign of first-rate weather.

As we passed our old hotel (Mont Blanc) we found a caravan of about eighteen mules and nearly as many guides, and all the Italian gentlemen pensioning there (no ladies) were going to the Col de la Seigne for the day.

I wish H.C. could have seen the shiftless southerners attempting to mount; four of them had actually got on a low wall to mount from while the guides were trying to poke the animals close enough for them. We hastened on, not wishing to get mixed up, and kept ahead the whole way, five hours, though we were alternately on foot, and got to the top just before them. We chose our spot to lunch, and they camped at a little distance, with many bows and "Bon appetit!" and other small foreign civilities as they passed us.

When we had finished and were moving off they shouted to us to stay, and all rose and came to us offering wine and fruit, and saying they wished to propose a toast and drink with us before we left. It was far too gracefully done to refuse; so red wine was poured, and all raised a most cordial "Vive l'Angleterre!" with great enthusiasm and clinking of glasses, to which we responded with "Viva l'Italia!" which seemed to please them. Then an old priest said, "Mesdemoiselles, êtes-vous catholiques? Viva Roma," to which I replied in Italian, "We can at least say, *Viva Roma capitale d'Italia!*" which response he quite understood and said, "Ah well, ah well! viva Christianity!" to which we of course responded *con amore*. Then two or three more, probably freethinkers I am afraid, said, "Oui bien, but no more popery," and other similar exclamations, at which we were very much astonished as at least three priests were in the party. Then we were allowed to depart with no end of hat wavings and good wishes. It was such a curious little episode, occurring too at such a superb spot, and close to the cross which marks the boundary and bears on one side "France" and on the other "Italia."

We reached Chapiu at two, and we hoped it might be possible to put on steam and get over the Col de Bonhomme this afternoon, but we found it could not be done before dark, so we were obliged to give it up and stay over Sunday at this funny little lonely inn.

It has been a glorious day, almost too clear, as it rather takes from the sublimity, the summits looking so near. We passed the Lac de Combat, all exquisitely soft tinted lake, pearly blue, but less intense than Geneva, reflecting a grand and lovely group of snow summits and ridges, more like a fairy fancy than a reality in its unique loveliness.

That lake was red in Napoleon's days, and a wretched garrison was kept freezing there four whole winters, guarding the pass at the boundary. The ruins of their rough fortifications are reflected in one corner, a melancholy contrast.

The col is 8,450 feet high, but the ascent was unusually gradual, and we were as fresh when we got to the top as when we started. But then we had ignominiously descended to having a mule between us, so it was only two hours and a half walking for each.

LETTER IX.

HOTEL GIBBON, LAUSANNE. Thursday, Aug. 3.

I actually have had no one half hour to begin this conclusion of my reports, for, in spite of all my resolutions, we have had three tremendous days. How was a mortal to resist doing all one could at Chamouni?

Sunday at Chapiu we turned out for a little air the first thing, came back in the rain, and had to stay in the rest of the day. We intended to have spent part of it in Scripture reading among the few scattered chalets within reach, as Costabel told us the inhabitants are mostly mere heathen, and not even looked after by any priest.

Monday dawned sulky, but not bad enough to stay at Chapiu, where the bread was sour and the other viands pale and greasy, and we, having the best room, were accommodated with one deal bench instead of any chairs. So we set off before sunrise, in hope, and after an hour's steep climb met the clouds, which were relieving themselves of sleet. We soon got to the highest chalet and took shelter. Such an interior! Fancy a good sized barn, one half consisting of a platform three steps high, the other with floor of bare earth. We were civilly invited to ascend the steps and sit on a box, which we thankfully did, for we dared not stir for dirt and fleas. On this platform, which had one window a foot square, were five beds, three of hay on the floor, covered with one filthy sheet and a great brown coverlet ditto, the other two a sort of boxes of hay. Presently the beds were made, and the process was simple, consisting of a shake and poke to the hay, which sent out a cloud of dust. Two children were awoke and dressed; their toilet, performed by the father, occupying about a minute, and chiefly consisting of putting on cap and shoes. We watched the proceedings on the earthen floor half of the house with amusement. The inhabitants all had breakfast in a desultory way, milk and curds and bits of black bread, supped out of great porringers with gigantic spoons. There were five men and a woman, all occupied with the milk and cheese business, and grouping themselves picturesquely in the light from the door, and a wood fire on the ground made near enough to a hole in the corner of the roof to give the smoke a chance. Over the fire a cauldron, at least four feet in diameter, swung about by a great creaking beam, a most witch-like affair. After nearly two hours the storm moderated, and the guide said we could go on.

When we had done all the worst of the ascent, the rain having happily ceased, I suddenly fell sick. It was a fix, for we were too high either to stop or go back, and I could not stir, but lay down on the wet stones, whereat the guide was frantic. "Madame serait malade, if she did not get up and walk." (They consider themselves as responsible for their travellers.) Most opportunely E. descried at some depth below two gentlemen and a mule; by the time they reached us I was rather better, and they were most amiable about lending me their animal, making out that it was only laziness to have had one at all. We continued the ascent; and, to my amazement, getting among the snow again so revived me that when we got as far as the mule could go (in about an hour) I felt all right. The "traversée," as they call it, of the Col de Bonhomme was the wildest of wild scenes, cutting across the west shoulder of the Mont Blanc chain, all rocks and snow, most formless and chaotic, and famous as being about the most difficult to find the way. Our benevolent friends had a Zermatt guide, who was supposed to know it well; but they quite lost the way, and were brought back by much racing and hallooing by the Chapiu man who was with me and the mule. A thick white icy fog had come on and made the col very characteristic, but we lost the grand views. We came down into the lovely valley of Contamines and dined at Nant Borrant, and after an hour's sleep we walked two hours more down to Contamines, which we reached about 5.30. Such a lovely place, luxuriant and bright, with snow summits closing the valley, and the rosy smile of a great white peak shining down at sunset through a cloud rift.

Next morning was another of the brilliant days of which we have had so many. It is eighteen miles to Chamouni, so we took a horse between us for the first six or seven miles, leaving less than eleven to walk. The top of the Col de Voza is glorious, it is too close under Mont Blanc to see the real summit, but the massive shining snow of the Dome and Aiguille du Gouté are close above; all the other aiguilles follow in a grand curve, and the fine sweep of the vale of Chamouni is nowhere seen to such advantage. The colouring was vivid, and the atmosphere keenly clear. We scampered down to Les Ouches, and then finished the walk with four miles and a half of level road to Chamouni, which was quite a rest after the mountain work. Having got our letters and looked about Chamouni, we took mules and started up the Bréven! Not all the way, as we could not reach the top before dark, but to Plampraz, about two-thirds of the way up, a firstrate place for sunset, rather higher up than La Flégère, and exactly opposite the great Glacier des Bossons and the very heart of Mont Blanc.

How we did triumph over the people whom we met going down to table d'hôte at Chamouni, just as the grand show up there was going to begin! There had been more than one hundred visitors at Plampraz, but all cleared down before sunset, and we had the little inn and the sunset all to ourselves. It seemed too much to have all alone; how I did want you and all! That whole magnificent range close opposite to us turned gold, and then fire colour, and then softened into rose, and then tenderly paled away into that most saintly colourless afterlight, which M. L. will remember we agreed in admiring most of all. The valley was quite dark below, and the black pine forests beneath, and the almost purple sky above, formed a wonderful setting for all that superb colouring.

Next morning, Wednesday, we were up just in time for a lovely clear sunrise; but there is no expanse of colouring in the morning, as the eastern tips are only seen sideways. The rose flush was very delicate and lovely, but all over in ten minutes. Then we had coffee, and soon after five started up the Bréven, which I did not intend to do at all, and meant to let E. go alone; but how could I help it on such a morning! It is much more difficult than I expected, as there are several snow slopes, and one where we should have been glad of an ice axe to cut steps; and near the top the "cheminée" is quite a hands and feet climb up a rock. The view from the very summit is a first class panorama, and quite a different thing from going only to the little inn which many do, and call it "going up the Bréven." We stayed an hour to take it in, then came down again to Plampraz and had another breakfast.

The next move was to march to La Flégère, about five or six miles, a more tiresome walk than we expected; as, instead of being nearly level along the slope, it was rather sharp up and down the whole way. It was delightful to see La Flégère again and compare impressions, as it was my first revisited scene. It was beginning to cloud over, and so looked just the same as when we saw it in 1869. I do not think the Mer de Glace part of the view lost anything by comparison with all we had seen; but the Mont Blanc part of it is very inferior to the Bréven view. We had only time to rest twenty minutes and drink some milk, and then set out again by a cross cut, which for part of the way was no path at all, down to Argentière. We had no guide, and occasionally made a bad speculation and made angles; however, we reached the Couronne where we breakfasted in 1869, ravenous!

After dinner we took mules for the Col de Balm at 4.30, rather annoyed at being reduced to this ignominy, but we had wearied ourselves in tracking the way to Argentière, and it was a close oppressive day. I had before inquired for Joseph Dévouassoud; he was off duty as guide; however he got wind of the inquiry and a description of the inquirer; whereby he arrived at the conclusion that it was the writer of the verses in his certificate book, which verses he seems to have considerably traded upon! So after dinner he came in delighted and gushing, quite amusing, and got leave from the guide chef to exchange his turn, and so came with us up the Col de Balm. It was cloudy and gloomy when we got up at nearly seven o'clock; we went immediately up the hill on the left, where H. C., M. L., and I went to get the panorama. It was really very grand; though I would rather have seen it in clear light, the sombre gloom was not a bad effect especially on the Tête Noire side, where the gulf was almost black and the mountains just awful, with the white Buet like a dim ghost overlooking them. The Mont Blanc range was a chaos of cloud and snow. We saw most where last time we saw least, *i.e.* down Martigny way; the Rhone valley mountains being clearer, and some vestiges of sunset light on them. No one else except a very fatigued German slept there; he had walked from Chamouni *viâ* Montanvert, and had quite exhausted himself; " it was far too much to attempt," he said. We were entertained, for we had done considerably more in the day, and were quite lively after it all.

It poured all night, but left off after seven a.m., so we prepared to start; our bill was simply scandalous. We decided to give up the Eau Noire gorge route, and go direct to Martigny. The P.S.G. calls it five hours and a half, but we scampered, wishing to catch the 12.30 train, and we actually did it in four hours, including five minutes' stoppage on the Col de Trient for a glass of wine and water.

Although it poured furiously part of the way, I never was more glad that we had no waterproofs; we could not have done it if we had, and if I come pedestrianising again I shall take none; getting wet is nothing in Switzerland, one gets dry again directly. It seemed quite too luxurious to get into such good paths again as the Col de Balm; Zermatt, etc., are half a century behind Chamouni in this respect.

It would have been tantalizing to go by rail down the Rhone valley if it had been fine; but it was all colourless and cloudy and rainy, so I was grateful to George Stephenson. The lake of Geneva can't help looking blue in any weather, but it was rough enough to make us glad we had not gone by steamer. Montreux, etc., looked astonishingly tame after the great scenes we have been in. We came on here (Lausanne), as our bags were to be at Poste Restante, otherwise it would have been

nicer to go on to Neuchatel. Even the smallest modicum of baggage is sure to be a nuisance first or last. Only fancy us at Hotel Gibbon! the first time we have been in one of these Swiss palaces in this tour, and we feel so out of place! The first thing I did on getting into this grand hotel was to tumble down full length on the polished gallery floor, owing to the nails in my boots. I never had a single fall on ice, snow, or rock! so it was rather odd.

Our evening coffee here under splendid chandeliers and mirrors and carving and gilding was a considerable contrast to the previous night. At Plampraz, which was lowest in the scale, we had no chair or table in our bedrooms, and the limited washing apparatus was on a very small shelf by the bed, which was a sort of wooden crib.

On the whole I set Courmayeur as A 1 of all, and I think Zermatt second, and Chamouni third. But there is no single scene more unique and characteristic than the Mer de Glace at Chamouni, and no panorama to compare with the Görner Grat. Courmayeur has far the most variety, whether for excursions or for strolls, and is quite the place for the longest stay. But Chamouni is the place to begin with, to get into training; Courmayeur to improve upon it; and Zermatt to use and tax all your Alpine powers. You can't think what easy walks all the Chamouni excursions seem to us now! N.B.—I read my letters over to E., so there is a guarantee against exaggeration!

Connie was the only person who addressed rightly to Chamouni; every one else put Switzerland, so causing delay and extra payment, as it is *France*. No one ever will believe that Chamouni is not Switzerland and never was, but Savoy, and now France.

Monday, 7.30 a.m.—Clapham Park. Just as uncomfortable a journey home as possible, a small counterbalance to our previous prosperity. I can't stay for details, but will write when I get to Perry Barr. Horrible crossing. Delightful Sunday here, splendid! most striking sermons, Rev. Aubrey Price; leave here 8.45. Could not possibly post on Saturday.

IV.

MY ALPINE STAFF.

MY Alpine staff recalls each shining height,
    Each pass of grandeur with rejoicing gained,
    Carved with a lengthening record self-explained,
Of mountain memories sublime and bright.

No valley life but hath some mountain days,
    Bright summits in the retrospective view,
    And toil-won passes to glad prospects new,
Fair sunlit memories of joy and praise.

Grave on thy heart each past "red-letter day"!
Forget not all the sunshine of the way
By which the Lord hath led thee: answered prayers
And joys unasked, strange blessings, lifted cares,
Grand promise-echoes! Thus thy life shall be
One record of His love and faithfulness to thee.

V.

HOLIDAY WORK.

I ONLY wish that all the tired workers at home would re-new their strength and spirits by such holiday work abroad as lies within reach of many who fancy it far out of their reach. I did not know till the summer before last what a combination of keen enjoyment and benefit to health, with opportunities of usefulness and open doors innumerable, was to be found in a *pedestrian tour by unprotected females!* This, too, without difficulties or discomforts worth calling such, and at a *very* much smaller outlay than is supposed possible by those who travel in the usual expensive way, and think that going to Switzerland for six or eight weeks means spending £50 at the least. Much less than half that sum will suffice for such a tour as ours. And lest it should be thought that exceptional strength is necessary, I may premise that both my friend and myself had been thor-oughly overworked, and were obliged to seek rest; that neither of us is very strong, and that a walk of a mile or two is the ex-tent of our English powers.

Of course we chose the inexpensive route, *viâ* Newhaven and Dieppe to Paris, and thence by night train to Belfort, on the frontier, where we arrived at nine a.m., June 29th, 1871. As we had slept pretty fairly, having had a carriage to ourselves by reason of the guard's natural sympathy for unprotected fe-males, and having been able to lie down full length by reason of going second class instead of first, we were not tired, and intended to proceed. But the train to Basle and Lucerne had just left. "*C'est une désorganisation complète!*" said a fatigued Frenchman, and rightly. No information whatever was to be had, either at Paris or at Belfort itself, as to trains beyond, unless you got hold of a German official. Moreover, every German train was arranged to depart just before the corresponding French one got in, and *vice versa,* apparently for the purpose of spite. And so it came to pass, as a result of the war, that we had nearly six hours to wait.

When there is no one to wait and be anxious for you, and no one to arrange for but your two selves, and no fixed plan beyond to-day, and that day and all its hours committed to a Father's guidance, disappointment becomes almost impossible, and the crossing of one's intentions constantly results in most evident guiding to something better. So it was with our detention at Belfort, which was no part of our own programme.

We set off through the town to the fortifications. "Why should we not begin at once?" said my friend, E. Clay. So, setting the example, she began offering French tracts and "portions" to almost every one we met. And a wonderful two or three hours we had! Such eagerness for the little books, such gratitude, such attentive listening as we tried to speak of Jesus, such tears as we touched the chord of suffering, still vibrating among these poor people, to whom war had been an awful reality! Surely God sent us! Not one to whom we spoke but told us of husbands, sons or brothers fallen in the siege or elsewhere; or else of terrible losses and poverty. Some to whom we gave tracts went away reading, and soon came back begging for another, "pour ma mère," "pour un ami." We went into a large room, where several wounded soldiers lay, while women sat at work; here again all was earnest attention and gratitude. *"Merci infiniment, infiniment!"* said one poor fellow.

At last we made our way up to the fortifications, where probably none but "unprotected females" would have been allowed! Our *petits livres* secured us the respect of the few soldiers and many workmen. We realized a little of what war means, as we wandered about the half ruined stronghold, and looked down upon a church with scarcely a square yard of roof intact, and houses in every stage of shatter and desolation, or, at best, poorly patched up for bare shelter.

Before we left, a deputation came to us from a party of workmen who had been reading our tracts during their dinner, to ask for a few more, that they might take them to some *camarades,* who were employed in another part of the town, and who "would be too happy to possess them."

As we returned through the town we found many waylaying us. At one point which they knew we must pass, at least thirty persons were waiting, and pressed round us, begging for more tracts. We had only a few leaflets left, with "Rock of ages" in French and German, and these they accepted eagerly. I have since regretted that it did not occur to me at the moment to *sing* it.

We reached Lucerne that night, and next morning steamed down the lake. It would have been contrary to our travelling principles to pay first-class fare for the privilege of sitting among the unsociable English, aft, with funnels and paddle-boxes right between us and the magnificent scenery opening out before us; so we took second-class tickets, thereby securing for half-price a clear front view, with nothing but transparent air between us and the increasing loveliness ahead, and also the advantage of being among the natives, who were all politeness to the English ladies. We thus had also the benefit of some charming Swiss songs, sung by a girls' school out for a holiday; they lent us their little song-book to follow the music, and were delighted at receiving little books in return, which might by His blessing put a *new* song in their mouths.

From Altdorf, at the other end of the lake, our long anticipated *real* pedestrian tour began. Our plan was as follows. Our luggage consisted of a *small* carpetbag apiece, every inch and ounce having been considered and economised, though even these were discovered on further experience to contain superfluities! These bags we sent on each morning by post or diligence if on *grandes routes;* by baggage mule, country cart, or small boy, if off the track: to whatever place we thought we could reach in the day without undue fatigue; and here we always found them all right; average expense, a few pence.

We started at four, or five a.m., walking on till we felt inclined, to stop and rest: our first halt being given to leisurely reading and prayer in some grand and lonely mountain oratory; a plan which we found more pleasant and profitable than devoting the whole time to it indoors before starting. Then we strolled on again, halting or taking refreshment, just as and when we felt inclined; resting for several hours in the heat of the day, and making another stage or two in the afternoon. We carried tiny knapsacks (bags are a great mistake, being more fatiguing to carry); these held tracts and "portions," a biscuit and a hard egg, and the barest necessaries in case of missing our carpetbags, or altering our plan for the night. As Switzerland is the land of hotels and travellers, such a tour as ours is easier than it would be elsewhere; unless you are in *very* out-of-the-way places, you seldom go three miles without some opportunity of getting a meal, nor six without a fair chance of beds.

We began very gradually; our first walk was only two miles, but in a fortnight we found ourselves doing from fourteen to twenty miles in the day without getting tired! Our early hours were part of the secret; one can do double the distance before seven am. that one can after; the invigorating effect of the crisp fresh mountain air from four to seven a.m. is indescribable. Those who think eight a.m. a pretty fair start never know what this atmospheric salvolatile is. But you cannot burn your candle at both ends, and must go to bed accordingly. If you resolutely and *regularly* retire at eight p.m., and make no scruple about taking a good siesta in the heat of the day; (and you may lie down on the grass with impunity in *such* open air), it will come quite natural to get up about 3.30 or 4 a.m. We felt sensitive about Dr. Watts and "wasting our hours in bed," if we were not out of it before 5.30 on Sunday mornings.

Oh the delicious freedom and sense of leisure of those days! And the veritable "renewing of youth," in all senses, that it brought! How we spied grand points of view from rocks above, and (having no one to consult, or to keep waiting, or to fidget about us) stormed them with our alpenstocks, and scrambled and leaped, and laughed and raced, as if we were, not girls again, but downright *boys!* How we lay down on moss and exquisite ferns, and feasted our eyes on dazzling snow summits through dark, graceful pines, with intense blue sky above, and the quiet music of little torrents coming up from the dell below, and with the "visible music" all round us, in every possible colour-key, of those marvellously lovely Alpine flowers, which people never see who go "in the season," a month or two later. How entirely, we were rid of that imp, Hurry, who wears out our lives in England! "No hurry!" It took us a long while to realize that delightful fact. And how we wished that a wish could have transported the whole Association of Female Workers and Young Women's Christian Association, whom we left in London, bodily to the spot, to share the wonderful rest and enjoyment which our Father was giving us! A *"holiday"* most certainly; but how about *"work"*? So much of that, that we never wanted more opportunities, but only more earnestness and faithfulness, and courage and love, to use them. If space allowed, one would like to give each day in order and detail, with its pleasant providences and openings. But we can only indicate briefly some of the different kinds of "opportunity" so thickly strewn in our path.

Our tour was entirely through Roman Catholic cantons; its roughly sketched outline being this: from Altdorf, over the Furca, down the Rhone valley to Viesch; a detour to Æggischhorn and Bel Alp; then to Zermatt; over the pass of St. Théodule into the Val d'Aosta; Courmayeur; over the Col de Bonhomme to Chamouni; thence to Martigny, where we took rail direct home, *viâ* Neuchatel. And all the way, no Bible, no gospel, but souls walking in darkness all around! Will not some of our workers try to go, and tell them of the True Light?

At the little inns where we slept, we nearly always found young waitresses. A few kind words and smiles secured their absolute devotion to us, and we were waited on like duchesses. (N.B.—How much nicer than going to big hotels, with waiters flying about, to whom you are merely No. 79 or No. 43!) They have "no time for religion in the summer," but attend extra masses in winter to atone for it. But they find time to listen with surprise as you speak to them of salvation. They are afraid to die; *"Ah, la mort, c'est terrible!"* And it is at least

something new to hear of a "sure and certain hope." We speak to them again in the morning before we go, and sometimes find that they have been lying awake thinking of what had been said. We give them a Gospel of St. John, and our own reading has not been less profitable because it has not been in our own Bibles, but in this "portion" for poor Thérése, marking as we read such bright star-texts as may catch her eye, and guide her to Jesus.

Here I may say that during our long mid-day rests we made it our special occupation to mark the most striking passages and texts in the "portions" we were going to give away. These were *chiefly* St. Luke and St. John, while to persons of superior intelligence and education we often gave Romans, but *always marked.* Even curiosity will induce people to look attentively at marked passages.

At Zermatt, where we stayed five days in the clean, cheap, and unpretending Hotel des Alpes (which we strongly recommend), there were two maidens, and we agreed each to make special effort with one. Alexandrine had evidently never thought about religion; but Marie, a singularly gentle and loveable girl, seemed an instance of "soil prepared." She had thought much of death, and with terror; she had tried to be worthy of heaven, and had failed, and wondered why she felt so bad when she really wished to be good. She said she knew that Jesus died for sinners, but had no idea what good that was to do for her, as of course she must gain her own salvation, and *then* He might save her. She had never seen a Testament, and no one of the many English ladies whom she had served had ever spoken to her about these things.

Every evening she contrived to come to my room, and we read the German Testament and prayed together. She listened eagerly, and as if it were indeed a matter of life and death. I cannot say that when we left she was able to *rejoice* in Christ, but I think that she had, though tremblingly, touched the hem of His garment; she was trusting to none other, and saw that it must be "Jesus only," and the whole desire of her heart seemed to be toward Him.

We often turned out of the path to go to parties of haymakers. They invariably received our books with pleasure, and their acknowledgments were most courteous. If we stayed to read a few verses, they never seemed to feel it an interruption. We gave them the book out of which we read, with a leaf turned down, that they might look again at the passage. One morning I sat down by an old woman, who was knitting, and watching goats. She was an "old maid," very poor and full of troubles. She often thought of heaven, she said, and how different it would be there, and she prayed that God would show her how to get there. She was sure she should be happy if she was where the good Lord Jesus was. It seemed to me that the poor old creature had some real love for Him, and was perhaps a true child of God, though with little light; so, acting on impulse, yet with misgiving as to its being the right choice, I read to her very slowly most of the 8th of Romans, pointing with my finger to every line as she looked over me, dwelling on and repeating the most comforting words. I was little prepared for the effect of the thought, so entirely new to her, *"no separation."* She took hold of it with unquestioning faith and with wonderful joy. "Has He said that, that I shall never be separated from Him? Ah, how beautiful; ah, how good! I can suffer now, I can die now." And the poor wrinkled old face was positively radiant. Her tears of gratitude, when, after a long talk, I said she might keep the little book which contained such precious words, were touching indeed. At my last glimpse of her she was poring over her Romans, heeding neither her goats nor her knitting.

Children were generally proud to be taken notice of by the *"Engländerinnen,"* and so were the parents, if, on making friends with a family group, we asked the little ones to show us how nicely they could read. As they mostly read clearly and well, this seemed to answer better than our own reading, for it gave additional motives for attention, and easy opportunities for questions and simple comments.

It is a good plan to learn by heart some of the leading gospel texts; even a very few, so learnt, prove valuable weapons, and without this one feels comparatively swordless, as one cannot give a rough and ready translation with the same confidence as the exact words of the French or German version. Sometimes we quoted such a text where we could have but a minute's conversation, and if our friends seemed at all struck with it, we gave them the portion containing it, telling them that if they would look carefully they would find those words in the little book. We sometimes, on looking back, saw them sitting down at once to search for it. *"My word shall not return unto Me void"* is a grand promise; and in the faith of that it was a comfort to quote and reiterate short and easily remembered texts, when our supply of "portions" ran short.

All very well; but what are those to do who speak little or no French and German? "Where there's a will there's a way," and plenty of ways too. You can mark the "portions"; you can offer them; you can point out passages, and get the person to *read it to you;* or you can set the children to read for you; and while that promise standeth sure, who shall say that such work shall be in vain? What does it matter about *our* words, if we can; even silently, give *His* words?

We never came upon ground trodden by any other sower, except among the guides, and we did find a few of them who had at least "heard of these things." They are intelligent and superior men, and seemed more often ready and disposed to converse *seriously* and *freely* on important subjects than any *class* of men there or elsewhere.

At Bel Alp, a mountain pension about seven thousand feet high, one of the loveliest spots in the darkest canton, we engaged a guide for the ascent of the Sparrenhorn, which is nearly ten thousand feet high. (Unless going above snow level, or crossing a glacier, we never required Swiss guides. A tolerable map and the "Practical Swiss Guide" were enough for all other routes.)

We started at 3.45 a.m., and from the stillness of the hill side overlooking the great Aletsch glacier watched an Alpine dawn. In the east was a calm glory of expectant light, as if something altogether celestial must come next, instead of a common sunrise. In the south and west, "clear as crystal," stood the grandest mountains, white and saintly, as if they might be waiting for the resurrection, with the moon shining in paleing radiance over them, and the deep Rhone valley, dark and grave-like, below. Suddenly the first roseflush touched the Mischabel, then Monte Leone was transfigured by that wonderful *rose-fire,* delicate yet intense. When the Weisshorn came to life (most beautiful of all, more *perfectly* lovely than any earthly thing I ever yet saw) the Matterhorn caught the same resurrection light on its dark and evil-looking rock peak. It was like a volcano, lurid and awful, and gave the impression of a fallen angel, impotently wrathful, shrinking away from the serene glory of a holy angel, which that of the Weisshorn at dawn might represent, if any material thing could. The eastern ridges were almost jet, with just a tinge of purple, in front of the great golden glow into which the "daffodil sky" rapidly heightened, till the sun rose, and the great dawn splendour was over. Would you not like to go and see such a sight?

During this excursion I had several little talks with our guide, Anton. In response to a remark, he quoted a verse from Hebrews to my surprise. He explained this by telling us that four years ago an English lady had spoken to him about his soul, and on her return to England had sent him a New Testament. This he had read daily. He had *no other help,* but found in it that he might pray for the teaching of the Holy Spirit, and from that time had constantly done so. He had learnt from it the need of a mediator, and that there is but *one* Mediator, and now prayed no longer to the Virgin or the saints, but only to and through the Saviour. He had no doubt but it was God's own word, because he felt its power and preciousness. "Life was a different thing to him now," he said, and it was evidently a life of faith on the Son of God. Possibly this may meet the eye of the faithful sower who dropped the incorruptible seed which has borne such "fruit unto life eternal."

What if but one of the words spoken or books given during a whole tour should be thus blessed! Would it not be worth all the effort, and the screwing up of courage, and the battles with shyness and nervousness and reluctance, which have to be fought again and again?

Ye who hear the blessèd call
   Of the Spirit and the Bride;
Hear the Master's word to all,
   Your commission and your guide:
"And let him that heareth say,
Come," to all yet far away.

.   .   .   .   .

Brothers, sisters, do not wait,
   Speak for Him who speaks to you!
Wherefore should you hesitate?
   This is no great thing to do.
Jesus only bids you say,
"Come!" and will you not obey?

VI.

AN ALPINE CLIMBER.

HO! for the Alps! The weary plains of France,
   And the night-shadows leaving far behind,
     For pearl horizons with pure summits lined,
On through the Jura-gorge, in swift advance
Speeds Arthur, with keen hope and buoyant glee,
On to the mountain land, home of the strong and free!

On! to the morning flush of gold and rose;
   On! to the torrent and the hoary pine;
     On! to the stillness of life's utmost line;
   On! to the crimson fire of sunset snows.
Short star-lit rest, then with the dawn's first streak,
On! to the silent crown of some lone icy peak!

'Twas no nerve-straining effort then, for him
   To emulate the chamois-hunter's leap
     Across the wide rock chasm, or the deep
   And darkly blue crevasse with treacherous rim,
Or climb the sharp arête, or slope of snow,
With Titan towers above and cloud-filled gulfs below.

It was no weariness or toil to count
   Hour after hour in that weird white realm,
     With guide of Alp-renown to touch the helm
   Of practised instinct; rocky spires to mount
Or track the steepest glacier's fissured length,
In the abounding joy of his unconquered strength.

But it was gladness none can realize
   Who have not felt the wild Excelsior-thrill,
     The strange exhilarate energies, that fill

The bounding pulses, as the intenser skies
Embrace the infinite whiteness, clear and fair,
Inhaling vigorous life with that quick crystal air.

That Alpine witchery still onward lures
   Upward, still upward, till the fatal list
     Grows longer of the early mourned and missed;
   Leading where surest foot no more ensures
The life that is not ours to throw away
For the exciting joys of one brief summer day.

For there are sudden dangers none foreknow;
   The scarlet-threaded rope can never mock
     The sound-loosed avalanche, frost-cloven rock,
   Or whirling storm of paralysing snow.
But Arthur's foot was kept; no deathward slips
Darkened the zenith of his strength with dire eclipse.

So year by year, as his rich manhood filled,
   He revelled in health-giving mountain feats;
     Spurning the trodden tracks and curious streets,
   As fit for old men, and for boys unskilled
In Alpine arts, not strong nor bold enough
To battle with the blast and scale the granite bluff.

One glowing August sun went forth in might,
   And smote with rosy sword each snowy brow,
     Bright accolade of grandeur! Now, oh now,
   Amid that dazzling wealth of purest light,
His long ambition should be crowned at last,
And every former goal rejoicingly o'erpast.

For ere the white fields softened in the glow,
He stood upon a long-wooed virgin-peak,
One of the few fair prizes left to seek;
Each rival pinnacle left far below!
He stood in triumph on the conquered height:
And yet a shadow fell upon his first delight.

For well he knew that he had surely done
His utmost; and that never summer day
Could bring a moment on its radiant way
Like the first freshness of that conquest, won
Where all had lost before. A sudden tear
Veiled all the glorious view, so grand, so calm, so clear!

VII.

LETTERS TO MRS. HAVERGAL,[1]

OF PYRMONT VILLA, LEAMINGTON,

IN 1873.

No. 1.

GRAND HOTEL, PARIS, Room No. 446.
May 30, 1873. 7 A.M.

THUS far all safe and well; but I must begin at the beginning, for the sake of M. and E., who will like details. We started May 28, in the morning, went to the Lord Warden at Dover, and crossed to Calais by the 9.35 boat. *Un beau ciel* enough, brilliant sun; but, alas! no enjoyment of it, as we were all ill.

The gangway on to the steamer happened to be pitched unusually steeply, so that it was quite an interesting speculation to Amy and me, whether Mrs. S. would come down or stay in England! and the steamer was tossing about very horribly; but E. did not hesitate an instant when her papa told her to go down it with his hand. When we got nearly to Calais, and Mrs. S., Ann, and I were not sufficiently recovered to stir, poor E., who looked just like a little white ghost, and could really hardly stand herself, would insist on trying to get to each of us with eau-de-Cologne; it was so pretty to see her. Ann is very sensible, and takes any little inconvenience more philosophically than I ever expected a maid to do.

I had an interesting talk with a young railway official, who came some distance in our carriage, getting in with cap off and *"Pardon, mesdames!"* (I do so like this foreign politeness.) He

was in Paris during most of the siege, and was "very hungry," and "souffrait affreusement"; at last owing to his railway position he had a sudden chance of getting out, which he only did that his mother and sister might have his share of rations; then when the armistice came he got into Paris by the very first train with bread and meat for the *"mère et sœur,"* and found them both so famished that they could not eat it! and it was weeks before his mother could digest a bit of meat, merely from the derangement of starvation. He thinks this generation won't want to go to war again! I asked him what he thought of the death of Napoleon. "It was the justice of God," he said. "Do you think the Prince Imperial will ever succeed?" "Not just yet, but events move in a circle, and his turn may come." He was very bitter about the war, saying, "And to think that we are all Christians, the French and the Germans!" This gave opening for a little further talk and a Gospel of St. John. He seemed extremely interested in watching me mark a number of passages before giving it to him.

Ceci met us at Paris; she has found nice accommodation for Amy in the house of a French pasteur, who is to give her lessons; it is near the Paumiers. This hotel, the "Grand," is supposed to be the finest in Europe; it is quite full, so we had to go *"au quatrième."* However we go up and down in a lift, and we have rooms with balconies, looking down into a fine boulevard, and so high up that we see over most of the roofs, and get less

---

[1] This was Caroline Anne Havergal, F.R.H.'s stepmother.

noise and dust. The inner court of the hotel is almost like an immense conservatory, tree rhododendrons in full flower and other things; the saloons are gorgeous, with enormous crystal chandeliers and mirror panels, so arranged as to make the place look interminable, quite a fairyland by gaslight.

HOTEL BELLEVUE, NEUCHATEL. Saturday Evening.

We could not start till twelve, and then went a drive round Paris, which looks its very best in spring foliage and costumes! We went over Notre Dame with a Napoleonist guide, who lost no possible opportunity of instilling Napoleonic ideas. "This is the altar where the Emperor was crowned, on the same spot the Prince Imperial was baptized, and here also he will probably be crowned!" We eschewed pictures, etc., because a general idea of Paris was the thing wanted. After dinner, Mr. and Mrs. S. and Amy went another two hours' drive to the Champs Elysées and the Bois de Boulogne, while Ceci and I went a walk in the Tuileries gardens.

Then comes an adventure! Express for Neuchatel left at eight p.m., and as it is a long way to the station and luggage had to be registered we ought to leave at seven, and the omnibus was ordered, but it never came till half-past seven, and then we had to tear like fire engines, and got to the station just as the doors were closing. Mr. S. undertook the live stock, and I the baggage. "Too late, too late!" raved four or five porters. However, by dint of most vehement pleading and a little bribery, I got it taken in and registered, while as I was obliged to have the tickets to show for this Mr. S. had a tremendous row with the platform officials because he had not the tickets to show. Finally, they wanted to bundle Mrs. S. and E. in, and the train was actually starting when E. came to the rescue by setting up such a howl of "I won't get in without papa; you shan't touch me!" and such floods of tears, that she actually moved the stationmaster to compassion, and he signalled the driver to stop a minute. Meanwhile, Mr. S. by main force held the door of the platform on one side, while an official struggled to close it on the other. Happily for me English muscle beat the French, and as I ran with my very utmost speed I got inside; Mr. S. loosed hold, and the door closed with such a slam behind me! Then we tumbled over each other into the carriage, and off for Neuchatel (at least so I supposed; the officials had told us we were all right without change till 9.40 next morning).

For the first hour a young man sat by me, who turned out to be "ancienne noblesse," son of a *duc,* a vehement legitimist, and apparently a leader among thirty thousand young men who "have inscribed themselves" on that side. He had just been laid up for a month through being wounded in a duel, a sword wound; and told me without the least compunction that his adversary had got the worst of it, and would not be able to walk for two or three years! Yet he was "bon Chrêtien," and always kept Fridays and other fast days!! I felt so sorry for him, for he was a fine intelligent fellow, but did not seem to have a glimmering of right and wrong! He turned out somewhere about Fontainebleau, and then we settled for the night (carriage to ourselves). E. proposed having prayers, so Mr. S. read a psalm and prayed. About 3.45 a.m. I roused up and thought somehow the country looked wrong (it was quite light), so I sat up in some anxiety for the next station. It came: Chalons-sur-Saone! on the line to Lyons and Marseilles! So I called to the stationmaster to know what was to be done; our party were all asleep, and rather astonished to be summarily bundled out. On went the train, and imagine the Snepps and I standing in a small French station at four o'clock in the morning, some fifty miles out of our route! Happily it was superb weather.

I soon made out what we could do, and it was a special providence that we roused when we did, for, like old Tiff's harness, it "broke in a 'straw'nary good place dis yer time!" and by omnibusing across the town we just caught a train to Dôle, a small town on the Neuchatel line. Then we proceeded across country for three hours in that serene leisurely way peculiar to continental trains, which might allow of the guard shaking hands with his friends along the road. As we all went to sleep it did not signify. At 7.30 we turned out at Dôle for ablutions and food.

Now just imagine Mrs. Snepp, etc., washing in large brown crocks, with unbleached towels, in the back room of a small French restaurant, the extempore washing apparatus on one table, and basins of coffee with tablespoons on the other (just like Belfort). However all was perfectly clean, and everybody was amused and liked the novelty. We had to change again at Pontarlier, and then a glorious two hours through the Jura gorge which I never appreciated before, because I was going away instead of coming. Mr. S. is delightful to travel with, he is so enthusiastic about the scenery; he regularly shouted when we came in sight of the snow mountains!

We got to Neuchatel at three, after eighteen hours' journey. E. is extraordinary; she has not flagged one bit yet, sleeps like a top, and is in firstrate spirits whenever awake, and not the least trouble, and seems to have left all her timidity behind her in England.

We are at the Hotel Bellevue here, where we were in 1869; one of the very choice Swiss hotels, quiet and elegant, on the edge of the lake. It is splendid weather, and Mont Blanc is perfectly visible, and last night (Sunday) was rosy in the sunset.

There are very few people yet, but Mr. S. finds work enough nevertheless; he had some most serious conversations yesterday, and seems to have made a wonderful impression on a Welshman, an M.P. and a dissenter. He seems so grateful for Mr. S.'s talk, and is quite staggered in his anti-Bible education views.

They went to English Service in the morning, and I went to French service, and dropped in for a confirmation of about ninety girls, all dressed in black with white caps and white folded handkerchiefs over them. Pasteur Nagles preached, and it was quite different to any foreign sermon I ever heard, "Lovest thou Me?" A most touching, personal, spiritual sermon, not at all the usual oration style, but simple and powerful and full of scriptural thought.

Late in the evening Mrs. S. and I went to try and find Madame Mercier, the Swiss representative of the Young Women's Christian Association, but she is gone away.

I routed Mr. and Mrs. S. up at four o'clock this morning to look at the dawn on the Alps from their balcony; it was very lovely, but not the "real thing," too distant for the grand effects. However we contemplated it for nearly half an hour, and then went to roost again.

No. II.

PENSION SCHWEIZERHAUS, LUCERNE. June 3.

I left off at Neuchatel, Monday. Well, we had views which I never before believed in, of the distant Alps, all the way by train along the lakes of Neuchatel and Bienne, and down the line to Berne.

We lunched at the Bernerhof, which M. will remember in 1869, and then I unmercifully dragged the whole party up one hundred and twenty-seven steps to the roof. It was so clear that it was difficult to realize the Jungfrau as more than ten or twelve miles off, though it was actually forty-five as the crow flies, and seventy-five by road! I believe Emily would wish to go up Mont Blanc at once if we proposed it. It is most amusing how she enters into the spirit of the whole thing, is quite certain she should be neither tired nor frightened to go anywhere, and is quite grand in her responsibility for a share of the small packages, generally marching in front with me, with as much as she can carry.

To return to Berne, we took a carriage and drove about. Saw the bears and fed them, all correct; waited for the big clock with its performances of cocks and bears and men with drums to strike the hour; and went into the cathedral. E. was very decided in her Protestant preference of it to Notre Dame at Paris, which she did not appear to feel quite safe in!

After a superb sunset we got to Lucerne at eight. I had written for rooms to the Schweizerhaus, a pension strongly recommended in the guidebooks, so the host was at the station to meet us. I advise any one staying more than a day at Lucerne to try this instead of the noisy and dusty town hotels on the quay. Fancy a house about two hundred feet above the lake (ten minutes' walk from the steamboats), looking down over everything, with no break to the lovely view of lake and moun-

tains, Pilatus right, Rigi left, and the snowy Titlis range in the centre; the foreground trees, etc., down to the lake; a small but pretty garden, a verandah with flower-stands and a balcony the same width over it, upon which all our rooms open.

Mrs. S. rather needed a quiet morning, so she very good-naturedly wished Mr. S. and me to "improve the shining hours" in some way. Unfortunately Pilatus is still snowed up, so we contented ourselves with the Rigi, and started by the 8 a.m. boat to Vitznau to go up by rail! The sensation and general effect are most peculiar. The "train" consisted of a single carriage, holding about fifty, with glass at the two ends, but open all down the sides where windows should be. Across this are rows of garden seats, bass instead of solid wood, all facing backwards, so that you all look downhill as you are being pushed uphill, and look uphill as you come downhill. The engine comes out of a den of a shed, and is hooked on behind, pushing, not drawing. Such an imp it looks, the drollest and most knowing thing you ever saw in the shape of machinery, with its little boiler stuck up on end, and slanting forward like the tower of Pisa, bunting and pushing in a most comical way, as if it were bending to the strain, with a determined shoulder to the wheel. Underneath are the massive cogged wheels in the middle, on which the whole affair depends, locking into a great toothed rail between the two ordinary rails. It is impossible to help laughing at the little fellow, as after a very small squeal or two off he goes. But one soon learns to respect him! The first fifty yards are a gentle incline, and then comes the first gradient, which produces what is mildly described as "sensation!" All at once the carriage seems as if it were going to be tilted up on end, and the people see over each other's heads just like an infant school gallery, and as we "back" uphill, those must be stolid indeed who can refrain from some sort of noise in expression of astonishment. I don't think I ever was more surprised. I expected some sort of gradual zigzag, a steep incline of course, but nothing beyond a carriage road; but this thing goes perfectly straight up a hill steeper than any I ever saw a wheeled carriage attempt, even the Lynton coaches. When you come to a station it is quite queer to feel the carriage go level again, with an odd little bump as the cog locks. The views as you rise are glorious. The rail is only open to Staffelhöhe, nearly an hour's walk from the top, and navvies are at work on the rest. I never was more sorry for not having brought more spiritual ammunition, for though I had tracts and "portions" for about forty, it was nothing like enough, and all would have accepted them had I had more.

The upper part of the Rigi was rather snowy, and somehow there is not the same pleasure in getting one's feet wet in commonplace snow that ought to be all gone by this time, as in the real thing above eternal snow level. It was very calm and bright and clear, but I never can see that panoramic views are so really beautiful as many others. Half way up, the view is nearly always the best. There is a piano in the inn at the top, so Mr. S. must needs have a hymn from "Songs of Grace and Glory," and a "Havergal Psalmody" tune, on it, at 5,900 feet high.

We only stayed about an hour and then came down by the Weggis path, which we did in a dense fog in 1869. Near the top the gentians, large and small, were in full beauty, and often on the very edge of snow patches.

The weather has quite suddenly cleared up. It was bitterly cold at Lucerne last week, and it snowed on the Rigi on Saturday, so that on Sunday morning there were three feet of snow! and on Tuesday gentians and positive heat! Just below the top we turned out of the path on to a lovely green plateau where the view is magnificent; and here we knelt on the very gentians, and Mr. S. prayed, or rather adored. It was so nice. It was a pretty fair first walk, being a spin of nine miles down, not reckoning the hour's walk up; but I hardly know anything lovelier in Switzerland, which is saying a good deal.

We went out for a nice drive in the evening with Mrs. S. and E., and saw the Lion, and drove up to the Pension Wallis, where the Queen stayed some days, a quiet unpretending house, quite five hundred feet above the lake.

Wednesday.—This morning we all set off by the 8 a.m. boat down the lake. For the benefit of those who have not been, I may elegantly describe the lake as three great sausages, the top sausage having two great arms! You sail out through a charming little strait into sausage No. 2, and seem to be quite in a new lake; and the same, only going sharp at right angles, into No. 3. The morning was beautiful; no wind, and bright sun; water, deep emerald. Just after entering sausage No. 3, Mr. S. called our attention to what looked like a most lovely rippling line of emerald and silver, about half a mile ahead. At the same moment the steamer men rushed on deck and hauled down the awnings, and in about a minute, just like a shot, the famous föhnwind was down upon us. We had just had some tea, and it blew a heavy cup and saucer clear off the table; everything loose went flying; the lake was covered with green and white waves all at once. The men helped the ladies down the stairs off the top-deck, and cleared away every footstool and loose seat; even turning a great strong table on its back with legs up, or that would have been blown over too! It must be awfully dangerous for little sailing boats. I never saw one of these curious lake storms before, and though not in the very least dangerous for a great steamer, yet it was most disagreeable, and on the return journey quite upset me for a little while. I could not have imagined such waves on a lake, and it certainly gave new force to the storm on Galilee. We drove from Fluellen a few miles along the opening of the St. Gothard pass, so well described as "solemnly beautiful"; the enjoyment was a little spoiled by the wind which came tearing down the pass, raising dense-clouds of dust. Mr. S., however, was in raptures, to my heart's content.

No. III.

HOTEL JUNGFRAUBLICK, INTERLACHEN. June 6.

We left Lucerne yesterday morning 9.40 (Thursday), under very doubtful appearances; Pilatus wrapped up in grey clouds, air damp and warm, and drizzle most of the morning. Still it was a new aspect of the pretty arm of the lake down which we steamed to Alpnacht (11.20).

The whole ride was charming, from 11.30 to 6.0, but the pass of the Brünig is exquisite. You wind up for an hour and a half, mostly through trees now in full beauty, with changing views first of the great valley behind you, then of a glorious opening upon the lake of Brienz deep below, then of smaller mountain valleys, and then of the white Oberland Alps and the grand valley of Meyringen. It had rained for a good while, and we feared it was hopeless for anything but driving up into grey clouds, when just as we began the ascent it left off, and kept fair all the way over the pass. Oddly enough it is the second time I have gone over the Brünig with the hope of staying at the top, which was part of our plan; it does seem such a pity to halt hardly five minutes, for one of the finest views in Switzerland, and then tear downhill again. If we could have been certain of the weather I think we should have stayed. We had great fun in hoisting Mrs. S. up to the banquette, for the spin downhill (only an hour); it was something quite new to see her perched up in that style. I believe she did it as much to entertain us as anything, which was very amiable of her.

The next possibility was to stay at the Giessbach falls at 6.30, and remain the night to see them illuminated, but unhappily it came on to rain again, so we steamed down the lake of Brienz to Interlachen, which we reached at 7.30. We are at my beautiful hotel; the card gives no idea of the views which are all around, so that there are no back and front rooms, but all have fine views. I have just been a little walk up the Niesen with Mr. S. and E.; it is a glorious morning after the rain, only the Jungfrau wears her veil of bright cloud, and I have only once caught a glimpse of the shining silver horn. But all the rest is as lovely as can be. It is very warm; too hot to go far out of the shade. I am writing out of doors on the terrace facing the Scheinige Platte and the lake of Brienz. I am so astonished at Mr. Snepp's French; he never gave me a notion that he knew a word, and now he comes out with all that is wanted for travelling or hotel talk quite fluently, and with a very good accent. But here French is no use at all; only German. He has a little pocket aneroid barometer, which shows the height above sea level exactly; it is so interesting,

June 7, Saturday.—Yesterday afternoon Mr. and Mrs. S. and E. went to the Giessbach falls; I stayed quiet, as I have not yet taken a blank day since leaving home, and I wanted to be very fresh for an early mountain start this morning, to the Scheinige Platte. We had all arranged overnight, guide and provisions; but it turned out a set-in soaking rain, with not merely the mountains covered with cloud, but the lower hills wreathed about with white veils almost down to the lake level.

HOTEL ROYAL, CHAMOUNI, HAUTE SAVOIE, FRANCE,
June 14. Saturday evening!

Actually not a line written for a whole week; but when I detail proceedings you will not be surprised that I found no time for writing. June the 8th was a queer Sunday, for though the whole place is Protestant, there is not a pretence at Sabbath observance, and the great annual shooting match of the canton Berne, lasting a week, began on Sunday at six a.m. by firing twenty-two cannons, one for each canton. The whole place was decorated with any amount of arches and other green erections, with mottoes and devices and flags innumerable, especially all over the hotels, both roofs and windows, while Swiss costumes thronged the streets and roads. As we went to church another cannonade of twenty-two rounds came off close by, so that we had literally to pass the cannons' mouths, and the rifle shooting begins with an occasional cannonade.

Our quiet sweet Communion service was a strange contrast to the scenes and noise outside. The reverberation of the cannon among the mountains was wonderful. I must tell you about little E.'s first missionary work, it was so very nice of her and entirely unprompted. A German lady in the hotel was a Protestant, but her husband a Belgian Romanist; they had one little girl, a most clever child, eight years old, speaking not only French and German, but English too with great fluency. She and E. played together all Saturday; and then, overhearing us talk about this poor little child being brought up a Romanist, which of course the priests had taken care to secure, E. got most interested and anxious. "Won't you give her a little tract?" "Won't you talk to her?" "Won't you tell her not to play with her dolls on Sunday?" So all Sunday E. was in a fever to get hold of her, and succeeded at last in bringing her up to my room with an air of great delight. So the little girls sat on each side of me, and we had quite a nice talk, little Célestine quite pleased and interested, and Emily playing into my hands in a very pretty way and quite helping me. However, as I did not say anything about the dolls, E. did that herself before going to bed, and also gave Célestine a little Gospel of St. John. E. enters most eagerly into distribution, comes to me for Gospels for waiters and chambermaids, and constantly asks me to give them to drivers or railway guards.

Monday, June 9, dawned promisingly, so we postponed

Grindelwald till the afternoon, and Mr. S. and I went up the Scheinige Platte, starting about 6.30; as it is five hours up (six thousand feet), and we were not fully in training, we had a horse, professedly between us, but I had the lion's share. The Platte was quite a surprise to me; it is not an inviting looking hill, a steep, sharp edged ridge, overlooking Interlachen, ascended by a path of three hundred zigzags through a steep forest; then another thousand feet among singular rocks and along the edge of sublime precipices (sheer down three thousand feet) and a cone of grass, flowers, and snow; and then you see on the north the whole of the lovely lakes of Thun and Brienz; and south, a superb snow amphitheatre: Wetterhorn, Jungfrau, Eiger, etc., with the two valleys of Grindelwald and Lauterbrunnen forking out in green depth of beauty several thousand feet below you.

It was fine and calm, and the grand snow range had just enough of cloud hanging about it to enhance the brilliance of the snow and the mysterious effect which those untrodden vastnesses always have more or less. We stayed about half an hour on the top to enjoy the view and the cold meat and red wine! and then scampered down, rather aggrieved to find that the horse and guide were great hindrances to speed. We started as soon as possible for Grindelwald, a grand drive of fifteen miles, in two little carriages.

No. IV.

HOTEL ROYAL, CHAMOUNI. JUNE 16.

I left off No. III. at Grindelwald, Monday, June 9. My second impressions of Grindelwald are far beyond my first. I cannot think how it was that it did not make more impression on me in 1869. I had no idea it was so beautiful: three immense mountains, Wetterhorn, Mettenberg, and Eiger; close to and full before one, with a grand snow view of the Viescherhörner through the glacier opening between them.

Our arrangement usually is that Mr. S. and I go off for an early excursion or walk, then Mrs. S. and Emily get more rest.

So on Tuesday. Mr. S. and I started about six, with the most stupid guide I ever had, for the Eismeer, the Grindelwald Mer de Glace. Of course I got my boots nailed over night, very knowing looking pyramid-shaped nails, which stick well into snow or smooth grass, and give a good cling to the foot when the slope is very steep; they are put in about an inch apart. The way was a little footpath under colossal rocks overhanging the edge of the glacier, and rising steeply till it brought us up to a level of 5,500 feet. From this point we looked down on a great basin of dirty ice, all over débris washed down from the heights. The motion of the glaciers is very wonderful; the whole mass moves down bodily, at rates varying on different glaciers from ten or twelve to four hundred feet per annum. The new snow keeps forming it above, and at the valley end it keeps melting and breaking away as it reaches the warmer level. It is a strong illustration of the might of silent influence; only the warm air, invisible and intangible; yet it forms an impassable barrier to these millions of tons of solid ice, which must otherwise pour down into the valleys and destroy all life. But the basin of dirty ice (two or three miles in extent) was not all we came to see. It was bounded by a magnificent and dazzling amphitheatre of snow, with only a protuberant dark rock here and there to throw up the brilliant whiteness, running up to over eleven thousand feet high; while the entrance of the gorge down which the glacier pours to the valley below is a great rock portal, of which the right doorpost consists of the celebrated precipice of the Eiger, which goes sheer up (too nearly perpendicular for snow to cover) to more than twelve thousand feet high.

Then we had a very stiff scramble of perhaps three hundred feet down to the glacier itself; and here, but for God's providence and Mr. S.'s watchfulness, I should have had a serious accident. Part of the descent was by two rough ladders against the face of the rock; the first was easy, but the second not only long but very steep indeed. The guide went first, and most culpably never warned me that the handrail of the ladder, consisting of two very long slender pine poles, pierced half way, was broken, so that the end of the upper pole was loose and ended in mid-air. Down I went (backwards), one hand adjusting my dress, and the other holding fast to the rail. As I could not see from above that it was broken, and suspected no danger, I was going comfortably down, face to the rock, and in another minute should have come to the sudden end of the rail to which I was trusting, when nothing but a miracle could have preserved me from a very severe fall of many feet on to the boulders below; but Mr. S. suddenly saw and shouted to me to stop; I instantly did so, and looking behind saw the broken rail in time not to trust it further. We went some distance over the glacier, and had the satisfaction of hearing several avalanches, and seeing one rather good one. My notion of an avalanche always used to be a gigantic snowball bounding down, but they are really rather a snow fall, just like a waterfall, only snow. This one started high up, and poured over several ledges of rock in succession, till it reached the edge of the glacier, where it formed in three minutes a great mound of snow, I should think thirty or forty feet high; the roar lasted nearly five minutes. It was rather pretty and elegant than grand, to see it come down. From the glacier we could see the ridge where the Rev. Julius Elliott was killed in 1869, within half an hour of the summit of the Schreckhorn (Horn of Terror).

We got to the hotel again at 11.30, and then went all together to see Mr. E.'s grave. There is a granite slab over it, and a tablet against the church wall with Hebrews 11:5, "For be-fore his translation," etc., and "To depart and be with Christ, which is far better." The Grindelwald people keep it in order themselves, and keep "edelweiss" planted round it, the Alpine flower *par excellence*, which is never found below eight thousand feet.

In the afternoon we drove to Lauterbrunnen; unfortunately, the Jungfrau was clouded, so we lost the special beauty of the valley. We pottered about up and down the village and to the Staubbach; and then I put some knowing guides up to beguiling Mrs. S. into just trying a chaise à porteur, which previously she would not hear of, and at last had the satisfaction of seeing her trotted out in one. This led to arranging for a small expedition next morning, which was to pave the way for something better.

Wednesday, June 11, accordingly we had a walk (about three miles) to the Trümlenbach, along the valley, spending most of the way in arguments and persuasions for Mürren, which Mr. S. and I were to have done alone, but which it would have been a thousand pities for Mrs. S. to have missed. At last, to my exultation, we won the cause, and Mrs. S. consented to come up to Mürren for the night, seeing that the porte-chaise somewhat exceeded her expectations. So we started directly after lunch and took it easy, and by 6.30 found ourselves at the pretty new inn, 5,500 feet high.

Though a fine and promising afternoon we got neither sunset or sunrise, *i.e.* veiled mountains and no tints at all. Still, unless absolutely buried in clouds, Mürren must always be grand, the mountains look more colossal and majestic than from any other place. It is just the right height to get the double effect of depth and height, the valley below so near and deep, and the giants opposite so close and precipitous. I enjoyed getting up into the colder mountain air; it is different from valley cold, and seems to brace and exhilarate without chilling.

Though Mürren was unknown not many years ago, there is now a good sized new hotel, with two "dépendances" besides, and an immense new rival is nearly finished, and there is talk of a railway up like the Rigi! Dreadful as that sounds, one really can't be selfish enough to grudge any means of facilitating the ascent, so that thousands may share the sublime view. Any one who has not been there will hardly understand the fact that, with this indescribably splendid mountain view, one is really distracted from it at almost every step by the flowers. No description can exaggerate these, either as to variety, loveliness, brilliance of colour, or number. The whole place is one mass of flowers, thicker than ever you saw the thickest daisy or buttercup field of monotonous yellow or white. Here and there in patches some special flower predominates, but generally all are mixed up together, perhaps twenty species in a square yard, and most of the colours intensely brilliant. I think we must have gone at the right time exactly, for I do not remember quite such splendour in 1869. Chief of all for attraction are the forget-me-nots, much brighter and larger than the English ones, whole spikes of living turquoise waving by myriads, then gentians and pansies, and large exquisite primrose-coloured anemones, and smaller white ones, and pink primula-like clusters, and purple bells most delicately fringed, and intense blue starflowers with a clear white eye, called "heaven flowers," and dozens of others. I brought in a nosegay which Mr. S. said was fit for a queen, only a queen could not purchase such a one unless she came to Mürren to get it; for they always fade long before we can get down to the valley again. However, even below there is a wealth of flowers which one never sees in England, only just a little commoner than this lovely aristocracy of flowers up above, so delicate and noble. It is worth any one's while to go early to Switzerland to see them; no one would believe it who only goes in July and August.

Sleeping at Mürren gave a fine chance for Mr. S. and me to go up the Schilthorn (nearly 10,000 feet), the finest nondangerous ascent in the Oberland. So we committed ourselves to a good guide, who put us through a catechism as to our capabilities and equipments, insisting on gaiters, veils, and dark spectacles, without either of which three he refused to take us! As Mr. S. had no veil, the guide first suggested that it would answer equally well to wet the face thoroughly and then blow flour over it! Fancy being done up in paste previous to being baked in the sun! But he said any *Anglais* would have his face skinned if he went up the Schilthorn without either veil or flour and water. As Mr. S. did not see the beauty of the latter plan, he offered to lend him a veil, and produced one, probably green originally, but resolved by weather and wear into its constituents of blue and yellow with a little surviving green. This he fastened on Mr. S.'s white hat in a style that would astonish Perry Barr. Then he agreed to call us at two a.m. and departed. So at two a.m. up we got, and soon after 2.30 had coffee, turning out, to poor Mrs. S.'s utter horror, a little before three. It was cloudy and dark, but quite hopeful, and might yet be magnificent. We toiled up for two hours, vainly hoping that a tantalizing glimpse or two of a speck of gleaming snow apparently up in the clouds might expand into a revelation of the whole range in dawn-beauty, but soon after we came to the first snow even that disappeared, and the clouds came down upon us with a very cool welcome to their domain.

We plunged on over a snow slope or two in pouring rain, and then the guide faced round, and after an ominous silence declared his mind, viz. that it was a great mortification and disappointment to him to fail, but he must tell us candidly that we must give up; the rain was hopeless, and had already so softened the snow that it would be entirely impossible for any mortal to get to the top, and we might as well turn back at once as struggle on for five hours more and then be defeated. Decision

is always better than uncertainty, so we scampered down again as fast as we could, and went to bed at 6.30, while our clothes were dried. It was a great disappointment to both of us, for the Schilthorn is a firstrate thing to do.

Happily it cleared up splendidly by eight at Mürren, though the Schilthorn remained wrapped in dense rain clouds. So after breakfast we had a very pleasant, though dirty, trot down again to Lauterbrunnen.

After some hurried soup we drove off to Interlachen, where the chief impediments (rightly so named) had been left, and, after a fatiguing scramble of packing and washerwomen and small bills, got off to the train which now, instead of omnibuses, meets the Thun steamers. It is a delightful little two-mile railway, with covered seats on the top of all the carriages, just from Interlachen to the landing place. We lost the lovely lake of Thun, just as in 1869; not a mountain top to be seen, driving rain all the way, and wind and motion enough to make us uncomfortable. We got to Berne (same hotel as in 1869), between seven and eight, a tiring day.

Next day, Friday, rail from Berne to Geneva, rain most of the way, so that we could see little of the views, which ought to be very interesting. Saturday (June 14) was just fair enough to justify starting, and at 7.15 we mounted one of those wonderful "diligences inversables" which are peculiar to this one road. They consist of a gigantic coffin below, which holds any quantity of luggage, and acts as ballast to the whole concern. Then over this are five rows of seats, rising behind each other like a deep gallery, so that twenty people (on emergency twenty-five) can all have a full front view at once. There is a peculiar board just over the horses' tails, on which two or three extra of the aborigines can sit if needs be, but the passengers' seats are luxurious with red velvet. Over our heads is a sort of canopy stretching across glazed sides; if neither wet nor sunny this canopy can be rolled back altogether, and as the whole of the glass sides can be let down, it then becomes an entirely open carriage, all except the coupé, which is boxed in at the very back with the worst view and the least air, and for which the wise English pay a good deal extra, in order to keep themselves to themselves and avoid the οἱ πολλοι. We had the whole front row, and I enjoyed it extremely.

But, alas! the grand views of Mont Blanc all clouded over, and finished up with a wet evening. I was particularly sorry for this, because the drive up to Chamouni is unsurpassable, and I think gives the finest "first impression" of Mont Blanc. The Swiss tell me that the weather for the last year or two has never been settled, and has baffled the calculations of the oldest guides. We had decided on the Hotel Imperial, and went, found the front door open and walked in, but rang bells in vain, and then discovered that it was void, nothing "open" except the entrance! It was so funny. Two others looked "fermés" also, so we went to the Royal and got a very cheerful set of rooms with good view, having choice of nearly all the rooms in the house, as it is so early yet for Chamouni. We all agree however that, though too early for high mountain excursions, it is much better on the whole than later, less heat and dust, cleaned up rooms everywhere, always a choice of apartments, much better attendance than when all is full, less noise and bustle, no crowded carriages, and the glorious Alpine flowers! It was quite pleasant to settle in here, after sleeping in different hotels for eight consecutive nights, and the last three days were more fatiguing than excursions, being travel, which implies "baggages et billets," and the still greater evils of smaller boxes, baskets, and bags, not to mention shawls, umbrellas, parasols, and alpenstocks.

Nothing like a carpetbag tour, with no packing and unpacking and registering and looking after and carrying about and counting up to do!

It was nice to find a notice up, that, for those who missed family prayer, the chaplain, Rev. J. F. Bickerdike, would hold it every evening, at 8.30, in the reading room. So of course we went, only "two or three," but it was very nice. Mr. B. is very earnest and spiritually minded; and Mrs. B. very nice too. She was at Mr. Pennefather's Deaconess Institution for some time, and has told us a good deal about Mildmay. She says that every one appeared to have been impressed with the singular heavenliness of Mr. P. during his last year. For many months before his death his special anxiety and interest had been prayer for real spiritual blessing upon the immense amount of machinery and organization which he had completed; work and workers all marvellously organized, and then his one thought seemed to be seeking for blessing upon it all.

Sunday, June 15, was a brilliant morning; Mont Blanc dazzling, though less grand from Chamouni itself than from any other point of view; one is too close under it to form any idea of its height. The little English church was bright and cheerful; every one likes it better than almost any other Sunday halt; and somehow they always manage to have excellent chaplains, who do not chill one by reading commonplace little sermons which were produced under totally different circumstances. It must be a poverty-stricken heart indeed, which can't speak out of its abundance in Switzerland. There is a small harmonium, which I played in the morning: Tallis, Worcester Chant, and Farrant for chants; Nottingham to "This is the day the Lord hath made"; and Hanover to "O worship the King all glorious above."

The responding and singing were capital, though the congregation only about eighty. There are a few French Protestant families here, who are visited twice a year by a distant pasteur; so Mr. B., who is a thorough French scholar, kindly visits and gathers them to a little French service, at 7 p.m. (English p.m.

service is at four), but after this is going to have them at 9 a.m. because that will suit them better. There is Holy Communion every Sunday morning. There was quite a nice gathering at the 8.30 p.m. "family prayers," and we sang Hymns 17 and 14 from "Songs of Grace and Glory."

Monday, June 16, we planned a grand expedition, the "Jardin," a wonderful glacier excursion which has long been an ambition of mine. It was fine after a wet evening, so Mr. S. and I started a little before six, and walked to Montanvert, overlooking the Mer de Glace (six thousand feet), reaching it soon after eight. We asked for a guide at once to take us up to the "Jardin," and were told by the innkeeper that we ought to have started not later than three a.m., and that the snow was far too soft to do it so late as eight, that nobody has been yet this year, and what with avalanches and slips and vagaries of ice and snow and crevasses and "éboulements," he couldn't say whether any of his garçons could find the way at all, and finally declined to sanction our going. This was sure to be right, because disinterested! for he sacrificed his own profits upon guide, provisions, and wine; and as a firstrate guide soon after endorsed the decision, we had no choice but to give it up. The chef des guides has since told us that he does not think the "Jardin" should be attempted till at least the end of next week. So we contented ourselves with a climb up the height on the right of Montanvert, and then down and across the Mer de Glace.

We were obliged to have a guide across the ice, and he says that at this time of year the route alters almost every day, crevasses safe to-day may be dangerous to-morrow; and he is responsible for inspecting the route every morning before any visitors cross, setting up little stone waymarks which the other guides understand.

The big "Moulin," which Mr. C. and M. will remember (a great hole in the glacier, down which you hear a tremendous roar of sub-glacial water hundreds of feet below), is all vanished since 1869. We said good bye to our guide, and trotted down the Mauvais Pas on the other side, striking off into a little path to get down to the Sources de l'Arveiron, where the river rushes out of the foot of the glacier; and then down into the road and back to Chamouni by about two o'clock.

Tuesday, June 17, a very doubtful morning, and not clear enough for the Col de Balm; so we started at six for the Col de Voza. It was damp and muggy; so, after walking nearly seven miles, I gave in and came straight back, while Mr. S. went on up the col alone. Just after I turned back it began a real mountain pour, so six miles walking in this was a tolerable soak; but nothing to Mr. S.'s state, who persevered through an amusing series of difficulties up to the top, and got back nearly two hours later.

This morning again (Wednesday) it is pouring, and seems likely to keep on at it. We have had more or less rain every day for a week now; no signs of fine weather yet.

I have written to see if Mr. S. can extend his tourist tickets beyond the month; if not, we get back to Birmingham on the evening of June 27 and I go on to Oakhampton next day.

I have not had much conversation with the natives, but have had plenty of opportunity of giving tracts and portions. Our driver to Grindelwald had a St. Luke; next evening he took it out of his breast pocket to show me that he had it, saying it was a treasure and he would never part with it. The evening before he had got it out at supper, and read it to the roomful of guides and drivers; most of them approved, and two or three wanted to buy it from him, but he said he would not give it up for anything. Then he read some more aloud, whereupon a godless guide began scoffing and blaspheming; not ten minutes after he cut his hand, or rather wrist, so fearfully that he was quite ill, and the driver said they thought he would be laid up for a fortnight, the loss of blood being so great as to be dangerous; I suppose it was an artery. The others were quite impressed, and said it was a judgment of God upon him. This old driver seemed to have the fear of God, and listened earnestly and responded warmly to all I tried to tell him.

———

No. V.

Hotel Royal, Chamouni. June 19.

We are not well off as to weather; Tuesday and Wednesday entirely lost, a continued pour. We reckoned on a probable fine morning after it, and early it was lovely; but we did not arrange to start till 10.30, and we had a hot and unprofitable tug up to the Montanvert, and a dull cloudy day, not the top of a single aiguille visible. The only fun was taking E. up; she is the strongest child I ever knew, and enjoys the whole thing deliciously.

At the little inn they brought us first a tureen of bright yellow soup, tasting like bad sour milk and oil, which even I could not touch! They call the compound "egg soup," and professed great astonishment at our not liking it. Then they produced a tureen of dish-water with a mild flavouring of broth, in which floated irregular slices and lumps of stale bread, with a few blacks and a good deal of smoke to improve the mess. So for once I really appreciated table d'hôte on our return, which is generally an unmitigated bore. Mr. Bickerdike always says grace from the head of the table, and the little gathering every night for "family prayers" is very nice.

Last evening looked very doubtful and heavily clouded; had any one guessed it would have turned out a glorious morning, we might have arranged for Col de Balm early, and might have been off at five or so. It is now (10.30), though still fine, quite clouded on the Bréven and Col de Balm; how curious it

is that only the early mornings, from four to nine, are ever really clear (with rare exceptions). This afternoon Mr. S. and I are going to make our last attempt at a good excursion; and having been disappointed of both the others (Schilthorn and Jardin), I do very much hope weather will keep up for this, the only remaining feather for our caps, Les Grands Mulets.

———

No. VI.

Hotel Royal, Chamouni.
Monday, June 23.

Hurrah! We have done it, and could not possibly have had a more successful or a more amusing excursion, "la première ascension" of the year, and consequently all Chamouni excited about it. We had inquired at the Bureau des Guides, and found that the regulation was two guides and a porter at an exorbitant tariff, being a "course extraordinaire." It did seem waste to spend six or seven pounds on one excursion, so we said it was out of the question. However, two strong young fellows not yet admitted as "guides," but only as "porteurs," who had formed part of Mrs. Snepp's carriers to Montanvert, talked to us about it. They had their testimonial books to show one had been seventeen times up Mont Blanc, and all seemed satisfactory. They undertook to take us up themselves without any further fuss, and so Mr. S. agreed to entrust them with our bones. Their eagerness and delight were comical; there is a certain éclat about "la première ascension," and they would go on any terms, so that they might have the glory of it, and take the shine out of their superiors, the sworn "guides." We saw that we could not be in better hands, as all their interest lay in making it a firstrate success. Our boots had to be fresh nailed, and a bigger spike put in my stick, and various arrangements made, all which they looked after.

On Friday, at 2.30 p.m., we set off, accompanied for the first stage by Mrs. S. and E. and the Bickerdikes, our fellows strutting in triumph with their great ice axes, called piolets, and a great coil of rope, and our small effects.

The first part was very hot, but we took it slowly; then came forest and ferns; then the path got worse, with tiny torrents crossing it, till by 5.30 we reached the first snow patches, alternating with flowers, and about six we reached Pierre Pointue, where we were to sleep. I had a little wooden room, with single boards between my head and the back den where the guides snored. Mr. S. had the salon converted into a tidy bedroom by the importation of trestles and boards as soon as our supper was cleared away. As there was no fire, we went into the little kitchen and warmed our feet in the oven, where also our boots were baked previous to being greased for the ascent.

As soon as our guides had eaten, they dashed off to collect wood and dried rhododendrons for a bonfire, for of course Chamouni must be apprised of our arrival, and as it got dark the flame blazed up well on a jutting rock in full view of the hotels below. Meanwhile we had a grand sunset, several sunset pictures in one, all thrown up by the dark depth of the valley below. On the right the Aiguille Verte and Aiguille du Dru formed an exquisite calm picture apart, both a delicate rose colour, partly veiled by floating mist of semi-transparent silver. Opposite, intense purple and very stormy-looking clouds massed densely all along the tops of the Bréven range; but their other side must have been gorgeous, for a weird light was reflected down from underneath it upon the upper slopes of rock and snow as from a great hidden fire, quite different from the *direct* sunlight. Then over the Pic de Varens were great rifts of gold, *quivering* with intensity and showing distant peaks of softer brilliance, changing every minute, as if series of golden gates were being unrolled, revealing gates of opal and pearl beyond them. Then to the left and behind the Dôme and Aiguille du Gouté, lit up with amber and scarlet, the Mont Maudit shone out as a cloud-tipped expanse of glowing snow; while the true summit of Mont Blanc just glimpsed through cloud, so rich in rose-fire and so beautiful that it was hardly tantalizing that the moment of full revelation never came, and all died away into white and grey as our bonfire blazed up just below us.

Of course I went to bed at once, and soon to sleep, spite of the snoring through the boards. In the middle of the night I heard a continued scratching, suggestive of rats, only it must be a snow species, as ours would not find the climate agreeable; after a while I found it proceeded from the salon, where Mr. S. was vainly scraping damp matches on the boards that he might see the time. Presently the host roused up and gave a light; it was 1.10 a.m., so we had yet fifty minutes to sleep. The men did not seem to mind being routed up, it was part of their business, and they subsided again quite good temperedly, and in three minutes the snoring recommenced. They made it up by overshooting two o'clock, when they should have called us, so Mr. S. himself gave the réveille at 2.10. I rushed anxiously to my window, and rubbed the frosty pane to look out, for it had been hard to distinguish between wind and torrents; to my exceeding delight it was the latter only, and the morning was perfect, the stars sparkling like winter, Mont Blanc cloudless, and just gleaming with that strange pale light preceding the dawn.

By a little after three we were off. The Cranes will remember the scramble to Pierre à l'Echelle well, a narrow path skirting a precipice; it is now all snow, up which we worked step by step, each foot planted with a firm poke to ensure the footing, and also improve the track for after comers. They will recollect the snow slopes down which Aristide Couttet glissaded; it was

up these we climbed. At Pierre à l'Echelle we roped, the guides and Mr. S. having leather belts with a metal ring like harness, too heavy for me; I was simply noosed round the waist with a firm knot. They insisted on a certain order: Désailloud first, then myself, then Payot, and Mr. S. last, saying this was the safest arrangement. About eight or ten feet of rope are allowed between each person; they showed us it was a real Alpine Club rope, known by a red thread in the middle of the three strands, and gave us distinct instructions what to do in case of one slipping, or snow giving way, and dangling in a crevasse. The sun had struck the summits with very beautiful colouring, something between amber and crimson; and Mr. S. called a halt and would have the Morning Hymn! It was very bad economy of wind, I sang two verses and then "struck." Sticking half way up a snow slope, holding on by a projecting crag at four a.m., is not the most favourable position for hymn-singing, however inspiring the sunrise may be. We worked up and across the great Glacier des Bossons, incomparably grander than the Mer de Glace; and if you want a good idea of it, study any of those snow stereoscopes, with people crossing crevasses and threading among blocks and pinnacles of ice and looking down into gulfs; they give an excellent idea of it. I could have fancied I had got into a stereoscope box in a dream.

The snow was in excellent condition, *i.e.* we did not often go in above our knees! and every now and then only went ankle-deep for a treat, and in a few very sheltered parts we could trot over the crust without breaking it.

Every few minutes Désailloud shouted "Attention!" "Faites tendre la corde!" (stretch the rope) and that signified a crevasse. Then we went very slowly, stretching the rope tight between us (which reduces the shock if anybody goes in), while Désailloud sounded the snow step by step, sometimes cutting away an unsafe bit, as it is safer to step or spring across an open fissure than a hidden one. There is so much snow now that most of the crevasses are well snowed over, and we needed no ladders, which are necessary in August. We had to pass close under the Aiguille du Midi, where the torn snow showed we were on the track of avalanches; and here Désailloud hurried us on, saying the sooner we got over that ten minutes the better, as there was no foreseeing an avalanche. All this time we had the advantage of being in the shadow of the immense heights, with sharp frosty air and crackling snow. About 7.15 we came out upon the steep snow slopes on the other side of the two glaciers we had crossed, and were not only in full view of the sun but of Chamouni. In three minutes the guides caught the sound of cannon, and listening we heard two more rounds. "On nous voit!" they shouted in a state of ecstasy, "Everybody in Chamouni can see us with the big telescopes!" They were so charmed, and I think we found it rather stimulating also, to know that we were being watched from below. Désailloud gave himself the trouble of hoisting a great shawl on his piolet as a flag, and carrying it up three steep slopes in triumph. And they were *very* steep, though not at all dangerous, as we got footing nearly knee-deep for every step.

A little before eight we reached the Grands Mulets, black desolate peaked rocks in the midst of an ocean of snow, and our arrival was signalled instantly by four more cannonades in Chamouni. There is a wooden cabin perched on a shelf of the rock; the guides knew where to find the key, and set out luncheon for us quite tidily, while we sat cross-legged on the two little beds to warm our feet. Payot acted lady's maid and took off my boots and stockings (I could not possibly get them off myself), and kindly lent me a pair of his own enormous worsted socks, warm and dry, which soon warmed me up beautifully, and then I sat upon my feet and handed the socks to Mr. S., who was very cold indeed, so that I was almost frightened for him till a little food and cognac warmed him up too. I did not feel the least tired all the way, and could have gone on much higher with ease; but as soon as I had eaten I went fast asleep for a quarter of an hour, which seemed rather grievous to do in such a scene, but I could not help it, and woke up as fresh as possible for the descent. In the meantime our guides had set off on their own account, scrambling and tearing about just like boys out of school, yelling madly, coming down again right over the roof of the cabin, which was all snow like the rest. The powerful sun during our halt had so softened the snow that our descent was a simple series of slides and plunges; after a few hundred feet we got quite used to the motion. Real glissades were not safe to attempt, with the glacier below. We had some lovely effects, such as I have never before seen, in passing the colossal ice blocks on the shady side; the sun behind them touching the transparent edges with a sort of aureole, and shining through a glittering drip from the overhanging ones. We wanted to stop and admire, but the guides said it was " not good " to stand there; the giants have an objectionable trick of tumbling over now and then, and it is as well to keep out of the way. The snow bridges required a little more caution than in the morning, but we passed them all quite safely.

At our first halt on the glacier about five a.m. Mr. S. dropped his spectacles (fortunately not the dark ones), and the slope being steep and the snow hard they went glissading down two or three hundred feet till they vanished in a hole, all in a few seconds. We could not have found the place again, but on our return the guides pulled up on the lower edge of a great hole about six feet wide, overhung by snow and rock, and announced that the spectacles were *there,* and they would fetch them up! They had made a different return track on purpose. Mr. S. entreated them to let it alone, but they declared there was no danger, and they would evidently have been desperately disappointed of their fun if he had insisted.

They untied me to give more rope, and then Désailloud lowered himself (Payot, Mr. S., and I holding the rope), and we roaring at him not to go, he only laughing in return out of the depths, and shouting that he could *see* the spectacles and meant to have them! There was luckily just rope enough for him to reach them, and up he came, like a monkey, with the spectacles safe between his teeth, all over snow.

They would not untie us when we got to Pierre à l'Echelle, because the snow slopes are so steep (though no more crevasses), which seemed to me the very reason why we should not pull each other down, as we soon proved, especially as I don't like glissading when roped, and one attempt thereat resulted in our all rolling over each other. Presently I thought we were come to a sufficiently easy part to go carelessly, whereupon I slipped, and Payot who was next me totally lost himself too, and we had just started a decidedly too rapid spin down a *very* steep incline, when instantaneously Mr. S. did the only possible thing which could have stopped all four of us; flung himself right on his back with his heels in the snow, the orthodox thing to do if only any one has the presence of mind to do it. This checked the impetus, and we quickly recovered our footing.

After this we were unroped, which I greatly preferred, as the roping is very hampering to individual action on the snow slopes, though splendidly safe for the glaciers. Being free I managed some nice long glissades by myself. Payot and Mr. S. did a magnificent glissade together, going down like a shot in less than two minutes, a descent which would have taken perhaps twenty minutes to get down any other way. I need not say that after these exploits there was not a dry inch on our clothes! I was not at all tired on reaching Pierre Pointue, so after settling the bill we raced down to Chamouni in considerably less than regulation time, owing to scampers and short cuts, as we were anxious to give Mrs. S. a pleasant surprise by being back much sooner than expected. It was very bright and hot, and we could never have done half the walking in the valley that we did on the mountains. We found we were not expected till five or six o'clock, so as we marched in before three the final salute was not ready, but our arrival was soon known, and the little cannon were blazing away again! About half a mile from Chamouni our guides passed their home and stopped for a minute; they might as well have left the heavy rope and ice axes as carry them to Chamouni and back again in the heat, but oh dear no, they could not possibly enter Chamouni without them, heat and weight being no consideration compared with getting the outward and visible credit of " la première ascension de 1873 "! So they shouldered it all again, and marched in in style.

Our reception was most amusing; even the waiters who are an unusually glum set were beaming, and Mr. S. was rushed at by the master of the hotel and the secretary of the *Journal de Genève,* all as frantic as if we had returned from the moon itself.

Refusals availed nought, and they positively insisted on treating us to champagne, which was taken with the usual foreign glass-clinking and ecstatic congratulations. Then came an humble request, would we write just a little article for the *Journal de Genève,* to appear on Tuesday? it would be such a favour, such a benefit (*i.e.* to the Hotel Royal), and so forth; and if we preferred writing in English, monsieur le secrètaire would speedily put it into French. So when I let them know I was not new at that trade, and graciously acceded, they congratulated *themselves* with fresh enthusiasm! I don't know when I ever laughed more, the whole concern was so funny and utterly novel. I had not a notion the ascent to the Grands Mulets was made such a fuss about, but the éclat was owing to its being the *first* ascent of the season, which had never before happened to be done by a lady.

But now for Mrs. S., who decidedly won her spurs while we won ours. To Mr. S.'s consternation she was out with E. and A. and the Bickerdikes, and no one gave the same version of her departure, the received one being that she had gone on a mule to meet us after being informed by the telescope that our descent had commenced. So we sent after her and at last when we were becoming really anxious the party drove into Chamouni at 6.30.

She was much disappointed and vexed at not being in time to receive Mr. S. She thought the expedition to La Flégère the B.'s asked her to take would only be for two hours. Up they toiled in the heat, mile after mile of those horrid zigzags; then the saddle slipped a little on one side, and the muleteer gave Mrs. S. such a counteracting push as nearly sent her over on the other, whereupon she dismounted and actually climbed all the rest of the way on foot. Then little E. would not ride, and they chartered a big boy who carried her two miles on his back! At last they reached the top, 6,500 feet! The report of our "ascension" had reached La Flégère, and the hostess was ready to embrace Mrs. S. on finding that she was wife of one of the "voyageurs," the whole neighbourhood seems to have been on the look out in a state of excitement. Presently up dashes E.'s boy: "Les voyageurs sont arrivés à Chamouni!" dancing and capering as if he would like to fly down to meet "les voyageurs." Pleasing intelligence for poor Mrs. S., on the top of La Flégère! So down she started full speed the four or five miles on foot, as it is so steep for riding down, and sent the aforesaid boy on to get a carriage to meet them at the bottom. So all ended well, and we had a *lively* table d'hôte at seven o'clock, as you may suppose, except that I was cross at having allowed myself to be beguiled into writing for the Geneva paper instead of taking a siesta as I intended.

They tell me I am *fully* equal to doing Mont Blanc *easily.* But now for a piece of wisdom: I really think it would not be worth while to do it, considering the great expense and the danger of being overtaken by bad weather, however delightful if continuously fine. We have had all the most interesting sights and doings of the ascent, and the only gain would be the being able to say we had done it.

Though not the faintest quiver of nervousness once crossed me to spoil the enjoyment, yet it certainly does not come within the promise I made in 1871 to attempt "nothing dangerous," for there is a certain amount of danger both from crevasses and avalanches which no surefootedness or precaution could entirely neutralise. Neither Mr. S. nor I thought of danger till we were actually up there, so I went with a clear conscience, which would not be if I were to go a second time, and I could not have the entire absence of fear and absolute trust in God's keeping which I had *this* time. Even as a matter of muscle and agility I would not recommend it to any but gentlemen, and by no means to all of those; it wants a light quick walker, good lungs, steady head and sure foot, and *light weight* and step for crossing the crevasses, The two days' splendid weather seemed just on purpose for us, it has changed again and been stormy all day.

Sunday was very pleasant, the number of English nearly double that of last Sunday. Mr. S. read prayers morning and afternoon. I played both times, and we had nice hymns and chants. At table d'hôte we met a Mr. Burns and his family who knew dear papa at Dunoon.

Our return is uncertain; probably we shall stay a Sunday at Boulogne, and perhaps get two or three days' sea bathing as a break in the long journey, and a *let down* out of the mountain air; I cannot give any certain address at all!

No. VII.

CHAMONIX. (How I hate spelling it French fashion! I never can reconcile my mind to considering it France.) June 25.

Weather continues to be "variable," so Monday we could do nothing, violent storms all day; once we saw a cloud come down into the valley two or three miles off, and then literally roll along the very ground as if it would swallow us up; and when it did reach the village, the pour beat any mountain storm I ever saw.

Tuesday we speculated would be fine, so Mr. S. and I started at 4.15 for the Col de Balm. We had a lovely walk along the valley to Argentière (six miles). We went on two miles more to La Tour, the highest village of the valley, nearly five thousand feet above sea level; and here I decided to stay, while Mr. S. went on to the top, four miles farther. As usual, the lovely morning failed, and clouds came down; and poor Mr, S. got no view at all, and had his tough climb all for nothing, up a path not yet "arrangé pour la saison," which means any amount of landslips and mud and snow and torrents and boulders to be walked over.

We got back to Chamouni at 1.30; the excursion is reckoned as nine hours' walking, five up and four down. So Mr. S. walked twenty-four miles, and I only about sixteen!

I never saw such an awful place for swindle without redress! All the hotels belong to a "Société Anonyme," so there is no competition and no *maître d'hotel*, whose personal interest it is to protect and please his guests. I have actually made them reduce our bill by nearly eighty francs; all such clear overcharges that they could not maintain them. One item beat anything I ever heard of, "a pencil, fifty centimes!" (*i.e.* half a franc) which turned out to be that a waiter had lent Mr. S. a pencil for half a minute to write a message with, the pencil not having been even asked for and returned on the spot! The only thing they don't swindle in is the guides and mules, which are all tariff, and though high are not utterly unreasonable, and are always exact.

Ann gives a sad report of the servants' table. I am glad she is a Young Women's Christian Association member, and she seems to have been brave and true to her colours. Of all the valets and ladies' maids she was the only one in Chamouni (for all the hotels dine together at present) who went to church, except one apparently well disposed man, who sided with her and spoke up for religion.

HOTEL DU PAVILLON. Saturday Evening.

I thought I should not have much to tell you, but we have had quite an adventure of a sort new to me! I wrote so far, early a.m. on Wednesday. As we wished to be at Geneva by Thursday evening, we ought either to have gone down direct on Thursday morning, or started not later than nine a.m. on Wednesday, to go by Tête Noire, which is nine hours. Although a little carriage road is open all the way, the ups and downs, etc., are so great that they allow just the same time as for foot or mule passengers.

We did not start till 12.30, and soon found that most of the way the carriage had to go even slower than we could walk! and we walked a good deal. I am not given to nervousness, but really in several places I was more easy in my mind out of the carriage than in; it always seems to me the most dangerous mode of progression, where a narrow road has only a slight and occasional fence of two fir poles, and there are torrents and real precipices below, especially in early summer when the edges often give way from the rains. Though not a bright day, it was tolerable till about half-past six in the evening, by which time we ought to have been safely housed at Vernayaz, instead of beginning the ascent of the Forclaz just beyond the Tête Noire hotel, which we did not leave till six.

For information of Maria, etc., I will just explain that the Tête Noire is a magnificent high level valley or gorge, winding for four or five hours at a good height among mountains, as picturesque a combination of heights and depths, rocks, torrents, cascades, pine trees, ferns, flowers, and precipices as exists anywhere. The upper end consists of an hour's stiff pull up to the Col de Forclaz, on gaining which you look down over the other side into the Rhone valley, deep below, reached by a rough zigzaging road of about seven miles down.

So we began the descent just as it was beginning to get dark! It reminded me of Astathes in that pretty little allegory, "The Spring Morning," who set out late on his journey and came in for storms and wild beasts, where Agape the early little traveller passed safely. After about ten minutes, in coming down a very steep bit, something went bang. The driver got out, pottered in the wet, and then "Faut descendre!" was his laconic information. So "descendre" we all did, in all the drench, and lo! the drag had broken, right in two. So he turned us all out, and we had to trudge seven miles down in the deepening dark!

Happily the rain ceased in a short time, or rather we came down out of the cloud, so it was only a question of tramp. It was pretty well at first, but as it got to nine and ten and eleven o'clock it was no trifle, and a sprained ankle would have been no marvel. We had to pick step after step with the utmost caution, among big stones and sudden dips and occasional streams, when we could trace anything; but when we passed under trees, which are luxuriant for the last mile or two, it was absolutely pitch dark, and we could only guide by each other's voices, or the jingle of the horse bells before us, or the rush of a little watercourse beside us. At last we got to the bottom, and were allowed to get into the carriage. I should say that I picked up two or three glow-worms, which were a material assistance in guiding those who walked behind me! By that time the wind had risen, and resisted all attempts to get a light while the re-harnessing took place. The arrangement is, one strong horse that goes all the way, and a mule that is tied on behind for descents, and brought to the fore for levels and ascents, running by the side of the shafts with two or three ropes and straps, which broke three or four times.

After we had our mule tied on we had to go nearly a mile at slow walking pace, "the police forbid any trotting through Martigny!" through wide roads and dead level. At last we got fairly out on the Vernayaz road, anticipating a good trot, when all at once a perfect hurricane came tearing down the lower Rhone valley to meet us, right in our teeth; it not only blew the clouds away, but bid fair to blow the stars out, and had it come broadside I believe it must have blown the vehicle over. And this lasted till some little time after midnight, when the great white new hotel of the Gorge du Trient loomed up ghostly and lightless under the rocks.

We were glad enough to see it, and soon rang the natives up, who were singularly amiable considering their sleepiness, stumbling down in various stages of costume and nightcap. Mrs. S. was very tired next morning, but no one else was a whit the worse, and Emily got in to Geneva the next night as lively as ever. In the morning we went up the Gorge du Trient, a colossal fissure from six hundred to one thousand feet deep, and often not six feet across, the only access being by a wooden gallery a quarter of a mile long, hung on iron cramps and supports above the roaring torrent, which fills up the bottom of the cleft, with no shore whatever, a narrow deep volume of mighty waters.

At the hotel they had a beautiful young St. Bernard, with her two splendid little puppies, a fortnight old. Mr. S. wants a dog badly as house-dog, and Emily wanted a puppy, and it seemed cruel to take such a little one away from the mother; so, as the people came to terms, he bought the whole family! The mother, Vinesse, is a beauty, with a grand head and gentle wistful expression, a dog that would die for you. The little fellows are sleek rotundities with big paws, supposed to be going to be very superb specimens. I am delighted with them of course.

———

[The last letter of this series is missing.]

———— ❀ ————

VIII.

JULY ON THE MOUNTAINS.

THERE is sultry gloom on the mountain brow,
    And a sultry glow beneath;
Oh for a breeze from the western sea,
Soft and reviving, sweet and free,
Over the shadowless hill and lea,
    Over the barren heath!

There are clouds and darkness around God's ways,
    And the noon of life grows hot;
And though His faithfulness standeth fast
As the mighty mountains, a shroud is cast
Over its glory, solemn and vast,
    Veiling, but changing it not.

Send a sweet breeze from Thy sea, O Lord,
    From Thy deep, deep sea of love;
Though it lift not the veil from the cloudy height,
Let the brow grow cool and the footsteps light,
As it comes with holy and soothing might,
    Like the wing of a snowy dove.

———— ❀ ————

IX.

THREE LETTERS,

(FROM A SERIES OF TWELVE) TO MRS. HAVERGAL IN 1874, DURING A TOUR CHIEFLY WITH CONSTANCE S. C.

THE INN ON THE FAULHORN.
6th July, 1874.

"SUNSET on the Faulhorn!" All day there had been strange rifts in the clouds, and sudden pictures of peaks or of abysses framed in white and grey; but towards seven o'clock the wind rose, and there was a grand outpour of colour upon everything, sky, clouds, and mountains.

Imagine yourself midway between heaven and earth, the sharp point of rock on which we stood hardly seeming more of earth than if we had been in a balloon, the whole space around, above, and below filled with wild, weird, spectral clouds, driving and whirling in incessant change and with tremendous rapidity; horizon *none,* but every part of where horizon should be, crowded with unimaginable shapes of unimagined colours, with rifts of every shade of blue, from indigo to pearl, and burning with every tint of fire, from gold to intensest red; shafts of keen light shot down into abysses of purple thousands of feet below, enormous surging masses of grey hurled up from beneath, and changing in an instant to glorified brightness of fire as they seemed on the point of swallowing up the shining masses above them; then, all in an instant, a wild grey shroud flung over us, as swiftly passing and leaving us in a blaze of sunshine; then a bursting open of the very heavens, and a vision of what might be celestial heights, pure and still and shining, high above it all; then, an instantaneous cleft in another wild cloud, and a revelation of a perfect paradise of golden and rosy slopes and summits; then, quick gleams of white peaks through veilings and unveilings of flying semi-transparent clouds; then, as quickly as the eye could follow, a rim of dazzling light running round the edges of a black castle of cloud, and flaming windows suddenly pierced in it; oh, mother dear, I might go on for sheets, for it was never twice the same, nor any single minute the same, in any one direction. At one juncture a cloud stood still, apparently about two hundred yards off, and we each saw our own shadows gigantically reflected on it, surrounded by a complete rainbow arch, but a full circle of bright prismatic colours, a transfiguration of our shadows almost startling, each moreover seeing only their own glorification! When the whole pageant, lasting nearly an hour, was past, we sang "Abide with me," and then the dear old joyous "Glory to Thee, my God."

ORMONT DESSUS. September.

This second month of my Swiss journey is altogether different from the first, for now I am making *writing* the first thing instead of idleness. I am doing it quite in moderation, and taking plenty of fresh air as well; one can be out half the day and yet get four or five good hours' writing as well, under these circumstances, when there are no other calls whatever upon time or strength; and this combination of work and leisure is very delightful. Besides, I feel as if I had got quite a fresh start with that month's rest; it seems as if nature had then walked into my brain and taken possession (turning *me* out meanwhile), and given a kind of spring cleaning! rubbing up the furniture, and fresh papering some of the rooms, and cleaning the windows! That perpetual "moving on," which some so delight in, does not suit me nearly so well as staying in a place, and taking it easy. The weather has been so much colder and more variable, since I changed my tactics, that the two things coincided beautifully; for, except two days, it has been too cold the last fortnight for any sitting out of doors.

I don't know why I always seem to shrink from writing much, or even anything, of the "under the surface" life (which is so much more than the "on the surface" and the mere surroundings), in my circulars. They would be much fuller if I told one tithe of the hourly bits of gentle guidance and clear loving-kindness which make the real enjoyment, or of the perpetual little opportunities of a "word for Jesus" which He seems to give me, and often of real work for Him, which yet seems to come so unsought so easily and naturally, so altogether without any effort, as to be not felt to be any working at all. Now I will give you an instance of how He took me at my word the other day. It was one of the few warm days, and I established myself with pen and ink in a shady nook by a little, steep, downhill torrent. I had suddenly got that sort of strong impulse to write on a certain theme, without which I never do my best, but with which I always do my best poems.

The theme was a grand one ("The Thoughts of God"); I had thought of it for months, and never before had this impulse to begin upon it; though, once begun, I expected it to be one of my best poems. I spent a little time in prayer first, and then the warning and the promise in Jeremiah 15:19 came strongly to my mind: "if thou take forth the precious from the vile, thou shalt be as My mouth." I felt that wanted looking into; I wanted Him to take forth the precious from the vile for me, and to reveal and purge away, then and there, all the self and mingled motive which would utterly mar the work that I wanted to be for His glory. After that the question came, was I—had He made me—just as willing to do any little bit of work for Him, something for little children or poor people, simple and unseen, as this other piece of work, which might win something of man's praise? Then I was intensely happy in feeling that I could tell Him that I had no choice at all about it; but would really rather do just what He chose for me to do, whatever it might be. However, there seemed nothing else to do, so I began my poem. I don't think I had written four lines when a labourer with a scythe came along a tiny path to drink at the stream a few yards below me. He did not see me, and started when I hailed him and offered him a little book. He climbed up to receive it, and then, instead of departing as I expected, deliberately sat down on a big stone at my feet, and commenced turning over the leaves, and evidently laying himself out to be talked to. So here was clearly a little call; and I talked to him for some time, he being very interested and responsive. Just as he was going to move off, two lads of about fifteen and eighteen, his sons, came crashing through the bushes; I don't recollect whether the father beckoned them or not, anyhow up they came, and he quietly sat down again, and they sat down too, and seemed quite as willing to listen to the "old, old story" as he had been, only I could not get so much out of them. At last the whole crew departed, and I was just collecting my thoughts and reviving the aforesaid "impulse," when in about ten minutes the younger lad reappeared, with his sister, a girl of about seventeen. They did not say a word, but scrambled straight up to me, and, seating themselves at my feet, looked up into my face, saying by their look as plain as any words, "Please talk to us!" What could one do but accede! and they stayed at least another half hour, so quiet and interested that one could not but hope the seed was falling on "good ground." The girl, Félicie, was more communicative than the lads, very simple, but intelligent. By the time they departed a good part of the morning was gone, and the "impulse" too! but I enjoyed the morning probably twice as much as if I had done a good piece of my poem; and it seemed so clear that the Master had taken me at my word, and come and given me this to do for Him among His "little ones," and that He was there hearing and answering and accepting me, that it was worth any amount of poem-power.

However, *next* day the "impulse" came again, which is by no means always the case when once interrupted; and once fairly started, I have worked out what I *think* is perhaps the best poem I ever wrote, so far as I can judge.

But this is only one of constant instances which I could tell. I do so feel that every hour is distinctly and definitely guided by Him. I have taken Him at His word *in everything,* and He takes me at my word *in everything.* Oh, I *can* say now that Jesus *is* "to me a living bright Reality," and that He really and truly *is* "more dear, more intimately nigh, than e'en the sweetest earthly tie." No friendship could be what I find His to be. I have more now than a few months ago, even though I was so happy then; for the joy of *giving* myself, and my will, and my all to Him seems as if it were succeeded, and even superseded, by the deeper joy of a conscious certainty that He has *taken* all that He led me to give; and "I am persuaded that He is able to keep that which I have committed unto Him": so, having entrusted my very trust to Him, I look forward ever so happily to the future (*if* there be yet much of earthly future for me) as "one vista of brightness and blessedness." Only I do so want everybody to "taste and see." Yesterday I somehow came to a good full stop in my writing much earlier than I expected, and asked what He would have me do next, go on, or go out at once? Just then a young lady came in; "Had I just a few minutes to spare?" So I went out with her at once. She had overheard a short chat I had had some days ago with another, didn't know *what,* but it had set her longing for something more than she had got. She had started out for a walk alone, thinking and praying, and the thought came to her to come straight to me, which she seemed to think an unaccountably bold step. Well, God seemed to give me exactly the right message for her, just as with Miss M. last week, the two cases starting from a very different level but the result the same, a real turning point. Don't conclude, however, from these that I am always seeing results, because I am not: but that I am entirely content about, just as He chooses it to be.

It has occurred to me that, as I profess to be "writing," you will expect a new book as the result, and will be disappointed; so I tell you simply what I *have* written, and what I am going to write.

"Our Swiss Guide." Article for *Sunday Magazine,* on the spiritual analogies in all sorts of little details of mountaineering.

"For Charity." Song for Hutchings and Romer.

"Enough." Short sacred poem.

"How much for Jesus?" A sort of little true story for children; for an American edition.[1]

"True Hearted." New Year's Address (in verse) for Young Women's Christian Association, for January 1875.

"Tiny Tokens." A small poem for *Good Words.*

---

[1] This manuscript we have no clue to; any information concerning it would be acceptable. [See page 225 of this book.]

"Precious Things." A poem.

"A Suggestion." Short paper for *Home Words*.

"The Precious Blood of Jesus." A hymn.

"The Thoughts of God." The aforesaid poem.

"Shining for Jesus." Verses addressed to my nieces and nephews at Winterdyne.

"New Year's Wishes," by Caswell's request, for a very pretty card.

These are all written, and copied, and done with. Next week (D.V.) [1] I set about what I have long wanted to do: "Little Pillows," thirty-one short papers as a little book for children of, say, twelve years old; a short, easily recollected text, to go to sleep upon for each night of the month, with a page or two of simple practical thoughts about it, such as a little girl might read every night while having her hair brushed. I think this will take me about a fortnight to write and arrange for press; adding probably a verse or two of a hymn at the end of each of the little papers. There are lots of little monthly morning and evening books for grown up people, but I don't know of one for children except those containing *only* texts. I dare say I shall get in somehow three other little poems that want writing (being on the simmer): "The Splendour of God's Will," "The Good Master," and (don't be startled at the transition) "Playthings"; also "Johann von Allmen," a little article for the *Dayspring*. I can clear off things easily here, especially through not having so many letters. If I could manage three months every year in a Swiss or Welsh valley, I should keep my printer going.

———

En route, September 29, 1874.

I don't know whether there will be enough of interest for a final circular, but when I am out I never feel inclined to do anything but write home. As I did not know your address, I had to write my last to Maria, at any rate part of my long letter to her was to do duty as circular.

I was nearly if not quite "the last rose of summer" at Ormont Dessus, the hotel shuts up on October 1. But the last week was the most perfect weather possible, and, without being unpleasantly hot, was warm enough for sitting out not merely in the sunshine but in the moonlight. My last day, Sunday, was one of the most exquisite days imaginable, brilliantly clear, the autumn tints throwing in touches of crimson and gold in splendid contrast to the pine woods; and, what is so rare in Switzerland, the noon and afternoon were as glowing as the morning, everything vivid all day,

At the little French service I soon saw we had "somebody" in the pulpit, and it was M. de Pressensé, who is, I have been told, one of the first French orators. His sermon was both eloquent and good. Madame de Pressensé, the well known

writer, was almost close to me, a sweet and handsome-looking elderly lady. Their daughter has married M. Bernus, the very charming young pastor of the Eglise Libre at Ormont Dessus, a curious change for this rather elegant and distinguée looking Parisienne to settle down in little wooden rooms over a little wooden chapel in this out of the way valley! M. Bernus is cousin to Helen Trench that was! I found this out when I went to get books at the Church Library. The people sing beautifully; it was a downright treat, in German choral style as to music, slow rich harmonies that bear dwelling on; one tune was Cassel, No. 190 in "Havergal's Psalmody." It was such sweet singing, every one keeping to *cres.* and *dim.*, neither instrument nor apparently any stated choir, but all the parts correctly sung by the peasant congregation.

I have finished not only "Little Pillows," but a companion to it for morning use, "Morning Bells," both manuscripts are ready for the press. I do not think it is nearly so easy to write for children as for adults; constantly I refrained from what I would most like to say about the texts I had chosen, because it would not be simple enough for the little ones. I have purposely avoided any stories or anecdotes, lest children should skim the book through in search of them, instead of reading them morning and night steadily; at least I know that is what I should have done. I do so hope these books will be really helpful to some of Christ's little ones.

On Monday morning I left Ormont Dessus at eight on foot, sending my bag "by post." By the bye the oddest instance of the Swiss way of sending all things by post was when one day Madame Treina apologised for giving me only chicken for dinner "because the beef had not come by post"! Instead of going direct to Montreux by diligence and rail, I went for a three days' walking tour. Please, nobody is to be shocked at this, because I quite came to the conclusion that it was not incorrect at all, and I found other ladies doing it. Besides who is any the wiser? If one is seen marching alone, one may have friends five minutes before or behind for aught any one knows! I have really had a good spell at writing, and I thought a three days' march would be a good thing to finish up with. It was a nice morning, and I walked till nearly twelve, and then "camped" till three in a mossy nook by a little stream, mended gloves, did my accounts, watched the water, and so forth. Then I walked on again and got to the little town of Saanen at five.

After crossing the Col de Pillon, an easy two hours pass out of the Ormonts valley into the Saanen-thal, it was all road, smooth and level, nothing exciting, but just a very quietly pretty valley, what one would call "peaceful"; the Ormonts always suggested the French term "*riante*"[2] to me. The whole way was musical with these pretty cow bells, as most of the herds have been brought down from the high alps, and instead of being

[1] D.V., Deo volente, Latin, meaning "God willing"   [2] *riante*: French, "laughing," "one who is laughing" (the feminine form of the word)

from one hundred to five hundred large, they are distributed among their owners for the winter. A herd on the mountains may belong to thirty or forty different people. The last fortnight my mountain rambles have been all the more enjoyable for the descent of the "bétail" from the "high alps," so that they were perfectly undisturbed. The high pastures or "alps," for the meaning is the same, where the cows are in summer, range from 5500 to 7500 feet; then in September they come down to the "middle alps," where hay has already been twice made; then in October they come down to the valleys, where generally there have been three crops of hay. It is very systematic, and a whole district acts simultaneously in these pastoral arrangements. The middle alps are enclosed with rough fencing, so I don't mind the beasts there; it is when two hundred or three hundred creatures are loose on the high alps, with no fences or retreat whatever, that I object to meet them.

This Saanenthal is more one's ideal of rural Swiss life than almost anything I have seen; no pensions, or any signs of foreign tourists, but pure aboriginal. No one would believe who has not seen it, the difference between the Protestant and Romanist valleys. Here in the Saanen-thal the chalets are beautiful, as spruce and pretty as the carved things one sees, and look roomy and comfortable, averaging about fifteen windows, in front! Nice little gardens are quite the rule, and in Ebuit, a small village, I saw several quite up to the mark of a "First Prize" at a Perry Barr flower show, which is saying a great deal; dahlias seem the pet flower just now. One never sees any "gentlemen's houses"; the land is all in small properties, and there is no Swiss nobility. The only things answering to our country houses are quite near the larger towns. A Swiss country pastor's life must be peculiarly isolated, often a day's journey from any one except peasants and peasant farmers.

At Saanen I put up at a queer old-fashioned inn, very comfortable and very cheap, with a capital piano, which was quite a treat, as it is a good while since I have even seen one. Tuesday morning was gloomy and suspicious, so I started at a quarter past seven, but it did not rain till the afternoon. I reached Chateau D'Oex by half-past nine, and was disappointed with it; it is pretty, but there are places ten times more so within reach; yet heaps of English stay there. Towards eleven I got to the Gorge de la Tine, a lovely narrow deep cleft, with an almost emerald river at the bottom, broken with white foam; I turned off and rested on moss nearly a foot thick, overlooking this beautiful gorge. Then I reckoned on some dinner at the village. At quite a large tidy-looking inn outside, I asked for some cold meat, and to be shown into the salon till it was ready.

Thereupon the very cheerful little waitress ushered me into their idea of a "salon," a room with one table covered with oil-cloth on which I was to dine, and another of sticks nailed across like an arbour table, a bed in one corner, a big box with three

puppies in another, and three chairs. The floor might have been washed last year or the year before! Then for the dinner, "they were sorry they had not what I asked for, but would do the best they could for madame." So in came a dish with four little squares of lukewarm lean bacon nearly black, and four ditto of fat. Another dish of two cold potatoes cut in half and dipped in some sort of brown juice, and *with these* half a dozen warm baked pears. Further, some very oily salad; however I am not particular, fortunately! Meanwhile the mother of the puppies aforesaid showed a positive determination not to let me leave the place without having a piece out of me; she watched every opportunity of the door being ajar to come in and make a rush at me; twice it came to a regular fight with my alpenstock! Every time they shut her up she got loose, and came at me again.

I have none of the nervousness about dogs that I have about bulls, still when I found she really meant mischief I thought, rain or no rain, I would push on to some more hospitable quarters. So I trudged on to Montbovon, rather out of my way; but it began to rain and I did not care to walk three miles in a pour to Allières, which is some way up the Col de Jaman. The Montbovon hotel folks, who were very pleasing, told me I should find accommodation in the auberge at Allières, not very luxurious, but I should be "very well" there. This being evidently disinterested advice, I relied on it and departed. However, for the first and only time in Switzerland, I found a strange contrast to the usual civility and even kindness of the people. I got there about a quarter past six, and found it just a remove better than the Sennbütte, which you will remember we camped at on our way from Mürren.

A tall, bold, rough girl, of twenty-five or so, let me in. "Yes, you can have a room when it's ready; not before. Here, in here!" And she ushered me into a dark dirty room with tables and benches, marched off, and shut the door. I did not like my quarters at all, but there was no help for it, as it would be impossible for me to cross the col or even get back to Montbovon in the dark. But of course I had been asking all along to be guided, so I was not uneasy, but expected I had been guided there for some good reason, perhaps some wandering sheep to be found. It got quite dark, and then five or six men came in, and she brought a candle, and they sat down at one of the tables and smoked. I hardly think they saw me. I asked if my room was ready. "No, you must wait!" and out she darted, slamming the door. So I waited, sitting on my bench in my dark corner for nearly an hour, she coming roughly in and out, talking noisily and bringing wine for the men. At last—"You can come upstairs now!" So I went, glad enough.

It was not quite so dirty as downstairs, but not brilliant. A jug and basin on the table was all the apparatus; the bed was barley straw, no pillow, but a pink cotton bolster. "Are you going to bed now?" she asked. I told her yes, very soon. About eight o'clock, just as I really was going to bed, came a sharp angry rap at my door. I was glad it was locked, for before I could answer the handle was rattled violently.

"What is it?"

"Are you going to burn the candle all night? How soon are you going to put it out, I should like to know! burning it all away 'comme cela!'" I considered it advisable to answer very meekly, so I merely said it should be put out in a few minutes, whereupon she banged downstairs. It seemed to me that this was an "opportunity," so I asked God that when morning came He would shut her mouth and open mine.

Wednesday morning I was up at daybreak, having gone to bed so early. At first the whole sky was clouded, and I feared I had lost my excursion, for the beautiful Col de Jaman is just one of those which it is worse than useless to cross except in good weather. However at sunrise the whole veil was withdrawn within a few minutes, and a more glorious morning could not be. I came down about half-past six; my friend was pottering over the fire with a big kettle. I asked her to get me some coffee. "Can't have coffee till it's made!" said she savagely. So I went and sat outside the door and waited patiently. In about half an hour she poked her head out. "Do you want anything besides coffee?" still in a tone as if I were a mortal enemy! I suggested bread and butter; "Butter!" (as if I had asked for turtle soup!) "there is none, but you can have a piece of bread if you like." So I had my coffee and a hunch of bread; but I don't pity anybody who breakfasts on Swiss bread and milk.

Then it was my turn! I went close to her, looked up into her wicked-looking eyes, and put my hand on her arm and said (as gently as possible): "You are not happy; I know you are not." She darted the oddest look at me; a sort of startled, half frightened look, as if she thought I was a witch! I saw I had touched the right string and followed it up, telling her how I saw last night she was unhappy, even when she was laughing and joking, and how I had prayed for her; and then, finding she was completely tamed, spoke to her quite plainly and solemnly, and then about Jesus and what He could do for her. She made a desperate effort not to cry. She listened in a way that I am sure nothing but God's hand upon her could have made her listen, and took "A Saviour for You" (in French), promising to read it, and thanking me over and over again. The remaining few minutes I was in the house she was as respectful and quiet as one could wish. I also got a talk with her old mother. So if God grants this to be the checking of this poor girl in what I should imagine to be a very downward path, was it not well worth getting out of the groove of one's usual comforts and civilities?

Then I trudged on up the col, and as I heard the bells of a large herd ahead I put myself under convoy of a little group of peasants, a woman, two men, and a lad; they were bright and intelligent, and seemed greatly to enjoy asking me questions about England, and were immensely gratified at my admiration of their own beautiful "patrie," so this made a nice opening for further talk about the more beautiful country above, and how to get there. I stayed some time on the top of the col, which I reached in about an hour and a half; the view was singular and fine; the lake of Geneva was hidden under an expanse of smooth white cloud, out of which the opposite mountains rose into an atmosphere as transparent as possible, while the farther heights above Lausanne loomed through a strange blue haze; all the rest of the view was vividly clear in splendid sunshine. It is about three hours down to Montreux; very pretty all the way, till you come through uninteresting vineyards, like the Rhine ones, three feet high, and not so pretty as raspberry beds.

I got here (Montreux) about noon, and turned into a hotel-pension conveniently close to the station.

A nice letter from Miss E. J. Whately, forwarded from Ormont, was awaiting me; she has been delayed in England, and is now staying at Spa, and cannot get here even if I waited a week for her, so we hope to meet another time. They are chiefly English in this pension, but not the sort who would care for me or I for them, I fancy. I have been a stroll this afternoon, and am now writing in my room before bedtime. I can't think how I shall do with English hours, after my early ones here. That reminds me, several have asked me to say how I am. Very well indeed, thank God. But I really do not feel sure whether I have "laid in a stock of strength," *i.e.,* whether I shall be able to do any more in England than I have done, without getting so very tired. For here I have been taking so much rest, and doing absolutely nothing to tire myself, and in every way setting health first, that I have had the best possible chance. Except at Sepey where I had two or three bad nights, I have been perfectly well the whole time, and now I really do mean to try and be very prudent with the health God has given me, only of course I do not mean to be idle; I seek to gain strength that I may use it. On the Col de Jaman I was greatly tempted to go up the Dent de Jaman, a most inviting rocky peak, commanding a splendid panorama; but it would have been two hours' extra exertion, and I thought I had better economise strength, and not run even a remote risk to finish up with.

Last Saturday week I was for a few minutes in (I believe) imminent danger, which I never was to my knowledge before. It was most utterly unexpected and unforeseen, or I should not of course have dreamt of putting myself in such a fix. I was having a higher afternoon scramble than usual, having waited for some time for a clear day to ascend a certain point (not a summit) on the great rocky mountain, Sex Rouge, from which I expected a peculiarly fine view. In two hours and forty minutes I reached my point, the edge of a shoulder over which I saw right into the midst of the great glaciers, and at the foot of a wall of great rocks which prevented further progress. It was merely a cow-track up to the highest alp most of the way, but beyond that came thirty-five minutes of very steep slope, partly poor grass and partly loose stones, but not so bad as to make me hesitate about climbing it. However, I found it more awkward coming down than I expected; so I scanned the place carefully, and fancied I could make out a much easier descent by making a certain angle farther down the edge of the shoulder, and then striking across the slope. I thought I had taken my bearings very accurately, a thing I seldom fail to find myself exact in; but somehow I lost them and trended too far to the left before ending the angle. It had certainly promised to be far easier than the other way, but after leaving the shoulder I found it getting worse and worse; still I thought every minute a few steps more would end the difficulty, so I crept on carefully across the small loose stones until I found it so steep that it would be nearly impossible to take any more steps without sliding down, stones and all. I had been so sure of my bearings that I had been only looking at my footing till then; but on pulling up to take a wider view of things, I was startled to see that instead of only a slope below me, which one might have slid down with impunity, there was a precipice not twenty feet below where I stood, a sheer edge with nothing whatever to catch at, not a bush or rock or boulder, nothing but the slipping stones which threatened to give way under my feet every instant. I believe that if I had felt the least confused or nervous I should have been lost, for the smallest wrong movement of foot or of balance would have been enough to send me and the stones down what must have been a fatal slope. I stood quite still, while I committed it all deliberately to Him who could keep my feet from falling, and then did what I could. I found it would be positively more dangerous to attempt to turn round; so the only thing was, as cautiously as possible, to *work* foothold with my alpenstock, moving one foot forward into it, and then working another, and so on. In less than five minutes I had passed the worst, and in about ten was beyond all danger. I cannot understand how I got there; there was some peculiar ocular delusion about the slope which altogether misled me; it looked as if every step must land me on a less steep slope, instead of which it was worse at every step. I have come across no parallel to it.

Connie and Elizabeth will recollect the steep shale slope where Abraham picked steps for us up the last part of the Dündengrat; it was much steeper than that, sharp rocky little stones instead of shale, and the precipice just below! Though God kept me perfectly calm and cool at the time, I could not think of it for days afterwards without shuddering, and it will certainly make me more cautious not only how I go, but where I

go; if ever I have any more mountaineering. Yet this was apparently a most innocent little excursion; not one I should ever have thought of taking a guide for, or expecting to find the least difficulty.

Dijon. October 2.

I left Montreux Thursday at noon. I determined to try the experiment of day instead of night travelling for a long journey. As one can only go first class by the night expresses, one actually saves, by sleeping on the way, as two nights at hotels do not equal the difference between first and second class, and the second class carriages are quite equal to our first. I think the home journey will be less tiring this way, as it is cool weather; if hot, then night is best. Besides, just now the homeward trains are all so very full that one could not have the least chance of room to lie down, and it would be intolerable to sit bolt upright all night. I can sleep anywhere if I can only lie down, but I can't do with sitting up.

So my Thursday's journey was only from Montreux to Dôle, which I reached at nine p.m. I waited from three to four at Auvernier, a tiny junction station near Neuchatel; the rest of the world goes on to Neuchatel and back again, getting the benefit of twenty minutes extra riding, and a great noisy station for hurried refreshments. By turning out at Auvernier I had an hour's quiet rest on a bench at a little table overlooking the lake, with a last view of the snow mountains gleaming among clouds. There were several countrywomen getting refreshment, café noir and vin du pays; and tracts were quite a new idea to them; they were uncommonly delighted, and wished me all manner of good things, nearly equal to Irish benedictions.

I had sunshine up to the last hour in Switzerland, but on entering the Jura heavy rain came on; nothing could have been more delicious, for it laid all the dust, which is so extra horrible on the way to Paris.

I seem to have a way of getting into queer situations, and always coming out of them all right; so at Pontarlier, where the train stops twenty minutes, I got out for some refreshment, and on coming back to what I felt sure was my carriage every vestige of my effects was gone, carpetbag, alpenstock, and all. Then ensued a hunt for pretty nearly half an hour, the train for some unknown reason stopping forty instead of twenty minutes, just as if for my private convenience. Now fancy me scampering at the heels of a man with a red light, it being perfectly dark, and no gas outside the station, all over a labyrinth of rails and trucks and empty carriages and live engines, hunting for various carriages which had been detached from our train, as the officials would have it I was mistaken about the carriage. I could not help laughing at the position, dodging full tear in and out of sheds and across turning tables, behind the red lamp, as if it were a will o' the wisp. I was about giving it up as hopeless, and decided on staying the night at Pontarlier, when an official suddenly shouted to me from behind a pump, "Est-ce là vos effets, madame?" And sure enough it all was, though nobody ever knew how it got there. So I went comfortably back to my own carriage and had no further adventures.

In the compartment were two respectable men from West Bromwich, who had been to Lucerne for a three weeks' holiday with Cook's tickets; they applied to me to interpret something for them, and this led to a little talk, which speedily drifted as usual into better things, to which I found a decided response. I had alluded to Christ's work for us, and the one to whom I was talking said quickly: "Yes, miss, it's a *transfer,* that's the word; the last three days I've had that word always in my mind; that's just what it is, a transfer. He takes our sins and makes over His righteousness to us." Then he told me that he had met on the Rigi an invalid Irish clergyman who seemed full of that one thing; "he began with the finished work and he ended with the finished work; and I never saw it so clearly before, though I have been, so to say, looking about for it this long time; it was worth all the journey there and back to get hold of this view." It seemed curious that such an excellent clergyman should be obliged to give up his living from ill health, and ordered abroad; but he was sowing the seed in fifty places instead of one. Yes, that great transfer, it is blessed! Was not this a nice instance of the real use of such seed sowing?

At Dôle I omnibused to the Hotel de Genève, where I was extremely comfortable.

Friday, a lovely morning, my train left at 9.27; but I had an hour's stroll about the town and suburbs, which I had specially planned to do, thinking it an unusually good opportunity for tract distribution, being not at all a likely place for other sowers to have been at work; so I finished up the rest of my supply.

It was not much more than an hour to Dijon, where I had to wait till 2.36; so, as I had only had one proper dinner since Sunday, I thought I had better come to this Hotel du Jura and have a long rest and a good meal at table d'hôte! I struck up with some lively English, who turn out to be relatives of Miss Weldon, of Kidderminster.

Travelling in cool weather does make an enormous difference in fatigue. I got to Paris at 10.36 p.m. It had rained most of the way, so it was a nice, clean, cool journey. On arriving I drove in a tiny open carriage, which was most refreshing, to Cook's Hotel, thinking it a better plan to go where heaps of Swiss tourists go than to any other hotel. I had a most paternal driver, really such a nice fellow, who told me I was " trop jeune " to travel " toute seule "! and wondered I was not afraid. So this led to a small sermon on God's care and love, which he seemed to think interesting. I was very comfortable at the hotel; and though I had a short night it was a good one, for I "paid attention to it," as Mr. Dowling says he does when he goes to bed for only three hours.

In the train I had one of those curious musical visions, which very rarely visit me. I hear strange and very beautiful chords, generally full, slow and grand, succeeding each other in most interesting sequences. I do not invent them, I could not; they pass before my mind, and I only listen. Now and then my will seems aroused, when I see ahead how some fine resolution might follow, and I seem to *will* that certain chords should come, and then they do come; but then my will seems suspended again; and they go on quite independently. It is so interesting, the chords seem to fold over each other and die away down into music of infinite softness; and then they unfold, and open out as if great curtains were being withdrawn one after another, widening the view, till with a gathering power and intensity and fulness: it seems as if the very skies were being opened out before me, and a sort of great blaze and glory of music, such as my outside ears never heard, gradually swells out in perfectly sublime splendour. This time there was an added feature: I seemed to hear depths and heights of sound beyond the scale which human ears can receive; keen, far-up octaves, like vividly twinkling starlight of music; and mighty, slow vibrations of gigantic strings, going down into grand thunders of depths, octaves below anything otherwise appreciable as musical notes. Then all at once it seemed as if my soul had got a new sense, and I could *see* this inner music as well as hear it; and then it was like gazing down into marvellous abysses of sound and up into dazzling regions of what to the eye would have been light and colour, but to this new sense was sound. Was it not odd? It lasted perhaps half an hour, but I don't know exactly, and it is very difficult to describe in words.

Saturday, the people called me at 5.30 a.m., saying the tidal train went at seven. So I was off at 6.35, and on reaching the station found the train that day was not till 9.10. However, it turned out for the best, of course. I went on to Boulogne by a 7.30 train, and thus had time for a two hours' rest and an unhurried meal, which I think was a better preparation for the crossing than a hurried scalding with soup or coffee and a rush to the boat. It was a bad look out in any case, for the wind was tremendous, so that it was positively difficult to walk along the quays, which are supposed to be quite sheltered, and even in this harbour the boat swayed so that it was not easy to get on board. But for being Saturday I almost think I should have waited; but I made up my mind to endurance, and went. I shall never forget the first stride of the vessel out of the harbour, I never felt anything like it as she met the first wave, it was just a sheer leap and a plunge! Now I take it to be a proof that I really must be very much stronger, for although it was so rough I was not nearly so ill as usual. I had not that horrible sense of utter illness which one fancies must be like actual dying; and I felt most thankful for the comparative exemption and the sign of strength. I should think there were three hundred people to watch the unfortunates come on shore! it was regularly running a gauntlet.

I came on to London, feeling quite well, and went straight to Clapton Square; I had telegraphed to them from Folkestone, and got in about 8.30, the boat being an hour late from the head wind.

It was rather nice that I had an opportunity of a last bit of "holiday work" in the very last five minutes before coming to anchor at the H.'s. I was looking for a boy to carry my bag; two poor little chaps were so eager that I chartered them both; one was a matchbox boy, and the other selling papers; they trotted on each side of me, as I divided my small burdens between them, not liking to disappoint either; and after having told the "old, old story" so many times in German and French, it was uncommonly pleasant to give a little of its sweet music in English to these poor little London lads; they were so attentive and apparently interested.

I wish you had seen and heard the welcome I got here! it was so nice, and altogether I was so happy. Curious that you should have sent me Psalm 103:1–3; my mind was specially full of it, only adding verses 4 and 5. I have so very, very much to bless Him for, and the beautiful sequence of five blessings seemed to sum it all up: "forgiveth," "healeth," "redeemeth," "crowneth thee with lovingkindness and tender mercies," and "satisfieth thy mouth with good things." What a great deal it is! And really I may add, "so that thy youth is renewed like the eagle's," for I feel so mentally fresh and unweary, and the H.'s all say they never saw me looking anything like so well. So herewith ends the "circular" series of 1874!

X.

GOLDEN LAND.

FAR from home, alone I wander
  Over mountain and pathless wave;
But the fair land that shineth yonder
  Claimeth the love that erst it gave.
Golden Land, so far, so nearing!
  Land of those who wait for me!
Ever brighter the vision cheering,
  Golden Land, I haste to thee!
On my path a golden sunlight
  Softly falls where'er I roam,
And I know it is the one light
  Both of exile and of home.
Golden Land, so far, so near,
On my heart engraven clear,
Though I wander from strand to strand,
Dwells my heart in that Golden Land.

PENSION WENGEN, 15th September, 1876.

XI.

OUR SWISS GUIDE.

Written in 1874.

(*Reprinted from the "Sunday Magazine."*)

NOT the least interesting part of mountaineering is the perpetual upspringing of lessons and illustrations and analogies. Sometimes an idea starts up which has, for one's self, all the delicious charm of a quite new thought, though very likely it may have flashed upon the minds of scores of other travellers; sometimes a very old and familiar one presents itself, and we have the pleasure of proving it, perhaps for the first time, by practical experience. In noting one little group of illustrations among many, those which cluster round the idea of a "Guide," we shall not be careful to steer clear of such old ideas, though we may hope to add some freshness to them.

The application throughout will be so very obvious to any mind accustomed to take the least interest in analogies of spiritual life, that we prefer giving the points of illustration only, leaving the reader to supply the "heavenly meaning" which shall underlie each sentence.

Curiously enough, the name of our favourite Swiss guide, the one who inspired us with most confidence, and to whom we should most like to entrust ourselves in any future tour, at once gave the keynote of thought; it was *Joseph*. While we instinctively trusted his sagacity and strength, it was additionally pleasant to find that our bright young guide was a believer in the Lord Jesus Christ, our true Joseph. He had remarked that his great physical strength and health was "the most splendid earthly gift," but on our mention of the most glorious Gift of all, our Saviour Christ himself, he rejoined fervently, "Ah, one can never estimate the value of *that* gift!"

But to proceed to our illustrations.

1. The first duty of a really firstrate guide, when arranging for a long snow or glacier excursion, is to see that we are properly provided with everything needful. He ascertains that you have snow spectacles, without which the glare of the snow is not simply inconvenient, but injurious; and veils, without which you stand a fair chance of finding your face completely flayed, if it should be a sunny day. He examines the spike of your alpenstock and the nails of your boots, and inquires after your wraps, and often gives curiously practical advice as to other points in your outfit. He not only tells you what you must have as to provision, but, if the excursion involves a night in some mountain hut, he sends on the necessary fuel and food, and sometimes even bedding. In all these matters you do not need to trouble at all; if you will only leave it altogether to him, he will think of everything, arrange everything, and provide everything; and when the time comes you will find all in order, your shoes fresh nailed, your alpenstock newly spiked, the porter sent on with provision, and the coil of strong rope and the ice axe all ready for the difficult places which you do not yet know of.

But many travellers do not even know that the guide is thus willing and competent; they do not ask, or perhaps they even decline, his aid and advice. Instead of throwing it all upon his responsibility, they take all the trouble themselves, and then generally find something gone wrong or something overlooked.

2. Before you start, the guide has disposed of all those heavier matters which you could not possibly carry for yourself. Very often they are taken completely out of your sight. Encumbered with these, you could not even set out on your journey, much less progress quickly and pleasantly.

But there are always plenty of little affairs which seem mere nothings at first, but which are soon found to be real burdens. The guide is perfectly willing to relieve you of all these. They are no weight to him; he quite smiles at the idea of its being any trouble to him to carry them, but they make a serious difference to you. He offers to take them at first; and if you decline, though he may not perhaps offer again, he will cheerfully take them when, later on, you feel their weight, and hand them one by one to him, till the very last is given up, and you walk lightly and freely. A beginner says she "would rather carry her little knapsack, it is really no weight at all!" and thinks a parcel or two in her pocket "can't make any difference," and prefers wearing her waterproof, because "it isn't at all heavy." But she has not gone far before she is very glad, if a sensible girl, to give up her knapsack, tiny though it be; and then she finds that a waterproof won't do for climbing, and she hands that over; and presently she even empties her pocket, and the guide trudges away with it all. Then she is surprised to find what a difference it does make, and understands why her friend, who knew the guide's ways better and gave up every single thing to him at first, is getting along so cool and fresh and elastically. But mark that the weight of a burden is seldom realized till we really are going uphill and in a fair way to make progress. Indeed, this very sensitiveness to weight is a quick test of increased gradient. We think nothing about it as long as we are walking on a level or slightly downhill; but as soon as we begin the real ascent the pull of the little burdens is felt at once, and the assistance, which before we did not crave, becomes very welcome. It is then that we feel we *must* "lay aside *every* weight."

3. One may almost certainly distinguish between a tyro[1] and an old hand by watching for a few minutes the style of march. A novice will walk at an irregular pace according to the irregularities of the ground, making little "spurts" when she comes to an easy bit, and either putting on steam or lagging behind for extra steep ones; stopping to gather flowers and poke at curious boulders; taking long or short steps according to circumstances, and never thinking of such a thing as noticing, much less imitating, the steady rhythm of the guide's walk. Probably she expresses her astonishment at his unexpectedly slow pace, and would prefer getting on a little faster; very likely she dashes ahead or aside, and presently has to be recalled to the track, which is not so easy to keep as she supposed.

One with more experience is quite content to take the guide's pace, knowing certainly that it pays in the long run, and saves an enormous amount of fatigue, and therefore of time also. Very short steps, slowly, silently, and steadily placed, but as regular as martial music, never varying in beat, never broken by alternation of strides and pauses—this is the guide's example for uphill work; and yet it is what one never believes in till one has learnt by experience that one gets through twice as much by it.

4. It is wonderful what a saving of fatigue it is if from the very beginning one obeys the guide implicitly and follows him exactly. You spy such a handy "short cut," you can see so precisely where you can join the path again, it will save you such a provoking long round, you can't think why the guide does not choose it! So away you go, exulting in your cleverness, straight uphill, instead of that tiresome zigzag.

But it is rather steeper than you thought, and you get just a little out of breath; and you find an awkward little perpendicular rock right in the way and you must go round it; and then you get into rhododendron bushes which are thicker than you thought, and you get very wet; and then you see your companions reaching the point you are making for, and you scramble and hurry. And by the time you have done with your short cut you find you have not only gained no time, but that the few minutes away from the guide have heated you and taken more out of you than an hour's steady following. Later in the day you recollect your short cuts of the morning, and wish you had economised your breath.

5. The full value of exact following is not learnt in the valleys or pastures. It is on the "high places" and on the unsullied snowfields that one discovers this.

It is when we are high away above the green slopes, seeing no track but our guide's own footsteps, that we learn its safety. He set his foot on that stone: there you must set yours, for the next is loose and would betray you; he planted his alpenstock on that inch of rock: there you must plant yours, for an inch either way would give no firm hold; he climbed by that jut of rock: so must you, for the other would be too hard a step; he sprang but half way over that torrent, and you must do the same at cost of wetting your feet, for he knew that the slab of rock which you could have reached at one bound was treacherously slippery and dangerous.

It is here also that we get into the way of instant and unquestioning compliance with every word our guide utters. I was struck with the remark of a Swiss Alpine Clubbist in a description of his ascent of the Tödi. His guide suddenly shouted to him, "Turn sharp to the right!" He saw no reason whatever for this, but obeyed instantly. The next moment an immense block of stone fell upon the spot where he would have been had he hesitated an instant or even looked round to satisfy himself. The quick and practised eye of the guide saw the trembling of the loosened mass which the traveller could not see. A query would have been fatal. He added, "In these high places one learns to obey one's guide without stopping to ask 'Why?'"

But when the snow slopes, so cool and pure and beautiful, are reached, another phase of following is learnt. There is not the excitement and effort of the rock climbing, and at first it seems very quiet and easy work, with a special exhilaration of its own, making one feel as if one had started quite fresh, all the rest of the journey counting for nothing. Once we set out on such a slope, tracking after our guide in a general sort of way, rather interested in making our own footprints, and hardly distinguishing his from those of our companions. If we turned to look back, it was surprising what a number of unconscious little curves our feet had made. But the snow was rather soft, and we soon found it much harder work than we expected. One of us was walking, as she always did, close behind the guide, because she was not quite so strong as the rest, and was therefore under his especial care. Suddenly she called out, "Oh, do set your feet *exactly* in the guide's footsteps, you can't think how much easier it is!" So we tried it, and certainly should not have believed what a difference it would make. All the difficulty and effort seemed gone; the fatiguing sinking and laborious lifting of our feet were needless; we set them now exactly where the guide's great foot had trodden, keeping his order of right and left, and all was easy, a hundred steps less toil than twenty before. But, to have the full benefit of this, one needed to keep also very near to the guide, for the last comers trod rather in their companions' footmarks, and were often misled by some false or uncertain treading of these, which marred the perfectness of the original steps.

[1] tyro (also spelled tiro): a novice or beginner

6. Thorough knowledge of the guide's language adds both to the enjoyment and safety of our following. He has much to tell us by the way, and is always ready to answer questions and give information. One who does not easily understand loses a great deal. A companion may be very willing to translate, but may do so incorrectly, and in any case the freshness and point of many a remark is lost; while it often happens that the usual interpreter of a party is not near enough for appeal or too tired to keep up the interchange. In sudden emergencies too it may be really important that each should personally understand, and thus be able instantly to obey, the guide's directions.

Moreover, it is very desirable not only thus to "know his voice," but to be able to speak to him for one's self. Once one of us slipped in a rather awkward place. She called out, "Stop a moment!" but the guide in advance knew no English, and therefore did not heed her, and but for the quick call in German of another who saw the slip, she might have been frightened and hurt.

7. When we come to really difficult places, or glaciers with hidden crevasses, we find the use of the coil of rope. This is fastened first round the guide himself, and then round the rest of the party, allowing a length of eight or ten feet between each. Once I questioned the strength of the rope, upon which the guide untwisted it a little, and showed me a scarlet thread hidden among the strands. He told me that this was the mark that it was a real Alpine Club rope, manufactured expressly for the purpose, and to be depended upon in a matter of life and death. It is remarkable that this typical "line of scarlet thread" should have been selected as the guarantee of safety.

Once roped thus, you have a sense of security in passing what would otherwise be very dangerous places, especially concealed crevasses. And not only a sense but a reality of security. You feel the snow yield beneath your feet, you sink in, and you have neither hand nor foothold; you get perhaps a glimpse of a fathomless blue depth below you. If you struggle you only break away the snow and enlarge the cavity. But you are in no real danger, and if you have confidence in your guide and the rope, you wait quietly, perhaps even smilingly, till you are hauled out of the hole, and landed on firm snow again. Why? Because you are firmly knotted to your guide, and also to all the rest of your party. You had not even time to call out ere he felt the sudden strain upon the rope, and instantly turned to help you, drawing you easily up to his side without hurt. Your friends felt the shock too but they could not do much to help, only they watched and admired the guide, and found their own fears (if they had any) lessened, and their confidence in him and his rope greatly increased.

But it is the guide himself who bears the brunt of these difficulties. He goes first, carefully sounding the snow, avoiding many a crevasse which we should never have suspected, and sometimes getting a fall which would have been ours but for his trying the way for us. If we really follow his steps exactly and patiently, the probability is that we never go in at all, for the snow that has borne his weight never gives way under ours. But if we swerve even a few inches from his footmarks, we may soon find ourselves in the predicament described above.

8. Sometimes we come to a slope of frozen snow so steep that it looks absolutely impossible to climb it. And so it would be, but for our guide. Our impossibilities only develop his resources. Now he unshoulders his ice axe, and with wonderful rapidity cuts steps by which we ascend even more easily than hitherto. And we notice that these extra-difficult slopes are a positive advantage to us, because while he has all the hard work we have time to take breath. When the steep bit is passed, we have gained greatly in height, and yet we feel quite freshened for further ascent, instead of fatigued.

9. The guide decides your rest as well as your progress, if you are wise enough to let him. He very soon measures your powers, and not only knows precisely when a crevasse is just too wide for you to leap without help, or a rock just too awkward for you to climb, but he also seems to know precisely when you had better make longer or shorter halts. Sometimes you are unwilling to rest when he proposes it, and perhaps he lets you have your own way and go on, and then you are quite certain to be sorry for it. But more often he insists, and then you always find he was right, and that he had timed the halt better than you would have done. Then, without waiting to be asked, he unfastens your wraps, contrives a seat upon the snow, and folds a shawl round you. It is no use saying you do not feel cold, he is responsible for you, and knows what is safe, and will not let you risk getting chilled by the subtle glacier wind. Then he gives you the provision he has carried for you, meat, and bread, and wine, and leaves no little stone unturned towards making your halt as refreshing and pleasant as possible. There is no need for you to be calculating time, and fidgeting about going on; he knows how much is yet before you, and he will tell you when it is time to be moving again.

10. I mentioned that the weakest of our party was specially cared for. Sometimes while the others had merely general orders, she had his strong arm, and thus escaped the slips which the more independent ones now and then made. Weakness or ailments proved his patience and care. On one occasion the "mountain sickness" which sometimes befalls travellers on great heights suddenly attacked one not accustomed to fail in strength, and then nothing could exceed Joseph's kindness and attention. He made a wonderfully comfortable couch on the snow, told us what was the matter, administered advice and wine, and waited patiently and sympathetically till his patient, completely prostrate for an hour, felt able to stand. Then in a firm decided tone he said, "*Ich* übernehme die Kranke!" (*I*

undertake the sick one!) and leaving the other guides to attend to all else, his powerful arm helped "die Kranke" down to a level where the less rarefied air soon set all to rights.

11. It is understood that a true Swiss guide is literally "faithful unto death," that he does not hesitate to risk his own life for the sake of his charge, and that instances are known in which it has not only been risked but actually sacrificed. We have never been in a position to prove this, but the undoubted fact completes the illustration. Yet this completion only shows the imperfection. For that poor faithful guide may perish *with* the traveller, and not *instead* of him; the sacrifice may be all in vain where the power and the will are not commensurate. In such illustrations we may learn as much by the contrasts as by the similiarities; and how often, as in this instance, does the very failure of an earthly type bring out the glory and perfection of the Antitype. Our glorious Guide, who has called us to the journey, and whose provision for it is "without money and without price," cannot fail in His undertaking. All who are in His covenant hands are "kept by the power of God through faith unto salvation," and "shall never perish." What He hath begun He will perform, for He "is able to keep you from falling, and to present you faultless before the presence of His glory with exceeding joy." He is not merely willing to lay down His life, but He hath laid it down for us, and now death cannot touch our Leader any more; He hath "the power of an endless life," and we are united to that life by the strong cords of His eternal purpose and His everlasting love, which no friction can weaken and no stroke can sever. However tremendous the gulf beneath us, if thus united to Him, He will lead us on till our feet, no longer weary, stand far above the clouds upon the mountain of our God, never to repass the toils and dangers of the ascent, never to return to the valley, never to part from the strong and loving Guide who has led us to such a Hitherto of rest and wonder, and to such a Henceforth of joy and praise.

XII.

A SONG IN THE NIGHT.

[Written in severe pain, Sunday afternoon, October 8th, 1876, at the Pension Wengen, Alps.]

I TAKE this pain, Lord Jesus,
 From Thine own hand;
The strength to bear it bravely
 Thou wilt command.

I am too weak for effort,
 So let me rest,
In hush of sweet submission,
 On Thine own breast.

I take this pain, Lord Jesus,
 As proof indeed
That Thou art watching closely
 My truest need;

That Thou my good Physician
 Art watching still;
That all Thine own good pleasure
 Thou wilt fulfil.

I take this pain, Lord Jesus;
 What Thou dost choose
The soul that really loves Thee
 Will not refuse.

It is not for the first time:
 I trust to-day;
For Thee my heart has never
 A trustless "Nay"!

I take this pain, Lord Jesus;
  But what beside?
'Tis no unmingled portion
  Thou dost provide.

In every hour of faintness,
  My cup runs o'er
With faithfulness and mercy,
  And love's sweet store.

I take this pain, Lord Jesus,
  As Thine own gift;
And true though tremulous praises:
  I now uplift.

I am too weak to sing them,
  But Thou dost hear
The whisper from the pillow,—
  Thou art so near!

'Tis Thy dear hand, O Saviour,
  That presseth sore,
The hand that bears the nail-prints
  For evermore.

And now beneath its shadow,
  Hidden by Thee,
The pressure only tells me
  Thou lovest me!

———— ❧ ————

XIII.

MEMORANDA OF

A SWISS TOUR WITH F. R. H.

BY HER SISTER M. V. G. H.[1]

IT was on a calm evening in the beginning of July, 1876, that we crossed by steamer from Newhaven to Dieppe. Some Mildmay deaconesses were on board, and others, who were leaving their work for needful rest and change. Frances said: "Of course we shall have a delightful passage! I find these dear deaconesses have been praying for it, and so have the dear boys at Newport." And so it was, and we landed at Dieppe before the usual time.

Frances walked with me along the quaint old quays, and it was curious to see one of my own names, that of my godmother, "Vernon," on an ancient stone building.

No need to describe the journey through Normandy and Paris to Lausanne, where we slept at the Falcon Hotel.

July 13.—By steamer on the lake of Geneva to Montreux, where Frances landed and took a mule to "Les Avants," to call on Miss E. J. Whately. I went on to the castle of Chillon to wait for Frances, and after exploring it I sat down by the lake. A poor Italian woman came with clothes to wash. She told me her husband was dead, and so she was alone, "alone always," and far from her own country. So I spoke of the one Friend and Saviour, ever near, ever loving, and who said, "I will never, never leave thee." She readily learnt a text, and then went on with her work. It was very hot. I took off my hat and rested on a bank; presently two young women came running to see what was the matter: "O madame, nous croyions que vous etiez morte! vous vous reposiez si tranquillement."[2] I thanked them, and explained I was only tired and the washerwoman was within call. They sat down, and I gave them some biscuits, and they told me about their homes and their fruit gatherings. Then I drew a little parable from their running so kindly to help a stranger; how the Good Shepherd, Jesus, saw us really perishing; how He pitied us, and came down close to us in

---

[1] Maria Vernon Graham Havergal (1821–1887).

[2] French: O madame, we believed that you were dead, you were resting so peacefully.

our souls' sleep. That He would not leave us lying there, but would bring us to His own safe fold, if we were only willing to "follow Him." Let me not forget to pray for this kind Pauline and Adelaide.

Frances returned to me beaming, saying, "Miss Whately is all and more than I expected. Only it was tantalizing to meet her, and yet see so little of her; we only had time to find out how much there was to talk about. Anyhow she is no longer one of my unknown specials!"

We went on to Vernayaz. It was late, but I went through the Gorge du Trient. Strange crypt-like aisles and ceaseless water music.

July 14.—Frances awoke me at four a.m., and we were ready before our guide and mule; and then Frances gave me my first lesson in Swiss slow paces, so unlike the Havergal speed.

The vivid colouring of the flowers was new to me; they seem always in Sunday dress here, bright and fresh. Halting at the Pension du Mont Blanc in the village of Finshauts, Frances was charmed with the utter quiet of the valley, and decided to stay a week. Valerie Longfat proved a most attentive waitress. We began our Swiss holiday by very early "rising and setting," as Frances wished me to get into good training before real expeditions came on. Our usual morning walk brought us in time to see the sunrise on Mont Blanc. Frances' favourite evening stroll was to a fairy glen of flowers and ferns, and few could arrange its spoils with so much taste. The little chalets around looked tempting to me, and one evening's visit led to many more. Two very aged women were sitting in their shady porch; one of them said she was "la vieillarde de Finshauts," and able to walk about with her "bon baton." I answered: "*One* good stick is enough, a dozen would only throw you down; now just as you lean on *one* stick, so do lean upon the one Saviour, the mighty One, the strong One. Some lean on a dozen angels and saints and mediators, but the Bible says, 'There is one God and one Mediator.'" She seemed to catch my meaning, and presently several of her neighbours joined us; so I proposed they should bring their chairs, and I read a chapter. These little open air services are very pleasant.

Sunday, July 16.—A brilliant cloudless day. Many peasants came by, going to early mass. I sat down on some logs of wood, and made a seat for any one who would like to rest. All returned my salutations, one and another chatting awhile, and taking tracts. A woman asked me why I did not go with them to mass. I told her I could not join in worshipping the host; that Jesus Christ ascended into heaven; that His glorified body was at the right hand of God; that Stephen saw Him standing there; so His body could not be in heaven and in a wafer too. "But," she said, "I think you love Him." "Ah, yes! and in England I do take bread and wine in remembrance of His great love

to me." She told me her name was Julie Zacharie, the familiar name of friends in Worcestershire; and it seems her ancestors were English!

After mass she called and invited me to see her home, a curious old chalet: thick stone walls, and the windows so narrow that I could only dimly see the variety of images and pictures. Julie showed me many of her old books. Before leaving I asked if I should kneel down and pray for God's blessing, that He would teach both of us.

"No, no, dear lady; I am just come from mass; I have taken Jesus there. Dear lady, you must believe our mass is a miracle; God can give our priest power to change the sign into the real body of Jesus."

"Show me in your Bible where God promises to do this."

"Oh, it is in our 'Instructions'! Madame, do you know them?"

"Yes, I was reading them to-day. The Epistles, Gospels, and Psalms are God's word, but not the 'Instructions.' Give me your book, and we will read exactly what the Lord Jesus said. Luke 22:19: 'Do this in remembrance of Me.' *What* did they then do? Ate bread, drank wine. The apostles could not *then* have eaten the Lord's body, for He was sitting alive by them; hence, as it was a sign, a memorial then, it must be the same now. Besides, whatever goes in my mouth never reaches my spirit, my affections; so, while taking bread, the outward sign, in my mouth, in my heart I feed on Him by faith with thanksgiving."

Julie listened and said: "Well, we do both love Him; will madame come with me this evening to my chalet by the river? I have cows there, and madame shall take cream."

I was resting upstairs in the evening, when a knock came at my door, and Julie appeared in my bedroom. We had a pleasant talk, and then she willingly knelt down with me: May the Spirit shine through all entangling webs!

Every day we found fresh walks, and the alpenrose blossomed where the snow was yet lingering. I tried crossing a snow slope, but gave it up, and watched Frances' agile steps, fearless and firm; now I can understand her glissades!

July 23.—Early this Sunday morning Frances wrote "Seulement pour Toi," and as our hostess and Valerie had often listened with pleasure to Frances singing, we told them they might invite any neighbours to assemble at three o'clock, for singing and Bible reading. But by two o'clock arrivals began, charming maidens and all the old peasants we had chatted with in the week. I would not disturb Frances, so produced pens and paper and the new French hymn for any who would like to copy it; this answered well. For the old women I proposed making some tea, but Valerie assured me no one ever cared for it! Lemonade seemed a more welcome idea, and was duly appreciated. There was one sprightly girl, Katrine, whose mischievous laughter betrayed her dislike to our plans. But even Katrine was interested when I produced the photographs of my Indian orphans in the Church Missionary school at Agurparah. The histories of little Daisy, Maria, and Monie (now called Frances, after Frances Ridley Havergal), and the novelty of some missionary information, awakened deep interest.

At three o'clock the room was full. Frances began by giving a free translation of her hymn, "Golden Harps," and singing it. Then came "Seulement pour Toi";[1] with Frances' lively encouragement, this was soon sung *en masse*. Frances read, in French, verses from the third, fourth, and fifth chapters of Romans, giving a few sweet linkings of the same, and then asked me to speak to them. I found it quite easy to address in French, and many thanked me afterwards.

No one seemed willing to kneel for the concluding prayer. I would not begin while all were sitting, so Valerie's father set the example, vigorously saying, "Mettez-vous tous à genoux." A few stayed to talk to us afterwards.

We welcomed our tea, though the old women did not. Frances said she wished she had a French Bible that she might put references to "Seulement pour Toi." *M.*: "Then I will go and ask monsieur the curè to lend us one, and certainly I shall give him your hymn." *F.*: "Whatever will you think of next! Marie, do you mean it?" *M.*: "I do; besides the curè has been on my mind all the week." *F.* (laughing): "Then ask him to correct my hymn."

Away I went to the priest's house, and who should open the door but the mischievous Katrine, evidently amused to see me! Giving my compliments to the curè and a request for the loan of a Bible, he returned with Katrine, inviting me to his study. He brought the Bible in four large volumes, inquiring which I required. I told him we had only French Testaments with us, and that my sister wished to put references to a hymn she had written that morning; possibly he would kindly correct it. After reading "Seulement pour Toi," he inquired if the writer was French, as only one idiom was incorrect. He was extremely pleasant, and I told him of our little service, adding a few words on the preciousness of Christ and the Holy Scriptures. Then he called Katrine and bade her carry the volumes home for me.

The next morning we walked to Argentière. While we were resting under a tree a lady, whom I had previously seen at our pension, and who wished to hear Frances sing, came by on her mule. She dismounted and joined us; and at my request Frances sang to her, thus ministering to one who seemed lonely and weary. I should like to have known the name of this solitary

traveller. We stayed some days at Argentière; Mont Blanc was just opposite our windows. What variety of rose and golden crowns descend on that kingly mountain!

July 31.—Frances walked with me part of the way to La Flégère; she returned to Argentière. No need for a guide, she gives me such clear directions. Instead of sunset on Mont Blanc sheet lightning kept up illumination of its height, while the aiguilles flashed as if cased in steel armour. A young lady from Denmark walked with me up and down the terrace. I told her how we all loved our beautiful Princess of Wales. She was interested to hear of the Bible, given her by the maidens of England, and that led to her accepting one from me. Her loyalty was as lively as mine.

The next morning was dense mist, but I went on to the Bréven by breakfast time. Turning over the tourist's book I found my sister's entry, Aug. 2, 1871: "F. R. Havergal and Elizabeth Clay. Felt exceedingly triumphant over all the tourists at Chamouni, and especially over those who had been here in the heat of the day. For from seven to eight p.m., while they were in the dusk of the valley and probably at table d'hôte by candle-light, we were enjoying a glory of gold and rose upon the whole chain of Mont Blanc, and watching it die into that strange, pale, holy after-light, which is almost more thrillingly beautiful than any more glowing effect. Furthermore at 4.30 a.m. we saw the first touch of rose-fire on the crown of the monarch."

It was useless to wait in the clouds, so I went down to Chamouni; suddenly, through the pine woods, Mont Blanc unveiled in silver. I walked on to Argentière, and Frances commended me for pushing bravely through the mist, and says I have the bump of locality.

August 3.—We left Argentière, walking part of the way with the Rev. J. H. and Mrs. Rogers, to the Tête Noire, where we lunched. I rested, but Frances as usual found ministering work. Then away to the Col de Forclaz, a satisfactory distance! The next morning we walked to the Croix de Martigny, and then turned up the road towards St. Bernard, and slept at Lembranchier.

August 5.—By diligence to Orsière, interesting ride; all the travellers joined in singing "Seulement pour Toi," and even the driver tried to sing the bass, whereon Frances jumped up by him; I do think she would make any one sing.

We reached the Hospice of St. Bernard on Saturday, and were gracefully received by the good Father Hess.

Sunday, August 6.—Clear cloudless sunshine. Sat under the rocks with Frances, reading Exodus 33:21, 22, of that rock and that cleft in the rock, where the glory "passed by," connecting it with John 17:24, the glory which will not pass away, but which we shall behold for ever.

---

[1] We give the words and music, as published by Messrs. Nisbet & Co. in leaflet form. F. R. H. also arranged the same melody to "Precious Saviour, may I live," published by Hutchings & Romer. [See the next page, 218.]

Seulement pour Toi.

[Written for and sung by some Swiss peasants at a Sunday afternoon Bible reading, July 23rd, 1876.]

Que je sois, O cher Sauveur,		*O that I be—May I be, O dear Saviour,*
Seulement à Toi!	Hosea 3:1*	* Only (wholly) Thine!*
Soit l'amour de tout mon cœur	Matt. 22:37	*Be the love of all my heart*
Seulement pour Toi.		* Solely for Thee.*
Je reviens à mon Père	John 14:6	*I come back to my Father*
Seulement par Toi,		* Only through Thee,*
Ma confiance entière	Psalm 118:8	*My confidence entire*
Sera en Toi,		* Will be in Thee,*
Seulement en Toi.		* Only in Thee.*
Le péché Tu as porté	I Peter 2:24	*The sin, Thou hast borne it*
Seul, seul pour moi;		* Alone, alone for me;*
Et Ton sang Tu as versé		*And Thy blood Thou hast shed*
Seul, seul pour moi.		* Alone, alone for me.*
Toute gloire, toute joie	Rev. 5:12	*All glory, all joy,*
Sera pour Toi;		* Will be for Thee;*
L'espérance et la foi	Acts 4:12	*The hope and faith*
Seront en Toi,		* Will be in Thee,*
Seulement en Toi.		* Only in Thee.*
Aujourd'hui, O cher Seigneur,	II Cor. 6:2	*Today, O dear Lord,*
Acceptes-moi!	Eph. 1:6	* Accept me!*
Tu es seul mon grand Sauveur,	Isaiah 19:20	*Thou art alone my great Saviour,*
Tu es mon Roi.	Psalm 44:4	* Thou art my King.*
Tous mes moments, tous mes jours	II Cor. 5:15	*All my moments, all my days*
Seront pour Toi!		* Will be for Thee!*
Jésus, gardes-moi toujours	Isaiah 27:3	*Jesus, keep me always*
Seulement pour Toi,		* Only for Thee,*
Seulement pour Toi.		* Only for Thee.*
Que je chante et que je pleure	Psalm 21:13	*O that I sing and that I weep*
Seulement pour Toi!		* Only for Thee!*
Que je vive et que je meure	Romans 14:8	*Let me live and let me die*
Seulement pour Toi!		* Only for Thee!*
Jésus, que m'as tant aimé,	Gal. 2:20	*Jesus, how Thou hast loved me,*
Mourant pour moi,		* Dying for me,*
Toute mon éternité	I Thess. 4:17	*All my eternity*
Sera pour Toi,		* Will be for Thee,*
Seulement pour Toi.		* Only for Thee.*

July 23, 1876

*Note: In F.R.H.'s posthumously published *Under His Shadow*, these Scripture references were given on these lines.

[hymn in French by Frances Ridley Havergal, set to her tune "Onesimus," English translation by David Chalkley]

When the chapel bells tolled for mass, Frances said that *for once* she should like to try joining in the service. I did not go, having tried it, and felt utterly wretched and the clearest conviction I was grieving God. In half an hour Frances returned distressed with the service, and expressed her grief that Protestant tourists often join in that form which involves downright error and idolatry. Nor did she find the music soothing or elevating, it was "just aggravating and monotonous." Just then five St. Bernard dogs came out; they barked at me, but immediately caressed Frances: instinctive discernment! There were many groups of peasants scattered about; they seem to make this a picnic pilgrimage, receiving food and lodging. We made sundry friends; even a large group of card players put their cards away and thanked us for civil warnings. Leaflets and portions were gladly received. At four p.m. Frances, a traveller from Boston, and I enjoyed a service in the very hush of those rocky aisles and vast icy temples. Frances chose Psalm 22:31 and Psalm 23, also Zephaniah 3.

After dinner Frances sang, by request of Father Hess, "Comfort ye," then "Seulement pour Toi," in which many joined. Being asked to sing her own music she gave, "Whom having not seen ye love." [1] It was evidently thrilling to all, and Signor Luigi and others expressed their admiration to me. They didn't know how Frances had prayed that her song might be a King's message.

August 8.—Walked back to Orsière.

9th.—Explored the Val de Feri. I will detail an incident illustrative of many others. I always carry a tiny kettle and tea, for our refreshment. The wind blew out my pine cone fire, so we went to a chalet for boiling water. The little maiden put brown bread, which required chopping, and goat's cheese on the table. She had never tasted tea, and did not seem to like it at all.

I asked Constance [2] if there was any one ill in the village.

"Yes, little Aline; she used to lie alone all day long, till I asked her father to put the key under a stone, that I might get in. Aline has no mother."

I followed Constance up some dark stairs into a room like a hay loft. A little tired face looked up from the rough bed:

"Oh, Marie! I am so ill; is father come? He went away so early."

Alone, alone, locked up in that cold loft, some greasy soup in a can, and a hard crust! Dear little Aline! I sat down by her and fed her with some jelly and biscuits, and sent Constance for some new milk. I took the thin hot hand and said in French:

"Dear Aline, there is One who loves you very much; the kind, good Jesus; do you know Him?"

Yes, she knew the name of Jesus, and that He died on the cross; but she did not seem to know it really was for her, in her stead. She seemed to drink in all that was said, and learnt this prayer: "Lord Jesus, wash me in Thy blood; take me in Thy arms."

I don't think Aline will be hungry again, for it was easy to arrange for a supply of milk. And Victorine, the daughter of our hotel keeper at Orsière, promised to go often and take her nourishing food. Meanwhile Frances had been at work in a chalet; I cannot recount half she does!

August 10.—Walked up to the Lac de Champé, and the next morning Frances found the way through the Gorge du Durnand; we always enjoy unknown routes. Thence to Martigny, and by diligence to Champéry, where we remained till August 28th.

At Champéry the delightful ministrations of Mr. Rogers, the chaplain, new friendships, and Frances' incessant ministries, whether by song, or conversation, or Bible reading, filled up every day. One evening, after playing the Moonlight Sonata, an aged German lady assured me that it quite recalled Beethoven's own rendering of it.

After leaving Champéry, *viâ* Berne and Interlachen, we stayed at the Pension Schönfels. The pressure of letters seemed to follow Frances everywhere, and I remember how good-naturedly she corrected roll after roll of poetical compositions by a stranger, although she was suffering extremely from the effects of being caught in a thunderstorm in an excursion from Champéry. While staying at the Pension Schönfels, the Baroness von Cramm, and Miss Carmichael, joined us, from Champéry. Poor Frances could not join in any excursions, nor did she attempt writing any circular letters, as in former tours. She told me that in writing those circulars she rather avoided expressing either the spiritual or the poetical ideas suggested; so she wrote "Holiday Work," and "Our Swiss Guide," as glimpses of her practical work for Christ, and those celestial revelations, which Alpine scenery constantly unfolded to her mind. It was at this time, however, that she wrote the following sonnet to her friend the Baroness Helga von Cramm.

TO HELGA.

COME down, and show the dwellers far below
　What God is painting in each mountain place!
　Show His fair colours, and His perfect grace,
Dowering each blossom born of sun and snow:
His tints, not thine! Thou art God's copyist,
　O gifted Helga! His thy golden height,
　Thy purple depth, thy rosy sunset light,
Thy blue snow-shadows, and thy weird white mist.

---

[1] Published by Hutchings & Romer.
[2] Marie Constance Jodant, in the village of Isere près d'Orsière.

Reveal His works to many a distant land!
    Paint for His praise, oh paint for love of Him!
He is thy Master, let Him hold thy hand,
    So thy pure heart no cloud of self shall dim.
At His dear feet lay down thy laurel-store,
Which crimson proof of thy redemption bore.

September 19th, 1876.

A letter has been sent to me, written about this time, which may interest some.

PENSION SCHÖNFELS.

MY VERY DEAR MARGARET:

I can't tell you how your letter touched me. I never thought He would let me give you a lift, who were already so bright and devoted. I tried to help other folks at Champéry, but I did not try with you, only just said what came uppermost. Oh I am so glad you see the "only for Jesus" in its special power. Having seen it, one wants to live it out, simply and entirely, and we can only go on trusting the Lord Jesus hour by hour to show us how. I wonder what He is going to show us next, dear M.! for He has so many things to say to us, as we can bear them. We have been guided to a wonderfully quiet pension, off the usual beat. Seven Germans here, only one of whom can speak any English. In answer to your query: well, I'll see about it; and if I can get a chance of being decently photographed I will send you a copy; but I am sure you won't like it, because the prevailing tone of my results under photographic torture is, "resignation under afflictive dispensations!" which a cheerful friend suggested as the most suitable inscription on my photos, of which she declined to accept one! Query No. 3: "This is not your rest" really does seem to be written on every attempt I make to find a quiet perch (as for a nest, I don't dream of that). If one set of fatigues is done with, another arises, personal or postal; but I really stand as good a chance here as anywhere, I think, so that will be a relief to your mind. And it has been enforced the last two days, because I left Champéry with a sharp sore throat, which developed into that sort of cold that has made me totally stupefied yesterday and to-day, and I have been in bed a good many extra hours. It was such a pleasure to meet you and dear Edith at C——; it is such a pleasure to recollect it, and will be ditto if we can some fine day come over and see you again. I think Maria is more likely to be free to do so than I. I am not quite so freely situated as she is, and have far more arrears to make up too, of long promised visits, as my long invalidism has thrown me far behindhand in that respect; and being seldom strong enough for any winter travelling limits my time for getting through my visits.

Yours lovingly,

F. R. H.

When she was better, we went to the village of Eizenflou, hoping for a fine sunrise on the Jungfrau. A feverish cold detained me there. Frances went to the village schoolmaster and secured the use of his schoolroom for a service the next evening, as her spirit was stirred up by finding no pastor ever came near these villages, and they were five miles from church. The evening was wet, and I wanted Frances not to go; but she said, "I may never come here again; and no man cares for these scattered sheep." The room was quite full. Frances addressed them in German from 1 John 1:7, and also led the hymns from their chorale book. Our hostess' report was: "Never, no never, had any one told them what the dear young lady did; it was wonderful! They never could forget her words; and surely she must be a born German!"

From Schönfels, we went to the Pension Wengen, above Lauterbrunnen, for several weeks.

October 1.—Unclouded sunshine. The Jungfrau and Silberhorn were radiant. Frances remarked, "It will be one of the new delights of heaven to be able to express all one's thoughts." The next day we took horses to the Scheideck Hotel. After resting, we rode up the Lauberhorn, with Hans Lauener for our guide. He seemed such a nice fellow, and sang some French hymns with Frances, on the top of the mountain.

I had the audacity to sketch the Silberhorn for Mary Fay. In the evening Frances called me to watch the singular effect of the moon rising behind sharp jutting rocks; the silver rays of an invisible but coming presence were most striking.

Another day we went to the Mettlen Alp, which Frances thinks the finest view in Switzerland, through pine woods, and then I stood with her on the silver steps of the Jungfrau's throne. What then? Avalanches and our silent Alleluias! Here it may be of interest to quote copy of the entry in the visitors' book, at Pension Wengen:

Summer returned; cloudless sky. Thermometer from 90° to 100° during our stay. Obliging attentions, honest charges, and tried truthfulness. The Mettlen Alp stands out in picturesque beauty. "All Thy works praise *Thee*." Avalanche Alleluias will long echo in English homes.

MARIA V. G. HAVERGAL.
FRANCES RIDLEY HAVERGAL.

Sept. 23rd till Oct. 16th, 1876.

This was Frances' last excursion; her health entirely failed.

October 8.—Frances in acute pain all day, and could not get up at all. She wrote the hymn, "I take this pain, Lord Jesus." They brought lukewarm water for fomentations, so I dived into the kitchen, and secured a saucepan, gathered pine cones and wood, and got leave to use the salon stove night and day.

October 9 and 10.—Frances moaning all day, but so wonderfully patient, even in sleepless nights. I could not say "Thy will be done," till she spoke so sweetly of texts that hush and gladden her. She verily exults in that declaration, "I love, I love my Master" (Exodus 21:5), connecting it with Revelation 22:3, "shall serve Him for ever."

October 12.—Tried camomile fomentations, at midnight, and darling Frances so grateful; I never nursed any one so uncomplaining. Reading to her, "Let Thy judgments help me," I asked her what it meant. She said, "I think God's judgments prove our faith, forcing us to trust more, to lean more. 'Help,' because He comes so very close, helps us when no one else can."

Madame Lauener, the mother of our host, often came up to Frances' room. She is intensely fond of Frances, and repeats Scripture in German, and prays most soothingly by her.

October 13.—Mrs. Simpson (English Pension) came all the way from Interlachen, bringing remedies, fruit and jelly for Frances; so extremely kind, as we are comparative strangers.

Frances sent for me to hear Madame Lauener repeat from memory the seventh chapter of the Revelation. Such a picture! through the window the glisten of the snowy Silberhorn,[1] on the pillow dear Frances and her golden curls; by her side the aged woman, who with beaming eye and waving hand emphasized those wonderful words; truly it brought a glimpse of

> "When robed in white before Thee,
> Without one stain or tear,
> Shall all Thy saints adore Thee,
> 'Midst wonder, love, and fear."
>
> (Rev. W. H. H.)

Sunday, October 15.—Frances was decidedly better, and able to take a few steps in the sunshine. Her comment on "For His mercy endureth for ever," was, "that is, every day." It seemed uncertain if we could leave next day, but it is impossible to fidget about anything when with Frances. She playfully said, "Now, Marie, can't you leave me entirely to our Father!" Another time I was anxious, and she put her hand on mine: "Marie dear, just trust! Jesus *is* with us, all must come right."

October 16.—Frances better, and able to leave in a chaise à porteur to Lauterbrunnen, from whence she enjoyed the drive to Interlachen. From the lake of Thun the snowy mountains of the Bernese Oberland brightened into sunset glory, and we saw them no more.

October 18.—Left Basle through Alsace; the Vosges mountains were dimly outlined, and then we went through a

pancake country with straight roads and fields, and straight poplars, to Strasbourg.

October 19.—Frances was too tired to go out, so I raced round Strasbourg. I was extremely interested in the flower market, and had sundry talks with the women. I took a diligence to get a sight of the Rhine, and, walking back by a short cut, got into the fortifications. The captain was most polite, and allowed me to speak to a few soldiers, giving them a rapid outline of what the Captain of our salvation did, and does.

The cathedral is magnificent, but it is so intensely grievous to see the shrines. One lady kept lighting little tapers at the Virgin's shrine, and another young girl seemed quite faint with kneeling; she came and sat by me, and I had an interesting talk with her.

We then left for Brussels, and arrived in England October 20th. The 21st from London to Winterdyne *via* Oxford. Just after leaving Oxford Frances startled me with: "Marie! I see it all; I can write a little book, 'My King!'"

That herald light was in her eye, which ever betokens some direct communication from her King. And the following letter to M. A. C. shows how prayerfully she afterwards wrote it, trusting for every word to be given her.

November 1, 1876. OAKHAMPTON.

I REALLY cannot let this be "gratis," though the next shall be. I am so delighted and thankful to hear that you really are going to give the whole winter to God's work, and that Miss de K. has joined you, and that you will be strengthening the hands of dear Miss Leigh, in Paris. Altogether, your letter has made me very happy and very grateful.

I am better now, but was far worse after you left us at Schönfels. Two attacks in succession, the second causing nearly a week of terribly prostrating pain. This day three weeks I could not even stand alone! So the only thing seemed to be to seize the very first day of being anyhow able to begin the journey from Pension Wengen, and get at least a stage or two nearer home, which we did; and though we had to take a week about it, and I was very ill on the way, we were brought safely to England. I am now at my eldest sister's, getting up my strength delightfully, and able for walks in the garden. Maria is quite renovated, and sleeps and eats properly, in spite of the really heavy strain upon her to have had to nurse me night and day while really very ill. Maria is not going to take to herself another wife at all! (since E. Clay's departure to India), so, after all, you won't have the pain of being superseded. She is going to live at Winterdyne for some time, and this is an immense satisfaction to us all.

Do you ever have time to pray for other people's work, now that you have so much before you? Because, if so, will you ask that He would give me special help in a little book which I want to write, as He may give me strength. The title will be simply "My King," and it will be little daily thoughts for a month, (uniform with the "Bells" and "Pillows," only for grown up folk) on thirty-one texts, all from the Old Testament, about our King. It is such a delicious subject, and I have so enjoyed the mere looking out of the texts about it, while not yet strong enough for serious writing; but I am not sufficient for these things, and never felt more deeply my own insufficiency. Only the idea of the book came so *very* forcibly to my mind that I could not but think He had sent it me; and so I have done what I never did before, shelved the little work I already had on hand, to do this first. I will send you one of the texts, because possibly you might not have thought of it, and it seems so nice for use. 2 Samuel 19:20: the knowledge that Shimei had sinned being the very reason, not for keeping away, but for coming the first of all to meet the king. I took it as the text for a little talk with the servants here, and never found a more telling one. The 2nd Book of Samuel is full of exquisite typical texts. The headings of the little daily portions will be such as "The Friendship of the King," "Decision for the King," "The Business of the King," "The Banquet of the King," "Speaking to the King."

It is so utterly bumptious of me to think of writing for grown ups at all, much more on such a theme, that I feel more entirely shut up to asking and trusting for every word of it, than I ever did before.

Please give my love to dear Miss Leigh. I owe her ever such a debt of gratitude for her kindness, and most helpful influence, with one of my dear nieces.

Good bye, dearest Margaret; Paris is not "among plants and hedges," but may you there dwell with the King, for His work. Love to dear Edith when you write.

Yours ever,

F. R. H.

Two years passed away, and I again visited the Pension Wengen, in 1878, with Mrs. Usborne and Miss Cowan. Knowing how much my sister F. R. H. was loved there, I took care, when writing for rooms, to say she was not coming, lest they should be disappointed. But they did not notice it, and so the grandmother eagerly expected her beloved Fraulein Fannie. When I arrived, there she stood, smiling a welcome, but pointed up, saying, "O mein Hans!" Then she went to meet the other horses, searching for F., till seeing she was not come, her wail was quite touching: "O my beloved, my Fraulein Fannie, where are you? why are you not come to comfort me?" Her countenance was still beautiful, but there was now a far off look in her eyes, sorrow for some one gone. And so it was; her son Hans, our bright young guide to the Mettlen Alp and the Lau-

berhorn, had met with an accident and died. His mother and brother gave me the following particulars.

All the winter Hans had been most active in relieving the peasants and going to their scattered chalets with soup and food, often through deep snow. There is a society here for that purpose, and Hans was its most useful member.

Some of the mountain land and pine woods, adjoining the Pension Wengen, belonged to him and his brother Ulrich. These pines are thinned, cut down, and taken into the valley beneath, and there sawn into planks. After the branches are cut off, the pines are brought to the glissade, which is formed by the freezing of some mountain stream, over which lies a deep bed of frozen snow. On the morning of March 5th, 1878, Hans, his brother Ulrich, and twenty men were thus at work. It requires great skill to steer the pine and keep it steadily in its torrent slide. Hans was ever the first, enjoying the dash of power requisite to guide the giant pine down that icy path. But in a moment the pine swayed out of its course, Hans was struck down, the whole weight of the pine crushing his side and leg. A mattress and pillows were brought, his brother wisely taking him at once to Lauterbrunnen, where he would be nearer a doctor than at home. Skilfully was he carried to the Hotel Staubbach, and a telegram soon brought doctors from Interlachen. But nothing could be done, the loss of blood was too great to allow of amputation. Hans was calm and patient, though in agony. He told them that "he had his passport all ready, that he saw the path of life before him, and he was quite sure he was in it."

He lived three days, during which the pastor, who was rationalistic, visited Hans, and the words of the dying guide spoke of a better hope. Hans told him that no works, no merit, no good and noble life, gave him any comfort now, but it was the sacrifice of Jesus on the cross, and the precious blood there shed to put away sin, that was his "passport."

"It is believing in Jesus Christ brings me this joy. Without the blood that atones for sin, I could not stand accepted before the throne."

The pastor heard and believed; this testimony brought new light and life to him, and a crown to the dying Hans. (Since then his sermons are quite evangelistic.) His only sorrow was to leave his mother and brother, but even then he comforted them: "God has prepared a place also for you my brother. Mother, my mother, there is only a short course for you to run." Hans spoke of F. R. H., and more than once sang the hymn in which they had joined on the heights of the Lauberhorn.

> "Vers le ciel, vers le ciel,
> J'entends, Jésus, Ton appel,
> O mon cœur, vers toi s'élance
> Dans la joyeuse espérance
> De se voir, Emmanuel!"

And then with the ancient passport of "the blood," the young guide passed upward, and entered in " through the gates into the city." He died March 8th, 1878.

It is now October, 1881, and in F. R. H.'s study there lies her motto card, "My own text," identical with the dying guide's " passport," "The blood of Jesus Christ His Son cleans*eth* us from all sin" (1 John 1:7).

XIV.

THE VOICE OF MANY WATERS.

FAR away I heard it,
 Stealing through the pines,
Like a whisper saintly,
Falling dimly, faintly,
 Through the terraced vines.

Freshening breezes bore it
 Down the mountain slope;
So I turned and listened,
While the sunlight glistened
 On the snowy cope.

Far away and dreamy
 Was the voice I heard;
Yet it pierced and found me,
Through the voices round me—
 Song without a word.

All the life and turmoil,
 All the busy cheer,
Melted in the flowing
Of that murmur, growing,
 Claiming all my ear.

What the mountain-message,
 I could never tell;
Such Æolian fluting
Hath no language suiting
 What we write and spell.

Rather did it enter
 Where no words can win,
Touching and unsealing
Springs of hidden feeling,
 Slumbering deep within.

Voice of many waters
 Only heard afar!
Hushing, luring slowly,
With an influence holy,
 Like the orient star.

Follow where it leadeth,
 Till we stand below,
While the noble thunder
Wins the hush of wonder,
 Silent in its glow.

Light and sound triumphant
 Fill the eye and ear;
Every pulse is beating
Quick unconscious greeting
 To the vision near.

Rainbow-flames are wreathing
 In the dazzling foam,
Fancy far transcending,
Power and beauty blending
 In their radiant home.

All the dreamy longing
    Passes out of sight,
In a swift surrender
To the joyous splendour
    Of this song of might.

Self is lost and hidden
    As it peals along;
Fevered introspection,
Paler-browed reflection
    Vanish in the song.

For the spirit, lifted
    From the dulling mists,
Takes a stronger moulding,
As the sound, unfolding,
    Bears it where it lists.

Voice of many waters!
    Must we turn away
From the crystal chorus
Now resounding o'er us
    Through the flashing spray?

————

Far away we hear it,
    Floating from the sky;
Mystic echo, falling
Through the stars, and calling
    From the thrones on high.

There are voices round us,
    Busy, quick, and loud;
All day long we hear them,
We are still so near them,
    Still among the crowd.

Yet athwart the clamour
    Falls it, faint and sweet,
Like the softest harp-tone,
Passing every sharp tone
    Down the noisy street.

To the soul-recesses
    Cleaving then its way,
Waking hidden yearning,
Unwilled impulse turning
    To the far away.

Far away and viewless,
    Yet not all unknown;
In the murmur tracing
Soft notes interlacing
    With familiar tone.

So we start and listen!
    While the murmur low
Falleth ever clearer,
Swelleth fuller, nearer,
    In melodious flow.

Voice of many waters
    From the height above,
Hushing, luring slowly,
With its influence holy,
    With its song of love!

————

Following where it leadeth,
    Pilgrim feet shall stand,
Where the holy millions
Throng the fair pavilions
    In the Glorious land.

Where the sevenfold "Worthy!"
    Hails the King of kings,
Blent with golden clashing
Of the crowns, and flashing
    Of cherubic wings;

Rolls the Amen Chorus,
    Old, yet ever new;
Seal of blest allegiance,
Pledge of bright obedience,
    Seal that God is true.

Through the solemn glory
    Alleluias rise,
Mightiest exultation,
Holiest adoration,
    Infinite surprise.

There immortal powers
    Meet immortal song,
Heavenly image bearing,
Angel-essence sharing,
    Excellent and strong.

Strong to bear the glory
    And the veil-less sight,
Strong to swell the thunders
And to know the wonders
    Of the home of light.

Voice of many waters!
    Everlasting laud!
Hark! it rushes nearer,
Every moment clearer,
    From the throne of God!

———— ✿ ————

(For the Episcopal Register.)

"HOW MUCH FOR JESUS?"

BY FRANCES RIDLEY HAVERGAL,
Author of "Ministry of Song," and other Poems.

A little group of boys and girls were gathered around me on a pleasant evening in the Easter holidays. We were talking about the Lord Jesus, and all the wonderful and solemn things which our Church services had so lately brought before us,—His agony and bloody sweat, His Cross and Passion,—His precious Death and Burial, and His glorious Resurrection. There was such a quieted and tender tone among them, such wistful looks and gentle voices, and the hearts of more than one were so evidently burning within them, that one could not doubt that "Jesus Himself drew near," and that while we spoke one to another, He not only hearkened and heard, but was really present in our midst. Then we spoke of what we owed to Him who had done so much for us. How much do we owe Him? And how much shall we give Him? Can there be any hesitation as to the answer? Shall it not be, joyfully and gratefully, "All! yes, *all* for Jesus!" But "all" means a great deal; it really does mean *all*; all our hearts, all our lives, all that we have, all that we are. And if truly "all," it must be for *always*, too; no reserve, and no taking back. I heard a little sigh by my side, as we spoke of this. Did it seem too hard? Could we ever hope to keep to it? Was it more than we dared say? Then we looked at the bright side of it,—the grand shining of gladness which Satan tries to hinder us from seeing. If we are "all for Jesus," He will be all for us, and *always* all for us, too. When we give Him all, He gives us all,—all His tender love, all His wonderful peace and joy, all His grace and strength. On His side there will be no reserve and no taking back. And with "all" this, we shall find, nay we *do* find that life is quite a different thing, ever so much happier than we imagined it could be, and that He does for us exceeding abundantly above all that we ask or think.

As this was dwelt upon, I saw a very bright smile on a face that was generally the merriest of the party. After a little while, "good-night" was said, and we separated. But I went up-stairs to two quiet rooms. In the first I found the author of that little sigh. She was, I had every reason to hope, a dear Christian child, who had for some time past "known and believed the love which God hath for us," and had tried to follow her Saviour in the little steps of home and school life. I put my arms round her and said, "Well, Alice, how much for Jesus?" The great dark eyes that just before had looked up so lovingly into my face fell, with such a mournful look that I shall never forget it. There was no answer. "How much, darling? Is it not *all* for Jesus?" Again came the little sigh, and a sad whisper, "I don't know!"

In the other room another warm kiss awaited me, and there was a something in the merry face which made me ask very hopefully, "Well, Meta, how much for Jesus?"

Oh, if I could describe to you the utter gladness in the bright eyes, and the very joy that seemed to overflow the lips, as she answered, not hastily, but very firmly and resolutely, "All, auntie, *all!*" That, too, was a look never to be forgotten—the words and the tone were sweet and strong, but the look told more than either. One could not but take knowledge of her that she had been with Jesus. She had given her heart to Him, and He had given His joy to her.

Let me put the question to you—"How much for Jesus?" Is your answer a sigh or a smile?

See the note at the bottom of page 204. "How Much for Jesus?" was later found, because Maria published it in the posthumous volume Ben Brightboots and Other True Stories, Hymns, and Music *(found on pages 372–373 of Volume III of the Havergal edition).*

This article, "A Memory of Miss Havergal" by E. H. H. (we do not know who E. H. H. was), was found in *The Sunday at Home Family Magazine for Sabbath Reading* 1887 (London: Religious Tract Society, 1887), pages 509–510.

A MEMORY OF MISS HAVERGAL.

AMONG the Swiss mountains in June. I had reached the Pension Alpenrose in the rain, very tired, and headachy, and had been much lamented over by the kind hostess, and the equally kind Marianne, the maid. "*Ach, armes Fraülein ! armes Fraülein*," [Ah, poor Miss ! poor Miss,] Madame kept repeating, as she and Marianne saw to my comforting in general, and put me to rest in the exquisitely white little wooden bower at the top of the house, reserved for me, I was told, because it was thought I should like to have the room Miss Havergal had had. From its window I could see the Jungfrau, and her fellows of mountains, and the pastures, and I could look right across the Lauterbrünnen valley, where the delicate mist of the Staubbach swept down the rock.

I got to know it all very well before my month's stay was over. It was wet a good part of the time, but when the sunshine came it was such wonderful sunshine, and one could lie out of doors on a waterproof cloak, with hosts of campanulas around one, and see the great mountains, and the etherealized water of the falls. And there I learned, as Miss Havergal had learned, the meaning of "whiter than snow." I had seen snow before, and often, but never such snow as the sheenful snow that lies in the rifts and clefts of the Alps.

The little peasant children would come and look at me, stopping in their progress, especially if I had a book or a note-book, and chatter to me and I to them, probably with much more good-will than understanding. But I believe I can say "*Gute Obe*" (*Guten Abend*) [Good night], with the purest Bernese Oberland accent.

One day I was sitting near the place where the hillside was cleft by a stream over which one passed by a little wooden bridge. Leaning over the bridge I have often drunk in the cool pureness of the water, and been refreshed as if I had tasted it with my mouth. A few yards off was a little cottage, and out of this cottage came a woman, who called out to me to know if I would not come and rest. So I went over and found in that little Swiss hut an old woman dignified and sweet, with a look of great peace on her face, and with the graceful ease of manner which we associate with the high breeding of a gentlewoman.

Despite my very defective German, I managed to have a little talk. I found out that my hostess was the mother of the master of the Pension where Miss Havergal stayed the last time she was at Wengen, and of the mistress of that at which I was staying, and where Miss Havergal had also at one time sojourned.

We talked a little about the "liebe Hans," [dear, or lovely, or beloved Hans] as his mother called him; the brave bright lad, so strong and good and kind, who met his death one winter by such a grievous accident.[1] And now the old Frau was living all alone, but her daughter sent one of her children to sleep in the grandmother's cottage every night. And she was not alone by day or night. You could not have seen her look as she spoke of God, *der liebe Gott* [the dear, or lovely, or beloved God], without knowing that He was to her a living presence, a Father of whom she was ever learning more and more. And one of the first questions she asked me was whether I knew Miss-Ham-Hammer-ley. I knew she meant Miss Havergal, and gave the name. "*Ach, ja*, Meess Haavurghall." It is impossible to symbolize the deep gutturalization of the name among the Swiss folk. A man who was staying at the Pension wanted me to teach him how to pronounce it, and I tried. I tried very, very hard, but I failed.

They cannot pronounce her name, but the love and reverence with which they speak of Frances Ridley Havergal are very great. She seems to have taken hold of their hearts by her personality. Ought I not rather to say by love and kindness and her earnest religion? But personality is a great deal too. And they evidently think of her as a famous English woman also, in very deed, and the old Frau loved Miss Havergal's memory very dearly, I think, as one feels sure that many do. One is glad to know a little of how she, who loved so much, was loved, and to think that her memory is a comfort as her presence was a gladness, on those far-off heights of the Bernese Oberland.

I saw the aged Frau more than once afterwards, and it will always be a pleasure to me to think of her, and her graceful and beautiful ways.

Do you say that faith in God is common, and that there is nothing unusual in an old woman living all alone and putting her trust in Him? Well, if it be so, it is very good. And if it be common to find faith, one is glad. But it is no reason why one should not dwell on it with great delight. Flowers are common, too; and the scent of fir-woods, and the live leaping of water. And yet who can speak of them too often or too much?

E. H. H.

---

[1] See Miss Havergal's "Swiss Letters." (See pages 222–223 of this book.)

These were four of F.R.H.'s correspondents. Top left: her sister, Ellen Prestage (Havergal) Shaw (see page 7). Top right: Elizabeth Clay, a very close and dear friend for twenty-eight years, from 1851 till Frances died (see page 4). Bottom left: Rev. Charles Busbridge Snepp, a friend and brother to her (see page 3 and pages 30–44, letters to the "Clerical Friend and His Wife"). Bottom right: Dr. John Tinson Wrenford, Vicar of St. Paul's Church, Newport, Wales (see page 66).

THE FRANCES RIDLEY HAVERGAL MEMORIAL, LIMERICK.

This print was the frontispiece of the original book Lilies and Shamrocks. *The photograph at the top shows the same building from a different position. See pages 236–237 and 245–246 of this book.*

LILIES AND SHAMROCKS.

BY

C. W. A.

AND

FRANCES RIDLEY HAVERGAL.

Fourth Thousand.

LONDON :

JAMES NISBET & CO.,

21, BERNERS STREET.

Tell it out!

Words and Music by
FRANCES RIDLEY HAVERGAL.

Tell it out among the heathen that the Lord is King! Tell it out! . . Tell it out! . .

out! . . . Tell it out among the nations, bid them shout and sing! Tell it out! . . . Tell it out! Tell it out with a-do-ra-tion that He shall increase; That the mighty King of Glory is the King of Peace; Tell it out with ju-bi-lation though the waves may roar, That He sitteth on the water-floods, our King for ev-er-more! Tell it

Tell it out among the heathen that the Saviour reigns!
Tell it out! Tell it out!
Tell it out among the nations, bid them burst their
Tell it out! Tell it out! [chains.
Tell it out among the weeping ones that Jesus lives;
Tell it out among the weary ones what rest He gives;
Tell it out among the sinners that He came to save;
Tell it out among the dying that He triumphed o'er
the grave.

Tell it out among the heathen Jesus reigns above!
Tell it out! Tell it out!
Tell it out among the nations that His reign is love!
Tell it out! Tell it out!
Tell it out among the highways and the lanes at home;
Let it ring across the mountains and the ocean foam!
Like the sound of many waters let our glad shout be,
Till it echo and re-echo from the islands of the sea!

[J. & R. Parlane, Paisley.

See pages 79–80 of this book. J. & R. Parlane published a number of her hymns in leaflets.

CONTENTS.

———— ❧ ————

This Irish harp with a wreath of shamrocks was painted by hand on a page in F.R.H.'s personal Album (containing poems, verses, illustrations, other items, and signatures by friends, from 1860–1868). The words are modern Irish, but written in an old form of lettering. The words are the first part of John 15:9: "As the Father hath loved me, so have I loved you."

Frances had planned to leave ("D. V." she wrote in a letter dated May 9, the initials for the Latin "Deo volente," meaning "God willing") on June 4, 1879, for a trip to Ireland for two months to tour the Irish Society Mission stations, and to write on what she observed and learned to raise awareness and support for that true work. The Lord had a better way: on June 3, her final illness ended, and she entered His presence.

PREFATORY NOTE.

THE following pages will explain themselves. They reveal to some extent F. R. H.'s interest in the Irish Society, and her formation of its Bruey Branch. The allegory of "The Lilies," written by Mrs. Ashby, was read and admired by F. R. H.; and her dear hand seems to bring, to her Bruey friends, lilies and shamrocks entwined. The lessons from the lily seem fragrant with humility and patience; while her own letters glisten, like the shamrock, with dewy freshness.

We bring this offering to our King, who "dwelleth in the gardens," and may we not claim for Ireland the fulfilment of His own promise, "The going in of Thy words giveth light, giving understanding to the *guideless*" (Psalm 119:130, Irish rendering).

MARIA V. G. HAVERGAL.

April 19th, 1883.

LETTER OF F. R. H. TO MISS TITTERTON.

PRYMONT VILLA,
1867.

DEAR MISS TITTERTON:

In case I do not *see* you I must scribble a few lines (excuse pencil, as I write reclining when I can, for my back is rather weak). I *write,* but I feel more inclined to give you a loving kiss. How kind of you to send me the allegory of "The Lilies"! It is touchingly sweet and true, and even had you not added to the interest by telling me about the writer, I should have felt that it was no mere fancy, but the transcript of truth graven deeply on a living and quivering, yet loving heart. "At any cost," the blessed Stranger waits patiently, and comes again and again to His children, till they can look up and say it, perhaps very tearfully, but unreservedly. How little will "any cost" seem when His work is perfected *in* us, and, by His work *for* us, we find the "abundant entrance" into His heavenly kingdom! That will be a glorious "nevertheless afterward," of perfect fruition of His chastening; but there is a sweet and precious "nevertheless afterward," in a nearer future, linked with every trial our Father's hand sends. I think we should look out hopefully and patiently for this corresponding light in even the lightest and smallest shadows of life; the least trial has its own "nevertheless afterward" if we only do not miss it by wrong use of it, much more than in the really dark and heavy ones.

Did you mean that you had copied "Lilies" for me? I should so much like to keep it if I may, and it will not lie idle. I know more than one to whom I believe it will be cheering. It did *me good really,* and I thank you so much for it.

Yours very sincerely,

FRANCES R. HAVERGAL.

LILIES.

AN ALLEGORY.

"My Beloved is mine and I am His; He feedeth among the lilies."—Song of Solomon 2:16.

IN the far east, in a land of sunshine and drought, a child eagerly watched for the growing of wonderful seed, which had been sown in her garden.

A stranger, with a face beautiful exceedingly, had sown the seed, and as he sowed, the child heard him speak to her, with a voice which was like the soughing[1] of the wind in the distant palm trees. He said: "These seeds must be watered, my child, or else they will not spring up." The child in her eager delight at the thought of the promised lilies listened not, as the stranger was going to tell her *how* to care for the precious seed; but, clapping her hands in ecstasy, shouted gladly: "I know, I know, I will care for them, and the flowers will be beautiful, oh! so beautiful." The stranger looked pitifully at her, but she heeded not, and he passed on his way.

Many gay plants bloomed in the child's garden. One she had sown grew up, and the flowers were bright and gorgeous. But the stranger's seeds sprang not up, and she was sorrowful, for she knew that his flowers would far exceed hers in beauty. She had, alas! forgotten even the few words she had heard him speak.

At last she saw him pass that way again, and with passionate earnestness she entreated him to teach her more about the seeds he had sown, and what she was to do with them.

"Wouldst thou have them bloom at any cost?" said the stranger gently; and as the child looked up into the face bending over hers, and saw that his eyes were filled with tears, involuntarily she echoed his words, "at any cost."

Silently she watched, as bending over her garden he pulled from thence her most cherished flowers. "Not that! oh, not that, I cannot part with it," she cried, as he was about to lay his hand on the flower she loved the best. So again the stranger passed on his way.

[1] soughing: whistling

It was a time of drought, and no rain or dew fell on the child's garden. She remembered the stranger's words, and daily watched the place where his seeds had been sown; but no tiny green shoot came to gladden the eyes grown weary with watching, and her heart was sad, for she loved the kind stranger, and had longed the next time he came that way to put into his hand some of his own lilies.

Eagerly she looked for his coming again. At last he stood by her garden, and this time she waited not for him to speak, but looking once more into his wondrous face, she whispered, "Yea, at *any* cost." In silence she saw her garden stripped of its beauty; at last all was gone, not one flower was left, and, without even speaking, the stranger left her.

She sat dumbly gazing, not heeding the pitiless sunbeams which were falling scorchingly upon her; she only saw the withered flowers in the pathway. Then she bent over the spot where the seeds had been sown, and her tears dropped quickly on the bare soil. She saw only dark brown earth, where once all was fair and beautiful. As she wept she fell asleep for very weariness, and in her sleep she saw a garden in which were rare flowers, such as she had never seen before, and her stranger friend was walking amongst them. Even in her sleep her tears fell fast. When she awoke the stranger was standing by her side, and she marvelled at the gladness on his face. He looked not at her, and her eyes followed the direction of his. They were resting on her garden, and she saw that it was no longer bare and desolate, but that, where her tears had fallen, tiny shoots were growing. Then the stranger spoke words of comfort to her. He looked lovingly at the child, and the words he spoke were these, only these, "*Watch* and *Wait*." So she waited; and at last, when many days were past, her garden was once more bright: very different was the brightness now. The lilies now blooming were dazzling in their pure whiteness, and far more lovely than her flowers had ever been. So she gathered the lilies he had given her, and stood waiting at her garden gate for the stranger. As she waited many travellers passed by, and as they looked at the child in her chastened gladness, with the lilies in her hand, so glorious in their purity, they smiled and passed on refreshed. At length the stranger came, and joyfully she put into his hands his own flowers. Once more he smiled, and sent her to work in the garden, which he said was his now, not hers.

And again he said "Wait," and as he passed on his way she thought she heard him say, "Yet a little while and I will come again and take you unto myself"; and they say she is still working among his flowers, and waiting till the stranger (now no stranger to her) comes to take her, with the flowers he calls his own, to that fairer garden which she saw in her dream.

"They that sow in tears shall reap in joy."

CAROLINE W. ASHBY

———

NOW AND AFTERWARD.

"Nevertheless, afterward."—Hebrews 12:11.

BY F. R. HAVERGAL.

Now, the sowing and the weeping,
    Working hard and waiting long;
Afterward the golden reaping,
    Harvest home and grateful song.

Now, the pruning, sharp, unsparing;
    Scattered blossom, bleeding shoot!
Afterward, the plenteous bearing
    Of the Master's pleasant fruit.

Now, the plunge, the briny burden,
    Blind faint gropings in the sea;
Afterward, the pearly guerdon
    That shall make the diver free.

Now, the long and toilsome duty
    Stone by stone to carve and bring;
Afterward, the perfect beauty
    Of the palace of the King.

Now, the tuning and the tension,
    Wailing minors, discord strong;

Afterward, the grand ascension
    Of the Alleluia song.

Now, the spirit conflict-riven,
    Wounded heart, unequal strife;
Afterward, the triumph given,
    And the victor's crown of life.

Now, the training, strange and lowly,
    Unexplained and tedious now;
Afterward, the service holy,
    And the Master's "Enter thou!"

———

GOD DOTH NOT BID THEE WAIT.

"Wait patiently for Him."—Psalm 37:7.

BY F. R. HAVERGAL.

GOD doth not bid thee wait,
    To disappoint at last;
A golden promise, fair and great,
    In precept-mould is cast.
Soon shall the morning gild
    The dark horizon rim,
Thy heart's desire shall be fulfilled,
    "*Wait* patiently for Him."

The weary waiting-times
    Are but the muffled peals
Low preluding celestial chimes,
    That hail His chariot-wheels.
Trust Him to tune thy voice
    To blend with seraphim;
His "Wait" shall issue in "Rejoice!"
    "Wait *patiently* for Him."

He doth not bid thee wait,
    Like drift-wood on the wave,
For fickle chance or fixèd fate
    To ruin or to save.
Thine eyes shall surely see,
    No distant hope or dim,
The Lord thy God arise for thee:
    "Wait patiently *for Him!*"

COPY OF LETTER.

From the Right Honourable the Earl of Shaftesbury, K.G., to the Ladies the Hon. Secretaries of the Bruey Branch.

May 19th, 1882.

Ladies:

I have been so occupied that I have, unpardonably I fear, long delayed to answer your letter.

If I can do any good to the "Bruey Branch" of the late admirable Frances Ridley Havergal, and show any respect thereby to the memory of that inestimable woman, I shall be most happy to become a Patron. You are good enough to say that you will have no other at your head. I bow to your decision, though, I think, I could give you better advice.

Your obedient servant,

Shaftesbury.

The Hon. Secretaries of the Bruey Branch.

LETTERS OF F. R. H.,

Linked by Emily Titterton.

THERE are a great number of people who have never heard of our "Bruey Branch," grafted into the parent tree of the Irish Society in 1877, by F.R.H.; or that we, as "workers for Christ," are working that the poor Irish-speaking people may have the word of God in their own language, and learn how to read it. Our beloved Queen says, "the cause of England's greatness is the open Bible." Ought we not then to give Ireland this "open Bible" and let Ireland have the opportunity of being great too?

In November 1872 dear F.R.H. wrote me: "Will you accept my new little book, 'Bruey,' and *use* it among your Irish subscribers. If I had written it ostensibly and obviously in support of the Irish Society, it would probably not have had much circulation, but as it is ostensibly *only* a story 'suitable for Christmas gifts' and so forth, it stands a much better chance of large sale, and thereby *wider* help to the Irish Society. The name and some of the incidents are real. It was only published last week, but I have already had a most strong notice of it in *The Christian,* which being the first, I take as an omen of success, if the Lord will."

In March 1876 she writes: "... I am so happy; have been adding up my Irish money, and find I have £61 and there are three cards yet to come in, yours, Miss Eve's, and a *little* new collector's, besides which *I* have three more *possible* contributors, so we shall run very near to £70, even if we don't quite touch it. Isn't this good? ..."

In the year 1877 the "Bruey Branch" was grafted into the Irish Society with the "little new collector" (Nony Heywood) as its first "twig." Again F.R.H. writes.

The Mumbles,
March 11th, 1879.

You have indeed done grandly. It is perfectly wonderful to me how you have done so much, and I take it as one of the "exceeding abundantly" answers to prayer. ... You see, I think that it is really important work that we are doing, far beyond the ordinary importance of collecting work, because I feel we are lengthening the cords and laying foundations for more extended work, and we don't know the end of it. That's why I am, as you see, aiming all along to get and keep it all organized from the very outset. Work so arranged is far more likely to be both permanent and increasing."

March 17th, 1879:—. . . I am almost frightened at the rate the Bruey Branch is growing at. Mr. Fitzpatrick says it quite astonishes them, that the movement seems to be so popular. It quite astonishes *me*, I must say, *although* we have asked it! I got a list of fourteen new collectors only yesterday.

March 22nd, 1879:—One can only say with all one's heart, Hallelujah! It is really wonderful. We may indeed thank God and take courage. I sent off £108 19s. yesterday from the Bruey Branch, which this time two years started with £20. And now you have sent in such a great increase for Leamington too, the whole thing is just a splendid answer to prayer. One only feels humbled, at any rate I do, for not having prayed more. The answer seems in such disproportion. . . .

Some people think the souls of the Irish-speaking people are not worth caring for, but dear F. R. H. was not of that number, neither is our Lord and Saviour Jesus Christ. I should like to tell you how He is gathering the poor hungry and thirsty souls into His fold, in the islands of Achill Sound, and Innisbegil.

A missionary clergyman, the Rev. M. Fitzgerald, lately appointed to these islands by the Irish Society, says in a letter dated Dec. 27*th*, 1882:

You are, I am aware, deeply interested in the good work of the Irish Society, and will, I feel assured, be pleased to hear that the Society is doing an excellent work here on the mainland, and on the islands of Achill and Innisbegil, and also at Castlebar. I examined 125 persons, including the boy and girl of ten, and the grandfather and grandmother of eighty and seventy, all in the Irish version of the Holy Scriptures. Of this number, about eighty were Roman Catholics, chiefly of the farming class, and the remaining forty-five, converts or children of converts. From forty-five to fifty, *mostly* Roman Catholics, committed the 19th chapter of St. John's Gospel, or the 20th chapter of St. Luke's Gospel, to memory, and repeated the chapter for me most accurately and correctly. In this parish alone several hundred persons are learning to read the Irish Scriptures, and before long I hope to have our Irish teaching, reading, extended to the neighbouring parishes. I may tell you that a brother clergyman attended one of these meetings here lately, on the 14th inst., and was, as he told me, greatly surprised to see a large schoolroom full of people, chiefly Roman Catholics, kneel down with me in prayer at the beginning and end of our meeting. The prayer was in Irish, and all audibly and heartily joined in the Lord's prayer. To God be all the glory.

I tell you this because I expect these islands, our F. R. H. Memorial Hall, Limerick, (that you see as our frontispiece) and the Bandon schools, etc., etc., will be given to us as our special work.

Dear F. R. H. wrote to me, March 16th, 1871:—

. . . Don't be discouraged about the Irish Society. I always reckon, in canvassing, to get at least eight or ten refusals to each success. *Your* doing anything at all is encouraging, and I never expected you

would meet *all* generous people and none of the other sort. And if you only got five shillings, remember that *that* teaches *one* poor dark heart to read and know the precious word of God. . . .

Did England cause a famine in Ireland—"Not a famine of bread, nor a thirst for water, but of hearing of the words of the Lord"?

Hear what the Right Rev. Christopher Wordsworth, D.D., the Lord Bishop of Lincoln, at his Triennial Visitation held in Nottingham in October, 1882, said:

Ireland was formerly called the "Island of Saints." For a thousand years the Church of Ireland was free. In the twelfth century England betrayed Ireland into the hands of Rome, and for four hundred years England tried to govern Ireland by means of Rome. No edition of the Common Prayer was provided in the Irish language in the sixteenth century, nor any portion of Holy Scripture. It was not till the year 1686 that the Old Testament was printed in that language, and during the whole of the eighteenth century not a single copy of the word of God was published in the mother tongue of Ireland. Notwithstanding all these disastrous hindrances and discouragements, the Church of Ireland was making steady progress, and might, by salutary measures of reform, have become a blessing to her people, and have been restored to her primitive place in Christendom. But England, twelve years ago, despoiled her of her revenues and disestablished her, and by so doing crippled her energies and diminished the number of her pastors, so that now, in 1882, there are five hundred less clergymen in Ireland than there were twenty years ago. England Romanized Ireland, and she ought to evangelize it.

It was Lord Nelson, beloved by all England, who said, "England expects that every man this day will do his duty."

If England *did* cast Ireland into darkness and into "the valley and shadow of death," by giving her into the power of Rome, is it not England's duty to try and lead her back into the glorious light of the gospel of our Lord Jesus Christ? *This* is the day for England to do her duty and make restitution for any wrong she may have done in former years. *This* is the time to work for poor Ireland. The Irish are emigrating by thousands. Give them the good seed, and they will scatter it wherever they go. If England's sons and daughters did do their duty, they would at once obey the command, "Go ye and preach the gospel to every creature in a language understood by the people," or else help to send others to do it for them.

Will you not, dear friends, as good enlisting soldiers, do your very best to get others to join our Bruey Branch, and help in the glorious work we have before us, that of restoring to the poor Irish-speaking people, England's *home* heathen, the light they say we took from Ireland. Oh that the cry may soon be heard, "Babylon the great is fallen, is fallen," and the joyous shout go forth, "The kingdoms of *this* world have become the kingdoms of our Lord and of His Christ and He shall reign for ever and ever."

Before I conclude I should like to tell you a little about our F. R. H. Memorial Hall, Limerick. It now contains 117 boys, who will be fed, clothed, and educated for Christ, and will not be lost sight of till they are put into some way of getting a living for themselves.

Dear F. R. H. wrote to me December 4th, 1878, and in a postscript said:

N.B.—*Every* Bruey Branch collector should have a report, to keep and make use of. I stipulated for myself that the Society must post them, to save me time and trouble, so I send up every name to be entered, and they send a report and papers by return. Thus, in case I died suddenly, they have always a complete list of names and addresses besides my private one. So every distant name you have sent me has had reports. But I did not send up the names of the new Leamington ones, because as you are constituted "Twig" Secretary, you will be responsible for seeing that they have reports, papers, etc. You can arrange this in any way you please; but I rather advise your supplying them with reports *yourself,* because the personal intercourse does so much to keep up interest.

This letter was the origin of the Frances Ridley Havergal Memorial Hall, Limerick!

Knowing our late dear Secretary's wishes on the subject, request was made for Bruey reports. The answer received was, the Irish Society is £1000 in debt, the committee cannot afford to give separate Bruey reports. So Leamington had a sale of work in a private house, to obtain the required money for printing the report. At the end of the day's sale it was found we had, together with donations, £175; and as that was more than we require for printing the report, a request was made to the committee of the Irish Society, that, if more money could be obtained, a substantial building should be erected in the way of a church or orphanage, as a tribute to the memory of our late beloved friend and secretary. I will leave others to tell why the Masonic Hall, Limerick, now called the "Frances Ridley Havergal Memorial Hall," was bought.

Dear friends, "the Lord *hath* done great things for us" and it seems as if He were saying "Thou shalt see *greater* things than these." So "be glad and rejoice, for the Lord *will* do great things." These three texts dear F. R. H. gave us to cheer us on in our work, in the very last circular letter she sent us. And does it not seem as if He were still saying, "Thou shalt see greater things than these"?

Yours very faithfully,

Emily Titterton,

General Hon. Bruey Branch Secretary for England, Scotland, and Wales.

The Lindens, Leamington.

CIRCULAR LETTERS

ADDRESSED BY FRANCES RIDLEY HAVERGAL TO THE COLLECTORS OF THE BRUEY BRANCH.

(*With Introduction by her Sister, M. V. G. H.*)

Our Motto—"For Jesus' sake only."

My dear little Collectors:

This Report will be different from the grown up people's Report, and so it must not be long or dry. You all know how pleasant it is when you or your brothers at school get a *good* report sent home after each term. Your papa opens the letter, and when he reads "good," "very good," "excellent," or "improved," "fair progress," how pleased your mamma looks, and the report is posted on to uncles and aunts. Does not this help you to work much harder next term? Now I do think your Bruey Report for 1879 must be "excellent"! But I have a brighter word still for you—"*splendid*"!

Yes, that was the very word my darling sister Frances said when she added up all your Bruey cards last March, and found that the sum (£117 11*s.* 10*d.*[1]) exceeded all her expectations. You can't think what pleasure it gave her to get all your cards! She seemed to me like your queen bee, and you the little workers bringing to her what had cost you diligent labour. And all you gathered together was given out again, in the honey of God's word, to many in Ireland, making them glad with the sweet news of salvation.

Are you quite clear why your Branch is called "Bruey"? Just this: some years ago my dear sister Frances went to a meeting for the Irish Society in Worcester. She was so interested that she at once began collecting for it, and hoped by trying very hard to get *one* pound the first year. And she did so, and every year she got more and more, so that altogether, from the first year she collected till last March, she had sent more than nine hundred pounds to the society! Of course she asked a great many other friends to help her; and the first little girl who took a card was Bruey!

Now I am going to copy for you what my dear sister wrote about Bruey to some friends in America.

Bruey was a *real* little girl. One of her names was Bruce, but "Bruey" was her pet name. The outline of her simple story is *true*. The sketch of her character is founded on recollections and inferences drawn from them. Bruey's Sunday school work, the affair of the hat, the Irish meeting, the cards and the forty-one names, her illness and early peaceful death, are all fact. I have kept the list of Bruey's forty-one names, and it is interesting to know *what* she did collect for. It was work for Christ that dear little Bruey undertook. I should like my dear little unknown American friends to know that I have heard already of many English children who have been stirred up by Bruey's example to wish to be "workers for Christ" too. Very many have asked their parents to tell them of something to do, like Bruey, "for Him." I am so far away that I shall probably never hear such pleasant news from America; but I send my little book across the ocean with a very earnest prayer that my heavenly Master may grant that by it many an American girl and boy may be led to become "a little worker for Christ."—F. R. H.

I will now tell you, that my dear sister's collectors so increased that she thought it would be well to make them, as it were, a *branch* of the Irish Society's tree. A branch grows and spreads, and has twigs and leaves and fruit. Because Bruey was her *first* collector she called it the "Bruey Branch."

Now you will like to know *who* was the *first* collector in the "Bruey *Branch*." Nony Heywood was the first collector. My dear sister knew and loved her very much. One day in March, 1877, she called on dear Nony's mamma, and mentioned the new Bruey Branch; and Nony immediately asked if she might have a card. I will copy Frances's note that same evening.

[1] The total, including the Penny Cards, amounted to £168 12*s.* 2*d.*

PYRMONT VILLA.

DEAR MRS. HEYWOOD:

When I mentioned my intended "Bruey Branch" of the Irish Society, I had no thought of anything so delightful as hearing then and there of a new little holder of a "green card." Your taking it up so kindly and *instantly* quite sent me on my way rejoicing! For I am extremely anxious to help on this good, and tried, and proved *old* agency of Bible work. Among so many *new* excellent agencies for home and abroad, the old established ones hardly get their fair share of support; and the enclosed appeal will show how great the need is. I have just written to the secretary to propose my "Bruey Branch." If your dear little Nony would like the idea of being one of the original collectors of the "Bruey Branch," do you think she could get a few shillings on the enclosed card by this day fortnight? For then she would literally be my *first* "Bruey Branch" collector, as I write her name on this card as belonging to the B. B. I will show dear Nony the *real* forty-one names which dear Bruey brought to me a little while before her last illness began. I trust Nony may do this little "work" really *for Jesus,* and then I am sure it will be a means of blessing to herself. Thanking you very much for what has been a real bit of encouragement in my work, and praying that the ever tender Hand may graciously close your eyes to-night, instead of holding them waking,

I am, yours cordially,

F. R. H.

A few days later my sister sent another short note.

LEAMINGTON, March 22nd.

The Irish Secretary tells me he wishes to have my accounts on Thursday the 29th. I am afraid your little Nony will not have had time to do anything, but if she *has* a few shillings on her card, would she bring it to me on Wednesday afternoon. The secretary has *warmly* taken up the idea of a "Bruey Branch," and I hope it will *grow,* but I should like my little friend Nony to be the *first* member! I hope she has received the report. Yours very truly,

F. R. HAVERGAL.

Dear little Nony entered with all her heart on this fresh work for the Master she loved. She wrote several letters to friends at a distance, besides asking contributions from friends near at hand. By the end of the fortnight she had the pleasure of taking rather more than two pounds to my dear sister, as her first collection for the "Bruey Branch." A few days later Nony received my sister's beautiful circular, in which she gave the "Bruey Branch" as their motto, "FOR JESUS' SAKE ONLY." We kept a copy of this circular, and as it was the *first* written for the "*Bruey Branch*," and some of the fresh members will not have seen it, I transcribe it here.

LEAMINGTON, April 2nd, 1877.

MY DEAR COLLECTORS:

Most of you do not know the great honour which has befallen you! I expect you to appreciate it immensely! You are the original members of the "BRUEY BRANCH"; for we have cut you off from the

Leamington branch, because we hope you will grow better as a separate bough! We begin with eight collectors, and a sum total of £20 9s. 1d.! Is not that good? But I hope it will be better next year. I want each of you to aim at two things by next March. *First,* to have more on your cards, even if it is only a shilling more, don't be satisfied without that; and, *secondly,* to get each of you one more "green card" taken; that would be worth several new contributors on your own. Sometimes when Swiss mountaineers are climbing a very difficult place, they throw their ice axe, with which they cut steps in the ice slopes, on to the ledge just above their heads. They then *must* climb up to it, for it would be death to try and get down without it, and, of course, they would not think of stopping quietly where they were. Now let us throw up our ice axe on to a higher ledge, and aim, God helping us, at getting £30 next year, and *twenty* collectors instead of *eight.*

I have visions of a "*Percy* Branch" some day, because boys can often collect where girls cannot; so please try and think of any cousins, or boys of any sort, who would take a green card. I have *one* already who is going to devote his Easter holidays to house-to-house collecting; *he* is the *first* new collector; now, who will find me the *second?* I have great hopes that our "Bruey Branch" will be a very "fruitful bough." Only, dear ones, I am praying that all the golden fruit it bears may be really and only "fruit unto God." Not fruit for *ourselves,* nor fruit sent to me, or to the Dublin office (for we are only counted "an empty vine" if that is all), but really fruit for *Jesus.* It is so easy to get quite interested in collecting, and forget this. Let us every one pray that we may always remember it. And this reminds me that I want to have a motto for our "Bruey Branch," a little watchword which we may always connect with the thought of it, something that shall help us, not merely to do a right thing, but to do it in a right way.

You remember how when the Lord Jesus was in Bethany many of the Jews came, but "not for Jesus' sake only." Now, let us cut off the "not," and take as our "Bruey Branch" motto,

"For Jesus' sake *only.*"

It will be such real help to our work to remember this, and to ask Him to write it on our hearts, "not with ink, but with the Spirit of the Living God."

One thing more I want you to do, and this most of all. Do try not to forget that we have agreed together to pray for our Irish work every Monday morning. I am not sure that all of you have *really* "agreed" about this yet; next time you write to me I wish you would tell me whether you do or not. It is a help if you put it down on a piece of paper and keep it inside the cover of your Bible; then you are not so likely to forget it. It will be so nice to know that you all, and I too, are always praying together on Monday mornings; and I am quite certain that our work will be blessed just in proportion to our praying about it.

I wish you would all just try and see how much God will help you if you will but ask Him. Three months ago I was at my wits' end, and could not think how in the world I was to get as much money as last year, so I prayed, "Lord, send me something quite unexpectedly," because you see I could not know who to expect anything more

from! and within a fortnight no less than £9 was sent me by different people, and every penny of it was "*quite unexpected!*" Altogether I got £83.

We are only beginning, but I hope we shall go on steadily until the whole work is done, and every poor Irish body who cannot speak English has had the tidings of great joy brought to them in their own native tongue. But work while you can; Bruey herself had only that one opportunity of collecting last summer. The one of all our collectors who had gone on most steadily, the one perhaps who *most* gave her very heart, first to the Lord, and then to this Irish work, was called away. She really did "what she could." Let us all ask our dear Master to help us to do the same.

"For Jesus' sake only."[1]

Yours lovingly,

Frances R. Havergal,

i.e. Aunt Fanny.

TO THE JUNIOR DIVISION OF THE BRUEY BRANCH OF THE IRISH SOCIETY.

The Mumbles, near Swansea.

My dear little Friends:

I have so many things to say to you, that I hardly know where to begin. Since my last circular it has pleased God to take my dear stepmother to Himself, after more than three years' illness. All the last year was very terrible suffering. So my old home at Leamington is broken up entirely, and I am come to live here at the seaside with my elder sister. Now will you please be very business like, and pay attention to what comes next. 1. Put down my new address on your green cards *at once,* before you forget it. 2. Mind you always address me "Miss *F. R.* Havergal," as I am not "Miss Havergal." 3. Please do not forget to send me your collections not later than the 1st of March. One collector did not appear in the Report at all this year, because he forgot to send in time. 4. If you send P. O. orders, make them payable to "F. R. Havergal," at "The Mumbles." 5. Remember that it is quite as convenient to me, or almost more so, if your parents write you a cheque for the money instead of a P. O. order. I mention this as two or three of you live far from a post-office. 6. I advise you all, instead of sending me your green card, to send me a copy of it, partly because it is likely to be easier for the printers to make out, and partly because it is nice for you to keep your old cards to refer to, and make sure that you have not forgotten to ask any one who contributed before. Now I shall see who is business like, and recollects all these six things!

You will be glad to hear, at any rate I am glad to tell you, that the Bruey Branch is growing famously. If everybody collects who did so last year, we shall have thirty-one collectors! To be sure, three of them have given out that they don't mean to collect again; but I won't believe that just yet! Surely they will not leave us! Perhaps when they

---

[1] When F. R. H. started the "Bruey Branch" Mrs. Heywood promised her that she would supply "Our Motto" to all the members. Should any new collectors be without it, Mrs. Heywood, Southwick Rectory, Brighton, will be happy to supply it on application.

have read to the end of this letter they will change their minds, and be willing to take the trouble again, "for Jesus' sake only." I would ask *you,* dear little friends, who are *not* tired of doing this little work for the Lord Jesus, to pray that they too may be kept from getting tired of it. But the B. B. is not only growing; it has taken to sprouting! for now we have got two "Twigs." The first was an Irish one, "The Bandon Twig," consisting of four girls, who are collecting, with a kind grown up friend at their head; the second is an English one, "The Lexden Twig"; and we should have had a third, a "Leamington Twig," but that one of my very best collectors has gone to live somewhere else, and so could not undertake to be its young secretary. Now what if some of you collectors could get up a "Twig" in your neighbourhood, and then be promoted to be "Twig Secretaries"? I shall be very glad to hear from any one who can get two or three near you to join, and then I will tell you what the little duties of a secretary will be. Nothing more formidable, only what any one of you can do! I think the *new* collecting cards, with spaces for 120 pence and the gift of a "Bruey" to every one who takes one from the society, ought to be a help in getting new collectors. See now, if you can't get just one taken!

We really must do our very best this year; for do you see at page 38 of the Report that England has sent more than £300 less than last year, and Ireland more than £400 less! I am sure my dear *Irish* members will be doing their best towards making up this sad loss, whatever the English B. B's may do! For just think what this means. It means not being able to pay nearly so many teachers, and not getting nearly so many poor Irish taught to read the Bible, and letting ever so many more die without hearing a word about the only Friend and Saviour who can take away the sting and the fear of death. Just you look at page 30 of the Report, about the poor old woman who thought Jesus was put to death in a stable, and who did not know what was done on Calvary; and think of her not having an idea how to be saved, and our dear Lord Jesus being *the last* she would think of as having anything to do with saving her! Don't you *want* to send some one to tell such poor creatures about Him? Don't you *want* to take a little trouble about the little bit of work He has given you to do for them? Tell your friends about her, and tell them there are eight hundred thousand poor people who cannot be got at at all except by the Irish Society. English folks generally have no idea there are so many who speak Irish. I hope you have looked at the map in the Report. Now why don't you take and show it to everybody you know, and ask them to help to send the "glad tidings" to all those coloured parts. Do you recollect our Monday morning prayer? I always hope that all of you are joining me then. Let us pray very much for the work and for each other these next three months, and then I hope the 1st of March will bring a good harvest. And please send up a little special prayer for the youngest of all our members; she has been not only very ill, but *very suffering* for a great many months, and is not able to walk or move; yet she has been very faithfully at work. "She hath done what she could." Could the Lord Jesus say that of all the rest of you, dear ones? Would you not like Him to be able to say it of you? But I really must leave off. Just one more thing—Will you, every single one of you, be so good as to send on this letter as soon as ever you can, putting the date when you get it and when you forward it? A kind collector will make three or four copies of it, so that each will not have

to go such a long round; but do *please* not forget to send it on, because it is not fair to others, *nor to me,* to keep it, and prevent the others from getting it.

Your very affectionate secretary,
FRANCES RIDLEY HAVERGAL.

POSTSCRIPT.—Since writing, I have had such good news from Leamington that I must send a postscript to catch the circulars. After all, we have our third "Twig," to be called "The Leamington Twig," with five new collectors. So we shall have, I do hope, no less than thirty-six collectors in the next Report.

———

The above circular was sent off on November 25th, 1878. The directions to send HER the cards and post-office orders can no longer be carried out, but the collectors may be as careful in sending the cards and post-office orders to those who now take the place of Miss F. R. Havergal. The collectors in England will please send them to Miss Emily Titterton, The Lindens, Leamington. At the request of F. R. H., Miss E. Titterton and Miss M. Fay will be the secretaries.

The next circular our little friends will read, though they have read it before, is full of sweet and wise words.

THE MUMBLES, SWANSEA:
April 2nd, 1879.

MY DEAR COLLECTORS:
God has given us one of the most splendid answers to prayer I ever knew. He has prospered our Bruey Branch ever so much beyond what *I* asked or thought, and so, maybe, it is beyond what you asked or thought either. So those of us who have been faithfully remembering to pray for our work on Monday mornings may have the joy of hearty thanksgiving for answered prayer; and if those who have been forgetting all about it will nevertheless join in thanking Him for doing what they did *not* ask, I think they will be glad to join in our prayers after this.

Two years ago we started with eight collectors, and sent up £20 9s. 1d.; last year we had eighteen collectors, and sent up £41 9s. 3d.; and this year we have seventy-eight collectors, and have sent up £108 19s. 1d.![1] Is not this grand? And this is not nearly all. Mr. Roe, one of the Association Secretaries, tells me that he has "hundreds of cards out, and is appointing 'Twig' secretaries in all directions," so that dear little Bruey's work is bearing most wonderful fruit, and it looks as if there would be a great deal more next year than this. We have five "Twigs" in the Bruey Branch, besides the Senior and Junior divisions; but it seems we shall have a *great* many more soon.

Now, as our faithful God has heard our poor little prayers so far, I want you to pray still more, and especially that He would not only help us in our collecting, but that He would send every great spiritual blessing on the work done in Ireland by means of the money collected. Will you join me in asking four things? 1. That God would give

---

[1] Collection, 1880: £850 16s. 9d.

His Holy Spirit to all the Irish teachers and their pupils. 2. That very many may during this year seek and find Jesus. 3. That those who find Him may be filled with love, and that the joy of the Lord may be their strength, especially in bearing persecution for His sake. 4. That every one who finds Christ may begin at once to bring others to Him. I wish you would just copy these four things out, and put them in your Bibles, so that you may be reminded every Monday morning *what* to pray for, and we shall see what gracious answers God will give us. "The Lord *hath* done great things for us," and it seems as if He were saying "Thou shalt see *greater* things than these," so "be glad and rejoice, for the Lord *will* do great things." Find these three texts out, and mark them in your Bibles.

Now for some business remarks. I wish you would all learn to be business like. Some of you did everything right, and I herewith offer my best thanks, as secretary, for their having saved me a good deal of trouble by doing *all* I asked. But how was it that I had to write to seven or eight of you, because the 1st of March went by, and you did not send your card in? Some of you even then kept me waiting, and thus I was defeated in a very nice little plan I had, which I meant to have written to each of you about, to reach you on St. Patrick's day, March 17th. I will see if I can do it next year.

One thing nearly everybody was very good about this time, and that was in forwarding the circulars. The Senior Division circular went round without one single day missed. But I want to explain that I *never* object to your keeping the circular another day or two, if it is really for a good purpose, if you want to show it to two or three friends who might be interested to see it, or if you are away from home and want some one there to see it, and so post it round by them. This is a very different thing from keeping it for nothing. Only when you do so, it would be a good plan if you wrote a word or two on the circular to explain why it was not sent on at once, and then I should know it was not carelessness, and perhaps should have the pleasure of seeing that it was doing a little more work. Just one thing more: now that I have so many collectors, I cannot undertake to recollect their addresses *offhand*, so when you write to me or to any one else who has a *great* many letters to write, please always put your *full* address at the top of your letter, and then I have not to stay to hunt it out in my address book.

Do you remember my asking you to pray for a dear little girl? Her mamma writes as follows: "I enclose £5, our darling Nony's collection for the Irish Society, and which in all probability will be her last, as the doctors say she is now past recovery and that it is only a question of *time*. What an unspeakable comfort and perfect rest it gives us to feel that our *times* are in His hand whose way is *perfect!* so that we cannot for one moment wish anything otherwise than as *He* orders it. The work sold was not *all* her own doing, but she worked a few minutes at a time as long as she was able. She has had two operations during the last month, and has a large wound in her thigh. Her sufferings have been terrible, but I have never heard a murmur. It was so kind of you to ask prayer for her, and seemed to please her much." Please remember, more, poor dear little Nony, and ask the Good Shepherd to deal very tenderly with His little suffering lamb. Surely He will send a special blessing on *her* work, "the few stitches" done "as long as she was able."

I am sending a copy of the February number of "*Day of Days*"

to each collector. If any one does not receive it, please let me know. I particularly want you *all* to take the little magazine in, and recommend it to your subscribers—it is only a penny a month,—for now we have arranged to have something about the Irish work in it every month, so that all collectors and contributors will be able to get fresh accounts, besides a great deal else that will be nice to read. The one I send contains a paper called "Novel kind of Schools." The March number (which I do hope you will get) has one called "How very Irish!" April will have—— Well, you get it, and see what! Next June I hope, please God, to go to Ireland myself, on purpose to go to the parts where our Society is at work, and then I shall write all about what I saw and heard, and have it printed in the magazine, which will be better than these short circulars, and I hope much more interesting. That's another thing I want you to pray for; ask that if it is God's will I should go and do this, I may be both blessed and made a blessing in doing it.

And now I will give you a text for your next year's work: "Be not weary in well doing." Perhaps some of you *are* a little bit weary in it; some have owned that they are, as they sent up a card not quite so full as last year. One loving elder sister writes of a younger one: "She is very sorry it is less than last year, but somehow the dear child has not been quite so mindful of it this last year, and she is terribly shy of asking strangers.[1] However, I do trust the loving Saviour will lay it on her heart with enduring power, that she may work for Jesus' sake only, and not get weary now the novelty has worn off." That is just what I pray for every one of you, dear ones, whether I know you personally or not. To that loving Saviour I commend you and your work for the coming year.

Your very affectionate secretary,
FRANCES RIDLEY HAVERGAL.

On receiving the £5 with the news that dear Nony had been very, very ill for some months, my dear sister sent her this sweet little note.

MY DEAR NONY:

I had no idea you were suffering so much all this time. I think Jesus must have been carrying you in His arms all the while, because you see when anybody can't even walk they *must* be carried. And I am quite sure He must be loving you ever so much; I mean with a very special and tender love, because it says, "Whom the Lord loveth He chasteneth." I thank you so much for the violets. I have such a number of new Bruey collectors that I hardly know how I shall manage them all. We shall have a famous report next year, I hope. . . .

Very much love from your loving friend,
F. R. H.

My dear sister also wrote to little Nony's mamma.

THE MUMBLES, February 28th.

DEAREST MRS. HEYWOOD:

Your letter does indeed bring sorrowful news. I can hardly realize that dear, little, sweet Nony is passing to the Better Land. How

---

[1] This collector's card is now one of the largest in amount.—M.V.G.H.

you will miss her! Yet the long terrible sufferings, making it the more manifest gain to her to depart, must make you less desirous to keep her from the perfect rest and gladness. I shall think much of her and you, and pray often for my dear little worker.

Would dear Nony like to send any message or text to the other little collectors? It might do good if she would, and be a very real bit of work for Jesus.

Surely her £5, which I find places her at the head of the list for this year, will be blest to bear some special fruit for God.

Yours, with most affectionate sympathy and fond love to little Nony,

F. R. HAVERGAL.

Nony never forgot the request for united prayer, and many were the simple, earnest petitions she offered on the appointed morning, that the poor Irish people might learn to read their Bibles and be led to the Saviour. Dear Nony was so pleased with the motto "For Jesus' sake only," she said she wished she had it printed to put up on her wall by her other motto, "What would Jesus do?" Then we thought it would be nicer still if *every* little Bruey collector had a printed copy of their motto. Accordingly, with F. R. H.'s consent, and to little Nony's delight, one hundred were ordered to be printed. It will please little Irish collectors to know that when we showed the proof to dear F. R. H., and asked if she approved of the colour selected (red and black), she said in her own animated way, "Oh, no, do let it be *green.* I should like it to be *regular Irish.*" When they were finished, and Nony was asked which she would have, she answered, "Oh, *of course* I would like a green one, like dear Miss Havergal."

Dear little Nony's work for Jesus, and long, patient suffering, ended on the evening of May 1st, 1879. The good Shepherd came and carried her to His own bright home. You will have received the lovely "In Memoriam" card of your dear little Bruey sister, sent by F. R. H.'s wish; but we reprint it here.

> "*Out of the mouth of babes and sucklings Thou hast perfected praise.*"—ST. MATT. xxi. 16.
>
> ---
>
> #### In Loving Memory of
> ## NONY OLIVIA HEYWOOD,
> Who, after fourteen months of intense suffering (borne without a murmur), entered into rest and the joy of her Lord,
>
> MAY 1ST, 1879,
>
> **Aged Ten Years and Eight Months.**

> "*My strength is made perfect in weakness.*"
> 2 *Cor.* xii. 9.
>
> ### SOME OF THE DEAR CHILD'S LAST WORDS.
>
> "O mamma, I feel so very, very happy; I don't seem able to tell you how happy I am!"
>
> "Little Nony is too ill and weak now to do anything but just trust Jesus, and that I'm doing all the time. 'Trusting Jesus, that is all!'"
>
> "I'm not in the least bit afraid to go. You know Jesus said 'Suffer little children to come unto Me'; and I'm quite sure He'll receive little Nony!"
>
> "Oh, how very nice it will be to see dear, good, kind Jesus!"

> "*Jesus Christ . . . hath abolished death.*"
> 2 *Tim.* i. 10.
>
> "They say she DIED! It seems to me
> That, after hours of pain and strife,
> She SLEPT at evening peacefully,
> And woke to EVERLASTING LIFE!"
>
> ---
>
> "O change, stupendous change!
> There lies the soulless clod;
> The Sun Eternal breaks,
> The new immortal wakes,
> WAKES UP WITH GOD!"

Only a month passed away, full of bright, busy work for Jesus, when rapid illness came on, and my darling sister Frances, and your loving friend, entered the golden gates, June 3rd, 1879. She looked so lovely and so glad to meet her King! I wish you could have heard her sing:

> "Jesus, I will trust Thee, trust Thee with my soul;
> Guilty, lost, and helpless, Thou hast made me whole.
> There is none in heaven or on earth like Thee;
> Thou hast died for sinners; therefore, Lord, for me!"

There are thousands in Ireland, who do not trust *only* in Jesus, as she did. You will carry on the work of sending them this good news by collecting for your Bruey Branch. Thus will you follow your bright, loving friend, Frances Ridley Havergal, even as she followed Christ Jesus our Lord.

In the desk of my dear sister Frances she left a paper, "Work for 1879, if the Lord will." But His will for her was "rest" not "work."

I know it was my sister's intention to write a memoir of little Nony, whom she knew and loved. The pleasant incident of Nony's willingness to become the first collector in the Bruey Branch of the Irish Society associates their names as fellow workers. My sister's loving sympathy followed her all through those sufferings which were the prelude to her glorious rest. The joy with which she rejoiced *for* her in her abundant entrance shall be given in her own words.

THE MUMBLES, May 5, 1879.

DEAREST MRS. HEYWOOD:

. . . Thank God for Nony! and thank God that *you* are *able* to thank Him! I *never* read anything sweeter than her welcome to her Lord's coming for her. . . . I have ventured to keep a copy of your beautiful letter to Miss B——. Would you let me make use of part of it in my next circular? I should so like to tell my dear little collectors about her whose name will be *highest* on the list in next Report. I feel it such a privilege to have been permitted to number this little saint of God among my band of collectors. One from the seniors (E. R. N.) and one from the juniors are "safe home" now, and both such abundant entrances. How beautiful Nony is now!

Yours in most loving sympathy,

F. R. H.

May 14.

Could I possibly have one hundred of those most exquisite memorials of dear Nony? If you did not mind kindly allowing me to send one to each of my other dear collectors, I would give anything to have them, for I think they *must* be a real blessing, and I never saw *anything* more beautiful, or more likely, under God's blessing, to touch little hearts.

Yours lovingly,

F. R. H.

May 19–20, 1879.

I should *very* much like to compile a little memoir of dear Nony, and could feel that it was real work for God to do so, for it might be blessed to many. But it would be *necessary*, if I do it at all, to come and spend a few days with you, as you kindly suggest, and hear all you can tell me, and so select material. . . . I am very glad I may have the cards. When ready will you kindly have them sent to Dublin, as I shall probably be in Ireland ere they arrive?

P.S., *May* 20.—On further consideration and prayer, I see that I cannot do this little work till *after* Christmas; at least not unless the autumn shapes itself quite differently from what God is at present indicating. *After* Christmas I should, in all probability, be free to decide on fresh work, and would then try to do my best. . . . But I *think* you would not like to postpone it so long, so decide just as you feel.

Very much love,

F. R. H.

This letter was one of the very *last* my sister Frances wrote. It seemed as if dear Nony entered the golden gates in time to welcome her.

On the 3rd of June, 1879, as just stated, the founder of the Bruey Branch of the Irish Society was called away to rest from working for Jesus upon the earth. Every working day must come to its closing hours, and end. So was it with the time given to my dear sister. But, though dead, she yet speaks to her little friends who helped her in the Bruey Branch. They will be pleased to read again F. R. H.'s circular letters to them. As she will never again write to them a new letter, they will be pleased to read once again the old letters.

May this little book[1] prove the loving Shepherd's call to every reader, showing His faithfulness, and that in the deepest suffering He carries the lambs in His bosom. How safe to be within His fold, ever following Him as Nony did!

Let me be your true friend,

MARIA V. G. HAVERGAL.

October, 1879.

[1] "Memorials of Little Nony." By her Mother. Nisbet & Co.

———— ✿ ————

HINTS FOR IRISH SOCIETY COLLECTORS.

BY THE LATE FRANCES RIDLEY HAVERGAL.

1. Never consider your work done; set your new card going the very week the old one is sent in.

2. At the beginning of your collecting year make a list of every one, near or distant, likely or unlikely, whom you could possibly ask during the twelve months, keeping the list where it may often catch your eye, adding names whenever they occur

to you, and marking off each as soon as you have applied.

3. Never be without a card; keep two in hand—one to be enclosed in letters, hoping for its return with stamps; the other should lie on the drawing-room table, and thus do some possible passive work when not in active use.

4. *Watch* for opportunities, and you will see them.

5. Ask unlikely people, and you will get delightful surprises.

6. Keep an eye to shillings, and even sixpences, as well as sovereigns.

7. Aim definitely at progress. Determine that, God helping, you will *never* retrograde, but always send an increase upon the last year.

8. Unless very sure of your ground, ask for a "contribution" rather than "subscription" or "donation." The former is alarming, because it implies continuance; the latter is objectionable, because it precludes asking next year. "Contribution" neither frightens the contributor nor hinders the collector, and nearly always results in a "subscription" in course of time.

9. Carefully read and *mark* your Reports or other papers, before lending, turning down leaves at the more important or attractive pages, and using the pencil freely. Persons who never touch an ordinary Report will and do seek out and read all your marked passages.

10. Lose no opportunity of gaining any information for yourself on the subject. Do not hesitate to talk about it and tell striking facts or statistics, even when you are not actually collecting. You may thus awaken interest in unexpected quarters, and seed, thus casually dropped, sometimes yields a golden harvest.

11. Remember that one collector is more real gain than several contributors; and, therefore, aim rather at getting others to undertake a card than to contribute to yours. This widens interest as well as increases funds, for persons always take more interest in what they work for than what they merely give to.

12. Be ready to sacrifice your own apparent results to the real gain of the society. We may often gain a new collector by handing over some of our own subscribers. They will shrink less from gathering in subscriptions already assured, and will generally double the amount thus transferred.

13. Pray, not occasionally, vaguely, and doubtfully, but (1) *Systematically.*—Fix one morning in the week all the year round for the praying part of your work. (2) *Definitely.*—Ask for exactly *what* you want and *all* you want in connection with your collecting; ask for faith, zeal, courage, and love; ask that names may be suggested to you, and openings made for you; ask *where,* and *when,* and *how* to appeal; ask that in each case you may be guided whether to write or speak, that hearts may be prepared before you come, and that the very words may be given you; ask beforehand, and ask at the moment, for wisdom, willingness, and, if it be His will, success. (3) *Expectantly.*—Do not look at *probabilities,* but at *promises*; work only for God's glory, and only in the Master's name, and then joyfully trust Him to "fulfil *all* thy petitions."

UNION FOR PRAYER AND PRAISE.

IN her Hints to Collectors, Frances Ridley Havergal urged thus the habit of prayer for the Irish Society: "Pray, not occasionally, vaguely, and doubtfully, but (1) *systematically,* (2) *definitely,* (3) *expectantly.*" She stated in a note that a few collectors had already "agreed together" to pray for the Irish Society, and for blessing, guidance, and success in their work for it, *every Monday morning.* Many collectors have joined in this Union. God has heard the prayers offered, and blessed richly those who thus united in supplication and intercession for this good work, and has blessed the mission field also. How precious the privilege of thus pleading with the Father of mercies, on behalf of sorely afflicted Ireland and the efforts to make known the gospel of peace and love among her misguided people! We know that if we ask believingly through our all-prevailing Intercessor, Jesus Christ, we shall receive. He will fulfil all our petitions. O Lord, teach all collectors for the Irish Society to pray as well as to work for increase of Divine blessing upon it! But it is a duty and happy privilege to unite *thanksgiving* with our prayers, and to praise God for all the funds collected, the Bibles circulated, the children taught to read the Holy

Scriptures, the old and the young who have heard in their own tongue wherein they were born the wonders of God's love, and all the souls to whom the Holy Spirit has revealed Jesus Christ and the efficacy of His blood which cleanseth from all sin—ignorant, superstitious, Irish Roman Catholics, brought from darkness to light.

All who will join in this Union for Prayer and Praise—union in spirit and holy exercise, however far apart their bodily presence—will oblige by sending their names to *Mrs. Heywood, Southwick Rectory, near Brighton,* who has kindly consented to act as *Secretary for this Union.*

———— ❧ ————

TO THE READERS OF " BRUEY."

THE following letter will be found interesting.

THE MUMBLES, SWANSEA:
March 16th, 1879.

DEAR MR. ROE:

I wanted to send you a line to supply you with a true defence, in case a certain objection against " Bruey " is brought up, as I hear you are kindly making good use of the little story. I am sometimes remonstrated with for " making Bruey die," and have only just had an epistle from Mr. Askwith on the subject. The answer is, I *didn't* make her die; she did die, and I could not help the fact. Had I been writing a fiction, I should have made her go to the seaside and collect triumphantly there, and " live happy ever after," as the fairy tales say. But dear little Bruey's collecting was no fiction, nor her calm, happy death.

Names and persons are disguised throughout, but all the facts are quite real, and I have now in my Irish drawer the copy of her own two cards with forty-two names, kept at the time. . . . I really do think it a rather remarkable instance of how a little bit of work undertaken by a little girl of twelve years old in simple love to Christ can be multiplied by Him far more than a hundred fold, as I think hers will prove to be, if the " Bruey Branch " goes on as at present. And I take it to be a lesson not to despise any day of small things, whether one's own or other people's. It struck me you might really find it useful to be able to assure people that Bruey was " a real little girl," as I tell the children.—Yours very truly, and with best wishes for your work,

FRANCES R. HAVERGAL.

———— ❧ ————

THE FRANCES RIDLEY HAVERGAL MEMORIAL HALL, LIMERICK.

AFTER F. R. H.'s death, those who knew and loved her in Leamington held a sale of work there, to form the beginning of a " Havergal Memorial Building Fund " in connection with the Irish Society. The result of this sale was £175. Various plans were suggested for the appropriation of this and any other sums that might be raised for the purpose of founding a permanent and useful Memorial, which would bear her name and aid the missionary work to which she was so devoted when living. The plan which the Committee of the Society decided to recommend to the contributors was the purchase of the Masonic Hall in the city of Limerick. This was effected. It is now styled "The Havergal Memorial Hall," and will be used for mission services, sermons or addresses in Irish, ragged and mission schools (Sunday and weekday), and other purposes of the Irish Society. The Masonic Hall is said to have cost £4000. As the latest owners were interested in Irish Society work, it was offered by them to the Society for *one thousand pounds*. The Boys' Ragged School has been transferred to it from the house in which it has hitherto been held, and which had become dilapidated and in many respects objectionable. In this School and the Girls' and Infant Schools, which occupy what is called the Roxborough Schoolhouse, are educated children of the very poorest class. The parents of some of the children are Roman Catholics; in other cases one parent is Protestant, the other Roman Catholic; in most cases one parent is intemperate, in some cases both parents are so. But in these three schools in the city of Limerick, under the same management, (that of the Rev. Canon Gregg and the Irish Society) there has been provided a shelter for the children of converts from Romanism in various mission stations, who are subject to persecution or in danger of being seduced whilst young and susceptible into the church of Rome. The children are protected, sheltered, supported, educated, and trained for God's service here and for heaven hereafter. This indeed has been for many years a "work of faith and labour of love," and God has very richly blessed it.

The applications are ever more than Canon Gregg has money to provide for. The number on school rolls now is 185; resident in dormitories, 122. Many who have been cared for in these schools are in the Navy, some have been sent to the Church of Ireland Training College to be trained as teachers; and nearly all those living are in respectable independence, who but for these admirable Schools might have added to the number of our criminal population.

The building, which was purchased as a memorial to that devoted friend of the cause, Frances Ridley Havergal, is now the property of the Irish Society, and vested in trustees nominated by the Committee of the Society. One thousand pounds was the sum paid for the building, and £110 was the cost of procuring possession of the yard, which had been let to an insurance company. The sums required for securing legal title to the premises, collecting the purchase money, and making known the object and nature of the memorial by printing, advertising, etc., have added considerably to the expenses.

When the purchase of this hall as a memorial of this gifted writer and friend of Ireland was proposed, it was confidently expected that her friends and admirers in England, Scotland, and Ireland, and the many who had been blessed by her friendship and her writings, would have come forward (without exceptions) to aid in making this building what its name really implies, a loving memorial of one who laboured most earnestly in the cause of Irish Missions, and who lost no opportunity to win the sympathy of all within the reach of her voice or pen, for the efforts of the Irish Society to give back to the Irish, in their own tongue, that Bible which their forefathers had given to England and Scotland.

The hope cherished when this memorial was proposed, and so warmly taken up by the friends of Frances Ridley Havergal, has been sadly disappointed, as the sum already contributed by them has been little above £700. Very nearly £500 are still due on the above accounts, including the original purchase. This is a heavy weight on the trustees. Of the sum just named, £428 is the amount due to the Irish Society Reserve Fund. The work of the internal alterations of the F. R. Havergal Memorial Hall, which has been carried on during the last twelve months, is now sufficiently completed to enable the building to be used for one of the purposes of the purchase, the valuable school, for which the Irish Society has for many years provided sound scriptural instruction. The internal arrangements have been superintended and provided for by the Rev. Canon Gregg, and he could not have accomplished so much had not one Christian friend in Dublin sent him for the purpose the liberal contribution of £800. It is not too much to ask or to expect from the friends, admirers, and those who have profited by the writings of the late Frances Ridley Havergal, that the debt should be at once cleared off. For this purpose, contributions may be sent to the Rev. Canon Gregg, Limerick; or to the Rev. William Fitzpatrick, Secretary to the Memorial Trustees, 17, Upper Sackville Street, Dublin.

P.S.—Profits from the sale of "Lilies and Shamrocks" will be sent to this fund and the Bruey Branch.

PRAYER FOR IRELAND.

GRACIOUS Saviour, look in mercy on this Island of the West,
Win the wandering and the weary with Thy pardon and Thy rest;
As the *only* Friend and Saviour let Thy blessèd Name be owned,
Who hast shed Thy blood most precious, and for ever hast atoned.

Blessèd Spirit, lift Thy standard, pour Thy grace and shed Thy light;
Lift the veil and loose the fetter, come with new and quickening might;
Make the desert places blossom, shower Thy sevenfold gifts abroad;
Make Thy servants wise and steadfast, valiant for the truth of God.

Triune God of grace and glory, be the Isle for which we plead
Shielded, succoured with Thy blessing, strong in every hour of need;
Flooded with Thy truth and glory (glowing sunlight from above),
And encompassed with the ocean of Thine everlasting love.

Oh, surround Thy throne of power with Thine emerald bow of peace;
Bid the wailing and the warring and the wild confusion cease.
Thou remainest King for ever; Thou shalt reign, and earth adore!
Thine the kingdom, Thine the power, Thine the glory evermore.

FRANCES RIDLEY HAVERGAL.

———— ✿ ————

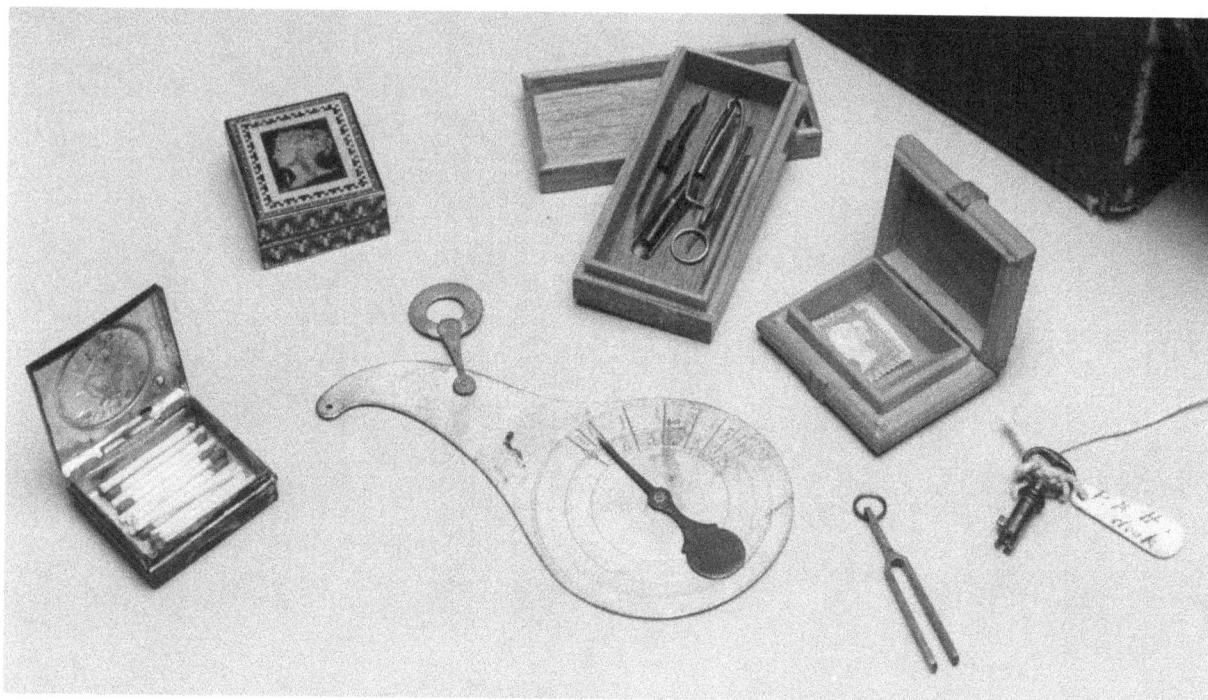

F.R.H.'s tuning fork, pen and pencil box, matches, desk key, other items, and the bottom corner of her portable travelling desk, when pens were dipped in ink and candles or oil lamps were needed to write at night.

Five objects of 1st Ep.
1. 3, 4; 2. 1; 5. 13.

CHAPTER I.

A.D. 90.

THAT which was from the [a] beginning, which we have heard, which we have seen [c] with our eyes, which we have looked upon, and our hands have [d] handled, of the Word of life;

2 (For the life was manifested, and we have seen it, and bear witness, and shew unto you that eternal life, [f] which was with the Father, and was manifested unto us;)

3 That which we have seen and heard declare we unto you, that ye also may have fellowship with us: and truly our fellowship [l] is with the Father, and with his Son Jesus Christ.

4 And these things write we unto you, that [n] your joy may be full.

5 This then is the message which we have heard of him, and declare unto you, that God is light, [r] and in him is no darkness at all.

6 If we say that we have fellowship with him, and walk in darkness, we lie, and do not the truth:

7 But if we walk [t] in the light, as he is in the light, we have fellowship one with another, and the blood [x] of Jesus Christ his Son cleanseth us from all sin.

8 If we say that we have no sin, [y] we deceive ourselves, and the truth is not in us.

9 If we confess [z] our sins, he is faithful and just to forgive us our sins, and to cleanse [b] us from all unrighteousness.

10 If we say that we have not sinned, we make him a liar, and his word is not in us.

CHAPTER II.

MY little children, these things write I unto you, that ye sin not. And if any man sin, we have an advocate [f] with the Father, Jesus Christ the righteous:

2 And he is the propitiation [g] for our sins: and not for our's only, but also for the sins of the whole world.

3 And hereby we do know that we know him, if we keep [k] his commandments.

4 He that saith, I know him, and keepeth not his commandments, is a liar, and the truth is not in him.

5 But whoso keepeth his word, in him verily is the love of God perfected: hereby know we that we are in him.

6 He that saith he abideth [m] in him, ought himself also so to walk, [n] even as he walked.

7 Brethren, I write no new commandment unto you, but an old commandment, which ye had from the beginning. The old commandment is the word which ye have heard from the beginning.

8 Again, a new [q] commandment I write unto you; which thing is true in him and in you, because the darkness [r] is past, and the true light now shineth.

9 He that saith he is in the light, and hateth his brother, is in darkness [s] even until now.

10 He that loveth his brother abideth in the light, and there is none [γ] occasion of stumbling in him.

11 But he that hateth his brother is in darkness, and walketh [u] in darkness, and knoweth not whither he goeth, because that darkness hath blinded his eyes.

12 I write unto you, little children, because your sins are forgiven you for his name's [y] sake.

13 I write unto you, fathers, because ye have known him [b] that is from the beginning. I write unto you, young men, because ye have overcome the wicked one. I write unto you, little children, because ye have known the Father. [e]

14 I have written unto you, fathers, because ye have known him that is from the beginning. I have written unto you, young men, because ye are strong, [g] and the word of God abideth [h] in you, and ye have overcome [i] the wicked one.

15 Love [k] not the world, neither the things that are in the world. If [m] any man love the world, the love of the Father is not in him.

16 For all that is in the world, the lust of the flesh, [o] and the lust of the [p] eyes, and the pride [q] of life, is not of the Father, but is of the world.

17 And [s] the world passeth away, and the lust thereof: but he that doeth the will of God abideth for ever.

18 Little children, it is the last [u] time: and as ye have heard [w] that antichrist shall come, even now are there many antichrists; whereby we know that it is the last time.

19 They went out from us, but they were not of us; for [a] if they had been of us, they would no doubt have continued with us: but they went out, that they might be made manifest [c] that they were not all of us.

20 But ye have an unction [d] from the Holy One, and ye know [e] all things.

21 I have not written unto you because ye know not the truth, but because ye know it, and that no lie is of the truth.

22 Who is a liar, but he that [h] denieth that Jesus is the Christ? He is antichrist, that denieth the Father and the Son.

23 Whosoever [i] denieth the Son, the same hath not the Father: [but] he that acknowledgeth the Son, hath the Father also.

24 Let [l] that therefore abide in you, which ye have heard from the beginning. If that which ye have heard from the beginning shall remain in you; ye also shall continue in the Son, and in the Father.

25 And this is the promise that he hath promised us, even eternal [o] life.

26 These things have I written unto you concerning them that seduce you.

27 But the anointing which ye have received of him abideth in you, and ye need not that any man teach you: but as the same anointing teacheth [p] you of all things, and is truth, and is no lie, and even as it hath taught you, ye shall abide in [β] him.

28 And now, little children, abide in him; that, when he shall appear, we may have confidence, and not be ashamed before him at his coming.

29 If ye know that he is righteous, [δ] ye know that [t] every one that doeth [t] righteousness is born of him.

CHAPTER III.

BEHOLD, what manner of love [v] the Father hath bestowed upon us, that we should be called the sons [w] of God: therefore the world [x] knoweth us not, because it knew him not.

2 Beloved, now are we the sons [z] of

Marginal reference column

a Jno. 1. 1, &c.
b chap. 1. 1.
c 2 Pe. 1. 16.
d Lu. 24. 39.
e Jno. 14. 7, 9.
f Jno. 17. 3.
g Ep. 6. 10.
h John 15. 7.
i Re. 2. 7, &c.
k Ro. 12. 2.
l John 17. 21.
m Mat. 6. 24.
Ga. 1. 10.
Ja. 4. 4.
n John 15. 11.
o 2 Pe. 2. 10.
p Ps. 119. 37.
q Ps. 73. 6.
r John 1. 4, 9.
1 Ti. 6. 16.
s Ps. 39. 6.
1 Co. 7. 31.
t John 12. 35.
u He. 1. 2.
w Mat. 24. 24.
1 Ti. 4. 1.
x Ep. 1. 7.
He. 9. 14.
1 Pe. 1. 19.
Re. 1. 5.
y 1 Ki. 8. 46.
Job 25. 4.
Ec. 7. 20.
Ja. 3. 2.
z Job 33. 27, 28.
Ps. 32. 5.
Pr. 28. 13.
a 2 Ti. 2. 19.
b Ps. 51. 2.
1 Co. 6. 11.
c 2 Ti. 3. 9.
d 2 Co. 1. 21.
e 1 Co. 2. 15.
f Ro. 8. 34.
He. 7. 25.
g Ro. 3. 25.
h chap. 4. 3.
i John 15. 23.
k Lu. 6. 46.
John 14. 15, 23.
l 2 John 6.
m John 15. 4, 5.
n John 13. 15.
o John 17. 3.
p John 14. 26.
q John 13. 34.
r Ro. 13. 12.
β or, it.
s 2 Pe. 1. 9.
γ scandal.
δ or, know ye.
t Je. 13. 23.
Mat. 7. 16, 18.
u Pr. 4. 25.
John 12. 35.
v Ep. 2. 4, 5.
w John 1. 12.
Re. 21. 7.
x John 17. 25.
y Ps. 25. 11.
Lu. 24. 47.
Ac. 10. 43.
z Ro. 8. 14, 18.

173

The first page of I John, in F.R.H.'s last Bagster study Bible that she read and studied at the end of her life.

www.ingramcontent.com/pod-product-compliance
Lightning Source LLC
Chambersburg PA
CBHW081254040426

42452CB00014B/2493